Cognitive Psychology

Applying the Science of the Mind

Gregory Robinson-Riegler
University of St. Thomas

Bridget Robinson-Riegler
Augsburg College

PEARSON

A and *B*

Boston ■ New York ■ San Francisco
Mexico City ■ Montreal ■ Toronto ■ London ■ Madrid ■ Munich ■ Paris
Hong Kong ■ Singapore ■ Tokyo ■ Cape Town ■ Sydney

Series Editor: Karon Bowers
Editorial Assistant: Carolyn Mulloy
Marketing Manager: Taryn Wahlquist
Editorial-Production Service: Trinity Publishers Services
Manufacturing Buyer: JoAnne Sweeney
Cover Administrator: Linda Knowles
Text Designer: Carol Somberg
Electronic Composition: Omegatype Typography, Inc.

For related titles and support materials, visit our online catalog at www.ablongman.com.

Between the time Website information is gathered and published, some sites may have closed. Also, the transcription of URLs can result in typographical errors. The publishers would appreciate being notified of any problems with URLs so that they may be corrected in subsequent editions.

Library of Congress Cataloging-in-Publication Data
Robinson-Riegler, Gregory.
    Cognitive psychology : applying the science of the mind / Gregory Robinson-Riegler, Bridget Robinson-Riegler.
       p.   cm.
    Includes bibliographical references and index.
    ISBN 0-205-32763-X
       1. Cognitive psychology. I. Robinson-Riegler, Bridget. II. Title.

BF201.R63 2004
153—dc21
                                                                          2003052281

Printed in the United States of America

10 9 8 7 6 5 4 3 2 1   RRD-VA   08 07 06 05 04 03

To our parents, Audrey and Roy Riegler and Ann and Frederick Robinson,
who instilled in us a passion for learning and teaching.
Here's hoping we're half the teachers they have been.

Contents

chapter 3

Early Perceptual Processing   72

chapter 4

Attending to and Manipulating Information   114

chapter 5

Identifying and Classifying Concepts   160

chapter 6

Encoding and Retrieval Processes in Long-Term Memory   208

chapter 12

Problem Solving 479

chapter 13

Reasoning, Judgment,
and Decision Making 523

Preface

To the Student

In this book you'll be reading about something with which you're intimately familiar yet haven't really stopped to think about. It's about something you engage in every day but rarely notice unless something goes wrong. You couldn't live without it, but you seldom stop to truly appreciate it. Is it TV? No. Coffee? No. Sleep? Nope. It's *thinking*. Ironically, although the mind is in constant use, most people take thinking for granted, only noticing when it misfires. Consider the following examples of annoying little disturbances in thought.

- Why did I just put the cereal in the refrigerator and the milk in the cabinet?
- Why did I just get a D on an exam when I thought I knew everything "cold"?
- Why are answers to exam questions right on "the tip of my tongue" but I can't quite "spit them out"?
- Why is that I can stare at the same problem for hours and make little or no progress?
- Why do I find it so difficult to listen to a professor lecture and take notes (not to mention stay awake) at the same time?

Your average Joe/Jane understands relatively little about how thought processes work and how to improve them. But take heart! Thousands of scientists (who call themselves cognitive psychologists) have made countless investigations on our everyday thinking processes and, as a result, have shed a great deal of light on the mechanics of thought. After reading this book, you will not be the average Joe/Jane.

What Is Cognitive Psychology?   Cognitive psychology is a subdiscipline of psychology that employs the scientific method to answer fundamental questions about how the mind works. By using controlled research (mostly experiments), cognitive psychologists attempt to explain the thinking processes we use every day. A cognitive psychologist would view the problems described above from an analytical and technical perspective—technical through the lens of a scientist. A cognitive psychologist might restructure the questions posed above as follows:

- What are the cognitive factors that underlie *action slips?* How does this relate to automatic processing?
- Why do people sometimes fail to monitor their own level of *comprehension?* What are the components of successful *metacognition?*
- What factors play a role in *retrieval blocks,* and how can these blocks be successfully resolved?

- What leads a person to exhibit *mental set*, and how is it related to convergent thinking? What are some strategies that can be employed to help people overcome mental set?
- How do people successfully *divide their attention* between multiple sources of stimulation, given the limited nature of attention?

Why Study Cognition?   The study of cognition has tremendous ramifications for an overall understanding of how you "tick" on a day-to-day basis. It is, in some ways, the most applied (and applicable) of psychology's subdisciplines. As noted above, cognitive psychologists attempt to understand the processes that you use every day: perception, attention, memory, language, and reasoning. Such understanding is key in knowing how people think and behave, which is the focus of psychology. And such knowledge is also important to us personally, in our everyday life—who hasn't been frustrated by the (sometimes more than) occasional "brain lapse" and other difficulties in attention, memory, and the like?

Let's broaden the point a bit. A full understanding of cognition is critical to an understanding of other subdisciplines in the field of psychology. This makes sense; psychology is typically defined as the scientific study of thinking and behavior, and questions of thinking are at the core of every other subdiscipline of psychology. Consider the following questions from other arenas of psychology:

- *Clinical psychology.* Do depressed people remember events from their lives differently than nondepressed people?
- *Neuropsychology.* What's happening in different areas of the brain's cortex as people engage in cognitive processes like memory and problem solving?
- *Developmental psychology.* How do cognitive processes like memory and problem solving change with age?
- *Personality.* Do a person's personality characteristics play a role in the types of decisions they make?
- *Social psychology.* What factors influence our ability to remember an individual?

These questions have quite a range, but there are two common threads. First, they are fundamental psychological questions; second, they all involve cognition. Unlocking and understanding the mechanisms that are involved in cognition is fundamental to psychological explanation.

Cognitive psychology can be a bit of a challenge to master, for a number of reasons. First, the subject matter of cognitive psychology (mental processes) can be difficult to grasp. You can't really see or touch cognitive processes, and most often they take place quickly and outside of conscious awareness. As a result, the discussion of mental processes often takes place on a somewhat abstract level, and discussions of findings from research on cognition are full of jargon that can be difficult to decipher. Second, cognitive psychology's roots are firmly planted in experimental methodology. So to understand cognitive psychology, you need to understand experimental methodology. Third, cognitive psychology is a sprawling field; no one has provided the one unifying theory of cognition, let alone of a simpler subprocess, like memory. Findings and theories tend to conflict, due to the relative youth of the field (experimental cognitive psychology has only been around for about 50 years). As a result, students don't gain a sufficient idea of "the big picture." This text offers a number of features designed to help you organize, integrate, and apply the material you'll be reading about cognition research.

First, the overall structure of the book parallels the progression of thinking. Take a simple cognitive process—looking at an animal in a zoo and recognizing it as a duck-billed platypus. This involves (1) perceiving the animal, (2) paying attention to the animal, (3) retrieving the matching label for the animal from your store of concepts in memory, and (4) saying "duck-billed platypus." Following this intuitive progression through the cognitive system, our text (after an initial foray into the history of cognitive psychology) proceeds from perception and sensory memory (initial perception of the animal), to attention and working memory (paying attention to the animal), to pattern recognition and concept representation (retrieving the label "duck-billed platypus" from memory). From there, the discussion moves on to higher-level mental processes, including autobiographical memory, language, problem solving, and decision making (relating the story of the summer we had a duck-billed platypus for a pet and, when it got too big, having to decide what to do with it).

A second feature of the text that will help you integrate the material is our inclusion of a number of recurring empirical "threads" in each chapter. These consist of topics that cut across all areas of cognition and serve as unifying themes for current research, namely:

- *Cognition and neuroscience.* Perhaps the most active and exciting frontier of cognition research is in *cognitive neuroscience,* which attempts to relate cognitive processes to process and structure in the brain. What is occurring in the brain as we sense, pay attention, remember, and decide? Each chapter of the text features a section that focuses on a neuroscientific investigation of the topic being discussed.

- *Cognition and consciousness.* Consciousness (which may be defined simply as one's awareness) is a mysterious concept that some may say defies explanation, having confounded philosophers, cognitive psychologists, and physiologists throughout history. Research in cognition has much to offer on the mystery of consciousness. To what extent do our everyday cognitive processes involve conscious awareness? How can we be influenced by things of which we are unaware? Each chapter of the text features a section that addresses the issue of consciousness within the context of the featured chapter topic.

- *Cognition and individual differences.* For the most part, research in cognition has focused on finding the *general* principles of how people think. *In general,* how do we pay attention? *In general,* how do we remember? *In general,* how do we solve problems? Focusing on the general tends to gloss over the fact that there are important differences in the ways that individuals think. These differences can be observed between women and men; between 6-year-olds and 60-year-olds; between those suffering from psychopathology, and those that are not; between folks from the Eastern Hemisphere and folks from the Western Hemisphere. Each chapter of the text features a study that investigates individual differences in the cognitive processes being discussed.

A third feature of the text that should help you gain a richer appreciation of cognitive psychology research is an entire chapter on research methods as they are applied to the study of thought. In this chapter, we explore the basics of experimental methodology within the context of cognitive psychology research. A chapter on research methods is a bit unusual for this type of text, but we think it's critical to your understanding and appreciation of the field.

A fourth device that will assist you in integrating and applying the material is a running story. Each chapter starts with a continuing installment in this exciting (?) tale. As the story progresses, you will gain an increasingly thorough idea of how each of the cognitive processes being discussed is an integral (yet often unnoticed) component of our lives.

In addition to features that assist you in organizing, integrating, and applying cognitive psychology research, our text provides several tools that we hope will help you in understanding and remembering the material. These features include:

- *Stop and Review!* To help you assess whether you've learned the important material from what you've just read, each major section of a chapter concludes with a short quiz. Following the quiz, a brief summary of the main points from the section (including the points covered in the preceding quiz) is presented.
- *Glossary.* To help you keep track of the myriad new and exciting terms to which you'll be introduced, we define each new term at the end of each chapter. Organizing glossary terms in this way helps you keep the important terms from the chapter in the appropriate context.
- *Stop and Think!* One of the best ways to understand and remember material is to become actively engaged with it. To help you accomplish this, each chapter features a number of exercises entitled "Stop and Think!" These exercises involve a number of hands-on and "mind-on" activities that will help you give closer consideration to the material being discussed. The exercises include demonstrations of cognitive processes and principles through "mini-experiments," questions about how you might design a study to investigate some cognitive process, opinion questions about controversial issues in the field, and questions that require you to examine your own cognitive processing on a day-to-day basis and evaluate it in the context of the topic being discussed.

As noted earlier, the newness, complexity, and breadth of cognitive psychology make it a challenging topic. However, these characteristics also make cognitive psychology an exciting and dynamic area of study. Its newness means that there are many exciting areas to explore and an endless array of questions waiting to be answered. Its complexity makes learning about it a great exercise in critical thinking. In reading this text, we hope that you will gain a firm understanding of how seemingly vague questions about mental processes can be translated into experiments that provide concrete empirical answers. The breadth of cognitive psychology makes it one of the most interesting of psychology's subdisciplines. Topics included in the text range from visual perception to eyewitness memory to language comprehension to problem solving, with many fascinating stops in between. Our sincere hope is that you will enjoy learning about cognitive psychology as much as we enjoy talking and teaching about it. Turn the page, and start thinking about thinking!

To the Instructor

Does the world really need another cognitive psychology text? We thought maybe it did. Between us, we've taught introductory cognition three or four dozen times, using seven different textbooks. The fact that we've used so many different texts reflects two things. Cognitive textbooks are at the same time satisfying and a bit wanting. All of the books we've used have their strengths: rigorous discussion of important empirical and theoretical principles, currency, real-world examples and application, good organization and pedagogy, engaging and student-friendly writing. The problem is, these texts all tend to be strong in two or three of these areas and not as strong in the other three or two. In our text, we're shooting for more.

Style.   We listened to the complaints, comments, and suggestions of nearly a thousand students. They often found the texts to be a little dry and boring. They didn't seem as "grabbed" by the field as we felt they should have been. We did our best to grab them (figuratively) in class, but we always sensed that something was missing. The books with the breezier writing style seemed to lack depth of discussion. The books that went into depth seemed to be somewhat obtuse. We've tried to write a text that strikes a balance: one that really grabs students and intrigues (even entertains) them while still capturing the theoretical and empirical elegance and rigor that characterize cognitive psychology research.

Research Methods.   Speaking of empirical elegance and rigor, we think that to gain a full appreciation of research in cognition, students need to have a firm foundation in research methods, particularly the experimental method. To this end, we've dedicated a chapter to the methods used in cognition research. While this may seem a bit unconventional, we feel that it's more than warranted. We are constantly faced with students who feel somewhat over their heads in the subject of cognition research because they don't have a firm hold on how experiments are conducted. To remedy this, Chapter 2 presents an overview of experiments and descriptive data analysis; importantly, we present these concepts *within the context of cognition research*. So even if students have had methods in a course, they haven't had it like we're presenting it. If you feel that your students are well beyond the need for such an overview, the chapter simply can be skipped, with no loss in organizational flow.

Organizational Structure.   In organizing the chapters of the text, we attempted to follow the flow of a piece of information that enters the cognitive system. The information is perceived, attended to and placed in working memory, identified, and committed to memory. Later, the information serves as the basis for the higher-level processes of language, problem solving, and decision making. This is an admittedly serial approach, but we think it provides for a satisfying intuitive description of cognition that will enhance understanding.

Although our text does feature a fairly standard approach to explaining the flow of cognition, there are a couple of notable exceptions. One is that attention and working memory are discussed in the same chapter. It always struck us (and our students) that when we discuss the control processes of attention and the control processes used in short-term/working memory, we are talking about many of the same things. The two seem to be (in many ways) flip sides of the same coin. This view is certainly not new; indeed, much of the work on working memory span (e.g, Engle, 2001) has emphasized attentional control as a key *component of* working memory. We thought it highly appropriate to discuss these components together. Another distinctive feature of our layout is that pattern recognition occurs after discussion of attention and working memory. We placed it here because conscious recognition of a stimulus only occurs as the stimulus is processed by working memory. In other words, pattern recognition can be viewed as the first task of attention/working memory.

We've also tried to provide some organizational structure by referring back to three important research themes in each chapter: neuroscience, consciousness, and individual differences. These research themes capture some of the most interesting and dynamic questions that currently define the field. In each chapter, we focus on a research investigation that has questions of the brain, levels of consciousness, or individual variation at its core. We hope that the inclusion of these themes will enhance students' sense of some of the overarching issues that currently define the field.

Finally, we've strengthened organizational flow by making the interrelatedness of cognitive processes very apparent. The separate discussion of perception, attention, memory, and so on is a descriptive convention; when it comes to everyday thinking, these processes are inseparable. We've tried to give students a sense of this by pointing out, whenever possible, the relationship between the cognitive processes currently being discussed and those already covered, and/or those to come.

Everyday Relevance.   Cognition is constant; thinking is what we do. Despite the obvious relevance of thinking to our everyday lives, we sensed that students didn't appreciate this relevance as fully as they should. To enhance this appreciation in class, we make liberal use of everyday examples and give students thought-journaling assignments and experiments to do outside of class. The students really enjoy these and often are surprised at how interesting this material can be (needless to say, we're never surprised). We've adopted this tack in our book, sprinkling the discussion with numerous examples and sprinkling each chapter with exercises entitled Stop and Think!—to entice students to do just that. These exercises can serve as homework assignments, as discussion generators for the classroom, or both. By the way, the instructor's manual for the text will include some ideas for elaboration and explanation of these exercises.

Another device we've used to enhance the everyday importance of thinking processes is a running story that describes several days in the life of some students and a professor approaching the end of a semester. Each chapter begins with another installment of this "thrilling" tale, and throughout the chapter we make a point of tying the cognitive processes being discussed back to what's happening (i.e., what and how people are thinking) in the story. (And it has a great "sixth-sense" ending!!)

Cool Experiments.   We also were never completely satisfied with the research presented in cognition texts. There are classic findings that merit extensive discussion, to be sure. But there are also some really intriguing empirical investigations, perhaps a little more off the beaten track, that merit mention and analysis. These investigations might be distinctive in their setting (e.g., transfer-appropriate processing on a basketball court) or in their empirical question (out-of-body experiences in touch caused by visual stimuli), but they still address fundamental questions of cognition. We've tried to include a number of studies like this, because they're likely to pique student interest and still convey the critical points.

Thanks for taking a look at our book. We hope your students enjoyed reading it as much as we enjoyed putting it together (we hope it didn't take them as long!) We'd love to get your feedback and suggestions. If you spot errors or misrepresentations, if you know of an interesting study that may merit discussion, or otherwise want to comment on the text, please feel free to e-mail us (Greg: glriegler@stthomas.edu; Bridget: robinson@augsburg.edu).

Acknowledgments

We wish to acknowledge a veritable legion of mentors and supporters who were instrumental in the preparation of this text or long before, as we began our academic careers.

First, we'd like to thank our undergraduate and graduate mentors, who fostered in us a passion for good research and good teaching. Bridget thanks her undergraduate mentors David Pisoni and Beth Greene at Indiana University. Greg would like to single out his mentors at the University of Cincinnati—R. J. Senter and especially Joel Warm—as well his graduate mentors at Purdue—Jim Neely, Gordon Logan, Roddy Roediger, Mark McDaniel, and James Nairne. Both authors wish to extend an especially warm and appreciative thank-you to James Nairne, a supportive mentor and caring friend whose skill as a researcher and writer has served as an inspiration to each of us. His guidance during our graduate training and his counsel during book preparation have proven invaluable. Thanks, Jim.

Thanks to our editor at Allyn and Bacon, Carolyn Merrill, who signed us for this project and provided calm and assured guidance and the freedom to create the book we wanted. We'd also like to thank editorial assistants Kate Edwards and Carolyn Mulloy. Thanks also to Marcie Mealia and Leslie Hill, who provided many a "shot in the arm" of enthusiasm.

This book would still be an unsightly 900-page manuscript were it not for the efforts of a devoted production team. We appreciate the efforts of Marjorie Payne, who coordinated the production of the book. A special thanks to goes to Evelyn and John Ward for the tremendous care they put into copy editing and producing the text. Thanks to Jay Alexander for neuroanatomical renderings and to Sarah Evertson for her photo research.

The authors also wish to thank several undergraduates who reviewed portions of the text: Sarah Gervais, Rachel Kohlman, Katie Pfeil, and Annie Stodolka. In addition, we'd like to thank our cognitive psychology classes at both Augsburg College and the University of St. Thomas for tolerating a unsightly 900-page manuscript as the class text. The book is better for their efforts. We also thank our colleague at Augsburg, Emily House, for her feedback on Chapter 13.

We'd also like to acknowledge the work of our colleagues that forms the basis for this text. A particular note of thanks goes to those who supplied us with sample materials and photos from their work: Cathleen Moore, Francesco Pavani, Sue Savage-Rumbaugh, and particularly Julian Keenan, who worked his morphing magic to turn Bridget into Marilyn Monroe.

And of course, the text is infinitely better due to the thoughtful reviews offered by our colleagues. Thanks to them for their careful consideration and insightful suggestions: Martin Bink, University of North Texas; Tom Busy, Indiana University; Darryl Dietrich, College of St. Scholastica; Jocelyn R. Folk, Kent State University; Gary B. Forbach, Washburn University; Gary Ford, Stephen F. Austin State University; Nancy R. Gee, SUNY–Fredonia; Barry Gholson, University of Memphis; Janet M. Gibson, Grinnell College; Anita Hartmann,

University of Alaska, Fairbanks; Jo Hector, University of Arizona; Andrew M. Herbert, University of North Texas; Douglas A. Hershey, Oklahoma State University; Lisa Isenberg, University of Wisconsin–River Falls; Paul W. Jeffries, SUNY–Stonybrook; Stephen Kitzis, Fort Hays State University; William Langston, Middle Tennessee State University; Andrew Lotto, Washington State University; Keith Millis, Northern Illinois University; Hal Pashler, University of California, San Diego; Danielle Polage, Pepperdine University; Christian Schunn, University of Pittsburgh; James Speer, Stephen F. Austin State University; Claudia J. Stanny, University of West Florida; Rick Stevens, University of Louisiana at Monroe; Evangeline Wheeler, Towson University; Stephen G. Yanchar, Brigham Young University; and Michael Young, Southern Illinois University.

1

An Introduction To Cognition

"This is Rowdy Ryan Davis at Thomas Augsburg's College radio. It's 6:30 A.M. and 30 degrees here in Minneapolis, 6 inches of snow already on the ground, and would you believe it?! 6 more on the way. Let's warm up with some hot tunes. Leading off, Michael Bolton, with 'When a Man Loves a Woman . . .'" Vince flails wildly for the snooze button. Can't . . . stand . . . Michael . . . Bolton, he thinks groggily. Whap! Whap! He gets lucky on his third slap. He picks up the clock, holding it close to his half-closed eyes, barely able to make out the numbers without his glasses, 6:33. Yawn.

Vince rolls over, sits on the side of the bed, and puts his feet on the cold wood floor. Ugh! Three classes today. He can barely stand the thought of it. And maybe 12 inches of snow . . . crazy drivers . . . sounds like a good day to be sick. Vince falls back into bed and shoves his feet well under the warm covers. I *am* feeling a little nauseous, he thinks. Of course, it could be the Michael Bolton. I should probably go in—but all that snow . . . and the traffic . . . and no one's gonna be in class anyway. He buries his head under his pillow. Geez, Michael Bolton . . .

It doesn't really seem like it, but Vince has accomplished a lot so far today. "Wait," you must be thinking, "he hasn't even pulled himself out of bed!" But consider what he's accomplished. He's focused his attention on the radio, perceived the words that were being said, held the words in his mind for a short time, and recognized the individual meaning of the words as well as what they mean together. He's even gone beyond what was said, figuring out that the traffic is probably going to be awful without actually hearing that it will be. He's tried to come up with a solution to that problem. And he's in the process of making a decision, based on the information that he's processed. All of this has occurred in the space of about a minute. What mechanisms underlie such an incredible accomplishment?

What Is Cognition?

Psychology is generally defined as the scientific study of mental processes and behavior. **Cognitive psychology** could be defined by eliminating the last two words of that definition—the scientific study of mental processes. Behavior is examined by cognitive psychologists, but primarily as an avenue into the underlying mental processes, in the same way that physicists infer the force of gravity from the behavior of objects in the world. And the study of *mental processes* covers a lot of ground. These processes include attention, remembering, producing and understanding language, solving problems, and making decisions. It is hard to imagine that we take such vital processes for granted. Thinking is something that is constantly happening, yet we rarely stop to . . . well, . . . think about it. However, for the past five decades, cognitive psychologists have done exactly that, using the methods of science to answer questions about the mind. With the experimental method as their primary tool, these researchers approach the mind as a type of machine, attempting to elucidate its inner workings. Given that thinking is at the heart of everything we do on a day-to-day basis, it's difficult to imagine a more important field of study.

The Omnipresence of Cognitive Processes

One of our goals in this text is to help you appreciate and understand the importance of the cognitive processes in which you are constantly engaged. As an exercise in thinking about thinking, consider the mental processes that you go through on the first day of class.

Perception and Sensory Memory.   As you listen to each professor outline the thrilling experiences you're about to have in their courses, you're engaging in perception—the basic set of front-end processes through which you organize and interpret incoming information. It would also be nice to have an information buffer to hold information to which you're not really attending, just long enough to determine whether it's some juicy gossip that seems worthwhile. This information buffer is sensory memory.

Attention.   Should you drift off in one of your classes, you may hear your professor bellow "Pay attention!" Attention is the set of processes through which you focus on

Sitting through the first day of class evokes a host of cognitive processes.

incoming information. Your ability to attend is flexible—you can divert your attention to that juicy gossip being discussed behind you. But it's also limited—if you shift your attention, you're not likely to remember much of what the professor has said.

Working Memory.   It's not enough to simply "zero in" on what the professor is saying at any given moment in time. In order to fully process and understand the facts and figures being discussed in class, you've got to perform a sort of mental juggling act. As the material is being presented, you've got to repeat it to yourself and/or jot it down in your notes. The on-line processor that makes this possible is working memory.

Pattern Recognition and Concept Representation.   "Be sure and read your syllabus carefully!" The words ring out in every college classroom on the first day. Everyone knows what this means, though they don't always follow the advice! Heeding this piece of sage wisdom requires that you *recognize* seven different letter *patterns* (the seven words in the instructions above) and that you do so instantly, without thinking about it. This requires (1) that patterns such as s-y-l-l-a-b-u-s are recognized as familiar, and (2) that encountering them leads to the activation of some concept in memory.

Long-Term Memory.   Let's go back to your juggling act. It's not over when the class winds to a close. When the class is finished, you must catch the balls you're juggling and put them in your pocket until the next juggling act. In cognitive psychology lingo, you have to store the information that you're taking in for later use. Taking notes helps serve this purpose—that is, if you take the note-taking process seriously and think about the concepts as you are writing them down. Through conscientious note taking, you start to commit information to long-term memory. In our discussion of memory, we'll examine some of the processes involved in remembering, at the point both where you are studying information and when you're trying to retrieve it.

Memory Distortion.   Memory's not perfect; far from it. It serves us well most of the time, but there are systematic ways in which it goes wrong. We're sure you've had the exasperating experience of completely blanking on or misremembering information that you thought you knew—especially on tests. We'll discuss some of the processes involved in forgetting and memory distortion.

Autobiographical Memory.   Chances are good that the first day of classes will be one of the better-remembered days of your entire school year. You can probably think of some reasons for this: you meet new professors, hear about new classes, get reacquainted with old friends, and make new ones. Research on how we remember our personal past has exploded, and the study of autobiographical memory has become one of the more dynamic and interesting topics within the field.

Knowledge Representation.   It is truly stunning how much you know. Think about it. You no doubt recognized and understood just about every word that every professor said in class. These words and concepts are just some of the pieces of knowledge that you possess. Cognitive psychologists would term these *mental representations*. Just like a jpg file of your family pet is a *representation* of your pet, mental representations are representations of your stored knowledge, and you access them when necessary. How is general knowledge like this stored and retrieved?

Language.   Your seamless processing of all the information from your first day is a testament to your skill in yet another important set of cognitive processes—those involved in the use of language. As the professor speaks, your implicit knowledge of and practice with sentence structure allows you to follow along just fine. What would happen if the professor came into class and said, "Class, and textbook turn your get page out OK to 28"? How about, "Pretty textbooks fly to the bookstore"? No doubt you'd be calling campus security. Your implicit knowledge of syntax (word arrangement rules) and semantics (rules for expressing meaning) allows you to comprehend instantly what makes sense and what doesn't. Your knowledge of language also allows you to ask questions that professors just love to hear, like "Do we have to know this?" or "Will this be on the test?"

Problem Solving.   After you've been to all of your classes, you've got another juggling act to perform. Somehow, you're going to have to fit studying for 15 to 20 tests, writing for 15 to 20 papers, and attending class for about 150 one-hour periods all into the space of 14 or so weeks. And you've got to do it well. This is a fairly hefty example of problem solving. Problem solving involves operating within constraints (such as time) and reaching a goal from a starting state that is nowhere near that goal.

Decision Making.   You're going to have to make many decisions throughout the semester. How much time should I devote to studying for each of my classes? If I miss class once in a while, am I going to pay for it in my final grade? (Do you really need an answer to that one?) The process through which you arrive at decisions involves a complex interplay among other cognitive processes such as attention, memory, and knowledge retrieval.

Stop *and* Think!   **THINKING ABOUT THOUGHT PROCESSES**

Look at the list of cognitive processes that begins on page 2. You engage in all of these in some manner every day. Come up with an example of each of these from your daily life.

An Interdisciplinary Perspective

Not only is cognitive psychology central to everything we do in our day-to-day lives, it is also central to psychology's quest to understand how people think and act. As noted above in the definition of psychology, cognition comprises half of the subject matter! Because cognition is so fundamental to understanding how humans "tick," it is crucial to psychology's other subdisciplines. Social psychologists investigate the mental processes involved in thinking about others. Clinical psychologists investigate the role that mental processes play in psychopathology. Developmental psychologists are interested in the ways that cognitive processes change throughout the lifespan. Neuropsychologists are interested in the association between mental processing and brain activity. Industrial/organizational psychologists are interested in how cognitive processes such as remembering and decision making play out in the workplace. Understanding the fundamental mechanisms of human cognition provides critical insights into the other subdisciplines that define psychology.

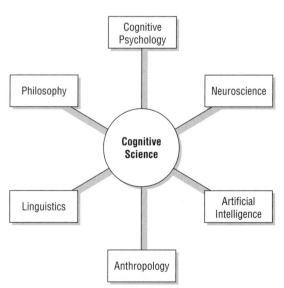

The study of cognition also lends insights beyond psychology. Cognitive psychology is a key player within the interdisciplinary field of study termed cognitive science. **Cognitive science,** simply defined, is an interdisciplinary effort to understand the mind. It includes a number of (seemingly disparate) disciplines, five of them plus cognitive psychology lying at its "core" (Gardner, 1985). Philosophy, the first discipline to systematically examine the mind, helps to formulate and examine the fundamental questions that define the field. Neuroscience attempts to specify the relationship between mind and brain. Artificial intelligence addresses issues of mind by modeling human thought processes with computer hardware and software. The field of linguistics investigates the structure of language and the specifics of language use and what they tell us about the mind. Anthropology explores the mind through quite a different lens—the lens of culture. How do our physical and cultural surroundings impact thinking? Since each of these disciplinary approaches is reflected to some degree in the work of cognitive psychologists, you'll be getting a taste of most of these disciplines.

S T O P *and* R E V I E W !

1. Define cognitive psychology.
2. Identify the major topics covered by cognitive psychologists.
3. True or false? Cognitive science is a specific field within cognitive psychology.
4. Identify the disciplines that comprise "cognitive science."

➤ Cognitive psychology can be defined as the scientific study of mental processes.

➤ Cognitive psychologists study a wide range of abilities—perception, sensory memory, attention, working memory, pattern recognition, concept representation, long-term memory, knowledge representation, language, problem solving, and decision making.

➤ Cognitive psychology lies at the core of an interdisciplinary approach termed *cognitive science.*

➤ Cognitive science attempts to bring together research from the fields of philosophy, neuroscience, artificial intelligence, linguistics, and anthropology in an effort to understand the mind.

Psychology B. C.
(*Before Cognitive* psychology)

As pioneering cognitive psychologist Hermann Ebbinghaus observed, psychology has a long past but a short history. Thinking has long been a topic of interest—no doubt since we, as humans, started thinking. It shouldn't be a surprise that philosophy is generally considered to be the primary disciplinary "parent" of psychology, particularly cognitive psychology. Ancient philosophers such as Aristotle were interested in the mechanics of mind. He (and others) sought to establish **laws of association** to explain why the activation of some concepts seems to automatically lead to the activation of others. Consider a word association task: What is the first word that pops to mind when we say "black"? How about "chair"? We'd be willing to bet that you thought of the concepts "white" and "table." Aristotle assumed, as do modern-day cognitive psychologists, that mental processes are lawful and predictable.

Although philosophers have long been interested in the mind, the subject was not thoroughly examined with the scientific method of controlled observation until the 1800s.

At this point a second disciplinary "parent" of psychology, physiology, had begun to establish itself as a legitimate area of scientific inquiry. Physiologists looked at the body as a sort of machine and employed scientific methods to determine its inner workings. How do nerve impulses travel? How does information from the outside world enter into our sensory systems? How is this information interpreted? These latter two questions bring physiology right to the doorstep of psychology because they are questions of human experience and thinking. Once physiologists started applying their methods to these types of questions, a complete science of mind was inevitable.

Stop and Think!

COMPARING COGNITIVE PSYCHOLOGY TO ITS FORERUNNERS

Philosophy and physiology are generally recognized as the parent disciplines of psychology.

- Do you consider cognitive psychology to be more like philosophy or more like physiology?
- Why do you think so?
- What are some of their similarities and differences?

Early Psychophysics

The scientific study of mind can be traced back to a number of origins, none more important than the work of early psychophysicists. **Psychophysics** refers to the study of the relationship between the physical properties of a stimulus and the properties taken on when the stimulus is filtered through subjective experience. For instance, suppose we see two lights in succession. The first light is double the luminance of the second light. Does the first light *seem* twice as *bright*? Note that while luminance is a physical measure of light intensity, *seem* is a subjective term and *brightness* is a psychological dimension, not a physical one.

Mapping out these sorts of relationships between the physical and the psychological was a primary concern of early psychophysicists such as Gustav Fechner (1801–1878).

Surrounding context plays an important role in determining what stimuli are perceivable.

One of Fechner's major contributions was his quantification of the relationship between incoming stimuli and corresponding perceptions. Fechner demonstrated that there is not a one-to-one relationship between changes in the physical intensity of a stimulus and changes in its *psychological* (or perceived) intensity. Think about it. If someone snaps their fingers at a rock concert, no one would notice. If somebody snaps their fingers in a quiet room, you notice it easily. Clearly, there is some process of translation occurring between the presentation of the physical stimulus and the actual experience of that stimulus.

Hermann von Helmholtz (1821–1894) influenced the newly developing science of mind primarily through his work on visual perception, which Helmholtz argued involved a process of **unconscious inference.** An inference is a conclusion that we arrive at through some type of evidence. According to Helmholtz, our visual systems are constantly making inferences about the external world based on the information gathered as well as the "evidence" of previous experience. Consider what happens when Vince picks up his alarm clock and holds it close to his face so that he can read it: the image picked up by the retina in the back of his eye gets larger as the clock moves closer. Does Vince recoil in horror at the sight of a giant clock? Of course not. Based on his life experiences, he has made an unconscious inference that alarm clocks (and other objects) do not spontaneously increase in size. Therefore, he knows that the clock is closer, not larger. Three important principles are highlighted by Helmholtz's concept of unconscious inferences. First, the perceiver plays an interpretive role in what is perceived; perception is not just a passive process of registering incoming physical energy. Second, perceptual and cognitive processes are influenced by previous experience. Third, perceptual and cognitive processes often occur outside of conscious awareness (as implied in the term *unconscious inference*).

Giant clock?

Stop *and* **Think!**

COGNITIVE PROCESSES—CONSCIOUS OR UNCONSCIOUS?

In proposing the concept of unconscious inference, Helmholtz helped make it clear that many cognitive processes occur outside of conscious awareness. Look again at the list of cognitive processes that begins on page 2. Rate each process on the following continuum and explain your rating.

1◄——— 2——— 3——— 4 ——►5
mostly unconscious   mostly conscious

It's not difficult to see why the work of early psychophysicists provided an important step toward a science of cognition. Psychophysicists were among the first to apply the scientific method to bridge the physical and the mental. Both psychophysicists and cognitive psychologists are interested in how stimulation and information in the outside world are linked with internal processes, representations, and conscious experience.

While psychophysicists tend to focus on the early stages of how we process information, cognitive psychologists focus on *all* stages of information processing. Let's turn our attention back to Vince. Psychophysicists might be interested in how bright the LED readout on the clock needs to be for Vince to read it, or on how loud the alarm has to be for him to hear it, or on whether Vince thinks the light is as bright as the alarm is loud—in other words, Vince's psychological interpretation of physical experiences. A cognitive psychologist, on the other hand, would be interested in these processes and more. How does Vince focus his attention on the radio? How does he recognize and understand the words coming from it? What are the processes that may lead him to decide to take the day off?

Structuralism: The Contents of Mental Experience

Although psychophysics may have helped lay the foundation, modern experimental psychology is generally traced back to1879, when Wilhelm Wundt (1832–1920) established the first psychological laboratory at the University of Leipzig in Germany. Wundt believed that a science of psychology should be concerned with how people consciously experience the world. Given that psychology was a fledgling scientific enterprise, some thought it wise to model psychology after a well-established science—chemistry. Simple chemical elements combine to form more complex compounds. The structuralists, as they would later be dubbed, wondered whether this approach could be applied to conscious experience. Perhaps the complexities of how we experience everyday events could be broken down into distinct and basic elements of consciousness. According to the structuralists, these elements could likely be classified into three broad categories: sensations (the basic sensory dimensions that we encode from a stimulus), feelings (emotions aroused by a stimulus), and images (purely mental impressions that seem sensory in nature).

Consider an example. Wundt and his colleagues might characterize looking at a sunrise as a complex experience made up of simpler ones. These would include simple sensations (e.g., warmth on the skin), simple images (e.g., hearing bird calls), and simple feelings (e.g., contentment). Wundt attempted to identify these simple components of complex experience through the use of **introspection,** a procedure that requires participants to provide a rigorous, unbiased report of every element of the conscious experience that accompanies the presentation of some stimulus (e.g., the presentation of a tone). It was hoped that applying this method of thorough, objective, journalistic analysis to a wide range of everyday experiences would yield the elemental sensations, images, and feelings that combine to produce everyday consciousness. One of Wundt's students, Edward Titchener (1867–1927), popularized this approach in the United States, terming it **structuralism.** While this early approach to the study of psychology may seem simplistic at best, you must remember the context in which it emerged. Psychology was new and trying to establish itself as a scientific discipline, so it made sense to emulate the approach used by another science.

Functionalism: The Functions of Mental Experience

At about the same time that structuralists were attempting to distill consciousness into its basic elements, a decidedly different approach was evolving. William James (1842–1910) and others were highly critical of the structuralist approach (see Kimble, 1985), contending that their atomistic approach to consciousness was wrong-headed. James invoked the well-known phrase *stream of consciousness* to capture the continuous, ever-changing nature of our experience. Analyzing it at any discrete point in time (as the structuralists did with introspection) violates its very nature. A related point is that the mere act of scrutinizing and analyzing one's conscious experience changes the experience. You're no longer studying consciousness.

Rather than using introspection to provide moment-to-moment snapshots of what was currently in mind, James thought psychology should devote itself to figuring out the *functions* of the mind—what it does in everyday life (hence the name given to this approach—**functionalism**). While a structuralist would attempt to determine the basic images, feelings, and sensations that comprise the conscious experience of being angry, a functionalist would study the emotion of anger by trying to determine the purpose or function of being angry. Given its emphasis on mental processing rather than mental structure, functionalism ultimately had a more profound influence on cognitive psychology than did structuralism. Indeed, the table of contents of James's famous text *Principles of Psychology* reads like a "what's what" of the study of behavior and cognition, including chapters on attention, remembering, emotions, and thinking.

RECURRING RESEARCH THEME
Cognition and Consciousness

The mystery of *consciousness,* or the subjective feelings and awareness that accompany every minute of our waking life, has long confounded philosophers, physiologists, and psychologists alike. What is the role of consciousness in everyday life? How can consciousness be explained physiologically? What is the relationship between cognition and consciousness? Psychologists have been particularly interested in consciousness, given its centrality in our moment-to-moment experience. As you've just seen, consciousness was a topic of primary interest for the first psychologists. To what degree does cognition imply, or require, consciousness? How do different states and levels of consciousness relate to our cognitive processing? Starting with Chapter 3, each chapter will present a detailed discussion of a research investigation that focuses on an investigation of cognitive processing that relates to these questions of consciousness.

Behaviorism: The Rejection of Mental Experience

While the structuralists and functionalists were debating the proper focus of a scientific study of consciousness, a storm was brewing. The study of the mind and conscious experience was entering what might be termed a sort of "dark age." Psychologist John B. Watson (1878–1958), intensely dissatisfied with psychology's lack of progress, suggested a shift that he believed would make the fledgling enterprise of psychology truly scientific. Watson's radical notion was the banishment of consciousness from scientific study, the hallmarks of which are observation, measurement, and repeatability. The study of conscious experience lends itself to none of these. It cannot be reliably observed or measured, and the results of an introspective analysis cannot be reliably reproduced. But behavior can be observed, measured, and repeated; hence, it should serve as the focus of a scientific psychology. Watson's approach, termed **behaviorism,** discarded both the subject matter and the approach of the structuralists and functionalists, instead emphasizing the study of observable responses and their relation to observable stimuli. Given its emphasis on observable stimuli and responses, it makes sense that behaviorism is sometimes referred to as **S-R psychology.** According to behaviorists, psychology should dedicate itself to discovering these S-R connections. Between stimulus and response is a "black box" that houses consciousness. Investigation of the contents of the black box is a futile enterprise, according to the behaviorists, because the contents do not lend themselves to scientific investigation.

The behaviorists were not denying that we experience consciousness; for example, they wouldn't have a problem with acknowledging that people have a conscious experience of hunger. They simply rejected the idea that this conscious experience could be meaningfully studied, owing to its inherently subjective nature. They also gave consciousness no causal role in producing behavior; we don't eat because we *feel hungry.* Eating is an observable response that occurs in the presence of some verifiable stimulus, such as low insulin levels or a plate of fresh-out-of-the-oven cookies. The complete rejection of consciousness from scientific study was a radical move, but it struck a resounding chord. In the United States, the behaviorist approach dominated experimental psychology for the first half of the 20th century.

Stop *and* Think!   ## THINKING ABOUT BEHAVIORISM

The behaviorists believed that all behavior and action could be understood purely in terms of observable stimuli and responses. Consider each of the following everyday activities:

hanging out with a friend

getting lunch

feeling nervous over an upcoming test

screaming for your team at a football game

going out to see the latest gross-out comedy film

working a crossword puzzle

telling a joke

going for a half-hour jog

For each activity, apply an S-R analysis by answering the following questions for each:

What would fit into the S box?

What would fit into the R box?

What would fit into the "black box" (that behaviorists would want to ignore)?

- Did you have any difficulties explaining these behaviors solely in terms of the S's and R's?
- If so, what were the difficulties?
- Which of the activities are most difficult to account for with an S-R view? (In other words, which activities involve a great deal of activity in the black box?)
- Does the S-R view of these activities offer any advantages?

Laying the Foundation for Cognitive Psychology

The rejection of consciousness as a topic for scientific study was not without good intent. The behaviorists wanted to establish psychology as a rigorous experimental science alongside other disciplines more readily acknowledged as "scientific," such as biology and chemistry. Their sincere belief was that the study of mind was never going to get us there. But scientists throughout the short history of psychology have demonstrated time and time again that rigorous observation and measurement of mental processes is possible. In fact, even before the behaviorists "threw down the gauntlet" to scientists interested in human behavior, Hermann Ebbinghaus was quietly conducting a strikingly methodical and precise series of experiments on remembering.

Ebbinghaus: Pioneering Experiments on Memory.   In the late 1800s, Ebbinghaus embarked on an investigation of his own memory—an investigation that demonstrated convincingly that complex mental processes could be submitted to experimental test. Ebbinghaus was a truly dedicated researcher; he served as his only participant, tirelessly testing and retesting his own memory under rigorously controlled conditions of presentation and testing. He did this by memorizing list after list of nonsense syllables—letter strings that do not form words (e.g., DBJ). For a given list, he would record the number of study trials it took to learn the list to perfection. Then, after varying periods of time, he would attempt to relearn the list to perfection again. As you might imagine, it took him fewer trials to relearn lists that he had memorized previously. Ebbinghaus coined the term **savings** to refer to this reduction in the number of trials it took to relearn a list. His previous experience in perfectly learning the material *saved* him some trials the second time he tried to learn it. Think about it: if you've already learned to do something well and then take some time off, you're not going to have to start from scratch when you attempt to redo or relearn the task.

Using the method of savings, Ebbinghaus revealed a number of fundamental principles of memory. He found that recall was more difficult as list length increased, a harbinger of later research that would investigate the limited nature of working memory. He found that his retention increased with the frequency of repetitions (if you study more, you'll remember more). And he captured the pattern of forgetting over time in what has been termed the **forgetting curve,** which relates the amount recalled to the time that has elapsed since study. Forgetting occurs rapidly early in the retention interval, then slows down considerably. This pattern has been replicated in countless investigations of memory, but as you'll read later, the precise function that relates what we remember and forget to the passage of time depends on myriad variables.

Ebbinghaus's research was significant for a number of reasons. First, it demonstrated that precise and well-controlled experimental methods could be applied to study complex mental processes, setting the stage for the experimental approach to cognition that was to follow. Second, it provided a well-conceived research paradigm for the study of verbal learning and memory that inspired a legion of later researchers. Finally, as noted above, it established a number of core principles of memory function that are still being replicated and extended in laboratory research today.

Bartlett's Memory Research.   Sir Frederick Bartlett objected to the use of tightly controlled laboratory procedures for revealing memory function. He believed that if psychological research was to be generalizable, it should be as naturalistic as possible. Following this principle, his procedure involved the presentation of materials that were meaningful rather than nonsensical. In assessing participants' memory for stories and folk tales, Bartlett (1932) discovered a fair amount of reconstruction. Some details were left out of the story; other details were inserted. Based on his results, Bartlett characterized memory as a reconstructive process rather than a reproductive one. This reconstruction was guided by what Bartlett termed *schemata,* generalized knowledge structures about events and situations that are constructed based on past experience.

Note that in contrast to the behaviorist explanations of the day, Bartlett was postulating that mental structures (schemata) exerted a causal influence over behavior. Bartlett's work was distinctive and important in a couple of ways. First, it provided an alternative to the mechanistic, S-R view of remembering as a group of simple verbal associations. Second, it showed incredible prescience, foreshadowing some major concerns that have taken center stage in present-day cognitive psychology—the reconstructive nature of memory. A social anthropologist at heart, Bartlett was interested in remembering as a dynamic, social process that helps us make sense of our daily lives. His classic book was titled *Remembering: A Study in Experimental and Social Psychology* (emphasis added). Cognitive psychology's current emphasis on the study of cognition within natural contexts owes much to Bartlett's early investigations.

It's interesting to note the strong contrast between the methods used by Ebbinghaus and Bartlett to study remembering. Ebbinghaus's method involved the precisely controlled presentation and remembering of lists of nonsense syllables, while Bartlett's method (though somewhat controlled) left more to chance, as participants were exposed to stories and asked to remember them. The tension between precise control and realism in procedures and materials will be discussed in Chapter 2.

Stop and Think! **LABORATORY AND ECOLOGICAL APPROACHES TO COGNITION**

Look at the list of cognitive processes that begins on page 2 (again!). For each process, give a brief description of how you would study it

- in the laboratory (with experimental control)
- in the real world (with high ecological validity)

Gestalt Psychology. The Gestalt perspective in psychology, developed in Germany and very active in the first half of the last century, emphasized the role that organizational processes play in perception and problem solving. Roughly translated, the German word *gestalt* means something like *configuration.* Psychologists who adopted the **Gestalt approach** were interested in the organizational principles that guide mental processing. So a Gestalt psychologist would be interested in investigating the way that you organize visual stimuli in your environment—do you see the items in Figure 1.1 as rows or columns of Xs? The Gestaltists believed that the answer to this question revealed something fundamental about visual perception.

X X X X X
X X X X X
X X X X X

Figure 1.1 Three rows or five columns?

The spirit of the Gestalt approach is captured well by their oft-cited credo "The whole is different than the sum of its parts." One cannot capture the essence of conscious experience by analyzing it into its elements, as the structuralists attempted to do. Experience is more than just a summary of elementary sensations, images, and feelings. When combined in a particular way, these elements of experience form a particular gestalt, or whole. And one cannot understand human experience and behavior by eliminating all talk of conscious experience, as the behaviorists attempted to do. Current cognitive psychology embodies the spirit of the Gestalt view by placing the mind center stage and viewing it as an active processor of information. In addition, the Gestalt approach still has a strong influence on how we view particular cognitive processes, most notably, perception and problem solving, as we'll see in Chapters 3 and 12.

STOP *and* REVIEW!

1. True or false? Philosophy provided the content of cognitive psychology, while physiology provided the method used by cognitive psychology.
2. True or false? Functionalism ultimately had a greater influence on psychology than did structuralism.
3. The behaviorist approach in psychology
   a. was theoretically aligned with Gestalt psychology
   b. followed the assumptions and methods established by structuralists and functionalists
   c. dominated psychology for decades
   d. focused on the role of mind in behavior
4. What are the basic ideas of Ebbinghaus, Bartlett, and the Gestalt approach to psychology?

➤ The scientific study of thinking has its roots in philosophy, which provides the basic questions that empirical research in cognition attempts to answer. The science of physiology provided a basic method for the investigation of perceptual processes. Modern attempts to understand the mind can be traced to the psychophysicists, who studied the relationship between physical stimulation and psychological experience.

➤ Psychology was established in 1879, when the structuralists began to formally investigate the elements of conscious experience. Their primary method was introspection, an intensive analysis of the contents (images, feelings, and sensations) of one's own consciousness. The functionalists were concerned with specifying the functions of consciousness, rather than its structure, and ultimately had a much larger impact on the field.

➤ Behaviorists favored the elimination of consciousness as a topic of study, given its subjective nature. Behaviorists believed a science of psychology should focus on observables like behavior. Behaviorism is sometimes referred to as S-R psychology, because of its emphasis on the analysis of observable stimuli and responses and their relation to one another.

➤ Ebbinghaus demonstrated that rigorous experimental work on cognition was possible. His research on memory for nonsense syllables established a number of key principles of memory that are still recognized today. Bartlett investigated memory for more realistic materials and, based on his results, argued that memory involves processes of reconstruction. Gestalt psychologists were interested in the organizational tendencies of the mind and had a significant influence on views of perception and problem solving.

The Emergence of Cognitive Psychology

Although behaviorism had struck a chord, to many it rang hollow, failing to capture the richness and diversity of human behavior and creativity. The challenges to behaviorism came from outside and from within and were both empirical and theoretical. From within the behavioristic camp, some studies of animal behavior were producing results that were problematic for S-R accounts, results revealing that rats could rightfully be described as "thinking" under some circumstances. The momentum from these research challenges began to build in the 1930s, posing a threat to the behaviorist stronghold on scientific psychology. In addition, psychologists were growing increasingly frustrated with the narrowness of explanations offered within the behaviorist paradigm, arguing that such explanations captured virtually nothing of what human beings do on a day-to-day basis, such as our use of language. Another major influence on the emergence of cognitive psychology was the development of new technologies like calculators, computers, and communication systems. These developments revolutionized how humans viewed machines and their capabilities. This, in turn, revolutionized the way humans viewed *themselves* and *their* capabilities.

S-R Explanations: *Seriously wRong?*

Failure to Account for Data.   As we've seen, behaviorists viewed reference to mental states or mental representations as useless, preferring to focus only on behavior, and using only the concepts of stimuli, responses, and the associations between them. Consider the following example. Suppose we have a rat that we place in a T-maze; the rat has to learn to run down the straightaway and choose the side with food in it. Over a series of trials, what do you suppose happens? As you might suspect, the rat starts to make the correct turn to obtain the food. Rats may not be the brightest of animals, but they can learn that simple association. A behaviorist would explain the rat's learning of the maze with three simple concepts: stimuli, responses, and reinforcement. Associations are formed between stimuli and responses, with reinforcement as the "glue" that holds the associations together. When placed in a particular *stimulus* situation (the feel and smell of a maze), the rat engages in a particular *response* (running forward in the maze). If it receives reinforcement at the end of the maze, this bonds the stimulus and the response together—an S-R association. The next time the rat is confronted with the feel and smell of the maze (the S), it will trigger the response of running (the R). Each time the rat is placed in the maze, this association plays itself out again and becomes stronger with each reinforcement. The rat runs faster. Over time, it zips down the alley and without hesitation makes the correct turn, without asking directions.

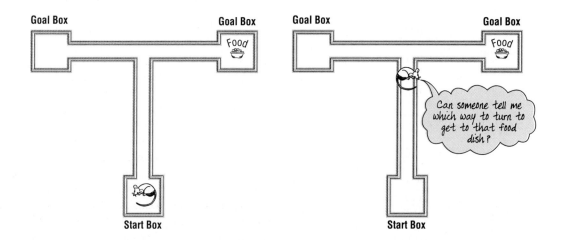

The behaviorist account of the learning process is simple and elegant and does not rely on reference to unobservable mental processes, like the rat *expecting* or *knowing* that the food is on the right. The rat doesn't "know" anything; it is simply executing a chain of S-R associations that have been built up over a series of trials. But the trouble is that there are too many scenarios in which this simple account doesn't work. Let's briefly review a few of these findings.

Learning without Responding.   According to the behaviorists, responding is absolutely essential for learning. It's the R in the S-R association link. Demonstrating that learning occurs in the absence of R would be difficult, if not impossible, to explain. A study by McNamara, Long, and Wike (1956) investigated whether learning would occur in this type of situation. Rats were tested in a T-maze, as described above. Some of the rats ran the maze themselves, eventually learning that they had to turn right to get to the food. Other rats were pushed by the experimenters down the alleyway in small carts. At the end of the runway, the experimenters turned the cart to the right and let the rat out to eat the food.

Which group of rats will know where the food is? "Isn't it obvious?" you must be thinking. They both will. They both saw the maze and saw that food was on the right. So now they *expect* the food to be on the right. But this is exactly the type of mentalistic explanation

that behaviorists rejected. Behaviorists would say only the group of rats that ran on their own would learn the correct response. Why? Because R is required for learning. The results failed to support the behaviorist prediction. When allowed to run on their own, the rats that had previously taken a ride to the food showed a preference for the right side, just like the rats that had run there on their own. Clearly, the hitchhiking rats learned—and without responding.

Learning without Reinforcement. Recall that, according to the behaviorist view, reinforcement is necessary for learning to occur; as described above, it's the "glue" that holds the S and the R together. If there is no reinforcement, stimulus and response will not be bonded, and there will be no learning. Tolman and Honzik (1930) tested this in a classic study. Over the course of two weeks, they placed three different groups of rats in a com-

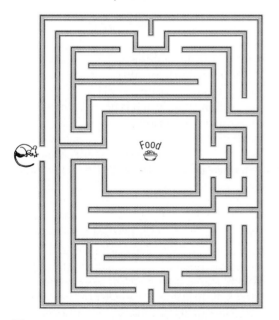

plex maze like the one in Figure 1.2 and had them explore it. One group of rats was reinforced every time they reached the goal box, starting on day 1. A second group was never rewarded. A third group was not rewarded during the first 10 days but began receiving a reward in the goal box on the 11th day.

Consider the prediction of the S-R view. The rats in group 1 should show a steady increase in running speed. The reinforcement in the goal box strengthens the response (R) of running when placed in the stimulus (S) of the maze. Group 2 rats should show no increase in running speed; they were never reinforced, so S and R were never bonded. Group 3 should look exactly like group 2 until day 11, when the rats see food in the goal box. Then, starting on day 12, group 3 rats should show the same gradual increase in running speed shown in group 1, as the goal box reinforcement starts to strengthen the S-R connection.

The findings were surprising, at least to those operating from an S-R perspective. The rats in groups 1 and 2 behaved exactly as predicted, showing

Figure 1.2 A complex garden-style maze used in some early studies of simple learning.

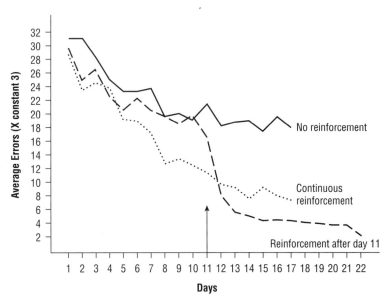

Figure 1.3 Latent learning; results from Tolman and Honzik's (1930) study. Rats who never received reinforcement until the 11th day nonetheless demonstrated that they had learned the maze. This is evident in the sharp decrease in errors immediately after reinforcement.

From Tolman, E. C., & Honzik, C. H. (1930). Introduction and removal of reward, and maze performance in rats. *University of California Publications in Psychology, 4,* 257–275.

a gradual increase in running speed and no increase in running speed, respectively. The results from group 3 proved problematic for the behaviorists. As you can see in Figure 1.3, starting on day 12, these rats ran as fast as rats in group 1. Clearly, they had been learning the maze all along, even without reinforcement. Tolman termed this phenomenon **latent learning.** This finding is difficult to handle from a behaviorist standpoint: How could learning occur if the stimulus and response were never associated? Once again, a cognitive explanation seems like a more reasonable one. The rats wandered around the maze for 11 days and picked up what Tolman (1948) termed a general "lay of the land." They were well aware of the maze layout, and once there was a reason to demonstrate what they had learned, they did.

Cognitive Maps.   In 1948, Tolman conducted a classic study that would put another fly in the behaviorists' ointment. In this experiment, rats were faced with a maze like the one pictured in Figure 1.4. There are three possible routes to the destination—three possible *responses:* path 1, path 2, and path 3. Which one would you pick, if you were hungry? The shortest one, of course, and this is what S-R theory would predict. In behaviorist terms, path 1 has the strongest S-R association because the reinforcement is obtained the most quickly and the less time that elapses between responding and reinforcement, the stronger the association. Following this logic, path 2 has the next strongest S-R association

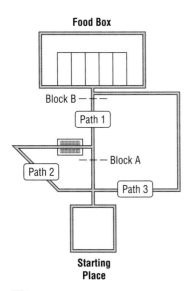

Food Box

Block B

Path 1

Path 2

Block A

Path 3

**Starting
Place**

Figure 1.4 Maze used to study latent learning. On different trials, blocks were placed at various places in the maze. Rats were able to figure out that if path 1 was blocked, path 2 must also be blocked, and therefore they should take path 3. The results suggested that the rats had stored a mental representation (i.e., a "mental map" of sorts).

From Tolman, E. C. (1948). Cognitive maps in rats and men. *Psychological Review, 55,* 189–208.

because food can be obtained quicker via this path relative to path 3. Path 3 has the weakest S-R association because taking this path would take the longest to get to the food.

The cognitive view of rat behavior in this situation is quite different. Recall Tolman's proposal that rats acquired a "lay of the land" as they explored the maze. Another way of putting this is that the rats formed a **mental map** of the maze layout and consulted it to determine which path would get them to the food most quickly. Note that this explanation is exactly the type of view that the behaviorists railed against because it appeals to the notion of mental representations (i.e., mental maps) and their influence on behavior. Behaviorists believed that behavior could be explained without any appeal to such factors.

In his study, Tolman allowed rats to freely explore the maze over a series of trials. True to S-R predictions, the rats preferred path 1, choosing it the most. Then, the investigators teased the rats by placing a block at point A. When rats ran into this block, they were forced to retreat to the choice point and go a different way. The S-R approach would predict that at this point the rats should behave according to the next-strongest S-R association and take path 2. The cognitive approach would also make this prediction, because when placed in this situation, the rats would consult their mental map and realize that path 2 was shorter.

The key condition was when a block was placed at point B. What is a rat to do? The behaviorist and cognitive predictions diverge in this case. According to the behaviorist view, the rats will take path 1, because path 1 has the strongest S-R association. When blocked, they will go back to the choice point and take path 2, which has the next-strongest S-R association. Finally, when blocked again, they should return to the choice point and choose path 3. The cognitive view gives the rats a little more credit. According to this view, the rats have a general mental map

for the entire maze arrangement; so when the rats see the block at point B, they'll realize that path 2 is also blocked. Therefore, they won't even bother with it. They'll run back to the choice point and take path 3. This is exactly what Tolman found. On the first trial with the block at point B, the rats chose path 3 over 90 percent of the time.

Because behaviorists claim that both reinforcement and responding are necessary for learning, they were bedeviled by the discovery of learning without responding and latent learning, as well as the seeming reality

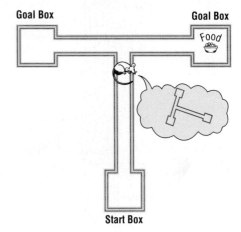

Goal Box   **Goal Box**

Food

Start Box

of mental maps. Theorists such as Clark Hull (1943) attempted to repair the damage done to behaviorist theory by postulating additional mechanisms and processes, but these changes (postulating unseen mechanisms) brought S-R theory perilously close to cognitive theory. Change was afoot: the failure of S-R theory was helping to set the stage for the new science of mind.

Lashley Lashes Out.   As the middle of the 20th century approached, the theoretical tide was shifting away from behavioristic explanations of action. In 1948, a group of scientists convened at the Hixon Symposium in what was to be a seminal event for the emergence of a scientific study of mind. As described by Gardner (1985), this conference featured a number of papers that championed a new approach to studying mind and brain and cast severe doubt on behaviorism's rigidity. One of the most devastating blows was dealt by Karl Lashley, who argued that any science of human behavior must be able to explain forms both simple (rats running in a T-maze) and complex (a human playing the piano). Complex behaviors, Lashley argued, could not possibly play out via a series of S-R connections, as the behaviorists claimed. Consider Jerry Lee Lewis playing "Whole Lotta Shakin' Goin' On," a breathlessly fast song. According to the behaviorists, the performance of this song can be explained through S-R connections. Jerry Lee's finger movements are the *responses* that are connected to the *stimuli* (the piano and the keys) by some type of *reinforcement* (be it audience applause, the sound of the music, or something else). The problem is, the sequence of movements involved in such a performance play out with such speed that there is no conceivable way that a chain of S-R connections could be the explanation. Complex behaviors like this need to be planned out and organized in advance, according to Lashley. Any complete science of behavior should have to address the question of internal mental plans for action. It was becoming more and more apparent that the banishment of mental representations from scientific explanations of behavior was threatening to lead psychology to a dead end.

Skilled performance: Amenable to an S-R analysis?

Chomsky's Challenge.   Challenges to standard behaviorist explanations came not only from inside the domain of animal learning research, but from disciplines outside of psychology, such as linguistics. Remember that behaviorism offered a general explanation of all behavior, animal and human. Indeed, renowned behaviorist B. F. Skinner termed language *verbal behavior* and applied an S-R analysis to the acquisition of language, arguing that even complex abilities like language could be captured in purely S-R terms. Skinner viewed language as the acquisition of a set of responses, explainable through the principles of reinforcement. Linguist Noam Chomsky (1959) wrote a scathing review of Skinner's analysis in what Leahey (1992) calls "perhaps the single most influential psychological paper published since Watson's behaviorist manifesto of 1913." In his review, Chomsky completely rejected the S-R view of language, characterizing it as more vague and unscientific than the very cognitive explanations that Skinner himself criticized (Lachman, Lachman, & Butterfield, 1979).

Behaviorists explained language, as they did all human behavior, in terms of stimulus, response, and reinforcement. When little two-year-old Jimmy drinks his favorite drink, looks up at Mommy, and happily says "Chocolate!" his mother says enthusiastically, "That's *right*, Jimmy!" Skinner applied a simple S-R account to such scenarios. The stimulus is the beverage Jimmy is drinking, the response is "Chocolate!" and the reinforcement is Mommy's smile and exclamation that solidifies the bond between the stimulus and the response. In Skinnerian terms, the *response* "Chocolate" comes under control of the *stimulus* of a glass of chocolate milk.

Chomsky challenged this conceptualization, pointing out gaping holes in Skinner's account. He argued that the concept of "stimulus control" has no meaning in language. Consider an example. If we hand you a glass filled with a brown-colored bubbling liquid (the stimulus), you could respond by saying "Coke?" or "cold" or "tasty." No matter what you said, a behaviorist would say that your response was elicited by some stimulus property, but there would be no way of predicting *which* stimulus property. Skinner would just say that whatever response you gave was elicited by a stimulus property. Chomsky pointed out that this explanation is no explanation at all. The term *stimulus* might mean something when a rat runs in a maze, but it loses virtually all meaning when applied to the subtleties and complexities of language.

Consider the following sentence: *After the storm, the sun came out, and the leprechaun started searching for the gold.* We just created this sentence. We've never heard it before. We've never been reinforced for saying it or writing it. It seems kind of silly to say that the *response* of typing it came about because of the *stimulus* of the laptop computer. The behaviorists really have no satisfactory explanation for how this sentence was created. They also have no explanation for the wonder of sentence comprehension—the process by which you understood the sentence and probably inferred that the leprechaun would first need to find a rainbow or his search would be unsuccessful. The term *reinforcement* doesn't hold up very well either. It's not really apparent what the reinforcement is for speaking. What's reinforcing about a person talking to themselves as they read or a child talking to one of her dolls? Skinner's explanation was *automatic self-reinforcement;* but once again, if such a slippery concept is allowed as an explanation of language, then we really have no explanation at all. Chomsky argued that Skinner's account of language learning was nothing more than a fuzzy, metaphorical description of language learning that happened to sound vaguely scientific.

Chomsky's critique of Skinner was so devastating that it was met by silence from the behaviorists for over a decade (Lachman, Lachman, & Butterfield, 1979); they simply didn't have an answer for it. The basic premise of Chomsky's account was that the productivity and novelty observed in language use can only be explained by appealing to mental representations—"rules in the head" that allow a person to produce and comprehend language. As you'll see throughout the text, the concept of mental representation is central to the study of cognition, and Chomsky deserves much of the credit for legitimizing it.

The movement toward a new science of mind now had undeniable momentum. Conceptually, behaviorism was failing as a satisfactory explanation of behavior. The issues discussed in the preceding sections were all converging on a single, very important point that lies at the heart of cognitive psychology—any satisfactory account of behavior must make reference to mental processes and mental representations. The time was right for a new approach to the study of mind to emerge. Behaviorism, the dominant explanatory paradigm, was failing. Around the same time that behaviorism was faltering, emerging technologies, such as communication systems and computers, provided useful models for describing the process of thinking and investigating its components.

Technological Influences

Communications Engineering.   Communication devices such as televisions, radios, and cell phones are all examples of information transmission systems. In 1948, Bell Telephone mathematician Claude Shannon developed a general theory of how such systems work. According to Shannon, any communications system has several key components, including an information source, a transmitter, a channel through which a message is transmitted, and a receiver. An effective communications system will transmit information with as much fidelity as possible, minimizing distortion and the effects of outside interference, or "noise." These issues are obviously of interest to engineers working with communications systems. But this description of a communications system is also a fairly good model of how humans process information. Consider Vince as he listens to his radio after waking up, taking in the weather report on the morning radio. The DJ is the information source, the radio is the transmitter; Vince is listening to the message via his auditory channel and receives the message, which he then interprets. The noise in the system could be static on the radio or the sound of a snowplow on the street outside of Vince's window. Shannon's concept of a communications system provided a fruitful metaphor for considering how human thought processes might work and suggested ways they might be analyzed and investigated.

Computer Science.   A second technological advance that had a dramatic impact on the newly developing science of mind was the development of the computer. It became apparent that machines could be programmed to perform some of the intelligent functions thought to be the exclusive province of humans. Simply put, computers could, in a sense, "think." It wasn't long before the analogy was more actively pursued. Could the way computers "think" be similar to the way humans think? After all, like communications systems, the computer provides a good descriptive model of how the mind might work. Computers handle information in three basic stages: input, some type of processing, and output. Humans can be thought of in exactly the same way. We take in information through our sensory systems, process it in some way, and respond to it in some way. A promising direction for a science of mind might be to specify the mechanisms whereby humans process data and how the data are stored, retrieved, and used. As you'll see, cognitive psychology research has these basic aims.

The computer has been a rich metaphor for conceptualizing mental processing.

Stop and Think! CONSIDERING COGNITION'S HISTORICAL INFLUENCES

Look over the developments that led to the decline of behaviorism and the ascendance of cognitive psychology and think about their relative importance. Provide a ranking of the following developments, from most important to least important, and explain your ranking.

Lashley's argument   learning-without-reinforcement study
Chomsky's argument   learning-without-responding study
cognitive map study   advances in communications engineering

STOP and REVIEW!

1. True or false? Research has shown that learning can occur without responding.
2. Explain Chomsky's objection to the behaviorist account of language learning.
3. True or false? Lashley argued that many behaviors are carried out too slowly for an S-R explanation to be correct.
4. Describe the ways in which technology was instrumental in the development of cognitive psychology.

➤ According to behaviorism, learning requires both a response and a reinforcement. Contrary to this view, research indicated that rats were capable of learning in the absence of reinforcement and in the absence of a response, suggesting that behavior is guided by mental representations like maps and expectations.

➤ Chomsky sharply criticized Skinner's simplistic S-R view of learning language, citing the tremendous novelty and generativity of language.

➤ Lashley pointed out the inadequacy of the behaviorist approach in explaining rapid behavioral sequences, like those involved in playing the piano.

➤ The development of new technologies such as computers and communication systems provided new models of how the mind might work and helped inspire the new science of cognition.

Psychology A. D.
(*A*fter the *D*ecline of behaviorism)

By the mid 1950s, cognitive psychology was well on its way to establishing itself as a legitimate paradigm within psychology. The failure of the S-R approach, coupled with the promise and excitement generated by new theoretical approaches and new technologies, fueled what some have termed the *cognitive revolution.* One of cognitive psychology's pioneers, George Miller (cited in Gardner, 1985), fixed the birthdate of cognitive psychology as September 11, 1956. On this date, psychologists interested in the study of mind gathered at the Massachusetts Institute of Technology for the "Symposium on Information Theory." As outlined by Gardner (1985), this conference featured a number of seminal papers that employed the new approach to mind. Chomsky presented his newly developed theory of language; computer scientists Allen Newell and Herbert Simon presented a paper detailing their "Logic Theory Machine"—a complete theorem proof carried out by a computing machine; George Miller presented his now-classic view of short-term memory as a limited information-processing mechanism that could hold approximately 7 ± 2 items. Clearly, times had changed.

Information Processing: A Computer Metaphor for Cognition

As cognitive psychology evolved, the **information-processing model** emerged as the preeminent paradigm in cognitive psychology. This model uses the computer as a model for human cognition and has dominated theory and research in cognitive psychology for its first five decades. Let's consider the similarities between humans and computers in more depth and, in so doing, review the basic assumptions of the information-processing approach. Lachman, Lachman, and Butterfield (1979), in a classic investigation of the information-processing metaphor, outlined a number of parallels between computer processes and human mental processes. First, both computers and humans are general purpose information processors. Both can perform a wide variety of different tasks based on the manipulation of internal symbols and representations. Both translate incoming information into a different form—computers, from the programmer's syntax into the machine's language; humans, from some sensory stimulus into mental representations and processes. Both have the capacity for executing a logical decision chain, such as "If condition A is true, then take action B." And finally, both humans and computers have the capacity to store programs and instructions as well as the data with which these programs work.

Lachman, Lachman, and Butterfield (1979) identified some of the major assumptions of the information-processing approach. The first assumption is that humans are *symbol manipulators* who encode, store, retrieve, and manipulate symbolic data stored in memory. Flowing from this is the idea of *representation;* the data of the human information-processing system consist of representations that correspond to information from the environment (e.g., objects and events) and processes (e.g., remembering and problem solving). Another assumption is that human thought is best characterized as a *system* of interrelated capacities and processes that all affect the other. The components cannot be fully understood in isolation from one another. This view also assumes that humans are active and creative information scanners and seekers; we don't just passively react to the environment. This idea contrasts powerfully with the behaviorist approach, which considers humans as passive responders waiting for the environment to elicit responses. According to the information-processing approach, thinking is a step-by-step process in which the products of a given stage serve as the input for the next stage, and so on. Each of these processes takes time and can be examined separately, to some extent. For example, we can attempt to isolate processes such as encoding, processing, and retrieval and estimate their duration. This assumption paved the way for using reaction time as a way to measure mental processing, something we will discuss in Chapter 2.

Stop *and* Think! | ## CONSTRUCT YOUR OWN INFORMATION-PROCESSING DIAGRAMS

As discussed in the chapter, you're constantly engaged in cognitive processing. According to the information-processing approach to cognition, thinking is a step-by-step process that can be broken down into a number of simpler subcomponents. For each everyday task (listed below), construct a simple flowchart that represents the information processing involved. See if you can take each subcomponent and divide it into smaller components, trying to get to the very basic elements of cognition. Here's an example to get you started:

Component tasks of doing a crossword puzzle:

- **read clues** ⇨ **figure out words that fit clues** ⇨ **write word in puzzle**
- **read clues**
  component tasks: perceive letters ⇨ recognize words ⇨ figure out what words mean together
- **figure out words that fit clues**
  component tasks: search for word that fits ⇨ retrieve word from memory
- **write word in puzzle**
  component tasks: perceive blank spaces ⇨ write each letter in blank space

Each of these component tasks can be subdivided into further components, which in turn can be further subdivided, and so on.

Try to break down the following processes in the same way:

taking notes in class
looking up and dialing the number of a pizza joint
ordering something at a restaurant
getting dressed for the day

Connectionism: A Brain Metaphor for Cognition

One might say that the information-processing approach would characterize the brain as the "hardware" of the human computer system and the numerous cognitive processes as the "software"; engaging in different mental operations is analogous to running different software packages. This analogy has proven to be a fairly appropriate characterization, as thousands of studies have helped to specify the "software" that is cognitive processing. However, some feel that the human-computer analogy has been taken to (perhaps beyond) the limits of its usefulness. Do humans really process information in a way similar to computers? It turns out there are some major differences between the two. The most important difference is that computers typically have some type of central processing unit that does things one at a time; that is, computers tend to operate in a serial (step-by-step) fashion. This is not how the human brain works. Investigations of the brain's basic function have failed to reveal any central processor and have made it apparent that much of the brain's functioning occurs in parallel, not serially.

Instead of a very rapid and serially operating computer, the mind seems better characterized as a set of slower computers that operate in parallel, all working on relatively specific tasks (Martindale, 1991). Computers can do things that humans find difficult (e.g., error-free calculation) and humans can do things that computers find difficult (e.g., recognizing variations in a familiar pattern). Unlike a computer, we can quickly recognize A, *A*, ᴀ, *A*, ₐ, **A**, *A* as all representing the same thing; consequently, it's clear that information is processed differently in each system. The inadequacies of the information-processing metaphor have led most psychologists to abandon it as a model for the way cognitive processes work. As you'll see throughout the text, however, this metaphor is employed as a descriptive device. Though there exist significant differences in how humans and computers process, certain similarities do remain.

In a continuing search for a good model, many cognitive psychologists have turned to structural aspects of the brain for answers to the riddle of cognition. A different model of cognitive processes has evolved and threatened to replace information processing as the dominant paradigm for exploring and explaining cognition. This approach, termed **connectionism,** uses the brain (rather than the computer) as a basis for modeling cognitive processes. Connectionist models (e.g., McClelland & Rumelhart, 1985; Rumelhart & McClelland, 1986) describe cognitive processing in terms of connections between simple units, which correspond to the basic unit of the brain, the neuron. The billions of neurons in the human brain form complex neural networks, which serve as the basis for knowledge

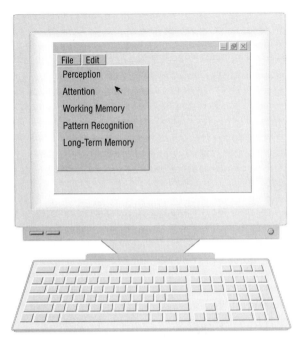

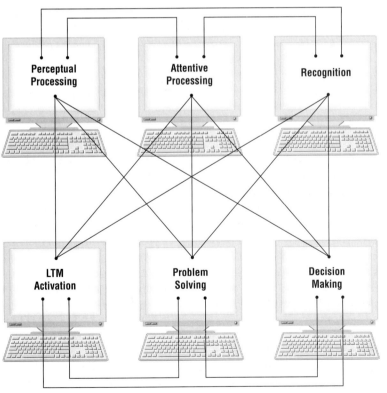

representation and cognitive processing. This model attempts to account for cognition solely in terms of the underlying "hardware" (in the computer terms used earlier) without the need to postulate extra "software" that "runs" on the hardware. In addition, psychologists (and scientists) prefer simpler theories to more complex ones, all things being equal. (The simplicity of a theory is termed parsimony.) Explaining cognition solely in terms of existing brain structure and function has a theoretically appealing simplicity—and it also makes a great deal of intuitive sense. It's not difficult to understand why these models generate a great deal of interest and enthusiasm.

Let's consider some of the key assumptions of the connectionist approach. The cognitive system (which corresponds to the brain) is made up of billions of interconnected nodes (corresponding to the billions of interconnected neurons in the brain) that come together to form complex networks. Nodes within a network can be activated, and the pattern of activation among these nodes corresponds to conscious experience. Connectionism is also referred to as **parallel distributed processing,** which lends a clue to how connectionists think mental processing takes place. Let's unpack this term and look at some basic assumptions underlying this approach. First, the approach proposes that the networks underlying cognitive processing operate largely *in parallel;* information processors throughout the brain work simultaneously on some specific component of a cognitive task.

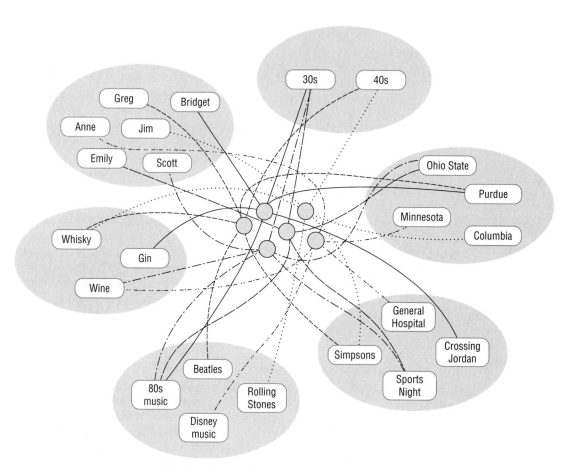

Adapted from Rumelhart, D. E., & McClelland, J. L. (1986). *Parallel distributed processing: Explorations in the microstructure of cognition.* Cambridge, MA: MIT Press. Reprinted by permission.

Second, the processing involved in a given task (e.g., retrieving a memory) does not occur in only one specific location. Rather, the networks involved in cognitive processing are *distributed* throughout the brain. This idea of parallel processing contrasts strongly with the idea of cognition as a serial (step-by-step) process, as proposed in the information-processing approach.

If cognition is characterized as the parallel activity of a complex series of networks distributed throughout the brain, you might be asking yourself "How are these networks formed?" The basic building block of these networks is a connection between two individual nodes. Once again, the dynamics of interconnection between nodes is modeled on the way neurons interact. The effect of one neuron on another may be excitatory, inhibitory, or nonexistent. So, within a neural network, nodes may have an excitatory connection (activation of one node makes activation of the other node more likely), an inhibitory connection (activation of one node makes activation of the other node less likely), or no connection (activation of one node has no effect on the other node). These connections are built up, solidified, and modified as we experience the world day to day, just as our memories, general knowledge, and skills are built up, solidified, and modified. Connectionist models postulate some type of learning rule to model this process. One intuitively sensible rule often employed is that connections between nodes are strengthened if they are activated at the same time.

Consider this simple example. Imagine that you meet Greg (one of your authors) at a party. It probably won't be more than about 15 minutes before he makes some reference to either the Simpsons ("Homer Simpson is the greatest comic creation in TV history") or the Beatles ("The Beatles are bigger than cognitive psychology"). From this encounter, you will have the beginnings of a connectionist network that corresponds to your memory of Greg—essentially, it *is* your memory of him. The nodes distributed throughout your neural network correspond to the bits of information you have about Greg and are connected one to another. There are excitatory connections between Greg's name, the Simpsons, the Beatles, and whatever other information you might pick up. Every time you meet Greg and he bores you with yet another piece of trivia about the Beatles, that particular connection gets stronger, along with any other one you encounter. When you are asked about him, all of the nodes in your network that are Greg are activated in parallel as you bring him to mind. From this simpleminded example, you can imagine how your brain might encode the thousands of memories and bits of information that you know and encounter.

Connectionist models have advanced far beyond simple accounts of how knowledge is represented. In recent years, cognitive scientists have developed connectionist models of everything from face recognition to problem solving to how we form attitudes about other people. These models are used to generate predictions, which are assessed with regard to existing and future experimental results. When predictions are correct, models are extended and elaborated; when incorrect, they undergo revision. Although connectionist modeling may hold an important key to truly understanding cognitive processes, most current research in cognitive psychology focuses on straightforward empirical investigations of cognitive processes and does not involve modeling, so our discussion of it will be limited.

RECURRING RESEARCH THEME
Cognition and Neuroscience

As the connectionist approach to cognition might imply, a primary aim of many cognitive researchers is the discovery of the links between cognitive processing and the underlying physiology of the brain. A complete understanding of how the mind works requires an understanding of the brain's underlying physiology; after all, cognitive processes are expressions of brain activity. The advances made by neuroscientists in understanding the brain rival (and may even surpass) those made by cognitive psychologists in understanding the mind. Perhaps the most exciting frontier of psychological research involves the interface of these two areas, sometimes termed **cognitive neuroscience.** Cognitive neuroscientists use tools like brain-imaging techniques to explore the complex relationship between cognitive processing, brain structure, and brain function. As a result, we know a great deal about what is going on in the brain when people pay attention, remember, speak, and solve problems. In Chapter 2, you will read about some of the techniques employed by neuroscientists, and throughout the text you will read about some of their important findings.

The Ecological Approach to Cognition

A trend in cognitive psychology research reflects the breadth of cognitive psychological inquiry. Since the late 1970s, cognitive researchers have been concerned with designing studies that produce results that can be generalized to everyday life, a characteristic often termed **ecological validity**. You've already read about cognitive research that varies in ecological validity. Recall Ebbinghaus's and Bartlett's investigations of memory. Ebbinghaus investigated memory by memorizing precisely timed lists of nonsense syllables. Bartlett investigated memory by presenting stories to his participants for later recall. Which of these methods seems more akin to what you do every day? Chances are, you're thinking "Bartlett's," and most would agree. This is not to say that Ebbinghaus's investigations are not generalizable; quite the contrary, they established several key principles of memory function. But they aren't as ecologically valid as those of Bartlett.

Why has ecologically valid research become especially prevalent? Think back to the dominance of behaviorism and the subsequent return to the study of cognition. The behaviorists rightfully criticized much of what early psychologists (structuralists and functionalists) offered in terms of understanding human behavior, because much of it was based on what behaviorists viewed as an unreliable source—introspective reports that can be neither verified nor repeated. The behaviorists emphasized strict control and objective measurement in their research. When the "new" study of cognitive processes arose in the 1950s, cognitive researchers threw out the strict reliance on observable behavior but retained the emphasis on precise definition, measurement, and laboratory control. So the first generations of cognitive psychology research were very tightly controlled laboratory investigations of clearly defined phenomena. Some might argue that experimental control was so tight it "squeezed" the meaningfulness right out of much of cognitive research.

By the mid 1970s, some researchers had started to shift toward topics that were more relevant to everyday life. And in the late 1970s, pioneering cognitive psychologist Ulric Neisser issued what turned out to be a "call to arms" for memory researchers, claiming that the field had made startlingly little progress in its first quarter century and urging researchers to study memory in more meaningful contexts. Given that Neisser's challenge focused specifically on memory, we will discuss it in more depth in Chapter 8. Neisser's challenge has been answered by other cognitive researchers in areas such as problem solving and decision making. This growing trend is reflected in many of the studies discussed in this text. Another outgrowth of the move toward more ecologically valid cognition research is a greater appreciation for the role that culture plays in cognition. It seems more than a bit presumptuous to assume that everyone around the world remembers, speaks, solves problems, and makes decisions in the same way. Therefore, current research is dealing more and more with the relationship between culture and cognition.

RECURRING RESEARCH THEME
Cognition and Individual Differences

Scientists are typically devoted to formulating generalities about how the world works. Cognitive psychologists also look for generalities but focus on discovering the general principles of how people think. There is a great deal of uniformity in some basic cognitive processes, but there is also considerable variation in others. How you think turns out to depend on who you are and where you are—woman or man, depressed or not depressed, Asian or Indiana Hoosier. In other words, cognition occurs within a given internal and external context and is significantly influenced by that context. Research on individual differences in cognition is in the spirit of the ecological approach described above. A complete understanding of everyday cognition depends critically on understanding the differences in how individuals think, because individual differences are an important feature of everyday life. In each chapter of the text, we'll have some discussion of how individual differences come into play.

STOP *and* REVIEW!

1. When did cognitive psychology develop as a field?
2. True or false? The information-processing model has been the dominant paradigm for explaining cognition since the 1950s.
3. Connectionist models use _____ as a model for how cognitive processing takes place.
   a. communication systems
   b. a library
   c. an interstate highway system
   d. the brain
4. True or false? Since the late 1970s, the trend in cognitive research is to emphasize ecological validity.

➤ Some call the emergence of cognitive psychology the "cognitive revolution." Some place the the birthdate of cognitive psychology at September 11, 1956, when psychologists interested in the study of mind gathered at the Massachusetts Institute of Technology for the "Symposium on Information Theory."

➤ The information-processing approach compares mental processing to the serial operation of a computer. Humans, like computers, encode and store information for later retrieval and use. This model has proven to be an extremely useful framework for investigating cognitive processes and has been the dominant approach to describing and investigating cognition since the 1950s.

➤ The connectionist approach uses the neural networks of the brain, rather than the computer, as a model for how thinking takes place. According to this approach (also termed parallel distributed processing), the interactive and parallel activity of neural networks distributed throughout the brain forms the basis for mental representations and processes.

➤ Since the late 1970s, the trend in cognitive research has been to feature investigations of cognition in ecologically valid contexts. In this spirit, more researchers are investigating cultural and individual differences in basic cognitive processes.

GLOSSARY

behaviorism: an early approach that eschewed the study of consciousness in favor of a scientific analysis of overt behavior (p. 11)

cognitive neuroscience: an interdisciplinary field of study, combining neuroscience and cognitive psychology, that attempts to relate cognitive processing to its neural substrates (p. 29)

cognitive psychology: the scientific study of mental processes (p. 2)

cognitive science: an interdisciplinary effort to understand the mind; includes the disciplines of cognitive psychology, philosophy, neuroscience, artificial intelligence, linguistics, and anthropology (p. 5)

connectionism (also **parallel distributed processing**): a model that uses a brain-based metaphor to describe cognitive processes in terms of complex and interconnected networks of individual processing units that operate in parallel (p. 26)

ecological validity: the degree to which results from a research investigation can be generalized to everyday situations (p. 30)

forgetting curve: a function relating memory to time passage. A good deal of forgetting occurs soon after study, then slows down over time (p. 13)

functionalism: an early approach to the study of consciousness that emphasized the discovery of the basic uses of consciousness and how it helps us adapt in daily life (p. 10)

Gestalt approach: an early approach to the study of consciousness that emphasizes the inherent organizing tendencies of the mind (p. 14)

information-processing model: a descriptive approach that likens the functioning of the mind to the operation of a computer (p. 24)

introspection: a rigorous and systematic self-report of the basic elements of an experience (p. 10)

latent learning: learning that occurs in the absence of any reinforcement (p. 18)

laws of association: principles that underlie the act of relating two ideas or concepts (p. 6)

mental map: a mental representation of a spatial layout (p. 19)

psychophysics: the study of the relationship between the physical properties of a stimulus and the properties taken on when the stimulus is filtered through subjective experience (p. 7)

savings: a measure of memory developed by Ebbinghaus that refers to the reduction in learning trials needed to learn some set of information due to previous learning trials (p. 12)

S-R psychology: another term for the behaviorist approach, emphasizing the observation of relationships between observable stimuli and responses (p. 11)

structuralism: an early approach to the study of consciousness that emphasized breaking it down in terms of its most elemental components (p. 10)

unconscious inference: an implicit assumption made by our perceptual systems about some characteristic of an incoming stimulus (p. 8)

2

Research Methods in Cognition

BEEP . . . BEEP . . . BEEP . . . The shrill shriek of the alarm nearly knocks Vince out of bed. He flicks the clock from Alarm to Radio ". . . so let's continue with our Block Party Thursday!" Vince closes his eyes again. The decision is made. I'm not going in, he thinks, falling back to sleep. Although Vince isn't actively thinking, let's take advantage of the opportunity and learn the nuts and bolts of psychology research as they apply to cognitive psychology.

In this chapter, we review the nuts and bolts of psychology research as it applies to cognitive psychology. As we discussed in the last chapter, cognitive psychology is the scientific study of mental processes. Consequently, cognitive researchers face a unique challenge: how to reach firm conclusions about a subject matter that is, for the most part, completely unobservable. As you learned in Chapter 1, the behaviorists didn't think this was possible and deemed the "scientific study of mental processes" a contradiction in terms. They believed that it was impossible to study something so hidden and subjective in a scientific way. And because the initial attempts to establish a science of consciousness were based heavily on introspection, the behaviorists' objections were largely on the mark. Try as they might, early pioneers of psychology could not completely remove the subjectivity and guesswork from their study of cognitive processes.

Much has changed from the late 1800s and the turn of the 21st century. The scientific study of consciousness was rejected and then reestablished as a legitimate field of scientific study, and technological and theoretical developments opened up a new world of possibilities for a controlled and methodical approach to the study of thinking. Today, research on cognitive processes is thriving. And the recently established field of cognitive neuroscience has added a new dimension to this research, seeking to delineate the connections between mind and brain. In this chapter, we'll introduce you to some of the basic issues confronted by researchers in cognition and cognitive neuroscience.

All scientific research seeks to describe, predict, explain, and modify some set of phenomena. Research in cognition is no different; it is designed to describe, predict, explain, and modify the processes that make up thinking. "Modifying thinking" doesn't mean sinister cognitive psychologists attempting mind control. This phrase basically amounts to efforts to improve cognitive skills like memory. Accomplishing the goals of description, prediction, explanation, and modification in the domain of thinking is a challenging task because the processes are wholly unobservable. You can't see what someone is thinking. So the existence of various internal representations (like mental images) and processes (like memorization or rehearsal) must be *inferred*, based on something that *is* observable—namely, behavior. As you'll see, cognitive psychologists have come up with some very creative methods for turning the processes of thought outward and making them observable.

Descriptive Research

Descriptive research techniques, as the name suggests, allow us to describe some set of phenomena. Descriptive methods include naturalistic observation, case studies, and self-reports. These methods can provide some interesting observations about behavior, but that's really all they provide. Descriptive research could indicate that factor A and factor B seem to go together but not how or why they go together. Typically, descriptive investigations serve as a sort of springboard for subsequent experimental research. Although their use in the study of cognition is limited, examples of each technique can be found.

Naturalistic Observation

Naturalistic observation involves the observation of behavior in its natural setting, uninfluenced by the researcher (hence the term *naturalistic*). As you might guess, this method is of relatively little use to cognitive psychologists. Mental processes are, by their very nature, unobservable. Simply watching someone do something tells you little or nothing about what they are thinking. You could try to infer what they're thinking based on their behavior, but this would be (at best) an educated guess, and probably a very general one at that. This is not to say that research in cognition has not benefitted from observational techniques. Quite the contrary; in Chapter 12 you'll read about pioneering cognitive researcher Wolfgang Kohler, who based much initial conjecture about problem-solving processes on systematic observations of chimpanzees. His observational studies helped spur human research on insight (the sudden realization of a problem's solution).

Stop *and* Think!

NATURALISTIC OBSERVATION OF COGNITION

Kohler (1925) used naturalistic observation to gain some insight into the way chimps solve problems. You can use the same approach with people:

- Identify a cognitive process.
- Observe people engaging in this type of mental activity. (Remember: the observation location must be public—the library, student union, local mall, etc.)
- Identify the inferences you are able to make about what people must be thinking based on what they are doing.
- List the limitations of the inferences you made.

Case Studies

Case studies involve an in-depth investigation of a single case or small number of cases. Typically, this method is used to study unique conditions that could not be created in a laboratory. Case studies of cognition have played a prominent role in one area in particular—brain research. (You'll read about this topic throughout this book in the sections on cognition and neuroscience.) A good deal of basic information relating brain systems to cognition and behavior is based on the study of individuals who have suffered some sort of brain damage. For instance, research on the brain mechanisms underlying memory have benefitted from work with amnesics, people who have lost much of their memory functioning due to brain trauma (discussed in Chapter 6). Although case studies add an important dimension to research on cognition, they are limited in one important way—**generalizability.** Because case studies are, by definition, based on a small number of unique cases, their results may not apply (be generalizable) to the majority of individuals. Basic cognitive functioning in those who have suffered brain damage may differ in important ways from basic functioning in normal individuals. Therefore, generalizing from one to the other can be tenuous. However, as you'll see at several points throughout the text, the usefulness of case studies in cognitive neuroscience is undeniable.

Self-Report

Another descriptive research technique involves individuals reporting on their own knowledge, attitudes, feelings, or opinions through some type of **self-report** questionnaire or interview. Within the realm of cognition, this might involve asking people about what they know or how they think. And indeed, some cognitive research has done just that. Think back to introspection (discussed in Chapter 1), one of the earliest tools for assessing the contents of the mind. This technique basically amounts to asking people to report what is currently in their consciousness. Introspection is a close cousin of one method that is sometimes used to investigate problem solving—the collection of verbal protocols (discussed in Chapter 12). A verbal protocol is literally "thinking out loud." Participants are given problems to solve and asked to provide descriptions of what they're thinking as they solve the problems. Some of the *Stop and Think!* exercises featured throughout this text involve self-report investigations of cognition and are designed to help you observe your own cognitive processes more analytically.

One benefit of observing your own thinking processes may be an improvement in metacognitive skills. **Metacognition** refers to people's understanding of their own cognitive processing and can be assessed using questionnaires or interviews. For example, a number of studies have investigated an interesting state called the "tip-of-the-tongue phenomenon," which occurs when you're sure you know some fact but you just can't seem to bring it to mind—the answer is on the tip of your tongue (discussed in Chapter 9). Cohen and Faulkner (1986) asked participants in their study to note any tip-of-the-tongue experiences they had over a period of two weeks. They found that the most common type of block (68% of the total) was for proper names of acquaintances or friends; the second (17%) was for names of famous people; and the third was for names of places (7%). Note that this study, while informative, is purely descriptive. It gives us some basic information about when tip-of-the-tongue blocks occur but doesn't really explain how or why they occur.

Stop *and* Think!   **USING THE INTERVIEW TECHNIQUE TO STUDY COGNITION**

Interview four friends and ask them about

- the study strategies they use
- which ones they use most frequently
- which ones are most effective and least effective

Based on their responses

- What do you conclude about the prevalence and effectiveness of these study strategies?
- What are the limitations of these conclusions?

S T O P *and* R E V I E W !

1. Why does the scientific study of cognitive processes present such a difficult challenge?
2. True or false? Descriptive research methods don't allow for assessing how or why two variables relate to each other.

3. What is naturalistic observation?

4. Why is the use of case studies valuable, and why is it limited?

5. How might self-report techniques be used in cognitive psychology research?

➤ Research in cognition is designed to describe, predict, explain, and modify the processes that comprise thought. Accomplishing these goals is a challenging task, because the processes are unobservable. The existence of internal representations and processes must be inferred based on behavior.

➤ Descriptive research techniques allow for simple descriptions of a phenomenon. They provide interesting observations about behavior but can't explain why or how something happens. Therefore, their use in cognitive research is limited.

➤ Naturalistic observation involves the unobtrusive observation of behavior in its natural setting. It is of little use for cognitive psychologists, because mental processing is, for the most part, unobservable.

➤ Case studies involve an in-depth investigation of a single case or small number of cases. This method is used to study unique conditions that could not be created in a laboratory, such as human brain trauma. Case studies, while valuable in cognitive research, are limited in generalizability.

➤ Self-report techniques involve individuals reporting on their own knowledge, attitudes, feelings, or opinions. In cognitive studies, this may involve asking people to describe their thinking process during different tasks.

Experimental Research

As stated above, descriptive methods are designed to do just that—describe. While these techniques have provided some useful information to cognitive psychologists, the information is limited. If cognitive psychologists want to provide *explanations* of cognitive processes rather than just educated guesses or *descriptions,* it's necessary to be more controlled and systematic when observing behaviors and inferring thought processes. To accomplish this, cognitive psychologists rely heavily on experiments.

Experimental research involves the systematic manipulation and measurement of variables and the observation of their effects on one another in controlled settings. The data yielded from experimental investigations go beyond simple descriptions of behavior and guesses about the underlying thought processes. A well-controlled experiment allows for causal statements to be made about the effects of variables on one another, a goal that even the most well-designed descriptive studies cannot reach.

The Importance of the Computer

In Chapter 1, you learned that the computer was central to the development of some of the ideas that remain at the core of current cognitive psychology. In addition to its role

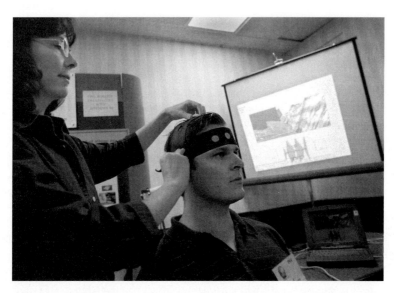

The computer has proven vital not only as a metaphor for cognition, but also as a research tool.

as a model for how thinking might take place, the computer has also been vital to actually conducting cognition research. Much of the research you'll read about in later chapters was conducted using a desktop computer. Computers are used for two primary reasons: automation and precision. Conducting an experiment on a computer allows for precision in exactly how stimuli are presented (e.g., presentation duration, time between stimuli, etc.) and how responses are recorded. This is not to say that all of cognitive research is conducted via computers; it is not. But certainly, the advantages offered by computer technology have had an enormous impact on how cognitive psychology research is done.

What Happens in an Experiment?

In an experiment, researchers manipulate factors they believe influence some mental process(es). Suppose we wanted to determine whether forming mental images is an effective technique for remembering information later. We could address this in a very simple experiment by having participants study a list of words, one group using mental imagery and the other group using simple mental rehearsal (repeating the items as they are presented). In the lingo of experimentation, we would be *manipulating* study strategy. Such manipulated variables (e.g., study strategy) are termed **independent variables.** Then, to find out if we're correct that imagery is an effective study strategy, we need to *measure* memory for each group and compare performance. Such measures are termed **dependent variables.** One measure could be the total number of words recalled. If we're right about the effects of imagery, then the participants who studied with imagery should recall more words than those who simply repeated the items silently.

The Advantages and Disadvantages of an Experiment

Experiments are the preferred method in cognitive psychology because of the explanatory power they offer. The results of a well-controlled experiment allow a researcher to state nearly definitively which of the manipulated variables had an effect on the measured variables and to describe the nature of these effects. In other words, experiments allow researchers to make statements about the "hows" and "whys" of mental processes, unlike descriptive studies, which limit researchers to simple conclusions about the "whats." Take the example of whether imagery helps memory. A descriptive study that addresses this question might involve interviewing individuals about their study strategies and whether they use imagery, or it might involve observing participants as they use mental imagery. This type of study might generate some interesting guesses about imagery and what it may do to help studying, but the conclusions remain guesses only. To really know the effect of a study strategy on memory requires a controlled series of experiments.

Do experiments have any disadvantages? One disadvantage is the artificial nature of the research. Well-designed experiments offer a great deal in the way of control and precision, which enhances their **internal validity.** However, they sometimes fall short in terms of naturalness, or how well they represent everyday life. In Chapter 1, we talked about this characteristic, termed **ecological validity.** Also in that chapter you read about the work of Ebbinghaus and Bartlett. We can look at the relationship between internal and ecological validity in the context of the research conducted by these pioneering cognitive psychologists. Ecological and internal validity typically have an inverse relationship; you trade off one to get more of the other. The addition of more realism to an experimental procedure often comes at the expense of experimental control. Bartlett's procedures and materials were not as tightly controlled as Ebbinghaus's, opening up the possibility that Bartlett's results may be the product of uncontrolled variables. However, if you impose too much control, you may create a situation that doesn't really mirror real life, thereby limiting your findings. Some might claim that Ebbinghaus's research, while rigorously controlled, is of limited value because nonsense syllables do not resemble the types of material that we encode and remember on a daily basis.

A problem with experiments arises if participants and/or experimenters have expectancies about what should or shouldn't happen in the experiment. These **expectancy effects** are typically controlled by keeping participants blind to the purposes of the study and keeping researchers blind to the particular treatment or condition being received by

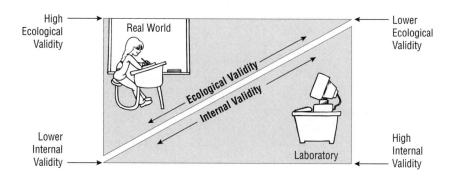

the participant. This is termed a **double-blind procedure**. Making researchers blind to the expected results of an experiment is quite difficult, given that they designed it, so experimenters have to take special care not to unintentionally influence the results of an experiment. Another way to control for expectancy effects is to minimize contact between experimenter and participants through the use of the computer to present instructions and stimuli.

STOP *and* REVIEW!

1. True or false? Cognitive psychology relies most heavily on experimental research.
2. Why are computers used in cognitive psychology experiments?
3. True or false? A well-designed experiment allows for causal explanations.
4. Discuss the relationship between ecological and internal validity in experimental research.

➤ Experiments are the preferred method in cognitive psychology because of their explanatory power.

➤ Conducting an experiment on a computer allows for precision in how stimuli are presented and in how responses are collected. Using a computer also minimizes contact between experimenter and participants, thus reducing expectancy effects.

➤ The results of a well-controlled experiment allow for causal statements to be made about the effects of one variable (the independent variable) on another variable (the dependent variable).

➤ Experiments offer control and precision (internal validity) but often at the expense of generalizability (ecological validity). Participant and/or experimenter expectancies can inadvertently influence research results. These unwanted effects can be controlled by keeping participants blind to the purposes of the study and researchers blind to the condition being received by the participant

The Cognitive Psychology Experiment

How Can We See Thinking? The Dependent Variable

Because cognitive processes are unobservable, researchers must come up with behaviors or measures of performance that reflect specific cognitive processes. In other words, the cognitive process in question, be it perception, attention, memory, decision making, or problem solving, must be given an operational definition. An **operational definition** involves defining a variable in terms of precise, measurable procedures that can be repeated by other researchers. Memory, a vague term, might be defined in terms of how many words can be recalled from a previously studied list. Problem-solving ability might be defined in terms of the time it takes for someone to solve a given problem. Following are some of the more common ways to operationalize mental processes.

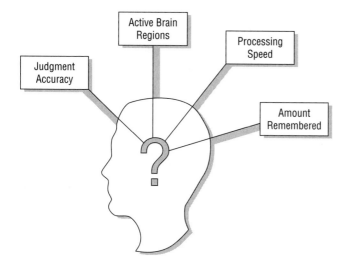

Judgment Accuracy

Active Brain Regions

Processing Speed

Amount Remembered

Speed and Accuracy. Cognitive processes take time, so a common measure of performance is **reaction time (RT)**. The speed with which someone engages in a particular cognitive process can provide useful information about how that process is being carried out. For example, people are quicker to respond affirmatively to the question "Is a robin a bird?" than to "Is a penguin a bird?" This is a consistent difference, and, as we'll see in Chapter 9, it lends insight into how categories are mentally represented.

F. C. Donders, a Dutch physiologist, was the first to realize that people's reaction times could be used to estimate the amount of time required to perform the component processes involved in a particular task (Donders, 1969/1868). Let's consider the three reaction time tasks needed do this analysis. The first, called a **B reaction** (or **choice reaction**) task, involves two stimuli and two responses. If stimulus 1 is presented, button 1 is pressed; if stimulus 2 is presented, button 2 is pressed. This task involves at least three components: stimulus discrimination (deciding which stimulus was presented), response selection (selecting which button to press), and response execution (making the response). If we want to determine the time needed to perform each of these components, we need to devise two additional tasks. The first is called an **A reaction** (or **simple reaction**) task. In this task, there is one stimulus and one response. If presented with the stimulus, a button is pressed. This task does not involve stimulus discrimination (there is only one stimulus) or response selection (there is only one button), but it does involve response execution. The other task is called a **C reaction** (or **go–no go**) task. In this task there are two stimuli but only one response. If stimulus 1 is presented, the button is pressed. If stimulus 2 is presented, no response is made. This task involves stimulus discrimination and response execution but not response selection (there is only one possible response).

With these three reaction time measures, one can determine the amount of time required to perform each component process in the B reaction task. If we want to know how long stimulus discrimination takes, we would take the reaction time for C minus reaction time for A. C involves stimulus discrimination and response execution. A only involves response execution. Therefore, subtracting A from C leaves the time needed for stimulus discrimination (see Figure 2.1a). If we want to know how long response selection takes, we would take reaction time for B minus reaction time for C. B involves stimulus discrimination, response selection, and response execution. C involves stimulus discrimination and response execution. Therefore, subtracting C from B leaves the time needed for response selection (see Figure 2.1b). By applying this sort of logic to the analysis of reaction times, cognitive psychologists have been able to tease apart and isolate various cognitive processes.

Another common measure is the **accuracy** of responding. If participants in a study are consistently less accurate in one condition relative to another, this may reveal important

	Stimulus Discrimination	Response Execution
A		
C		
C–A		

(a)

	Stimulus Identification	Response Selection	Response Execution
B			
C			
B–C			

(b)

Figure 2.1 Graphic depiction of the subtraction logic employed by Donders. In panel (a), the simple reaction time task (A) requires only response execution, once the stimulus has been registered. However, the choice reaction time task (C) involves an extra stage in which the person must decide which of the two possible stimuli are present. This process is termed *stimulus discrimination.* Because both tasks involve response execution but only task C requires stimulus discrimination, subtracting the reaction time of task A from that of task leads to an estimate of how long the stimulus discrimination process takes.

The two-choice reaction time task (B) in panel (b) adds a stage of response selection, as a person must discriminate between the stimuli and then select the appropriate response. By the same logic as in panel (a), subtracting reaction time C (stimulus discrimination and response execution) from reaction time B (stimulus discrimination, response execution, and response selection) leads to an estimate of how long the response selection process takes.

information about the thought processes involved. For example, when you try to attend to two different things, you make more errors than when your attention is focused on only one. As we'll see in Chapter 4, this gives us important information about the nature of attention. Often, speed and accuracy have a reciprocal relationship. That is, as responses get faster, the accuracy of those responses sometimes suffers, a relationship termed the **speed-accuracy trade-off.** Researchers need to keep this trade-off in mind in interpreting the results of any study using speed and accuracy as their dependent variables.

Stop *and* Think!   ## A SPEED-ACCURACY TRADE-OFF

Get ready for a typing test. Go to a keyboard and type out this tried-and-true sentence (which includes every letter in the alphabet):

The quick brown fox jumps over the lazy dog.

Try typing this sentence five times under two different conditions:

1. Type it at a moderate pace five times, maybe a little slower than you normally do.
2. Type it as fast as you possibly can five times.

Count the number of errors you made in conditions 1 and 2.

- Did your results show a speed-accuracy trade-off?
- Why?

Note any problems with the "design" of this experiment?
- What are they?
- How could you fix them?

Other Characteristics of Responding.   Speed and accuracy serve as general and useful indicators in nearly all areas of cognitive research, but there are a myriad other dependent variables that researchers use to assess mental processing. For the most part, the particular dependent variable used depends on the cognitive process being studied. A researcher interested in reading might measure reading comprehension. A researcher interested in problem solving might look at the level of creativity in the solution to the problem. A researcher interested in decision making might assess the types of choices that are made in particular situations.

Physiological Measures.   Recent advances in neuroscientific technology have introduced a whole new class of dependent variables into the study of cognition. Researchers in cognitive neuroscience investigate not only the characteristics of mental processing, but also the corresponding brain activity as revealed by physiological measures like positron emission tomography (PET), functional magnetic resonance imaging (fMRI), or event-related potentials (ERP). These dependent variables will continue to play a critical role as researchers bridge the gap between mind and brain. We'll talk more about these dependent variables later in this chapter.

What Variables Influence Cognition? The Independent Variable

As you might imagine, cognitive processes can be influenced by a host of variables, which are called the independent variables in an experiment. An independent variable has at least two levels; the levels of the independent variable determine the **experimental conditions.** The simplest experiment involves one independent variable with two levels and therefore with two conditions. For example, suppose we wanted to look at how the type of memory test affects the amount that people can remember. We can study a real-world analog—the tests you take in class. Which would you prefer—a test where we give you a term and ask for a definition, or a test where we give you a term along with four possible definitions and you have to pick the correct one? Chances are you'd perform differently in each situation.

How would we test this idea in the laboratory? We would present you with a list of words and test your memory of the list in different ways. The independent variable in this simple experiment would be the type of test. This variable has two levels—recall (you are given a blank sheet of paper and asked to write down everything you remember) and recognition (you are given a list of words and asked to circle the ones you saw before). In experimentation, there is no real difference between the terms *level* and *condition.* When you're talking about the design of the experiment, you talk about *levels* of the independent variable. When you're actually testing participants, you assign the *conditions* that correspond to these levels. What are the important independent variables in studies of cognition? Jenkins (1979) proposed a classification of independent variables that could be investigated in a memory experiment. However, this scheme is quite useful for classifying variables in all sorts of cognition experiments.

Participant Variables.   Not everyone thinks in the same way, so it should come as no surprise that many cognition studies focus on how thinking is affected by *who* is doing the thinking: man or woman, young or elderly, Asian or European. Studies using **participant variables** will be featured in the *Cognition and Individual Differences* sections that appear in each chapter. Participant variables are unique in that the experimenter does not assign participants to a condition. For example, we can't tell Bob that he's in the female condition in our experiment. Participants are "assigned" to different conditions by virtue of circumstances. A study by Channon and Baker (1996) investigated the participant variable of depression, assessing its influence on problem solving. The problem-solving task was to review electrical wiring diagrams and find errors. The investigators' primary interest was strategy differences that might exist between nondepressed and depressed participants. The results showed that depressed participants were no less accurate than nondepressed participants but were slower and tended to carry out more redundant tests of the wiring.

Material Variables.   The way that people think also depends on *what* it is they're thinking about. Cognitive processes vary depending on whether people are processing individual words, stories, pictures, computer screens, pieces of general knowledge, or brain-teasing puzzles. So a great deal of cognitive research manipulates what might be termed **material variables.** Consider a study by Kemp (1988) concerning a person's ability to date events. For example, do you know what year the space shuttle *Challenger* exploded shortly after takeoff? It was 1986. Kemp investigated individuals' ability to date events and varied the material, comparing participants' recall of recent events (like the *Challenger* disaster) to more remote events (like the year Abraham Lincoln was assassinated). Kemp's study revealed that people tend to underestimate the age of remote events (i.e., they think the Lincoln assassination occurred later than it did) and to overestimate the age of recent events (they think that the *Challenger* disaster occurred earlier than it did).

Experimental Context Variables.   Cognitive processing may be influenced by many aspects of the experimental context. For example, a researcher may manipulate the instructions given to participants (e.g., having them use different study strategies), the situation in which an experimental task is performed (e.g., having participants perform a task under time pressure or no time pressure), or the situation in which a particular material is encountered (e.g., having participants identify the perpetrator of a witnessed crime when a weapon was used and when a weapon was not used). A study by King (1991) provides a good (and relevant) example of the use of **experimental context variables.** In this study, the effect of listening strategy on lecture comprehension was investigated. Some students simply listened to the lecture, while other students used self-questioning during the lecture. The results demonstrated an effect of listening strategy. The group that engaged in self-questioning was superior in their comprehension of the lecture material to that of participants who simply listened to the lecture.

Performance-Measure Variables.   These variables are a bit more subtle than the others. Basically, the dependent variable is used as an independent variable, because sometimes cognitive processing depends on exactly how you measure the particular cognitive process. Andersson and Roennberg (1996) provide an example of the use of **performance-measure variables.** These authors were interested in the process of collaborative memory in dyads. Put more simply, what happens when two people (a dyad) remember an event, and does this recall depend on the type of memory test? The researchers investigated these questions by comparing dyads' performance on two different types of tests: one that requires recall of a story presented earlier and one that involves answering general information questions. The results showed that the type of memory test made a difference. Recall of the story suffered when participants recalled in pairs relative to when they recalled on their own. However, on the fact retrieval test there was no such difference. The way in which memory was queried proved to be an important factor.

Stop *and* **Think!** ## IDENTIFYING AND LABELING VARIABLES

For the following descriptions of actual studies, identify the independent variable(s) and dependent variable(s). For each of the independent variable(s), determine which of the four types of independent variable it is and specify the levels of the variable.

1. Bauer and Johnson-Laird (1993) were interested in whether diagrams could improve reasoning with different types of disjunctive logic problems (type A and B). They investigated people's ability to solve these types of problems, comparing conditions in which the problems were presented with a diagram to conditions in which the problems were presented verbally.
2. Holtgraves (1997) was interested in people's memory for the exact wording of remarks made in everyday situations. Participants heard statements that were made by a high-status (e.g., a professor) or equal status (e.g., another student) person. Holtgraves compared recall and recognition memory for these statements.
3. Forsterlee and Horowitz (1997) were interested in the effects of taking notes on mock jurors' decisions in a complex trial. Participants saw a complex trial on videotape, and either did or did not take notes. Performance was measured by looking at the amount of compensation awarded to the plaintiff.
4. Coleman and Shore (1991) were interested in how people who varied in their knowledge of physics would vary in problem solving. They compared experts (graduate students in physics) high achievers from a high school class, and average achievers from a high school class. Coleman and Shore looked at performance by classifying and counting the types of statements made by these participants as they were solving the problems.
5. Schmidt (1994) was interested in the effects of humor on people's ability to remember sentences. In one experiment, he presented both humorous and nonhumorous sentences and tested recall of these sentences with either free recall or cued recall.

After the independent and dependent variables have been chosen and operationally defined, other issues must be addressed. Let's examine some of the major concerns we should have in designing a study comparing performance on tests of recall and recognition.

Confounding Variables

Confounding variables are factors that vary along with the independent variable, making the results difficult to interpret. For example, in the memory test experiment, we would want to make sure that everything is as equivalent as possible in the two conditions being examined—the participants, the testing conditions, the words presented—everything. The only difference between the two conditions being compared should be the type of memory test participants get (i.e., the independent variable). If something else is different (say we give milk and cookies to the participants in the recall condition but not to the participants in the recognition condition), then we won't know if it was the food or the type of memory test that caused the difference in results. A researcher must ensure that the conditions being compared are as equivalent as possible. Once we have anticipated possible confounding variables, we have another decision to make. Should we use different participants in each of the conditions (i.e., a between-subjects design) or the same participants in each condition (i.e., a within-subjects design)?

Assigning Participants to Conditions

In practice, a wide variety of factors are likely to influence a given behavior. Therefore, many experiments in cognitive psychology will examine more than one of these factors. However, for the sake of simplicity, we will limit our discussion to a **single-factor experiment,** which examines the influence of a single **factor** on behavior. In other words, there is one independent variable in the experiment; the terms *factor* and *independent variable* are synonymous. Each independent variable in an experiment must have at least two levels. Again, for simplicity's sake, we will limit our discussion to independent variables with only two levels. Our memory test experiment is an example of a simple single-factor experiment. We are manipulating one independent variable (memory test) with two levels (recall and recognition) and investigating its effect on one dependent variable (the amount remembered).

Within-Subjects Designs.   In a **within-subjects design,** the same participants take part in each condition of the experiment. Suppose we have 12 participants in our memory test experiment. If we are using a within-subjects design, we would have each of the 12 participants perform both the recall and recognition tests. Testing the same participants in all conditions offers a big advantage. Remember that the conditions of an experiment should be as similar as possible (with the exception of the independent variable). When we use a within-subjects design, the participants in the conditions are *identical,* which eliminates one possible difference between the conditions. However, this design suffers from some disadvantages—namely, **practice effects** and **carryover effects.** When participants take part in more than one condition, there is a strong likelihood that participation in one condition will affect performance in the other one, either by giving the participants practice on the task (practice effect) or by giving them a strategy that influences performance in the other conditions (carryover effect). Let's look at our memory test experiment. Suppose we test a participant in recall first, then in recognition. It's quite likely that the initial act of attempting to recall all of the words is going to influence how the participant does on the recognition test. This influence could be characterized as a general practice effect: taking one memory test helps you on a second one. This influence could also be characterized as a strategy carryover effect: taking the first memory test may change the way you approach the second one. In either case, we are not really getting a pure comparison of these two conditions.

Between-Subjects Designs.　In a **between-subjects design,** different participants are assigned to each condition of the experiment. So if we recruit 12 participants to be in our memory test experiment, we would assign six of them to each of the two memory test conditions. One major advantage of a between-subjects design is that there is no danger of performance in one condition influencing performance in another condition, because each condition involves different participants. A between-subjects design is preferable when there is a strong likelihood of carryover from one condition to another. Carryover is very likely in the memory test experiment. If participants attempt to recall words, then there will probably be a contaminating effect of this recall on a later test of recognition. Therefore, it's preferable to use a between-subjects design in such cases.

Between or Within?　If possible, researchers prefer to use within-subjects designs, because fewer participants are required. Also, within-subjects designs have more statistical power than do between-subjects designs. That is, an effect is more likely to be revealed using a within-subjects design. A statistical test determines if the independent variable was responsible for the difference found between the conditions. Reducing other differences between the groups makes the difference due to the independent variable more likely to be detected (i.e., gives the test more statistical power). As we just noted, in a within-subjects design, the participants in the conditions are identical, thus eliminating a major source of variation between conditions. While within-subject designs are typically the design of choice, the chance of practice or carryover effects occurring from one condition to another makes the choice of a between-subjects design preferable in many cases.

Let's review the four types of independent variables in the context of the between-subjects versus within-subjects choice. *Participant variables,* by definition, involve a between-subjects comparison, because the comparison of interest involves different groups of participants. Recall that Channon and Baker (1996) compared depressed and nondepressed participants on their problem-solving ability. *Experimental context variables* are often manipulated in between-subjects designs. This was the choice made in the King (1991) study that investigated the effect of listening strategy on lecture comprehension. Because different participants were used in the each of the strategy conditions, the experimenter did not need to worry about a strategy in one condition carrying over to another condition. When experimenters vary *materials,* they commonly do so using a within-subjects manipulation; the same participants experience each type of material. As you read earlier, Kemp (1988) was interested in comparing people's ability to date historical and recent events and presented each participant with both types of events. It is unlikely that there would be any influence of one type of event on the other, so the choice of a within-subjects design was appropriate. Studies that manipulate *performance-measure variables* do so either within or between subjects, depending on the particular issue being investigated. A between-subjects manipulation is often used when the two measures are likely to influence each other, obscuring their comparison (like recall and recognition of the same information). However, when the two measures are unlikely to influence each other, a within-subjects design is chosen. As you may remember, this was the choice of Andersson and Roennberg (1996), who used a within-subjects design to compare dyadic memory performance in different retrieval situations. Recalling facts from a story you just read is unlikely to influence the way in which you recall general information facts. Therefore, the added power of a within-subjects design was the obvious choice.

The decision about whether to manipulate a given variable within- or between-subjects is dependent on the particular experimental question being investigated and must be made with caution and a clear understanding of previous research. In fact, choosing a within-subjects or between-subjects design can determine whether you get an effect or not. For example, forming bizarre images of a concept helps you remember it, but only when participants see both bizarre images and common images. Bizarre images are remembered better when they contrast with more common images in the same context (e.g., Cox & Wollen, 1981; McDaniel & Einstein, 1986). On the other hand, if you give one group of participants a bunch of bizarre images and the other group a bunch of common images (i.e., if you manipulate bizarre imagery between-subjects), you get no effect. There is nothing for the bizarre images to clash with in this design, so they aren't very well remembered. Clearly, the decision to manipulate a particular variable between or within subjects is a critical one. Researchers must consider the variables being manipulated and their impact on one another.

Stop *and* **Think!**

MANIPULATING VARIABLES—BETWEEN OR WITHIN?

Below are some independent variables that might be of interest to a cognitive psychologist. For each, identify the levels of the independent variable and identify whether you assign participants to the conditions in a between-subjects or within-subjects manner. Be sure to justify your choices.

1. the effects of the type of word people are trying to remember—positive (i.e., wedding) or negative (i.e., funeral)
2. the effects of the way in which a problem is presented on people's ability to solve a problem
3. the effects of modality (whether something is presented visually or auditorily) on memory for words
4. the effects of gender on the ability to form mental images
5. the effects of listening to Mozart or Britney Spears on people's reaction time and accuracy in a cognitive task
6. the effects of TV commercials on people's memory for the commercial itself and on brand preference

STOP *and* REVIEW!

1. Identify and define the four types of independent variables.
2. True or false? The terms *independent variable* and *factor* mean the same thing.
3. What is RT and the speed-accuracy trade-off?
4. True or false? Operational definitions are vague and imprecise explanations about how a variable is measured.

▶ The dependent variable in an experiment must be given an operational definition, which involves defining a variable in terms of precise and replicable measurable procedures. Independent variables have at least two levels that determine the experimental conditions. There are four types of independent variables. Participant variables involve groups of participants who differ on some critical factor. Material variables involve varying the nature of the material being processed. Experimental context variables involve varying the nature of the instructions given to participants. Performance-measure variables involve varying the response measures given to participants.

➤ A factor is another name for an independent variable. A single-factor experiment has one independent variable. Researchers attempt to make experimental conditions as similar as possible, except for the manipulation of the independent variable. Confounding variables can obscure the interpretation of experimental results, because they inadvertently vary along with the independent variable.

➤ Reaction time (RT) is the time taken to respond to a stimulus. A speed-accuracy trade-off refers to the tendency for decreases in response time to be associated with increases in error.

➤ In a within-subjects design, the same participants participate in each condition. Possible problems are practice effects (performance changes as a result of continuous participation in the study) and carryover effects (specific effects of processing in one condition affect processing in another condition). In a between-subjects design, different participants are assigned to each condition. Generally, within-subjects designs are preferable because they require fewer participants and are more likely to reveal an effect.

The Factorial Design

As we noted earlier, a wide variety of factors can influence a given behavior or cognitive process. Because of this, cognitive psychologists often conduct studies that investigate more than one factor. Let's go back to our memory test experiment. Suppose that we are interested not only in how the type of test affects memory, but also if there is any difference in how well we remember high-frequency words like *house,* and low-frequency words like *aardvark.* We could accomplish this by conducting another experiment in which we compare words that are encountered frequently in the English language (high-frequency words) to those that are encountered less frequently (low-frequency words). By conducting these two independent studies, we could determine how memory is affected by the type of memory test employed and word frequency.

However, it is possible that these variables may have a different effect on memory performance when they are examined together, relative to when they are examined in isolation. For example, the effect of word frequency might vary based on whether the memory test is free recall or recognition. In other words, the effects of one variable may *depend on* the other one. Manipulating both independent variables in the same study allows us to look at the joint effects of these variables, as well as the effect of each variable in isolation. This is called a **factorial design**—a design that completely crosses each level of one independent variable with each level of the other independent variables. In order to conduct our experiment, we would completely cross each level of the memory test variable (recognition and

		Memory Test	
		recall	recognition
Word Frequency	high	high/recall	high/recognition
	low	low/recall	low/recognition

Figure 2.2 In a factorial design, each level of one independent variable is crossed with each level of the other independent variables.

recall) with each level of the word frequency variable (low and high word frequency) to produce four conditions: high-frequency words/recognition test, high-frequency words/recall test, low-frequency words/recognition test, low-frequency words/recall test (see Figure 2.2).

A factorial design may employ any number of independent variables, each having any number of levels. To keep our discussion clear, we'll consider the simplest case: a factorial design with two independent variables, each with two levels (e.g., the memory test/word frequency experiment). For each of these independent variables, the researcher has the choice of manipulating it between subjects (using different participants for each level of the independent variable) or within subjects (using the same participants for each level of the independent variable). In a **between-subjects factorial,** both variables are manipulated between subjects. Participants are assigned to one of the four conditions. In a **within-subjects factorial,** both variables are manipulated within subjects. Each participant experiences all four of the conditions.

The best design for our study would probably be a hybrid between the two just mentioned: a mixed-factorial design. In a **mixed-factorial design,** some variables are manipulated between subjects and other variables are manipulated within subjects. For the present study, all participants would see a list that includes both high- and low-frequency words (a within-subjects manipulation of word frequency). The independent variable of word frequency is a *materials* variable, which is commonly manipulated within subjects. The independent variable of memory test is a *performance-measure* variable and should probably be manipulated between subjects in this situation. If we were to use a within-subjects design and test recognition followed by recall (or vice versa), the second test will be affected by the first, because it's a second attempt to remember the same words. So, half of the participants would be tested with recall, and the other half would be tested with recognition. Mixed-factorial designs like this are extremely common in cognition research. Once the data from a factorial design have been collected, a researcher needs to summarize, analyze, and present the results. This involves a number of statistical procedures that are beyond the scope of this text, but we'll briefly review some of the highlights.

Analyzing and Presenting Results

Researchers submit data to a number of statistical procedures in order to determine whether their hypotheses have been supported. **Descriptive statistics** are used to provide a thumbnail sketch of the data. The major class of descriptive statistics we will discuss is called central tendency. Measures of **central tendency** (the *mean* is the most commonly used) give an idea of the typical score for a given condition. Common practice is to present means in the form of data graphs or data tables. However, descriptive statistics do not provide a complete picture of the data. For example, in our memory test experiment we may find that recall percentages for the two conditions are 40% and 50%. It seems as though these are different levels of performance, but differences such as these can arise purely through chance, and this possibility needs to be assessed. This involves the use of **inferential statistics,** which go further than simply summarizing the data. Inferential tests allow a researcher to determine how likely it is that a difference between conditions occurred due to chance. And if it is unlikely that the difference occurred by chance, the *inference* is that it must have occurred due to the differences in the levels of the independent variable. In other words, the differences between conditions are "real" and the effect is said to have achieved **statistical significance.**

Main Effects. Let's say that we carried out our memory test/word frequency experiment. As described above, the experiment is a mixed-factorial design with four conditions. The four conditions are yielded by crossing a two-level independent variable (memory test) with another two-level independent variable (word frequency). This design allows us to assess if either of the independent variables influences performance and whether the variables interact. Given the proposed design, two **main effects** would be assessed, one for each of the independent variables. We can assess the effect of memory test on memory performance by examining recall and recognition scores regardless of the type of word. We can also assess the effect of word frequency on memory performance by examining memory for high- and low-frequency words regardless of memory test.

These data can be presented in the form of a table like the one in Figure 2.3a, which presents the main effect data for our hypothetical memory experiment. The overall means for the levels of each independent variable are presented at the bottom (for type of memory test) and far right (for word frequency). A statistical comparison of the means for the memory test variable reveals a statistically significant main effect: overall, recognition leads to better memory than recall. Now, shifting to the side of the table, we can assess whether there is a main effect of word frequency. We see that there is not a statistically significant difference between these two conditions; high- and low-frequency words are remembered equally well. The same data can be captured in the form of a graph, as displayed in Figure 2.3b. Take a look at the pair of bar graphs for the memory data. The graph on the right shows the bar representing recognition is higher than that representing recall. The graph on the left shows the bar representing

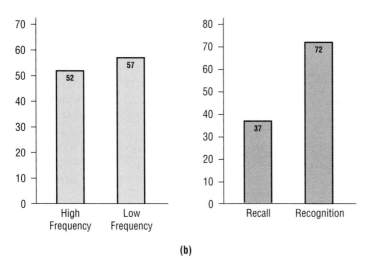

		Memory Test		
		recall	recognition	
Word Frequency	high			52
	low			57
		37	72	

(a)

(b)

Figure 2.3 Main effects are assessed by looking at the overall means for each of the conditions, often displayed in the margins of the table. The table (a) shows the main effect data from the hypothetical memory experiment. The graphs (b) show the main effect data for the hypothetical memory experiment.

memory for high-frequency words and low-frequency words are nearly identical in height, indicating equivalent performance.

Interactions.   If you want to know whether these two independent variables influence one each other, we need to look at the means for *each* of the four conditions created by the factorial design. Take a look at Figure 2.4a, which shows the means for all four conditions in our hypothetical memory experiment. Looking at these means reveals that the previously stated conclusions based on the main effects do not ring completely true. This is because the data indicate a statistically significant interaction between the two variables. When examined in isolation, the independent variable of word frequency seems to have no influence on remembering; but when you look at the means for all four conditions, this overall effect is quite misleading. The ability to remember high- and low-frequency words depends critically on how memory is tested. High-frequency words are remembered better in recall, while low-frequency words are remembered better in recognition. In other words, there is an **interaction** between the effects of memory test and word frequency.

An interaction might be described as a "difference of differences." In Figure 2.4a, it's apparent that this is exactly what we have. In recall, there is a 14% advantage for high-frequency words; in recognition, the difference is reversed, with a 24% advantage for low-frequency words. So the high-frequency/low-frequency difference is different for the two memory tests. The same interaction can be viewed from a different angle. Compare memory for recognition and recall. Recognition is superior to recall overall, but the superiority is much more evident in the case of low-frequency words. Once again, we see a difference between differences; the difference between recognition and recall is 54% for low-frequency words but only 16% for high-frequency words. So viewed either way, the effects of word frequency and memory test *depend on* each other. This interaction also emerges from the bar graph in Figure 2.4b, which includes all four conditions. Compare the pattern observed in each half of this graph. In the recall panel, the bar representing high-frequency words is higher than the bar representing memory for low-frequency words. The converse can be seen in the recognition panel, demonstrating the interactive effect of word frequency and memory test.

		Memory Test	
		recall	recognition
Word Frequency	high	44	60
	low	30	84

(a)

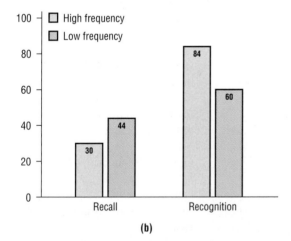

(b)

Figure 2.4 Hypothetical data showing an interaction between word frequency and type of memory test, presented as a table and a bar graph. Both displays reveal an obvious difference of differences, with high-frequency words better recalled than low-frequency words, and low-frequency words being better recognized than high-frequency words.

Stop *and* Think!   SPOTTING MAIN EFFECTS AND INTERACTIONS

Below are some hypothetical experimental designs and results. Look at the patterns and determine whether the results indicate main effects and/or interactions. Given that the data have not been submitted to inferential statistics, the assumption about statistical significance is given with each experimental example.

Dependent measure: Comprehension rating for a baseball story presented in different formats. Rating is on a scale from 1 to 10. Following are scores averaged across participants. (Assume that a difference of 2 is statistically significant.)

		Presentation Format		
		Video	Written Story	
Baseball Expertise	High	6	6	6
	Low	4	2	3
		5	4	

Dependent measure: Reaction time (in seconds) for solving word puzzles and math puzzles that are either simple or complex. (Assume a difference of eight is statistically significant.)

		Difficulty Level of Problem		
		Simple	Complex	
Puzzle Type	Word	4.9	13.1	9.0
	Math	6.6	23.8	15.2
		5.8	18.5	

Dependent measure: Percentage accuracy in detecting odd and even digits presented visually or auditorily. (Assume that a difference of 10 is statistically significant.)

	Odd Numbers	Even Numbers	
Distracted	55	56	55.5
Full Attention	93	92	92.5
	74	74	

Dependent measure: Knowledge of material (% correct on either a fill-in-the-blank test or essay test) from a textbook chapter for different study strategies (memorization of terms and outlining). (Assume that a difference of 10 is statistically significant.)

		Test Type		
		Fill-in-the-Blanks	Essay	
Study Strategy	Memorize	60	42	51
	Outline	50	66	58
		55	54	

A Sample Experiment

Let's put all of the pieces together and dissect a classic experiment by Chase and Simon (1973). These authors were interested in the cognitive processes involved in playing chess and how these processes might depend on a player's skill level. One process they were interested in was memory; more specifically, memory for chess pieces laid out on a board. As you might guess, they postulated that people at different skill levels would differ in their memory for chess positions.

Variables and Design.   Let's restate the research question: How does level of expertise influence memory for chess pieces placed on a board in various configurations? Chase and Simon compared master chess players to beginning chess players. The players were exposed to chessboard configurations that were either typical of a game situation or randomly rearranged versions of these typical configurations. Participants looked at a given board arrangement for five seconds. Then the board was covered and they were asked to reconstruct what they had seen by placing pieces on an empty chessboard.

The dependent variable in this experiment was performance on the chessboard reconstruction task, measured in terms of how many pieces could be replaced on the board in the correct position. Can you guess the independent variables? There are two. One is level of participant expertise, which is a *participant variable* with two levels (master and beginner). By definition, participant variables involve *between-subjects* comparisons. One person cannot simultaneously be an expert and a beginner. The other independent variable is chessboard configuration, a *materials* variable with two levels (game configuration and random configuration). This variable was manipulated *within-subjects*—all participants saw both types of board configurations. So this investigation was a *mixed-factorial* that featured four conditions. This design allowed Chase and Simon to examine the *interactive* effect of expertise and board configuration. It wouldn't be surprising to find that masters remember chess positions better than beginning players, but would this advantage depend on type of board configuration?

Results and Conclusions.   Chase and Simon analyzed the number of pieces correctly placed by the participants as a function of expertise level and chessboard configuration. The results are pictured in Figure 2.5. First, let's examine the main effects of the two independent variables. There was a significant main effect of expertise; overall, masters were better at remembering the piece positions than novices. There was also a significant main effect of board configuration; configurations that represented actual game positions were much better remembered than random board configurations.

But once again, the main effects don't tell the whole story. The results reveal a significant interaction between expertise and board configuration: the pattern of results differs starkly between the two conditions. When it comes to actual game positions, masters are markedly better than novices. But there is *no difference* between masters and novices in remembering chess pieces randomly strewn about the board; in this condition, expertise offers no memory advantage. Chase and Simon explained this result by suggesting that when viewing the chessboards, experts categorized the pieces on the board into groupings that were familiar from their own experience. This categorization allowed for easier encoding and retrieval of the information. However, since the categorization was based on actual

		Expertise Level		
		experts	novices	
Chessboard Configuration	random arrangements	3	4	3.5
	game arrangements	16	4	10
		9.5	4	

(a)

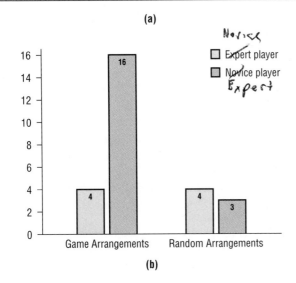

(b)

Figure 2.5 Data from Chase and Simon's (1973) experiment, presented as a table and as a bar graph. Main effects of expertise level and chessboard configuration are apparent, as is an interaction between the two variables.

From Chase, W. G., & Simon, H. A. (1973). Perception in chess. *Cognitive Psychology, 4,* 55–81. Copyright 1973 by Elsevier Science (USA). Reprinted by permission.

game experience, it was only possible for board configurations from actual games. So expertise led to benefits in memory performance, but only for game configurations. Once again, the simultaneous investigation of more than one variable allowed for more elaborate conclusions than could have been gathered from investigating the variables in isolation.

Stop *and* Think! IDENTIFYING THE VARIABLES THAT AFFECT THINKING

You no doubt realize that what you think and do on any given day is affected by a host of variables. For example, Greg's memory for a joke from "The Simpsons" can be affected by (1) the fact that he's a big fan, (2) what time of day it is, (3) whether he's just seen the episode that has that particular joke, (4) whether a friend is helping him remember it . . . you get the idea. Pick a cognitive ability that you use on a daily basis and come up with five variables that affect it (based on your intuition).

For two of the variables that you identify, create a factorial design to determine the effect of the variables on that cognitive ability. Then follow these steps:

1. Identify and operationalize your independent variables (with the levels).
2. Operationalize your dependent variable.
3. Identify and state how you would attempt to control for any confounding variables.
4. Identify and justify whether the design should be a within-subjects, between-subjects, or mixed factorial.

STOP *and* REVIEW!

1. True or false? Factorial design experiments involve more than one independent variable.
2. Identify and define the three types of factorial designs.
3. Briefly describe the purpose of descriptive and inferential statistics.
4. An interaction can only be assessed if
   a. a researcher uses more than one dependent variable
   b. a researcher uses only between-subjects variables
   c. a researcher uses only within-subjects variables
   d. a researcher manipulates more than one independent variable

➤ A factorial design involves the manipulation of more than one independent variable, completely crossing each level of one independent variable with each level of the others. Factorial designs allow researchers to determine how different variables affect one another.

➤ Within-subjects designs involve exposing each participant to all levels of the independent variable(s). Between-subjects designs involve exposing different groups of subjects to the various levels of the independent variable(s). Within-subjects designs are generally preferred because they require fewer participants and are more likely to reveal an effect of the independent variable. One problem with within-subjects designs is the possibility of a carryover effect from one condition to another.

➤ In a between-subjects factorial, all independent variables are manipulated between subjects. In a within-subjects factorial, all independent variables are manipulated within subjects. A mixed factorial involves the joint manipulation of at least one between-subjects variable and one within-subjects variable. Mixed-factorial designs are extremely common in cognition research.

➤ Descriptive statistics are used to summarize the data. Measures of central tendency (most commonly, the *mean*) give an idea of the typical score for a given condition. Inferential statistics are used to determine how likely it is that a difference between conditions occurred due to chance. If this likelihood is low, the effect is said to be statistically significant.

➤ A main effect refers to an overall effect of an independent variable on the dependent variable. An interaction occurs when the effect of an independent variable depends on the level of the other independent variable(s).

Cognitive Neuroscience
Investigating Mind and Brain

There is little doubt that the most rapidly expanding research frontier within psychology is cognitive neuroscience, which involves relating cognitive processes to their neural substrates; in other words, what the brain is doing when the mind is thinking. Gazzaniga, Ivry, and Mangun (1998) describe cognitive neuroscience as a coalescence of biology and psychology. According to these authors, cognitive neuroscience began to emerge in the 1970s out of necessity. At this time, neuroscientists began to move beyond the simple method of destroying brain tissue and relating the destruction to behavioral function and to use increasingly sophisticated methods to address more complex questions, such as how visual cells process and combine information to produce percepts. As neuroscientists advanced beyond simple approaches, so did psychologists. Recall that by the 1960s, psychologists were developing theories and models of cognition and action that were based on mental representations (whose basis, ultimately, was the brain). Given that the interests of many neuroscientists were getting more cognitive and the interest of many cognitive psychologists was turning toward brain representation, a union of the two approaches was inevitable.

An Overview of the Nervous System

Throughout the text, we'll be discussing cognitive neuroscience research. Before we do, it would be helpful to review some basics about the nervous system. We'll start at the most basic level with a discussion of the basic nerve cell, the neuron. We'll then proceed to the brain, highlighting its structure and discussing some of the important questions posed by cognitive neuroscientists, as well as their tools of investigation.

The Neuron.   The nervous system is the body's system for processing information, and the **neuron,** or nerve cell, is its basic unit. It is estimated that there are about 100 billion neurons throughout the nervous system. Many of these are located in the brain's cerebral cortex, the seat of complex thought. A simple neuron is pictured in Figure 2.6. This is a general representation; there are many different types of neurons, with different sizes, shapes, and functions. Given that there are billions of them, you might imagine that they're interconnected in incredibly complex networks. Indeed, this aspect of brain structure forms the basis for the connectionist approach to cognition, discussed in Chapter 1.

Neurons are electrochemical information processors. Within a neuron, communication is basically an electrical process whereby a signal travels from the dendrites to the cell body down the length of the axon. This process is called an **action potential,** and it occurs in an all-or-none fashion if the stimulation of the neuron reaches some critical value, or threshold. At this point, the communication process becomes chemical; the action potential causes the release of neurotransmitters into the tiny gap between neurons, the synapse. The neurotransmitters released into the synapse interact with dendrites of many receiving neurons, leading to their excitation or inhibition. This system of excitatory and inhibitory connections between these basic units of the nervous system underlies all thinking and behavior. Indeed, many believe it *is* thinking (e.g., LeDoux, 2002), although this assertion generates some philosophical argument.

Hebb (1949) suggested a basic principle of neuronal functioning. According to Hebb, "when an axon of cell A is near enough to excite a cell B, and repeatedly takes part in firing it, some growth process or metabolic change takes place in one or both cells such that A's efficiency as one of the cells firing B is increased" (Hebb, 1949 p. 62). In other words, the association between neurons can become stronger with experience; neural networks can learn. Hebb's suggestion has been supported by research and has served as a partial basis for the connectionist approach to mental processes, which attempts to explain thinking in terms of strengthening and weakening (i.e., the changes) in association among

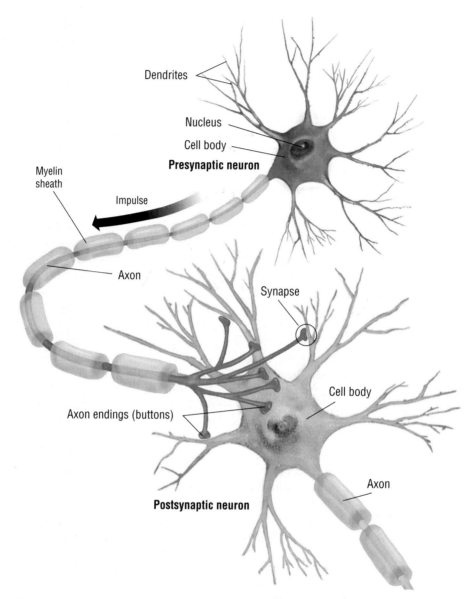

Figure 2.6 A neuron and its major structures.

simple units. These simple units and their interconnections correspond to the brain's neurons and neural networks. Researchers have attempted to simulate thinking tasks like problem solving or pattern recognition with computer models that have an architecture similar to that of the brain, in hopes that these models might provide some insight into how the microstructure and activity of the brain subserve cognitive processes.

Research in cognitive neuroscience has not progressed to the point of explaining cognition in terms of how individual neurons and neural networks actually do work in their seemingly infinite complexity and variety. But researchers have come a long way in modeling how cognition *might* work, given the properties of neurons (e.g., Pinker, 1994). So while we can't map out the exact grouping and activity of neurons that underlie the cognitive processes that occur as we're deciding what to watch on TV tonight, we are fairly certain where in the brain the relevant activity takes place and how some of the component processes may play themselves out in a system modeled on the neural networks of the brain. So some of the pieces of the puzzle about how the brain works are in place, while cognitive neuroscientists continue to look for the remaining ones.

The Brain.   The brain serves as the primary focus of cognitive neuroscience because the brain is the center of information processing. Cognitive neuroscientists examine a number of questions about brain structure and its relation to cognitive processing. A great deal of research has investigated exactly what brain areas are active during different mental processes. Based on this general information, researchers can pinpoint more specifically the brain substrates of cognition.

A Terminology Tour.   Neuroscience can be a challenging topic, in part because of the sheer volume of new terminology one encounters: anterior commissure, parahippocampal gyrus, anterior thalamic nucleus—it's enough to give one dorsal-ventricular cerebral distress (i.e., a headache). Knowing some of the standard terminology will help you understand some of the neuroscience research you'll read about throughout the text. As a convention, anatomists (and neuroscientists) use certain terms to refer to different areas of the brain (see Figure 2.7). The term **anterior** (or **rostral**) refers to the front portion of

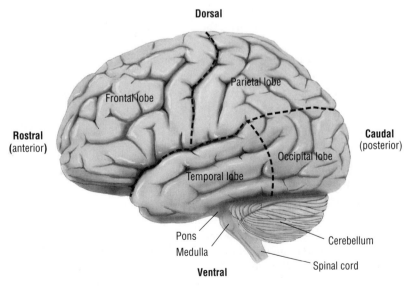

Figure 2.7 The major divisions and anatomical regions of the brain.

the brain or brain region, while **posterior** (or **caudal**) refers to the back portion. **Dorsal** (or **superior**) refers to the top surface of the brain or brain region (like the dorsal fin of a shark), while **ventral** refers to the bottom. Other general terms you might hear in conjunction with specific brain structures are **lateral** (referring to brain structures closer to the periphery) and **medial** (referring to areas closer to the brain's midpoint).

The seat of cognitive functioning is the brain. Neuroscientists commonly distinguish between three major areas in the brain. The **hindbrain** is located at the base of the brain, just above the spinal cord, and its primary function is to monitor, maintain, and control basic life functions such as breathing and heartbeat. Just above the hindbrain, a relatively small area termed the **midbrain** contains areas that are involved in some sensory reflexes and helps to regulate brain arousal. The remainder of the brain, the forebrain, is what serves as the primary interest for cognitive neuroscientists. The **forebrain** comprises most of the brain and includes the **cerebral cortex,** the familiar wrinkled outer shell of the brain, which is actually a sheet of billions of neurons. The cerebral cortex is the primary neural substrate for what might be termed higher cognitive functions—remembering, planning, deciding, communicating—essentially, all the things you'll be reading about in this text. Beneath the cortex lies an array of important structures that are involved in basic processes such as the regulation of memory and emotion.

The Cerebral Cortex. The cerebral cortex consists of two nonsymmetrical hemispheres, which are made up of layered sheets of neurons that form tremendously complex interconnections and networks. Each hemisphere can be subdivided into four major areas, or *lobes* (shown in Figure 2.8). Some areas within each of the lobes are specialized for particular functions. The frontal lobe is the anterior portion of your cortex, located immediately behind your forehead, running back to about the middle of the top of your head. The posterior area of the frontal lobe, the motor cortex, plays an important role in carrying out voluntary movements. Areas in the anterior portion of the frontal lobe (commonly called the prefrontal cortex) are important in higher aspects of motor control, such as planning and executing complex behaviors. The frontal lobe also includes Broca's area, an important area related to the physical production of speech. Behind the frontal lobe lies the parietal lobe, centered more or less under the crown of your skull. In the anterior portion of the parietal lobe resides the somatosensory cortex, which controls the experience of bodily sensations such as touch, temperature, and pain. In terms of cognitive processes, the parietal lobe houses areas important in regulating (among other things) the processes of attention and working memory. Beneath the parietal lobe in the posterior portion of the cortex is the occipital lobe, which contains the primary visual cortex, the area of the brain primarily responsible for vision and the ability to recognize visual patterns. (So we really do have "eyes" in the back of our head!) Finally, the temporal lobe is appropriately located behind the ears. It contains the auditory cortex, the brain's primary sensory area for audition. It also includes Wernicke's area, which is involved in speech comprehension. Many areas of the cortex are not specifically devoted to motor or sensory function and have been dubbed association areas. Association areas of the cortex are believed to integrate the processing of other brain areas, serving as the basis for higher mental processes that require such integration, such as language processing, problem solving, and decision making.

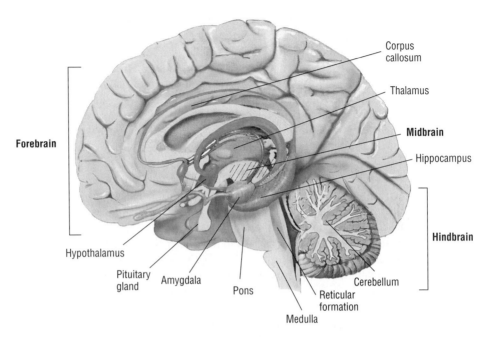

Corpus
callosum

Thalamus

Midbrain

Hippocampus

Hindbrain

Forebrain

Hypothalamus

Pituitary
gland Amygdala

Pons

Cerebellum

Reticular
formation

Medulla

Figure 2.8 The cerebral cortex and major subcortical structures.

Ten Percent of Our Brains? Given that the brain is the center for cognitive processing, it's not surprising that you hear claims about "unleashing your brain power" or "tapping into the unused portion of your brain." One of the more flaky claims is that we only use 10% of our brain. There is no evidence whatsoever for this assertion (except maybe the fact that people make it), yet it persists like the weeds in our front yard. Radford (1999) notes this idea may have originated from the functions of the different cortical areas and the prevalence of association areas. Some have misinterpreted the lack of specialization of the association areas of the brain as a lack of function, wrongly thinking that if these "unused" areas were tapped we could enhance our "brain power." The assumption may be that the association areas are just sitting there doing nothing. Nothing could be further from the truth. There are no unused areas in the brain. Areas that are not specialized for particular functions are critical for combining and integrating information from other brain areas.

The Brain's Hemispheres. The cerebral cortex is made up of two hemispheres, the right and the left. The hemispheres appear more or less symmetrical in their appearance, but as we'll see, each features some interesting processing differences. In general, the operation of the hemispheres is lateralized. The left hemisphere receives information from and controls the right side of the body, while the right hemisphere receives information from and controls the left side of the body. The two hemispheres communicate primarily by means of the corpus callosum, a nerve bundle located in the center of the brain above the limbic system.

Research investigating the differences in the brain's hemispheres has revealed some asymmetries of processing (though not the extreme differences often portrayed by "pop" psychologists when they talk about right brain and left brain). The main distinction between the hemispheres relates to verbal ability. In most people, the left hemisphere is specialized for verbal processing, while the right hemisphere is relatively nonverbal. One major source of evidence for this asymmetry has been research on **split-brain patients,** people who have had their corpus callosum severed to alleviate the severity of epileptic seizures. While successful in alleviating seizures, cutting the main source of communication between the right and left hemispheres does lead to some oddities in processing that have illuminated some of the differences in hemispheric function. These oddities are only apparent under special conditions in the laboratory. Were you to meet a split-brain person on the street, you would notice nothing different in their behavior.

Split-brain research takes advantage of the "wiring" of the visual system, which is structured so that if you were to stare dead ahead, information to the right of center would go predominantly to the left hemisphere, while information to the left of center would go predominantly to the right hemisphere. When split-brain participants are presented with a stimulus (e.g., a word) that is left of center fixation, the information goes to the right hemisphere but cannot get to the left due to their severed corpus callosum. (See Figure 2.9.) If these participants are asked to read the word aloud, they will have a great deal of

Figure 2.9 Testing procedure for revealing hemispherical asymmetry in split-brain patients. When a stimulus is presented to the right hemisphere, vocalization is difficult, yet the stimulus can be identified with the left hand. When a stimulus is presented to the left hemisphere, it is easily identified through speech.

difficulty, because the right hemisphere is relatively limited in its verbal ability. But interestingly, if asked to reach with their left hand behind a screen to pick up the item that the word names, they are able to do so, because the right hemisphere directs the left hand. The right hemisphere "knows" the word it saw but cannot demonstrate this knowledge verbally. However, if a word is presented to the right of center fixation, the information goes to the left hemisphere, and these participants have no trouble reading the word aloud, because the left hemisphere is specialized for verbal processing.

Differences in left- and right-brain function can also be seen in people with an intact brain. Research has revealed that the left hemisphere is specialized for language processing, while the right hemisphere is specialized for spatial tasks, such as assembling the pieces of a puzzle or orienting oneself within the environment. There are some other asymmetries in processing, some of which you'll hear about in subsequent chapters. But one should be careful not to overgeneralize about brain function. The two hemispheres of the brain form an elegantly integrated system that involves close interaction between right and left.

Subcortical Structures.   Beneath the cerebral cortex lies a complex system of structures that play an important role in a variety of cognitive processes. Most of the structures are grouped together and termed the limbic system. The **limbic system** is integral to learning and remembering new information as well as the processing of emotion. Important structures in the limbic system include the hippocampus, which is vital for encoding new information into memory. The amygdala plays a key role in regulating emotions and in forming emotional memories. The thalamus serves primarily as a relay point that routes incoming sensory information to the appropriate area of the brain (directing visual information to the visual cortex and so on) and also seems to play a role in attention. Below the thalamus lies the hypothalamus ("hypo" means "under" in Latin), which controls the endocrine system (the body's system of hormones) and plays an important role in emotion as well as the maintenance of important and basic survival processes, such as temperature regulation and food intake. Together, the thalamus and hypothalamus are termed the diencephalon. The basal ganglia play a critical role in controlling movement and are important for motor-based memories, such as the procedures involved in riding a bike.

Although brain areas and brain structures are to a considerable extent specialized for certain types of functions, it is important not to lose sight of the brain as an integrated system. No function (particularly cognitive functions like remembering) takes place in a single brain structure or area. While some subcomponents of cognitive processes may be localized in one area, complex cognition involves an intricate interplay between brain areas and brain structures distributed throughout the brain.

Stop *and* Think!

USING BRAIN TOPOGRAPHY TERMS

Let's have some fun with your newly acquired brain terminology! See if you can fill in the blank with the appropriate anatomical term. Here are your choices:

dorsal   ventral   posterior (caudal)   anterior (rostral)

1. The hypothalamus is on the _____ side of the thalamus.
2. The motor cortex is in the _____ portion of the frontal lobe.

3. The limbic system is _____ to the cerebral cortex.
4. The occipital lobe is _____ to the temporal lobe.
5. The somatosensory cortex is in the _____ portion of the parietal lobe.

The Tools of Cognitive Neuroscience

Cognitive neuroscientists rely on a number of investigative techniques to discover the neural underpinnings of cognition. Before the development of sophisticated technologies, much of the information we know about the brain, and what happens where, was discovered through investigations of people who had suffered brain damage. In the last 25 years, there has been an explosion in the development of brain investigation techniques. Some of these techniques involve the assessment of the electrophysiological activity occurring in the brain during cognitive processes, while others involve "taking a picture" of the brain activity that accompanies mental processing.

Brain Trauma.   Much of the early knowledge about what brain areas underlie various cognitive functions came from studies of patients who had suffered some sort of trauma to the brain through injury or disease. A prominent example relevant to cognitive psychology is the work of Paul Broca, a neuroscience pioneer in the mid 1850s. Broca had a famous patient who was dubbed "Tan" because this syllable was all he could say. In spite of this inability to speak normally, Tan's ability to understand was relatively unimpaired. Broca discovered that this patient had damage to the left frontal lobe. Later, in the 1870s, Carl Wernicke had a patient who could speak but what he said was gibberish. Furthermore, he was unable to understand written or spoken language. Wernicke discovered that this patient had damage to the left temporal lobe. Based on these and other patients with language impairment, researchers were able to more clearly delineate the role of left hemisphere areas in language processing.

The most severe limitation of using cases such as these to study cognitive processes is that they allow absolutely no control. A researcher can't map out the human brain by systematically damaging different areas and observing the associated deficits. (How would you like to volunteer for that study?) Studies of brain trauma cases also suffer the limitations in generalizability that we discussed in Chapter 1 in conjunction with case studies. There may be critical differences in the functioning of a normal and a damaged brain. And finally (and this is true of most brain investigation techniques), the evidence yielded is purely descriptive. It provides a relatively simple sketch of the relationship between brain areas and cognitive function.

Single and Double Dissociations.   So what modes of assessment do cognitive neuroscientists use in studying individuals with brain damage? Often they will compare performance on two tasks that differ in the use of one proposed mental operation. Let's consider an example from Coltheart (2001). Suppose we find a person who has brain damage in area X and exhibits deficits in comprehending written language (i.e., reading) but has no deficits in comprehending spoken language. This would be an example of a **single dissociation**—performance deficits in one task and no performance deficits in another task. Based on this data, it's tempting to conclude that area X is responsible for written comprehension but not for spoken comprehension. Perhaps spoken comprehension depends on some other area Y. Do you see a problem with this conclusion? Maybe area X is responsible for *both* written and spoken comprehension, but the damage is not severe enough to reveal the deficits in spoken comprehension. (We use this example for discussion purposes only; whether this is a reasonable argument will depend on the nature of the differences between spoken and written comprehension.)

So what can researchers do? They could examine patients with different areas of brain damage—X *and* Y. Suppose we found a patient with damage to area X who shows deficits in reading but not in understanding spoken language *and* a patient with damage to area Y who has deficits in understanding spoken language but not in reading. This pattern is termed a **double dissociation** and serves as stronger evidence for the claim stated above— that area X is responsible for written comprehension and area Y is responsible for spoken language comprehension. Although double dissociations are quite informative, they still do not conclusively show that written and spoken comprehension are based on *completely* different brain processes and structures. However, the double dissociation in this case certainly suggests that written comprehension and spoken comprehension are partially independent and controlled by areas X and Y, respectively.

The EEG allows a researcher to record summed action potentials from different brain sites.

The value of double dissociations extends well beyond cognitive neuroscience. Double dissociations have also been used to argue that the performance on two different experimental conditions or tasks relies on different mental processes, or different cognitive systems. Let's consider the memory test/word frequency experiment we discussed to explain the basic principles of a factorial design. As you'll recall, high-frequency words were better recalled than low-frequency words. However, low-frequency words were better recognized than high-frequency words. This double dissociation indicates that recall and recognition are influenced, at least to some extent, by different factors. Throughout this text, you'll encounter numerous examples of dissociations that indicate the operation of distinct brain systems, or distinct sets of cognitive processes.

The Electroencephalograph. Remember the way neurons work—they are electrochemical information processors. Because the activity of neurons is electrical in part, some research techniques involve recording the electrical activity of the brain and relating it to cognitive functioning. The **electroencephalograph** (EEG) uses electrodes placed on the scalp to pick up the electrical current being conducted through the skull from the activity of neurons underneath, essentially providing a global recording of the action potentials occurring in the brain. Although researchers have used this method to localize the brain processes underlying cognition, the results have been somewhat disappointing. The electroencephalograph simply records a combination of the activity of millions of neurons at the brain's surface, making it difficult to pinpoint specific areas underlying cognitive processes. Also, because the neural impulses are traveling over the brain and through the skull and scalp, some distortion in the recorded signal is inevitable, further confounding attempts to localize where the important brain processing is occurring. Some have likened this use of the EEG to trying to diagnose a computer malfunction by holding up a voltmeter in front of it. As we'll see, neuroscientists have developed much better techniques for mapping out brain function.

Event-Related Potentials.   Although electroencephalography leaves something to be desired in terms of brain-mapping precision, it does have one advantage over some other techniques. It has fairly good temporal resolution, or precision, in specifying the time course of events. Researchers can observe EEG tracings over time and look for *changes* in the brain's electrical activity at certain critical points, like when something surprising occurs. These changes are termed **event-related potentials** (ERP) because they represent the action *potentials* that occur in *relation* to some *event*. These potentials allow researchers to plot out *when* (as opposed to *where*) important brain activity is occurring.

Functional Imaging Techniques: PET and fMRI Scans.   The greatest strides in cognitive neuroscience have been made by using functional imaging techniques. These imaging techniques have proven much more successful than EEGs in precisely localizing the brain areas associated with various cognitive processes. Unlike EEGs, imaging techniques do not involve the direct measurement of neural activity. Rather, changes in blood flow are used as indices of where brain activity is occurring during various cognitive processes, essentially providing a map of brain activity.

Imaging techniques involve a comparison between an active and a (relatively) inactive brain. In a test scan, researchers present some type of task thought to reflect a given cognitive process. For example, to investigate how we access words from our mental dictionary, researchers might have participants generate synonyms for words as they are presented. Brain activity would be monitored as participants engage in this task, and the results would yield an *image* of what the brain is doing. But this image isn't enough to highlight the brain centers important for performing the task. These brain centers might be active anyway, because the brain is never simply "turned off." Therefore, researchers must also get an image of the brain activity that's occurring when the brain is at rest or is involved in some simpler task. This image is termed a baseline, or control scan. By comparing the *difference* in the two images, researchers can extract the areas of the brain that seem to be consistently associated with the task in question. Let's take a closer look at the two major brain-imaging techniques: positron-emission tomography (PET) and functional magnetic resonance imaging (fMRI).

A **positron emission tomography scan (PET scan)** uses radioactive substances ingested (in harmless amounts!) by a willing participant to trace brain activity. The technique is based on a feature of brain metabolism: active areas of the brain are associated with increased blood flow, and a decaying radioactive substance can serve as a gauge of

A PET scanning machine.

where this blood flow is occurring. Detectors pick up this blood flow and convert it into a visual image. The image is essentially a map of the brain in which "hot" colors, like red and yellow, indicate increased activity and "cool" colors, like blue and green, indicate less active brain areas.

Functional magnetic resonance imaging (fMRI) is similar to a PET scan in that it reflects brain activity through changes in blood flow. But fMRI picks up this activity with magnetic detectors that are sensitive to hemoglobin levels in the blood. Basically, a magnetic scanner picks up on differences in hemoglobin that is oxygenated (carrying oxygen) or nonoxygenated (no longer carrying oxygen). The larger the difference, the more neuronal activity is occurring in that area (Gazzaniga, Ivry, & Mangun, 1998). This activity is displayed in much the same way as in PET scanning—as a multicolored map of more and less active brain areas.

fMRI offers a number of advantages over PET scanning. First, it's noninvasive. In other words, no foreign agent has to be introduced into the body, like the radioactive substance used in PET scan studies. Functional magnetic resonance imaging is also cheaper. Equipment that's already present in many hospitals and clinics can be modified to do it, whereas PET scanning equipment is relatively exotic. A third advantage of fMRI is a little more subtle, and relates to how the brain scans are collected over time. Because a PET scan uses a radioactive substance to trace brain activity, some time must

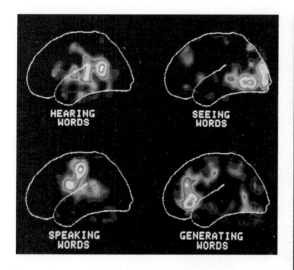

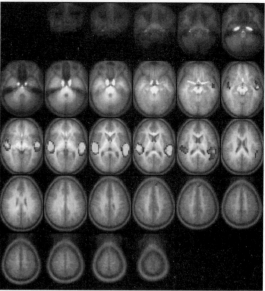

Both PET scans and fMRI images allow researchers to note active and less active areas of the brain.

be allowed between test and control scans to allow the substance to dissipate; the next scan needs to start with a "clean slate." Therefore, over a given period of time, only a limited number of scans can be taken, and these scans are combined into an average image.

In fMRI research, there is no decaying radioactive tracer to worry about, so test and control scans can be interspersed with much greater frequency. In other words, researchers can collect many more control scans and many more test scans in a given period of time. Why is this important? Common sense probably tells you that the more participants in an experiment, the higher the likelihood is that the results of the experiment will be valid and representative. The same principle applies here; the more scans that are obtained, the more likely it is that a researcher is getting a valid and representative idea of brain activity.

Limitations of Imaging.   Imaging techniques such as PET and fMRI have led to crucial insights about where the neural substrates for cognitive activity may lie. These techniques do have a number of limitations. One major limitation is their relative inability to provide a time-based analysis of cognition. Most basic cognitive processes occur on the order of fractions of a second, and the temporal (time) resolution of imaging techniques is nowhere near this fine, so what we get is only a global picture of brain functioning. Another disadvantage is that functional imaging provides only *descriptive* information about where the brain activity that accompanies mental activity is taking place. It doesn't tell us about anything at the level of individual neurons and how their complex interplay is related to cognitive processing. However, this technique has allowed researchers to isolate important subsystems of the brain where these neurons do their work.

STOP *and* REVIEW!

1. What is the basic unit of processing? What are the major divisions in the brain?
2. Which of these terms would be used to describe activity occurring toward the back of the brain?
   a. ventral
   b. posterior
   c. medial
   d. lateral
3. True or false? Distinct processing differences are evident when comparing the activity of the left and right hemispheres.
4. What do brain imaging techniques such as PET scanning allow researchers to do? What are two limitations to imaging techniques?

➤ The basic unit of processing in the brain is the neuron. The brain provides the physiological machinery used in thinking and can be subdivided into the hindbrain, midbrain, and forebrain.

➤ Anatomical terms used in discussions of brain structure and activity include anterior and posterior (front and back), dorsal and ventral (top and bottom), lateral and medial (to the side or toward the midpoint).

➤ The left and right hemispheres of the cortex are specialized in their processing capacities. The most prominent example is a left-hemisphere specialization for language.

➤ The EEG involves recording brain potentials (through the scalp) from different sites in the cerebral cortex. Event-related potentials can reveal the time course of brain activity in response to stimuli. Brain-imaging techniques (PET scanning and fMRI) allow researchers to pinpoint brain regions active in conjunction with various cognitive tasks but are limited to simple descriptions of the localization of brain activity.

GLOSSARY

A reaction (simple reaction): an RT task that involves simple registration and response to one stimulus (p. 41)

accuracy: the percentage of trials on which a subject is correct (p. 41)

action potential: an all-or-none reaction of a neuron that occurs when stimulation reaches some critical threshold value (p. 57)

anterior: (rostral): toward the front (of the brain) (p. 59)

B reaction (choice reaction): an RT task that involves discerning between a number of presented stimuli, each of which is mapped to its own appropriate response (p. 41)

between-subjects design: an experimental design in which different participants receive each level of the independent variable (p. 47)

between-subjects factorial: a factorial design in which different participants are assigned to each of the experimental groups created by the factorial design (p. 50)

C reaction (go–no go): an RT task that involves discerning between two presented stimuli, only one of which requires a response (p. 41)

carryover effects: occur when processing or strategy effects from one condition influence processing in a subsequent condition (p. 46)

case studies: intensive investigations of a single case or small number of cases (p. 35)

central tendency: a descriptive measure that gives an indication of a typical score (p. 50)

cerebral cortex: the outer shell of the brain that comprises the majority of the forebrain and is made up of billions of neurons (p. 60)

confounding variables: the factors that vary in conjunction with the independent variable (p. 45)

dependent variables: the variables measured in an experiment that are influenced by changes in the independent variables (p. 38)

descriptive statistics: the numbers that provide an overview of basic characteristics about some set of data, such as central tendency (p. 50)

dorsal: (**superior**): toward the top (of the brain) (p. 60)

double-blind procedure: a technique for preventing expectancy effects by keeping both the participants and the experimenter naive as to the purposes of the study (p. 40)

double dissociation: occurs when two measures of performance are affected in an opposite fashion by different experimental variables (p. 65)

ecological validity: the degree to which the experimental methodology simulates the real world (p. 39)

electroencephalograph (EEG): a brain investigation technique that involves recording summed action potentials (through the scalp) from different areas of the brain (p. 65)

event-related potentials (ERP): changes in the brain's electrical activity at critical points that are measured to show the temporal relationship between stimulus presentation and brain response (a technique used in conjunction with the EEG) (p. 66)

expectancy effects: the influence of participant or experimenter beliefs on the results of a study (p. 39)

experimental conditions: the groups being compared in an experiment; the circumstances formed by the manipulation of the independent variable (p. 43)

experimental context variables: varying the nature of the instructions given to participants or the situations in which participants are tested (p. 44)

experimental research: the systematic manipulation and measurement of variables in a controlled setting, designed to allow for causal explanations (p. 37)

factor: a synonym for the independent variable in an experiment (p. 46)

factorial design: an experimental design that involves completely crossing the levels of one independent variable with the levels of all other independent variables (p. 49)

forebrain: the largest region of the brain, surrounding the midbrain and dorsal to the hindbrain; controls higher-level processes involved in sensation, emotion, and thought (p. 60)

functional magnetic resonance imaging (fMRI): a brain-imaging technique that traces brain activity through the use of magnetic detectors sensitive to blood hemoglobin levels (p. 67)

generalizability: the extent to which research findings apply outside of the research context (p. 35)

hindbrain: the brain region that lies under the base of the skull and controls basic life functions (p. 60)

independent variables: the variables manipulated in an experiment that are assumed to cause changes in the dependent variables (p. 38)

inferential statistics: statistical tests that provide an indication of the probability that the results obtained were due to chance (p. 50)

interaction: occurs when the particular influence of one independent variable depends on the level of another independent variable (p. 52)

internal validity: the degree to which extraneous variables are controlled (p. 39)

lateral: toward the periphery (of the brain) (p. 60)

limbic system: system of structures in the lower forebrain that is important in learning, memory, and basic emotion (p. 63)

main effects: the overall effects of an independent variable on the dependent variable (p. 51)

material variables: varying the nature of the material being processed by participants (p. 44)

medial: close to the midpoint (of the brain) (p. 60)

metacognition: one's awareness of one's own cognitive processing tendencies and abilities (p. 36)

midbrain: a small brain region dorsal to the hindbrain that controls some sensory reactions and relates to overall brain arousal (p. 60)

mixed-factorial design: a factorial design that involves the joint manipulation of at least one between-subjects factor and at least one within-subjects factor (p. 50)

naturalistic observation: watching and recording a behavior of interest in its natural setting (p. 35)

neuron: a nerve cell; the basic building block of the nervous system (p. 57)

operational definition: defining a variable in terms of precise, measurable procedures that can be repeated by other researchers (p. 40)

participant variables: varying the nature of research participants (e.g., female or male, young or old, etc.) (p. 44)

performance-measure variables: varying the nature of the response measures given to participants (p. 44)

positron emission tomography scan (PET scan): a brain-imaging technique that traces brain activity by observing the distribution of an ingested radioactive substance (p. 66)

posterior (caudal): toward the rear (of the brain) (p. 60)

practice effects: the general improvement in participant performance that occurs over the course of participation in an experiment (p. 46)

reaction time (RT): the time taken to respond to a stimulus, usually measured in milliseconds (p. 41)

self-report: the use of interviews or questionnaires to gather participant data (p. 36)

single dissociation: occurs when some change influences the operation of one particular process but leaves another unaffected (p. 64)

single-factor experiment: an experiment in which the effects of only one independent variable are assessed (p. 46)

speed-accuracy trade-off: the tendency for (all other things being equal) faster responding to be associated with higher error rates (p. 42)

split-brain patients: people whose corpus callosum has been severed, usually as a treatment for severe epilepsy (p. 62)

statistical significance: a term used to describe results that are unlikely to have arisen through simple chance variation (p. 51)

ventral: toward the bottom (of the brain) (p. 60)

within-subjects design: an experimental design in which the same participants receive each level of the independent variable (p. 46)

within-subjects factorial: a factorial design in which the same participants partake in each of the conditions created by the factorial design (p. 50)

3

Early Perceptual Processing

While Vince snores through the day, Ryan, the announcer who's been keeping Vince awake, finishes up his radio show and quickly leaves the building, anxious about the snow. The plow is coming down the street, ready to bury his car, so he quickly jumps in and starts it up. He pulls away just as a 16-inch pile of snow piles up on the cement rectangle that had been his parking spot.

Ahh . . . I have about an hour and a half before I pick up Sherry for lunch, Ryan thinks. She's so excited about me meeting her friend William. I hope he lives up to expectations. Ryan slips and slides around the slick city streets. He pulls in at the media store, looking to spend the $35 that is burning a hole in his pocket. Let's see, a little classical, maybe some jazz, he thinks. He puts on the headphones to sample some classic jazz. Getting into the music, he sways his body as the piano separates from the other instruments into a searing solo.

Suddenly he feels as if he's being watched . . . he is! A couple is eyeing his improvised choreography with amused curiosity.

As he scans the CDs, his eye is caught by an instructional video on golf. What's this doing here, he thinks. Improve your golf game subliminally while listening to authentic ocean sounds recorded at Pebble Beach? Hmph! I wonder if it has tips on how to find your ball when it becomes subliminal. He goes to the check-out counter and picks what turns out to be the slowest line; he seems to have a gift for that.

Finally, it's his turn. The cashier looks at him sideways and says something Ryan doesn't quite get. Oh, wait . . . he said, "Nice dance moves." He must have seen my performance, Ryan thinks, embarrassed. He avoids eye contact, pays for the discs, and hustles out of the store. He stops dead in his tracks. What's that funny smell? he thinks. Smells like . . . hmmm . . . Teen Spirit? No . . . hmmm . . . can't put my finger . . . er, my nose on it. He laughs at his little joke. We DJs are so funny.

He fishes his keys out of his pocket and jumps into his car, eager to play his new CD. After what seems like 15 minutes, he finally manages to remove the cellophane and pops it into the player. Ahh . . . now I can enjoy this in the privacy of my own car. His head starts swaying . . . suddenly the car in the next lane is way too close, and Ryan swerves away. Idiot! talking on his cell phone . . . hang up and drive, he thinks, glaring at the other driver.

Basic Perceptual Processes

Given that cognition is often characterized in terms of information processing, it makes sense to say that cognition begins as soon as information enters the cognitive system. Therefore, any complete understanding of cognitive processes requires an understanding of how we register information—our basic sensory and perceptual processes. Psychologists usually distinguish between *sensation* and *perception*. Although the distinction is somewhat artificial, there are a number of reasons for making it. The most relevant one for our purposes is a distinction between the physiological and the psychological. The term *sensation* is sometimes loosely associated with the physiological processes that underlie information intake. In contrast, the term *perception* refers to the psychological processes involved in the immediate organization and interpretation of those sensations. Perception can be affected by factors inherent in the stimulus as well as those not inherent in the stimulus. What we perceive is importantly influenced by our previous knowledge, expectations, and biases.

The processes of perception are the result of what are commonly termed bottom-up and top-down processes. **Bottom-up processing** basically refers to a flow of information that proceeds from the stimulus, to the neural activity driven by this stimulus, to its eventual identification. Bottom-up processing is sometimes termed **data-driven processing**, because it refers to the processes whereby the stimulus itself (i.e., the *data*) leads to the sensible percept. **Top-down processing** refers to the processes whereby we bring previous knowledge to bear in determining what it is we see or hear. Because it refers to the application of concepts to perception, top-down processing is sometimes labeled **conceptually driven processing**.

Before we begin, let's revisit a concept you learned about in Chapter 1. Psychophysics involves the study of the relationship between the physical properties of a stimulus and how the stimulus is perceived. One concept of psychophysical interest is the **absolute threshold**—the amount of stimulus energy needed to perceive a stimulus 50% of the time. This is the point at which we're squarely on the fence (or on the threshold) regarding whether a stimulus is present or not. The **difference threshold** refers to the *change* in the intensity of a stimulus that is detectable 50% of the time. The difference threshold for a given stimulus depends on the intensity of the original stimulus—a simple demonstration of the effects of context on perception. For example, if you light a match in a room that is completely dark, you will notice a change in brightness. However, if you walk outside in broad daylight and light the same match (well, a match from the same pack), you would not notice any change at all.

You might imagine (quite correctly) that your ability to detect a stimulus, as well as a change in that stimulus, depends on how sensitive an observer you are. But it turns out that sensitivity is only one dimension of perceiving. Perception also involves the knowledge that something was perceived—**sensitivity**—and a willingness to report it—**response bias.** Think about bumps you may have heard in the night. Did you really perceive them, or were they a product of your imagination? The important point here is that, in addition to a discrimination process based on sensitivity, perception involves a *decision* regarding whether a stimulus was perceived. This important insight forms part of the basis for **signal detection theory,** an approach to psychophysics that characterizes perceptual experiences as the joint product of sensitivity and response bias. Two people may succeed and fail to perceive some stimulus (e.g., a sound) because one observer is more sensitive than the other or because one observer is more willing to report that they perceived the stimulus.

Vision and Audition

The research you'll be reading about in the remaining chapters will deal almost exclusively with information taken in by the visual and auditory senses. Most of the complex information we process and respond to (most notably, events going on around us) taken in through our eyes and ears. As such, vision and audition are the most thoroughly investigated sensory modalities in perception and cognition research.

Perception of Depth and Relative Location.   An important aspect of perceptual processing is the ability to locate objects in space. Knowing the distance between you and objects in the environment is critical information to encode correctly, if you are to ambulate about the world without bumping into things. Seeing the world in three dimensions may *seem* trivial, but it is important to remember that the image on the retina is two-dimensional. How is information about depth (for vision) and location (for audition) extracted from a stimulus?

Visual Cues to Depth.   Three cues to depth are a consequence of the physiological processing of the visual system. **Accommodation** refers to the change in the shape of the eyeball's lens with changing distance from a visual stimulus. The physiological process underlying this change provides information about depth. A second cue is **convergence,** which refers to the degree to which the two eyes turn inward toward each other when brought to fixation on a common point. When looking at a very close object, your eyes turn inward quite a lot, but when looking at an object that is not so close, your eyes turn inward to a lesser extent. In combination with accommodation, convergence provides reasonably accurate information about the depth of relatively close objects in the environment; these two cues alone support reasonably accurate depth perception to a distance of about 10 feet (Rock, 1984).

A third cue inherent in the physiological structure of the visual system is retinal disparity. When we view objects with both eyes open, a slightly different view of the objects appears on each retina due to the fact that the eyes occupy two different positions on your head. The eyes are in slightly different positions relative to the scene you're looking at. As a result, the relationships among the objects in your field of view are different for the two retinas. You can prove this to yourself by staring straight ahead, sizing up two objects of differing distance from you, and alternately closing one eye and opening the other. You'll notice that the apparent relationship between the two objects changes as you alternate eyes. **Retinal disparity** refers to the differing views of the scene offered by each retina. Fusion of these images leads to stereopsis, or 3-D vision.

The last two cues discussed rely on the fact that we have two functional eyes, but it's a simple exercise to demonstrate to yourself (by closing one eye) that not all depth perception relies on this fact. The environmental depth cues that only require the use of one eye are appropriately termed **monocular cues.** Many of these cues are evident in Figure 3.1.

Figure 3.1 What cues in this picture give it a three-dimensional feel?

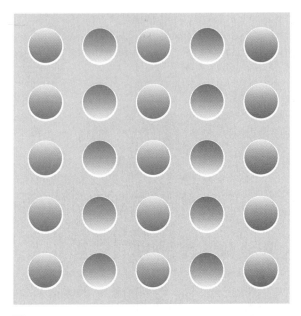

Figure 3.2 Shading and perception of depth. Depending on shading, the dots will look sunken or raised.

The simplest of these cues is **interposition:** objects that overlap other objects are perceived as nearer in space. A second environmental cue is **relative size:** if two objects are known to be similar in size, yet one is smaller in the picture, the smaller object is *perceived* as more distant.

A number of environmental cues can be placed under the general rubric of perspective. **Perspective cues** to depth are those that arise from the changes in information received by the eye as our distance from and/or perspective on the objects change. The most striking perspective cue is **linear perspective,** in which two parallel lines seemingly converge as they recede from the viewer. Another cue that depends on viewer perspective is **texture gradient,** which refers to the variations in the perceived texture that occur as we move closer and farther away from an object. The closer we are to an object, the more of its texture we see. A third perspective cue is **aerial perspective.** Because of the way light scatters throughout the atmosphere, objects that are farther away appear hazy and unclear. A final perspective cue is **shading.** Take a look at Figure 3.2. Some of the circles in the figure look like bumps, while others look like craters. Now turn the book upside down; the craters are now bumps, and the bumps are craters. The fact that there is shading in the figure means that the visual system will perceive depth. Two-dimensional surfaces don't cast shadows, so this must be a three-dimensional surface. Also, light almost always comes from above. Working under this assumption, the visual system assumes that when the bottom half is shaded, we are looking at a convex surface (i.e., a bump). When the top half is shaded, we assume we are looking at a concave surface (i.e., a crater).

A final environmental cue is unique in that it provides depth information only if we are in motion. **Motion parallax** refers to the differences in the relative motion of objects as you pass them or as they pass you. The apparent motion of near objects is more rapid than for far objects.

Stop *and* Think!   **DEPTH**

Right now, stop reading, look up, and make a list of all of the depth cues that are assisting you in depth perception. If you're near a window, walk to it and see if any other depth cues seem apparent.

Sound Localization.   Our ability to localize sound is an important aspect of auditory perception and might be considered an analog to depth perception. You need to know where the blaring car horn is coming from in order to respond effectively. Teachers need to know where the whisperers are in their classrooms so they can turn in the right direction to tell them to be quiet. Unlike vision, there is no information inherent in the stimulus itself that allows us to place sounds in space. It turns out that sound localization depends critically on the fact that we have two ears. One source of information is the **inter-aural time difference (ITD)**—the discrepancy in time of arrival of a sound at each ear. The greater the discrepancy, the easier it is to localize the sound on the side where the sound first arrived. A second source of information is the **inter-aural intensity difference (IID)**—the difference in a sound's intensity as it enters each ear. Greater intensity in one ear indicates that the sound is closer to that ear. Interestingly, the use of these sources seems to vary in effectiveness as the frequency of sounds changes. A classic study by Stevens and Newman (1934) demonstrated that for low-frequency sounds, localization depends on ITD, while for high-frequency sounds, localization depends on IID. Most sounds involve a mix of frequencies, however, so both cues are important in just about every situation. It's important to note that any particular ITD or IID specifies a range of possibilities about where the sound is coming from but doesn't uniquely specify an exact location. You've probably had the experience of knowing from which general direction a sound is coming but not being able to pinpoint the exact source.

Perceptual Grouping and Perceiving Form. One vital characteristic of perceptual processes is the tendency to segregate and group things in the environment so that the percept, rather than being a jumbled mess of randomly arranged stimulus patterns, ends up being a neat orderly package. We do this so seamlessly that we're not even particularly aware of it, though we are, of course, aware of the results.

Gestalt Principles of Grouping. Much of the work on how we group the elements of our stimulus environment was done by the Gestalt psychologists, who were briefly introduced in Chapter 1. The Gestalt psychologists were interested in the processes underlying perceptual and mental organization. Perhaps most notable were their proposed **principles of visual organization.** These principles account for most of the "order" we see in our visual environment. The Gestalt psychologists believed these principles were the cornerstone of perception.

The most fundamental principle of organization, termed **figure-ground,** refers to our tendency to segregate visual scenes into a background and a figure that appears to be superimposed against it. Several cues allow for us to parse figure from ground. Regions picked out as figure tend to be smaller and have more symmetrical features than regions designated as background (Palmer, 2002). Recent findings by Vecera, Vogel, and Woodman (2002) add another feature to the mix. Elements in the lower region of the visual field are more likely to be seen as figure, relative to elements in the upper region of the visual field. According to Vecera and colleagues, this tendency develops with visual experience. In most natural scenes, regions below the horizon line are closer and do comprise the figure. Experience tunes our visual systems to parse the scene in this way, yet another indication of top-down processing.

Some of the other Gestalt grouping principles are depicted in Figure 3.3. **Proximity** refers to the tendency for objects that are near one another (i.e., *proximal*) to be grouped.

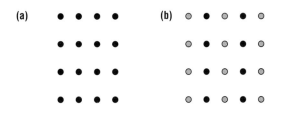

Figure 3.3 The Gestalt grouping principles that guide perceptual organization.

The elements of Figure 3.3a look like rows rather than columns because the row elements are closer to one another than are the column elements. The principle of **similarity** dictates that items be grouped to the degree that they are similar to one another. The elements of Figure 3.3b appear as columns rather than rows because the columns have like elements. The principle of **good continuation** refers to our tendency to perceive lines as flowing naturally, in a single direction. For example, the letter X appears as two lines that cross rather than two connected 45-degree angles. According to the principle of **closure,** we tend to complete the incomplete, perceptually connecting contours that are almost, but not quite, connected. Finally, **common fate** refers to our tendency to group elements together if they are moving in the same direction or at the same speed.

Two additional principles are discussed by Rock (1984) and are shown in Figure 3.3c and 3.3d. The first is **uniform connectedness**—elements that are connected in some way will be grouped, even if this grouping conflicts with the other Gestalt principles, such as similarity (see Figure 3.3c). The second is **common region**—elements that seem to belong to a common designated area, or region, will be grouped. Once again, this principle may overrule other *classic* Gestalt principles. For example, in Figure 3.3d the principle of common region dominates the principle of similarity.

Stop *and* **Think!** **GROUPING**

Right now, stop reading, look up, and make a list of all of the Gestalt grouping cues that are assisting you in organizing your visual environment. If you're near a window, walk to it and see if any other grouping cues seem apparent.

Although the Gestalt principles are most easily demonstrated with visual examples, there is no doubt that they play an important role in the way we analyze what Bregman (1990) terms *auditory scenes.* Auditory grouping plays a fundamental role in our perception and enjoyment of music (Sloboda, 1986). As Iverson (1995) notes, the music listener's task is to take a jumble of sounds arriving at the ear simultaneously and group them in terms of the instrument that is producing them. This grouping might be done along the dimensions of loudness, pitch, or timbre. For example, the highly pitched piccolo is relatively easy to "pick out" from a marching band or orchestra. Brass instruments such as trumpets and trombones differ in timbre (and usually loudness) from woodwind instruments like clarinets and saxophones. These instrument classes are easily separated and grouped (and the full enjoyment of music also involves their recombination). The figure-ground principle is at work in our opening vignette as Ryan listens to the jazz piece and the soloist's playing emerges from the background, serving as an auditory "figure."

GROUPING WHILE LISTENING

Put on a favorite piece of music or turn on the radio to a music station and attempt to analyze the song you're listening to in terms of the Gestalt cues. Pay particular attention to figure-ground and similarity, although other cues might be discernible.

Global Precedence. When we hear a symphony or look at a painting, it seems that (phenomenologically, at least) we tend to blend the elements into an integrated whole rather than isolating separate elements. The Gestalt credo that "the whole is greater than the sum of its parts" nicely states this phenomenological experience. The Gestaltists viewed perception (and thinking in general) as a process of apprehending whole configurations or relationships—and this apprehension is more than just the sum of a group of independent sensations and thoughts. Basically, the Gestalt view is that apprehending wholes or configurations is a primitive. It's the natural tendency of our perceptual system and, as such, is done fairly easily and automatically. In other words, the "forest" is apparent before the "trees."

A classic study by Navon (1977) provides some support for this perspective. Navon was interested in how people process visual displays. More specifically, would this processing be dominated by the specific and individual features within the pattern (i.e., local features), or would it be dominated by the overall pattern (i.e., global features)? Navon (1977) addressed this question rather cleverly, by composing stimuli that could be perceived in one of two ways, depending on whether participants were more influenced by global or local features. He pitted these two modes of processing against one another to see which would dominate by using stimuli like those pictured in Figure 3.4. When viewed globally, the figure is an H; however, the local features are made up of a different letter (S). When you glance at this figure, what do you notice first?

Navon (1977, experiment 3) investigated this question with a fairly straightforward procedure. Participants viewed letters like the one in Figure 3.4 under different instructional conditions. In the *global-directed* condition, the task was to indicate whether the global figure was H or S; in the *local-directed* condition, the task was to indicate whether the component letters were H's or S's. The big letters presented to participants were of three types: (1) the global and local features were consistent (a big H made of little H's); (2) the global and local features conflicted (a big H made of little S's); (3) the global and local features were neutral with respect to one another (a big H made from little rectangles). If global processing takes precedence, then conflicting letters should only pose a problem in the local-directed condition, because in this condition, one can't help but see the big letter. Also, in this condition, where the large letter conflicts with the one participants have to identify, responses should be slower and more prone to error.

The results are shown in Figure 3.5. The first thing you see in the graph is that the reaction time (RT) for the big letters (global-directed) was much less than for the small ones (local-directed). This

```
S         S
S         S
S         S
SSSSSSSS
S         S
S         S
S         S
```

Figure 3.4 Sample stimulus from Navon's (1977) study of global precedence.

From Navon, D. (1977). Forest before trees: The precedence of global features in visual perception. *Cognitive Psychology, 9,* 353–383. Copyright 1977 by Elsevier Science (USA). Reprinted with permission.

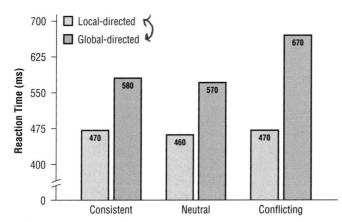

Figure 3.5 Results from Navon's (1977) study. Less time is required to identify global letters than to identify local letters. More important, interference from a conflict between the global and local letters is apparent only in the local-directed condition, supporting the notion of global precedence.

From Navon, D. (1977). Forest before trees: The precedence of global features in visual perception. *Cognitive Psychology, 9,* 353–383. Copyright 1977 by Elsevier Science (USA). Reprinted by permission.

demonstrates that perceptually it's easier to "get" the whole rather than its component parts. This could be due simply to the size of the stimulus—it's easier to identify something that's bigger. This explanation would suffice, were it not for the striking interaction that's apparent in the graph. Interference from the conflicting letter had markedly different effects on global-directed and local-directed conditions. When participants were directed to notice the global aspects of the presented stimulus (identify the large letter), it didn't matter whether the local (small component) letters were consistent, conflicting, or neutral. The global (large) letter was easily apprehended. Such was not the case for the local (small) letters; whether the global letter was consistent or conflicting made a huge difference. If the large letter conflicted, participants' RT was slowed by 100 milliseconds (relative to the neutral condition), a sizable inhibition effect. This implies that even when instructed to look for the local letters, participants couldn't help but encode the global one.

Based on these results, Navon proposed a sequence of processing whereby the global features of a scene are registered first, followed by a systematic analysis of the local features. Basically, Navon's results and analysis suggest that perception of the whole of a scene is an example of a **visual primitive**—a feature of the visual environment that is registered automatically, without the need for higher-level interpretation or analysis. Navon's oft-replicated **global precedence** effect fits well with the Gestalt notions of organization. Segregating visual scenes into parts based on cues such as figure-ground, similarity, and proximity is very much a global approach to explaining how we visually encode the environment.

Somesthesis

Although the focus of much cognition research is on visual and auditory information, it would be a serious misstatement to say that cognition is limited to information processing through these modalities. For example, consider the oft-overlooked perceptual and cognitive characteristics of touch, or **somesthesis.** It's easy to understand why touch is taken for granted. Everyone can imagine what it's like to be without vision or audition—you can just close your eyes or cover up your ears. And you know what it's like to be without taste or smell if you've ever had a bad head cold. However, it's difficult to imagine what it's like to not feel something physically. Craig and Rollman (1999) begin their review of somesthesis with the story of Ian Waterman, a man who lost all sense of light touch and **kinesthesis** (the ability to sense the position and movement of one's body parts) below his neck, probably due to a virus. Because of the complete loss of kinesthetic feedback from peripheral nerves, the only way he could monitor all of his movements was visually (Cole, 1995). Therefore, if the lights went out unexpectedly, he would fall down! Clearly, somesthesis is a critical and underappreciated capacity.

Let's begin our discussion of touch with a simple question: Are there basic dimensions of touch perception analogous to our visual sensitivities to color and brightness? Hollins, Faldowski, Rao, and Young (1993) had participants tactually encode a variety of everyday objects and then performed a detailed analysis of their descriptions. This analysis yielded three fundamental dimensions of touch perception: roughness/smoothness, hardness/softness, and sponginess.

Another distinction relevant to somesthesis is between active and passive touch. **Passive touch** refers to just that—touch that does not involve active exploration. Through passive touch, we gather basic information about the stimuli impinging on our skin receptors. So what are some of the factors that affect our ability to sense through passive touch—that is, our **tactile acuity**? Body area is a major factor, due to the difference in cortical area devoted to somesthesis in different regions of the body. Your face is extremely sensitive; your upper arm, less so. In addition, tactile acuity is enhanced when stimulus probes are warmer or cooler than the skin (e.g., Stevens and Hooper, 1982), and it seems to decrease with age (e.g., Stevens, 1992).

The acuity of somesthesis is affected dramatically by activity. More specifically, you pick up much more information from **active touch** than you do from passive touch. In fact, such active touch is associated with fairly complex information processing. Active touch involves the addition of information from the kinesthetic sense (in this case, information about hand position and movement) to the information gathered from passive touch. The combination of the relatively simple information gained through the skin senses with the information gained from hand position and movement is termed **haptics.**

Given our incredible proficiency as visual perceivers, we fail to notice how much information is available through touch (Gibson, 1966). We tend to think of vision as the primary mode for environmental exploration and information intake. However, haptic sensing provides useful and distinct information that is often taken for granted. Klatzky, Lederman, and Reed (1987) suggest the following thought experiment: think of what you would likely see if you were looking at a cat. Chances are this visual image includes a head, pointy ears, whiskers, four legs, and a tail, along with the respective sizes and layout of these features. If you were asked to think of how a cat feels to the touch, you'd likely come up with quite different attributes: furriness, warmth, or softness. There's a great deal of information about objects in the environment that you can't get just from looking. In our opening story, Ryan has no problem fishing his keys out of his pocket, in spite of the fact that his pockets also contain coins, paper money, tissue, lint, and who knows what else. Nonetheless, he manages to identify and remove his keys in about a second.

So how do you gain this information? Klatzky, Lederman, and Metzger (1985) coined the term **exploratory procedures (EPs)** to describe the precise motor patterns performed by the hands in exploring an object. They asked participants to identify 100 common

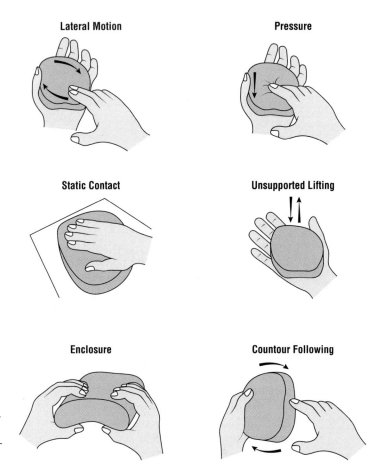

Figure 3.6 Exploratory procedures used in active touch. From Klatzky, R. L., Lederman, S. J., & Metzger, V. A. (1985). Identifying objects by touch: An "expert system." *Perception & Psychophysics, 37,* 299–302. Reprinted by permission of the Psychonomic Society, Inc.

objects using nothing but their hands. It may seem surprising that participants were able to identify each object in a matter of one to two seconds, with virtually no wrong identifications. Clearly, we can gather an incredible amount of information with what Klatzky and Lederman (1995) call a *haptic glance.*

Based on their observations of participants' haptic exploration, Klatzky, Lederman, and Metzger (1985) identified six exploratory procedures (depicted in Figure 3.6): static contact, unsupported lifting, lateral motion, pressure, contour following, and enclosure. Each of these EPs is directed specifically toward obtaining information about a specific characteristic of an object. Static contact is used to ascertain the temperature of an object; unsupported lifting helps ascertain information about weight; lateral motion is used to extract information about texture; pressure is used to extract information about hardness; contour following provides information about shape; and enclosure provides information about object size. Lederman and Klatzky (1990) found that haptic exploration proceeded in a quite orderly manner. The first EPs performed by participants tended to be enclosure and unsupported lifting. In other words, participants began their exploration by grasping and hoisting the object to determine its basic shape and weight. Subsequently, the rest of the EPs described above were used in further exploration to determine such things as size, shape, and function.

Stop and Think!   ## EXPLORING EPs

Gather up a few objects that can be easily held and keep them out of view. Recruit a couple of friends and have them attempt to identify the objects through haptic exploration. You'll have to direct your "subjects" to close their eyes or otherwise divert their gaze from the objects. Take careful note of what their hand movements are doing.

- Do the EPs discussed cover the span of movements done by the identifiers' hands?
- Which of the EPs are the most common?
- Do the EPs seem to take place in any particular order?

Chemosenses

The cognitive correlates of **gustation** (taste) and **olfaction** (smell), sometimes collectively referred to as the **chemosenses,** have received even less research attention than those of touch. However, there is no doubt that they are intimately involved in our daily information processing. For example, smells are often cited (anecdotally) as one of the strongest cues to remote memories of childhood. We'll discuss this particular power of odors further in Chapter 8. For now, we'll take a look at some the fundamental aspects of taste and smell perception and their relation to basic cognitive processing.

Gustation.   As with the other senses, one fundamental issue in taste perception relates to the basic dimensions of taste. You're probably familiar with the four basic tastes—salty, sweet, bitter, and sour (some add a fifth, savory). You're probably also well aware that just about anything you taste involves a complex interaction among these basic categories. As a fan of single-malt scotches, Greg (your first author) can certainly attest to this. And that's not all; the basic tastes combine with a number of other factors to produce the complex perception of flavor. **Flavor** includes the combination of the four basic tastes along with other factors, such as smell, texture, and temperature.

Two major issues in taste perception relate to the idea of these basic tastes. First, how many tastes are there? Many agree on the four we mentioned above, but this is still controversial. Can all of the complex flavors we experience be boiled down to these four tastes? Another issue relates to the way the basic tastes are combined in our perceptual experience. When we taste something complex, say, some hot apple cider, are all of the basic tastes discernible? Can you experience the *sour* of apple cider in isolation? McBurney (1974, 1986) contends that we can, due to the fact that there are receptors in the tongue that are maximally sensitive to each of these four basic tastes. Others disagree, arguing for what might be termed a Gestalt approach to taste, contending that component tastes fuse together to produce a singular sensation that can't be described in terms of basic elements (Erickson, 1982; Erickson, Priolo, Warwick, & Schiffman, 1990). Another fact about taste is its strong reliance on smell. In fact, as Rozin (1982) notes, taste and smell are so inextricably linked that smells are often mistaken as tastes.

TASTES LIKE . . . CHICKEN?

Try to scrutinize your taste experiences a bit (or pester friends while they're eating and have them introspect about the experience). As you (or your friends) eat, attempt to describe the taste (flavor) of the food. Take note of the following:

- Are the four basic tastes evident?
- Do the four basic tastes seem to fully describe the experience?
- What aspects of the flavor don't seem to fit the four basic tastes?

Olfaction.   A fundamental question about smell rings familiar: Are there primary or basic smells? This has proven difficult to answer. As Lawless (1997) points out, there is tremendous variation in people's sensitivity to smells and their ability to discriminate different smells, as well as in their ability to recognize and label a given smell. The difficulty in easily capturing the perceptual characteristics of smell is also demonstrated by what Lawless terms the **olfactory-verbal gap.** Like Ryan in our opening story, people tend to have difficulty describing odors and identifying them correctly. In fact, studies show that participants often label as few as 50% of presented odors correctly (e.g., Cain, 1979; Desor & Beauchamp, 1974). The picture changes considerably if odor identification is tested with a choice of labels. Under these conditions, odors are quite reliably named, and for reasons not yet completely understood, women are better at labeling smells than men. Another indicator of the olfactory-verbal gap is sometimes termed the **tip-of-the-nose phenomenon** (Lawless & Engen, 1977), which refers to a frustrating inability to come up with the verbal label for an odor in spite of a strong feeling that one knows what the odor is. The "smeller" can describe the odor and name similar ones, but the label is stuck on the "tip of the nose."

WHAT'S THAT SMELL?

Similar exercise, different sense. Gather up some basic household stuff (such as peanut butter, chocolate, baby powder, rubbing alcohol, garlic, onion, vanilla, deodorant, household cleaner, pencil shavings, crayons). For each smell you choose to present, come up with some alternatives you could give on a multiple-choice labeling test.

Again, recruit your friends. Place the smell substance in a small paper cup so the "smellers" can't see the items as you present them. Have them take a good whiff of the item and then attempt to identify it. Try to test both males and females. First, have them describe the smell; then ask them to identify it. If they cannot, give them the multiple-choice options you created.

- Were there any signs of the olfactory-verbal gap?
- Were they able to readily identify the smells? Was the tip-of-the-nose phenomenon evident?
- Did providing choices aid in their identification of the smells?
- Did you find a difference between males and females in identification ability?
- Did you find that any taste terms (e.g., salty) were used to describe the smells?

RECURRING RESEARCH THEME
Cognition and Individual Differences

Nonvisual Sensory Acuity in the Blind

One common belief about blind individuals is that due to their visual deficits, their other sensory systems are more sensitive or highly refined. This speculation does make some intuitive sense, but is there any empirical evidence to support it? It turns out there is. Stevens, Foulke, and Patterson (1996) were interested in whether the experience of blind individuals in reading Braille would be associated with an increase in tactile acuity. In particular, they were interested in whether the decrease in tactile acuity with aging might be less for Braille readers, who have made more active use of their fingertips. As expected, the results of their study demonstrated that blind readers of Braille have greater tactile acuity than do sighted individuals, but only in their fingertips. Tests of similarly sensitive areas (e.g., lips) showed no differences between the groups. And for all participants (blind and sighted), tactile acuity decreased with increasing age.

The possibility of differences in chemosensory acuity in the blind has been addressed in a couple of studies. Smith, Doty, Burlingame, and McKeown (1993) compared blind and sighted participants on a number of tests of smell and taste acuity. They also tested experts—people who worked for the Philadelphia Water Department on a water quality evaluation panel. On measures of taste and smell acuity, the researchers did detect some differences but not in favor of the proposed hypothesis. The experts outperformed the other two groups (blind and sighted), and these latter groups did not differ from one another. Converging evidence for the comparable chemosensory acuity of blind and sighted individuals was also found in a study by Rosenbluth, Grossman, and Kaitz (2000). This study showed no enhanced sensitivity to olfactory stimuli in blind children relative to sighted children. However, this study did reveal one interesting difference: the blind children were better at retrieving verbal labels for smells (i.e., they weren't as likely to suffer from the tip-of-the-nose phenomenon). So although the ability to detect smells does not appear to differ, there may be some enhancement in more general cognitive functioning (i.e., retrieval from memory).

Finally, a number of studies have assessed the possibility of enhanced auditory acuity in blind individuals and these studies have yielded mixed results. Although absolute sensitivity in detecting auditory stimuli does not seem to differ in blind and sighted individuals (e.g., Bross and Borenstein, 1982), there is evidence that blind individuals are particularly good at localizing sounds in space. This is somewhat surprising, because as you'll read later, visual cues play an important role in auditory perception. In spite of the lack of availability of these visual cues, enhanced proficiency in localizing sounds is found (e.g., Arias, Curet, Moyano, & Joekes, 1993). Lewald (2002) suggests that blind individuals may enjoy enhanced processing of proprioceptive and vestibular information (i.e., information about body and head position), which in turn supplements the purely auditory information they use in sound localization. In sum, there is some evidence for enhanced function of nonvisual senses in blind individuals, although the effects appear to be subtle.

STOP *and* REVIEW!

1. What are the two factors that play a role in whether someone reports a stimulus?
2. Name three cues to depth.
3. Name three grouping principles in vision and perception of form.
4. Distinguish between active and passive touch. What is an EP?
5. Name the four basic tastes.

➤ People's perception of sensory events is a reflection of both their sensitivity and their willingness to respond. Perception involves both bottom-up processes (analyzing sensory data) and top-down processes (imposing expectations and knowledge on incoming data).

➤ In vision, perception of depth is based on the physiological cues of accommodation, convergence, and retinal disparity. Monocular (single-eye) cues to depth include pictorial cues like shading, perspective, interposition, and texture gradient. In audition, sound localization depends on inter-aural time and intensity differences.

➤ Gestalt principles of visual grouping indicate a global precedence effect, or a tendency to note the gross features of a visual scene before we notice the details. Perception of form is guided by fundamental principles of organization. Scenes are naturally segregated into a figure and background. Similar elements and elements that are close to one another tend to be grouped perceptually.

➤ Passive touch can be contrasted with active touch, which involves the combination of skin senses with kinesthesis. Active touch is also termed haptics. Exploratory procedures used during active touch include lateral motion (to determine texture), contour following (to determine shape), and enclosure (to determine size). The basic dimensions of tactile sensation are roughness, hardness, and sponginess.

➤ Some controversy exists over the idea of basic tastes, which many cite as sweet, salty, sour, and bitter. It's unclear whether complex taste experiences can be analyzed into these basic components. Taste is closely linked with smell. Smell is a complex sensory experience, and smells tend to be difficult to describe and label, as evidenced by the olfactory-verbal gap.

Interactive Effects in Perception

Interactions between Sensory Systems

One of the continuing themes in the study of cognition is the degree of interrelatedness among cognitive processes. Treating perception, attention, memory, and so on as separate topics is largely a matter of descriptive convenience. The same is true (albeit on a lesser scale) for perceptual processes. For example, what we see affects what we hear; what we see also affects our sense of touch. In addition, the same sensory stimulus can be experienced in more than one modality, leading to the puzzling phenomenon known as synesthesia (which we'll cover a bit later).

Vision and Audition.   A great deal of information processing involves the joint intake of visual and auditory stimuli, so it's not surprising that there are some powerful interactions between the two. You'll see that in each, vision tends to dominate audition. Two examples of such interaction involve the process of sound localization. In a movie theater, the sound appears to be coming from the appropriate sources on the screen—the actors, the ringing phones, and so on. But in reality, the sound is coming from speakers positioned around the theater. Ventriloquism relies on the same effect; the voice seems to be coming from the dummy, not from the ventriloquist.

Another example of visual dominance in audition comes from a study by Saldana and Rosenblum (1993). They presented one group of participants visually with a video of a cello being either plucked or bowed in conjunction with a corresponding auditory stimulus— a tape recording of a cello being plucked or bowed. Other participants were presented with only the auditory stimulus. Participants in the visual-plus-auditory condition tended to "hear" what they saw rather than what was presented auditorially. In other words, if the participants in both conditions heard a cello pluck, those in the auditory-only condition indicated that they heard the pluck. However, those participants who heard the pluck and saw a cello bow indicated that they heard a bow, not a pluck.

MacDonald and McGurk (1978) investigated the role of visual information in speech perception. In their study, participants were presented with speech sounds (e.g., /bə/); simultaneously, they were presented with a (silent) visual display of a speaker pronouncing a different speech sound (e.g., /gə/). That is, the auditory and visual information were in conflict. What "wins" in this case? Interestingly, a sort of "average" of the two speech sounds (/də/) is the resulting perception. This phenomenon has been dubbed the **McGurk effect.** Some neurological evidence provides further support for the importance of visual information in speech perception. Calvert and colleagues (1997) performed functional magnetic resonance imaging (fMRI) on individuals who were watching a speaker's lips in the absence of any auditory stimulation. Intriguingly, simply watching these speech-related lip movements led to the activation of the auditory cortex of the brain. This activation didn't occur for just any type of facial movement. The auditory cortex was only activated when facial movements were linguistic in nature. This neurological evidence converges with laboratory evidence indicating an important role for visual cues in speech.

Vision and Touch.   Vision and touch allow us to gather richly elaborated information about objects in the world. But what happens when these two are placed in conflict? Evidence indicates that vision exerts undue influence, just as it does in the cases of conflict between vision and audition.

Pavani, Spence, and Driver (2000) devised a unique test of the possible dominance of vision in touch. They placed participants in the setup pictured in Figure 3.7a. In this experiment, participants wore rubber gloves, and their hands were placed out of sight. A small sponge cube was held with the thumb and forefinger of each hand. The cubes were equipped with tiny vibrators that could either vibrate the thumb or forefinger position. Directly above the hand-held sponge cubes were two visible sponge cubes. These sponge cubes were equipped with an LED at the top and bottom that would light up simultaneously when the respective hand-held cube below was vibrated. The relationship between which LED was activated (top or bottom) and which position received the

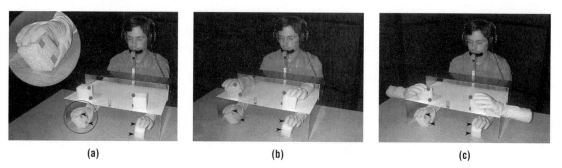

(a) (b) (c)

Figure 3.7 Interaction between vision and touch; setup for the Pavani, Spence, and Driver (2000) phantom hand study.

From Pavani, F., Spence, C., & Driver, J. (2000). Visual capture of touch: Out-of-body experiences with rubber gloves. *Psychological Science, 11*, 353–359. Copyright 2000 by Blackwell, Inc. Reprinted by permission.

vibration (forefinger/top or thumb/bottom) was random on any given trial; sometimes they matched, and sometimes they mismatched. But activation of the lights and vibration always occurred at the same time. The participants were to identify the source of the vibration, and reaction time for this judgment was recorded. A question of interest is the possible facilitatory or inhibitory effect of the light. Would the location of the light on the cube (top or bottom) being viewed affect the reaction time to identify the source of the vibration (top or bottom)?

Here's where the fun starts. On half of the trials, dummy hands in rubber gloves were placed on the visible cubes (the ones with the LEDs). Participants' hands (situated below, and out of sight) were in identical rubber gloves, and the fake hands were positioned so that they looked like they could have been participants' hands (see Figure 3.7b). Imagine what participants would experience in this condition. They'd be looking at "hands" that are holding cubes; the LEDs on these cubes would light up at the same time as they'd feel a vibration directly underneath. *Now* what happens when the visual cue and tactile stimulation match or mismatch?

The results are presented in Figure 3.8a. Participants' speed in identifying the source of the vibration is plotted as a function of whether the viewed light matched or mismatched the position of the vibration, and whether or not there were dummy hands holding the cubes. As you can see, the reaction time to identify the source of the vibration was slower when the light mismatched the vibration position than when it matched. More important, however, is that the dummy hands significantly accentuated this interfering effect! In the dummy hand condition, participants were even slower (reaction time was greater) at identifying the source of the vibration when the light mismatched the vibration position. Seeing the light at a given position on the dummy hand gave rise to an illusory sensation of feeling that vibration was occurring in the corresponding position below.

Perhaps, you might think, participants were confused because they were seeing another set of hands. In a second experiment, Pavani and colleagues (2000) replicated the same procedure but with misaligned dummy hands that were clearly fake (see Figure 3.7c). The results, shown in Figure 3.8b, make it clear that the dummy hands had no effect under

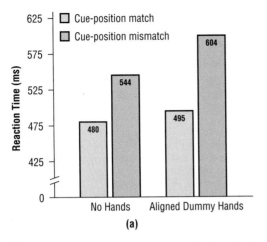

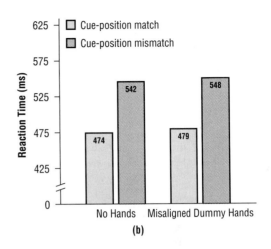

Figures 3.8 Results from the Pavani, Spence, and Driver (2000) study. Interference arising from a cue-position mismatch was more pronounced in the condition where dummy hands were aligned.

From Pavani, F., Spence, C., & Driver, J. (2000). Visual capture of touch: Out-of-body experiences with rubber gloves. *Psychological Science, 11,* 353–359. Copyright 2000 by Blackwell, Inc. Reprinted by permission.

these conditions. Therefore, the results of the first experiment show that participants experienced the dummy hands as their own (to some extent). The results of this and a number of other studies underscore the fact that tactile sensations are the result of a complex blend of tactile, kinesthetic, and visual information.

Synesthesia.   An intriguing example of interactions among sensory systems is found in the phenomenon known as synesthesia. **Synesthesia** refers to experiences in which input from one sensory system produces an experience not only in that modality but in another as well. For example, synesthetes (as they're termed) might experience a particular musical chord as green. These cases, termed *strong synesthesia* by Martino and Marks (2001), are very rare (occurring in less than one out of every 2,000 individuals); interestingly, female synesthetes outnumber males about six to one (Baron-Cohen, Burt, Smith-Laittan, & Harrison, 1996). This disproportionate distribution, combined with the fact that synesthesia runs in families (Baron-Cohen et al., 1996), indicates that the phenomenon may have a genetic basis.

Synesthetic experiences are not as exotic or uncommon as they may seem. Most people have cross-modal experiences in which stimuli from one sensory modality are experienced in terms of another. Martino and Marks (2001) call these garden-variety synesthetic experiences *weak synesthesia*. For example, people commonly blend somesthesis and vision in distinguishing between "warm" and "cool" colors. Weak synesthesia is also evident in controlled laboratory settings. For example, in studies requiring participants to match the pitch of a presented tone with an appropriate color, people reliably place higher-pitched tones with lighter colors (Marks, 1987). In another study by Martino and Marks (2001), tones were presented, and participants were to rapidly classify them as high or low. Tones were accompanied by either a black or white square. Results indicated a cross-modal

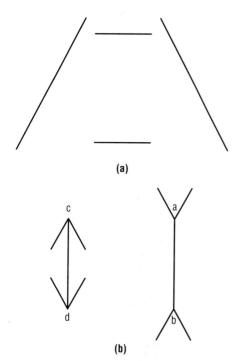

Figure 3.9 Ponzo and Müller-Lyer illusions.

interaction (weak synesthesia); high-pitched tones were more quickly classified when presented along with white squares than when presented with black squares. The opposite pattern held for low-pitched tones. This pattern is termed a *congruence effect.*

What leads to synesthetic correspondences, and do similar mechanisms underlie the strong and weak varieties? We don't know yet. Some believe that these effects derive from the way we process sensory data at lower levels. Others believe that these effects derive from the way we think about the sensory dimensions. One explanation of the first sort appeals to the notion of "sensory leakage" (Harrison & Baron-Cohen, 1997), such that information from one sensory modality is miscoded and/or misprocessed by another modality. In strong synesthesia, this could be due to some abnormality in the development of neural connections. A similar explanation can be applied to weak synesthesia. For example, the congruence between high-pitched tones and light colors could occur due to low-level sensory processes. That is, processes that convert stimulus energy into neural activity may transduce low tones and dark colors in a similar manner, leading the two to be perceptually associated.

Conversely, Martino and Marks (1999) propose that synesthetic effects arise from higher-level mechanisms. More specifically, they propose that the associations between sensory modalities that give rise to synesthetic effects are the product of knowledge. Synesthetic effects derive from the way we think about and linguistically code our sensory experiences. According to Martino and Marks (1999), as we experience and describe our perceptions, we build up an abstract network of concepts that applies to these experiences. With further experience, some of these concepts become strongly associated (e.g., light and high pitched, dark and low pitched) such that one concept can automatically activate the other. So the experience of light blue activates a related concept (at least within this network)—coolness.

Interactions with Experience and Context

Recall the notion of top-down processing discussed at the beginning of this chapter. Top-down processing refers to the imposition of context, knowledge, and expectations on what we take in through our sensory systems. Most of the time, top-down processing adds speed and efficiency to analysis of the environment. But occasionally, this increase in speed and efficiency comes at the expense of perceptual accuracy.

Illusory Percepts.   Our perceptual systems do a breathtakingly good job of decoding the complexities of the sensory environment, yet there are some rather striking cases when we are misled. The occurrence of illusions underscores the importance of context and inter-

RECURRING RESEARCH THEME

Cognition and Neuroscience

Blindsight

Research on the neural mechanisms underlying vision has provided some intriguing evidence regarding the nature of visual consciousness. Consider the fascinating case of blindsight, detailed in a case study by Weiskrantz (1986). His patient, D. B., was blind on the entire left side of his visual field as the result of surgery to remove enlarged blood vessels in his right visual cortex. The wiring of the visual system is such that information to the left of center goes to the right part of each eye and ends up being processed in the right visual cortex. The reverse is true for visual information to the right of center. So the right hemisphere receives information from the left visual field, and the left hemisphere receives information from the right (see Figure 3.11). Further visual mapping

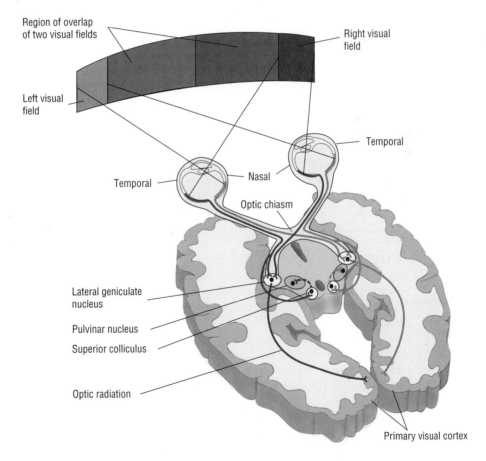

Figure 3.11 Visual pathway from retina to visual cortex.

with D. B. revealed that his blind spot (or scotoma) comprised the entire left half of the visual field for each eye. Consistent with this, D. B. reported no awareness of objects or events on his left. However, there were some intriguing suggestions that he had some knowledge of them. For example, he could accurately reach for a person's outstretched hand in order to shake it. He attributed this type of success to lucky guessing, swearing up and down that he didn't see the hand—that is, he was visually unaware. In Block's terms, he was demonstrating access consciousness in the absence of phenomenal consciousness.

To investigate D. B.'s deficits and abilities more systematically, Weiskrantz placed him in controlled visual settings and presented a variety of stimuli to his left and right visual fields. Whenever stimuli were presented to the left visual field, D. B. reported seeing nothing; his self-reports indicated blindness. Weiskrantz employed a *forced-choice procedure* to find out what, if anything, D. B. knew about the stimulus he claimed not to see. In a forced-choice procedure, participants are given two alternative answers and are "forced" to choose the correct one; "I don't know" is not an acceptable answer. After presenting visual stimuli, Weiskrantz asked D. B. to make a forced choice about some aspect of the stimulus, such as where it occurred or, in the case of stimulus lines, the orientation of the lines. D. B.'s performance under these conditions was quite surprising; his responses were well above chance accuracy. In spite of his lack of visual awareness, he was able to process some information about the stimuli. Weiskrantz termed the phenomenon **blindsight,** underscoring the seeming contradiction between the capacity to classify a presented stimulus in some respect while being unaware that it has been presented.

Subsequent research on blindsight (along with other research on the visual system) has indicated that there are two distinct neurological systems underlying vision that are dissociated in the case of blindsight. One of these systems, based primarily in the visual cortex, is responsible for identifying, recognizing, and becoming aware of visual stimuli. This is often termed a *what system.* The other system, an earlier point in visual processing (i.e., a subcortical system), is concerned with detection and localization (i.e., a *where system*). Researchers are still investigating the neural basis for the preserved functioning demonstrated in patients with blindsight, which may lead us closer to discovering the neural basis for awareness.

Perception without Awareness?   An issue that has been the subject of hot debate in both the public arena and in cognition laboratories is the relative influence of stimuli of which we are unaware. You saw that such stimuli can have an influence in cases of blindsight. In the lay literature, the effects of **subliminal perception** can allegedly be seen in many different guises. Many proponents (e.g., Key, 1973) claim that ice cubes in vodka ads, heavy metal rock songs, and the frames of movies contain insidious subliminal messages that exert an influence on our behavior. One of the most famous examples of supposed subliminal influence (the example most students relate when they claim that subliminal influence is for real) was reported by advertising expert James Vicary in 1957, who (self-) reportedly embedded the messages "eat popcorn" and "drink Coke" in a movie, resulting in a rush of movie watchers to the concession stands to buy refreshments. Almost everyone has heard some version of this story. However, almost no one knows that Vicary later admitted that it was a hoax—a story he cooked up to generate some publicity for a struggling advertising firm (see Weir, 1984). But based on stories like this, and other anecdotal evidence, people tend to believe in the reality of subliminal influence.

Contrary to popular belief, there's no reason to believe that subliminal messages in music influence behavior; they may not even exist at all!

Cognitive research has revealed extremely subtle (though consistent) effects of subliminally presented stimuli, but not the large-scale effects claimed by Vicary and others. One reason for the gulf between popular opinion and research results is a lack of precision in definition. When your local newscaster or your Aunt Edna says something about subliminal perception, the term *subliminal* could simply mean "not attended." This is unfortunate, since the difference between "not attended" and "not perceived" proves to be critical when assessing whether a stimulus is likely to affect processing. As you'll see in Chapter 4, it's clear that unattended stimuli can exert an influence on behavior. In Chapter 6, you'll see that information we don't remember can also influence our behavior. But subliminal means literally "below threshold"—that is, it cannot be perceived. So the sound of people murmuring behind you in class is not subliminal; it's simply not attended to (hopefully!). The real question of subliminal perception is whether stimuli that aren't even judged as being present at all can influence behavior. As you'll see, there are even subtler definitional shadings to the notion of subliminal.

Subliminal Perception Research.   Marcel (1983) conducted a series of studies to investigate the possibility of subliminal perception. The procedure involved a Stroop task; in this task, one must name the color of ink when shown a word written in a conflicting ink color. (That is, when shown the word *red* written in green ink, the task would be to respond "green." (We'll discuss this task in more detail in the next chapter.) In Marcel's experiments, participants had to name quickly the color of a presented color patch. The interference was created by presenting a conflicting color name before the color patch. For example, the word *orange* would be presented, followed by a green color patch, and participants were to respond "green."

What makes this a test of subliminal perception? The catch was that the word presented before the color patch (called a *prime*) was (on some trials) presented subliminally—that is, participants could not see it. The subliminal presentation of the prime was accomplished by presenting it for an extremely short period of time and visually masking it after presentation. Visual masking involves following a stimulus immediately with a jumble of other stimuli, effectively obliterating the stimulus that was just seen. To ensure that participants could not see the prime, Marcel adjusted the length of time between the prime and the mask for each subject, to a point where they achieved only slightly better-than-chance performance in guessing whether the prime was present or not.

Would a prime presented at a level where participants had reported not seeing anything at all produce an effect on responding? Marcel's results showed that it did. If the prime word was consistent with the color of the patch, it facilitated (speeded) responding; if inconsistent, it inhibited (slowed) responding. (Both the facilitation and the inhibition were relative to a condition with a neutral prime word, like *table*.) The prime words influenced the speed of color naming, even if the primes were presented at a level where participants reported not being aware of them.

Subjective and Objective Thresholds. A great deal of consternation in studies of subliminal perception has centered on exactly how to define *subliminal*. Marcel (1983) defined it in terms of what participants said they perceived. *Subliminal* was defined as the conditions under which participants guessed that there was a prime presented about half the time; he then used these stimulus conditions for the unaware conditions. You might say that Marcel defined the threshold subjectively—in terms of the participants' phenomenological experience. Others (e.g., Cheesman & Merikle, 1984) have emphasized the importance of what is termed an *objective threshold*—that is, the level at which performance on some task (not participants' self-reports) indicates that the prime was not perceived. These researchers point out that in the Marcel procedure, where awareness was defined subjectively, participants may have perceived the prime but were conservative in saying that they had. So even though they said they were unaware, they may have been aware. This relates to two concepts of psychophysics discussed earlier. When participants reported that they hadn't perceived the subliminal prime, it may have been a matter of *sensitivity* (they truly did not detect it) or a matter of *response bias* (they were conservative in their reporting).

Cheesman and Merikle (1984) used the same task as Marcel (1983)—a primed color identification task—but they were more stringent about the way they determined that a prime was presented subliminally. Recall that in a pretest, Marcel presented primes under different masking conditions and defined subliminal as the level at which participants said that a word had occurred about half the time. Cheesman and Merikle defined *subliminal* differently. In a pretest, they presented prime words under different masking conditions. After each presentation, participants were asked (as they were in the Marcel study) if they had seen anything. They almost always reported a lack of awareness of any prime word. Then they were presented with four color names and forced to choose which they had seen. If their guessing performance matched their self-report, they shouldn't have been able to guess the color more than 25% of the time (chance-level performance). But even under conditions where participants reported seeing nothing, they guessed the color they had seen at a level much higher than chance. This demonstrates that some information about the stimulus must have been processed; otherwise, participants' guessing would have been at chance levels.

Using this pretask, Cheesman and Merikle tested the effects of prime words presented under the conditions identified in the pretest. In the objective threshold condition, primes were presented under conditions that had led to chance levels of performance in the pretest. The authors believed that this was the condition that truly involved subliminal presentation, because at this level of exposure, participants couldn't guess what color had occurred with any level of proficiency. Thus, this condition was termed an **objective threshold.** In a second condition, roughly equivalent to Marcel's, they presented primes under conditions that had led to 55% accurate guessing in the pretest. This latter condition used what Cheesman and Merikle termed a **subjective threshold.** Participants reported that they couldn't see the prime words, yet their guessing performance indicated otherwise.

The results of this study are presented in Figure 3.12, which shows the reaction time to name the color of the patch for prime-target congruent trials and prime-target incongruent trials relative to a neutral-prime condition. As you can see, primes presented below an objective threshold failed to influence performance (reaction time did not differ from a neutral prime). But primes that were presented below a subjective threshold (primes that were presented at a level that allowed 55% detectability in the pretest) produced inhibitory priming (slower reaction time than the neutral prime condition) for prime-target incongruent trials and facilitatory priming (faster reaction time than the neutral prime condition) for prime-target congruent targets. Note that the effects in this latter condition occurred even though participants reported not being aware of the prime. Cheesman and Merikle concluded that the reality of subliminal perception, or *subliminal semantic activation* as it's sometimes called, depends on how one defines the threshold of awareness below which the stimuli presented are deemed subliminal. Defined subjectively, the answer is yes; objectively, the answer is no. It's important to note that even when subliminal influences are found, they tend to be small effects, on the order of 1/20th of a second.

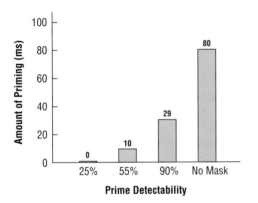

Figure 3.12 Results from the Cheesman and Merikle (1984) priming study. The bars indicate priming scores, which reflect the difference between reaction times on trials that included a prime and trials that did not include a prime. As you can see, no priming occurred below an objective threshold (defined by 25% prime detectability). However, a small but reliable priming effect did occur below a subjective threshold (defined by 55% prime detectability).

From Cheesman, J., & Merikle, P. M. (1984). Priming with and without awareness. *Perception and Psychophysics, 36,* 387–395. Reprinted with permission of the Psychonomic Society, Inc.

Subliminal Self-Help?   Do the subtle effects reported in laboratory studies of subliminal influence translate into any real effects? One common application of what might be termed *subliminal perception technology* involves presenting subliminal messages on tapes. Such tapes claim to offer assistance with everything from weight loss, to alleviating depression, to curing acne (see Druckman & Bjork, 1991, for a more complete list). There may even be a tape, like the one Ryan found in the opening vignette, that gives subliminal aid for one's golf game. Is there any evidence that such tapes work? Usually, their advertisers cite the evidence of testimonials from satisfied customers. Even if these testimonials are real, they aren't very compelling evidence. Satisfied customers represent a biased sample; people who listen to self-help tapes are certainly motivated to make the change targeted by the tape. Any observed behavioral change may simply be the result of these motivational factors.

Stop *and* Think!   ## SUBHELPFUL SUBLIMINAL PROGRAMS

Search the Internet and magazines for advertisements and descriptions of subliminal self-help programs (or other subliminal claims). Take note of what they claim and how the subliminal message is delivered.

To separate the possible effects of subliminal self-help messages from motivational effects, one needs to conduct a double-blind study of the effects. Greenwald, Spangenberg, Pratkanis, and Eskenazi (1991) conducted a double-blind study on the effectiveness of subliminal message tapes. They used commercially manufactured tapes that had subliminal messages embedded within classical music, popular music, or nature sounds. In a clever procedure, they gave participants one of two tapes with an embedded subliminal message; the message was designed to improve either self-esteem or memory. However, the label on each tape was randomly assigned. A tape labeled "memory improvement" was actually a self-esteem tape for some participants, and a tape labeled "self-esteem improvement" was actually a memory improvement tape for some participants. Participants were given pretests that included measures of memory and self-esteem and were then instructed to listen to their tapes every day for one month. They then returned for a series of posttests, including retests of memory and self-esteem. Participants were also asked to rate whether they believed their self-esteem and memory had improved.

The results were clear: the posttest measures of self-esteem and memory showed none of the expected improvement over the pretest measures in any of the conditions. The only consistent effect that emerged was a subject-expectancy effect. When asked about their perceived improvement, participants were generally of the opinion that they had improved in whatever quality (memory or self-esteem) was on the tape label (even if the tape had been labeled incorrectly). For example, participants who saw a self-esteem improvement label on their tape thought that they had made improvements in their self-esteem, regardless of what was actually on the tape.

Merikle (1988) applied the logic of Cheesman and Merikle and attempted to find out whether subliminal message tapes even met what he termed the *minimum stimulus conditions* necessary for subliminal influence. Recall that subliminal influence only occurs in conditions where (1) participants report there is no stimulus, but (2) demonstrate on some objective (forced-choice) measure that they are sensitive to its presence. Merikle set out to determine whether subliminal message tapes fit this pattern. Certainly, condition 1 is met: people who hear nature sounds with an embedded subliminal message report no subjective awareness of that message. But for this subliminal message to have any chance of influencing behavior, it must fit condition 2: on some objective measure, participants should be able to pick which of two tapes has a subliminal message with above-chance accuracy. Merikle found that participants could not do this. They showed no ability whatsoever to distinguish between commercially produced tapes that did and did not have embedded messages. Since these tapes fail to meet the minimum stimulus conditions necessary to demonstrate subliminal perception, subliminal message tapes do not work (at least not through subliminal influence).

Subliminal Perception and Top-Down Processing.   Subliminal messaging is also challenged by another line of research, one that indicates that messages embedded in various media (e.g., print ads and rock music) are actually creations of the lookers' or listeners' imaginations. Vokey and Read (1988) demonstrated this in an informative series of studies. In one of their studies, they investigated the phenomenon of backmasking—the alleged presence and influence of messages on record albums (which were all the rage before CDs) that are supposedly discernible if the records are played backward. According to some, messages embedded in rock albums are capable of eliciting negative effects in listeners. Somehow, these backmasked messages exert an influence on behavior. In an especially tragic case, the heavy metal band Judas Priest was sued by the parents of two teenagers who jointly attempted suicide. Sadly, one of the boys succeeded; the other died from drug complications a few years later (Moore, 1996). The plaintiffs alleged that subliminal messages in the music played a role in prompting this tragedy. After hearing expert testimony on both sides, the judge ruled in favor of the defendants. (See Moore, 1996, for an excellent discussion of this case, as well as an informative discussion of lay and legal belief about the effectiveness of subliminal messaging.)

Vokey and Read demonstrated that you can hear just about anything in a garbled message, as long as you have an expectation that you're going to hear something. In one of their studies, they made backward recordings of Lewis Carroll's *Jabberwocky* ("Twas Brillig and the Slithy Toves . . .") and the 23rd psalm ("The Lord is my shepherd . . ."). The experimenters did some (in their words) "creative listening" to these backward tapes and detected a few sequences that could be heard as something meaningful. Among these were "Saw a girl with a weasel in her mouth" and "I saw Satan." Now mind you, these messages weren't really there; the garbled noise that was there could be construed into these messages by the creative (or as it turns out, expectant) listener. The experimenters found six such passages for each of the two recordings. They then gave participants a simple task: they were to listen to the backward recordings to see if they could hear the messages designated by the experimenter. Each participant was given only the six messages for one of the passages; for the other passage, they listened without any prior prompting about what they might hear. As Vokey and Read suspected, participants were very good at hearing the backmasked messages, but only the ones that they were told to expect. The six messages in the control passage, extracted by the experimenters but not mentioned to the participants, were never heard by the control group. So in essence, the participants created the backmasked messages because they expected to hear them; when they didn't expect them, they didn't hear them. Clearly, top-down processing is at work here: the data are garbled, but expectations and knowledge impose order on this garbled data.

To sum up: the only solid evidence for subliminal influence consists of smallish re-action time and accuracy effects on laboratory tasks. The empirical evidence for success-ful application of subliminal messaging in real-world situations is extremely weak, almost nonexistent.

S T O P *and* R E V I E W !

1. The McGurk effect is an example of
   a. the influence of speech perception cues on vision
   b. the influence of visual cues on speech perception
   c. the influence of visual cues on tactile perception
   d. the influence of tactile cues on vision
2. True or false? Synesthesia is the lack of sense perception.
3. Distinguish between the constructive and direct views of perception.
4. Distinguish between access and phenomenological consciousness.
5. Can we be influenced by subliminally presented stimuli? Explain, relating your answer to the distinction between objective and subjective thresholds.

➤ Vision tends to dominate both audition and touch. Visual information can influence speech perception (McGurk effect) and can lead to illusory tactile perceptions.

➤ Sensory experiences can combine in the form of synesthesia, cases where input in one modality is experienced in another modality. Synesthesia can be strong or weak.

➤ The constructive view of perception emphasizes the role of inference and expectations on perception. This view is supported by the fact that illusory percepts arise when environ-mental cues lead to a misinterpretation of a stimulus. The direct view of perception em-phasizes the richness of information provided directly to sensory systems, without the need for interpretation.

➤ Several senses of consciousness can be distinguished. Two types are access consciousness, which refers to the manipulation of mental representations, and phenomenological con-sciousness, which refers to one's subjective feeling or state.

➤ The subjective threshold refers to the level of stimulation below which stimuli are not reported as perceived but can affect performance. The objective threshold is the level of stimulation below which stimuli are not perceived and do not influence performance. Stimuli presented below a subjective threshold can influence behavior if they're above the objective threshold. Practical applications of subliminal influences of stimuli are extremely limited.

Sensory Memory

One of the most influential theories that employs an information-processing approach has been the Atkinson-Shiffrin model of memory (Atkinson & Shiffrin, 1968). The model posits that incoming information is (potentially) processed by three different storage systems, one of which is perceptual in nature and hence relevant to our discussion of early information processing. Figure 3.13 presents a basic sketch of the model. In this model, incoming information is briefly held and processed by a sensory store, or **sensory memory**. From there, the information is passed on to short-term memory, an information buffer in which incoming material is identified and held for further processing. The final "box" proposed by the model is long-term memory, which is made up of everything we know about our lives and about the world in general. (The two latter "boxes" proposed in the model will serve as the subject of discussion in Chapters 4 through 9.)

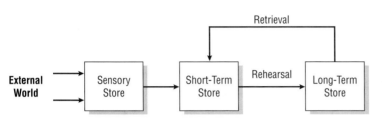

Figure 3.13 The information-processing model.

Here, we are interested in the first stage of information processing called *sensory memory*—the initial reception and early processing of incoming information. Theoretically, we have a sensory memory for each of our major senses; however, almost every investigation has focused on vision and audition.

Visual Sensory Memory

The proposed processing buffer in which we initially take in and briefly store visual information has been termed *visual sensory memory,* or **iconic memory.** An *icon* is a visual image or symbol; iconic memory is a fleeting image of a stimulus that was just presented but is no longer present. It may strike you that applying the term *memory* to this phenomenon is a bit of a misnomer. Indeed, iconic memory seems more like a phenomenon of perception rather than memory (though many would argue that it's hard to separate cognition this way).

Whole Report versus Partial Report.   Actually, the concept of iconic memory predates Atkinson and Shiffrin's information-processing model. It was proposed and thoroughly investigated in an extremely influential doctoral dissertation by George Sperling (1960). Sperling was interested in how much information could be taken in during a glance at a briefly presented stimulus. He presented participants with matrices (rows and columns) of letters, as pictured in Figure 3.14a. Stimuli were presented with a *tachistoscope* (or *t-scope*). A tachistoscope allows for the rapid presentation and removal of a stimulus without any fade-out. (With current technology, a computer would be used for stimulus presentation, but in the early 1960s, computers and computer technology were not nearly as advanced and easy to access and employ as they are today.)

F	P	Z	D
C	M	R	B
W	N	J	T

(a)

F	3	Z	9
2	M	R	5
W	1	8	T

(b)

Figure 3.14 Stimulus matrices employed by Sperling (1960).

From Sperling's results, as cited in Crowder, R. G. (1976). *Principles of learning and memory.* Hillsdale, NJ: Erlbaum. Reprinted by permission of Lawrence Erlbaum Associates.

In one study from his 1960 series, Sperling presented matrices containing three rows of letters, with four letters in each row. The presentation was a brief 50-millisecond flash. (To give you an idea of just how fast 50 milliseconds is, clap your hands as fast as you can; the time between each "clap" is about 100 milliseconds!) After the 12-letter matrix disappeared, a tone signaled participants to report every letter in the matrix (a procedure termed *whole report*). Typically, no more than three or four letters could be reported. But it seemed unlikely to Sperling that nothing else was available from the matrix. See for yourself—look straight ahead and quickly shut your eyes. Chances are you retained an image of the entire scene in front of you (albeit extremely briefly). Similarly, Sperling suspected all 12 letters in the matrix had been available for an extremely brief period after the matrix disappeared. However, by the time participants were able to report three or four of the letters, the rest of the information was gone; but this did not mean it wasn't there in the first place. To reveal that it was there, Sperling needed a different reporting condition.

Using an ingenious condition he termed *partial report,* Sperling eased the load of recalling by requiring participants to report only part of the display. For example, a high tone would signal recall of the top row in the matrix. How would this procedure provide a truer test of the information available in the icon? The key was that participants were not informed about which row to report until after the display was gone. If the entire display is indeed available for a short time, then participants should be able to report most or all of the elements in any row. However, if the capacity of sensory memory is limited to approximately four items (that indicated from the whole-report technique), then only a small subset (maybe one item) could be reported from the designated row. Sperling found that in the partial-report condition, about three out of the four letters in any row could be reported. This suggests that immediately after stimulus offset, participants were "looking at" a more-or-less complete image of the matrix and could "read out" any row when given the signal.

In order to plot the time-course of the icon's fade-out, Sperling varied the delay between the offset of the letter matrix display and the onset of the cue. The results are presented in Figure 3.15. As you can see, iconic storage is quite fleeting. Although 80% of the matrix could be reported when the cue was presented immediately, only about 50% could be reported after a quarter of a second. After about half a second, recall had fallen to the rather meager levels seen in the whole-report condition. Sperling surmised that although the entire matrix was available initially, it faded rapidly and was gone within about 500 milliseconds.

Other Methods of Assessing Iconic Memory.   Early research using a variety of methods provided converging evidence for Sperling's view of iconic memory. These methods involved variations in the characteristics of the presented display and different responses from participants.

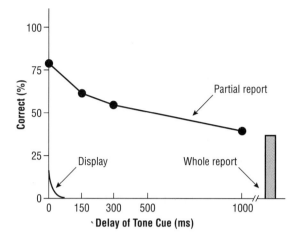

Figure 3.15 Recall in the whole-report condition and in the partial-report condition, as a function of delay between display offset and partial-report cue.

A popular technique for assessing the properties of the icon employs a procedure discussed earlier in this chapter—visual masking. Recall that the presentation of a mask immediately following a visual stimulus can essentially wipe out what's left of the visual stimulus. Varying the time between the presentation of a stimulus and the presentation of the mask provides an estimate of how long the icon lasts. The logic is as follows: if a mask is presented immediately after a visual stimulus, it will destroy the icon; as the delay before the mask is increased, the effect of the mask is decreased. Finally, after about 300 milliseconds, the mask has no effect, suggesting that there is no icon left to be interfered with. Estimates of the duration of the icon from visual masking studies (i.e., 300 milliseconds) converge nicely with those from partial-report studies (i.e., 500 milliseconds) (Massaro & Loftus, 1996).

Another method for estimating the duration of the icon, in phenomenological terms (i.e., in terms of how it's experienced), is by having a person estimate its duration. A general procedure for doing so is outlined by Massaro and Loftus (1996). In this procedure, participants perform a synchrony-judgment procedure in which a stimulus (i.e., a letter matrix) is followed by a second (auditory) stimulus, such as a tone. The period between the two stimuli is termed the ISI, or interstimulus interval. The ISI is under the control of the participants, who are instructed to vary it until it seems like the tone occurs just as the icon has completely faded. Estimates using this method indicate that the phenomenology of the icon matches its visual characteristic; subjectively, it seems to have faded within a third to a half a second, just as the ability to extract information from it fades within a third to a half a second.

The Precategorical Nature of Iconic Memory?   A great deal of early research on iconic storage focused on the nature of the partial-report task. More specifically, a number of studies varied the nature of the partial-report cue in an attempt to specify the nature of the information represented in the icon. Sperling himself addressed this in his classic 1960 study. Recall that in the original study, Sperling essentially cued participants to report certain locations from the matrix, given a certain type of cue. In a follow-up study, he cued participants to report certain types of items from the matrix. To do this, he presented a matrix filled haphazardly with letters and numbers (see Figure 3.14b, p. 104). He presented these matrices in the same way described earlier, but once the matrix had disappeared, he cued participants to report the letters or the numbers. Note that to do this successfully, the characters in the display had to have been identified. Perhaps surprisingly, the partial-report cue "report the numbers (or letters)" did not help participants; performance with this type of cue didn't even surpass performance in the whole-report condition. From this result, Sperling surmised that the iconic representation is *precategorical*—that is, meaning has not yet been extracted from it; it has not yet been categorized. A study by von Wright (1972) replicated this result, demonstrating that position (row) and color (red versus black) were helpful partial-report cues, while category (letter or number) was not.

By the 1970s, a fairly clear picture (pardon the pun) of iconic memory had emerged. An icon

- is the first representation of a visually presented item.
- has a fairly large capacity that includes everything in the visual scene.
- has an extremely brief duration of about 300 to 500 milliseconds.
- is a relatively raw, unprocessed residual of the visual stimulus.
- can only be sorted based on physical characteristics.

As you're about to see, this view has undergone a great deal of revision over the past quarter century.

Scrutinizing the Icon.   There can be no doubt that Sperling's study stands as one of the classics in cognitive psychology and paved the way for much important research and theory regarding the early stages of information processing. But the 1980s saw a reevaluation of the concept, both on philosophical and empirical grounds.

Iconic Memory: Who Cares?   Perhaps the idea of iconic memory may not seem particularly noteworthy to you. After all, how important can what amounts to a visual afterimage be? We don't look at the world in short bursts, so what's the big deal about iconic memory? Haber (1983) agreed and launched a broadside attack on the notion of iconic memory and its ecological validity (the generalizability of research findings to real life, as discussed in Chapter 1). Basically, Haber argued that the notion of iconic memory was not an appropriate topic for scientific investigation, owing to what he viewed as its lack of importance in everyday life. Haber noted (tongue planted firmly in cheek) that the only everyday circumstance in which iconic memory might prove useful is "reading during a lightning storm."

A number of researchers attempted to come to the rescue of iconic memory, supplying various proposed applications. One promising suggestion was that iconic memory is important in integrating what one sees from one eye fixation to the subsequent one. Such memory would provide stability to a visual world that is constantly changing. Unfortunately, further research on iconic memory (e.g., Irwin, 1992; Rayner & Pollatsek, 1983) failed to support this conjecture. In fact, information taken in during the subsequent eye fixation, rather than being integrated with information from the previous one, serves to mask it.

The idea that iconic memory is simply a fading visual buffer was also challenged. A number of researchers (e.g., Bowen, Pola, & Matin, 1974; Di Lollo, 1980) varied the duration of visual displays and then measured the duration of the icon. They found something rather puzzling: the longer the display, the less durable the icon! This **inverse duration effect** doesn't really fit with the simple notion of an icon as an afterimage that remains after visual stimulation. There's no conceivable reason why a longer-lasting display should lead to a shorter-lasting icon. This finding, in part, has led some to reconceptualize iconic memory.

Reframing Iconic Memory.   The notion of a rapidly decaying iconic memory store has become a bit outmoded, in the view of many researchers (e.g., Massaro & Loftus, 1996; Nairne, 2002). Rather than viewing iconic memory as a passive buffer, or "box," that holds information for a brief time, iconic memory is usually conceived of as a phenomenon of **visual persistence** that results from the way the visual system processes stimuli over the course of time. Put another way, the decaying icon is simply a by-product of the way our neural systems process visual information. For example, when a visual stimulus is presented, the presentation will begin a neural response that lasts for a few hundred milliseconds. If the stimulus is removed immediately after presentation (as it is in many studies of iconic memory), the neural response will continue to its natural end; this continuation is experienced as the fading icon. If the stimulus lasts longer, then it may outlast this initial neural response. Reconsider the inverse duration effect—the finding that the icon diminishes more rapidly as the initial display increases in duration. The inverse duration effect fits perfectly with this interpretation of visual persistence. A longer-lasting display will overlap more of the initial neural response just described; hence, the experience of the icon will be correspondingly brief. Modern research has tended to focus more on the neural responses to visual stimuli and the phenomenon of visual persistence and less on the notion of a "storage box" called iconic memory.

Auditory Sensory Memory

The proposed processing buffer in which we initially take in and briefly store auditory information has been termed *auditory sensory memory,* or **echoic memory.** The need for such a store is perhaps more apparent than for iconic memory. The nature of speech is transient; it's there and gone, whereas visual stimulation is continually present. Thus, a briefly held buffer, or auditory "echo," seems needed if we are to hang onto the stimulus being processed (i.e., the beginning of the sentence that's just now ending). But as you're about to see, the picture is a bit muddled. Some of the "muddlement" has resulted from the different methodologies researchers have used to investigate echoic memory.

Partial Report versus Whole Report.   People have approached the study of echoic memory in pretty much the same way as they have iconic memory. For instance, Darwin, Turvey, and Crowder (1972) used a "three-eared man" procedure in which three different sequences of mixed letters and digits were presented. One sequence was presented to each ear, while the third sequence was presented to both ears, giving rise to the perception that it was coming from midway between the ears. In the whole-report condition, participants were to report each of the letters after receiving the recall cue. In addition to reporting the letters, they were to report the location of each letter (e.g., right ear, midpoint, etc.). In the partial-report condition, participants were cued to report just one of the three sets of stimuli. Darwin and colleagues' findings paralleled those of Sperling (1960) in that partial report led to greater re-call. In addition, the partial-report advantage became increasingly small as the delay between presentation and cue increased. This pattern is basically the same as for iconic memory, but the time-course is different—the partial-report advantage lasts about two seconds for echoic memory, considerably longer than it does for iconic memory (500 milliseconds). This finding was taken as evidence that echoic memory is pretty much analogous to iconic memory: it's a raw, unprocessed version of the just-presented stimulus, but it's longer lasting. In our opening scenario, Ryan isn't really paying attention as the cashier makes his sarcastic quip, but the "echo" of what the cashier has just said sticks around long enough for Ryan to get it.

The partial-report advantage in echoic memory is a little hard to interpret, as it turns out. In the Darwin and colleagues study, the whole-report condition required participants to report the letters and their location; the partial-report condition didn't have this extra requirement (neither did the partial-report condition in Sperling's study of iconic memory). This difference may have inflated the difference found between whole and partial report. Consistent with this, a partial-report advantage in echoic memory has been a difficult finding to replicate.

Modality and Suffix Effects.   Further evidence of a relatively long-lasting "echo" that lingers for several seconds after the presentation of an auditory stimulus comes from quite a different paradigm, one that's commonly used in studies of short-term memory. When participants are presented with a short list of items (e.g., numbers or letters) in either visual or auditory mode, their recall of the last few items is much better for the words presented in an auditory mode than for words presented in the visual mode. This finding is termed the **modality effect**—memory for recently presented items depends on the modality of presentation. This relates to one of the more robust phenomena of memory: when presented with a list of items to remember, people tend to remember the first few and last few items better than the middle ones. These are termed *primacy effects* and *recency effects,* respectively. Collectively, they're known as the *serial position effect.* (We'll discuss this effect in more depth in Chapter 6.) The modality effect refers to a larger recency effect for auditory material relative to visual material.

The enhanced recency effect for auditory material has been taken as evidence for an auditory echo that lasts for several seconds after stimulus presentation—auditory lists feature the echo, while visual lists do not. The echo could be consulted on the memory test, leading to an advantage in remembering the last few items presented. An ancillary finding that supports this interpretation comes from an experiment by Conrad and Hull (1968), who found a much larger recency advantage for words spoken aloud relative to words read silently. The importance of an echo in producing this effect is supported by a companion finding termed the **suffix effect.** The suffix effect refers to the finding that an auditory signal, or suffix, presented at the end of a list wipes out the modality effect. The suffix can be just about anything: any spoken word, backward speech, a vocal grunt—all of these serve to obliterate the advantage seen in the modality effect. Why? Ostensibly because the suffix wipes out the echo on which the advantage is based.

The Precategorical Acoustic Store.   Based primarily on the findings of modality and suffix effects, Crowder and Morton (1969) proposed a *precategorical acoustic store (PAS).* In their view, the PAS is a sensory storage system capable of holding a few pieces of auditory information for a few seconds following presentation. This relatively intact auditory trace could be consulted in tests of immediate recall, leading to an advantage for the last few items presented. Presenting another (irrelevant) stimulus at the end of a list interferes with the information already in the limited buffer, thus obscuring the recency advantage for auditory information. The fact that any vocal noise can obscure the modality effect supports the notion of a precategorical acoustic store.

The notion of PAS had a fair amount of success in accounting for many early findings from studies of echoic memory. But, as with iconic memory, a number of later findings served to challenge this traditional view. For example, Nairne and Walters (1983) had participants silently mouth visually presented words and found large recency effects. This finding cannot be accounted for by the PAS. Since the stimulus list was not auditory (the participants were silent), no echo remains after presentation. Hence, there should be no recall advantage for the last couple of items. The same inexplicable finding was obtained by Campbell and Dodd (1980), who had participants lip-read stimuli. Once again, a recency advantage was obtained for nonauditory stimuli. In addition to these problematic findings, the suffix effect was found to be sensitive to conceptual aspects of the suffix (e.g., Neath, Surprenant, & Crowder, 1993). According to the PAS notion, the acoustic store should be insensitive to meaning (i.e., it's precategorical).

This notion of a relatively long-lasting acoustic echo also took a hit from some other research designed to investigate the characteristics of the auditory trace. One of these methods is analogous to visual masking (which you'll recall was one of the techniques for investigating iconic memory). The auditory version of the procedure involves presenting a high or low tone, which is immediately masked by another tone. The task is simply to classify the pitch of the first tone. Accuracy in classification increases as the presentation of the mask is delayed, up to a delay of about 250 milliseconds (Massaro, 1972); at this point, accuracy levels off. Researchers infer from this that an auditory image of the target stimulus exists for about 250 milliseconds, after which it becomes unavailable for further processing. So the results of auditory masking studies lead to an estimate of about 250 milliseconds for the duration of echoic memory, an estimate that fits well with the estimates of iconic memory. Estimation techniques, which require participants to make some type of judgment that reflects the decay of the auditory trace, yield similar estimates. So is echoic memory a long-lasting buffer that holds an echo of an auditory stimulus or an extremely brief afterimage of the same that is gone within about 250 milliseconds?

Reframing Auditory Sensory Memory.   You may notice that the question just posed is similar to that faced by researchers of iconic memory. Based on this similarity, some researchers (e.g., Cowan, 1995; Massaro & Loftus, 1996) characterize echoic memory in terms of sensory persistence. Just as it does in vision, **auditory persistence** refers to the rapidly decaying trace of an auditory stimulus that remains for about a quarter of a second after the stimulus is gone. Just as in vision, an auditory stimulus tends to persist in the form of a brief afterimage.

Perceptual Memory

We've now reached the same conclusions about visual and auditory sensory memory. Both seem to be describable in terms of a general persistence phenomenon that extends the experience of the stimulus for a brief period after its removal. But what about much of the evidence we've just discussed—evidence that points to a longer-lasting auditory memory trace, one that lasts anywhere from two to 10 seconds? Some researchers (e.g., Massaro, 1975; Massaro & Loftus, 1996; Cowan, 1988) have proposed the notion of **perceptual memory** to refer to a more stable and (relatively) long-lasting representation of information that retains the perceptual characteristics of the stimulus. An auditory perceptual memory might range anywhere from replaying the last thing said by a friend in conversation a few seconds ago (a short-term memory) to replaying your favorite song from the Broadway show you saw last month (a long-term memory). A visual perceptual memory could take the form of visually running through the last few places you've looked for your lost keys (a short-term memory) to recalling the horrible sight of the 9/11 attacks on the World Trade Center (a long-term memory). Indeed, the latter memory is very likely to be what researchers term a *flashbulb memory,* a type of perceptual memory that we'll discuss in much more depth in Chapter 8.

Note the similarities and differences between perceptual memory and sensory memory. While both retain modality-specific characteristics present when the event was encoded, sensory memory is an extremely fragile and transient replica that's present for just a fraction of a second. Perceptual memories, on the other hand, can last for seconds, days, and even years.

S T O P *and* R E V I E W !

1. Iconic memory lasts about
   a. 1 minute
   b. 1 second
   c. 1/4 second
   d. 1/8 second
2. True or false? The longer a visual display is presented, the shorter lasting the icon.
3. Describe the modality effect and the suffix effect.
4. What is perceptual memory?

➤ Sensory memory refers to the relatively brief, modality-specific trace of a stimulus that remains immediately after its presentation. Research on visual sensory memory (iconic memory) suggests that we retain most of a visual display for a very brief period after its presentation—about 250 milliseconds. Other methods for estimating the duration of iconic memory converge on this estimate

➤ Iconic memory has been reframed as a phenomenon of visual persistence, whereby the neural response to a visual stimulus continues for a short time after its presentation. The dissipation of this neural response is experienced phenomenologically as a fading icon. This interpretation fits well with inverse duration effect—the finding that as exposure time increases, the duration of iconic memory decreases.

➤ Auditory sensory (echoic memory) refers to the proposed processing buffer in which we briefly store auditory information. This "echo" is suggested by the finding of a modality effect (good memory for the final items of an auditory list), which is disrupted by the presentation of an auditory suffix at the end of the list (suffix effect). The notion of echoic memory has undergone a reframing similar to that for iconic memory. Both are conceptualized as phenomena of persistence that last for about 250 milliseconds.

➤ Some researchers have proposed the concept of "perceptual memory" to refer to representations of events experienced through any sensory modality that retain the sensory characteristics of that modality for seconds, minutes, even days.

GLOSSARY

absolute threshold: the amount of stimulus energy needed to perceive a stimulus 50% of the time (p. 74)

accommodation: the change in the shape of the eyeball's lens with the changing distance of a visual target (p. 74)

active touch: the tactile and kinesthetic sensation that arises from active exploration (p. 81)

aerial perspective: the view of very distant objects as unclear and hazy (p. 76)

auditory persistence: the tendency for the auditory processing of a stimulus to persist for about a quarter of a second after the stimulus has gone (p. 109)

blindsight: a neurological disorder characterized by a lack of visual awareness but the preserved ability to report on some aspects of a stimulus (p. 96)

bottom-up (data-driven) processing: the identification of a stimulus through the assembly of its component features (p. 73)

chemosenses: a term referring to the senses of taste and smell (p. 83)

closure: a tendency to perceptually complete incomplete objects (p. 78)

common fate: a tendency to group elements together if they are moving in the same direction or at the same speed (p. 78)

common region: a tendency to group elements that seem to belong to a common designated area or region (p. 78)

constructive view (of perception): emphasizes the role of active construction and interpretation in arriving at a 3-D percept of the world (p. 93)

convergence: the degree to which the two eyes focus inward toward each other when brought to fixation on a common point (p. 74)

difference threshold: the change in the intensity of a stimulus that is detectable 50% of the time (p. 74)

direct view (of perception): emphasizes the direct pickup of information from the environment, and deemphasizes the role of constructive processes in producing a percept (p. 93)

echoic memory (or auditory sensory memory): the proposed processing buffer in which we initially take in and briefly store auditory information (p. 107)

ecological approach: another term for the direct view of perception, because it emphasizes in real-world contexts (p. 93)

exploratory procedures (EPs): the precise motor patterns performed by the hands in exploring an object (p. 81)

figure-ground: a tendency to segregate visual scenes into a background and a figure that appears to be superimposed against it (p. 77)

flavor: the combination of the four basic tastes and other factors such as smell, texture, and temperature (p. 83)

global precedence: a tendency to encode the overall features of a scene before apprehending scene details (p. 80)

good continuation: a tendency to perceive lines as flowing naturally, in a single direction (p. 78)

gustation: the sense of taste (p. 83)

haptics: the combination of information gained through the skin senses and information gained from hand position and movement (p. 81)

iconic memory (or visual sensory memory)**:** a proposed processing buffer in which we initially take in and briefly store visual information (p. 103)

inter-aural intensity difference (IID): the difference in intensity of a sound as it enters each ear (p. 77)

inter-aural time difference (ITD): the discrepancy in time of arrival of a sound arriving at each ear (p. 77)

interposition: the overlapping (or perceived overlapping) of one object by another (p. 76)

inverse duration effect: a negative relationship between the duration of a briefly presented visual stimulus and the duration of the icon (p. 107)

kinesthesis: the ability to sense the position and movement of one's body parts (p. 81)

linear perspective: a depth cue whereby parallel lines seem to converge at a far point as they recede away from the viewer (p. 76)

McGurk effect: a speech perception effect in which visual information conflicts with auditory signals, changing the perceived speech sound (p. 87)

modality effect: the larger recency effect for auditory material relative to visual material (p. 108)

monocular cues: the environmental depth cues that require the use of only one eye (p. 75)

motion parallax: the differences in relative motion of objects passing by or being passed by an observer (near objects appear to move faster than distant objects) (p. 76)

objective threshold: the level of stimulus energy below which participants report not seeing a stimulus; forced-choice procedures also indicate a lack of awareness (p. 99)

olfaction: the sense of smell (p. 83)

olfactory-verbal gap: difficulty in labeling and describing smells (p. 84)

passive touch: tactile sensation that arises in the absence of active exploration (p. 81)

perceptual memory: a relatively stable and long-lasting representation of information that retains the perceptual characteristics of the just-presented stimulus (p. 110)

perspective cues: the cues to depth that arise from the changes in information received by the eye as our distance from and/or perspective on the objects change (p. 76)

principles of visual organization: the principles followed by our perceptual system to organize incoming sensations in a sensible and simple manner (p. 77)

proximity: a tendency for objects that are near one another (i.e., *proximal*) to be grouped (p. 77)

relative size: the difference in perceived size of two objects that gives rise to a perception of depth (close objects are seen as larger than distant objects) (p. 76)

response bias: a participant's willingness to report the presence of some stimulus (p. 74)

retinal disparity: the differing views of a visual scene as encoded by each retina (p. 75)

sensitivity: one's perceptual acuity; the ability to detect the presence or absence of a stimulus or a change in a stimulus (p. 74)

sensory memory: an extremely transient, modality-specific memory of a briefly presented stimulus (p. 103)

shading: the manner in which light seems to fall on different regions of a scene (brightly lit objects appear closer than shaded objects) (p. 76)

signal detection theory: an approach to psychophysics that characterizes perceptual experiences as the joint product of sensitivity and response bias (p. 74)

similarity: a tendency for objects that are similar to one another to be grouped (p. 78)

somesthesis: the sense of touch (p. 80)

subjective threshold: the level of stimulus energy below which participants report not seeing a stimulus; forced-choice procedures indicate some minimal awareness (p. 99)

subliminal perception: the purported tendency to be influenced by stimuli presented below the level of awareness (p. 96)

suffix effect: the finding that an auditory signal presented at the end of a list eliminates the modality effect (p. 108)

synesthesia: experiences in which input from one sensory system produces an experience not only in that modality but in another as well (p. 89)

tactile acuity: the sensitivity of passive touch (p. 81)

texture gradient: the variations in perceived texture that occur as we move closer and farther away from an object (closer objects appear to have more texture than distant objects) (p. 76)

tip-of-the-nose phenomenon: difficulty in retrieving the verbal label for a familiar odor (p. 84)

top-down (conceptually driven) processing: the identification of a stimulus with the help of context, previous knowledge, and/or expectations (p. 73)

uniform connectedness: a tendency to group visual elements that are connected in some way (p. 78)

visual persistence: the tendency for the visual processing of a stimulus to persist for about a quarter of a second beyond its presentation duration (p. 107)

visual primitive: a feature of the visual environment that is registered automatically, without the need for higher-level interpretation or analysis (p. 80)

4

Attending to and Manipulating Information

"Are you driving?!" Sherry demands. "I can't stand it when you call me when you're driving—-it's so danger-ous. You can't pay attention to me and the road." She's right, William thinks. I almost hit that car.

"OK." William pulls over into a nearby parking lot to finish the conversation. "I need directions to Pattaya."

"I don't know how to get there. Ryan's picking me up. I can't wait for you to meet him!"

Her new boyfriend. I'm really curious to meet this dreamboat, William muses. "Well, can you give me Anne's number? I think she knows where the restaurant is."

"Sure, it's 779-246-5649."

"Whoa! Slow down—I'm not good at phone num-bers—especially with the area codes. Tell me again."

"I've got an easy way to remember this one. The numbers actually spell out p-s-y-c-h-o-l-o-g-y, if you can believe it. That's how I remember it."

"Hey, that's pretty good! See you in about half an hour."

Better play it safe, William thinks, as he hooks up his hands-free cell phone device. He dials "psychology" and then pulls out of the parking lot.

"Hi, Anne."

"Oh, hi, William!" Anne says. "How's it going?"

"Not bad," he replies. "Say, I need to get directions to Pattaya. I'm meeting Sherry and her new boyfriend. I know how to get downtown, but after that I'm lost."

"I think you'll like Ryan. He's a disc jockey at the college's radio station. Speaking of which, did you hear how he handled that crank caller? It was so hilarious . . . " William sighs. "I couldn't believe he was so funny . . . " This time William has relatively little trouble keeping his attention on the road. " . . . I just love the winter . . . everything is so crisp and . . . "

"Hey, I'm sorry but I really need to get going, so, maybe, those directions to Taco Bell?"

"Taco Bell?"

William laughs. "Did I say Taco Bell? I just passed one! That's funny. Anyway, I don't mean to be short, but I really need those directions to Pattaya."

William slows down, listening intently as Anne tells him how to find his way through the downtown maze of one-way streets.

Just like William, each of us is constantly being bombarded by information moving in and out of our conscious awareness. As he searches for the restaurant, William simultaneously registers and acts on various sensory input—avoiding other cars, calling on his cell phone, listening to directions, suppressing his impatience with Anne's chatter. There is a nearly constant need to monitor the events occurring in our external environment as well as the "events" in our internal environment (i.e., our thoughts and feelings). Cognitive psychologists term this monitoring process **attention.** In addition, these events must be examined, considered, manipulated, and responded to appropriately. These processes are generally referred to as **working memory (WM).**

Attention is one of the many processes that make up working memory. Not only that, it probably could be considered the most important. Why? Because if we conceive of working memory as a sort of mental work space, attention can be viewed as the *gateway* that allows information in. Attention might also be conceived of as a *reservoir of mental resources* that we can draw on to accomplish our daily thinking tasks. Information on which we've chosen to focus our attention is then further analyzed by other working-memory processes.

Attention

This section of the chapter should be pretty short, if William James (1890) was correct in his assertion that "everyone knows what attention is." James was confident about people's lay knowledge about attention because (provided we're awake) we are constantly engaged in this monitoring process. Our waking existence involves a continuous focusing and refocusing of what might be termed *mental effort.* On the other hand, this chapter might be quite lengthy if modern-day attention researcher Harold Pashler is correct that "no one

A formidable problem of selective and divided attention.

knows what attention is." Pashler (1998) and others lament that the concept of attention is thrown around so frequently and used to describe so many different phenomena that it really isn't a very useful concept (e.g., Pashler & Carrier, 1996). What exactly attention is remains hard to pin down.

While it may be difficult to state exactly what attention is, it has two notable features (Pashler, 1998). First, attention allows for *voluntary control* of how we deal with incoming information. This feature is the basis for the conceptualization of attention as a gateway into working memory; we can choose which aspects of the environment we wish to attend to or not attend to. Second, attention is *limited in capacity;* we simply cannot (effectively) monitor all of the events occurring around us simultaneously. The notion of limited capacity serves as the basis for conceptualizing attention as a reservoir of mental resources; there is a limit to the attentional resources we have to devote to performing tasks.

At any given moment, there are a multitude of events going on in your environment, only some of which require a response on your part. Unless we are able to select those events we need to deal with, we will experience sensory overload. British psychologists Donald Broadbent and Colin Cherry did much of the pioneering work on sensory overload. Their interest in this topic was based on the experiences of World War II pilots who were faced with increasingly complex control panels having a bewildering combination of visual and auditory displays. Monitoring these panels and responding appropriately presented an incredible challenge. Coping with challenging situations is involved in the first feature of attention: voluntary control over how we deal with incoming information.

When dealing with multiple streams of information, we have two choices. We can engage in **selective attention**—monitoring and responding to one event at the exclusion of others. Alternatively, we can engage in **divided attention**—monitoring and responding to multiple events.

Theories of Attention

Theories of attention attempt to explain how our cognitive systems operate under conditions of potential sensory overload. When William is driving and talking on his cell phone, what mental processes allow for the selection and division of attention? The theories proposed to account for these types of scenarios tend to focus on one of the two conceptualizations we mentioned earlier—a gateway into working memory or a reservoir of mental resources. The first few theories we discuss view attention as a gateway—a sort of filtering mechanism that allows some information to come into conscious awareness while keeping other information out. Consequently, the studies addressing these theories utilize selective attention tasks in which some information must be processed and responded to and some must be ignored. The later theories we discuss view attention as a set of mental resources—a sort of limited-capacity store that can be devoted to the completion of different tasks. Consequently, the studies addressing these theories will utilize divided-attention tasks in which all information must be processed and responded to, taxing the resources of the attentional system.

Attention as a Gateway.   Before we consider the different theories of attention as a gateway, let's take a look at one of the classic selective attention tasks. Cherry (1953) had participants put on specially rigged headphones that presented a different message to each ear; this is termed **dichotic listening.** But simply having someone listen to two messages doesn't tell us anything about attentional processing. To address this, Cherry had participants repeat one of the messages word for word, which is termed **speech shadowing.** Speech shadowing forces the listener to selectively attend to one message (the *attended message*) while ignoring the other (the *unattended message*). Participants were fairly successful in their attempts to shadow the attended message. However, they seemed to know very little about the content of the unattended message, though they were aware that a message was being played and did notice such things as changes in pitch (e.g., whether the speaker was male or female). But as for what was actually said, they could remember practically nothing. This basic pattern—minimal processing of information presented in an unattended channel—was a common finding in early studies of selective attention (e.g., Moray, 1959).

Early-Selection Theories.   One of the first theories of how we selectively attend under conditions of sensory overload was Broadbent's (1958) *filter model* of attention. This account, often termed an **early-selection theory,** is depicted in Figure 4.1a. While reading about it, try to figure out why such theories are termed "early selection." Multiple streams of information all make it into sensory memory. This initial processing encodes each source of information in terms of its physical characteristics. At this point, the information sources are filtered based on this information, and only one source is selected for further processing (i.e., identification and manipulation in working memory).

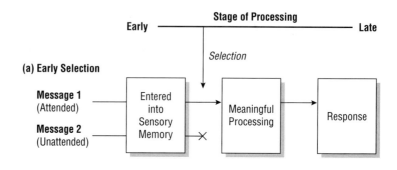

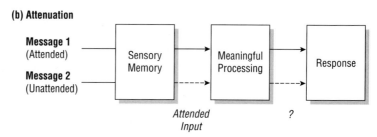

Figure 4.1 Attentional processing according to (a) early-selection theory, (b) attenuation theory, and (c) late-selection theory. Note the differences in whether stimuli can be identified according to each view.

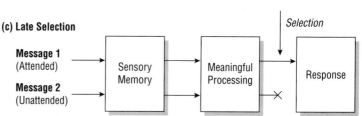

So, did you figure it out? Broadbent's approach is termed *early selection* because the selection process whereby we designate information for further processing occurs early in processing, as the information is first registered by the senses. The process of early selection accounts for Cherry's results: the only things that participants seemed to notice about the message in the unattended channel were its physical characteristics, which is exactly what would be expected if all messages were processed only to an early stage of analysis. After the selection of the attended message, the other messages are essentially discarded.

Problems with Early-Selection Theories. Although an early-selection theory provides a neat explanation of the early returns from selective attention studies, there are some problems with this approach. One problem is evident when you consider the **cocktail-party phenomenon.** You've no doubt been at a party where there are many conversations occurring all at once, yet you have little or no trouble focusing on only one. This is an everyday example of selective attention. According to early-selection theories, the unattended conversations are like static; you're not really processing much of them. Yet (and this is where the problem lies) if someone in another conversation says your name, you are

Right Ear

Psychology is a really interesting / walk on the beach.

Left Ear

On our vacation we went for a / major for students.

"an interesting — uh — major for students"

Figure 4.2 The procedure employed in the Treisman (1960) selective attention study. Contrary to the predictions of early-selection theory, participants followed the meaning of the message, even when it switched to the unattended channel.

Adapted from Treisman, A. (1960). Contextual cues in selective listening. *Quarterly Journal of Experimental Psychology, 12,* 242–248.

very likely to notice. Based on a strict interpretation of early-selection theories, this shouldn't happen; the analysis of unattended information stops early, at the point of noticing only sensory characteristics. Therefore, you shouldn't be able to recognize your name (or anything else), because this requires analysis at the level of meaning (i.e., analysis occurs at a later stage of processing). This demonstration doesn't necessarily give one cause to toss out the theory. Perhaps you notice your name because of a lapse in your attention or because you switch your focus of attention. Perhaps, when you are truly attending to a given conversation, early selection is the rule.

The result of a classic (not to mention ingenious) study by Treisman (1960) gives more substantive cause to doubt a strict early-selection approach. Treisman employed dichotic listening in her study but with an interesting twist. Participants heard different messages in each ear and were required to shadow one of them. Occasionally, the meaning of the shadowed message switched ears, as depicted in Figure 4.2. The critical test, then, is whether the person shadowing will say, "Psychology is a really interesting walk on the beach" (the correct response) or "Psychology is a really interesting major for students" (the meaningful response). If selection of attended material is done early, participants should say the first response; the attentional system isn't processing meaning in the unattended channel. But as you might have anticipated, shadowing mistakes like the second response were quite common. This result demonstrates clearly that analysis of unattended messages goes beyond just registering physical characteristics like pitch.

RECURRING RESEARCH THEME
Cognition and Consciousness

A Shocking Failure of Early-Selection Theory

The previous two studies indicate that unattended information can be meaningfully identified, given that it is personally meaningful (as in the cocktail-party phenomenon) or that it is relevant to the immediate semantic context (as in the Treisman study). In both of these examples, the shifts in attention are marked by rather obvious behavioral changes. Perhaps analysis of the unattended message occurs even more often than these demonstrations imply. Might this be revealed with more subtle indicators of message processing?

Corteen and Wood (1972) conducted a two-phase study to find out. In the first phase, participants were asked to listen to a series of words. Each list contained three city names (e.g., Minneapolis, Lafayette, Cincinnati), and each name was followed by a slight electric shock. The shock produced an autonomic nervous system response called a *galvanic skin response (GSR)* (which involves a slight sweating of the fingertips). In the second phase, participants performed a dichotic-listening-and-shadowing task. The unattended message was a list of words that consisted of 12 critical words—six words presented in phase 1 (the three shock-associated city names plus three nouns not associated with shock) and six words not presented in phase 1 (three new city names and three new nouns). When the dichotic-listening-and-shadowing task was complete, some of the participants reported that they had heard words in the unattended ear, but they were unaware that some of these words were city names. Seemingly, the words had not been identified.

Or had they? During the dichotic-listening task, the three shock-associated city names from phase 1 produced a higher galvanic skin response relative to that produced by the three nonshock associated nouns from phase 1 (37.7% versus 12.3%). As noted earlier, these words were not consciously identified (or at least they weren't remembered shortly after presentation). But contrary to the predictions of early-selection theory, they must have been meaningfully identified in order to produce a GSR. The contention that the city names were indeed identified is supported by an additional finding. The three new city names not presented in phase 1 produced a more intense GSR than the three new nouns not presented in phase 1 (22.8% versus 8.7%). The fact that the heightened GSR generalized to control items from the same semantic category (i.e., city names) is further evidence that the city names presented in the unattended channel in phase 1 were indeed identified. This finding flies in the face of strict early-selection theory, indicating that unattended stimuli are often processed well beyond their physical characteristics.

Attenuation Theory.   To account for our tendency to process information meaningfully, even in the absence of full attention, Treisman (1960) proposed the **attenuation theory,** essentially a slight modification of early-selection theories. This theory is depicted in Figure 4.1b. According to this model, unattended information is not completely blocked from further analysis beyond sensory memory. Rather, it is attenuated, or "turned down," if you will. Thus, the early filtering of messages is partial, not complete. Unattended information (albeit weak) can make it through to working memory. So how does this weak trickle of information allow for identification? Treisman proposed that some words in our "mental dictionary" are permanently more available than others because of their personal importance (e.g., your name). Similarly, other words are temporarily more available due to the current circumstance (e.g., the context of the sentence in Treisman's ear-switching study or words that might indicate the arrival of a shock in the Corteen and Wood study). Therefore, even the small trickle of information that makes it through the attenuating filter might be enough to trigger recognition. To put it in the terms we introduced in Chapter 3, some stimuli require less information from bottom-up processing to trigger recognition because of the facilitatory effect of top-down processing (e.g., personal importance or current circumstances).

Late-Selection Theories. Of course, Treisman's attenuation theory is only one of many ways one might account for the identification of unattended information; another way is **late-selection theory** (e.g., Deutsch & Deutsch, 1963). This theory is depicted in Figure 4.1c. According to late-selection theory, all incoming information (attended and unattended) makes it past sensory memory and enters working memory for identification. After the information is identified, only the selected piece enjoys further cognitive processing (conscious responding or entry into long-term memory). The nonselected information is quickly forgotten due to the limited capacity of working memory, which you will read about shortly.

The late-selection approach easily accounts for the identification of unattended messages. This explains the cocktail-party phenomenon: since unattended stimuli are identified, one's name certainly would be, leading to an attention switch. The experimental demonstrations of Treisman and Corteen and Wood are also explained using this theory. All incoming information (the unattended passage in the Treisman study and the word list in the Corteen and Wood study) is identified. This identification leads to an attention switch (as in the Treisman study) or an emotional reaction (as in the Corteen & Wood study). But attention, according to the late-selection account, is limited, and this limitation operates at a late stage—working memory. Although all incoming information is identified, we cannot reason about, respond to, or remember all of it.

You might find it difficult to differentiate between attenuation and late selection, because both theories seem to make similar predictions, allowing for the identification of unattended information. Driver (2001) provides a useful way to distinguish the two approaches. Attenuation theory proposes that identification of unattended information is the exception rather than the rule. Whether information is identified depends on the context or the exact nature of the information. Conversely, late-selection theory argues that the identification of meaning is the rule rather than the exception. The identification of meaning is obligatory; all information (attended and unattended) is identified. So which is correct? Driver (2001) indicates that neurological studies of attention are more consistent with an attenuation-type account. While the attenuation theory proposed by Triesman may be a bit simplistic, it is clear that attention is influenced by the type of top-down processing (e.g., context, current task demands, goals of the attender, etc.) proposed by attenuation theory.

Attention as Capacity. An attentional gateway is not the only way to conceptualize attention. The idea of attention as a sort of limited capacity or resource has been suggested by many researchers (e.g., Kahneman, 1973; Norman & Bobrow, 1975; Wickens, 1984). According to **capacity theory,** attention is limited and must be allocated according to the particular demands of the situation. Some tasks require more of the attentional "budget," leaving less attention for the performance of other tasks. In the opening vignette, William has no trouble driving and listening to Anne when she's rambling about irrelevant information. However, when she finally starts giving him the directions, he has to devote more attentional capacity to the conversation and must slow down to complete both tasks (driving and listening). The fact that trade-offs are quite often observed when two tasks are shared suggests that the capacity approach might be an appropriate way to conceptualize attention.

Stop and Think!

THE PRICE OF ATTENDING

Imagine that all of the attention you could possibly focus on some everyday task has a value of $100. That is, the most mentally challenging task in the world costs $100. Based on this idea, "price" each of the following tasks.

watching TV
listening to music
taking notes in class
talking on the cell phone
walking
driving in an unfamiliar location
driving a familiar route
listening to a professor lecture
eating

Based on your "pricing system,"

- Which pairs of tasks would not send you "over budget"?
- Which combinations would?
- What makes tasks easy or difficult to combine?

Capacity or Capacities?   One issue that has been bandied about within the context of capacity theories is whether or not attentional capacity is unitary. In other words, do we have one general type of resource we draw on to perform attentional tasks, or do we have multiple specific resources? If there are multiple resources, what differentiates them? Consider your ability to balance two tasks at once: you have no doubt noticed that this ability depends on the nature of the two tasks. For example, you probably find it relatively easy to talk and drive at the same time. However, you would find it much more difficult to drive and read at the same time (although we have seen people reading their paper while driving!). Performing two visual monitoring tasks seems more difficult than performing one primarily visual task along with one primarily auditory task. No doubt a great deal of the ease or difficulty relates to the physical operations required by each of the tasks, but some researchers (e.g., Navon & Gopher, 1979; Wickens, 1984) have proposed that there is likely a difference in the type of mental resource required.

What differentiates these different types, or pools, of resources? Wickens (1984) suggests that these pools are differentiated according to a number of factors, such as whether the input modality is visual or auditory and whether the response required is vocal or manual. According to this view, tasks interfere to the degree that they tap into the same pool of resources. For example, an auditory and a visual task or tasks requiring a vocal and a manual response will interfere less with each other than will two visual tasks or two tasks requiring a manual response. Take driving while using your cell phone. Since driving relies primarily on the visual modality, while talking on the cell phone relies primarily on the auditory modality, you might decide that these tasks will not interfere with each other. However, it is important to note that less interference does not mean no interference.

A study by Strayer and Johnston (2001) indicates that Sherry's concern about William's driving while he's talking on his cell phone is well-justified. Participants in the

Strayer and Johnston study performed a simulated driving task, having participants move a joystick to keep a computer cursor aligned with a moving target. Participants performed this task alone (single-task condition) or in conjunction with a cell-phone conversation, using either a hand-held or hands-free device (dual-task condition). Periodically a red or green light would appear, and participants were to respond appropriately on the joystick task, stopping in response to the red light or continuing in response to the green light. Participants in a control group listened to the radio instead of carrying on a cell-phone conversation.

The number of light signals missed and the reaction times to respond to the signals were compared in the single- and dual-task conditions. The results didn't support commercials touting the advantages of hands-free cell phones: using a hands-free device was shown to be no better than using the hand-held phone. More important, participants carrying on a conversation were twice as likely to miss a signal in the dual-task than the single-task condition (7% to 3%), and RT was elevated as well. Responses to the "traffic light" in the dual-task condition took 50 milliseconds longer than did responses in the single-task condition. When the second task was simply listening to the radio, there was no performance deficit. So in our opening story, William may feel safer because he's switched to his hands-free cell phone, but his confidence is unfounded.

What Are Mental Resources? In spite of the general success of the notion of capacity as a descriptor of task sharing, the concept has some pretty harsh critics (e.g., Logan, 1997). Whether there is a general resource from which we draw or multiple specific resources begs a more fundamental question: What exactly are mental resources? *Mental resources* is a vague term used to explain attention, but it doesn't really explain anything; it simply redescribes attention. In addition, the definition of *resources* is circular. That is, the notion of limited resources is used to explain why sharing two tasks is difficult; but the fact that two tasks are difficult to share is used as the demonstration that there are limited resources! Using a concept to explain some phenomenon and then using the phenomenon as evidence of the original concept is shoddy theorizing. There needs to be some concrete measure or definition of *resources* that is independent of increases in the difficulty of a task. A satisfactory definition has not emerged, and therefore some theoreticians (e.g., Logan, 1997) have urged restraint in using this term.

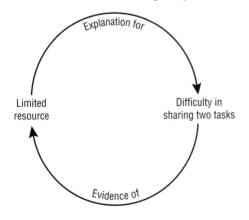

Limited resource — Explanation for → Difficulty in sharing two tasks — Evidence of →

The Multimode Theory of Attention. So is attention a gateway or a limited resource? As is so often the case in psychology, the answer appears to be either, depending on the situation. On balance, the evidence indicates that both approaches have some validity. A hybrid of the gateway and capacity approaches provides a useful way to look at attention. A series of investigations by Johnston and Heinz (1978) provides evidence for this **multimode theory** of attention. According to Johnston and Heinz, attention is flexible in that people can shift from early modes of attention (processing only the physical characteristics of incoming stimuli) to late modes (processing the meaning of incoming stimuli). Given that we have voluntary control over how we deal with incoming information, we are capable of determining the basis on which we select information for further processing (an early- or late-processing mode). However, attending in each of these modes has an associated set of costs. As selection proceeds to a later point in the information-processing system, more mental capacity is required.

To test the multimode theory of attention, Johnston and Heinz developed a clever divided-attention task. Participants were given two tasks: dichotic listening in the experimental conditions and simple detection. Participants were required to shadow one of the presented messages while ignoring the other. During the presentation of these messages, they also had to watch for a light signal and were to press a key as quickly as possible when they saw it. This light-detection task was included to assess the mental effort or capacity expended on the dichotic-listening task. If a great deal of capacity was being used in the dichotic-listening task, this would leave less capacity to perform the light-detection task and reaction time would be slowed. Alternatively, if the dichotic-listening task didn't require much in the way of attentional resources, there would be more capacity left to perform the light-detection task, resulting in faster reaction times.

Recall Johnston and Heinz's basic idea that attention can operate in different modes but that there are corresponding costs. These researchers varied the mode of attention (early versus late) by manipulating the nature of the two presented messages and hence the difficulty of the listening task. In what might be considered the easier condition, the two messages presented were different physically: one was read in a female voice; the other, in a male voice. Shadowing one of these passages could be done with a simple discrimination of their physical characteristics; in other words, only early-selection processing was required. In a more challenging condition, the two passages had similar physical characteristics (i.e., they were read by speakers of the same gender), but the meaning of the information presented in the two messages was different. Therefore, the listening task required the much more difficult discrimination between the meaning of each of the messages—that is, late-selection processing was involved.

(a) Late-Selection Condition

Resources taken by dichotic-listening task
Resources available for light-detection task

(b) Early-Selection Condition

Resources taken by dichotic-listening task
Resources available for light-detection task

The difference in capacity required by the different listening tasks was assessed by examining how they affected the light-detection task. According to the multimode theory, early and late selection are both possible, but late selection costs more in terms of capacity. The condition in which the messages were physically similar and differed only in meaning required late selection; in order to selectively listen, participants had to pay attention to what was being said. This is costly in terms of attentional capacity. Therefore, there would be little capacity left to perform the light-detection task, and reaction time should increase. The condition in which the messages differed physically required only early selection; in order to selectively listen, participants only had to note the physical characteristics of the messages. This is less costly in terms of attentional capacity; more capacity is left to perform the light-detection task.

The results, presented in Figure 4.3, support these predictions. The figure plots RT cost, which is calculated by comparing single-task (only light detection) reaction time to

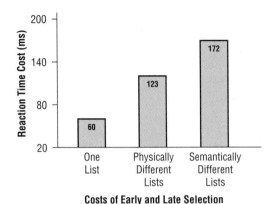

Figure 4.3 Results from Johnston and Heinz (1978, experiment 4). In the single-list condition, the cost to simple RT was small. In the two-list condition, in which participants were required to shadow, RT costs were much higher. Note that the most "expensive" condition in terms of RT to the secondary task was the shadowing condition that required late selection.

From Johnston, W. A., & Heinz, S. P. (1978). Flexibility and capacity demands of attention. *Journal of Experimental Psychology: General, 107,* 420–435. Copyright 1978 by the American Psychological Association. Reprinted by permission.

dual-task (both light detection and a listening task) reaction time. As you can see, the presence of a listening task exacts a cost in reaction time. More important, the "price" was different depending on the nature of the listening task. In the control condition, participants simply listened to and shadowed one message. This exacted a slight cost on RT, as you can see. The requirement to shadow one of two messages was much more challenging—and more costly in terms of attention. Consistent with Johnston and Heinz's analysis, the cost was greater in the late-selection condition, where participants had to discriminate between two messages on the basis of meaning. These findings support Johnston and Heinz's view that both early and late selection are possible, but late selection requires a greater amount of mental effort or capacity.

STOP *and* REVIEW!

1. Distinguish between tasks requiring selective attention and tasks requiring divided attention.
2. True or false? Early-selection theory and attenuation theory both place the filter early in cognitive processing.
3. Explain the difference between late-selection theory and attenuation theory.
4. According to the mutimode theory of attention, an early mode of selection (based on identification of physical characteristics) seems to demand _____ attentional capacity than a late mode of selection (based on meaningful identification).
   a. more
   b. less
   c. the same amount
   d. no

➤ Attention refers to the processes we use to monitor and respond to ongoing events. Tasks requiring selective attention involve monitoring one message and excluding others. Tasks requiring divided attention involve dealing with several sources of information simultaneously. Theories characterize attention as a gating mechanism or as a limited resource that must be allocated to different tasks.

➤ Early-selection theory contends that attended information is selected early in cognitive processing, based on physical characteristics, and unattended information is processed only to this level. However, research indicates that unattended information can be processed beyond physical characteristics.

➤ Attenuation theory suggests a process that attenuates (rather than rejects) unattended messages early in cognitive processing. Late-selection theory suggests that all information (attended and unattended) is processed to the point of identification. No attentional limitations are evident until late in processing. Neuroscience data seem more consistent with the attenuation account.

➤ The notion of capacity has enjoyed popularity as an explanation of attention, although it tends to be too liberally applied, and is circularly defined. According to multimode theory, attenders can choose to attend in either early- or late-selection "modes," but this choice has consequences in terms of the capacity that is needed; late selection involves more attentional capacity.

Automaticity

You have probably noticed that many of your daily activities seem to involve little or no attention. These tasks involve *automatic processing*. This **automaticity** typically develops as the result of extensive practice. After years of repeatedly engaging in a set of processes, such as those involved in driving a car, these processes occur with relatively little effort. Posner and Snyder (1975) note three features of automatic processes. First, they occur without intention; in other words, they seem to be obligatory. Consider the motions you go through as you start your car in the morning; the movements seem to practically "come out of you," with little or no deliberate effort. Second, automatic processes are not open to conscious awareness. That is, you don't reflect on automatic processes (indeed, you almost can't reflect on them) as they are occurring. As a result, actions performed automatically are often difficult to recollect consciously. Do you often find that after driving to work or school, you remember nothing at all about the trip? Finally, automatic processes consume very little in the way of mental resources. When you're doing something automatic, it seems relatively easy to combine it with another task.

The Stroop Effect

Perhaps the most celebrated demonstration of automatic processing is the Stroop effect. First demonstrated by J. Ridley Stroop (1935), the **Stroop effect** refers to the finding that the ability to name the ink color in which a word is printed is inhibited if that word happens to name a conflicting color. For example, if the word *red* is printed in blue ink, it's quite difficult to name the ink color (blue) without suffering some interference. How does this demonstrate automatic processing? One common explanation for this effect is that reading is an automatic process; as stated earlier, it's obligatory—you can't *not* do it. Therefore, the ability to name the ink color of the word suffers tremendous interference because you are automatically reading a color word that conflicts with the ink color. It is important to note that this effect is not limited to the traditional task of naming color words. Words that are closely associated with a given color can also have an inhibitory effect on naming a conflicting color. For example, if the word *grass* is written in red, it's very difficult to name the color red because you are thinking of the color of grass—green (Klein, 1964).

Stop *and* Think! STROOPING

Try these variations on the Stroop task. Find a friend to take part in each version.

Version 1: For each of the two lists, have your friend name the number of characters in each grouping as quickly as possible. Test the lists separately, and time how long it takes to finish each of the lists.

List 1	List 2
FFF	222
GGGGGGG	8888888
PPPPP	66666
VVVVV	555555
JJ	33
DDDDD	44444
NN	11
LLLLLL	777777
SSSSSSSS	99999999

Version 2: Treat each of the following as "cards." The participant's task is to say the position of each word on the card using one of these four labels: up, down, right, or left.

List 1

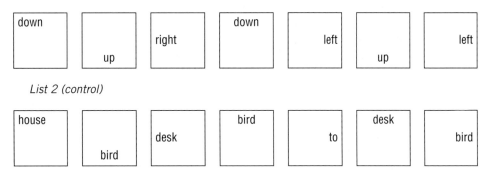

List 2 (control)

- How did your participant's reaction time for the lists vary with the type of list?
- What two processes seem to be competing with each another?
- Can you map these versions of the Stroop effect onto the traditional version (color naming)?

The Stroop Effect Reconsidered.   Work on the Stroop effect by Besner and colleagues (Besner, Stolz, & Boutilier, 1997; Besner & Stolz, 1999) casts some doubt on the automaticity interpretation of the Stroop effect. Besner, Stolz, and Boutilier (1997) tested this interpretation with a disarmingly simple task. Participants were presented with words in the center of a computer screen. Either one letter of the word (randomly chosen) was colored, or the whole word was colored. Participants' task was to name the color they saw—of the entire word or the single letter. According to the automaticity interpretation of the Stroop effect, there should be equal interference in both conditions, because in both conditions, participants should be automatically drawn to read the word. However, findings from this study revealed that the Stroop effect was greatly reduced in the letter condition.

These researchers' explanation of the Stroop effect is markedly different from the over 500 articles that chalk it up to the automatic reading of words. They claim that the Stroop effect is an instance of *mental set*. Mental set refers to our tendency to revert to well-practiced and routine mental processes when faced with a cognitive task. (We'll be talking more about mental set in Chapter 12.) In regard to the Stroop effect, participants fall into a familiar mental set when faced with a word—namely, they read it. But they don't have to read it, as the automatic reading view suggests. Given an alternative mind set—asking them to search the letter strings for the colored letter—they are able to disregard their familiar mind set and not read the word. This is contrary to what the automaticity view would predict (Besner, Stolz, & Boutilier, 1997).

Automaticity with Practice

Schneider and Shiffrin (1977) provide another oft-cited example of automatic processing based on extensive research with a visual search task. Visual search involves scanning a display for certain critical items. Here's a simplified description of the procedure. Participants were to encode a memory set that consisted of a series of letters. While holding this memory set in mind, they were required to search a retrieval frame to determine if any of the items they were holding in mind were present. The retrieval frame could include a target (i.e., a member of the memory set) and/or distractors (items not in the memory set). Figure 4.4 provides an overview of the procedure.

In the easy version of this task, letters always appeared in only one role—as targets (i.e., the distractors in the retrieval frame were never letters, only numbers). Because letters and numbers played consistent roles across all of the experimental trials (always targets and distractors, respectively), this condition was termed *consistent mapping*. In the more difficult version of the task, letters could appear as either targets or distractors. In other words, the role of a given letter varied across trials. (Sometimes it was a target and sometimes it was a distractor.) Hence, this condition was termed *varied mapping*. Consider the difference in what was required in these two conditions. In the consistent-mapping conditions, participants needed simply to determine whether there was a letter there or not. If there was a letter in the display, it had to be a target and the response had to be yes, because letters never served as distractors. So the consistent-mapping task boiled down to "Does this display have a letter?" Now consider the varied-mapping task; in this case, it wasn't enough to find letters in the retrieval frame, because letters could also be distrac-

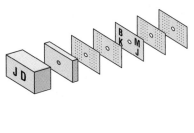

Varied Mappings

Memory set size = 2
Frame size = 4

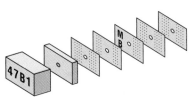

Consistent Mappings

Memory set size = 4
Frame size = 2

Figure 4.4 Procedure from the Schneider and Shiffrin (1977) study. Participants were first presented with a memory set of items to keep in mind. Then they had to decide whether each of the subsequent target displays included any items from the memory set.

From Schneider, W., & Shiffrin, R. M. (1977). Controlled and automatic human information processing. I: Detection, search, and attention. *Psychological Review, 84,* 1–66.

tors. Participants were forced to consider the exact letters being held in memory and determine whether any of these particular letters were in the retrieval frame.

Which of the conditions do you think was associated with automaticity? Performance over the course of trials was radically different for the two conditions. Consistent-mapping performance started out much faster than varied-mapping performance, and the gap between the two became even wider over the course of trials as the consistent-mapping task became less and less effortful. The varied-mapping task, on the other hand, never really got any easier. Trial after trial, participants had to painstakingly compare the items they were holding in memory to the items that were displayed in the retrieval frame to determine whether any of them matched.

One of the critical variables manipulated by Schneider and Shiffrin was the size of the memory set—the number of items participants had to hold in mind. You can probably guess how this affected (or didn't affect) performance in the consistent- and varied-mapping conditions. As you can see in Figure 4.5, the number of items to be held in memory (i.e., memory set size) didn't matter much in the consistent-mapping condition. This was particularly true after the task was well-practiced. After all, participants only had to determine whether the retrieval frame had a letter or not. But memory set size mattered tremendously in the varied-mapping condition. Here, every item in the memory set had to be compared to every item in the retrieval frame. The more items in the memory set, the more comparisons to be made, thus increasing reaction time.

Schneider and Shiffrin also manipulated the number of items to be searched on the retrieval frame (i.e., frame size). This manipulation yielded a parallel result. Frame size didn't matter in the consistent-mapping condition; no matter how many items there were on the retrieval frame, participants needed only a glimpse to see if there was a letter present or not. But because the varied-mapping condition required a careful examination of all items in the retrieval frame, more items required more examination time. Each of the items was a potential target or distractor, and this determination required an item-by-item

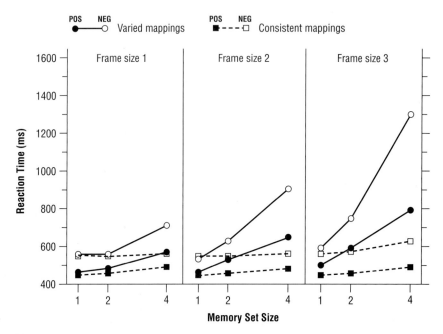

Figure 4.5 Results from the Schneider and Shiffrin (1977) study. In the consistent-mapping condition, the number of items in the memory set did not have much influence on RT. However, in the varied-mapping condition, the number of items in the memory set had a strong effect on RT.

Based on Schneider, W., & Shiffrin, R. M. (1977). Controlled and automatic human information processing. I: Detection, search, and attention. *Psychological Review, 84,* 1–66.

search. According to Schneider and Shiffrin's interpretation, searching through the items became automatic in the consistent-mapping task. After many trials of practice, participants were able to search the entire display in *parallel;* all items were encoded simultaneously, so the number of items on the retrieval frame or in the memory set didn't matter. In essence, the task became effortless. In contrast, varied mapping involved *serial processing* that never really got any easier; each item in the memory set had to be compared with each item on the retrieval frame.

Reevaluating Automaticity

Not everyone agrees in terms of what exactly is happening as a task becomes automatic. As described above, Shiffrin and Schneider's (1977) interpretation of the results from the consistent-mapping condition was that the visual search task was undergoing a transition. Participants were always doing the same thing—they were searching the visual display. However, when they started, they were searching step by step (i.e., serially); after a great deal of practice, they were searching all at once (i.e., in parallel). Essentially, the search process became much faster with a great deal of practice.

Logan (1988) has a different interpretation of what is going on as a task becomes automatic. According to his view, termed the *instance-based view,* there is a fundamental change in the way tasks are performed as people get more and more practice. Performance of a task in the early stages tends to be conscious and deliberate, involving effortful memory search and information manipulation. Each encounter with the task leads to the formation of a new memory trace, so after a great deal of practice, there are countless *instances* of having performed the task stored in memory. After sufficient practice, performance of the task switches from the deliberate algorithmic mode to the quick and simple retrieval of an instance from memory. So after a great deal of practice, instead of having to rely on repeating a mental computation, a person performs the task by quickly retrieving relevant information from memory.

The experience of Greg (your first author) as a mail clerk serves as a good example of this transition from algorithm to memory retrieval. One of the many exciting tasks that mail clerks get to perform is the tabulation of mail charges for bundles of mail. When Greg was a mail clerk, a piece of presorted mail cost 17 cents to mail (yes, he's that old). His first few months on the job, he would painstakingly multiply 17 by any and all numbers, rather laboriously in his head, or sometimes on paper. But after two years of clerking, he was extremely fast at multiplying any number by 17 (a feat that now serves no useful purpose, but boy, does it impress his friends!). What accounted for this incredible gain in performance? According to Logan's view, after years of practice, the way Greg was accomplishing this task had changed fundamentally. Instead of carrying out the actual multiplication each time he was holding 23 envelopes ($3.91!!), he was instantly and directly retrieving an instance from his hundreds of memories of having multiplied 17 by 23. This transition from computation to memory retrieval is what is happening as a task becomes automatic.

Costs of Automaticity

Although the nature of automaticity is still debated, there is little doubt about the practical implications of automatic processing. Automaticity seems to be largely a good thing; after all, we perform tasks more quickly and efficiently and are better able to share attention between tasks. But there is a downside to automaticity. Automatic processes can be quite difficult to abort or modify, due in part to the fact that they involve relatively little in the way of conscious monitoring. Therefore, it's often the case that people make absentminded mistakes when they are engaged in automatic processing. These mistakes can range from the amusing to the downright dangerous. Norman (1981) coined a term for these all-too-common bouts of absentmindedness—**action slips.**

Action Slips.   We've all done it—put the cereal in the refrigerator; gone to a room to fetch something only to return with the wrong object; called someone on the phone and forgotten who it was we were calling. Norman (1988) would label each of these as an action slip. Action slips tend to occur in the absence of attention (hence the term *absentmindedness*). Recall that one characteristic of automatic processes is that they are performed with relatively little conscious awareness. Given this, it's not surprising that many action slips occur in the context of automatic processing; quite literally, when we do things automatically, *we aren't thinking.*

Norman (1988) proposes that highly learned action sequences (like driving a car) are controlled by organized memory structures termed *schemas*—an organized body of knowledge (or set of movements) that guides motor activities. Each schema is assumed to cover only a limited range of knowledge. Therefore, a given action sequence must be made up of a number of hierarchically organized schemas. The highest-level schema is called the *parent schema* and consists of a series of *child schemas* that are initiated by the parent schema at the appropriate times. A sample parent schema might be driving to school in the morning, which is made up of many child schemas, such as walking to the car, starting the car, and parking. Norman contends that once an action becomes highly skilled, only higher-level (parent) schemas need be activated to set a behavior chain in motion; once set in motion, it basically "runs off" fairly mindlessly.

Action slips can occur at any time during this schema activation. Table 4.1 lists the various types of action slips. Let's take a look at each one. Some action slips can occur when schemas are triggered inappropriately. One type of slip, termed a *capture error,* occurs when some sequence being performed is similar to one that is very familiar and well-practiced. The schemas controlling the well-practiced action sequence may become activated and take over. For example, if you were a hockey player for your college team, you would be very familiar with the way you stop while on ice skates. When on roller skates, you might try to stop in the same manner, because the ice-skate-stopping action is more familiar than the roller-skate-stopping action. Consequently, you might find yourself on the ground rather than on your feet!

A *data-driven error* occurs when external events cause the (inappropriate) activation of a schema and force some type of unwanted behavior. William's error in the opening vignette is an example; as he is driving past a Taco Bell he asks Anne for directions to Taco Bell instead of the restaurant he intended. An *associative activation error* occurs when your intention to do or say something activates a strongly related but inappropriate schema. For example, you might respond to a friend's question "What's up?" with "Great!" This happens because what might be termed a *greeting schema* activates a number of *reply schemas* that are closely associated, and the wrong one wins.

Given that the associative activation error, the capture error, and the data-driven error all occur because an inappropriate schema is activated, you may find it difficult to differ-

---

Table 4.1   **Chart of Action Slips**

Capture error	A well-practiced, but unintended, action takes over when it shares initial sequence elements with a more unfamiliar action.
Data-driven error	External events cause the (inappropriate) activation of a schema and force some type of unwanted behavior.
Associative activation error	The intention to do or say something activates a strongly related but inappropriate schema.
Loss-of-activation error	Error lies in forgetting an intention to do something or remembering the intention but forgetting what to do.
Description error	The desired action is carried out but with the wrong object.

Adapted from Norman, D. A. (1981). Categorization of action slips. *Psychological Review, 88,* 1–5. Copyright 1981 by the American Psychological Association.

entiate them from one another. To distinguish them, think about the familiarity level and the nature of the intruding action sequence. If the intruding action sequence is more familiar than the intended action sequence, then a capture error has occurred. If the intruding action sequence is not more familiar but simply related to the intended action sequence, then an associative activation error has occurred. If the intruding action sequence is initiated by some aspect of the environment, regardless of whether it was more familiar or less familiar, then a data-driven error has occurred.

Activation of inappropriate schemas isn't the only route to an action slip. Some slips involve a failure to completely activate or maintain the activation of a schema. One of the most frustrating types of slips is the *loss-of-activation error,* which basically involves going to do something and forgetting what it was you wanted to do. This occurs when an activated schema loses activation because of decay or interference (two mechanisms for forgetting we'll discuss later in the chapter). Some slips can occur because an intention to do something is formed, but not correctly or completely. In other words, an incomplete description of what to do is formed, leading to what Norman terms a *description error.* This is when you carry out the action you wanted to but on the wrong object. For example, in a rush to put things away in the kitchen, you may find yourself putting cereal in the refrigerator and milk in the cupboard. The actions are appropriate, but they're performed on the wrong objects.

Stop *and* Think!

ABSENTMINDEDNESS

Start a diary of all the absentminded mistakes you make over the next couple of weeks. Classify each error according to the scheme discussed in the text. Write them down in detail, including what happened, what should have happened, and what was going on externally (i.e., in the environment around you) and internally (your own thoughts, how you felt).

- When do these slips seem to occur?
- Relate their occurrence to the characteristics of automatic processing.

According to Norman (1981), all of these action slips occur because their prevention and/or detection require feedback from the information-processing system about ongoing processing. Because such conscious monitoring is at a relatively low level when actions are automatic, slips are more likely to occur. Slips are prevalent in other situations that involve lowered conscious monitoring of behavior, such as when you're tired, stressed, or doing too many things at once.

STOP *and* REVIEW!

1. List the three processes that characterize an automatic process.
2. How have researchers explained the Stroop effect?
3. True or false? According to one account of automaticity, there is a transition from parallel processing to serial processing.
4. Explain why action slips are more likely to occur during automatic processing.

5. George was making pumpkin bread for his wife. He usually makes her banana bread but today he decided to make pumpkin bread. When it came time to put in the pumpkin, he found himself peeling bananas. What type of action slip is this?
  a. associative activation error
  b. capture error
  c. data-driven error
  d. loss-of-activation error

➤ Automaticity characterizes tasks that have received extensive practice and, as a result, seem to operate without intention, outside of conscious awareness, and with a minimum demand on attention.

➤ Some attribute the Stroop effect (interference in color naming when presented with a word of a conflicting color) to automatic reading of the color word, which interferes with naming the conflicting color. Recent research suggests that it may be an instance of mental set, or a tendency to revert to well-practiced mental processes (like reading) when faced with a cognitive task (like seeing a word).

➤ One interpretation of automaticity is that the processes used for a task undergo a transition from slow and serial (step by step) to fast and parallel (all at once). An alternative is that as a task becomes automatic, there is a change in the nature of the processes underlying performance. For example, tasks that are initially performed with a rule or algorithm are eventually performed with simple memory retrieval.

➤ Automatic processes are likely to give rise to action slips because their prevention requires conscious feedback about ongoing processing, and conscious monitoring is reduced when actions become automatic.

➤ Action slips include capture errors (a sequence being performed gives way to another one that's similar but more familiar and well-practiced), data-driven errors (external events cause the activation of an inappropriate schema), associative activation errors (an intention activates related but inappropriate ones), loss-of-activation errors (forgetting what you wanted to do), and description errors (carrying out an intended action with the wrong object).

Short-Term Memory

At several points in our discussion of attention, we said that once information has passed through the limited-capacity gateway of attention, it receives further processing. What is the nature of this further processing? These processes are referred to collectively as short-term memory, or working memory. The distinction between a temporarily activated, conscious form of memory and a nonactive, nonconscious store of knowledge that can be brought into an active state when necessary is not a new one. William James (1890) himself proposed such a distinction, labeling the former primary memory and the latter secondary memory.

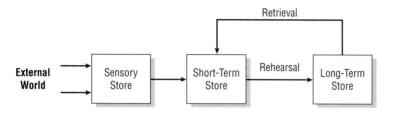

Figure 4.6 The modal model: An information-processing view of memory.

Waugh and Norman (1965) and Atkinson and Shiffrin (1968) formalized and popularized this distinction, making it a centerpiece of their information-processing views of memory. The Atkinson-Shiffrin view has been so influential that it is often termed the *modal model* of how memory works. The **modal model** (also called the information-processing model) is summarized in Figure 4.6. As you can see, the model is clearly in the tradition of information-processing models, postulating a series of chronologically arranged stages through which incoming information passes. Although current researchers are unsure about this stagelike progression, not to mention the idea of three distinct memory stores, the model provides an extremely useful way to describe what phenomenologically seem to be different types of memory processing.

As you can see in Figure 4.6, Atkinson and Shiffrin propose three different types of memory storage. The first, sensory memory, is a briefly held representation of a just-presented stimulus (as was discussed at length in Chapter 3). The centerpiece of the theory has proven to be the other two memory stores and the postulated distinction between them. Long-term memory (LTM) contrasts powerfully with the fading buffer that is sensory memory. Long-term memory can be conceptualized as a vast repository that houses all of the experiences, knowledge, and skills we have accumulated throughout our lifetimes. (Keep in mind that this simple spatial metaphor is only a convenient description of LTM and fails to capture anything about LTM storage on a physiological level.) We'll address issues of LTM in more depth in Chapters 6 through 9.

So what lies between the transient sensory buffer and the long-term storage of everything we know? **Short-term memory (STM)** is the set of processes that we use to hold and rehearse information that occupies our current awareness. This temporary form of memory can be conceptualized as a sort of mental workbench we use to rehearse or recycle information. You'll notice that in Figure 4.6 there are arrows running from STM to LTM, and vice versa. This signifies that rehearsal in STM is thought to result in LTM storage. And when information in LTM is appropriate for dealing with present circumstances, it is brought back into STM.

One of the major theoretical issues within the study of memory is whether it is useful and valid to distinguish between short-term and long-term memory stores. Many (e.g., Crowder, 1993) suggest that this distinction is useful in terms of description only and that in reality STM and LTM are both expressions of the same underlying unitary memory system. However, most would agree that the distinction is still quite useful at a descriptive level. Following this popular convention, the remainder of this chapter will deal primarily with the operation of this immediate form of memory. We will return to this issue regarding the distinction between STM and LTM in Chapter 6.

Since the inception of the modal model in 1968, research on short-term memory has exploded, and many investigators' conceptualization of it has gone well beyond the original idea of STM as a holding and recycling buffer. Short-term memory is often investigated in the context of other more complex cognitive processes, such as reading and problem solving. There is no doubt that these abilities are critically dependent on the elaborate processing of information that currently resides in consciousness, not just on temporarily holding a set of items in mind. In discussing this expanded conceptualization of short-term memory, researchers often use the term *working memory (WM),* a concept we'll examine in more detail later in the chapter. It is important to note that the term *working memory* is now the modal terminology used by cognitive researchers (and will be used throughout this book). However, from a historical perspective, investigations into this area began with what was traditionally termed STM. Therefore, we'll start our discussion in the same manner, by examining the basic characteristics of STM.

Limited Duration

When keeping track of your instructor's riveting lectures, you've no doubt experienced one of the defining characteristics of STM—the fact that it has a limited duration. The information seems gone nearly as quickly as it is presented. Information is active in STM only temporarily; in order to maintain information in STM, it needs to be rehearsed. In Chapter 6, you'll read more about the rehearsal of information in STM (termed *maintenance rehearsal*) and its effect on long-term retention.

The limited duration of STM has been most often demonstrated with the **Brown-Peterson task** (Peterson & Peterson, 1959; Brown, 1958). In this task, people receive a brief presentation of a consonant trigram (e.g., JDL) immediately followed by the presentation of a three-digit number. Participants must count backward by threes from that number. The purpose of the counting task is to prevent the participants from thinking about the material. The amount of time they're required to count defines the **retention interval.** The amount of time that lapses between encoding and retrieval is a common independent variable in memory experiments. Peterson and Peterson's results are presented in Figure 4.7. As you can see, forgetting was quite extreme and quite quick; within about 20 seconds, the probability of recalling the trigram was only 0.10 (or 10%).

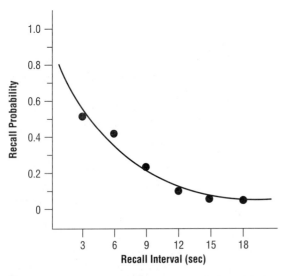

Figure 4.7 Short-term memory fades with time.
From Peterson L., & Peterson, M. J. (1959). Short-term retention of individual verbal items. *Journal of Experimental Psychology, 58,* 193–198.

Limited Capacity

A loose analogy can be drawn between STM and the functioning of a tape recorder. One similarity is their limited capacity. A tape recorder can only record a finite amount of information, depending on the tape's length. Analogously, the amount of information we can hold in STM is also limited (we'll return later to this analogy). Limitations in STM capacity were noted by George Miller, one of the leading figures in the cognitive revolution of the 1950s. In a classic paper, Miller (1956) notes the prominence of what he coined the **magical number, 7 ± 2.** He was referring to a strikingly consistent limitation in the number of items we can hold in STM. Miller notes that this number is applicable across a wide array of different stimulus types, from letters, to numbers, to words, to musical notes. So "magical" was this number that it was the basis for our seven-digit phone numbers. Based on the early work investigating STM capacity, seven digits were chosen as the most reasonable load an individual could remember that would still allow for various phone number combinations. This is also the reason why (in the opening scenario) William has so much trouble with phone numbers that include area codes—10 digits tax the capacity of STM.

The limited capacity of STM is most often assessed through **memory span,** the longest string of information (e.g., numbers, letters) that a person can immediately recall. A legion of research findings from studies of STM memory span confirm what Miller originally proposed: that we have a fundamental limit in our ability to keep track of incoming information (e.g., Baddeley, 1993; Shiffrin & Nosofsky, 1994). Nairne (1996) likens the limited capacity of STM to the capacity of a juggler. Just as a juggler can keep only so many balls in the air at a time, our STM can keep only so much information "in the air" at a time. Miller puts the limit at 7 ± 2 items. Now the question is, what exactly constitutes an item?

Chunking in STM. It turns out that our STM is considerably more powerful than the magic number would imply. Although there is no doubt that there is a limit in memory span, we can functionally increase the limits by recoding information, combining it into larger and larger "chunks." Through this process, called **chunking** or **recoding,** you translate incoming information into a more manageable form. In our story, William has a tough time handling a 10-digit phone number. But once he knows that the 10 numbers correspond to the letters in *psychology,* he has no problem managing it. The capacity limits of STM never get beyond the magic number, but with efficient use of recoding strategies, we can functionally increase the capacity. In the juggling analogy to STM, we can think of this as being able to juggle seven large balls or seven small balls, but seven is all that can be juggled.

Our ability to chunk or recode information is affected by a number of variables. First, because STM has a relatively brief duration, the rate of presentation can be a limiting factor in chunking. For instance, when someone tells you a phone number too quickly, with no pauses, this *characteristic of presentation* has a significant effect on your recoding. Recoding is also profoundly affected by *knowledge base.* When you're taking notes based on a professor's lecture, you are recoding the information. This ability is enhanced the more you know about the topic; previous knowledge aids your reorganization of the information. (That's why it helps to read the material from the textbook before you come to class!)

A powerful demonstration of the role knowledge can play in STM was provided by Chase and Ericsson (e.g., Chase & Ericsson, 1982; Ericsson, 1985; Ericsson, Chase, &

Faloon, 1980), who investigated the chunking abilities of a normal everyday college student much like yourself. But this student (S. F.) had spent two years essentially "exercising" his STM, engaging in memory-span practice a few days a week for about an hour a day (and you thought physical exercise was tough!). The general procedure he used was to read a digit sequence at a rate of one digit per second and then test himself on the sequence; if he recalled the sequence perfectly, he increased the next sequence by one digit. After nearly 300 hours of testing himself in this way, S. F. had increased his memory span from a measly seven items to nearly 80 items.

How was S. F. able to complete this prodigious feat of memory? He was a very skilled long-distance runner, and he used his expertise with distance running to build a scheme that allowed him to chunk the incoming digits in a meaningful way. He encoded them as running times and groups of running times. The ability to recode information quickly and effectively within a meaningful scheme is an important component of expertise. According to skilled-memory theory (e.g., Chase & Ericsson, 1982), expertise in a given domain allows for the direct storage of information in LTM; in essence, S. F.'s rich recoding scheme allowed him to practically bypass STM. We'll talk more about the role of memory in expertise when we talk about problem solving in Chapter 12.

Effects of Word Length.   Because the information in STM seems to be lost relatively quickly, it shouldn't be surprising that the longer an item takes to pronounce, the fewer such items you can hold in STM. Since Miller's (1956) original formulation of the magic number, research has demonstrated that this number may not be as "magic" as was first thought. Short-term memory span seems to be limited not necessarily by the number of items being encoded but by the time it takes to encode a given set of items. Consider again the tape recorder analogy: the amount of information that will fit on a tape is not only determined by tape length, but also by how fast you talk. (The faster you talk, the more information you can get on the tape.) Similarly, retaining 7 ± 2 long items (e.g., hippopotamus) in STM proves to be much more difficult than retaining 7 ± 2 short items (e.g., cat). This **word-length effect** is a consistent finding in studies of STM (e.g., Baddeley, Thompson, & Buchanan, 1975; Schweickert, McDaniel, & Riegler, 1993) and serves as another illustration of the time-based nature of STM.

Stop *and* **Think!**

WORD LENGTH AND STM CAPACITY

Find two friends to serve as cognitive guinea pigs. For each participant, pick one condition, and test their short-term memory of each list by reading each item at a rate of about one second per item and having them recall after each list.

Condition 1	Condition 2
1. ham	1. mystery
dog	vanilla
gem	bicycle
skill	pyramid
heart	condiment
bag	television
ring	automobile

2. cat
   beef
   stone
   tin
   job
   fruit
   blue
3. shoe
   bow
   book
   jaw
   song
   can
   jug

2. gigantic
   anatomy
   octopus
   factory
   ladybug
   metallic
   cabinet
3. tornado
   animal
   martini
   surgery
   radio
   cantaloupe
   barbaric

- Did the participant in each condition demonstrate the same or different results?
- Did the results fit Miller's "magic number"?
- If not, what factor(s) may have led to the discrepancy?
- Why?

Coding in STM

How is information typically coded in STM? When you're listening to something, whether it's a phone number or an important fact from class discussion, how do you keep track of it in consciousness? For one thing, you probably repeat it to yourself. A great deal of research indicates that *auditory coding* is the dominant mode of processing in STM. That is, we "hear" information as it is being rehearsed via a sort of "inner voice." One piece of experimental evidence supporting this idea is the **phonological similarity effect,** the finding that lists of similar-sounding items are more difficult to keep track of in STM than are lists of different-sounding items. This basic effect has been replicated many times (e.g., Baddeley, 1966; Conrad, 1964; Schiano & Watkins, 1981). It even occurs when material is presented visually, strongly implying that visually presented information is quickly converted into an auditory form. The word-length effect, described earlier, is also cited as evidence for auditory coding in STM: the longer it takes to say an item, the fewer such items can be held. STM depends on the characteristics of pronunciation. Since we recycle information by repeating it, it makes sense that when it takes a long time to say something, more strain will be placed on our STM.

Stop *and* Think!

PHONOLOGICAL SIMILARITY AND STM

Same instructions as last time. Find two friends to serve as cognitive guinea pigs. For each participant, pick one of the list conditions (1 or 2) and test memory of each list by reading each item at a rate of about one second per item and having the subject recall the items.

List 1a: f, z, k, w, r, p, m
List 1b: e, g, z, b, t, p, v, c
List 2a: cat, chair, joy, hat, book, run, tree, lamp, house, egg
List 2b: cake, lake, bake, sake, take, make, rake

- Did you notice any differences in participants' ability to recall the two lists?
- If so, what factor(s) seemed to relate to this difference?

But is audition the only modality in which information can be coded in STM? Simple introspection tells us that STM processing is not limited to some type of auditory rehearsal. The processing of material in your conscious awareness also allows for visual coding. The use of a visual code is easy to demonstrate. Look up from this book (yes, we know that's hard to do), close your eyes, and think about the steps involved in getting to your first class in the morning. It's a good bet that you aren't verbally saying "Walk out door, turn right, turn left, enter elevator, go outside." It's more likely that you're visualizing the path you take; this is a simple example of visual coding in STM.

A study by Brandimonte and Gerbino (1993) provides an interesting demonstration of auditory and visual coding in STM. Their experiment made use of reversible figures (pictures with two possible interpretations that alternate as you're viewing it). One question that emerges from the investigation of these figures is whether mental images (i.e., visual codings) of these reversible figures can be ambiguous—that is, interpreted in two different ways. For example, if you briefly view a reversible figure and then simply hold it in memory, does it reverse just as it does when you're actually looking at it? If the answer is yes, this provides strong evidence for the presence of a visual coding mechanism in STM.

Brandimonte and Gerbino (1993) reasoned that image reversal in STM probably is possible, but only under certain conditions. Consider what might happen if you were presented very briefly with the reversible picture depicted in Figure 4.8. Chances are, if your inner voice says "duck," the image being held in STM will look like a duck. (Or conversely, if your inner voice says "rabbit" the image being held in STM will look like a rabbit.) But (and this is the important point) if the image is quickly labeled as either a duck or a rabbit, seeing the other version will be much less likely. In other words, the auditory code that enjoys such prominence in STM leads to a particular interpretation of the figure and blocks the other interpretation. But if the auditory processing of STM is somehow prevented, both interpretations might remain equally viable and allow for a spontaneous figure reversal.

Figure 4.8 Rabbit or duck?

From Brandimonte, M. A., & Gerbino, W. (1993). Mental image reversal and verbal recording: When ducks become rabbits. *Memory and Cognition, 21,* 23–33. Reprinted by permission of the Psychonomic Society, Inc.

To test this idea, Brandimonte and Gerbino trained participants using a couple of reversible figures so they would be familiar with the general idea and experience the image reversals that can occur. After this training phase, they were presented with a new reversible figure (the duck/rabbit figure); the presentation duration was brief (two seconds) to prevent participants from experiencing the reversal while actually viewing it. But this brief presentation was sufficient for an auditory coding of the stimulus. During this brief presentation, half of the participants remained silent; the other half was required to say "la, la, la" (which helps prevent auditory rehearsal). After the image was taken away, participants were asked what they had seen. Next, in an imagery phase, participants were told to hold the figure in mind and attempt to reverse it in order to reveal the second possible interpretation. The investigators wanted to see if image reversals would depend on whether or not participants were able to use an auditory code during the initial encoding.

An interesting aspect of this study is that Brandimonte and Gerbino investigated both children and adults. Citing other experimental evidence that young children tend to rely on a visual code in STM tasks, they argued that young children's ability to imagine the reversals would not differ in the silent and "la, la, la" conditions. That is, since young children don't rely on auditory coding, it should not matter whether they are allowed to rehearse or not. But because older children and adults tend to code information in an auditory form, they should be affected by the prevention of auditory rehearsal and therefore imagine more reversals in the "la, la, la" condition.

The results from the study are presented in Figure 4.9. Consistent with the researchers' analysis, reversals of the mental image were much more likely to occur when auditory rehearsal was prevented; for example, preventing participants from silently saying "rabbit" when they first saw the item made it more likely that they would be able to see a "duck" when they imagined it later. Clearly, we have the ability to encode information in a visual format in STM. Interestingly, the effect did depend on age. As predicted by the investigators, young children experience just as many image reversals when auditory rehearsal is prevented as when it isn't, suggesting that auditory coding isn't that important in their initial encoding. The Brandimonte and Gerbino study is just one in a number of studies that supports the existence of visual coding in STM. In other words, our STM seems to feature both an "inner voice" and an "inner eye."

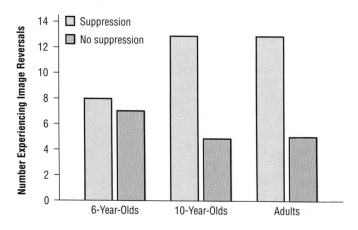

Figure 4.9 Results from the Brandimonte and Gerbino (1993) study. Articulatory suppression interfered with the verbal recoding of the ambiguous item. As a result, image reversals were more prevalent. Young children were not influenced by articulatory suppression, suggesting a lack of articulatory processing.

From Brandimonte, M. A., & Gerbino, W. (1998). Mental image reversal and verbal recoding: When ducks become rabbits. *Memory and Cognition, 21*, 23–33. Reprinted by permission of the Psychonomic Society, Inc.

RECURRING RESEARCH THEME
Cognition and Individual Differences

Sex Differences in Visual STM

Visual coding is an important form of representation and processing in STM. As noted by Loring-Meier and Halpern (1999), the ability to use STM for simultaneously maintaining a representation of visual/spatial information, as well as imagining what objects would look like when viewed from another perspective, is critical in a number of fields, such as architecture, design, and carpentry. A good deal of evidence reveals that there may be sex differences in this aspect of STM processing. According to Dror and Kosslyn (1994), visuo-spatial processing in STM can be conceptualized in terms of four component processes (image generation, image maintenance, image scanning, and image transformation). How do sex differences in visual/spatial processing map onto each of these components? Loring-Meier and Halpern did a study to examine the possibility of sex differences in each component of visuo-spatial processing proposed by Dror and Kosslyn.

The first component is called *image generation*—bringing an image from LTM into STM. In the image-generation task used by Loring-Meier and Halpern, participants committed 10 different block letters to long-term memory through extensive encoding and drawing practice. Then testing began. Participants were presented with a lowercase script version of a letter, and then an X was presented in a certain place on the screen. The task was to imagine the uppercase version of the presented lowercase letter and decide whether this letter would cover the X. To do this, participants had to retrieve from long-term memory one of the images they had just learned. The RT for the yes/no decision served as a measure of image-generation time. The second component is called *image maintenance*—holding the image in STM once it has been formed. The image-maintenance task was similar to the image-generation task; participants encoded a presented pattern and held the image in STM when it was removed. Then an X appeared on the screen, and they were to indicate whether the image they were maintaining would have covered the presented X. The speed of this decision indicates the proficiency of image-maintenance processes. The clearer the maintained image, the quicker the decision.

The third component is called *image scanning*—searching the image being held in STM for some feature. In the image-scanning task, participants memorized a pattern of small squares that formed a large square; some of these squares were filled, and some were not. After memorizing the pattern, it was removed, and an arrow appeared, pointing to one of the small squares. The task was to indicate whether the arrow pointed to a filled or unfilled square. To do this, participants essentially had to scan around their mental image, so the RT for this decision served as an indicator of image-scanning time. The final component is called *image transformation*—actively manipulating an image being held in STM. In the image-transformation (actually, image-rotation) task, participants were presented with two figures side-by-side and had to decide whether the two were identical. The figure on the right differed from the one on the left by varying degrees of rotation. Making this decision required mental rotation of the right-hand figure to see if it matched

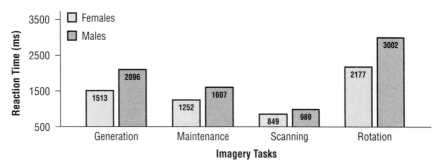

Figure 4.10 Results from the Loring-Maier and Halpern (1999) study. Males were faster than females on each of the four imagery tasks.

From Loring-Meier, S., & Halpern, D. F. (1999). Sex differences in visuospatial working memory: Components of cognitive processing. *Psychonomic Bulletin and Review, 6,* 464–471. Reprinted by permission of the Psychonomic Society, Inc.

the left-hand figure; in this condition, reaction time serves as an indicator of mental rotation speed.

The results (shown in Figure 4.10) revealed men to be faster than women in each of the four components of visual/spatial processing. You may be wondering whether the men's speed came at the expense of accuracy; perhaps women made fewer errors. Good thinking, but the error rate did not differ between men and women for any of the four tasks. Loring-Meier and Halpern concluded that women are generally slower in tasks that utilize the visual and spatial processes of STM and that this slowness cannot be isolated in any one component. The authors point out an interesting implication of their result for standardized tests such as the *Graduate Record Examination* (GRE). Many of the items on these tests involve visualization processes—generating, maintaining, and manipulating images—that no doubt correspond to those investigated in the Loring-Meier and Halpern study. The results of these tests indicate that women and men do equally well (in terms of accuracy) on tasks requiring these components of STM. However, these tests are also speeded; test-takers must complete them within a limited time frame. Given the study's results, it would seem that making the tests speeded would have a differential negative impact, potentially lowering women's performance more than men's. According to Loring-Meier and Halpern, this may provide at least a partial reason for men's' overall superior performance on standardized tests like the GRE (Willingham & Cole, 1997).

The investigation by Loring-Meier and Halpern provides strong evidence that sex differences in the speed of visual STM processing exist, but it doesn't provide information about the origins of these differences. The question of the relative role of biological (i.e., brain structure and hormonal) and environmental (i.e., experiences and training) factors in producing these differences is still a matter of some debate. There is evidence that both types of factors play a significant role (see Halpern, 2000, for a review of the evidence).

Forgetting in STM

As stated before, one of the most palpable characteristics of STM is the fact that information is lost fairly quickly. Two mechanisms have received a great deal of attention as the primary culprits in this loss of information: decay and interference. Let's examine each of these in more detail.

Decay.   The loss of information from STM due to the passage of time is referred to as **decay.** The initial evidence for this rather simple view consists of findings from early studies that employed the Brown-Peterson technique. Forgetting in this task seemed to occur even with minimal interference. It was assumed that counting backward did not interfere with the maintenance of information in STM, because the corresponding stimuli (letters and numbers) are so dissimilar. Therefore, any forgetting that occurred was attributable to decay.

The decay view of forgetting may be seen as a little wanting. As everyone knows, time passes, and we forget. As noted by Nairne (1996) in a critique of the decay account of forgetting, the fact that iron rusts over time does not mean that the rust was caused by time passage. It's caused by something that happens over the time interval—namely, oxidation. In the same way, many researchers believe that a better account of STM forgetting must involve the specification of the events that happen during the retention interval. The most likely candidate is interference.

Interference.   According to the notion of **interference,** information is lost from STM because information currently being processed is negatively influenced by the presentation of other information. In a broad sense, interference can occur in one of two basic patterns. When earlier information interferes with the ability to retain information that comes later, it's termed **proactive interference.** The complementary case, where later information interferes with the ability to retain information that occurred earlier, is termed **retroactive interference.** These two can be distinguished by considering the temporal relationship between the to-be-remembered information and the interfering information. Figure 4.11 should help you distinguish between the two.

So what causes forgetting in STM—a simple process of erosion, or the confusion that arises when we encode additional information? There still exists a fair amount of disagreement on this score, although most researchers probably look to interference as the more likely culprit. There are a number of findings that cast serious doubt on simple decay theory. For example, Keppel and Underwood (1962) used the Brown-Peterson task to assess forgetting and found that there was virtually no forgetting on the first trial of a set of Brown-Peterson trials. Not only that, it didn't matter how long the delay interval was; even with long delays, there was almost no forgetting on the initial trial. There seemed to be little or no effect of longer retention intervals until trials started to accumulate. Put another way, there seemed to be little or no effect of delay until there was significant potential for interference to occur. Hence, interference is implicated as the more important cause of forgetting. What type of interference did Keppel and Underwood find—proactive or retroactive? Use the information in Figure 4.12 to figure it out.

Here's a scheme that should help you discriminate between retroactive and proactive interference. Imagine that you've spent your weekend studying for two tests—psychology and sociology. You studied psychology on Saturday and sociology on Sunday.

Which information was learned first? Write it down:

> *psychology*

Which information was learned second? Write it down to the right of the item that was learned first; it was learned after the first item:

> psychology   *sociology*

Which of the two pieces of information is trying to be remembered? Let's say you're taking your psychology exam. Underline that item and draw an arrow from the nonunderlined item (i.e., the item that is not being remembered) to the underlined item (i.e., the item that is being remembered).

If the arrow is pointing in the backward direction (pointing backward in time from what was learned second to what was learned first), the type of interference is *retroactive* (*retro* means "backward"). Sociology information is retroactively interfering with your ability to remember information for your psychology exam.

Now let's imagine you are in your sociology exam.

If the arrow is pointing in the forward direction, the type of interference is *proactive* (*pro* means "forward"). Psychology information is proactively interfering with your ability to remember information for your sociology exam.

Figure 4.11 Scheme/mnemonic for distinguishing retroactive and proactive interference.

From Robinson-Riegler, G., & Robinson-Riegler, B. (1999). *Instructor's resource guide* for J. Kalat, *Introduction to psychology* (5th ed.). Belmont, CA: Wadsworth. Copyright 1999. Reprinted by permission of Wadsworth, a division of Thomson Learning.

Trial 1	*Recall*	Trial 2	*Recall*	Trial 3	*Recall*	Trial 4	*Recall*
daisy		tulip		orchid		plum	
rose		sunflower		carnation		peach	
daffodil		hyacinth		marigold		banana	

Figure 4.12 A rendition of the Wickens et al. (1976) procedure for demonstrating release from proactive interference. Test a friend; have them read each list, followed by a three-digit number (e.g., 843), and have them count back by 3 from the number for 10 seconds. Then have them recall that three-item list. Continue until all lists have been read and tested. Did you find evidence of proactive interference, followed by a release from PI?

Adapted from Wickens, D. D., Dalezman, R. E., & Eggemeier, F. T. (1976). Multiple encoding of word attributes in memory. *Memory and Cognition, 4,* 307–310.

Although interference may be the explanation of choice for STM forgetting, the exact manner in which it inhibits STM is a matter of some debate (Nairne, 1996). The negative effects of interference on STM could result from a problem in storing information in STM or in retrieving information out of STM.

Stop and Think!   INTERFERENCE AND FORGETTING IN STM

Go back to the results you gathered from the Stop and Think! on the word-length effect. Better yet, rerun the experiment, this time with a different set of questions in mind.

- Should the number of words recalled change from group 1 to group 3, regardless of condition?
- If so, how should it change? Why?
- What did your results show? (Think about it in terms of interference.)

Interference may have damaging effects on STM because it makes storage of information difficult. The *displacement view* suggests that when a new item enters STM, it "bumps out" (or displaces) a previously stored item. The *overwriting view* assumes that when a new item enters STM, it overwrites a previously stored item. A study by Proctor and Fagnani (1978) indicates that the overwriting view may be a better description of the effects of interference. These researchers found more interference in a Brown-Peterson task if newer information was presented in the same modality as previously stored information (i.e., both visual or both auditory) than if the two were presented in different modalities (i.e., one visual and one auditory). If the interference effect was due to items being "bumped out" of STM, the new information would bump the old material out, regardless of presentation modality. The fact that the similarity of the information led to more interference indicates that similarity caused confusion among the items, whereas the lack of similarity reduced confusion. Reduced confusion leads to more effective storage, hence more effective retrieval.

On the other hand, it is possible that interference does not affect how information is encoded but instead makes retrieval of information more difficult. Anytime you're required to remember something, a process of retrieval is involved. And as you'll see in Chapter 7, long-term memory retrieval is not perfect; it is a reconstructive, rather than a reproductive, process. The same is true in STM; the rememberer must reconstruct the information that has just been presented in order to report it. Some accounts of interference place the locus of its effects at the point of information recovery or retrieval (Nairne, 1992). According to the notion of *blurring* and *deblurring*, items in STM can blur into one another and become difficult to tell apart (or "deblur") at retrieval.

Let's examine these views by taking a look at a classic experiment by Wickens, Dalezman, and Eggemeier (1976). In this study, Wickens and colleagues employed the Brown-Peterson task but used categorized lists instead of letters. On a given trial, participants would read three professions—lawyer, nurse, custodian—and then be required to count backward for 18 seconds. After this distractor period, they were asked to recall the professions. Four trials were performed, each using three more items from the same category.

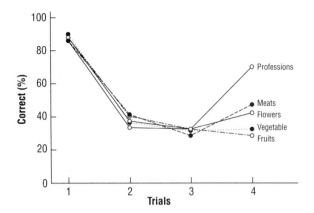

Figure 4.13 Trial-by-trial recall in the Wickens et al. (1976) study. Note that recall decreases over the first three trials due to proactive interference. However, recall recovers on a fourth trial, but only under conditions where the items in the final word lists differ semantically from the items in the previous lists (i.e., fruits).

From Wickens, D. D., Dalezman, R. E., & Eggemeier, F. T. (1976). Multiple encoding of word attributes in memory. *Memory and Cognition, 4,* 307–310. Reprinted by permission of the Psychonomic Society, Inc.

Can you imagine what happened over the course of these three trials? Try it and see, referring to Figure 4.12.

You probably found that as you tried to remember the words on the third and fourth trials, you became more and more confused about what words were on these lists, largely because the earlier items were interfering with your ability to remember the later items; this is proactive interference (the same type of interference found by Keppel and Underwood a few paragraphs ago). As you can see in Figure 4.13, the participants in this study were profoundly affected by this interference; recall fell by 60% from the first to third trials. But the most intriguing finding from this study emerged on a fourth Brown-Peterson trial. Recall that participants had received three successive lists from the same category. On the fourth trial, they were presented with three items but this time from a different category—fruits. (A control group received fruits on all four trials.) The last data point in the figure shows the surprising result: recall bounced back up. This bounce-back effect is termed **release from proactive interference.** Interestingly, the greater the difference between the original lists and the final list, the greater the release.

Imagine what might be happening in this experiment according to the different notions of interference. Let's look at the memory performance for the first three trials. If interference is a storage problem, new items entering STM get confused with the old items already encoded. As a result, these newer items are poorly encoded. Confusion can also make it difficult to retrieve or reconstruct information from STM. So many items are associated with the STM retrieval cue "professions" that it no longer serves as an effective hint when the rememberer thinks of it (Nairne, 2002). On the fourth trial (when the category switches), the confusion is greatly reduced. New words interfere less with old words, because the new words come from a new category. An astute reader may be asking why should they be less interfering? After all, the words were presented in the same modality.

As it turns out, the Wickens study is a classic, not only for its demonstration of proactive interference and release from proactive interference, but also for revealing another dimension of STM: STM is also (at least somewhat) sensitive to meaning. When the category shifted, the words were less likely to be confused with old ones because the meaning had changed. Furthermore, the cue that the rememberer thinks of (fruits) is fresh and new and has only been associated with three items, so the cue "fruit" does a better job of cuing the items from that trial. So confusion at storage and/or retrieval results in proactive interference, and a reduction in that confusion results in the release-from-proactive-interference effect.

STOP *and* REVIEW!

1. The duration of STM
   a. is about two minutes
   b. is less than one second
   c. is about 20 seconds
   d. depends on the length of the word
2. True or false? The capacity of STM is determined solely by the number of items that must be remembered.
3. Would it be hard or easy to keep a list of similar-sounding items in STM? Explain.
4. True or false? Retroactive interference occurs when earlier information makes it difficult to remember later information.
5. Distinguish between displacement and overwriting.

➤ STM refers to the processes that are used for temporarily holding, rehearsing, and responding to information currently in consciousness. STM is limited in duration, lasting less than 20 seconds without rehearsal.

➤ STM capacity is limited (7 ± 2 items), but can be functionally increased by chunking incoming information. Ability to recode information is affected by rate of presentation and the person's knowledge base. Capacity is taxed by long words, relative to short words, as indicated by the word-length effect. (It's easier to keep track of short words than long words in STM.)

➤ Information in STM is processed predominantly in auditory (sound-based) form as indicated by the phonological similarity effect (similar-sounding items are more difficult to keep track of in STM than are different-sounding items). Visual coding is also possible in STM.

➤ Information loss from STM is thought to result from decay (the simple passage of time) or interference (inhibition from other sources of information)—proactive interference (earlier information interferes with the ability to retain information that comes later) and retroactive interference (later information interferes with the ability to retain information that occurred earlier). Researchers prefer interference as an account of STM forgetting.

➤ Interference can affect memory through displacement (a new item enters STM and "bumps out" out a previously stored item) or overwriting (a new item enters STM and overwrites a previously stored item). A change in meaning from a series of lists to a final list leads to a release from proactive interference, indicating that STM codes information semantically.

A Modular Approach to STM: Working Memory

Three decades of research on STM have liberated it from its conceptualization as a simple information recycler, as conceived of in the early days of information-processing theory. Based on years of research demonstrating the richness and variety of STM processing,

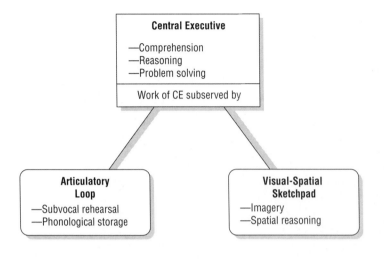

Central Executive

—Comprehension
—Reasoning
—Problem solving

Work of CE subserved by

Articulatory Loop

—Subvocal rehearsal
—Phonological storage

Visual-Spatial Sketchpad

—Imagery
—Spatial reasoning

investigators have proposed increasingly elaborate models of STM function, the most popular of which is a model termed *working memory (WM)* (Baddeley, 1986, 2000; Hitch & Baddeley, 1976). The model has captured researchers' fancy to such a degree that working memory is how many psychologists refer to the collective set of processes we've been discussing. According to this model, working memory is actually a number of closely interacting subsystems that combine to subserve a host of higher-level mental processes, including language comprehension, problem solving, and reasoning. Two of the subsystems incorporate notions of auditory (articulatory loop) and visual (visuospatial sketchpad) coding in STM. A third component (the central executive) serves as the "boss" of STM, supervising the operation of the other subsystems and carrying out important duties of its own.

The Articulatory Loop

Intuition, along with the results of many investigations of STM, tells us that information can be temporarily held in some type of active form and that the dominant mode for holding the information is based on some type of auditory code (the "inner voice" discussed earlier). According to the working memory model, this is accomplished by the **articulatory loop.** This component is actually made up of two subcomponents: a *phonological store* that holds information temporarily and an articulatory process, which Baddeley terms the *subvocal rehearsal mechanism,* used to rehearse information. According to this model, the effects we discussed earlier (of word length and phonological similarity) result from the mechanics of the articulatory loop. The word-length effect derives from the fact that information in the phonological store is extremely limited in duration. Our difficulty remembering similar-sounding items results from the subvocal rehearsal mechanism.

The name "sub*vocal* rehearsal mechanism" and research indicating the dominance of auditory coding in STM (the "inner voice") may make you think that the WM system is based solely on audition. But what about deaf individuals? They lack normal auditory sensory capabilities, but it seems unlikely that they have no rehearsal mechanism. Therefore, the mechanism must be more general in nature, allowing for internal rehearsal in whatever mode the rehearser is accustomed to using.

The name of the working memory (WM) subsystem that contains the subvocal rehearsal mechanism provides a hint—it's called the articulatory loop. Articulation requires the coordination of various motor movements to produce the basic units of the communication system, whether those units are sounds (in the case of speech, which we'll discuss

All uses of language—including American Sign Language—involve the articulatory loop.

further in Chapter 10) or hand movements, for users of American Sign Language (ASL). The prominence of auditory coding discussed earlier occurs because the participants in these studies used speech to communicate. So while it is functionally accurate to say that the dominant mode is auditory (most people use speech to communicate), this fact may lead one to have an oversimplified view of WM. Audition is prominent not because the basic mechanisms of WM rely on the auditory modality but because WM relies on articulatory processes, which happen to be auditory in hearing adults. With this revised viewpoint, let's reconsider some of the findings we discussed earlier.

For users of speech, researchers find a phonological similarity effect: similar-sounding words are more difficult to keep track of than different-sounding words. But the critical factor is not that the words sound similar, but that similar motor movements are required to articulate the words. Given that the important dimension is the particular mode of articulation rather than sound itself, we should expect to obtain an analogous finding for users of ASL in their articulatory mode—namely, signing. In other words, deaf signers of ASL should show a sign-based similarity effect. Similar-looking signs should be more difficult to keep track of than different-looking signs, because similar-looking signs share similar motor movements. This has been found by several investigators (e.g., Hanson, 1982; Beluggi, Klima, & Siple, 1974; Wilson & Emmorey, 1997); signs that share the same hand movements are more difficult for deaf signers to retain in WM than are signs that vary in hand movements.

Second, one would expect to find a word-length effect; long signs should be just as difficult to keep straight for deaf signers as long words are for hearing speakers. To test this idea, Wilson and Emmorey (1998) presented deaf users of ASL with signs that varied in terms of the movement features. Long signs were ones that featured movements that were large and circular, covered distance, or featured a change in direction; short signs involved short movements, with no change of direction. Importantly, the long and short signs were

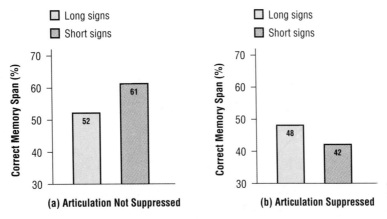

Figure 4.14 In panel a, a word-length effect is apparent for sign language. When articulation is required (panel b), the word-length effect is eliminated. This is identical to the pattern observed in hearing participants.

From Wilson, M., & Emmorey, K. (1998) A "word-length effect" for sign-language: Further evidence for the role of language in structuring working memory. *Memory and Cognition, 26,* 584–590. Reprinted by permission of the Psychonomic Society, Inc.

matched for other features, such as the hand shapes used. The signs were filmed and presented to participants via videotape. At the end of each sign sequence, a probe sign was presented that signaled participants to recall the list. The results are presented in Figure 4.14a. As you can see, the researchers did indeed find a word-length effect for sign language. Signs involving more distance, changes in direction, or large circular motions were more difficult to remember.

Effects of Articulatory Suppression. Given that articulation is the critical factor in the operation of the articulatory loop, what would happen if we prevent a person from articulating the information they are attempting to rehearse? Remember the "la, la, la" distractor discussed in the rabbit/duck study? Well, it has a name—**articulatory suppression task.** The task is designed to prevent a person from using articulation mechanisms to recycle information by tying up the "inner voice" of speech-using participants with other matters. As you might expect, this makes the retention of information in WM much more difficult, decreasing memory span (Murray, 1968).

Articulatory suppression also influences the effects of phonological similarity and word length. Recall that even visually presented stimuli (e.g., printed words or nameable pictures) seem to be quickly translated into an auditory form (Posner and Keele, 1967) and therefore are subject to the negative effects of phonological similarity. However, something interesting happens when you introduce articulatory suppression during the encoding of visually presented items: there is no negative effect of phonological similarity (e.g., Murray, 1968; Coltheart, 1993). It makes sense if you think about it. Seeing a picture of a tiger, or the printed word *tiger,* will lead you to silently rehearse *tiger* using the subvocal rehearsal mechanism—unless I prevent you from doing so through articulatory suppression. In this case, the item cannot be coded in terms of the articulatory mode of your communication system—sound—so the way the words sound doesn't influence performance. So it doesn't matter whether the items sound alike or not; you can't use articulation mechanisms anyway.

Articulatory suppression has similar effects on the word-length effect. An articulatory suppression task prevents rehearsal with the subvocal rehearsal mechanism. Therefore, it makes no difference whether the incoming information is long or short; it can't be rehearsed through articulatory mechanisms anyway. Indeed, articulatory suppression tends to eliminate the effects of word length on recall from WM (e.g., Baddeley, Lewis, & Vallar, 1984).

In investigations of the word-length effect in users of ASL, participants were presented with hand signs that were either long or short. Would articulatory suppression make this effect go away, as it does with hearing participants? And what would articulatory suppression be for deaf participants? Wilson and Emmorey (1998) looked at the effects of suppression in a second condition of their study. To do this, half of the participants had to engage in a suppression task. These participants were required to touch their middle fingers to their respective thumbs (the ASL 8 hand shape) while at the same time having their hands circle one another, with contact at the end of each circle (this is the sign for "world"). Just as saying "la, la, la" prevents a hearing person from using the "inner voice" to vocally rehearse, making hand motions should prevent a nonhearing person from using what might be termed the "inner hands" to manually rehearse. As you can see in Figure 4.14b, this is exactly what Wilson and Emmorey found: suppression not only disrupted WM performance overall, it also eliminated the effects of sign length. And interestingly, an earlier study by Wilson and Emmorey (1997) produced the corresponding finding: articulatory suppression eliminated the sign-based similarity effect. So whether you're dealing with the spoken word or ASL hand movements, it's pretty clear that there is an articulation mechanism that immediately codes incoming information in terms of one's customary language and developmental experience (Wilson & Emmorey, 1998) and that this articulation mechanism can be blocked.

R E C U R R I N G   R E S E A R C H   T H E M E
Cognition and Neuroscience

PET Scanning the Articulatory Loop

Partial support for the existence of separate subsystems in working memory comes from investigations of brain function. A series of investigations by Awh, Jonides, Smith, Schumacher, Koeppe, and Katz (1996) provides further evidence for the subtle distinction discussed above. As we pointed out, the articulatory loop is actually thought to be made up of two components: a phonological store and a subvocal rehearsal mechanism. Awh and colleagues had participants perform various WM tasks in an attempt to separate these two components and isolate the brain areas underlying each.

In one study, participants were tested in one of three conditions, which were cleverly designed to involve or not involve the two components of the articulatory loop. In the two-back condition, participants saw a string of letters presented one at a time on a computer screen.

On the presentation of each letter, their task was to determine whether that letter matched the one presented two items back by clicking a mouse button. This task is fairly challenging, in terms of WM processing. Both components of the articulatory loop are necessary for this task; participants must constantly manage a WM load (which uses the phonological store) and silently repeat each letter as it is presented (which uses the subvocal rehearsal mechanism). To find the brain areas that correspond to the workings of the articulatory loop as a whole, these investigators performed PET scans on participants while they performed the two-back task.

In a search-control condition, participants saw the same stimuli and made the same physical response (clicking a mouse), but the task was far simpler. All they had to do was judge whether each presented letter matched the first one they had seen in the sequence. This task severely minimizes, if not eliminates, the need for either component of the articulatory loop. Very little must be held in the phonological store (the same letter), and there is really no need to continually rehearse the one letter; therefore, the subvocal rehearsal mechanism is not needed. The only brain activity in this task is clicking the mouse and watching digits. Looking at the difference in brain activation between these two conditions—subtracting them, if you will—allowed the researchers to find the brain areas involved when the articulatory loop is active. Awh and colleagues found that the important cortical areas were the speech areas in the frontal lobe (Broca's area, which is involved in speech planning and execution) and the posterior regions of the parietal cortex (which are involved the storage of verbal information). (See in Figure 4.15.)

The researchers didn't stop there. Other comparisons allowed them to tease apart the phonological store and subvocal rehearsal mechanism of the loop. In a rehearsal-control condition, once again participants saw the same stimuli and made the same physical response (clicking a mouse), but they had to repeat each letter they saw silently until the next letter appeared. This task was designed to isolate the brain areas active during the use of the subvocal rehearsal mechanism. This task does not require the use of the phonological store, because there is essentially nothing to store (one letter). Subtracting this area of activation from the total area of activation involved in the articulatory loop leaves only a view of the brain areas involved in the phonological store. This subtraction revealed that activation in the parietal regions seems to be the basis for the phonological store, while activation in the frontal lobe is associated with the subvocal rehearsal mechanism. Based on this result, the authors suggest that the subvocal rehearsal mechanism depends on articulatory mechanisms similar to the ones used in overt speech (i.e., Broca's area). This provides further support for the idea that the subvocal rehearsal mechanism is based on articulation rather than sound.

Visuo-Spatial Sketchpad

Based on findings that indicate visual coding in STM, Baddeley (1986) proposes a corresponding subsystem within WM, termed the **visuo-spatial sketchpad**. This component of WM is responsible for the storage and manipulation of visual and spatial information and seems to operate (in large part) independently of the other subsystem (the articulatory loop). In other words, visual/spatial encoding and articulatory coding do no interfere with one another.

This lack of interference was demonstrated in a study by Brooks (1967). Brooks manipulated the task mode (visual or verbal) and the response mode (visual or verbal).

Areas involved in verbal working memory, phonological storage, and subvocal rehearsal

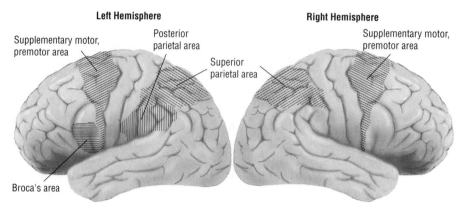

Areas involved in phonological storage

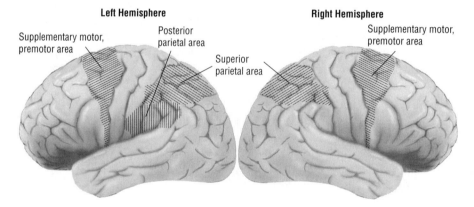

Area involved in subvocal rehearsal

Left Hemisphere

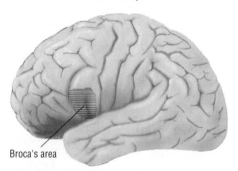

Broca's area

Figure 4.15 Cortical areas involved in articulatory processing in working memory.
From Awh, E., Jonides, J., Smith, E. E., Schumacher, E. H., Koeppe, R. A., & Katz, S. (1996). Dissociation of storage and rehearsal in verbal working memory: Evidence from positron emission tomography. *Psychological Science, 7,* 25–31. Copyright 1996 by Blackwell, Inc. Reprinted by permission.

His results showed that while participants had a great deal of difficulty when the task mode and the response mode were in the same modality—if they were both visual (i.e., both engaging the visuo-spatial sketchpad) or both verbal (i.e., both engaging the articulatory loop)—they had little difficulty if the task mode and response mode were different. It seems that the visuo-spatial sketchpad and articulatory loop can operate together with little loss in performance efficiency. If this discussion of the visuo-spatial sketchpad makes you think about the study on sex differences in visual STM from earlier in the chapter, give yourself a pat on the back. In fact, the title of the Loring-Meier and Halpern study is "Sex Differences in Visuo-Spatial Working Memory," so it is exactly these sorts of processes they were considering.

The Central Executive

The third component of Baddeley's WM system is a central controller, termed the **central executive.** Recall that earlier we noted that the attentional system could be conceptualized in two ways: as a gateway or as a pool of resources that is allocated to the tasks of consciousness. Baddeley's central executive might be conceived of as the "gatekeeper" or "capacity allocator" for the attentional system. When a particular task demands extensive involvement of either the articulatory loop or the visuo-spatial subsystem of working memory, the central executive deploys the necessary resources. The central executive is also thought to be responsible for the higher-level thought processes involved in reasoning and language comprehension. Because the capacity of the attentional system is limited, the central executive only has so much to give; if a task is too demanding, the central executive's resources will be drained, and complex thinking will suffer.

Stop *and* Think!   **WORKING WITH WORKING MEMORY**

Return to the tasks from the Stop and Think! The Price of Attending and reconsider them in light of Baddeley's model of working memory. For each of the tasks (relisted below), determine how each of the three subcomponents of working memory might be involved, and how they are.

watching TV
listening to music
taking notes in class
talking on the cell phone
walking
driving in an unfamiliar location
driving a familiar route
listening to a professor lecture
eating

As you did earlier, consider these questions:

- Which pairs of tasks would be easy to share?
- Which would be difficult to share?
- Why are certain combinations more or less manageable, given Baddeley's view?

Let's take a look at how the working memory system might be operating during William's drive to pick up Sherry. The articulatory loop figures prominently in his processing of what's being said in the conversations he's having. The phonological store allows him to temporarily hold the information, and the subvocal rehearsal mechanism allows him to repeat silently what's being said. The visuo-spatial sketchpad is the basis for whatever visual or spatial processing needs to be done as William is thinking. In this example, such processing is likely as he negotiates his way along his driving route, particularly so when he is listening to the directions that Anne gives him. In fact, it's likely that as William drives, he's going to have difficulty visualizing the directions he's getting on the phone. These demands will likely overload his sketchpad and drain his central executive, perhaps leading to less-than-optimum performance (i.e., poor driving).

Evaluation of Working Memory

Baddeley's model has served as an extremely useful heuristic for organizing and explaining much of what researchers have found about the duration, capacity limitations, and coding mechanisms in STM. It certainly does a better job of describing STM than the relatively simple mechanisms proposed in the original modal model, which characterized immediate memory as a static holding place for information. The working memory model represents immediate memory as a dynamic set of processes used not only for storage but also for active manipulation and consideration. A great deal of evidence has accumulated indicating that working memory is an extremely important skill that serves as a sort of foundation for more complex abilities such as reasoning and language comprehension. The importance of working memory in subserving more complex processing has become especially evident in recent years, as researchers have developed measures of working memory span and related performance on these measures to other aspects of cognitive processing.

Recall that *short-term memory span* is a simple measure of how many items can be held in immediate memory. Just as working memory provides a more dynamic and valid characterization of immediate memory, *working memory span* provides a more dynamic and valid characterization of immediate memory's capacity. Consider one of several tasks used to measure WM span, a task termed *operation span*. In this task, participants receive trials like the following (see Engle, 2001):

Is $(8/4) - 1 = 1$? bear

Is $(6 \times 2) - 2 = 10$? dad

Is $(10 \times 2) - 6 = 12$? beans

Participants are to read the problems aloud and solve them. After each of the three problems in a trial has been presented, they are to recall the words that accompanied each problem. Operation span is essentially a divided-attention task; participants must process and answer the simple math problems while at the same time keeping track of the words. As Engle (2001) notes in his review of WM span and its relation to complex thinking tasks, performance on operation span tasks (as well as other measures of WM capacity) has proven to be a strikingly good predictor of a broad range of more complex abilities, including spoken and written language comprehension, writing, note taking, vocabulary learning, and even bridge playing!

Why is WM such a good indicator of other more complex abilities? According to Engle (2001), it's because the tasks involved in WM span are a microcosm of what is required during complex cognitive processing. We must process multiple streams of information, keeping some of it active and easily retrievable even in the face of interference from other material that may be more relevant at the time. Consider the operation-span task; participants need to somehow keep the words fresh and active even as they're performing those annoying little calculations. You have to do this in class if you have professors like us, who put notes up on a projector and then lecture at the same time. You somehow have to get down what's in the notes (which seems a lot like doing a rote math problem) while tracking what the professor is saying (which seems a lot like remembering *bear*, *dad*, and *beans*).

The predictive power of working memory span underscores the important role that attention and information manipulation play in more complex cognitive processing. A quote by Engle (2002, p. 302) sums it up quite neatly and serves as a fitting ending for this chapter:

> Working memory capacity is about attention in the service of memory. Greater WM capacity means that more items can be maintained in the focus of attention, but it also means that information can be effectively blocked from the focus of attention.

STOP *and* REVIEW!

1. Identify and define the two subcomponents of the articulatory loop subsystem of the working memory model.
2. The word-length effect is due to the
   a. phonological store
   b. subvocal rehearsal mechanism
   c. visuo-spatial sketchpad
   d. central executive
3. True or false? The processing of the articulatory loop and the visuo-spatial sketchpad depend on each other.
4. How is the working memory model different from the original conceptualization of short-term memory?

➤ Working memory is made up of three closely interacting subsystems that combine to subserve a host of higher-level mental processes, including language comprehension, problem solving, and reasoning. The first subsystem is called the articulatory loop and is made up of two subcomponents—the phonological store (which allows one to hold information temporarily) and the subvocal rehearsal mechanism (which allows for articulatory rehearsal).

➤ The word-length effect derives from the characteristics of the phonological store, and the phonological similarity effect derives from the characteristics of the subvocal rehearsal mechanism. If we prevent the use of the subvocal rehearsal mechanism through articulatory suppression, the effects of word length and phonological similarity are eliminated, because these effects depend on articulation. Brain-imaging studies indicate that articulatory mechanisms of WM are similar to those involved in overt speech.

➤ The second subsystem is called the visuo-spatial sketchpad, which is responsible for the storage and manipulation of visual and spatial information in immediate memory and is largely independent of the articulatory loop. The third subsystem is the central executive. The central executive is responsible for higher-level thought processes and allocating attention.

➤ The WM model provides a more elaborate conceptualization of immediate memory processing than does the earlier notion of a simple STM buffer. Measures of WM span provide strikingly good predictions of performance on a wide range of more complex thinking tasks.

GLOSSARY

action slips: absentminded actions that are often the result of automatic processing (p. 131)

articulatory loop: a subcomponent of working memory that allows for the mental rehearsal of incoming information (p. 149)

articulatory suppression task: a task designed to prevent the rehearsal of information in the subvocal rehearsal mechanism of the articulatory loop (p. 151)

attention: limited-capacity processes devoted to the monitoring of internal and external events (p. 115)

attenuation theory: a theory positing an attenuation mechanism that minimizes, but does not eliminate, analysis of unattended information; salient or context-relevant information can be recognized (p. 120)

automaticity: the tendency for cognitive processes to occur nonintentionally, unconsciously, and with little effort after extensive practice (p. 126)

Brown-Peterson task: a sequence of letters is encoded, followed by a counting-backward distraction task, followed by recall of the letter sequence (p. 136)

capacity theory: a theory of attention positing a limited-capacity pool of attentional resources that is allocated to different tasks (p. 121)

central executive: a limited-capacity control mechanism for working memory responsible for the higher-level thought processes involved in planning, reasoning, and language comprehension (p. 155)

chunking (recoding): regrouping items in STM (p. 137)

cocktail-party phenomenon: a tendency to notice highly relevant stimuli presented in an unattended channel (p. 118)

decay: the loss of information from memory with the passage of time. (p. 144)

dichotic listening: simultaneous listening to two different messages, one in each ear (p. 117)

divided attention: monitoring and responding to more than one source of information (p. 117)

early-selection theory: a theory positing a sensory processing filter for incoming messages; limitations in attention occur immediately after sensory processing (p. 117)

interference: information currently in memory is negatively influenced by the presentation of other information (p. 144)

late-selection theory: a theory of attention positing that selection occurs after all incoming stimuli have been identified; limitations in attention are at the stage of response (p. 121)

magical number: 7 ± 2, the number of items we can hold in STM (p. 137)

memory span: the capacity of STM; the longest string of information a person can immediately recall (p. 137)

modal model: the information-processing view of memory that postulates a series of chronologically arranged stages through which incoming information passes (sensory memory, STM, and LTM) (p. 135)

multimode theory: a theory of attention positing that we can engage in early or late selection depending on the situation; late selection requires more attentional resources than early selection (p. 123)

phonological similarity effect: the finding that lists of similar-sounding items are more difficult to keep track of in STM than are lists of different-sounding items (p. 139)

proactive interference: occurs when earlier information interferes with the ability to retain information that comes later (p. 144)

release from proactive interference: the release from the cumulative effects of proactive interference when there is a change in the nature of the stimuli being encoded (p. 147)

retention interval: the amount of time between encoding and retrieval (p. 136)

retroactive interference: occurs when later information interferes with the ability to retain information that came earlier (p. 144)

selective attention: monitoring and responding to only one source of information (p. 117)

short-term memory (STM): the set of processes that we use to hold and rehearse information that occupies our current awareness (p. 135)

speech shadowing: repeating a message word for word (p. 117)

Stroop effect: the ability to name the ink color in which a word is presented is inhibited if the word happens to name a conflicting color (p. 126)

visuo-spatial sketchpad: a subcomponent of working memory that allows for the processing of spatial information and manipulation of visual images (p. 153)

word-length effect: the finding that STM span is negatively related to the length of encoded items (p. 138)

working memory (WM): the processes involved in examining, considering, manipulating, and responding to internal and external events (p. 115)

5

Identifying and Classifying Concepts

After getting off the phone with William, Anne heads to the campus rummage sale. She sees Lance and another guy looking at a strange object. "Hey Lance! What's that?"

"Hi, Anne! I don't know . . . looks kind of like a cross between a screwdriver and a spatula."

"What do you think it's for?"

"Dunno . . . but if you tried to cook with it, you'd probably screw up dinner."

"Very funny. Hi, I'm Anne," she says to Lance's companion.

"I'm Irv. Nice to meet you."

"Sorry we have no time to chat—we gotta run," Lance says as he tosses the unidentified implement back in the box.

As Lance and Irv make their way through the adjacent gym, they stop to watch a cheerleading practice. The cheerleaders are practicing handstands. Lance and Irv move closer. When the cheerleaders pop upright, Lance recognizes one of his classmates.

"Oh, hey, Tom. I didn't recognize you. I had no idea you were on the team. You don't seem like the cheerleading type."

"What's the cheerleading type?"

"Oh, I dunno . . . I guess I was surprised to see you here."

As Irv and Lance walk on, Irv says, "You know, Tom is kind of loud and outgoing . . ."

"Yeah, but he just doesn't seem like a cheerleader."

Irv grunts noncommitally. "Did I tell you I'm thinking of getting an animal?"

"Oh Yeah? What?"

"A Lhasa apso"

"A what?"

"A dog"

"Oh. Why didn't you just say so?"

Irv is pretty sure he did.

In this chapter, we continue our "tour" through the early components of the information-processing system. Up to this point, we've talked about how we look or listen, pay attention, and hold information in our immediate memories for further processing. The first step in further processing involves *identifying* and *classifying* what it is you've latched onto through attentional processing. The process of identification is typically labeled **pattern** or **object recognition**—the processes whereby we match an incoming stimulus with stored representations for the purpose of identification. The things we identify every day can be classified into three broad categories: patterns (letters and numbers), objects (everything in the environment around you), and faces. Accordingly, we'll be using the terms *pattern recognition, object recognition,* and *face recognition.* (And, as you'll see, the processing underlying these three can be quite distinct.)

The fact that we can look at a pattern of stimulation and say "bird," "football," "tree," or "chair" begs the question of how we know what birds, footballs, trees, and chairs are. That is, how do we represent these *concepts,* and how did we arrive at these representations? What is a tree, exactly? You've probably never thought too much about questions like this (unless you major in philosophy), but this chapter will introduce you to some of the answers that cognitive psychologists have proposed to these questions.

In Chapter 3, we discussed the basic processes of visual perception through which an incoming stimulus is translated into a percept. In order to deal with these incoming stimuli, we need to identify them (*recognize* these patterns and objects). It turns out that a distinction we introduced in Chapter 3 is critical to an account of pattern recognition—namely, the notions of *bottom-up* and *top-down processing.* Bottom-up processes employ the information in the stimulus itself (what you might call "data") to aid in its identification. That is, we build and identify stimuli "from the bottom up." For example, you recognize the capital letter A because of the data of two slanting lines connected near the middle by a third line. It's not difficult to see that bottom-up processing is necessary for recognizing patterns. It's obvious that we can't identify something without any data at all; there would be nothing there to identify. But while bottom-up processing may be necessary to account for pattern recognition, it isn't sufficient. A fundamental fact about pattern recognition is that both bottom-up and top-down processes play an important role.

The importance of top-down processes may not be as obvious, but they do play a vital role in our ability to recognize what we see. Quite often, incoming data are incomplete or obscured in some manner and are thus unidentifiable. In these cases, we must rely on expectations, knowledge, and/or surrounding context to supplement the data (i.e., top-down processing). Even if the aforementioned letter A were partially obscured, chances are you'd be able identify it, because you are familiar with this letter. You would be even more able to recognize the A if it were in a familiar context (e.g., C A T); our knowledge of the word *CAT* enhances identification of the obscured A. In other words, we identify what things are "from the top-down."

Stop *and* Think!   ## BOTTOM-UP AND TOP-DOWN PROCESSING YOUR ENVIRONMENT

Recognizing patterns is a matter of both bottom-up processes (the processing of data) and top-down processes (bringing previous knowledge and context to bear on the data). Look at the objects within view and make note of (1) the data that comprise them—what are the component elements that allow you to know what the thing is? and (2) the contextual elements in the scene that may be aiding your recognition—what is it about the situation that you're in that aids in your identification of the patterns you see?

- Are there any patterns for which you lack data yet can still identify the pattern?
- What aspects of the situation or your previous knowledge allow you to do that?

The number of patterns and objects we are able to recognize is nothing short of phenomenal. Look around you and identify all of the things you can. Chances are you were able to name at least 10 or so things in the space of 10 or so seconds. A computer recognition system can't touch this level of performance. Decades of work in artificial intelligence have not cracked the problem of getting computers to "see" in the rapid, flexible, and accurate manner that we can. Consider what has to happen during the process of visual recognition. A tiny distorted image received by the visual receptors is translated into a three-dimensional percept (Chapter 3) and labeled accurately (i.e., the *pattern* is *recognized*), all in less than a second. This occurs even if the stimulus is partially blocked, misoriented, or obscured in some other manner. What's the basis for this rapid and efficient recognition?

Bottom-Up Views of Pattern Recognition

Given that pattern and object recognition involve the processing of the actual "stuff" that makes up what we see, it's not surprising that views of pattern recognition differ primarily on the mechanisms by which this stuff is analyzed—that is, they differ primarily in their characterization of bottom-up processes. Explanations for how we recognize patterns in the world can be sorted into two broad categories. These two categories of explanation differ in terms of how the object being identified is matched against information in memory. The basic question is this: As I look across the room and quickly engage in object recognition (it's a couch), what am I doing with my view of the couch? And to what am I matching the information in memory?

The answers to these questions differentiate two major approaches to how we recognize patterns and objects. According to a *view-based approach*, I am comparing the whole image of the couch, in the orientation in which I'm viewing it, to a representation of the whole couch in memory. When I find the corresponding representation, I identify it. According to a *structural-description-based approach*, I am breaking the couch into the fundamental shapes of which it is composed. I then compare this set of components to information in memory and recognize that this set of basic components in this particular combination equals a couch.

It turns out that one particular factor helps distinguish these two basic approaches: What happens when the pattern or object we're looking at is distorted in some way? According to a view-based approach, there should be some cost to recognition in these circumstances, because the image of the object must be "normalized" in some way—that is, it must be transformed to a view that can be recognized. This normalization process takes time. Alternatively, current versions of a structural-description-based approach propose that visual recognition does not suffer from changes in orientation because the incoming pattern is immediately coded in terms of its basic subcomponents and their interrelationships, which remain basically the same no matter what the orientation. These components and relations allow for recognition. Let's look at these models.

Structural-Description-Based Approaches

According to a **structural-description-based** (SDB) **approach** to pattern and object recognition, we compare patterns to a *structural description* stored in memory. This structural description includes a list of the visual features of the pattern, as well as the relationships between these visual features. Given the emphasis on features, it may not surprise you that SDB approaches are often given the label **feature analysis.**

An important feature of SDB approaches is that the representation stored in memory is not visually or spatially analogous to the pattern being recognized. Rather, we compare the features of the incoming visual stimulus to an abstract description of those features in memory. Pattern recognition based on structural descriptions offers an obvious advantage; the particular orientation or view of the pattern is not important. No matter what the perspective, patterns are broken down into component parts and compared to a structural description in memory. So orientation or transformation of patterns doesn't matter, as long as the component parts are still identifiable. Therefore, these approaches are also termed *viewpoint independent*, because identification of the pattern does not depend on the particular view of the pattern that we have; it only depends on the component features of the pattern itself.

The Pandemonium Model.   One fanciful SDB approach, proposed by Selfridge (1959), is termed the **pandemonium model.** This name reflects Selfridge's view that pattern recognition is the result of hierarchically organized chaos (see Figure 5.1). Within the metaphor of pandemonium, the processes of feature analysis are carried out by *demons,* entities that each carry out different jobs that culminate in the recognition of the pattern. In true information-processing style, each set of demons passes their information on to the next set for further analysis. Let's consider the pattern of the letter A. First, the *image* demons are responsible for the initial encoding of the pattern. Next, *feature* demons analyze the stimulus in terms of its component elements (e.g., /, -, and \); different feature demons look for each of these elements. *Cognitive* demons monitor the work of the feature demons, looking for evidence that supports a specific pattern; each cognitive demon represents a different pattern (e.g., A, V). Cognitive demons "shout" with each piece of evidence (i.e., information from feature demons like /, -, or \) that supports their designated pattern. Therefore, multiple cognitive demons will be shouting if the to-be-identified pattern shares features with several cognitive demons. So for the pattern A, the A cognitive demon plus the V cognitive demon will be shouting, because both have diagonal line segments (/ and \ that combine differently to form the letter V or part of the letter A). Finally, *decision* demons assess the shouting of the cognitive demons. They evaluate which one of the cognitive demons (e.g., A or V) is "shouting the loudest" (i.e., has detected the most evidence supporting its designated pattern) and use that information to decide what the pattern is.

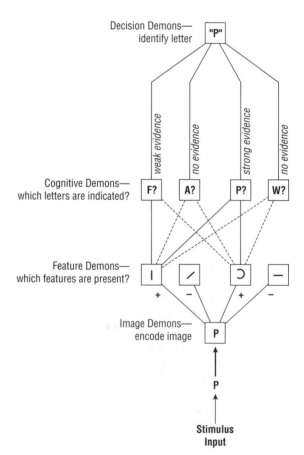

Figure 5.1 A rendition of the pandemonium model of visual pattern recognition. As you can see, recognition is a hierarchical process that begins with the identification of the most simple elements of a pattern. After these elements have been identified, higher-level detectors identify combinations of the elements, and still higher-level detectors identify the pattern itself.

From Selfridge, O. (1959). Pandemonium: A paradigm for learning. In D. V. Blake and A. M. Uttley (Eds.), *Proceedings of the Symposium on mechanisation of thought processes* (pp. 511–529). London: H. M. Stationary Office.

How quickly can you recognize the patterns?

Now this may all seem a bit silly, but it's just a metaphor for the process of pattern recognition as it might proceed if it involved the hierarchical analysis and combination of component features. This general approach fits fairly well with much of what we know about lower-level perceptual processes. True to the model, different components of the visual system are specialists in the recognition of certain features. The pioneering work of Nobel Prize–winning physiologists David Hubel and Torsten Weisel (e.g., Hubel & Weisel, 1979) demonstrated that cells in the visual cortex are maximally sensitive to lines of certain lengths, orientations, directions of movement, and so on. So it makes sense to characterize pattern recognition as a gradual process of evidence accumulation based on a feature-by-feature analysis of the incoming information. The pandemonium model oversimplifies matters to be sure, but it serves as a useful sketch of the pattern-recognition process.

Like the pandemonium model, many simple SDB approaches to pattern recognition are limited to explanations of how we recognize simple patterns like letters. Letters are easy to define in terms of their component features. But how do we recognize the infinite variety of objects we encounter, like baskets, wreaths, shoes, ceiling fans, doorknobs (all objects currently within my view)? Surely, there isn't a cognitive demon for each feature of these objects! Another problem is specifying the features to be analyzed: What are they? Here, feature analysis runs into a problem—representational economy. It seems unlikely that we have a near-infinite number of feature analyzers to analyze a near-infinite number of features.

Marr's View.   A much more sophisticated and extremely influential SDB approach was proposed by Marr (1982). According to Marr, the goal of the visual system is to transform a two-dimensional retinal image into a three-dimensional percept that is quickly and easily identified. To realize this transformation, Marr proposed a progression of processing stages. A detailed exposition of these processing stages is well beyond the scope of our discussion, but we'll provide a brief sketch of the general approach.

According to Marr's approach, the first stage in visual recognition is to register the information contained in the retinal image; the specific features of this retinal image depend on the particular view of the object. The image includes information about light intensity, boundaries, discontinuities, edges, and groupings. This information is extracted and used to form a **primal sketch**—a rough rendition of the most primitive elements of the object. Next, information from the primal sketch is used to construct what Marr termed a **2½-D sketch** (think of this as halfway between a two-dimensional and three-dimensional image). The 2½-D sketch includes information about the orientation and relative depth of the visible surfaces as well as information about discontinuities in depth and orientation. The information derived from the primal sketch and 2½-D sketch forms the basis for the construction of a **3-D model** of the object. The parts of this model are termed *volumetric primitives* but are basically generalized 3-D cylinders. We construct a sort of "pipe-cleaner version" of the object we're looking at, as you can see in Figure 5.2. Unlike the primal sketch and the 2½-D sketch, which will differ depending on the perspective of the observer, the 3-D model is not view specific. Rather, the representation is *viewpoint independent.* Marr's model is infinitely more complex than the primal sketch provided here, but the general theme of this model—that object recognition is based on a viewpoint-independent structural description of the object—made it the prototype for an entire class of approaches to object recognition.

Recognition-by-Components (RBC) Theory.   Another influential theory, inspired by Marr, has been proposed by Biederman and colleagues (e.g., Biederman, 1987; Biederman & Cooper, 1991; Biederman & Gerhardstein, 1993). Its name—**recognition-by-**

Figure 5.2 According to Marr's view of visual recognition, a final step in object identification involves specifying objects in terms of volumetric primitives, or generalized three-dimensional cylinders.

From Marr, D., & Nishihara, H. K. (1978). Representation and recognition of the spatial organization of three dimensional structure. *Proceedings of the Royal Society of London, 200,* 269–294. Reprinted by permission.

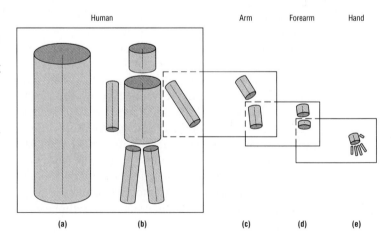

Human   Arm   Forearm   Hand

(a)   (b)   (c)   (d)   (e)

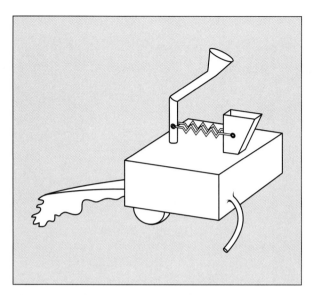

Figure 5.3 Can you label this object? What seem to be its components?

From Biederman, I. (1993). Visual object recognition. In D. Osherman (Ed.), *Visual cognition: An invitation to cognitive science* (pp. 121–165). Cambridge, MA: MIT Press. Reprinted by permission.

components—makes the general approach pretty clear. Object recognition is a matter of separating, analyzing, and recombining the features of whatever we're looking at. Take a look at Figure 5.3. Chances are you won't be able to name what it is, but Biederman reports that people are near unanimous in their description of its components. We all tend to parse the object at the same places and then use simple everyday volumetric terms (i.e., cone, cylinder, cube) to describe them. And although it isn't a familiar object, we can say what it looks like—a hot dog cart. As Biederman (1987) describes it,

A New York city hot dog cart, with the large block being the central food storage and cooking area, the rounded part underneath as a wheel, the large arc on the right as a handle, the funnel as an orange juice squeezer, and the various vertical pipes as supports or umbrella supports. (p. 116)

According to Biederman, we analyze all objects, both familiar and unfamiliar, by segmenting and analyzing them into their component features. In our opening scenario, Irv is able to parse up the parts of the unnamed object and suggest that it's a spatula-screwdriver hybrid.

Stop and Think! | **WHAT THE HECK IS THAT?**

Present the object in Figure 5.3 to some of your friends, and ask them to label it as an object. Take note of their responses. In addition, ask them to describe the object in words and note whether they parse it according to the principles outlined in Biederman's recognition-by-components theory.

Unlike the pandemonium approach, the analyzed features are not simple line segments, angles, and curves; the features are basic 3-D shapes that Biederman terms **geons** (derived from the phrase "geometrical ions"). A sampling of these shapes is presented in Figure 5.4, along with a variety of ways in which they might combine to form everyday objects. According to Biederman's theory, there are a total of 36 geons that serve as *visual primitives*—simple shapes that can combine to form most other more complex shapes. Importantly, these geons are viewed the same way regardless of orientation; a cylinder almost always looks like a cylinder, no matter what visual perspective you happen to have on it.

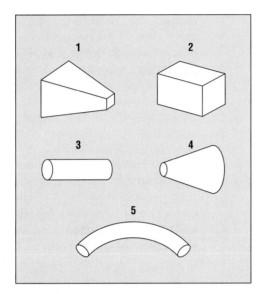 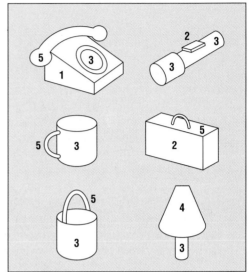

Figure 5.4 Some of the 36 geons proposed by Biederman (1987) and how they combine to form simple objects.

From Biederman, I. (1985). Human image understanding: Recent research and a theory. *Computer Vision, Graphics, and Image Processing, 32,* 29–73. Copyright 1985. Reprinted by permission of Elsevier Science.

Stop *and* **Think!**   ## SPOTTING GEONS

From where you're sitting, look around at all of the various objects you are able to easily identify.

- How many basic parts (i.e., geonlike parts) make up each object?
- How do the objects break down into component parts?

Also note whether anything in your field of view is difficult to identify.

- Why is it?
- Is the object at an odd angle?
- Is most of it blocked?
- Are geons unidentifiable?
- Are there any objects that seem confusable?
- Does it seem like orientation would influence your ability to recognize any of these objects?

RBC theory is similar to Marr's (1982) approach in that it proposes a series of hierarchically arranged stages whereby information about component features is used to identify the object. First, information about edges is extracted from the retinal image. This edge-extraction process looks for differences in features like texture, luminance, and color and results in a simple line drawing of the object. Following this edge extraction, we encode the *nonaccidental features* of the retinal image. Nonaccidental features are those that are almost sure to be actual features of the stimulus rather than some accident of the perspective the observer has on the object. Put simply, we detect features of the stimulus and assume they don't vary with the particular viewpoint. This should sound familiar. Recall from Chapter 3 that Gestalt psychologists were particularly interested in how cognitive processes impose organization on incoming information. A basic theme underlying their principles of organization is *simplicity;* we tend to parse objects in the simplest way possible. The segmentation of objects, as proposed by RBC theory, is guided by this basic assumption (Biederman, 1987).

Concurrently with this search for regularities, the visual system is also parsing the object at areas where there appear to be boundaries between the parts of the object. Next, with the information gained to this point, the components of the figure (the geons) are determined, and this set of components is matched with object representations in memory. When a match is found, the object is identified. You may be wondering whether 36 geons is a sufficient number, given the incredible variety of objects we view on a daily basis. Biederman argues that it is; he estimates that humans are familiar with up to 30,000 visually discriminable objects (see Biederman, 1987, for more information on how this estimate was derived). This estimate is no match for the number of objects that could be formed by the 36 geons. Given only two geons—and considering differences in their size, where they join together, and their position relative to one another—over 50,000 shapes are possible. Add a third geon to the mix, and the estimate goes to over 150 million! Clearly, 36 geons provide enough representational power to account for the power of object recognition.

RBC theory makes a couple of critical predictions. First, objects should become less identifiable the harder it gets to recover their components. That is, if the stimulus is obscured in a way that makes it difficult to discern the object's main parts, then the object will be rendered unidentifiable. A second prediction is that rotation of objects should not hinder their recognition too much; most changes in orientation do not influence the basic components of the object and their relationships to one another. If rotation does obscure some of the geons or the fundamental relationships between them, it will make recognition more difficult. However, minor changes in orientation should not matter.

The first prediction was put to the test by Biederman and Cooper (1991). In their study, participants were presented with sketches of objects in which 50% of the contours had been deleted. However, the way in which the contours were deleted varied among the figures. For some figures, the contour deletion disrupted the figure at the points of segmentation that would be used to carve the object into its component geons. For other figures, the contour deletion did not prevent recovery of the geons (although the same amount of the contour was deleted). According to the RBC approach, object recognition should suffer in the first condition but not in the second one. Only when observers are unable to recover the components of the figure should object recognition be deleteriously affected. The findings were consistent with RBC theory: object recognition was unaffected when contour deletion preserved the components of the figure and was more difficult when it did not.

The second prediction—that object recognition should not be hampered much by the particular view of the object—was tested in a study by Biederman and Gerhardstein (1993). In this experiment, participants were presented with a series of objects like the ones pictured

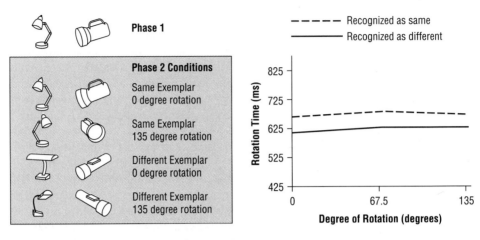

(a) Sample Stimuli from Experiment   (b) Effect of Rotation on Object Recognition

Figure 5.5 Sample stimuli from the Biederman and Gerhardstein (1993) study, and graph of the major results. These results suggest that object recognition is not affected by rotation and are consistent with the recognition-by-components approach.

From Biederman, I., & Gerhardstein, P. C. (1993). Recognizing depth-rotated objects: Evidence and conditions for three-dimensional viewpoint invariance. *Journal of Experimental Psychology: Learning, Memory, and Cognition, 19,* 1162–1182. Copyright 1993 by the American Psychological Association. Reprinted by permission.

in Figure 5.5 and were simply to name each one as quickly as possible. In a second phase of the experiment, they were once again presented with a series of objects to name. This series of objects included some of the items named in the first phase, along with some new items. In addition, the items from the first phase were presented at varying degrees of rotation. According to RBC theory, recognition of the objects shouldn't be affected by rotation, because the particular orientation of the object doesn't influence geon extraction—that is, object recognition is viewpoint independent. The results of the study are also presented in Figure 5.5. Plotted are reaction times for judging whether the objects presented in phase 2 were the same objects that had been seen in phase 1. As you can see, the degree of rotation of the figures presented in phase 2 had a negligible effect on the participants' ability to judge them as same or different, consistent with a major prediction of the RBC approach.

View-Based Approaches

In contrast to an SDB approach, a **view-based (VB) approach** to pattern recognition contends that patterns are recognized wholistically through a process of comparison with a stored analog. When a match is found, the pattern is recognized. In contrast to SDB approaches, VB approaches are considered *viewpoint dependent,* because identification of a pattern or object depends critically on the particular perspective the viewer has. To identify the pattern/object, an image matching this particular view must be found, or the incoming stimulus image must be manipulated in some way (e.g., rotated) until a match is found with images represented in memory.

An Early Attempt: Template Matching. The first systematic attempt to account for pattern recognition in the early history of cognitive psychology was proposed by Neisser (1967), who suggested that pattern recognition was a process of *template matching.* According to this **template-matching theory,** our store of general knowledge includes a set of **templates,** or copies, of every pattern that we might encounter. You may have seen (or used) plastic stencils that allow you to trace perfect forms (provided you have a steady hand). You might picture templates this way—as perfect forms or replicas of a pattern. The basic notion behind template-matching theory is that when we encounter some pattern that needs to be identified, the mind quickly rifles through its set of templates, and then when a match is found, the pattern is given the label stored with the template (i.e., the pattern is recognized).

Template matching is a VB approach in that pattern recognition involves a comparison with a stored analog. Many simple computer-based recognition systems are based on this sort of process. For example, the somewhat odd-looking numbers at the bottom of your checks are rigidly structured such that they fit the templates that computers use for recognition. These recognition systems are "stupid" in that even the slightest change in the pattern will lead to a recognition failure. This strict version of the template view is too limited to even begin to account for the tremendous flexibility of human pattern recognition. We have no problem recognizing patterns that are distorted, upside down, backward, tilted, partially blocked, bent, twisted . . . you get the idea. Another problem is the lack of economy implied by the template approach. To recognize all of the patterns we are able to, we'd need countless templates. Also, we'd need different templates for different versions of patterns (tilted, upside down, partially blocked). This means we'd have to have an essentially infinite number of templates, something that just doesn't seem feasible.

Modern Versions of the View-Based Approach. The strict version of the template theory described above is really a sort of straw-man argument that's not very difficult to dismiss. But this general approach is not without its merit. The basic mechanism—matching our view of an object with a representation of that view stored in memory—is quite sensible. The problems arise from the rigidity implied in the original approach. Based on our overwhelming "hit" rate in correctly identifying objects in the world, it seems pretty apparent that misorientation and distortion don't seem to hurt visual recognition as much as the template-matching view would imply. Biederman and Gerhardstein lent empirical support to this intuition in their research, as discussed earlier, revealing minimal effects of orientation on object recognition.

But actually, our recognition of patterns can be affected by misorientation. Consider a study conducted by Tarr and Pinker (1989) in which participants were taught names for shapes like the ones in Figure 5.6. These shapes were always presented in the same orientation during training. During a test phase, these shapes were presented for recognition. Participants responded quickly if the shapes were presented at the same orientation as in training, but their responses were successively slower as the degree of rotation from the original position

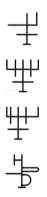

Figure 5.6 Sample stimuli from the Tarr and Pinker (1989) study.

From Tarr, M. J., & Pinker, S. (1989). Mental rotation and orientation-dependence in shape recognition. *Cognitive Psychology, 21,* 233–282. Copyright 1989, Elsevier Science (USA). Reprinted by permission.

increased, indicating that perception is viewpoint dependent. However, after training on the new orientations, participants eventually became equally fast, regardless of the orientation.

Tarr and Pinker propose that this pattern of results parallels the everyday recognition of objects. We start with one representation of objects (often termed the *canonical representation*), and through experience with objects in many different orientations and viewed from many different perspectives, we develop multiple representations, or *views*, of the patterns/objects. These *multiple views* serve as the templates for later recognition. The reason orientation tends not to affect our visual recognition under most circumstances is that everything we must recognize has received extensive exposure from different perspectives. For example, think of all the different perspectives from which you've viewed your car. Based on extensive exposure to these different perspectives, you've developed multiple views of your car that you use in recognizing it.

The view-based approach is consistent with some findings from studies of basic visual processing in monkeys (who have visual systems comparable to our own). Logothetis, Pauls, and Poggio (1995) taught monkeys to recognize novel 3-D objects from a variety of different perspectives, and like humans, the monkeys eventually became equally proficient at recognizing these objects, given any of the rotations. Especially compelling was the neural activity associated with recognition during a later testing phase; different sets of cells responded most strongly to certain objects, indicating that certain networks were devoted to certain objects. More important, a given set of cells responded most strongly when that object appeared in the same orientation as it had during training. The responses of these cells decreased systematically with increases in the rotation from that perspective. Consistent with the basic assumption of a view-based approach, these monkeys seemed to have what might be termed *physiological templates* that were devoted to recognizing a specific object in a specific orientation (Tarr, 2000).

Object Recognition: Views or Structural Descriptions?

By no means is the issue of object recognition settled. The view-based and structural-description-based approaches are both alive and well, and their respective proponents are engaged in lively debate about which approach is the right one. Much of the debate centers on the basic question of whether object recognition is truly independent of the particular view. Evidence that this independence does exist (e.g., Biederman & Gerhardstein, 1993) supports the SBD approach. But there is also considerable evidence that recognition of objects is not so generalizable across different viewpoints—that it does depend on the particular perspective we have on the object (e.g., Hayward & Tarr, 1997; Tarr & Pinker, 1989). So what's going on?

Tarr and Bülthoff (1995) offer a possible resolution of the viewpoint-dependent/viewpoint-independent debate. They suggest that object recognition be conceived of as a continuum. At one end are heavily viewpoint-dependent mechanisms that are used for making subtle discriminations among similar exemplars. For example, the subtle discriminations required to distinguish between a crow and a sparrow are likely made by viewpoint-dependent mechanisms (i.e., images or templates). At the other end of the continuum are heavily viewpoint-independent mechanisms. These mechanisms will be recruited when more gross categorical judgments are required, such as distinguishing a hammer from a sparrow. In this sort of judgment, orientation is not likely to matter nearly as much.

The processes used to distinguish between two similar objects may be different than those used to distinguish between two very dissimilar objects.

This continuum of object recognition and the mechanisms that underlie it may help explain the discrepant findings regarding the effects of orientation and transformation on object recognition. The experiments conducted by Biederman and colleagues employ everyday objects that are very distinct from one another (i.e., they require fairly gross discriminations—see Figure 5.5). As a result, the object recognition process appears to be viewpoint independent. The investigations of Tarr and colleagues employ unfamiliar objects that tend to be similar to each other (i.e., they require fairly subtle discriminations; see Figure 5.6). Therefore, the mechanisms that accomplish recognition are viewpoint dependent. Similar continua for object recognition have been proposed by other researchers (e.g., Farah, 1992). Given the complexities of vision and object recognition, it makes sense to assume that there may be a number of mechanisms responsible rather than just one.

But by no means is the matter settled. Notwithstanding the possible resolution proposed by Tarr and Bülthoff (1995), both sides of the debate are driven by the more parsimonious alternative—that a one-mechanism explanation is better than a two-mechanism explanation. So each camp continues to present evidence for the validity of its approach as *the* set of mechanisms for pattern and object recognition (e.g., Biederman, 2000; Tarr, 2000).

STOP *and* REVIEW!

1. True or false? Models of pattern/object recognition differ on their characterization of bottom-up processing.
2. Discuss the main process by which patterns/objects are identified according to a structural-description-based approach.
3. Discuss the main process by which patterns/objects are identified according to a view-based approach.
4. Discuss how the view-independent/view-dependent controversy may be resolved.

> ➤ Pattern/object recognition is the process whereby we match an incoming stimulus with stored representations for the purpose of identification. Pattern recognition is influenced by both bottom-up and top-down processes. Theories of pattern recognition differ primarily on their characterization of bottom-up processes.

> ➤ Structural-description-based approaches contend that stimuli are recognized by comparison to structural descriptions stored in memory. These approaches are termed viewpoint independent; identification does not depend on the perspective of the viewer. Examples of this type of approach include the pandemonium model, Marr's view, and recognition-by-components.

> ➤ Image-based views contend that stimuli are recognized wholistically through a process of comparison to a stored analog. These approaches are termed viewpoint dependent, because they contend that identification depends on the perspective of the viewer. Template-matching and the multiple-views theory are two examples of this type of approach.

> ➤ The view-based/structural-description-based controversy can be resolved by conceiving of pattern/object recognition as a continuum. At one end of the continuum, stimulus recognition involves viewpoint-independent mechanisms (à la structural-description-based approaches), and the other end involves viewpoint-dependent mechanisms (à la view-based approaches). The nature of the identification task will determine which mechanisms are used.

Top-Down Processing in Pattern Recognition

Think of all of the situations in which you were able to read a smudged line of print or managed to figure out something someone had mumbled. In both of these cases, the surrounding context probably helped in your identification—that is, pattern recognition proceeded (in part) from the top down. It is a trivial exercise to demonstrate that our analysis of incoming visual data is based on more than just the data itself. Take the phrase depicted in Figure 5.7; you probably had little hesitation in recognizing the patterns THE and CAT. Given this easy interpretation of ambiguous data, it's clear that something other than bottom-up processing is occurring. In this case, your knowledge of the English language makes it clear that the other options, TAE and CHT, aren't options, because they aren't words. This is a clear example of top-down processing—the application of context and previous knowledge to aid in pattern recognition.

TAE CAT

Figure 5.7 Read this quickly. You probably had no problem in recognizing THE and CAT, even though the H and A are the same symbol.

The Word-Superiority Effect

An important demonstration of the role of top-down processing in pattern recognition was provided in a classic study by Reicher (1969). Reicher was interested in the effects of

WORK → K D   ORWK → K D

Figure 5.8 Display used in studies of the word-superiority effect. The word on the left is presented very quickly, followed by a choice of two letters. The participant is to respond with which letter appeared in the underlined position. Letters presented in the context of a word (left panel) are more easily identified. From Reicher, G. (1969). Perceptual recognition as a function of meaningfulness of stimulus material. *Journal of Experimental Psychology, 81,* 275–280.

different contexts on the recognition of letters. In his study, participants were briefly presented with letter strings that either did or did not form a word (e.g., OWRK or WORK, respectively). Following a rapid display of such a letter string, participants were queried about the component letters, as depicted in Figure 5.8. Two alternatives were presented, and participants were required to pick the one they had just seen. Reicher found that identification was easier if the letter had been presented in the context of a word relative to when it had been presented in the context of a nonword. This finding has been replicated in a number of studies and has been termed the **word-superiority effect** (e.g., Krueger, 1992).

The word-superiority effect demonstrates the importance of top-down processing. If letter identification had been based solely on bottom-up processing, then letter-identification accuracy should have been equivalent in the two conditions. The data that make up the letter D do not vary depending on the context in which D appears; a D is a D. Given that letter identification did differ with the surrounding context, it's clear that this context played a role in the identification. In other words, top-down processing engaged by reading a familiar word aided in the identification of the components of that word.

Stop and Think!   ## TESTING WORD SUPERIORITY

Recruit two friends and have them identify the underlined letter in each letter string as quickly as possible. Have one friend do this for list 1 and one friend do it for list 2.

List 1	List 2
hou<u>s</u>e	ohe<u>s</u>u
ti<u>g</u>er	rt<u>g</u>ie
televisi<u>o</u>n	tievesin<u>o</u>l
d<u>a</u>isy	y<u>a</u>sid
windo<u>w</u>	nwiod<u>w</u>
boo<u>k</u>	obo<u>k</u>
<u>c</u>ouch	<u>c</u>uhco
pape<u>r</u>	epap<u>r</u>
shi<u>r</u>t	tih<u>r</u>s
r<u>o</u>ad	a<u>o</u>dr

According to the word-superiority effect, which list of letters should be identified more quickly? Is this what you found?

An Interactive Approach to Recognition.   It's clear from the word-superiority effect that context has a facilitatory effect on the recognition of letters. But this effect is not just due to top-down processing. It is the result of an interplay between the bottom-up processes that an-alyze the incoming data and the top-down processes that apply what we know. Basically, this means that the lower-level, more basic features (i.e., the letters) aid in the identification of the whole word. In addition, high-level features (i.e., the word) aid in the identification of the let-ters. So the three different levels of representations for a given word (i.e., its features, letters, and the word itself) interact with one another to aid in the word's identification. One very in-fluential model of these interactive effects was proposed by McClelland and Rumelhart (1981).

One assumption made by the model is implicit in the simple analysis we just sketched: words are represented in our *mental dictionaries* at three different levels—as sets of features, as groups of letters, and as whole words (see Figure 5.9). The McClelland and Rumelhart model uses a connectionist approach. We discussed the fundamental assumptions of this approach in Chapter 1. One of the key assumptions is that cognitive processes occur largely in parallel. According to the model, combining this parallel-processing assumption with our representations of words means that each type of information about a word is being ana-lyzed simultaneously, and information about the word's identity accumulates. That is, when you read the word *chair,* analyses of the individual features, the letters, and the word pat-tern converge to allow for identification of the word. Not only that, the analysis on each level influences the analysis at other levels. The connectionist approach provides a realization of a distinction we've discussed several times already—bottom-up and top-down processing. In the McClelland and Rumelhart model, the two interact and converge on a solution.

Recall one other assumption of the connectionist approach: nodes (which correspond to features, letters, and words) are connected via either excitatory or inhibitory connections. If two nodes have an excitatory connection, activation of one leads to activation of the other. If two nodes have an inhibitory connection, activation of one leads to the inhibition of the other. For example, let's consider the letter A. Activation of the A detector will excite nodes repre-senting words that have an A but inhibit nodes representing words that don't have an A. Note that this particular type of processing is bottom up; lower-level information is feeding into the analysis of higher-level information. Working in the other direction (from the top down), activation of the A detector will excite nodes representing features that are part of the letter A (e.g., slanted lines) but inhibit nodes that are not part of the letter A (e.g., a curved line).

So how does this account for the word-superiority effect? When we read a word (like *work,* as in the example from Reicher), information about the component letters leads to the activation of representations at the word level that include these letters. This height-ened activation at the word level then feeds back to the letter level, enhancing activation of component letters of the word activated. But only the letters in the word WORK are re-ceiving the top-down activation. Therefore, evidence for these particular letters will ac-cumulate the fastest, facilitating their identification. Finally, because nonwords don't have representations at the word level, the letters in the nonword (e.g., OWRK in the Reicher example) don't receive this additional top-down activation. Therefore, speed of identify-ing a letter in a nonword will be slower.

A Scene-Superiority Effect

A parallel to the word-superiority effect has been obtained using scenes that contain pre-dictable objects. The idea is that identifying an object within a scene is facilitated when the

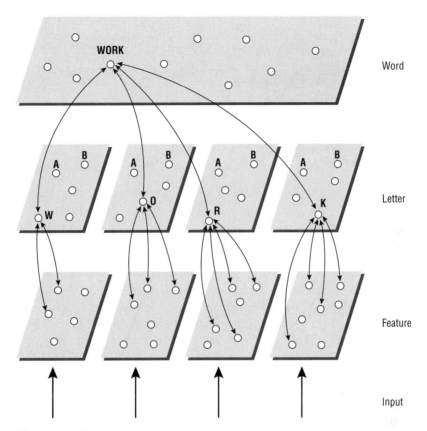

Figure 5.9 Distributed representation of a word in memory. Note that the word is represented at three different levels: in terms of the individual features that comprise each of its letters, in terms of the letters themselves, and in terms of the entire word. These levels are interconnected such that excitation of a representation at one level leads to the excitation of representations at other levels. In the word superiority effect, activation from the whole-word representation facilitates the identification of the individual letters.

From McClelland, J. L. (1985). Putting knowledge in its place: A scheme for programming parallel processing structures on the fly. *Cognitive Science, 9,* 113–146. Copyright 1985. Reprinted with permission.

object is consistent with the scene (e.g., a refrigerator in a kitchen) relative to when it is inconsistent (e.g., a refrigerator in a farm scene). This effect has been demonstrated by a number of researchers (e.g., Biederman, Mezzanotte, and Rabinowitz, 1982; Boyce & Pollatsek, 1992; Palmer, 1975). For example, Biederman, Mezzanotte, and Rabinowitz (1982) used a procedure similar to that depicted in Figure 5.10a. Participants saw the name of a common object, followed by a real-world scene, then a mask that included a location cue. The participants were to determine whether the object had appeared at that location in the scene. Biederman and colleagues found that detection performance was better when

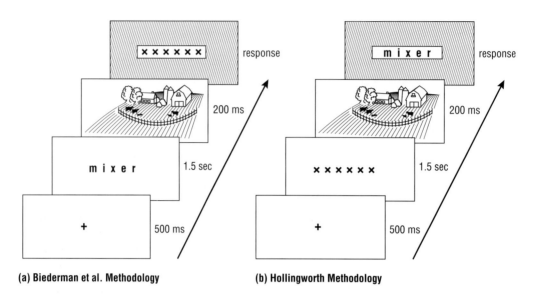

(a) Biederman et al. Methodology   **(b) Hollingworth Methodology**

Figure 5.10 Display sequence used by (a) Biederman et al. (1982) and
(b) Hollingworth (1998). In (b), the final display is followed by a forced-choice of which
object occurred. Under these conditions, context provides no identification advantage.
From Hollingworth, A. (1998). Does consistent scene context facilitate object perception? *Journal of Experimental Psychology:
General, 127,* 398–415. Copyright 1998 by the American Psychological Association. Reprinted by permission.

the object was consistent with the scene (e.g., a sheep in a farm scene) relative to when the
object was inconsistent (e.g., a coffee maker in a farm scene).

Not all agree that scene context facilitates the recognition of scene-consistent objects.
For example, Hollingworth (1998) notes that a subtle response bias (discussed in Chapter 3) may have been at play in the Biederman procedure. Participants were told what to
look for in the scene prior to the scene's presentation. This set up an expectation of what
would likely be in that scene and may have also influenced participants' response. Seeing
the word *sheep* might lead to an expectation of a farm scene; if that scene is indeed presented, then participants will have a bias to respond yes. However, when an inconsistent
scene is presented (e.g., an office), participants will demand a lot of visual evidence (i.e.,
bottom-up information) before they'll acknowledge that a sheep was in the office; in other
words, they will have a bias to respond no.

To test this response-bias interpretation of the scene-superiority effect, Hollingworth
(1998, experiment 4) employed a procedure much like the one used by Reicher (1969) to
investigate the word-superiority effect. To eliminate any expectation or bias effects, they
rearranged the basic sequencing of the Biederman study. Their version of the task is
presented in Figure 5.10b. Do you see the difference? In this version of the procedure,
participants don't know which object they'll be asked about in advance. This eliminates
an expectation bias. After the presentation of a scene (e.g., farm), participants were given
a forced-choice recognition test in which two alternatives were presented—either both

scene-consistent (sheep, pig) or both scene-inconsistent (coffee maker, mixer). Participants had to pick the one that was in the scene. If scene context truly facilitates recognition, then in the scene-consistent trials, participants should successfully choose the correct option most of the time. However, if the previous effect had been due to a guessing bias, then this procedure should eliminate the scene-superiority effect. When faced with two alternatives that both fit with the context, neither item will have an advantage; they're both likely choices. Under these conditions, Hollingworth found no scene-superiority effect. Participants were just as good at choosing which of two scene-inconsistent objects had occurred as they were at guessing which of two scene-consistent objects had occurred.

Hollingworth (1998) concluded that scene context does not facilitate the recognition of scene components. The processes underlying object recognition seem to be isolated from information about objects that might occur in any given scene. In fact, Hollingworth proposes that the lack of an effect of contextual knowledge on object recognition is probably a good thing. Consider that at almost every single waking moment, you're looking at a scene. If identification of objects in each of these scenes involved consulting general knowledge about objects both relevant and irrelevant to the scene, we would get bogged down. In this case, top-down processing would be an unnecessary drag on the system. But if this is the case, why does top-down information facilitate the recognition of letters? According to Hollingworth, one possibility centers on the fact that our experience with any given word is not as extensive as our experience with a given natural scene. Also, the letters that can appear in a word are much more constrained by context (i.e., context provides more information about the component letters of a word) than are the objects that can appear in a scene. Therefore, in the context of words, top-down processing is not a drag on the system.

Two-System Views of Object Recognition

In the last 10 years, a different class of models for object recognition has been proposed by a number of investigators. These approaches expand on the basic issue of how objects are represented by proposing multiple modes, or systems, of representation. One version of this approach (Cooper & Schacter, 1992) proposes that objects are represented in two separate systems: a *structural description system* and an *episodic system*. The structural description system includes information about the global shape of an object as well as the relationships among the object's parts. The episodic system encodes specific semantic (i.e., meaning) and visual information about the objects, such as their identity, their function, and specifics of their visual presentation.

As support for the existence of multiple object-representation systems, Cooper and Schacter (1992) present evidence of *dissociations* (presented in Chapter 2) in object recognition—cases in which different object-recognition tasks are influenced by different classes of variables. Their basic experimental paradigm involved an encoding phase in which participants were asked to make a judgment about possible and impossible objects (see Figure 5.11). *Possible objects* are ones whose surfaces and edges are configured such that they could exist in a 3-D world. *Impossible objects* are those that could not exist in three dimensions. In a later phase of the experiment, participants are given two different object-recognition tests. In one test, they are asked whether they saw each figure earlier. In another

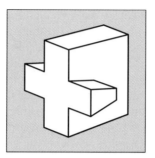
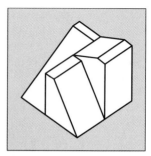

(a) Possible Objects

Figure 5.11 Sketches of possible (a) and impossible (b) objects, employed in the studies by Cooper and Schacter (1992).

From Cooper, L. A., & Schacter, D. L. (1992). Priming and recognition of transformed three-dimensional objects: Effects of size and reflection. *Journal of Experimental Psychology: Learning, Memory and Cognition, 18,* 43–57. Copyright 1992 by Blackwell. Reprinted by permission.

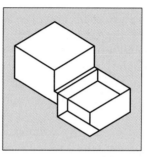
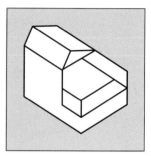

(b) Impossible Objects

test, they are asked to rapidly classify a series of objects as possible or impossible. As you may have guessed, some of these objects were presented earlier. The dependent variable of interest in this test is whether participants have an easier time making the possible-impossible judgment for figures that they had seen before. Any benefit from having seen an object before is termed *priming.*

That's the basic procedure—now for the demonstration of dissociations. Across a series of experiments, Schacter and his colleagues (e.g., Schacter, Cooper, & Delaney, 1990; Schacter, Cooper, Delaney, & Tharan, 1991) varied the way in which participants encoded the figures and observed the effects on the two object-recognition tests. The different encoding tasks were designed to get participants to concentrate on different aspects of the objects. (Look at the figures and try these tasks yourself.) The *global-structure task* required participants to decide whether the object faced right or left; the investigators believed this task would induce participants to encode the global properties of the objects and the interrelationships between the parts. The *meaningful-properties task* required a meaningful elaboration of the object; participants were to name something that each object resembled (much like Biederman's label of "hot dog cart" for the object in Figure 5.3).

It turns out that the two object-recognition tests—recognizing objects and rapid classification of objects as possible or impossible—yield strikingly different patterns of performance for the two encoding conditions. That is, there were *dissociations* between performance on the two tests. Take a look at Figure 5.12, which presents a sampling of the results gathered by Schacter and his colleagues. When participants had to recognize the ob-

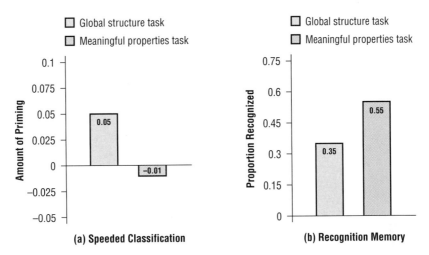

Figure 5.12 Results from studies of object recognition by Schacter and colleagues. Note that performance in speeded classification is better when figures are encoded for their global structure rather than in terms of meaning. The opposite pattern holds for recognition memory.

From Cooper, L. A. & Schacter, D. L. (1992). Dissociations between structural and episodic representations of visual objects. *Current Directions in Psychological Science, 1,* 141–146; Schacter, D. L., Cooper, L. A., & Delaney, S. M. (1990). Implicit memory for unfamiliar objects depends on access to structural descriptions. *Journal of Experimental Psychology: General,* 5–24; Schacter, D. L., Cooper, L. A., Delaney, S. M., & Tharan, M. (1991). Implicit memory for possible and impossible objects: Constraints on the construction of structural descriptions. *Journal of Experimental Psychology: Learning, Memory, and Cognition, 17,* 3–19. Copyrights 1992, 1990, 1991 by Blackwell, Inc. Reprinted by permission.

ject as one they had seen before, the most effective encoding was to think about it in meaningful terms (the meaningful-properties task). This finding foreshadows a fundamental finding and principle of memory termed the *levels-of-processing effect* (to be discussed in Chapter 6). We remember material much better when it's processed at a deeper level—that is, in terms of its meaning rather than its physical structure. Conversely, when participants had to rapidly classify objects as possible or impossible, the most effective encoding was to notice the global structure of the object (the global-structure task).

According to Schacter and colleagues, these dissociations in performance reveal some important facts about how we represent and perceive objects and provide compelling evidence that two different systems are at play in object recognition. These two systems seem to correspond to bottom-up and top-down processing and help to highlight the importance of both types of processing in object recognition.

Structural Descriptions.   The first system, the *structural description system,* includes a stored representation of the overall structure of objects and is used as the basis for their rapid recognition. This is the representational system that subserved performance on the speeded possible-impossible objects classification test. The only encoding method that primed the representation in this system was the global structure task (which induced participants to notice the overall structure of objects). Processing of the information in the structural description system could be viewed as analogous to bottom-up processing in that this system contains the actual data that we analyze.

Episodic System.   The second system, the *episodic system,* includes a stored representation of the identity of the object and its distinctive physical characteristics. This system is the basis for our memory of and knowledge about objects and is the system that subserved performance on the recognition test. Since this system stores information about what objects are, recognition was most affected by the encoding task that required participants to say what each object resembled. Processing of information from the episodic system could be viewed as analogous to top-down processing in that this system includes our conceptual knowledge about the objects that we need to identify.

An interesting side note to the findings: as noted above, global judgments primed representations in the structural description system. However, this was only true for possible objects; the rapid recognition of impossible objects showed no benefit from the global-structure judgment. According to Cooper and Schacter (1992), this indicates that the structural description system is incapable of representing objects that could not exist in three dimensions. This would seem to indicate the importance of top-down processing in object recognition: even the structural description system, which provides the data for bottom-up processing, is influenced by our previous experience.

RECURRING RESEARCH THEME
Cognition and Consciousness

Subliminal Visual Priming

The findings from the studies just discussed demonstrate a fundamental fact of pattern recognition: people process patterns more efficiently to the degree that they have processed them before (i.e., priming). Can priming of a stimulus be observed in the absence of conscious awareness? In other words, if we are presented with something so quickly that we can't even guess what it was, does it still facilitate identification of that stimulus on a later presentation? And if so, do we obtain priming in both the structural description system (bottom-up processing) and the episodic system (top-down processing)?

A study by Bar and Biederman (1998) tested for subliminal visual priming in a relatively straightforward manner. The general methodology is presented in Figure 5.13a. Participants viewed line drawings (e.g., a desk lamp) at one of nine different locations for an extremely brief duration (approximately 50 milliseconds). Following stimulus presentation, participants had to name the item. If they couldn't, they were given four alternatives and were to guess which one was the presented item (termed a 4AFC test—four-alternative forced-choice test). This served as a test of whether the participant was consciously aware of the stimulus and whether any information could be consciously extracted from it. Failure to exceed a chance guessing level of 25% would indicate a lack of conscious awareness and the failure to consciously extract any information from the stimulus. Would the presentation of a stimulus that participants were unaware of benefit the recognition of the same item presented later? Important to note here is that participants were never informed that some of the items would

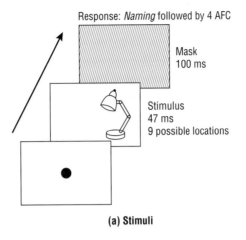

(a) Stimuli

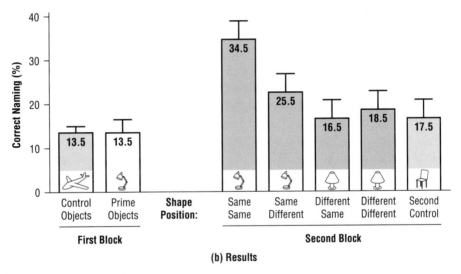

(b) Results

Figure 5.13 Subliminal visual priming; stimuli (a) used in the Bar and Biederman (1998) study and the results (b), which indicate that stimuli presented at below threshold intensity can have a sizable effect on recognition.

From Bar, M., & Biederman, I. (1998). Subliminal visual priming. *Psychological Science, 9,* 464–469. Copyright 1998 by Blackwell, Inc. Reprinted by permission.

be repeated, and on average, about 15 to 20 minutes elapsed between the first and second presentation of an item.

Across experimental blocks, some of the items were repeated in one of four different ways: the same item in the same location, the same item in a different location, a different but semantically related item in the same location, or a different but semantically related item in a different location. These different types of repetitions allowed for an assessment of the boundary conditions of subliminal priming. Would any observed benefits of priming extend to stimuli presented in different locations? And would priming be semantic in nature, extending to a similar example from the same category?

The results are presented in Figure 5.13b. The first bar represents the percentage of never-repeated control objects that could be named at the beginning of the experiment. General improvement in the ability to perform the naming task can be determined by examining the presentation of new items (i.e., never previously presented) at the end of the experiment. An increase in the percentage of items named would indicate a general improvement. As you can see, this benefit was about 4% (13.5% increasing to 17.5%); any benefit statistically greater than this serves as evidence of priming. The second bar on the graph indicates the percentage of to-be-repeated (prime) objects that could be named at first presentation (13.5%). The other 86.5% of the objects could not be named, and the ability to recognize them in the 4AFC test did not exceed chance (i.e., no information about the object was consciously extracted). Therefore, any increase in naming accuracy that statistically exceeded 4% (i.e., priming) would be subliminal.

Subliminal priming was observed in the same-object/same-position condition; ability to name the item increased by 21% on the second presentation. Subliminal priming was disrupted by repeating the same item in a different location; the benefit of repetition here was only about 12% (still statistically greater than the 4% increase for control objects). No other conditions of repetition yielded significant priming. Therefore, it seems that identification of a picture can be primed by the subliminal presentation of a structurally similar picture but not by the subliminal presentation of a semantically similar picture. This suggests that a fair amount of the bottom-up processing in object analysis (i.e., the structural description system) occurs outside of awareness and that the products of this analysis can last for some time.

STOP *and* REVIEW!

1. According to the interactionist approach to word recognition:
   a. the word-superiority effect is the sole result of bottom-up processing
   b. the word-superiority effect is the sole result of top-down processing
   c. the word-superiority effect is the result of both top-down and bottom-up processing
   d. letters should be especially identifiable when they're presented in the context of nonwords
2. True or false? The scene-superiority effect has been shown to be the result of a response bias.
3. Discuss how the two-system view of object recognition corresponds to bottom-up and top-down processes.
4. True or false? Viewing an object subliminally can prime later identification of a semantically similar object.

➤ Top-down processing (previous knowledge and expectations) plays an important role in pattern recognition and is evident in the word-superiority effect (the tendency for word context to aid in letter identification). According to the interactionist approach, this effect is the joint product of bottom-up and top-down processes.

➤ Some research suggests the existence of a scene-superiority effect (a parallel finding to the word-superiority effect). However, later research suggests this advantage is the product of a response bias.

➤ The two-system view of object representation proposes that objects are represented within two systems. The structural descriptions system provides a description of the structure of the object; the episodic system includes specific information about object identity and characteristics.

➤ Subliminally presented objects prime later presentations of identical objects but do not prime semantically similar objects.

Recognizing Faces

If there's one class of patterns for which recognition is the most important, significant, and frequent, it's the recognition of faces. Without the ability to recognize familiar faces, we would be awash in a sea of strangers. Indeed, this is the disconcerting dilemma faced by those suffering from **prosopagnosia,** an inability to recognize familiar faces. Consider the experience of a prosopagnosic described by Farah (1992). She recounts a story of a prosopagnosic who was sitting in a country club wondering why another gentleman was staring so intently at him. He asked one of the servers to investigate and found that the man staring at him was his own reflection in a mirror!

The Face-Inversion Effect

Let's take a closer look at face recognition and an interesting dissociation that reveals that inversion (turning something upside down) has different effects on the recognition of faces and objects. The deleterious effect of inversion is disproportionately great for faces (Yin, 1969). Look at the man in the photo on page 186. Do you recognize him? He is the same man seen in the photo on this page. You may not have recognized him. If you didn't, it is because he was upside down. In our opening scenario, Lance fails to recognize his friend Tom, who happenes to be upside down, doing a handstand. This disproportionate effect has been cited by many as evidence for the existence of a special face-recognition mechanism.

What if you couldn't recognize your own face?

Familiar or not?

Does inverting a dog's face make it harder to recognize?

What makes the recognition of faces so different from that of other objects, and how does this lead to the inversion effect? Diamond and Carey (1986) propose that to recognize objects, we need *first-order relational information*—that is, information about the parts of an object and how those parts relate to one another. For face recognition, this would involve an analysis of the person's facial features and the relationship among those features. However, first-order relational information is not enough to recognize faces; simply noticing that two eyes are above the nose, which is above the mouth, may be enough for recognition that something is a face but doesn't allow for recognition of who the face is. To recognize faces, we need what Diamond and Carey term *second-order relational information.* Second-order relational information involves comparing the first-order analysis to facial features of a "typical," or "average," face. This typical face is built up through experience and serves as an implicit standard against which we compare the faces we see. When a face is inverted, this disrupts the encoding of second-order relational information. Since this information is most important for recognizing faces, inversion disproportionately harms face recognition.

Diamond and Carey (1986) performed an interesting test of their hypothesis. In addition to replicating the basic inversion effect with human faces, they also investigated recognition of dog faces (not ugly people—actual dogs). The twist was that they compared dog experts with dog nonexperts. Their reasoning was as follows: Everyone is an expert at recognizing faces. Through countless *practice trials,* we've formed views of the "typical" face, and we encode the faces that we see relative to this example in terms of second-order relational properties. The same should be true of dog experts: they're so experienced with dogs that they should encode dog faces in terms of second-order relational properties. This leads to an interesting prediction. Inversion should have adverse effects on the dog nonexperts' recognition of human faces but not of dog faces. To a nonexpert, a dog is like an object, and inversion should not harm recognition. But inversion should have adverse effects on dog experts' recognition of both human faces and dog faces. This is exactly what occurred. Further evidence supports the idea that inversion has a disproportionate effect on the encoding of spatial and relational information, and because this information is so important for face recognition, inversion disproportionately disrupts it (Murray, Young, & Rhodes, 2000).

Wholistic Processing of Faces

The inversion effect underscores the fact that faces have strong configural properties. Because of this, some (e.g., Farah, 1992) contend that faces are encoded, stored, and retrieved from memory as whole configurations rather than as a set of features or parts. This contention was supported by the results of a study by Tanaka and Farah (1993). These authors reasoned that to the degree that a given object (e.g., a face or some other object) is stored as a set of features, then those features ought to be useful cues in retrieving the remaining information about the object. However, if a pattern is stored as a whole configuration (as seems to be the case with faces), then presenting part of that whole will not be particularly helpful in recognition.

To test their hypotheses, Tanaka and Farah presented participants with sketches of faces and sketches of houses, both decomposable in terms of distinct features. Each face and house was given a label, such as "Larry's house" or "Larry's face." On a later recognition test, participants were asked about the faces and houses in either an isolated-part condition or a whole-object condition. In the isolated-part condition, they were given a choice of two object parts and had to pick which one of them had been part of an object presented earlier (e.g., "Which of these is Larry's nose?" or "Which of these is Larry's door?"). In the whole-object condition, they were given a choice of two whole objects and had to pick out the one they had seen earlier (e.g., "Which of these is Larry's face?" or "Which of these is Larry's house?").

The results are presented in Figure 5.14. As you can see, the type of question asked didn't matter for recognition of houses; participants were just as good at recognizing parts of houses as they were at recognizing whole houses. But for faces, the type of question did matter. Participants were not as good at recognizing face parts as they were at recognizing whole faces. This fits with the view that faces are encoded and retrieved as whole configurations and that disrupting this configuration harms recognition. Sound familiar? The finding in this study hearkens back to a difference between view-based approaches and

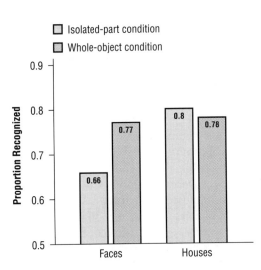

Recognition of Faces and Houses

Figure 5.14 Results from Tanaka and Farah (1993). In the face-recognition condition (left two bars), the whole stimulus served as a better cue than an isolated part. This difference was not found for object (house) recognition (right two bars).

From Tanaka, J. W., & Farah, M. J. (1993). Parts and wholes in face recognition. *Quarterly Journal of Experimental Psychology, 46A*, 225–245. Copyright 1993. Reprinted with permission of Psychology Press, Ltd.

structural-description-based approaches to pattern/object recognition. Is face recognition more similar to a VB or SDB approach? Recall that VB approaches assume wholistic processing of patterns/objects, whereas SDB approaches assume an analysis of component features. The processes involved in face recognition seem to be more reminiscent of a view-based approach than a structural-description-based approach.

Dissociations and Associations in Face Recognition

As you have just read, there is good reason to believe that there may be a special mechanism for recognizing faces, but some researchers posit at least two distinct subsystems for recognizing letters, objects, and faces rather than a special mechanism for face recognition. What's the evidence for this dual-system approach? Some of the evidence comes from consideration of visual recognition deficits that tend to be specific to only one or two of the classes of stimuli just mentioned. At the beginning of this section we discussed prosopagnosia (the inability to recognize faces). Let's consider two more visual recognition deficits. **Alexia** refers to deficits in the ability to recognize printed words or letters. **Object agnosia** refers to a deficit in the ability to recognize everyday objects.

In a review of cases of visual recognition deficits, Farah (1992) notes some intriguing patterns of association and dissociation among alexia, agnosia, and prosopagnosia. There are three interesting features of these case studies. First, deficits in recognizing faces are associated with at least some deficits in recognizing objects. Second, deficits in recognizing letters and words are associated with at least some deficits in recognizing objects. These two findings indicate that object recognition does share some mechanisms with both letter/word and face recognition. The third and most intriguing feature is what is almost never found. Deficits in object recognition with no deficits in face and letter/word processing or the opposite pattern (deficits in face and letter/word processing with no deficits in object recognition) are rarely found. None of the case studies Farah reviewed demonstrated these patterns.

Is your head spinning? Let's pause to consider what this implies. The fact that face recognition and letter/word recognition are almost never spared together (with object recognition being impaired) or impaired together (with object recognition being spared) indicates that face recognition and letter/word recognition rely on quite distinct mechanisms. And the fact that problems in object recognition quite often line up with problems in either face or letter/word recognition indicates that object recognition shares some common mechanisms with each. Based on these patterns, Farah proposes that visual recognition involves two primary mechanisms. One mechanism is used for the representation and combination of parts. This system is critical to letter/word recognition, because printed words and letters are very much the combination of distinct parts. A second mechanism is used for the representation and combination of complex wholes. This system is critical for face recognition. As you read earlier, faces are processed and remembered as whole patterns; they tend not to be easily decomposed into parts. Therefore, the first mechanism is not important for the recognition of faces, and the second mechanism is not important for the recognition of letters and words. A combination of both mechanisms is involved in object recognition. This two-system theory accounts for the patterns of associations and dissociations described above.

RECURRING RESEARCH THEME
Cognition and Neuroscience

The Right Hemisphere and Self-Recognition

Let's return to the plight of the man in the anecdote related by Farah (1992) who failed to recognize his own face. His visual recognition deficit is striking, reminding us of the degree to which we take this ability for granted. Our knowledge of our own face seems inseparable from our general knowledge of self—who we are, our likes and dislikes, our personal history. Whether face recognition involves a special mechanism or shares some processes in common with object recognition, there does seem to be evidence to suggest that recognition of one's own face may be particularly special. One indicator of this is that although nonhuman primates have shown face recognition ability, they fail on tests of self-recognition even after extended training (Keenan, Wheeler, Gallup, & Pascual-Leone, 2000). Might our own face recognition rely on different brain areas than general face recognition?

Both case-study and brain-imaging evidence suggest that the area of the brain called the fusiform gyrus (located in the temporal lobes) is specialized for recognizing faces. Prosopagnosics (those with an inability to recognize faces) show selective damage to this area (e.g., Sergent & Signoret, 1992), and brain-imaging studies with normal individuals demonstrate increased activation in this area during face recognition (Kanwisher, McDermott, & Chun, 1997). However, relatively little research exists regarding the neural substrates of self-face recognition. Recently, Keenan and colleagues (Keenan, Freund, Hamilton, Ganis, & Pascual-Leone, 2000; Keenan, McCutcheon, Freund, Gallup, Sanders, & Pascual-Leone, 1999) found some intriguing evidence that self-recognition may involve the right prefrontal area of the cortex. This evidence is especially intriguing in light of what others have found—that this same area is especially active during other tasks involving the self, such as recalling the events from one's own life story (Fink, Markowitsch, & Reinkemeier, 1996). (We'll talk more about recall of one's life story—autobiographical memory—in Chapter 8.)

Consider an investigation by Keenan, Freund, Hamilton, Ganis, and Pascual-Leone (2000). Their first study employed a simple recognition task. Participants were presented with pictures of faces and had to identify each face as quickly as possible as their own face, the face of a coworker, or the face of a stranger. For half of the trials, they used their left hand to respond; for the other half, they used their right. Why the hand switch? This was actually a critical component of the study given the contralateral organization of the brain's hemispheres: a left-hand response is controlled by the right hemisphere of the brain, and the converse is true for a right-hand response. If the right hemisphere is specialized for self-recognition, then one might expect to find a left-hand reaction time (RT) advantage. This is exactly what happened. RTs for recognizing one's own face were faster than those for recognizing the other two types of faces; more important, this advantage was seen only when participants responded with their left hand! This result would be expected if the right hemisphere enjoys an advantage in processing of one's own face relative to the faces of others.

Keenan and others' follow-up study bolsters this conclusion. In this study, participants saw a series of rapidly presented faces—a sort of "face movie." The series of faces began with the person's own face and ended with the face of a famous person (e.g., Bill Clinton or Marilyn

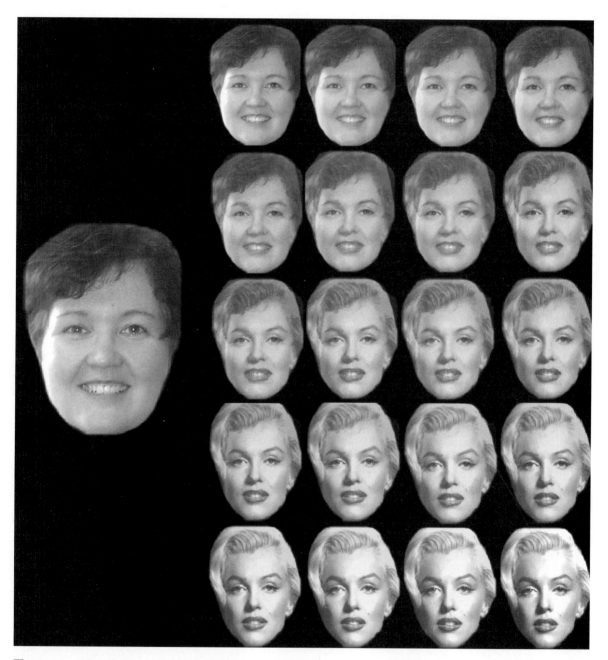

Figure 5.15 Facial morph like that used by Keenan et al. (1999). Over a series of pictures, a participant's face morphs into a famous face.

From Keenan, J. P., McCutcheon, B., Freund, S., Gallup, G. G., Sanders, G., & Pascual-Leone, A. (1999). Left-hand advantage in a self-face recognition task. *Neuropsychologia, 37,* 1421–1425. Copyright 1999. Reprinted by permission of Elsevier Science.

Monroe). In between was a sequence of morphed pictures that were combinations of the two (see Figure 5.15). Imagine yourself watching a gradual sequence of pictures in which you turn into Marilyn Monroe or Bill Clinton. (The researchers also used the opposite sequence, where the famous face would gradually morph into your face.) Participants were told to watch the series and press a key when they felt that each picture had become more "not themselves" than "themselves" (or vice versa, in the reverse condition). Once again, they used either their right or left hand to press the key. When participants responded with their left hand, the transition from "me" to "not me" was judged as occurring significantly earlier than when participants responded with their right hand. This again seems to confirm that the right hemisphere (which controls the left hand) has an advantage in self-recognition.

STOP *and* REVIEW!

1. Describe the face-inversion effect and what it indicates about face recognition.
2. Which of these two sets of stimuli seem to depend on quite different recognition mechanisms?
   a. faces and objects
   b. faces and letters
   c. objects and letters
3. True or false? The right hemisphere seems especially proficient at recognizing one's own face.

➤ Prosopagnosia refers to an inability to recognize familiar faces. The face-inversion effect refers to the finding that upside-down presentation makes face recognition quite difficult. This indicates that face recognition is reliant on second-order relational information, which is disrupted by inversion. In addition, components of faces do not serve as useful retrieval cues for an entire face. These findings indicate that faces are stored and recognized in terms of their configural properties, rather than in terms of their components.

➤ Prosopagnosia, along with other recognition deficits (alexia—the inability to recognize printed words or letters—and agnosia—the inability to recognize familiar objects), provides further evidence of the uniqueness of face recognition. Patterns of association and dissociation among these deficits indicate that face and letter recognition rely on distinct mechanisms. A combination of these mechanisms is thought to underlie object recognition.

➤ Some evidence indicates that self-face recognition—or the ability to recognize a face as one's own—is largely a right-hemisphere function.

Concepts and Categories

We've seen that pattern recognition involves the identification and classification of some object. The process whereby we arrive at a decision about what something is—the process of pattern recognition—begs a basic question: What makes a thing what it is? In other words, what is it about a poodle, a Lhasa apso, and a Great Dane that would lead us to look at all of them and apply the same label—"dog"? And why would animals that seem similar enough to belong to the dog category (e.g., a Minnesota timber wolf—the animal, not the basketball player) be classified in a different category? In this section of the chapter, we'll discuss some fundamental work on concepts and categories. A **concept** can be defined as "a mental representation of a category serving multiple functions, one of which is to allow for the determination of whether or not something belongs to the class," and **category** can be defined as "the set of entities picked out by the concept" (Medin & Coley, 1998, p. 404). We'll follow a common convention and use the terms *concept* and *category* interchangeably to refer to both the mental representation and the examples that fit this representation.

Concepts are extremely important in our everyday thinking; they serve as a sort of "mental shorthand" that allows for quick and efficient understanding. The lack of a concept results in processing difficulties, as indicated in our opening vignette by Lance's unsuccessful attempt to name the object at the rummage sale. But Lance's description of a cross between a screwdriver and a spatula was probably helpful in enabling you to imagine such an implement, given that you're familiar with each component concept. Similarly, when I say that my favorite TV show is a sitcom, I probably don't need to add that the show is funny, that it lasts 30 minutes, that it's on at night between 7 P.M. and 9 P.M., or that I watch it on a little box that projects color images. The term *sitcom* immediately evokes all of these ideas. Put another way, our ability to form concepts allows us to infer knowledge not explicitly stated. Similarly, knowledge of a given concept allows for *generalizations* across category members. Knowing that carrots, broccoli, and celery are all no-fat, healthy, and bland-tasting foods leads one to assume the same characteristics for other lesser-known members of the category "vegetable," like okra, rutabaga, and turnip. In the story that opens this chapter, it's obvious that Irv and Lance both have a concept of "cheerleader" and some idea of what does and doesn't fit the concept.

Types of Categories

Natural and Artifact Categories and Nominal Kinds.   There are a number of different schemes one might use to distinguish between category types (see Medin, Lynch, & Solomon, 2000, for an extensive consideration of this issue). One commonly cited distinction is between what are called natural categories and artifact categories. **Natural categories** are those that occur (naturally) in the world; they in essence define themselves. For example, all flowers are grouped into a single category by virtue of the naturally occurring attributes they share. These naturally occurring concepts are labeled only after their discovery (Medin & Heit, 1999). Two other types of categories are the product of human design, invention, and language. **Artifact categories** include objects or conventions designed or invented by humans to serve particular functions (e.g., tools, sports, furniture). Finally, **nominal kinds** are linguistic conventions that involve the arbitrary assignment of a label to entities that fit a particular set of conditions. For example, "triangle" and "bachelor" are arbitrary labels that apply to concepts that have been defined by society as a matter of convenience. They are not naturally occurring things that were discovered and only subsequently given a label.

Different, but the same. What allows us to classify each of these as members of the same category?

Ad Hoc Categories.   The way we categorize can be strongly influenced by context. If I ask you to name a sport on Super Bowl Sunday, chances are good that you'll say "football." Context can also determine whether a category even exists; some categories are only formed when there's a need for them—a goal to be served. For example, we doubt that "things to take on vacation" has the same presence in your knowledge representation as does the natural category "fruit." Nonetheless, asking for "things to take on vacation" would lead to consistent responses across individuals within a particular cultural context, suggesting that we can form categories "on the fly," given a particular goal. Such categories have been labeled **ad hoc categories,** because they're formed only for a purpose (Barsalou, 1983).

Levels of Categorization.   Rosch (1978) notes that categories vary along both horizontal and vertical dimensions. The horizontal dimension reflects our knowledge about a host of different categories that vary a great deal from one another—animal, furniture, weapon, bird, game. A category may also be organized along a vertical dimension, representing different levels of specificity. Take, for example, the categories to which the three little four-legged creatures in our house belong. I could give them a *superordinate-level* category label—"animal." I could get more specific and give them what is termed a *basic-level* category label—"cat." I could get still more specific and call them "overweight tabby house-cats"—the *subordinate-level* category label.

How do these hierarchies map onto our everyday use of categories? Rosch (1978) notes that given the limited-capacity nature of information processing, categories should maximize information while minimizing cognitive effort. Rosch terms this principle *cognitive economy.* Which level fills that bill? The basic level, as it turns out. We're less likely to speak in terms of vegetables, animals, weapons, and pieces of furniture (too general) or baby carrots, fat tabby cats, Smith and Wessons, or rocking chairs (too specific) than we are of carrots, cats, guns, and chairs (just right). This gradation in the usefulness of the categories is evident in the conversation between Irv and Lance. Lance has no idea what Irv means by a Lhasa apso until he hears the basic category label "dog."

Approaches to Concept Representation

A number of approaches have been proposed to explain how we represent and think about everyday concepts. Central to these accounts is the question of what makes category members *cohere,* or stick together. Approaches to concept representation can be classified into two broad categories (see how pervasive categorization is!): similarity-based approaches and explanation-based approaches.

Similarity-Based Approaches.   **Similarity-based approaches** to concept representation assert that categorization is a matter of judging the similarity between the target object and some standard in long-term memory. That standard might be a clearly specified set of features or characteristics, an abstracted "best example" version of the category, or all of the other members of the category. We now examine each of these possibilities.

The Classical View.   The earliest and perhaps most straightforward account of how we use concepts is termed the **classical view.** According to the classical view, items are classified into particular categories if they have certain features or characteristics. These features are both necessary and sufficient for defining the concept. For example, the concept "triangle" is a closed, three-sided figure whose angles sum to 180 degrees. Shapes that have these characteristics are triangles; shapes that don't are not. This view fares pretty well with nominal kinds, like "triangle," "even number," or "bachelor." Each of these concepts has a set of features that are necessary and sufficient for inclusion. The classical view is considered similarity-based, because categorization is based on whether the set of features that characterize a given entity is similar to the features that define the concept.

Stop and Think!

DEFINING CONCEPTS WITH RULES

Consider the following concepts:

gemstone
sport
square
plant
grandmother
furniture
spice
game

For each of these concepts, try and come up with a list of features that define it—a set of features that, if possessed by some object or person, would make them a member of the category. After you've defined each concept, try and think of exceptions to the "rules" you just made.

- Which set of concepts had the most exceptions (i.e., "problem concepts")?
- Which concepts didn't have any?
- Can you refine your definitions of the "problem concepts" to accommodate more examples?
- What are they?

Although the classical view provides a ready description of how we might classify concepts that have clearly defined properties, closer inspection reveals some serious flaws. The most significant criticism gets at the very core of the approach: it's very difficult to specify many concepts in terms of features that are both necessary and sufficient. For example, take the concept "game," which can include Ring around the Rosie, Monopoly, football, and cribbage—what on earth are the common features that define them as games and make them members of the category? Which features are necessary and sufficient for something to be called a game?

Graded Structure and Fuzzy Boundaries. Another serious problem with the classical approach is that it can't explain a fundamental characteristic of categorization—the fact that our representations of categories have a **graded structure.** When we think of a category like "furniture," it's not the case that all furniture is created equal. The vast majority of respondents, when asked to name a member of the category "furniture," will say "table," "chair," or "couch." The classical view of concepts has no way to deal with this finding. According to the classical view, if something has all of the features that define "furniture,"

Sport, or not a sport?

then it's a piece of furniture; if it doesn't, then it's not. The view has no mechanism that explains why certain category members (e.g., tables) are more "furniturey" than others. An interesting side note: even members of ad hoc categories, like "things to take on vacation," vary in their typicality (typical: "swim suit"; less typical: "deck of cards"). The graded nature of category representation is evident from many research studies, most notably the work of Rosch and colleagues (e.g., Rosch & Mervis, 1975). When participants are asked to rate which members of categories are typical, there is overwhelming agreement about which members are more and less typical.

A second problem with the classical approach is the implication that categories are separated by absolute, clear-cut boundaries. If something has the necessary and sufficient features of a category, then it's a member; if not, it's not. Were the categories of "game" and "sport" well-defined, it would be a trivial task to classify "bowling." But in reality, categories have what have been called **fuzzy boundaries;** one person's game is another person's sport. When we invite opinion from our students regarding whether bowling is a sport, we invariably get a split. Bowling is "kind of" a sport; like other sports, it requires well-coordinated motor movements, and it's shown on the sports channel. But still, it seems (at most) like "sort of" a sport. But the classical view doesn't allow for this "sort of" view of categories. Something is a sport or it isn't. This absolute view fails to capture many of the categories we think about every day.

The Prototype Approach. The **prototype approach** to categorization provides a more flexible view of categorization. Rather than specifying necessary and sufficient features that each category member must have, the prototype view contends there are features of the category that members are likely to have. Instances of the category are evaluated and classified based on their resemblance to other members. Instances that have a high family resemblance (i.e., those that share many features with other category members) are classified as typical members of the category and serve as the standard to which other category members are compared. Those with a low family resemblance are seen as less typical members. For example, typical bird features might be the following: flies, chirps, has feathers, has a beak. The instance "robin" is perceived as more typical, because it is characterized by all four of these features, than "penguin," which is characterized by only two. (Penguins are one of the aberrations of the bird category.) This is why the prototype approach is classified as similarity-based: category membership is determined by an item's similarity to the prototype.

The prototype view solves the problems encountered by the classical view. First, it avoids the rigidity of the classical approach. One doesn't need to come up with the set of features that absolutely defines a category. The prototype view contends that there are features that tend to be present. The second problem—the fact that some category members are perceived as more typical, or "better," members than others—certainly poses no problem. In fact, its the very basis for prototype theory. Finally, the fuzzy boundary issue isn't really a problem for the prototype approach. The fuzzy boundary between the categories of "game" and "sport" fits well with this view. "Bowling" is difficult to classify because it lies near the boundaries for each category (about equidistant from each prototype), and the category boundaries aren't really clear.

Stop *and* **Think!**

AND THE NUMBER 1 FRUIT IS . . .

Recruit a few willing friends as participants, and give them this concept task. Give them the following category names and have them generate the first four examples that come to mind.

fruits
games
weapons
beverages
things you'd save in a fire

Tally up the responses and consider the following questions:

- Did prototypes emerge from the categories? What were these prototypes?
- Did your "participants" have any trouble with the "ad hoc" category? Did generation of members of this category take any longer than the more "traditional" categories?
- Is the graded nature of category structure apparent from the responses?

How does a category member become a prototype? Prototypes are thought to be abstracted through repeated experience with category members. Through repeated encounters with birds, we arrive at a representation of a "bird" that includes the features we've seen the most often; smallish, flies, builds nests, has feathers, and so on. A particularly compelling demonstration of prototype formation is provided by Posner, Goldsmith, and Welton (1967). These investigators used an unusual sort of category—dot patterns—to investigate prototype formation. Figure 5.16 presents some sample patterns. Unbeknownst to participants, all of the dot patterns presented were statistically generated distortions of a prototype; the presented examples differed from the prototype by varying amounts. However, the prototype itself was never presented. During a test phase, participants were presented with both old (previously presented) and new dot patterns and were to determine whether or not they had seen each pattern in the earlier phase.

The most compelling result came from test trials on which the prototype pattern was presented. Participants tended to confidently confirm that they had seen the prototype pattern, even though they never had. They were considerably less likely to make this same mistake with other new patterns. Later in the session, after only the one test presentation, the prototype was recognized just as well as patterns that had been presented throughout the experiment, almost as if the prototype itself had been repeatedly presented. In a sense, it had, according to prototype theory. Throughout the initial presentation trials, participants were abstracting a prototype that represented the average of all the patterns they were observing.

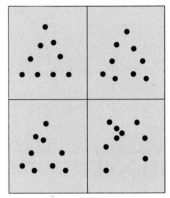

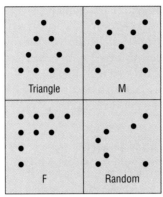

Figure 5.16 Stimuli used in the Posner et al. (1967) study of prototypes.

From Posner, M. I., Goldsmith, R., & Welton, K. E. (1967). Perceived distance and the classification of distorted patterns. *Journal of Experimental Psychology, 73,* 28–38. Copyright 1967 by the American Psychological Society. Reprinted by permission.

(a) Prototypical Pattern   **(b) Triangle Distortions**

Characteristics of Prototypical Category Members. The term **prototype** refers not only to the theoretical approach to concept representation but also to the most representative member (or members) of a given category. These *anchoring,* or *standard,* category members are afforded advantages in processing (similar to the processing advantages enjoyed by basic-level categories).

Let's take a look at some of the processing advantages enjoyed by prototypes (reviewed by Rosch, 1975a). First, *speed of access* is quicker the more prototypical the category member. In reaction time studies, people are quicker to verify the category membership of prototypical category members like "hammer" relative to less prototypical members like "T-square." *Ease of access* to prototypes is also indicated by the fact that when asked to generate members of a category, the order in which people generate the items (e.g., Battig & Montague, 1969) corresponds closely to prototypicality ratings (Rosch, 1975a). In other words, the more prototypical the word, the earlier it is listed. *Rate of learning* also seems to be faster for prototypical category members. Rosch (1973) compared children's and adults' ability to verify category membership of prototypes and nonprototypes and found a much larger difference in children relative to adults. Children were much slower at verifying the category membership of nonprototypes relative to prototypes, implying that the prototypes had been more quickly learned. Prototypes are also more likely to be *primed* by presenting the category name. Rosch (1975a, b) found that presenting the name of a category (e.g., "weapon") speeds the recognition of a prototypical member (e.g., "knife"), but can inhibit the recognition of a nonprototypical member (e.g., "brick").

Prototypical category members also have some primacy in terms of how they're used linguistically—that is, how they're used when we communicate. Take the example of a *linguistic hedge* (Lakoff, 1972) in which we qualify what we're saying with phrases like " technically," "in essence," or "when you come right down to it." For example, we're more likely to say that "when it comes right down to it, a penguin is a bird," than we are to say "when it comes right down to it, a robin is a bird" (cf., Rosch, 1975a). The latter sounds preposterous, because "robin" and "bird" seem nearly synonymous.

Problems with the Prototype View. There is no question about the descriptive value of the term *prototype.* As just discussed, the idea that certain category members serve as the basis to which other members are compared is not in doubt. But *prototype* as a theoretical explanation for how we represent concepts has fared less well than *prototype* as a descriptive term. One problem is that people's representations of categories and their characteristics seem to be much more complex than would be implied by the prototype approach. Categorical knowledge extends beyond the simple average representation suggested by the prototype approach. Evidence indicates that people are sensitive to the ways in which certain properties of category members do and do not go together. For example, people are sensitive to the fact that small birds tend to sing but large birds tend not to sing (Mervis & Rosch, 1981); furthermore, they use this type of information in classifying objects. It's not clear how an average representation could allow for this rather sophisticated representation of object properties and their intercorrelations.

The prototype view also fails to capture another key feature of category representation—the fact that it's sensitive to context (Roth & Shoben, 1983). Research shows that what we view as a typical category member depends on how we think about the category. For example, if I ask you to name a musical instrument, you're quite likely to say "piano"; but if I ask you to name a "campfire musical instrument," you're likely to say "guitar" or "harmonica." If our representation of a category is centered on one (or two or three) typical member(s), it's not clear why context should matter at all. A similar problem arises when one considers the conjunction of two concepts (Hampton, 1993). Take the concept "pet fish," for example; most people would say "guppy" or "goldfish" if asked for an example, but neither of these is prototypical of either individual concept ("pet" or "fish").

The Exemplar Approach.   Partially in response to the problems encountered with the prototype approach, some researchers have proposed the **exemplar approach,** which suggests that we represent categories in terms of examples, or category exemplars. According to this view, there is not a single representation of a category that gets abstracted over time.

Exemplars of the concept "guitar."

There are a number of different versions of exemplar theory (e.g., Brooks, 1978; Hintzman, 1986; Nosofsky, 1984). The extreme version of the exemplar view proposes no abstraction or generalization process. Rather, our representation of a concept (i.e., "guitar") consists of every single encounter we've had with it. When we think about the concept, we retrieve one of these encounters (e.g., Brooks, 1987). Note that like the prototype view, the exemplar view is similarity based: objects and events are assessed in terms of their similarity to a standard. But in this case, the standard is a specific example of the category rather than a generalized representation. Also, the standard that is used (i.e., the particular example) will depend on circumstances. When asked if an eagle is a bird, the instance retrieved will be some relatively large bird of prey (Ross & Spalding, 1994).

Stop and Think!

REPRESENTING CONCEPTS

Bring each of the following categories to mind.

vegetable
vehicle
tool
four-footed animal
type of reading material

Take note of what it is you think about when you retrieve the category name or when you think about what the category represents.

- Does it seem like a general prototype or a specific exemplar comes to mind?
- If it's a specific exemplar, why might this particular exemplar have been brought to mind?
- Was it seen recently?
- Was it appropriate to the context you're in?

Do the same demonstration with some friends, and ask them the same questions.

- To what degree are their responses influenced by contextual elements such as the situation in which you ask them or their own life experiences or habits?
- Do people seem to think in terms of specific examples or in terms of prototypes?

Like the prototype approach, the exemplar view can deal readily with the difficulties of the classical view. The effect of typicality poses no problem for the exemplar approach. The reason we're most likely to think of "robin" when we encounter the concept "bird" is because the majority of our stored examples of birds are robins (or similar to robins). When we retrieve an instance, we're more likely to retrieve one that's been encoded frequently.

The exemplar view can also deal quite readily with some of the problems encountered by the prototype view. The biasing effect of context ("harmonica" as an example of "a campfire musical instrument") is no problem for exemplar theory, which claims that a particular context can activate certain exemplars, essentially *priming* their retrieval. When we're in the middle of the Christmas season, for example, Christmas songs abound. So if asked in December to give an example of the category "song," "Jingle Bells" may well be the answer; in this case, temporal context serves to make this particular exemplar especially retrievable. Exemplar theory also has no problem with the finding that people are sensitive to correlations in the properties of category members (Malt & Smith, 1984). (Remember the previous example that little birds chirp and big birds don't?) Since we store every single encounter with category members, all information about the category's members is available. So although you may not be particularly aware that small birds tend to chirp and big birds tend to squawk, you are able to arrive at this conclusion if asked. (Of course, who would ask but a cognitive researcher?)

But alas, it seems every theory has its problems, and exemplar theory is no exception. For one thing, it seems that in some circumstances people are truly using an abstracted representation—one that's constructed from repeated encounters. Think back to the dot-pattern classification study conducted by Posner and colleagues (1967). In this study, people were very likely to say they had seen the prototype they had never seen, so there was no corresponding exemplar. Obviously, exemplar theory has no explanation for these results. How would one recognize an exemplar that was never encoded? Another problem with the more extreme versions of the exemplar approach is one of economy (Komatsu, 1992). It strains credulity to think that every single encounter with every single object is stored in memory. (This recalls the problem of economy faced by the template view of pattern recognition.) Even if only some exemplars are stored, what determines the ones that are? As is often the case in theoretical debates, it appears that both the prototype view and the exemplar view have some merit and that both may serve as accurate descriptions of concept representations. Malt (1989) demonstrated that under different circumstances, people may classify based on either exemplars or prototypes. It seems that the boundary between these two categories of theories is definitely fuzzy!

Perhaps both?

Explanation-Based Approaches.   Similarity-based approaches to categorization take what might be termed a bottom-up approach to categorization. These approaches emphasize the processing of the particular features possessed by members of the concept; a robin is a bird because it has the features of a bird, or is similar in features to some prototypical bird or to an exemplar. Alternatively, an **explanation-based approach** to categorization is more of a top-down approach; categorization is based not so much on encoding the particular properties of entities in the external world and comparing these properties to those of stored exemplars or prototypes. Instead, categorization of external entities is based on a person's general idea (or "theory") regarding the essence of the concept.

One of the strongest pieces of evidence for the explanation-based approach comes from a dissociation between two different judgment tasks: judgments of category membership and judgments of similarity. Rips (1989) presented participants with stories that involved hypothetical organisms. Given their properties, participants were likely to label these organisms as a member of a familiar category, like a bird or an insect. (However, these labels were never presented to participants.) (See Figure 5.17 for example stories from each condition.) The researchers compared two conditions. In the accident condition, the organism (a birdlike creature called a sorp) underwent a catastrophic accident that resulted in many of its external features being altered such that it now looked like a member of different category (an insect) but still behaved like a member of its original category (a bird). In the essence condition, the sorp underwent the same type of external change (looked like an insect rather than a bird). But now it behaved like its new category rather than its old category (like an insect rather than a bird) and was given a new name (a doon). So in one

There was an animal called a sorp which, when it was fully grown, was like other sorps, having a diet which consisted of seeds and berries found on the ground or on plants. The sorp had two wings, two legs, and lived in a nest high in the branches of a tree. Its nest was composed of twigs and other fibrous plant material. This sorp was covered with bluish-gray feathers.

The sorp's nest happened to be not too far from a place where hazardous chemicals were buried. The chemicals contaminated the vegetation that the sorp ate, and as time went by it gradually began to change. The sorp shed its feathers and sprouted a new set of wings composed of a transparent membrane. The sorp abandoned its nest, developed a brittle iridescent outer shell, and grew two more pairs of legs. At the tip of each of the sorp's six legs an adhesive pad was formed so that it was able to hold onto smooth surfaces; for example, the sorp learned to take shelter during rainstorms by clinging upside down to the undersides of tree leaves. The sorp eventually sustained itself entirely on the nectar of flowers.

Eventually this sorp mated with a normal female sorp one spring. The female laid the fertilized eggs in her nest and incubated them for three weeks. After that time normal young sorps broke out of their shells.

During an early stage of the doon's life it is known as a sorp. A sorp's diet mainly consists of seeds and berries found on the ground or on plants. A sorp has two wings, two legs, and lives in a nest high in the branches of a tree. Its nest is composed of twigs and other fibrous plant material. A sorp is covered with bluish-gray feathers.

After a few months, the doon sheds its feathers, revealing that its wings are composed of a transparent membrane. The doon abandons its nest, develops a brittle, iridescent outer shell, and grows two more pairs of legs. At the tip of each of the doon's six legs an adhesive pad is formed so that it can hold onto smooth surfaces; for example, doons take shelter during rainstorms by clinging upside down to the undersides of tree leaves. A doon sustains itself entirely on the nectar of flowers.

Doons mate in the late summer. The female doon deposits the eggs among thick vegetation where they will remain in safety until they hatch.

Figure 5.17   Transformation stories used in the study by Rips (1989).
From Rips, L. J. (1989). Similarity, typicality, and categorization. In S. Vosniadu & A. Ortony (Eds.), *Similarity and analogical reasoning* (pp. 21–59). Cambridge, UK: Cambridge University Press. Reprinted by permission of Cambridge University Press.

condition, there were accidental changes in the organism; in the other, there were essential changes in the organism.

After reading these stories, participants were given a categorization task in which they were to rate the degree to which the sorp (or doon, in the essence condition) fit into the category of "bird" on a scale from 1 to 10. They were also given a similarity-rating task in which they were to rate the similarity between sorps and birds (or doons and birds) on a scale from 1 to 10. If the basis for categorization is similarity—as both the prototype and exemplar views contend—then the accidental changes and the essential changes should influence judgments of similarity and judgments of categorization in the same manner. Since the basis for categorization is similarity to a prototype or exemplar, any manipulation that increases similarity ratings for an item should also make that item seem like a better member of the category.

The results were striking. Take a look at Figure 5.18. Presented here are ratings of category membership in and similarity to birds, relative to a control group who only read the description of the birdlike sorps. In the accidental change condition (eventually looked like an insect but behaved like a bird), the change lowered similarity ratings more than categorization ratings. In the essential change condition (eventually looked and behaved like an insect), the change lowered categorization ratings more than similarity ratings. So similarity ratings were affected more by accidental changes than by essential changes, while categorization ratings were affected more by essential changes than by accidental changes.

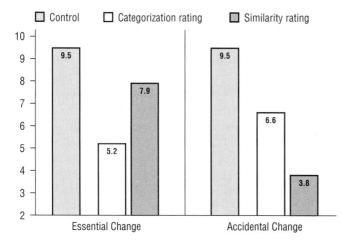

Effects of Changes on Categorizing and Similarity Ratings

Figure 5.18 Data reported by Rips (1989). The far left section presents participants' ratings of the target stimuli (e.g., "birdlike" stimuli) prior to any changes. As you can see from looking at the control ratings, the fictional organism was easily categorized as a bird and rated as highly similar to a bird. Similarity ratings were affected more by accidental changes than by essential changes, while the opposite was true of categorization judgments. This suggests that similarity judgments and categorization judgments are based on different mechanisms.

From Rips, L. J. (1989). Similarity, typicality, and categorization. In S. Vosniadu & A. Ortony (Eds.), *Similarity and analogical reasoning* (pp. 21–59). Cambridge, UK: Cambridge University Press. Reprinted by permission of Cambridge University Press.

This intriguing dissociation between judgments of similarity and judgments of category membership suggests that the two are fundamentally different. This, of course, poses a serious challenge to the prototype and exemplar views, which basically say that judgments of category membership and judgments of similarity are one and the same. Clearly, they aren't.

These findings led Rips and others to propose explanation-based views of categories. According to these views, representation is a matter of what might be considered a *personal theory* or *explanation* about what a concept represents. Our views of categories are based on implicit theories about what makes a thing what it is; in other words, what is the essence of a bird? In our opening scenario, Lance's categorization of Tom as a cheerleader clearly doesn't amount to a simple comparison of Tom's characteristics with those of a typical cheerleader. Lance's comment to Tom, "You don't seem like the cheerleader type," indicates that Lance's concept of "cheerleader" is perhaps better conceived of as an explanation.

Stop and Think! **WHAT'S THE ESSENCE OF . . . ?**

Consider once again what makes a thing what it is and what makes a category cohere. Think about the following items and what makes each of them a member of their respective category. Also think of why the third example isn't a member of its category although it might share some features with the other two.

- What makes a brick a weapon? What makes a chain a weapon? Why isn't a sponge a weapon? What is the essence of a weapon?
- What makes water a beverage? What makes tomato juice a beverage? Why isn't motor oil a beverage? What is the essence of a beverage?
- What makes a bus a vehicle? What makes a bicycle a vehicle? Why isn't an escalator a vehicle? What is the essence of a vehicle?
- What makes a piano a musical instrument? What makes cymbals a musical instrument? Why aren't two garbage can lids a musical instrument? What is the essence of a musical instrument?

In answering each set of questions, what should emerge is your own explanation-based view of the category——the "essence" of the category. Try the same demonstration with your oh-so-patient friends.

Explanation-based views do a better job of explaining the notion of *category coherence* than do the exemplar and prototype views. When asked to list examples of the category "weapons," how do disparate items, such as guns, knives, missiles, candlesticks, and baseball bats, all gain membership in this category? What is it about these objects that allows them to "hang together," or cohere, as members of the same concept? They certainly don't look similar, yet we have no trouble grouping them together. And conversely, what is it about two seemingly similar animals—a shark and a dolphin—that leads them to be placed in different categories (Ross & Spalding, 1994)? They look similar but we categorize them differently. According to the explanation-based view, a category is not the set of common features that objects share. So the fact that guns and knives don't look like each other and don't share an identifiable set of features doesn't matter; it's our idea about the essence of a weapon that must be similar. And our idea about the essence of a weapon is consistent with guns, knives, and baseball bats; consequently, they are placed in the same category. Also, the fact that dolphins and sharks share structural similarities doesn't matter. What matters is that our knowledge of dolphins and their essence (they're mammals) is not similar to our knowledge of sharks and their essence (they're fish). Based on these essential differences, these two do not cohere and are categorized differently.

Komatsu (1992) notes that a couple of problems arise in considering the explanation-based approach. Given the view's relative recency, it remains underspecified. The notion of psychological essence is rather vague, and it's not yet clear exactly what types of explanations and theories do and do not make up the essence for any given concept. A related problem noted by Komatsu is how to distinguish between what one knows about a concept and one's representation of a concept. For example, consider once again the concept "dolphin." An explanation-based view of this concept might include the following: they look like fish but aren't; they're intelligent and friendly enough so that you can swim with them (like Bridget, your second author, did one summer); "Flipper" was a 1960s TV show about a dolphin; and Greg (your first author) had a "Flipper" lunch box when he was a child. But now we've blurred the line between a concept of a dolphin and everything we know about dolphins. What's the difference? Where does one leave off and the other begin? Failure to draw this line clearly might make the notion of a concept meaningless for anything other than a descriptive term for what we know about something.

RECURRING RESEARCH THEME
Cognition and Individual Differences

Causal Similarity, Perceptual Similarity, and Children's Categorization

According to the pioneering developmental theorist Jean Piaget (1929), young children categorize things according to their superficial similarity. Rather than classifying objects in terms of causal power (i.e., what the object does), children focus on perceptual attributes (i.e., size, color, shape). However, recent research indicates that children may not be so limited to the superficial characteristics of things in the world and may be capable of using the causal structure of objects in order to classify them. In other words, children have theories of what things are and how they work. These theories, in turn, guide categorization and inferences based on categories (as in the explanation-based view of categorization).

In a series of investigations, Gopnik and Sobel (2000) examined the impact that causal similarity and perceptual similarity have on judgments of category membership. They did so in a somewhat whimsical manner. They "invented" a machine termed a *blicket detector.* This machine would light up and play music when certain objects were placed on it. These objects were termed (of course) *blickets.* Although activation of the blicket detector was under the control of an unseen confederate, children didn't suspect this at all. They accepted the machine and its capabilities at face value.

To find out the basis for children's categorization, Gopnik and Sobel (2000) tested three- and four-year-old children on a category-inference task. The children were shown the blicket detector (they weren't told its name at this point) and the four blocks (A and C were square, B and D were rectangular) presented in Figure 5.19. The experimenter told the child that blocks A and B were blickets and blocks C and D were not blickets. Then block A was placed on the blicket detector, which went off. At this point, the experimenter simply exclaimed, "Look! See, this one set the machine off." Then the experimenter asked the child to indicate which of the other objects (blocks B, C, or D) would set the machine off.

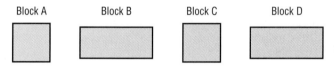

Block A   Block B   Block C   Block D

Figure 5.19 Stimulus blocks used in the Gopnik and Sobel (2000) study. Blocks A and B were labeled as "blickets," while blocks C and D were labeled as "not blickets."

From Gopnik, A., & Sobel, D. M. (2000). Detecting blickets: How young children use information about novel causal powers in categorization and induction. *Child Development, 71,* 1205-1222. Reprinted by permission of the Society for Research in Child Development.

As you can see, Gopnik and Sobel pitted perceptual characteristics against causal characteristics, placing them in conflict to find out which one was more salient to children as they made their classification decision. As just noted, the two blickets are different in shape: one is square and one is rectangular. The question of interest is this: On being informed that block A and B are blickets and then seeing block A set off the blicket machine, which property of block A would they apply to the experimenter's question? A focus on perceptual characteristics would lead the children to choose the perceptually similar object (block C); a focus on the concept that block A is a blicket would lead them to choose the other blicket (block B). The results demonstrated that the fact that something was called a "blicket" meant much more than perceptual similarity. On 73% of the trials, children chose the item that had the same label (block B) but had a conflicting shape. The perceptually similar item (block C) was chosen on 15% of the trials; and on 12% of the trials, children chose block D, which was neither causally nor perceptually similar.

These results demonstrate that even very young children have the ability to go beyond appearance and use information about causal power to classify objects. A blicket was conceived of not as an object with certain physical properties, but as a causal agent that influenced other entities in predictable ways. Placing items into categories, then, is not a simple judgment of physical similarity; such information can be overridden by deeper conceptual relations, supporting the explanation-based approach to categorization.

STOP *and* REVIEW!

1. Discuss the three different types of categories. How are they different? Provide an example of each.
2. Which of the following level of categorization is most often used when describing objects?
   a. superordinate level
   b. basic level
   c. subordinate level
3. Compare and contrast the classical, prototype, and exemplar views of categorization.
4. Describe the explanation-based view of categorization and how it differs from similarity-based views.

➤ Natural categories refer to groups of naturally occurring entities (e.g., insects). Artifact categories refer to groupings of human-made objects (e.g., furniture). Nominal kinds refer to arbitrary labels applied as a convention to some set of objects or events (e.g., bachelors).

➤ Categories are represented at varying levels of specificity. The most general is the superordinate level (e.g., tools); the most specific is the subordinate level (e.g., ball peen hammer); the most useful level is the basic level (e.g., hammer).

➤ Similarity-based approaches to categorization assume that categorization is a matter of judging the similarity between the target and a representation stored in long-term memory. According to the classical view, we compare targets to a set of features that defines the concept. The classical view is too rigid to account for the graded structure of categories and fuzzy boundaries between them. The prototype approach assumes that we compare objects to a best example from the category. This approach does not account for the variability of categories with context. The exemplar approach proposes that we think of concepts in terms of specific examples. This approach has problems with economy of storage.

➤ Similarity and categorization judgments (which should be the same, according to the similarity-based approaches) behave quite differently under some circumstances. This has led to the explanation-based view of categories, which contends that concepts are represented as explanations or theories about the essence of a concept rather than as instances of the category or a prototype.

GLOSSARY

2½-D sketch: in Marr's theory, an intermediate stage in object identification in which we encode information about the orientation and relative depth of the visible surfaces as well as information about discontinuities in depth and orientation (p. 166)

3-D model: in Marr's theory, a viewpoint-independent construction of a viewed object (p. 166)

ad hoc categories: categories formed "on the fly" in the service of a goal (p. 194)

alexia: a neurological disorder characterized by a deficit in the ability to recognize printed words (p. 188)

artifact categories: categories that include objects or conventions designed or invented by humans to serve particular functions (p. 192)

category: the specific examples designated by a concept (p. 192)

classical view: the view that items are classified into particular categories if they have certain features or characteristics. (p. 194)

concept: a mental representation that allows for determination of whether or not something belongs to the class (p. 192)

exemplar approach: a view of categorization that suggests that we represent categories in terms of examples, or exemplars; when we think about the concept, we retrieve one of these examples (p. 199)

explanation-based approach: the view that categorization is based on a person's general idea or explanation of the essence of a particular concept (p. 201)

family resemblance: the degree of overlap between members of a category (p. 196)

feature analysis: one version of SDB; contends that we recognize patterns (particularly letters) via an analysis and recombination of their component parts (p. 163)

fuzzy boundaries: the notion that separation between some categories (e.g., "games" and "sports") is indistinct (p. 196)

geons: the basic 3-D shapes that form the basis for object recognition, according to the RBC approach (p. 167)

graded structure: the fact that category members differ in how well they present the category (p. 195)

natural categories: categories that naturally occur in the world that, in essence, define themselves (p. 192)

nominal kinds: linguistic conventions that involve the arbitrary assignment of a label to entities that fit a particular set of conditions (p. 192)

object agnosia: a neurological disorder characterized by a deficit in the ability to recognize everyday objects (p. 188)

pandemonium model: one view of feature analysis; postulates hierarchical recognition of component features, building from feature to letter recognition (p. 163)

pattern/object recognition: the processes whereby we match an incoming stimulus with stored representations for the purpose of identification (p. 161)

primal sketch: the first stage in Marr's approach to recognition whereby we encode a rough rendition of the most basic elements of the scene (p. 166)

prosopagnosia: a neurological disorder characterized by an inability to recognize faces (p. 185)

prototype: the most representative member (or members) of a given category (p. 198)

prototype approach: a view of categorization proposing that we categorize by judging similarity between a target concept and a best example from the category (p. 196)

recognition-by-components (RBC): Biederman's view of object recognition; contends that recognition is a matter of separating an image into a structural description and using this description for identification (p. 166)

similarity-based approaches: the view that categorization is a matter of judging the similarity between the target object and some standard in long-term memory (p. 194)

structural-description-based (SDB) approach: contends that we recognize objects by comparing incoming visual information to stored structural descriptions of the objects (p. 163)

template-matching theory: a view of pattern/object recognition whereby we compare incoming patterns to stored whole patterns in memory until we find a match (p. 171)

templates: the stored replicas of patterns that need to be identified (p. 171)

view-based (VB) approach: contends that we recognize objects by comparing incoming visual information to stored whole-object images representing the objects (p. 170)

word-superiority effect: the finding that letters are more easily identified if presented in the context of a word relative to when they're presented in the context of a nonword (p. 175)

6

Encoding and Retrieval Processes in Long-Term Memory

After cheerleading practice, Tom goes back to his apartment and takes a shower. Feeling refreshed, he decides to do a few errands. Gotta run to the grocery store, he thinks, grabbing a piece of paper and a blue pen out of his desk to make a list.

Opening the fridge, Tom grimaces. "Uff-da! I should make a list of what I need to throw away. Oh well, maybe next week. OK, let's see . . . I need milk, cheese, butter, soda . . . "Giving his nose a break, he closes the fridge and checks the cabinets. "Wow! I'm out of everything—spaghetti sauce, pop-tarts, mac 'n' cheese, potato chips, rice, don . . . Darn pen!" Tom says disgustedly, shaking it up and down. He charges into his bedroom, grabs a red pen out of his desk, and heads back to the kitchen to finish the most critical item on the list—donuts.

Catching sight of the TV, he remembers that he needs to return the video he watched last night—"Ferris Bueller's Day Off." Great movie, he thinks. Please be kind; always rewind, he chuckles silently as he pops the video out. Hmmm . . . wanna make sure I don't forget this . . . Aha! Brilliant, he thinks, as he leans the video against the front door.

OK, I'm outta here . . . Drip. What the . . . Drip. Oh, yeah, that faucet I told the landlord about a month ago, he sighs. Guess I should remind him about it . . .

Tom puts on his winter coat and heads for the door. Practically tripping over the video, he picks it up, smiling at his own ingenuity. He bursts outside into the cold.

"Hi Tom! Cold one, huh?"

"Hey, Mr. Scully." Tom shivers. "Yeah . . . a real cold one," he says, hustling away. Once in the car, Tom pounds his head with his hand. The faucet! I forgot to tell him about the faucet! And now he's gone. Oh well . . . next time.

First stop—the video store. Tom fumbles the video into the slot, noting the muffled "plunk." He hustles over to the adjacent grocery store. So what do I need? Tom wonders, reaching for his grocery list. "Oh, no!" he says a little too loudly, furiously tapping his pockets. Should've leaned the list against the front door, too, he muses disgustedly.

Let's see . . . what was it I needed? Milk, cheese, butter, donuts . . . rats!!! That's all I can remember.

After collecting these items, Tom approaches the express checkout, quickening his pace to beat another shopper. Ha! Made it! Just as he sidles into line, the cashier pulls down his microphone. Oh. Not a . . . "Price check on lane 1," echoes through the store. Never fails, Tom despairs.

Gee that cashier looks familiar, Tom thinks. He decides to be friendly. "Don't you attend Thomas Augsburg College?"

"Yeah, but with this weather, I may not be attending today."

"Yeah, I know what you mean. Hey, did you hear they're changing the state motto of Minnesota?" The cashier looks up blankly.

Darn it! Can't remember it. Tom ponders. Let's see, James told me last night when we were studying. Oh yeah! "Minnesota—glove it or leave it!" The cashier chuckles politely and continues to scan the items. Tom, still puzzling about the guy's familiarity, asks, "What's your name?"

"John," the cashier says, still scanning. He's got John Lennon glasses, Tom observes. That should be an easy way to remember him, since I'm a Beatles fan. If I see him on campus, he'll be impressed that I remembered his name.

It would be difficult to overestimate the importance of memory. It serves as the cornerstone of cognition, informing and assisting every process in our cognitive arsenal. As discussed in Chapter 4, working memory is critical for on-line processing of incoming information. Another vital component of memory is our long-term memory. In previous chapters (and subsequent ones) the importance of long-term memory is readily apparent. Long-term memory forms the database for pattern recognition (Chapter 5), language (Chapters 10 and 11), problem solving (Chapter 12), and decision making (Chapter 13). Memory is also important from a personal standpoint; it houses our autobiographies, the personal histories that give us our sense of identity and place in the world (Chapter 8). In this chapter, we're going to take you through the basic workings of long-term memory, including the processes by which you manage to store and retrieve the countless bits of information that form the core of thinking. Just think of all of the manifestations of long-term memory in Tom's afternoon errands. If Tom didn't have long-term memory, he wouldn't have remembered that he had watched a video last night. He wouldn't have remembered who Mr. Scully is. He wouldn't know how to get to the store. He'd be completely lost, existing in a world with no mental reference points.

Fundamental Distinctions

Short-Term and Long-Term Memory (Revisited)

As discussed in Chapter 4, the modal model of memory (Atkinson & Shiffrin, 1968) proposes three memory stores (sensory memory, short-term memory, and long-term memory). The distinction between short-term memory (STM) and long-term memory (LTM) has proven to be controversial. What might be termed a *multiple stores view* (e.g., Cowan, 1995; Pashler & Carrier, 1996) argues that there is good reason for making such a distinction. Alternatively, some theorists (e.g., Crowder, 1993; Nairne, 1992) espouse a *unitary view,* suggesting that short-term and long-term memory are manifestations of the same underlying memory system. While a complete discussion of these theoretical alternatives is beyond the scope of this text, let's briefly consider a phenomenon at the center of the debate—the **serial position effect.** This refers to the finding that items at the beginning of a list (**primacy effect**) and items presented at the end of the list (**recency effect**) are remembered better than items presented in the middle of the list. The existence of this phenomenon is not in question (the general prominence of information that comes first and last is a common pattern in many areas of cognition, as you'll see throughout this book), but the explanation for the recency effect has served as a sort of flashpoint for the STM/LTM debate.

Waugh and Norman (1965) were early proponents of the multiple-stores view. By their account, the recency effect occurs because the items currently being rehearsed (i.e., the items currently in STM) are easily retrieved. Essentially, they're "dumped out" immediately in response to a recall cue. This explanation runs into problems when one considers another finding: there are recency effects in long-term memory (Bjork & Whitten, 1974). Long-term recency effects would seem to provide partial support for the unitary view. However, it is important to note that recency effects in immediate recall are indeed greater than those found in delayed recall. This indicates that there may be different bases for the two recency effects, which is consistent with the multiple-stores view. Currently, the debate continues. Cowan (1995) suggests that future research attempting to resolve the issue should focus on the neural mechanisms underlying short-term and long-term memory processing. Whatever the resolution of the STM/LTM debate turns out to be, there is certainly enough evidence to justify using the distinction as a descriptive device. We will adopt this convention in our subsequent discussion.

The STM/LTM distinction certainly fits well with our conscious experience of memory. Clearly, memory exists in both a limited, immediate, "thinking about it right now" form as well as a more vast "warehouse of information" form that is largely removed from conscious awareness. Let's review some of the characteristics that distinguish our temporary working memory from our more permanent long-term memory. Probably the most salient differences are the limitations (or lack thereof) of the respective systems. Working memory is quite limited, in both duration and capacity. Information can only be held by working memory for a limited period of time, and doing so requires mental rehearsal. Working memory also has severe capacity limits; one can only do so much in the "mental work space." There are ways to get around these limits, to be sure, but the limits are there. Contrast this with long-term memory, which is virtually limitless, both in terms of capacity and duration. Consider all of the important and inane information your friendly author Greg knows. He knows where he lives, how to drive a car, the lyrics to every Beatles song, what he did last night, and what he did on the Fourth of July in 1976. Information in long-term memory has the potential to last a lifetime. In addition, there is always room for more information—a testament to long-term memory's tremendous capacity.

Episodic Memory and Semantic Memory

Tulving (1972, 1983) suggests that there are two distinct types of **long-term memory (LTM):** episodic memory and semantic memory. **Episodic memory** refers to one's memory for personally experienced events that include contextual elements like the time and place of the event's occurrence. **Semantic memory** refers to knowledge of information about the world that does not include contextual elements like the time or place the information was learned. Greg's memory of his first rock concert (the Doobie Brothers on their first of three farewell tours) is an episodic memory. He experienced it in a specific time and place (August 30, 1982, in Colorado). Greg's knowing that the Declaration of Independence was signed on July 4, 1776, is a semantic memory. It's just something that he knows. He wasn't at the signing, so he has no personal memories of it. Tulving (1983) outlines several other key differences between episodic and semantic memory (see Table 6.1). The retrieval of an episodic memory is typically associated with a recollective experience. Greg's memory of his first concert is accompanied by a strong feeling of recollection, almost as if he can place himself there. Semantic memories feature no such recollective experience. They involve the simple retrieval of an isolated fact. Episodic memories are more vulnerable to forgetting. Many of the details of Greg's first concert have faded over time. Semantic memories are relatively resistant to forgetting. Greg will never forget that particular fact about the American Revolution. Episodic memories often include an affective

Table 6.1 Contrasting Characteristics of Episodic and Semantic Memory		
	Memory System	
Characteristic	**Episodic**	**Semantic**
Likelihood of forgetting	High	Low
Usefulness	Low	High
Recollective experience	Present	Not present
Sensory component	Present	Not present
Presence of emotion	Present	Not present

Based on information in Tulving, E. (1983). *Elements of episodic memory.* New York: Oxford University Press.

(emotional) component. Seeing his first rock concert was an exciting experience and is a positive memory. This contrasts sharply with semantic memories. Greg has no emotional connection to the historical fact of the signing of the Declaration of Independence.

As with the distinction between short-term and long-term memory, not all researchers agree that episodic and semantic memory represent two different memory systems; many believe the same memory system underlies both. They point out that there may be as many similarities as differences in the two. Still, as with the STM/LTM distinction, there does seem to be good intuitive and empirical evidence to use the distinction on a descriptive level. In this chapter, we will be dealing primarily with episodic memory, discussing the processes that are used to encode and retrieve events. Semantic memory, our general knowledge base, will be discussed further in Chapter 9. We should note that most of the research in this chapter is tightly controlled laboratory research, so the remembering done by participants (on the face of it) might not always bear a close resemblance to the way you remember every day. As you'll see in Chapter 8, research on episodic memory has expanded considerably, and how we remember everyday life episodes has become the focus of many research studies. In this chapter, we'll be discussing the basic laboratory work that serves as the foundation for this research.

Stop and Think!   **DISTINGUISHING EPISODIC AND SEMANTIC MEMORIES**

Come up with examples of episodic memories (episodes from one's life) and semantic memory (general knowledge about the world). Then examine Table 6.1, which summarizes the key distinctions between these two types of memory. Assess the distinction between these types of memory by analyzing your examples.

- How well does each example fit each of the characteristics listed?
- Do episodic and semantic memories seem truly distinct?
- Why or why not?

A Descriptive Framework: Encoding, Storage, and Retrieval

When memory researchers discuss the processes involved in memory, they often appeal to a disarmingly simple and useful description of memory proposed by Melton (1963), who suggested that the processes of remembering can be characterized in terms of three stages: encoding, storage, and retrieval. **Encoding** refers to the processes involved in acquisition of material. Encoding processes are what you engage in when you're studying material for your next test. You study the material repetitively, generate notes based on what you read, relate it to other material you already know, and/or form a silly picture of it in your head, all in the hope of remembering it later. **Storage** of information involves the formation of some type of memory representation, or *memory trace.* If you've encoded some event (like a class lecture) successfully, there should be some remnant of the study experience. (And to do well on an exam, it had better be a pretty big remnant!)

But simply having this stored remnant of experience is no guarantee that you're going to remember it. Memory depends critically on the final process in this sequence—retrieval. **Retrieval** refers to your ability to get something out a memory once it has been encoded and stored. Think of all the times you've been frustrated while you're taking a test, thinking "I *know* this, but I just can't think of the answer right now!" This is a retrieval failure, and unfortunately, professors don't give partial credit for retrieval failures (although you never know—check your syllabus).

Encoding and Storage.　　The distinction between encoding, storage, and retrieval provides a useful thumbnail sketch for discussing how memory works. In this chapter, the focus will be on the processes of encoding and retrieval and how these processes interact. What about storage, you ask? The term *storage* is used to refer to the state of information once it has been encoded; it doesn't really describe a process. *Encoding* is the term typically used to describe processes of study and retention and is really inseparable from the notion of storage. If something is processed effectively at encoding, then it will be stored. In this chapter, we'll examine exactly what comprises effective processing.

Encoding and Retrieval.　　We're going to discuss encoding processes and retrieval processes separately, but discussing them in this way is mostly a matter of convenience. It turns out that remembering depends critically on the interaction between the two. You no doubt have some intuitive sense that this is the case. You study differently based on the type of test you're going to take. In other words, you change how you encode based on how you'll have to retrieve. As you'll see, memory research has borne out that this intuitive strategy is based on solid empirical ground. The first major section of this chapter will deal with how various encoding factors influence memory. To enhance your understanding of these effects, you should be aware of the explicit-implicit retrieval distinction.

Explicit versus Implicit Memory Tests.　　Remembering is a more complex concept than you might suspect. Memory researchers have drawn a critical distinction between explicit and implicit memory tests. **Explicit memory tests** (or *direct memory tests*) involve conscious recollection of some specific event from the past. The first few decades of cognitive psychology research focused on explicit tests, and the first several sections of this chapter will focus on how encoding processes influence remembering in these sorts of situations.

Sometimes however, experiences and events have an influence on our behavior in the complete absence of conscious memory for that event. Tests that assess these implicit influences have been collectively termed **implicit memory tests** (or *indirect memory tests*). Consider a story from the French neuropsychologist Edouarde Claparede (1911/1951). Claparede had a patient who suffered from **amnesia,** or memory loss due to brain damage. One day, Claparede hid a pin in his hand and greeted this patient with a prickly handshake. The incident was quickly forgotten by the patient. The next time the two met, the amnesic denied having met Claparede. But when Claparede held out his hand for the customary shake (this time without the pin!), the patient refused. When pressed for the reason, she insisted that she had the right to not shake hands. This is quite remarkable; the amnesic demonstrated that she both did and did not remember what had happened previously. In other words, the amnesic demonstrated a failure of explicit memory by failing to recall having met Claparede but showed successful implicit memory in refusing to shake hands with him. As you'll see, the distinction between explicit and implicit memory tests has proven to be essential for describing how various encoding factors affect remembering.

STOP *and* REVIEW!

1. The unitary view assumes
   a. that STM and LTM are distinct memory stores or processes
   b. that STM and LTM are based on the same underlying memory system
   c. that episodic and semantic memory are distinct memory stores or processes
   d. that episodic and semantic memory are based on the same underlying memory system
2. Define semantic and episodic memory.
3. Name the three general stages of remembering and briefly describe each.
4. True or false? Implicit memory tests require the conscious recollection of previous events.

➤ The unitary view contends that one underlying memory mechanism is responsible for STM and LTM processing. The multiple-stores view contends that STM and LTM are distinct systems, with distinct underlying processes. Serial position effect (better memory for the initial and final items in a list) is sometimes offered as evidence for the distinction.

➤ Long-term memory is often subdivided into episodic memory (memory for personally experienced events that include context) and semantic memory (context-free general knowledge about the world).

➤ There are three basic stages involved in memory: encoding refers to the processes whereby events are taken in; storage refers to the retention of these events over time; retrieval refers to the processes whereby information is recalled.

➤ Explicit tests of memory (often termed *direct*) require the conscious recollection of a specific event, while implicit tests of memory (often termed *indirect*) do not.

Encoding Processes in Explicit Long-Term Remembering

It's obvious that your ability to remember something depends on what you do as the information is coming in. Think about the steps you take when you really want to remember something. What do you do to increase your chances of remembering? In this section, we'll talk about some of the fundamental encoding factors that influence LTM. Keep in mind that the research discussed in this section deals primarily with explicit memory tests—memory tests that require conscious recollection. The rules may be different for implicit memory tests, as you'll see later.

Attention

As you learned in Chapter 4, attention is the gateway to conscious processing. So it should come as no surprise that attention plays a critical role in long-term memory. Quite simply, you're more likely to recollect something to which you've paid attention. Think about sitting in class, listening to your professor. You're not going to recollect much of anything from the lecture if you're tuning in to the juicy gossip behind you instead of to what the professor is saying. A simple-minded explanation might be that attention leads to a longer-lasting and more retrievable memory trace. The role of attention is considerably more complex than this simple statement would imply. But there is little doubt that focused attention is necessary for explicit and detailed recollection of some event.

Repetition

Another factor that affects retention is **repetition.** Material that is presented more than once is easier to remember. This principle is so fundamental that Crowder (1976) notes, "If any generalization is basic to the field of learning it is that an experience that occurs twice is more likely to be remembered than a single experience" (p. 264). But the picture gets a bit more complex when we consider the issue of exactly how material is repeated. One important distinction involves how repetitions occur over time. **Massed repetition** involves repeated presentations that occur closely together in time, while **distributed repetition** involves repeated presentations spread out over time. Which do you think works better?

The advantage of distributed repetitions over massed repetitions has been termed the **spacing effect,** and this effect has been found in numerous empirical investigations (Melton, 1970; Glenberg, 1974). Why should repetitions spaced out over time be better than repetitions that are crammed together? Researchers have proposed two likely explanations, both of which have some empirical support (Greene, 1992). These accounts place the locus of the spacing effect at different stages of the remembering process. The *deficient-processing view* focuses on encoding, suggesting that massed repetitions lead to deficient processing of the second presentation—you simply don't pay much attention to the later presentations relative to the first (Hintzman, Block, & Summers, 1973). As a result, you only have one fully encoded memory representation rather than many. The *encoding variability view* is similar in that it contends that massed presentations amount to little more than one presentation, but it places the locus of the effect at retrieval. According to this view, under massed presentation conditions, there is little or no variation in how the repeated events are encoded into memory, so the corresponding memory representations will be similar and relatively indiscriminable. This will make them more difficult to "find" in a memory search relative to when presentations have been distributed. When repetitions are distributed in time, each encoding will be relatively distinct from the others, so you're more likely to "stumble on" one of them during your memory search.

It's not difficult to find an everyday example and a practical application of the spacing effect. Think about how you study. Does it seem more akin to massed or distributed

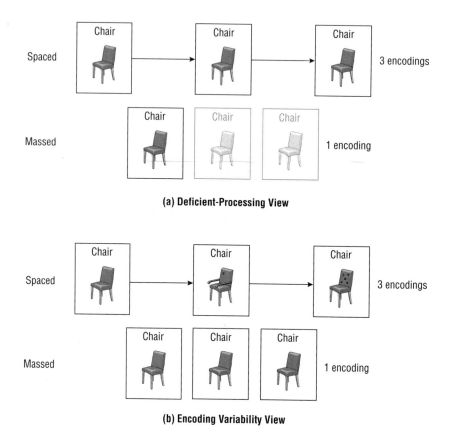

(a) Deficient-Processing View

(b) Encoding Variability View

repetition? If you're like many students, you cram more than you should. Cramming—trying to learn material with massed repetition within a relatively short time span—is a relatively ineffective study technique if your goal in college is to learn what is being taught (a sensible goal, given that you're investing a not-so-small fortune in it!). Research on the spacing effect suggests that your study time would be better spent spread out over a longer period. That is, when presenting yourself with stimuli from your classes (i.e., studying your notes and your text), you should distribute your presentations. But if you have tuition money to burn and are only interested in learning information for the next test, then massed repetitions are the ticket. But get your tuition dollar's worth—you never know, you may need the information on a cumulative final, in a later class, or (gasp) in real life!

Rehearsal

It should come as no surprise to you that **rehearsal,** which is basically mental practice, improves memory. It's easy to confuse the concepts of repetition and rehearsal, because they are closely related. Repetition refers to the fact that an item is experienced more than once, whereas rehearsal refers to how that item is thought about internally. Let's consider the processes involved in the mental practice of information and how these processes relate to remembering.

Maintenance Rehearsal.   To a large extent, memory follows the old axiom "Practice makes perfect." As discussed in Chapter 4, rehearsal is important for maintaining information in working memory and, according to some early models of memory (Waugh & Norman, 1965; Atkinson & Shiffrin, 1968), may be instrumental in encoding it permanently in LTM. But as was the case with the seemingly straightforward variable of repetition, simple rehearsal isn't as effective as you might think. An experiment by Craik and Watkins (1973) demonstrates how truly ineffective it can be. Participants were presented with lists of words, and their task was to keep track of the words that began with a specific letter (e.g., *p*). At the end of each list, participants were to report the last word that had begun with that letter. If you were a participant, you might be presented with *cherry, plow, tiger, desk, house.* After presentation of the list, your job would be to say "plow." How would you accomplish this fairly simple task? Probably by mentally rehearsing the word *plow* over and over until you got another *p* word or until you had to report the word *plow*, whichever came first. Consider this list: *tree, peach, carpet, table, igloo, garlic, bird, clock.* Your response would be *peach.* In this case, you would have to rehearse the word *peach* approximately twice as many times as the word *plow.* At the end of the experiment, when asked to recall all of the words from each list, you might think that this increase in rehearsal would make it more likely that you'd remember the rehearsed word. It doesn't. Craik and Watkins varied the number of intervening items (and hence the amount of rehearsal) from 2 to 12 items, and found no difference in later recall.

The type of rehearsal employed in this situation is aptly termed **maintenance rehearsal,** because all you're doing is maintaining the item in consciousness, with little or no embellishment. Trying to memorize information from your class notes by simply repeating the information over and over is not a very effective technique. Certainly, repeating it once is better than not repeating it at all, but after one presentation there seems to be little in the way of additional memory benefit. So if you use maintenance rehearsal to study, one thorough exposure is as good as several. Based on your experience with college tests, you're probably thinking that one simple rehearsal would not be sufficient to pass most class tests.

But the story on maintenance rehearsal isn't quite so simple. Recall the earlier discussion about the importance of the interaction between the stages of encoding and retrieval. Whether or not you get any benefit from maintenance rehearsal depends on the retrieval task. Let's take a short detour and talk about the two most common explicit retrieval tasks, recall and recognition. Suppose you're a participant in a memory experiment and you're presented with 48 words, followed by a memory test. If you're tested with **recall,** you are given little or nothing to work with in terms of hints, and the task is to come up with as many of the 48 items as you can. In **recognition,** the task is a bit easier. You're presented with a large set of items that includes the items presented earlier and some other items. Your task is to distinguish the two. Usually, recognition proves to be easier than recall, because in recognition you actually get to see the correct answers—you need only recognize them.

Now, back to the effects of maintenance rehearsal. While maintenance rehearsal is relatively ineffective in enhancing one's ability to recall information, it does lead to some improvement in the ability to recognize it. Successful recognition depends on the degree to which you've thoroughly processed an individual item, whereas recall depends more on making associations between the to-be-remembered items (Anderson & Bower, 1973; Gillund & Shiffrin, 1984). When you consider this, it's not difficult to see why maintenance rehearsal helps recognition but not recall. Repeating an individual item over and over will lead to more thorough processing of that individual item but will do little or nothing to build associations between items on a list (Nairne, 1983).

Let's consider the practical implications of these findings. In general, maintenance rehearsal is a relatively ineffective way to remember something. It helps in laboratory tests of recognition where you have to answer the question "Did you see this concept before?" But real-world memory situations are never this simple. Professors never ask "Do you remember the term *rehearsal* from your reading?" If they did, everyone would get 100% on every test. You're more likely to be asked "What's the difference between rehearsal and repetition?" Simply recognizing the word *rehearsal* isn't going to help you answer this question. So although maintenance rehearsal may be effective in certain laboratory settings, it is a relatively inefficient technique for committing information to memory (Greene, 1992). There are much better uses for your study time.

Elaborative Rehearsal. A better alternative to maintenance rehearsal is **elaborative rehearsal.** This involves thinking about the meaning of the information that is to be remembered, as well as making associations from that information to information already stored in memory.

An early study by Hyde and Jenkins (1969) demonstrates the effectiveness of this type of processing. Participants encoded single words by making a simple judgment about each. They were to rate the pleasantness of the word, estimate the number of letters in the word, or determine whether the word had an *e*. Hyde and Jenkins were interested in how well the words themselves would be remembered. The results were clear-cut. Memory was much better when participants were required to judge the pleasantness of words relative to when they were noticing *e*'s or counting letters.

Consider the differences in these tasks. Judging the pleasantness of words requires that you think about what the word means and may even make you think about some associated information. For example, judging whether Jello is pleasant or unpleasant requires you to think about what Jello is and may even trigger a thought about the red-white-and-blue-layered Jello salad you enjoy at family picnics on the Fourth of July. Counting the number of *e*'s in Jello would produce nothing like this. You would give the word a simple read but little quality thought.

One surprising aspect of this finding is that this advantage occurred in both incidental learning and intentional learning. Under **incidental learning** conditions, participants are not told that memory will be tested. Instead, they are under the impression that the encoding task is the sole focus of the experiment. Under **intentional learning** conditions, participants are explicitly told that they are participating in a memory experiment and that the encoded material will be tested later. Hyde and Jenkins found a memory advantage when participants were just reading words and making simple judgments about the words, as long as the judgments made participants consider the meaning of the concept. It didn't even matter if participants were trying to remember the words. They just did, because they gave the words quality processing. Given these findings, memory research began to focus on the effects of different types of processing on memory.

Stop *and* Think!

MASSING, DISTRIBUTING, MAINTAINING, AND ELABORATING

You've read about the benefits of repetition and rehearsal as well as their variations. Suppose you combined these two variables and came up with the following four encoding conditions:

1. massed repetitions/maintenance rehearsal
2. distributed repetitions/maintenance rehearsal
3. massed repetitions/elaborative rehearsal
4. distributed repetitions/elaborative rehearsal

Rank each these four conditions in terms of the quality of memory you think they would produce. Explain your ordering. Test your predictions by getting 4 friends, and giving them each one of the list versions below, along with the appropriate instruction. The numbering of the following instructions corresponds to the numbering of the conditions presented above: Did you find your predicted results?

1. *Instruction:* As each word is presented, repeat it over and over silently. (Use list on left.)
2. *Instruction:* As each word is presented, repeat it over and over silently. (Use list on right.)
3. *Instruction:* As each word is presented, think of an associate of the word. For example, if presented with the word *tiger,* you might think of *lion.* (Use list on left.)
4. *Instruction:* As each word is presented, think of an associate of the word. For example, if presented with the word *tiger,* you might think of *lion.* (Use list on right.)

List for 1 and 3	*List for 2 and 4*
earth	earth
earth	ambulance
spinach	cotton
spinach	square
ambulance	spinach
ambulance	earth
cotton	machine
cotton	nutmeg
machine	oxygen
machine	cotton
square	square
square	ambulance
nutmeg	spinach
nutmeg	oxygen
oxygen	machine
oxygen	nutmeg

Levels of Processing

The notion that memory depends on how information is processed at encoding served as the foundation for Craik and Lockhart's (1972) landmark **levels-of-processing theory.**

This theory serves as an alternative to the modal model of memory. Recall that the modal model focuses primarily on structural aspects of memory, proposing the existence of separate storage systems along with principles regulating the transfer of information between memory stores. How the incoming information was processed was not ignored by this model, but it was not central.

Craik and Lockhart made processing the focus of their approach, proposing that how incoming information is processed is the critical determinant of whether that information is remembered. According to their theory, analysis of incoming information proceeds from a shallow and superficial analysis of structural features to a more deep and thorough analysis of meaning. The primary determinant of whether information is remembered is how far processing gets on this continuum. Information that is processed to a deep level will be better remembered than information processed only to a shallow level. Craik and Tulving (1975) propose that maintenance rehearsal has relatively little impact on later memory, because processing never gets beyond the superficial level. They propose *elaborative rehearsal* as a superior alternative. During elaborative rehearsal, the analysis of incoming information proceeds to a deeper, more meaningful level.

Let's apply this analysis to Hyde and Jenkins's (1969) study. According to the levels-of-processing approach, the different encoding tasks led participants to process information to different levels. Simply noting *e*'s or estimating the number of letters in a word can be accomplished with only a superficial level of analysis. Deciding whether a word is pleasant requires more; you need to proceed all the way from encoding the physical features of the word to thinking of the word's meaning and whether or not it is a pleasing concept. This more extensive level of analysis leads to a more enduring and retrievable memory trace.

As fresh and popular as the levels-of-processing approach was when it was introduced, its vagueness was troublesome to many. For example, the word *mouse* is remembered better when it's presented with the question "Is this an animal?" relative to when it's presented with the question "Does this word rhyme with house?" Why? Because the first condition leads to a deeper level of processing. But how do we know the first question leads to deeper processing than the second? There seems to be no clear answer other than "Because you remember it better." Depth of processing is used as an explanation for memory performance, and then memory performance is used to define depth of processing. This circular definition is really no definition at all. (You may remember the notion of a circular definition from our discussion of capacity in Chapter 4.) In order to avoid this circularity, we need something else (besides memory performance) that indicates a deep level of processing.

Depth of Processing or Transfer-Appropriate Processing?

In general, research inspired by the levels-of-processing paradigm has told us a great deal about the nature of encoding processes and how they relate to remembering. However, the levels-of-processing paradigm is a bit narrow in that it emphasizes encoding processes as the primary determinant of memory, failing to discuss retrieval at any length. Morris, Bransford, and Franks (1977) propose the notion of **transfer-appropriate processing** as an alternative. According to these authors, no encoding task is inherently better than another in terms of leading to retrievable memory representations, as the levels-of-processing paradigm implies. According to the notion of transfer-appropriate processing, what qualifies as memorable processing at encoding is defined by what is required at retrieval. In other words, the information gained in the study phase is going to have to transfer to retrieval situation, so the processing performed at encoding should be appropriate for how it's to be retrieved. That is, processing should be transfer-appropriate.

Morris, Bransford, and Franks disagree with the levels-of-processing notion that a deep encoding task generally leads to a durable and retrievable memory trace. They claim that the memory that results from a surface encoding task might indeed be durable, but the typical memory test doesn't pick up on the information that was encoded (i.e., structural information about the word). According to this analysis, if the memory test did make use of this information, then shallow processing might actually lead to better performance than deep processing.

The authors tested their hypothesis in a clever series of experiments. In one experiment, participants encoded words either semantically (deep processing), by judging whether a word (e.g., *train*) fit in a sentence (The _____ had a silver engine), or phonologically (shallow processing), by judging whether a word (e.g., *eagle*) rhymed with a second word (*legal*). They tested memory with either a traditional recognition test (described earlier) or a *rhyme-recognition test*. In the rhyme-recognition test, participants had to recognize words that rhymed with the words they encoded. For example, the word *regal* would appear on the recognition task, and participants had to indicate if this word rhymed with one of the studied words. According to the levels-of-processing approach, a more durable memory trace is created in the semantic condition, so participants in this condition should remember more words, regardless of the test. According to transfer-appropriate processing, both encoding conditions create durable memory traces, but ones that contain different information. Semantically encoded words should be better remembered on the typical recognition test, which requires access to the concepts represented by the words. Conversely, phonologically encoded words should be better remembered on the rhymeing recognition test, which requires access to phonological information—that is, the spoken label for the word.

The results, displayed in Table 6.2, support the transfer-appropriate-processing analysis, demonstrating what might be termed a reverse levels-of-processing effect. On the rhyme-recognition test, words processed less deeply were remembered better. What mattered the most was not depth of processing but whether the encoding process was appropriate for the memory test. The notion of transfer-appropriate processing reflects the move of memory research away from the simple analysis of encoding variables toward a focus on the interaction between encoding and retrieval. You'll read more about this later.

Organization

In our discussion of depth of processing, we noted that the degree to which we think about the meaning of an event is important for memory. Conversely (or perhaps we should say

Table 6.2 Data from Morris, Bransford, and Franks (1977) Study

	Rhyme Recognition	Standard Recognition
Semantic Encoding	0.33	0.84
Rhyme Encoding	0.49	0.63

From Morris, D. C., Bransford, J. D., & Franks, J. J. (1977). Levels of processing vs. transfer-appropriate processing. *Journal of Verbal Learning and Behavior, 16,* 519–533. Copyright 1977, Elsevier Science (USA). Reprinted by permission.

"In a complementary manner"), memory also depends on the degree to which individual events are organized or structured. The term **organization** can refer to either the characteristics of the incoming information (i.e., whether this information is structured in some way) or to the strategic orientation of the encoder (i.e., whether a person attempts to organize the incoming information).

Stimulus Organization. The degree to which incoming information is structured exerts powerful effects on memory, as demonstrated in a study by Bower, Clark, Lesgold, and Winzenz (1969). It's extremely unusual for participants in a memory study to achieve perfect recall, but that is exactly what happened in this study. Bower and colleagues presented participants with four different lists of items to be encoded. Each set of items belonged to a particular category. For example, a list of items could belong to the category "minerals," and the subcategories "metals" and "stones." The experiment featured a very simple design. Participants in the organized condition saw the items organized into their respective taxonomic categories (e.g., "precious stones"), while participants in the unorganized condition were presented with the items in a random arrangement. Memory was tested with *multitrial free recall*. Participants attempted to learn the lists and then recall them; this learn-and-recall cycle was done three more times (four total cycles). The results were striking: participants in the organized condition recalled over 90% of the items by the second trial and were perfect on the final two trials. In contrast, the unorganized group never got up to 70% recall, even after studying the same lists four times.

Organization could have played a role in Tom's memory for the items on his grocery list. He left his list at home but remembered to get four items on the list. He may have remembered three of those items (milk, cheese, and butter) because they could be easily organized into a category (e.g., "dairy products"). Later, we will learn why he may have remembered the fourth item (donuts).

Strategic Organization. In addition to the organizational structure inherent in the to-be-remembered information, deliberately imposing structure on incoming information can also be a powerful determinant of effective encoding. Such organization might be considered a close companion to chunking in working memory (discussed in Chapter 4). Recall that chunking refers to recoding information into meaningful groupings of information, thereby lightening the load of what must be recycled in working memory. Imposing structure while encoding the information for later recall accomplishes the same thing. The organizational scheme employed facilitates the rehearsal and/or formation of associations between the bits of information as they are being encoded. It also serves as a structure that can be used for later retrieval as we retrace the associations formed at encoding.

We are such resourceful information processors that we will use organization to aid our memory even in the absence of an obvious list structure. Tulving (1962) was interested in the degree to which participants would impose their own organizational schemes on incoming information, so he used lists of words that had no inherent structure; the list items were unrelated to one another. As in the Bower and colleagues (1969) study, memory was tested with multitrial free recall. Over the course of the first two presentations, Tulving thought that participants would form idiosyncratic categories. They would think of certain words together and use this subjective organization to impose structure on the unstructured list. And, in keeping with the finding that organization helps memory, he hypothesized that people who showed more of these idiosyncratic categories (i.e., people who employ subjective organization) would recall more on the third recall trial. The results support his hypothesis. The patterns of recall for the first two trials revealed that participants consistently grouped certain items together, and participants who did this to a greater degree remembered more. So, even when the materials do not lend themselves to organization, we impose our own organization in order to help us recall the information.

Distinctive Encoding

Intuitively, it seems as though concepts or events that "stand out from the crowd" are especially well-attended to and well-remembered. This intuition receives further empirical support from memory research focusing on the effects of distinctiveness on remembering. **Distinctiveness** refers to the degree to which an event contrasts with other events in a surrounding context (although there are a number of other ways to define distinctiveness; see Schmidt, 1991). A classic demonstration of the effects of distinctiveness on memory, the **von Restorff phenomenon** (von Restorff, 1933), was studied extensively in the early days of cognitive psychology. Early investigations of the phenomenon involved presenting a list of items with one item that "stuck out like a sore thumb" (e.g., in a different color); the "isolated" item is often particularly well-remembered (Wallace, 1965). You've already read about an example—Tom's grocery list. All of the items on the list were written in blue ink except for (do you remember?) *donuts.* You'll note that this was the other item he remembered to get at the grocery store. The fact that *donuts* was written in red may have made it slightly more attention grabbing, resulting in enhanced rehearsal.

Self-Reference

As we've seen, research on levels of processing has demonstrated that words processed deeply (i.e., in terms of their meaning) are remembered well. Later research by Rogers, Kuiper, and Kirker (1977) revealed an encoding condition that seems deeper than deep. In their experiment, participants encoded words (e.g., *happy*) with different types of encoding questions, as in the levels-of-processing studies, with one exception: they added an encoding condition they termed "self-reference." Words in this condition (e.g., *generous*) were encoded with the question "Does this term describe you?" The results demonstrated the standard levels-of-processing effect, with a twist: words that were self-referenced were remembered even better than those deeply processed. Over the last quarter-century, many studies have replicated and extended this basic **self-reference effect,** establishing it as a robust memory phenomenon (Symons & Johnson, 1997).

Why is relating information to yourself such an effective technique? In their review of studies on the self-reference effect, Symons and Johnson (1997) conclude that self-reference promotes good memory through elaboration and organization. Because the self is such an elaborate, well-developed, and well-practiced network of knowledge, it offers incredible potential for both elaborative and organizational processing. The implications for your own memory are clear. Chances are that you'll increase the likelihood of remembering something to the degree that you can relate it to yourself. Processing in this way encourages both organization and elaboration of the incoming information, and this, in turn, makes it more likely that you'll remember it.

You have already seen an example of the self-reference effect. Tom wanted to remember the cashier's name just in case he ever saw him on campus. Therefore, he made a connection between the cashier and one of his favorite music artists—John Lennon. By relating the clerk's name to something already stored in LTM and making that connection personally relevant (i.e., using self-reference), Tom made it much more likely that he'll be able to retrieve the name.

Visual Encoding

Visual encoding is another factor that has a powerful impact on memory. As with organization, the use of visual encoding can be either an aspect of the information being encoded (pictorial stimuli) or an image-based encoding strategy (imagining something as you study it). Information that is encoded in pictorial form or with the use of image-based rehearsal processes tends to be well-remembered. This basic finding has been demonstrated in a couple of different experimental contexts. First, a number of studies (e.g., Paivio & Csapo, 1969; Yuille & Paivio, 1969) have compared memory for concrete and easy-to-imagine concepts like "candle" with memory for abstract and difficult-to-imagine concepts like "truth." As you might expect, concrete concepts are more likely to be remembered than are more abstract ones. In a similar vein, Madigan (1974) demonstrated what has been coined the **picture superiority effect.** In his experiment, participants either read simple concepts (e.g., "tiger"), or viewed simple line drawings of the same concepts (e.g., a picture of a tiger). Concepts were more likely to be remembered if they were presented as pictures rather than as words.

What accounts for the advantage in memory for easily visualized material? According to Paivio's **dual-code theory** (Paivio, 1971), there are two distinct representational systems in memory. One system is verbal and includes symbolic codes corresponding to the verbal description of an event. The other system is imaginal and includes symbolic codes that correspond to the actual physical object. Concrete concepts and concepts presented as pictures are encoded into both systems, while abstract concepts are encoded only verbally. Memory is enhanced when a concept is encoded by two systems rather than just one. Once again, the ramifications for your own memory are clear. Visualization is an extremely powerful strategy for improving your own memory. Indeed, as you'll see in a while, it serves as the primary basis for a number of effective memory improvement techniques. However, using visual imagery is a bit difficult, because much of what you have to remember on a daily basis doesn't lend itself very well to visualization. But to the degree that you can translate information into an image or visual representation, your memory will be enhanced. We'll revisit the question of whether a special code or mode of processing exists for mental images in our discussion of knowledge representation in Chapter 9.

Stop *and* **Think!**   **YOU'RE THE PROFESSOR!**

Congratulations! You've just been designated "Professor for a Day." (Prepare for a pay cut!) Imagine you have to teach a class of college freshman about what cognitive psychology is (some of the basic information from Chapter 1) and make sure that the information sticks. What techniques could you use to develop an effective and memorable presentation of the important concepts? (Give specific examples.)

STOP *and* REVIEW!

1. True or false? Distributed repetition is more effective than massed repetition.
2. How does transfer-appropriate processing differ from the levels-of-processing approach?
3. This technique is thought to aid memory by activating two different memory codes:
   a. self-reference
   b. imagery
   c. distinctiveness
   d. generation

➤ Attention brings information into conscious awareness, enhancing the likelihood that the information will be stored for the long term. The repetition of information is more effective if distributed over time rather than massed. The advantage of distributed repetition probably derives from producing more easily retrievable memory traces. Elaborative rehearsal is more likely to result in long-term memory storage than maintenance rehearsal.

➤ The levels-of-processing approach emphasizes how information is processed at encoding as a key determinant of memory. Processing involving the analysis of meaning (i.e., deep processing) is more likely to lead to long-term storage than processing that involves a more superficial analysis (i.e., shallow processing). Transfer-appropriate processing cites retrieval as a critical factor, emphasizing that the effectiveness of a study technique will depend on how memory is tested.

➤ Material that is organized tends to be better remembered. Organization can be inherent in the information encoded or used strategically by the encoder. Distinctive encodings (i.e., that stand out from other events) are more likely to be remembered. Visual encoding may enhance memory through a richer (perhaps dual-code) representation in memory. Relating information to oneself (self-reference) enhances memory through elaboration and organization.

Retrieval Processes in Long-Term Memory

Successful encoding and storage of information is necessary but not sufficient to guarantee later memory. Remembering also involves the processes of retrieval, whereby we regain access to encoded information. Of course, as mentioned early in the chapter, retrieval does not occur in isolation from encoding and storage. The effectiveness of retrieval depends on the effectiveness of those two processes as well as on whatever reminders (i.e., **retrieval cues**) are present. This section will focus on the effectiveness of various retrieval cues and will consider how various retrieval tasks and situations interact with the encoding variables discussed earlier.

Availability and Accessibility

It's interesting to note that the process of retrieval went relatively unnoticed in the early days of memory research as investigations focused on encoding and storage (Roediger & Guynn, 1996). Retrieval tasks were seen basically as means to an end, namely, revealing the contents of storage. Failures to retrieve information were seen as failures of encoding (e.g., the material was not processed deeply enough) and/or storage (the material was lost due to disuse or interference). Retrieval itself was never really varied and investigated systematically. The research tide began to turn in the 1960s when Tulving and Pearlstone (1966) asserted that failure to remember information was not necessarily due to encoding or storage failure. These investigators thought it likely that a great deal of information had **availability** in memory but not **accessibility**. Speaking figuratively, the information is sitting there waiting to be retrieved, but the lack of appropriate reminders (i.e., retrieval cues) renders the material unreachable.

You've experienced this distinction every time you've stared at a test question as the critical information fails to come to mind. The problem is not necessarily that the information isn't stored; the information may be there (i.e., it's available), but you can't get to it given the information (retrieval cues) in front of you (i.e, it's inaccessible). The problem is, this is still forgetting, and you're still going to lose points on the test. **Retrieval failure** is now widely recognized as a primary cause (perhaps *the* primary cause) of forgetting.

An investigation by Tulving and Pearlstone (1966) provides a simple illustration of the distinction between availability and accessibility. In this study, participants encoded categorized lists that contained two target words from each of 24 categories. If you were a participant, you might be presented with "type of spice: garlic, parsley." Participants were instructed to remember the target words for a memory test. Some participants were tested with *free recall.* Under these conditions, participants recalled substantially less than half of the items. Tulving and Pearlstone suspected that this failure of recall was not necessarily a complete failure of memory. It's conceivable that all 48 encoded items are available in memory but that a blank piece of paper and instructions to recall the words are not good enough cues to allow access to the information. In other words, memory failure in this situation was due largely to problems in accessibility, or retrieval failure. To test this notion, the authors had other participants take a *cued recall test* in which information is presented to assist the retrieval process. Tulving and Pearlstone provided these participants with the category names (i.e., type of spice) as retrieval cues. Incredibly, in this condition, participants recalled nearly three-quarters of the words. Clearly, they had successfully encoded and stored the information. The locus of the problem had indeed been at retrieval. The information was available, and the right retrieval cues made it accessible.

Encoding Specificity

It's clear that retrieval cues are critical to remembering. This begs another question: What types of cues are most effective? What types of cues helped Tom as he was trying to remember a joke a friend told him? He wanted to relay the joke to the grocery store cashier and was having trouble remembering. His forgetting was quite likely a retrieval failure, because the joke was recently attended to, comprehended, and enjoyed. What did Tom do to jog his memory? He tried to place himself back in the situation where he'd heard the joke. This was a good idea; memory retrieval is aided by a cue to the extent that the cue helps reconstruct the encoding situation. In other words, memory depends on the amount of overlap between what's happening at retrieval and what happened at encoding. This fundamental retrieval principle is termed *encoding specificity*. According to this principle, the appropriate retrieval cues for the joke Tom heard are determined by what happened as he encoded the joke, because all of this information was stored as part of the memory.

Let's consider a classic investigation by Thomson and Tulving (1970) that demonstrated the **encoding specificity principle.** Participants encoded weakly related word pairs, like *plant-bug,* where the word *bug* was the word that had to be remembered (i.e., the target). After encoding a list of such pairs, a cued-recall test was given in which a cue was presented for each of the targets. Thomson and Tulving compared two retrieval conditions. In one condition, a strongly related word was presented to cue the target. For example, the participant would see *insect* as a cue for *bug*. In the other condition, the word from the original word pair was presented as a cue for *bug* (i.e., *plant*). Intuitively, which word do you think would be a better cue for *bug*? It seems as though *insect* would be; it's a synonym for the target and a very strong associate. But as it turns out, it was a relatively ineffective cue for recall relative to *plant*. Consider why this was the case in light of the encoding specificity principle. The event that has to be retrieved is encountering the pair *plant-bug*. The best retrieval cue will be one that helps reactivate that specific encoding situation, and *plant* is much more effective for this purpose because it was *part* of the encoding situation. If I wanted you to simply say the word *bug, insect* might be a good cue, but if I want you to remember an episode in which you saw the words *plant* and *bug* together, then *plant* is much more effective.

You may have noticed a similarity between the encoding specificity principle and the transfer-appropriate processing principle discussed earlier. The two are quite similar in that they emphasize the overlap between encoding and retrieval as the key determinant of remembering. You might consider them to be opposite sides of the encoding-retrieval coin. The transfer-appropriate processing view focuses on encoding, emphasizing that the encoding processes one uses should be appropriate for how memory is going to be tested. The encoding specificity principle focuses on retrieval, emphasizing that the best retrieval cues are those that tap into how something was encoded. For example, knowledge of the transfer-appropriate processing principle should influence the way you study for a test: you should study in a manner appropriate for the type of test you will be given. Conversely, knowledge of the encoding specificity principle should influence the type of retrieval cues that will be helpful for that test, given the way you studied.

Stop *and* Think!

STUDY SKILLS COUNSELING

Suppose your friends are worried about how to effectively study for their finals. Use the encoding principles and the retrieval principles discussed to generate some study tips that may help. Be specific about what you think your friends should do.

- Would you emphasize encoding or retrieval more?
- Why?
- What specific factors would you emphasize as extremely important?
- Why?
- What factors do you consider less important?
- Why?

Extensions of Encoding Specificity.   Clearly, the nature of retrieval cues is a critical determinant of memory. You might be wondering about how wide-ranging this principle is. Does it extend to the physical environment? Since you learn much of the information in your class in a particular room, should you be in the same room when you're tested? Does the principle extend to how you feel? If you've had a couple of drinks and then meet some new friends, are you more likely to remember their names at the next party after you've had a couple of drinks? Evidence indicates that the encoding specificity principle is quite general. Studies manipulating physical context (e.g., Smith, 1979), presence or absence of music (e.g., Balch, Bowman, & Mohler, 1992), odor (e.g., Schab, 1990), drug or alcohol intake (e.g., Goodwin, Powell, Bremer, Hoine, & Stern, 1969), and mood (e.g., Eich & Metcalfe, 1989) at encoding and retrieval have all revealed **context-dependency effects.** That is, given a particular encoding context, memory is better when retrieval reinstates that context.

The general structure of a context-dependency experiment is outlined in Table 6.3. These experiments generally involve four groups of participants. Some participants encode in context A and also take their memory test in context A. A second group of participants encodes in context A but is switched to context B for their memory test. A third group encodes in context B and is switched to context A for their memory test; and finally, a fourth group encodes in context B and is tested in context B. The prediction from the encoding specificity principle is that for a given encoding condition, memory will be better if the same context is reinstated at retrieval. So condition AA should be better than condition AB, and condition BB should be better than condition BA. It is important to point out that these comparisons are the only ones relevant to the encoding specificity principle. While it may seem reasonable to infer that AA should also be better than BA, this won't necessarily be the case. The encoding specificity principle states that *for a given encoding condition,* memory is best when the retrieval condition matches the encoding condition. A comparison between AA and BA involves different encoding conditions,

Table 6.3 General Format of a Context-Dependency Study

	Retrieval Condition A	Retrieval Condition B
Encoding Condition A	AA—match	AB—mismatch
Encoding Condition B	BA—mismatch	BB—match

Table 6.4 **Results of the Godden and Baddeley (1975) Study**

		Retrieval Condition	
		Under water	On land
Encoding	Under water	32	22
Condition	On land	24	37

From Godden, D. R., & Baddeley, A. D. (1975). Context-dependent memory in two natural environments: On land and underwater. *British Journal of Psychology, 66,* 325–331. Copyright the British Journal of Psychology. Reprinted with the kind permission of the British Psychological Society.

so any differences in memory performance can't necessarily be attributed to the encoding specificity principle.

External Context. If the physical environment in which an event occurs is truly part of the memory representation for the event, then a switch of environments between encoding and retrieval might result in poorer memory due to an encoding-retrieval mismatch. Godden and Baddeley (1975) tested this idea in a unique situation by having deep-sea divers participate in an underwater memory experiment. Divers encoded words in one of two conditions: on a beach or under several feet of water. Later, recall was tested in the same environment in which they had encoded the information or in the other environment. As you can see in Table 6.4, the results revealed a context-dependency effect. If divers had been on the beach during encoding, they were better off on the beach at retrieval. If they had been underwater during encoding, they were better off underwater during retrieval. Consider why this was the case. The divers' memory did not just consist of the encoded words. It also featured the physical environment in which the encoding took place. When this physical environment was presented as a cue at retrieval, memory was enhanced. This general finding has been found across a variety of experimental situations (Smith, 1988).

Internal Context. Rather than manipulating the external context in which items are encoded and retrieved, other studies have manipulated a person's internal context—that is, how they feel internally. In these experiments, some type of internal context (e.g., intoxication, sad mood) is induced in participants, who are then presented with information to remember. The memory test is given to participants in the same context as encoding or in a different context. In these studies, memory tends to be better when the retrieval context matches the encoding context.

A recent study investigated whether context-dependent memory might extend to the internal context associated with aerobic exercise. Miles and Hardman (1998) manipulated the encoding context by having some of their participants pedal an exercise bike vigorously enough to double their heart rate. The other half of the participants simply learned the words while at rest (sitting on the bike but not pedaling). Physiological context was manipulated in the same way at retrieval. The results, displayed in Table 6.5, revealed a context-dependency effect. If

Table 6.5 **Results of the Miles and Hardman (1998) Study, Demonstrating State-Dependent Learning with Aerobic Exercise**

		Retrieval	
		Exercise	At rest
Encoding	Exercise	8.1	6.3
	At rest	7.2	8.2

Adapted from Miles, C., & Hardman, L. (1998). State-dependent memory produced by aerobic exercise. *Ergonomics, 41,* 20–28. Copyright 1998 by Taylor and Francis. Reprinted by permission.

participants had been sweating it out during encoding, they were better off sweating it out during retrieval. If participants had been taking a breather during encoding, they were better off taking a breather during retrieval. Miles and Hardman point out that the findings may have implications for athletes who need to retrieve information in the context of competition. If such retrieval is necessary, it would behoove athletes to encode the information under competitionlike conditions, to enhance the encoding-retrieval match.

Effects of Test Type.   A theme that's becoming increasingly obvious is that various memory phenomena depend on exactly how memory is tested. It should come as no surprise then, that the context-dependency effects discussed above vary with the type of memory test given. Research has shown that context-dependency effects are more likely to occur in free recall than in cued recall or recognition. For example, in the Baddeley (1975) underwater memory experiment, a context-dependency effect was not found when memory was tested with recognition. According to Eich (1980), the more direct the contact between the retrieval cue and the memory trace, the less likely it is that context will be needed as a cue. Cued recall and recognition both offer this direct contact and typically do not show context effects. Basically, the use of context as a cue is a last resort that you'll turn to only when better cues are unavailable. Smith (1988) proposed a similar notion, terming it the

Mismatch between encoding and retrieval.

outshining hypothesis. Basically, it claims that context serves as a useful cue for memory when those cues are most needed. In recall, there are no retrieval cues, so context reinstatement provides some aid to the retrieval process. But in recognition, the retrieval cues are extremely strong (you get to see the item itself), so context reinstatement is not critical. In other words, on recognition tests, test items themselves "outshine" context as a cue.

What are the practical implications of this principle? Students often hear about these dependency effects and worry that perhaps they should eat, sleep, and (mostly) study in the room where they're going to be tested. The results are mixed on whether switching classrooms between study and test has any impact on performance. Metzger and colleagues (1979) found a negative effect of room switching, but other studies (e.g., Saufley, Otaka, & Bravaresco, 1985) have found no effect. There's a few reasons why you needn't worry about taking a test in a different location than where you studied. First, most of the studies demonstrating context dependency use lists of unrelated words as the material to be remembered, which is hopefully not what you're learning in class (see the dean if you are!). Second, context almost certainly gets outshined by other more useful retrieval cues. Smith (1988) suggests that processing information in a meaningful way produces retrieval cues that are likely to outshine context. In other words, if you know the material well, you won't need to rely on the physical context for retrieval help. Also, many tests provide a good many cues (multiple-choice stems, definitions) that would outshine context at retrieval.

Table 6.6 Results from Grant et al. (1998)

a. Percentage correct on short-answer test

		Test Condition		Row Mean
		Silent	Noisy	
Study Condition	Silent	67	46	56.5
	Noisy	54	62	58.0
Column Mean		60.5	54.0	

b. Percentage correct on multiple-choice test

		Test Condition		Row Mean
		Silent	Noisy	
Study Condition	Silent	89	79	84
	Noisy	79	89	84
Column Mean		84	84	

From Grant, H. M., Bredahl, L. C., Clay, J., Ferrie, J., Groves, J. E., McDorman, T. A., & Dark, V. J. (1998). Context-dependent memory for meaningful material: Information for students. *Applied Cognitive Psychology, 12,* 617–623. Copyright 1998, John Wiley & Sons, Ltd. Reprinted by permission.

Although the effects of context dependency may be slight or nonexistent in many classroom situations, a study by Grant and colleagues (1998) suggests that the principle should not be dismissed altogether. If you're like many students, you study under conditions of distraction. The TV or stereo is on, your roommates are talking, or there's a buzz of activity at the library. But you're not tested in the presence of the TV, your stereo, your blabbing roommates, or the noisy library; you're tested in a completely silent room. Is there an effect of this mismatch of conditions (studying with background noise and activity and testing in silence)? To test this, Grant and colleagues followed the standard research design, manipulating the presence or absence of general background noise at both encoding and retrieval. They had participants encode a two-page article on psychoimmunology and tested them with a fill-in-the-blank test followed by multiple-choice questions. The results, shown in Table 6.6, are intriguing; there was no main effect of distraction at encoding. Distracted participants remembered just as much as undistracted participants, which seems to support many a student's claim that studying with background music does not hurt memory. However, this main effect is mediated by an interaction: whether or not participants were distracted at encoding, they were better off in the same environment at retrieval. Consider the ramifications for test performance. Because tests are given in quiet conditions, studying should occur under quiet conditions, maximizing the encoding-retrieval match.

Stop and Think! ENCODING SPECIFICITY AND FOND MEMORIES

Go somewhere you haven't been for a while—a place on campus, a restaurant, anyplace—and see if any memories spontaneously pop into mind. Use the encoding specificity principle to explain why this might have happened.

Retrieval: An Effective Encoding Strategy?

Retrieval is necessary to demonstrate that information has been effectively encoded and stored in memory. However, retrieval itself can also be utilized to enhance your ability to retrieve information at a later point in time. In other words, while studying information that you need to remember, it is useful to periodically attempt to retrieve the information you are trying to encode. This **testing effect** has been found in tests of free recall (Hogan & Kintsch, 1971), cued recall (Allen, Mahler, & Estes, 1969), and recognition (Wenger, Thompson, & Bartling, 1980). Let's take look at a typical study.

In the first phase of a study by Carrier and Pashler (1992, experiment 2), pairs of words were presented to participants for 20 seconds. Each pair consisted of a stimulus term (i.e., the first word was a St. Lawrence Island/Yupik Eskimo language word) and a response term (i.e., the second word was the English equivalent of the stimulus term). The second phase involved a mix of two different trial types. On the pure study (PS) trials, the word pairs were presented once again but for 10 seconds. On the test trial/study trial (TTST) trials, participants were presented with the stimulus word for 5 seconds, and then the response term was added for an additional 5 seconds. On both types of trials the participant was instructed to give the response term associated with each stimulus word as quickly as possible. On the pure study trials, the response term was presented so participants simply had to read it. However, on the TTST trials, participants had to retrieve the response term from memory. In the third phase, participants were given the stimulus words from each pair presented in phase 2 and asked to recall the corresponding response word. The next day, participants returned and were again given the same cued recall test. The results revealed that more words were recalled from TTST trials in both an immediate test (6.4 versus 5.7) and a delayed test (4.6 versus 3.9). This was true despite the fact that in the pure study condition, the response items were physically presented for twice as long (10 seconds) as in the TTST condition (5 seconds).

The Carrier and Pashler findings suggest that the act of retrieving an item was more effective than passive reading. The implications for your studying should be clear; after some level of initial learning has been achieved, you should test yourself on the material by attempting to retrieve the information. For example, when trying to learn new terms, the use of flashcards should be particularly beneficial, because it forces you to attempt to retrieve the definition before flipping over the card and reading the definition. Similarly, generating the answers to questions on a review sheet is a much better strategy than simply reading the section of your text that provides the answer to a review question. So testing yourself proves to be a much more effective study strategy than simply reading a definition or a text section over and over and over . . .

Sound familiar? The latter situation is basically maintenance rehearsal, which as you read earlier in this chapter is a relatively ineffective method for storing information in LTM. The testing effect may give you some insight on how to increase the benefit of maintenance rehearsal. First, read terms and their definitions (or review questions and their answers) a few times to reach some level of initial competency. But then follow these maintenance rehearsal trials by attempts at retrieving the definitions and answers, using the terms and questions as cues. This method should enhance your ability to retrieve information at a later point in time. In addition, retrieval failures will give you an idea of which terms and concepts you know well and which ones need further study.

RECURRING RESEARCH THEME
Cognition and Neuroscience

Encoding, Retrieval, and Brain Hemispheres

As you read in Chapter 2, research on brain functioning has revealed asymmetries in the functioning of the right and left hemispheres, with each half of the brain specialized for different types of processing. Recent research has revealed that this asymmetry in processing extends to the two fundamental processes that we have just discussed: encoding and retrieval. Tulving and his colleagues (Nyberg, Cabeza, & Tulving, 1996; Tulving, Kapur, Craik, Moscovitch, & Houle, 1994) have proposed the HERA (hemispheric encoding/retrieval asymmetry) model.

The HERA model is based largely on the results of neuro-imaging studies. As you know, neuro-imaging techniques such as positron emission tomography (PET) and functional magnetic resonance imaging (fMRI) allow researchers to observe which areas of the brain are more and less active during cognitive processing. Let's take a look at some of the evidence reviewed by Nyber, Cabeza, and Tulving (1996). One task that has been employed extensively in neuro-imaging studies of cognition is a verb-generation task (e.g., Petersen, Fox, Posner, Mintun, & Raichle, 1988), where participants are presented with nouns, one at a time, and are required to generate an appropriate verb. For example, when presented with the word *joke,* the correct response would be "laugh." (Unless it's a joke a professor tells in class, in which case you would say "groan.") This task involves *retrieval from semantic memory.* Knowing the verb that goes along with *joke* is a fact that you just know. It also involves *encoding into episodic memory.* Seeing words like *joke* and thinking of their associates while you're being PET scanned is an event that you'll remember later. Neuro-imaging evidence from the verb-generation task indicates greater activation in the left prefrontal area relative to the same area in the right hemisphere, indicating that the left is instrumental in retrieval of information from semantic memory and encoding of episodic memories. It's also interesting to note that left hemisphere activation is influenced by exactly *how* incoming information is processed. Kapur and colleagues (1994) found that processing items deeply at encoding led to greater left hemisphere activation than processing them shallowly.

Let's contrast this with circumstances in which the right hemisphere is more active than the left hemisphere. Nyber, Cabeza, and Tulving (1996) reviewed evidence from neuro-imaging studies of episodic retrieval. These studies have investigated a wide range of retrieval situations (e.g., free recall, cued recall, recognition) and a wide range of material to be remembered (words, sentences, objects, locations, odors). These situations all involved *episodic retrieval,* because the task was to recollect a specific encoding episode—what happened at some point in the past. Imaging studies of episodic retrieval have produced pretty consistent results. Nearly all of the studies reviewed demonstrated that when recalling or recognizing the occurrence of some past event, there tends to be more intense activation in the prefrontal area of the right hemisphere than in the left.

STOP *and* REVIEW!

1. What does it mean to say that a memory is available but inaccessible?
2. The encoding specificity principle indicates that retrieval will be best when
   a. encoding conditions and retrieval conditions are different
   b. encoding conditions and retrieval conditions are the same
   c. multiple retrieval attempts are made
   d. the person's mood at encoding matches their mood at retrieval
3. True or false? If you test memory with recognition, you're more likely to find a context-dependency effect than if you test it with recall.
4. In studying for a Spanish test, would it be more beneficial to repeatedly read a Spanish word and its English translation, or present yourself with the Spanish word and try to retrieve its English translation? Why?

➤ Information stored in LTM (i.e., it's available) may not be remembered because the retrieval cues are insufficient (i.e., it's not accessible). Retrieval failure is a common cause of forgetting.

➤ According to the encoding specificity principle, a retrieval cue will be effective to the degree that it overlaps with the information provided at encoding. A closely related finding is that memory tends to be better when the context present at retrieval matches the context that was present at encoding. This applies to both external (i.e., physical surroundings) and internal (i.e., mood, body state) contexts.

➤ Context-dependency effects depend on how memory is tested. According to the outshining hypothesis, context-dependency effects are more likely to found on free recall tests (few retrieval cues) than in cued recall or recognition (more retrieval cues), because the presence of other retrieval cues tends to outshine the context cue.

➤ The testing effect indicates that periodic retrieval of to-be-remembered information during acquisition is more beneficial for later retention than simply studying the to-be-remembered information for more time. Retrieving information from semantic memory seems to be associated with left frontal activity in the brain, while episodic retrieval is associated with right prefrontal activity.

Implicit Memory

For the first part of the chapter, we've been talking about memory retrieval as a deliberate, conscious process. All of the retrieval situations we've discussed involve people consciously thinking back to some previous experience (an encoded list or story) and remembering everything they can. These retrieval situations require conscious recollection of a previous episode for successful performance. Free recall, cued recall, and recognition all have one thing in common—an explicit instruction to mentally reinstate a previous experience and recollect what happened. Over the past 20 years, it's become apparent that this is only part of the retrieval story. Even if something isn't remembered explicitly, it may still have an impact on your attitudes, feelings, or behavior. In other words, you may "remember" something without really "remembering" it. Memory tests that reflect this type of remembering are termed *implicit memory tests* and do not require conscious recollection of a previous episode for successful performance. Memory is reflected implicitly—as an improvement or change in some task that occurs even if the participant remembers nothing about the original event.

Here's an example of implicit memory in everyday life. We were moving into our new house, carrying box after box into the house and up the stairs. Later that day, Greg found that a song was running through his head. He was whistling and humming it, and he had no idea why, much to his frustration (you know the feeling). The song was "Handle with Care" by the Traveling Wilburys. After thinking about it for a few hours, it finally came to him why he was whistling that song. Most of the boxes he had carried up the stairs earlier had "Handle with care" printed on the side, which in turn had led him to whistle that song. Although throughout the day, he had no explicit memory of reading that phrase, his whistling of the tune was a reflection of implicit memory.

Schacter (1996) and other researchers (e.g., Brown & Murphy, 1989) suggest that implicit memory may lie at the heart of **unconscious plagiarism.** In some instances, you come up with what you think is a brilliant idea—that is, until the friend you're describing it to informs you that they had the same idea and discussed it with you three months ago. Your failure to recall that it was your friend's idea is a failure of explicit memory. Yet you do remember the encoding episode implicitly, as reflected by your generating the idea you encountered in your earlier conversation. Former Beatle George Harrison (who was one of the Traveling Wilburys, by the way) may have been an unwitting victim of implicit memory. The melody for Harrison's song "My Sweet Lord" sounded a little bit too much like "He's So Fine," an earlier hit by the Chiffons. Harrison acknowledged being aware of the song but denied copying it. The court found the similarity between the tunes too great to be an accident and ruled against Harrison. Interestingly, the actual ruling included language basically stating that in composing the song, Harrison must have been "subconsciously" primed by the earlier song (Schacter, 1996).

Schacter (1996) also suggests that implicit memory may lie at the heart of déjà vu experiences. Déjà vu occurs when we have the distinct impression or feeling that we've been in some place or had some experience before, when in reality we have not. Berrios (1995) claims that (in keeping with the encoding specificity principle) some piece of a memory gets activated by a cue, but the entire memory is not retrieved. Instead, one is left with a feeling of familiarity that cannot be readily explained. Hence, déjà vu may be an expression of the encoding specificity principle in the form of an implicit memory.

Experiments that investigate implicit memory start out the same way as the studies we've been discussing: participants study some type of information, most commonly a word list. Later, memory is tested. Just as explicit memory is assessed with a battery of different retrieval tasks (free recall, cued recall, and recognition), a number of different tasks have been developed to assess implicit memory. In **word-fragment completion,** you're faced with a word where some letters are there and some aren't, and your task is to come up with the appropriate word. (Think of the game show "Wh_ _l of F_rt_ne.") In **word-stem completion,** the initial three letters of a word are presented, and your task is to complete the stem with the first word that comes to mind.

A participant in an implicit memory experiment encodes a list of words. Later, when given the implicit memory test, there is no mention of these previously encoded words. But presenting the word earlier primes the person to come out with it later, either by successfully completing the word fragment with the previously seen word or by blurting out the previously seen word, given a stem that could be completed by several possibilities. For example, if you've seen the word *garlic* in a list an hour ago, when you see the word stem *gar_____*, you're quite likely to respond "garlic" (rather than "garbage," "gargoyle," "garden," or some other nonpresented word).

Implicit memory is typically measured in terms of **priming,** or the benefit in performance from previous exposure to a word. Let's consider an example, depicted in Table 6.7. Say you encoded a list of 5 words and were tested a week later with 10 word fragments that included those 5 words, and 5 other words. Let's say you successfully complete 4 of the 5 fragments with words you saw earlier, or 80%. For the other 5 word fragments, you only manage to complete 1, or 20%. In this example, priming is 60%—there is a 60% benefit in performance from having seen the words earlier. And it's important to note that you may not be able to consciously recollect any of the words you saw; still, having seen them will help you complete a word fragment. So a memory benefit can occur from previous exposure to a word in the absence of conscious recollection of the word.

Table 6.7 A Word-Fragment Completion Study

Words are encoded, and fragments based on these words are given at the test. Completion rates for these encoded words are compared with completion rates for new words. The difference provides an estimate of priming.

	Test	
Encode	Encoded words	Control words
giraffe	g-r-f--	t-b--
assassin	-ss-ss--	c-n-l-
paper	p-p--	-tt-m-n
chapel	-ha--l	e-e-ha--

Note: priming = % of encoded words completed − % of control words completed.

Stop *and* Think!   **WHEEL OF FORTUNE!!**

See if you can complete the following word fragments. Spend only about 5 to 10 seconds on each fragment. *Do not read below the fragments until you are done.*

1. c_rt__n   3. p_ _sl_y   5. ca_p__   7. c__dl_   9. c_v_r_
2. d_nu_   4. b__em_n_   6. c_nt_x_   8. h__ve_   10. a_s_ss__

Take note of the fragments you successfully completed. Calculate the percentage you got correct for questions number 2, 3, 6, 7, and 8. Do the same thing for the other five items (questions number 1, 4, 5, 9, and 10). Questions number 2, 3, 6, 7, and 8 were "studied," because you saw them earlier in the chapter. Questions number 1, 4, 5, 9, and 10 were "nonstudied"—you didn't see them earlier.

- Did you show any priming?
- What is your explanation?

1. curtain (or cartoon) 2. donut 3. parsley 4. basement 5. carpet 6. context 7. candle 8. heaven 9. cavern 10. assassin

---

Laboratory research on implicit memory began its rise to prominence in the 1960s, as researchers investigated memory functioning in amnesics (people with severely impaired memory function). For a while, it was believed that many amnesics lacked the ability to move things into long-term storage. This was based on the observation that amnesics demonstrated relatively normal working memory ability but suffered profound long-term memory deficits. So it seemed that working memory was intact but the mechanism whereby new information is transferred to long-term memory was nonfunctional (and, indeed, this dissociation was cited as evidence for a distinction between a short-term and long-term memory store). But as it turned out, the story wasn't so simple. (Recall that STM/LTM memory distinction has suffered a similar fate.) In spite of their inability to consciously recollect previous events, the amnesics showed signs of long-term retention.

Let's consider an early investigation by Warrington and Weiskrantz (1970), who compared memory functioning in amnesics and nonamnesics. In one study, a list of words was presented, followed by an explicit memory test (recognition). Faced with this test, which required them to consciously think back to the earlier episode, amnesics were relatively lost, recognizing far fewer words than nonamnesics. This finding came as no surprise. But testing retrieval with an implicit test yielded some surprising results. When their memory was probed indirectly with word stems or word fragments, amnesics demonstrated priming, just like nonamnesic participants. Amnesics were better able to complete stems and fragments that corresponded to words they had seen earlier *even though they could not consciously recollect many of those same words.* Clearly, the words were represented in long-term memory but were simply not retrievable with explicit memory instructions. This general pattern—equal performance between nonamnesics and amnesics on implicit memory tests—has been replicated in countless investigations, and the investigation of implicit, nonconscious manifestations of memory has been one of the most active frontiers of memory research.

Retrieval Dissociations

One of the most fascinating things about implicit memory tests is that they seem to follow a different set of rules than do explicit tests. Over the years, study after study has demonstrated dissociations between implicit and explicit tests. A **dissociation** occurs when some variable influences performance in different ways, depending on how performance

Table 6.8 Conditions of the Smith and Branscombe (1988) Study (phases 1 and 2)

Phase 1 (encoding)	Targets	Phase 2 (retrieval)
(No cue):	generous	Free-recall targets or
Read from the Bible to his children daily:	r_____	g-n-r–s r-li-io-s

From Smith, E. S., & Branscombe, N. R. (1988). Category accessibility as implicit memory. *Journal of Experimental Social Psychology, 24,* 490–504. Copyright 1988, Elsevier Science (USA). Reprinted by permission.

is measured. Early studies revealed dissociative effects of amnesia on memory. The ability to remember explicitly is impaired in amnesics, while remembering implicitly is unaffected.

Dissociations between implicit and explicit memory are not limited to remembering in amnesics. These intriguing patterns have been revealed in many studies of non-amnesics. One variable that produces a dissociation between implicit and explicit memory is stimulus generation. The **generation effect**—the finding that information generated from some incomplete stimulus is better remembered than material that is simply read—turns out to depend on whether memory is tested directly with an explicit memory test or indirectly with an implicit memory test. Several studies (e.g., Jacoby 1983; Smith & Branscombe, 1988) have found the reverse of the generation effect (i.e., read items remembered better than generated items) on tests tapping implicit memory.

Let's take a look at a social psychology study by Smith and Branscombe (1988). An overview of their general procedure is presented in Table 6.8. In phase 1 of the experiment, participants encoded trait words. Some of these words were simply read, while others were generated from clues and an initial letter. In phase 2, participants were tested in one of several ways. Some participants had a free recall test in which they tried to remember as many of the trait words as possible. Other participants were tested implicitly with word-fragment completion. The results, presented in Table 6.9, reveal a dissociation between an explicit memory test (free recall) and an implicit memory test (word-fragment completion). When tested explicitly, generated words were more likely to be remembered than read words. Conversely, when tested implicitly, read words were more likely to be remembered than generated words.

Explanations for Explicit-Implicit Dissociations.   Early research comparing performance on explicit and implicit tests of memory revealed a number of other dissociations

Table 6.9 Conditions of the Smith and Branscombe (1988) Study (phase 2)

	Free Recall (CD retrieval, explicit)	Word-Fragment Completion (DD retrieval, implicit)
Read (data-driven encoding)	45	62
Generate (conceptually driven encoding)	61	43

From Smith, E. S., & Branscombe, N. R. (1988). Category accessibility as implicit memory. *Journal of Experimental Social Psychology, 24,* 490–504. Copyright 1988, Elsevier Science (USA). Reprinted by permission.

involving classic encoding and storage variables, including levels of processing, visual encoding, organization, and retention interval. Two major frameworks have emerged to explain the dissociations observed between tests of implicit and explicit memory (Roediger, 1990).

Memory Systems Account.   According to the *memory systems account* (e.g., Tulving, 1983; Schacter, 1989; Squire 1993), LTM is not a unitary entity. Rather, it is made up of a number of subsystems. According to Squire, the major distinction is between conscious forms of memory, such as retrieving memory for facts and events (**declarative memory**), and nonconscious forms of memory, such as priming and the learning of skills and habits (**procedural memory**). These two types of LTM are mediated by different brain systems (Squire, 1993) with different neurological underpinnings. Because performance on explicit and implicit tests is based in different brain systems, these two LTM memory types are affected by different variables. The dissociation between conscious and nonconscious forms of memory in amnesics suggests that the brain systems underlying these types of memory have been differentially affected by the associated brain damage. The structures associated with declarative memory have been damaged, but the structures underlying procedural memory have been spared.

Let's take a look at the distinction between these two memory systems. Declarative memory is the long-term memory system responsible for retention of factual information about the world and one's personal past and serves as the basis for performance of such explicit memory tasks as recalling and recognizing that some event occurred earlier. Knowledge based in the declarative system is sometimes informally described as "knowing that" something is so. Greg *knows that* on August 30, 1982, he saw his first rock concert. He *knows that* the U.S. Declaration of Independence was signed on July 4, 1776. Do these examples sound familiar? You may recall that earlier in the chapter, we classified Greg's rock concert memory as an *episodic memory* and Greg's knowledge about the Declaration of Independence as a *semantic memory.* Many researchers consider episodic and semantic memory to be subsystems within declarative memory.

Whereas declarative information can be characterized as "knowing that" something is the case, procedural memory can be characterized as "knowing how" to do something. Procedural memory, in contrast to declarative memory, is difficult to verbalize. Imagine you're teaching someone to tie their shoe. Chances are you'd have a difficult time verbally describing the steps, so you'd probably demonstrate it by going through the motions. (Really, try it yourself.) Examples of procedural knowledge include skills (tying your shoe, typing, swinging a golf club), the priming involved in word-fragment completion, and the formation of simple associations (like a classically conditioned taste aversion). Results indicating that these forms of learning are spared in amnesia suggest that amnesia affects the declarative memory system but spares the procedural memory system.

Once again though, the story gets a bit more complicated. Comparison of nonamnesic and amnesic performance on implicit tests of memory does not always show equivalent performance. Ostergaard and Jernigan (1993) reviewed a large number of findings that showed that the distinction between implicit and explicit memory was not so clear-cut; in many instances, implicit memory performance actually mirrored explicit memory, with nonamnesics outperforming amnesics. The fact that similar effects can be revealed on explicit and implicit tests indicates that the same memory system may underlie both.

Ostergaard (1999) proposes just such an account. In his model, priming effects are based on episodic memories for previous exposures to the item. The retrieval of episodic memories involves conscious remembering, complete with the contextual elements present at encoding. Ostergaard proposes that this conscious remembering might be used in implicit memory tasks. Let's consider the implicit memory task proposed by Ostergaard. It's a simple one: participants are simply instructed to name visually presented words as quickly as possible. In order to name these words, participants must use whatever information is available to them (prior experience with the word, information from the stimulus itself, or prior exposure to the word during the experiment). Priming occurs when naming a word becomes faster after previous exposure.

Words are presented in one of two conditions. In condition 1, the words gradually appeared over a period of 5 seconds. On the first presentation, the only information available to name the word will be information inherent in the stimulus itself (i.e., the "data" that provide for bottom-up processing). In this condition, naming speed will be slow because of the slow accumulation of data. On a second presentation, nonamnesics will be able to add top-down processing to their arsenal, relying on their previous exposure to the word (i.e., an episodic memory for a previous presentation) in order to help identify it. Therefore, the improvement in naming speed from presentation 1 to presentation 2 (i.e., priming) will be large for nonamnesics. Conversely, amnesics will not be able to fully use the information from top-down processing because of their impaired ability (not complete inability) to retrieve prior episodes. Therefore, priming will be small. The comparison of amnesics to nonamnesics will reveal the same pattern found on explicit memory tests— nonamnesics do better than amnesics.

In the second condition, intact words are presented instantly to participants. At the first presentation, naming speed will be fast, because information from the stimulus is completely available; this information is the basis for naming the word (i.e., bottom-up processing). On the second presentation, top-down processing from having previously seen the word will be less important because of the ready availability of the data for bottom-up processing. Nonamnesics will still get some small benefit from top-down processing, but given that initial naming speed is so quick, the priming effect will be small. Given the reduced role of top-down processing in this condition, amnesics will not show as much of a deficit, and differences in priming will also be small or nonexistent. This is the traditional pattern found on implicit memory tests. Indeed, much of the research that demonstrates this pattern utilizes retrieval tasks that are more akin to condition two of the Ostergaard study.

The account proposed by Ostergaard does not rely on the distinction between declarative and procedural memory to explain differential performance on implicit and explicit memory tests. Both types of tests are based in the declarative system, more specifically, on memory for previous episodes. Dissociations between implicit and explicit performance arise simply because of how the retrieval task allows (or doesn't allow) the use of these past episodes.

Transfer-Appropriate Processing Account.   According to the *transfer-appropriate processing account* (e.g., Roediger, 1990), dissociations between implicit and explicit memory tests occur because these tests typically depend on different sorts of processing. Implicit retrieval tests, such as word-fragment and word-stem completion, are *data driven* in that they rely on reading and perceptual operations for successful performance. Explicit memory tests, such as free recall and recognition, are *conceptually driven* in that they rely on elaboration and organization for successful performance. Performance on a given test will depend on how the material was processed at encoding. Successful performance will result if the encoding processes successfully transfer to retrieval. Because implicit retrieval tends to be data driven, it will be aided by data-driven encoding processes. Explicit retrieval tends to be conceptually driven, so it will be aided by conceptually driven encoding processes.

Consider the dissociative effects of generation on implicit and explicit memory found by Smith and Branscombe (1988). According to the transfer-appropriate-processing account, generation is a conceptually driven encoding process that will transfer better to a conceptually driven retrieval task like free recall. This explains why participants recalled generated items better than read items—the encoding and retrieval processes matched. Alternatively, reading is a largely perceptual (i.e., data-driven) process that should transfer well to a data-driven retrieval task like word-fragment completion. Consistent with this prediction, priming in word-fragment completion was higher for words that had been read, relative to words that had been generated.

According to this view, whether a test is implicit or explicit is not critical to explaining dissociations (as it is in the memory systems approach). The critical factor is whether there is a match or mismatch of encoding and retrieval processes. This view would not predict that generating would help only explicit memory. It would predict that generating (which is a conceptually driven task) would help any conceptually driven task, explicit or implicit. Let's return to the Smith and Branscombe (1988) study and look at one other memory test used in phase 2, a *category accessibility test*. In this test, participants considered descriptions of ambiguous behaviors and provided a one-word description of the person. Note that this task is implicit, because no reference is made to the trait words encoded earlier. It is also conceptually driven, relying on meaning and association. This condition pits the memory systems and transfer-appropriate-processing views against each other. The memory systems approach would predict that the pattern of results from category accessibility should be similar to word-fragment completion (read items are remembered better), because both are implicit tasks. Alternatively, the transfer-appropriate-processing approach would predict that the results from category accessibility should look like free recall (generated items are remembered better), because both are conceptually driven. The results presented in Table 6.10 support the transfer-appropriate-processing approach. As you can see, performance in the category accessibility test paralleled performance in the

Table 6.10 Conditions of the Smith and Branscombe (1988) Study (phase 3)

	Free Recall (CD retrieval, explicit)	Word-Fragment Completion (DD retrieval, implicit)	Category Accessibility (CD retrieval, implicit)
Read (data-driven encoding)	45	62	45
Generate (conceptually driven encoding)	61	43	52

From Smith, E. S., & Branscombe, N. R. (1988). Category accessibility as implicit memory. *Journal of Experimental Social Psychology, 24,* 490–504. Copyright 1988, Elsevier Science (USA). Reprinted by permission.

free recall condition; priming was higher for generated items relative to read items, just as free recall of generated items was higher than for read items.

These results, in conjunction with Ostergaard's (1999) assertion that performance on implicit memory tests is not necessarily preserved in amnesics, might lead you to conclude that the transfer-appropriate-processing approach is the preferred account of implicit-explicit memory differences. However, the theoretical debate goes on—many researchers (Bowers & Schacter, 1993; Squire, Knowlton, & Musen, 1993) still advocate the memory system approach. In addition, some researchers (Kelley & Lindsay, 1996; Tulving & Schacter, 1990) believe that the final answer may lie in some convergence of these two accounts.

Stop *and* **Think!**   TRANSFER-APPROPRIATE PROCESSING VERSUS MEMORY SYSTEMS

Imagine the following two hypothetical experiments:

Experiment 1

Encoding: Participants encoded a set of 20 words. They encoded half of the words with a data-driven task by simply reading them off of a computer screen (e.g., *white*). The other half were encoded with a conceptually driven task by coming up with the opposite of a presented word (e.g., *black*).

Retrieval: Participants were tested in one of two ways:
  a. free recall (conceptually driven, explicit task)
  b. anagram solution—that is, rearranging scrambled letters to form a word (data-driven, implicit task)

Experiment 2

Encoding: The same as experiment 1

Retrieval: Participants were tested in one of two ways:
  a. free recall (conceptually driven, explicit task)
  b. word-association game—that is, given a word, come up with first association that pops to mind (conceptually driven, implicit task)

For each retrieval task, the result could be

a. A word that was generated at encoding would be "better remembered" than a word that was read.

or

b. A word that was read at encoding would be "better remembered" than a word that was generated.

(*Keep in mind that something can be "better remembered" explicitly or implicitly.*)

For each experiment, predict the results based on the transfer-appropriate processing account and the memory systems account.

- Why would each account make that prediction?
- Was a memory dissociation predicted?
- Why was a dissociation predicted or not?

RECURRING RESEARCH THEME

Cognition and Consciousness

Conscious and Nonconscious Access to the Past

In recent years, the question of how consciousness relates to memory has become a question of intense interest. This stands in stark contrast to 20 or 30 years earlier, when the mystery of consciousness seemed too subjective to assess with the scientific method and remained outside the realm of experimental psychology. The tide began to shift with research on implicit memory, which made it apparent that questions of consciousness could be addressed scientifically. Tulving's (1972, 1983) proposal of distinct memory systems also focused researchers' attention on questions of consciousness. As you'll recall, one of the major factors that distinguishes episodic from semantic memory is whether retrieval is accompanied by an experience of recollection, or a *reliving* of the past experience. In the past decade, investigators have developed methods to assess directly the relationship between consciousness and memory.

One of the more popular approaches for separating the conscious and nonconscious components of memory is to ask about one's state of awareness during the retrieval of a previous experience. This has been termed the **remember-know paradigm** (Gardiner, 1988). In this paradigm, participants are asked to recognize events (typically words) that occurred in an earlier list. For items that are recognized, another judgment is made. Participants are asked if they remember seeing the word, or do they just know that they saw it earlier. A *remember judgment* means that participants can vividly recall the presentation of the word, basically reliving the experience. They can consciously recollect that the word was indeed presented (Rajaram, 1993). A *know judgment* means that although the participant knows the word was part of the study list, there is no experience of recollection or reliving; the participant just "knows" the word appeared earlier. So if we remember that an event occurred, this reflects conscious and effortful retrieval. If we just know that an event occurred, this reflects nonconscious, automatic memory retrieval.

Research employing this task has demonstrated a number of dissociations. Remember and know judgments are influenced by different variables. For example, both Gardiner (1988) and Rajaram (1993) found that levels-of-processing manipulation had different effects on these two types of judgments. Rajaram (experiment 1) presented words (e.g., *cat*) to participants and had them generate either a rhyme associate (*bat*) or a semantic associate (*dog*). Memory was tested with recognition. If a word was recognized, participants also made a remember-know judgment. Based on what you've read about the levels-of-processing effect, you might correctly anticipate that words for which a semantic associate was provided were remembered better. So overall, there was a levels-of-processing effect. But when the conscious and nonconscious components of memory were teased apart, an interesting pattern emerged. The levels-of-processing effect was limited to remember judgments. In fact, as you can see in Table 6.11, the effect was reversed in know judgments.

Research employing the remember-know paradigm has revealed that many of the encoding factors that improve performance in explicit memory tasks (i.e., recall and recognition) also influence remember judgments. These factors include attention (Gardiner & Parkin, 1990), picture presentation (Rajaram, 1993), and stimulus generation (Gardiner, 1988).

Table 6.11 Data from Rajaram (1993, experiment 1) Study

	Percent Correct Responses		
	Overall Recognition	Remember Judgments	Know Judgments
Shallow Processing	62	32	30
Deep Processing	86	66	20

From Rajaram, S. (1993). Remembering and knowing: Two means of access to the personal past. *Memory and Cognition, 21,* 89–102. Reprinted by permission of the Psychonomic Society, Inc.

These same encoding factors exert relatively little influence on know judgments. You may note that the dissociations between remember and know judgments mirror the dissociations obtained between tests of explicit and implicit memory. Indeed, some have used the concept of memory systems to account for the remember-know results (e.g., Tulving, 1983; Gardiner & Parkin, 1990), suggesting that remember judgments are based on the episodic memory system, while know judgments are based on the procedural system.

STOP *and* REVIEW!

1. What's the primary difference between explicit and implicit tests of memory?
2. True or false? Dissociations between explicit and implicit memory tests are observed only in amnesic subjects.
3. Discuss the connection between implicit/explicit memory tests and procedural/declarative memory systems.
4. Discuss the connection between implicit/explicit memory tests and data-driven/conceptually-driven processing.

➤ Explicit memory involves deliberate and conscious retrieval of information. But remembering is not always conscious. Memory for events can be reflected implicitly, in feelings, attitudes, and behaviors. Implicit memory is reflected in priming.

➤ Many variables seem to affect explicit and implicit memory differently. One such variable is amnesia, which seems to affect explicit remembering more so than implicit remembering. Dissociations can also be observed in nonamnesics, with standard encoding variables (e.g., stimulus generation) influencing explicit and implicit memory differently. The variables that affect explicit memory also seem to exert more influence on remember judgments within the remember-know paradigm.

➤ According to the memory systems view of dissociations, implicit and explicit memory tests rely on different memory systems and so are influenced by different variables. Implicit memory performance is thought to be based in the procedural memory system, and explicit memory performance is thought to be based on the declarative memory system.

➤ According to the transfer-appropriate-processing view, implicit and explicit tests typically depend on different sets of processes at retrieval. Implicit memory tests tend to depend on data-driven processing. Therefore, memory performance on implicit tests is facilitated by data-driven encoding tasks. Explicit memory tests tend to depend on conceptually-driven processing. Therefore, memory performance on explicit tests is facilitated by conceptually driven encoding tasks. The critical distinction is not the type of test but the match between the processing required at encoding and the processing required at the test.

Memory Improvement

When people hear that we're psychologists who do research on memory, the first response we get is invariably "Oh! I have the worst memory," followed by some type of specific memory complaint. And everyone wants to know how to improve their memory. It's important to note that there are no magic tricks or shortcuts that you can employ to improve memory. Memory improvement is hard mental work and requires application of the basic principles discussed earlier in the chapter: attention, organization, elaboration, and imagery.

Another way to improve memory is through the use of memory aids. Harris (1980) makes a distinction between internal and external memory aids. **Internal memory aids** are the internal encoding strategies we employ to make information more memorable and involve the practical application of the encoding factors discussed earlier. Memory research has focused almost exclusively on the effectiveness of these internal aids. But people also make extensive use of **external memory aids,** which are the physical reminders that we create and place in the external environment. These might include a note to yourself, a list, or the proverbial string around the finger. *Combination aids,* such as the notes you take in class, combine the features of internal and external memory aids. Taking notes in class involves the mental rehearsal of information as you write it down (an internal memory aid) and provides you with a valuable external source of reminders (the notebook that you open for a final review the night before the test).

Internal Memory Aids

While studying, you no doubt make extensive use of internal memory aids, also termed **mnemonic techniques.** These techniques range from the mundane (yet effective) techniques that we use every day, such as elaborative rehearsal, to the slightly bizarre procedures involved in structured mnemonic techniques. Searlemann and Herrmann (1994) make a distinction between naive mnemonics and technical mnemonics. *Naive mnemonics* are the internal memory strategies we employ spontaneously, with no need for formal instruction. The techniques you employ to remember your notes for an upcoming test would be considered naive mnemonics. These techniques typically take advantage of the tried-and-true principles of memory discussed earlier: rehearsal, elaboration, and organization. A common technique that you've almost certainly put to good use is the first-letter mnemonic, which involves forming an acronym using only the first letters of a set of important concepts. For example, you might remember the colors of the rainbow by the acronym ROY G. BIV, and the five Great Lakes of the United States by the acronym HOMES. Another version of the first-letter technique is to take the initial letters of each concept and form a sentence in which each word begins with one of them. This technique is known to every beginning musician who remembers the notes of the musical staff (in the treble clef) using the sentence "Every good boy does fine." Use of the first-letter mnemonic imposes a simple organizational scheme on the material you have to re-member, essentially reducing it to one chunk. It also provides cues for retrieval—the ini-tial letters of each concept.

Unlike naive mnemonics, *technical mnemonics* are not used every day. Indeed, most people probably don't even know about most of them. Bellezza (1982) terms these devices *technical* because in order to use them you need to commit some technical information to memory. Each of these techniques involves some type of scheme that must be memorized, a scheme that usually involves organization and imagery. This scheme serves not only as a framework for encoding the material, but also as a valuable set of retrieval cues that allows you to access the information when you need it. Let's examine a few of these techniques.

The **method of loci** technique can be illustrated with a rather gruesome story, related by Yates (1968). In 477 B.C., the Greek poet Simonides was addressing the attendees of an indoor banquet when he was called outside by some messengers. While he was outside, the roof of the banquet structure collapsed, killing everyone inside and mangling their remains beyond recognition. However, Simonides was able to identify them based on his memory of the banquet. Can you guess how? During the banquet, he had paid enough attention to everyone so that he knew where they were all sitting. So he imagined the banquet table and mentally went around it, naming the person who had been sitting in a given position. In other words, he used the method of loci, or location. This method involves memoriz-ing a set of familiar locations (like landmarks on your college campus), taking a mental stroll through these locations, and placing a piece of information that must be remem-bered (such as items on a grocery list) at each location. When it comes time to remember the information, you simply take another mental stroll and pick up each item. The tech-nique sounds a little flaky, but can be quite effective. Think about why, in terms of the fac-tors that promote successful encoding and retrieval. The method of loci promotes (spatial) organization and visualization of the material to be remembered, and the locations used at encoding serve as ready-made retrieval cues. A good deal of research demonstrates the effectiveness of this technique (e.g., Roediger, 1980; Groninger, 1971)

The **peg-word technique** is similar to the method of loci in that it relies heavily on using imagery at encoding. But instead of a set of locations, the encoding framework is a set of prememorized *peg words*. The technique involves taking each item or concept to be remembered and relating it to a peg word (the first concept to the first peg word and so on) by forming an interactive image. Put another way, each concept to be remembered gets "hung" onto a "peg" with visual imagery. So the encoded items enjoy the benefits of visual encoding, and as in the method of loci, the peg-word method provides a ready-made set of retrieval cues—the peg words. Retrieval of the encoded list involves mentally review-ing the peg words, which trigger the encoded images, which then allows retrieval of the as-sociated concept.

The **keyword technique** is similar to the peg-word technique and has proven effective in enhancing the retention of foreign language vocabulary. Let's take a look at how it would help you remember the Spanish word for donut, *bunuelo*. (This information would come in very handy when you stop at the Buñuelos De Dunkin (Dunkin' Donuts) in Mexico City.) The first step in the keyword method is to think of a concept that sounds like the foreign vocabulary word to be learned. In this case, the word might be *bun*. You then imagine this concept interacting with the target word (*donut*). So in this case, you might imagine a *donut* on a hamburger *bun* (looks tasty, doesn't it?). When you are cued with the word *donut*, the image will be retrieved and will lead you to the concept "bun," which will hopefully cue recall of *bunuelo*. Note the similarity to the peg-word method. The word that must be remembered is imagined interacting with some other concept. This concept serves as a later cue for the word. The keyword technique has proven quite effective in learning foreign vocabulary terms (McDaniel, Pressley, & Dunay, 1987) as well as other material, such as medical terminology (Troutt-Ervin, 1990).

Stop *and* **Think!**

NMEMORIZING WITH MNEMONICS

Find a couple of friends willing to be guinea pigs and give them the following set of words to remember:

Items: apricot   piano   sweater   wrench   piccolo
       tractor   cannon   castle   puzzle   falcon

Vary the instructions you give them. Tell one friend to simply repeat the items over and over silently. Instruct the other friend in one of the technical mnemonic systems (your choice) to use in encoding the items.

- Who recalled the list of words better?
- Did you notice any other differences in the way the items were remembered?
- What do you think accounts for these differences?

After reading about these memory aids, you're probably wondering why you don't hear much about them, much less use them to study your textbooks and notes. Although late-night infomercials may tout the value of these memory devices, they really aren't terribly useful in most practical situations. Even people that are "in the know," memory researchers themselves, rarely use them (Park, Smith, & Cavanaugh, 1990). Searlemann and Herrmann (1994) note a couple of reasons why technical mnemonics are almost never used. First, the methods do not apply very well to the information you typically encounter. Most of the research demonstrating the power of technical mnemonics has investigated memory for word lists, which aren't too much like anything you try to remember on a day-to-day basis. Technical mnemonics aren't readily applicable to jokes, stories, daily events, or other things you want to remember. Another problem with these technical mnemonics is the effort it takes to use them. What would you rather do to remember the eight things you need to buy at the store: "hang" them all on peg words using interactive imagery, or just get a piece of paper and write the items down, as Tom did in our opening story? The latter technique, an external memory device, is probably the more cost-efficient choice.

External Memory Aids

External memory aids are environmental reminders or cues, like having a friend remind you to do something, making a note to yourself, or placing something in a location where you're sure you won't miss it. A study by Intons-Peterson and Fournier (1986) revealed two facts about external aids: (1) external memory aids are used more extensively than internal aids, and (2) external memory aids are used more to remember to do something in the future (e.g., like Tom did to make sure he didn't forget to return the video), whereas internal memory aids are used more to remember information from the past (e.g., like Tom did to remember the cashier's name).

These two primary findings uncovered by Intons-Peterson and Fournier are quite telling, because they imply that a sizable proportion of memory failures involve people forgetting not what happened in the past but what they have to do in the future. The ability to remember future activities and plans is termed **prospective memory.** Thus far, this chapter has dealt exclusively with **retrospective memory,** or memory for past events. But as you know from personal experience, this is only part of the memory picture. Forgetting what you wanted to get from a particular location, missing an appointment, and forgetting to perform some action are very common memory problems, and each represents a failure of prospective memory. Prospective memory, simply put, is remembering to do things. Little research has been conducted on prospective memory, relative to retrospective memory. This is surprising, as failures of prospective memory are common memory complaints.

One fundamental difference between retrospective remembering and prospective remembering seems to be the event that triggers retrieval. In retrospective memory (recognition and free recall), retrieval is initiated by some external cue that initiates a search of memory, such as "Tell me all of the words that appeared on the previous list." In prospective memory there is no cue; retrieval tends to be self-initiated. Suppose you see a friend to whom you have to deliver a message. When you see the friend, there is no external cue urging you to give them the message. The idea must spontaneously occur to you. And once you realize that you have to give a message, you must remember the content of the message. This is similar to retrospective memory; once you are given the cue "Recall all the items on the list," you must recall the content of that list. So prospective memory seems to involve a different component than retrospective memory—"remembering to remember." External memory aids are used primarily to assist this unique feature of prospective memory. Writing notes or putting something in a special place provides the cues that are lacking in prospective memory. These cues initiate retrieval so you won't have to, serving as effective safeguards against "forgetting to remember." In order to remember to return the video, Tom put it in front of the door. This external aid facilitated his memory, reminding him to perform the task. However, he had no such external aid to help him remember to tell the landlord about the leaky faucet. As a result, he forgot to deliver the message.

Stop *and*
Think!
USE TWO MEMORY AIDS AND CALL ME IN THE MORNING

Think of some of the memory aids that you commonly use and list them, along with the memory problem you're trying to solve. Evaluate whether each memory aid is internal or external.

- Which do you seem to use more often?
- Which seem more effective?

RECURRING RESEARCH THEME
Cognition and Individual Differences

Aging and Prospective Memory

As you might expect, memory ability declines somewhat as we age. But this statement is vastly oversimplified; the interactions between aging and remembering are complex. Craik (1986) proposes that age-related memory declines reflect the degree of self-initiation required by a memory task. That is, these deficits will be observed to the degree that a memory task requires a person to initiate and drive their own retrieval processes. Can you guess which memory test—recall or recognition—is most likely to show memory deficits? If you guessed free recall, rather than recognition, you're correct. In free recall, virtually no assistance is given at the time of retrieval; the only cue available is a prompt to recall the previous list. Contrast this with recognition, in which the retrieval process is initiated by a strong cue (the item itself) and does not rely as much on self-initiated search of memory. In line with this analysis, Craik and McDowd (1987) found greater age-related decrements in free and cued recall, relative to recognition. Does this pattern ring a bell? It should. Recall the outshining hypothesis, described earlier in conjunction with context-dependency effects. A mismatch in encoding and retrieval environments can have a detrimental effect on memory that can be overcome (e.g., outshined) if more effective cues are available. Similarly, advancing age produces declines in memory that can be overcome if cues are sufficient.

Consider the self-initiated retrieval required by prospective memory. Because prospective memory involves the distinctive feature of having to "remember to remember," a person must initiate the memory process completely on their own. Based on this line of reasoning, one might expect large age-related decrements in prospective memory. Einstein and McDaniel (1990) examined this prediction in a series of studies. They compared college-age and elderly participants in a laboratory-based prospective memory task. Participants saw lists of words that were to be recalled immediately (a short-term retrospective memory task). In addition, they were told to watch for certain target words. If any of these target words appeared, they were to press a special response key (the prospective memory task). The results were surprising. Although the typical age-related deficits were found in retrospective memory performance, no deficits were found in prospective memory. The elderly participants were just as likely as the younger participants to notice and respond to the target words.

So, is prospective memory an exception to the memory deficits observed in the elderly? It turns out that the answer is fairly complex. Einstein and McDaniel (1990) propose that prospective memory tasks vary in the degree of self-initiated retrieval required, just as retrospective memory tasks do. They suggest a distinction between event-based prospective memory tasks and time-based prospective memory tasks. In *event-based prospective memory* tasks, the action that must be taken is triggered by some event. For example, you must give your friend a message when you see her. Seeing your friend is the event that triggers the action. The procedure used in the study discussed above was event-based. When a particular event (e.g., a word) occurred, participants were to make a special response. In *time-based prospective memory* tasks, an action must be taken at some specific point in the future. For example, you must remember to go outside and turn off the water sprinkler in two hours. Which of these two situations do you suppose involves more self-initiated retrieval? Time-based prospective memory tasks do; there is no cue to remind you that you have to do something.

Based on this distinction, Einstein and McDaniel (1990) suggest that the elderly may be more likely to show deficits in time-based prospective memory because it requires more self-initiation: you have to remember to remember without any external cue. This idea has been put to the experimental test by a number of investigators (e.g., Einstein, McDaniel, Richardson, Guynn, & Cunfer, 1995; Park, Hertzog, Kidder, Morrell, & Mayhorn, 1997), and the results have generally supported the prediction. Deficits in prospective remembering are more pronounced on tasks that are time-based relative to those that are event-based.

STOP *and* REVIEW!

1. Distinguish between external and internal memory aids and give an example of each.
2. What is prospective memory, and how does it differ from retrospective memory?
3. True or false? Older adults perform less well than younger adults on all prospective memory tasks.

➤ Internal memory aids refer to the mental strategies we use to improve memory. External memory aids refer to physical reminders, such as notes. Internal memory aids make use of basic encoding principles—such as elaboration, organization, and imagery—and include technical mnemonics—such as the method of loci, the peg-word technique, and the keyword method.

➤ External memory aids are more commonly used than internal aids and are typically used in the service of prospective memory, which refers to our ability to remember future activities and carry them out. Prospective memory is self-initiated in that there is no explicit cue to remember. This contrasts with retrospective memory, which is defined by an explicit cue to recall some past event.

➤ Elderly adults seem to be particularly deficient in self-initiated memory tasks, in which a person must initiate and drive their own retrieval processes. Due to this deficiency, older adults suffer in time-based prospective memory tasks in which self-initiated retrieval is critical; no event occurs to cue retrieval. However, older adults show little or no deficit in event-based prospective memory, in which the requirement to perform some action is cued by an event.

GLOSSARY

accessibility: the degree to which a piece of information can be recalled, given certain retrieval cues (p. 226)

amnesia: memory loss due to brain damage (p. 213)

availability: whether or not information is actually stored in memory (p. 226)

context-dependency effects: the finding that, given a particular encoding context, memory is better when retrieval reinstates that context (p. 228)

declarative memory: the conscious forms of memory, such as retrieving memory for facts and events (p. 239)

dissociation: occurs when some variable influences performance in different ways, depending on how performance is measured (p. 237)

distinctiveness: the degree to which information is distinguished from other information in memory (p. 223)

distributed repetition: repeated presentations that are spread out over time (p. 215)

dual-code theory: proposes two distinct representational systems in memory, one verbal and one imaginal (p. 224)

elaborative rehearsal: the formation of links between material to be remembered and information already stored in memory (p. 218)

encoding: the processes involved in the acquisition of material (p. 212)

encoding specificity principle: the retrieval of information in memory will be effective to the degree that the cues present at retrieval match the information that was present at encoding (p. 227)

episodic memory: the memory for personally experienced events that include contextual elements (p. 211)

explicit memory tests: memory tests that involve the conscious recollection of some specific event or episode from the past (p. 213)

external memory aids: the physical reminders that we create and place in the external environment (p. 245)

generation effect: the finding that information generated from some incomplete stimulus is better remembered than material that is simply read (p. 238)

implicit memory tests: memory tests in which successful performance does not depend on conscious recollection of some specific event or episode from the past (p. 213)

incidental learning: conditions in which a memory test is not expected (p. 218)

intentional learning: conditions in which a memory test is expected (p. 218)

internal memory aids: the internal encoding strategies we employ to make information more memorable (p. 245)

keyword technique: a mnemonic technique often used to memorize foreign language vocabulary; the foreign word to be learned is encoded as a base language word or phrase, which is then associated with its meaning through an interactive image (p. 247)

levels-of-processing theory: a theory emphasizing the notion that memory depends on how information is processed at encoding (p. 219)

long-term memory (LTM): the permanent store of information (p. 211)

maintenance rehearsal: mental practice that consists simply of repeating information over and over (p. 217)

massed repetition: repeated presentations that occur closely together in time (p. 215)

method of loci: a mnemonic technique that involves relating each item to be remembered to a location along a well-practiced route or set of locations (p. 246)

mnemonic techniques: memory improvement techniques (p. 245)

organization: the degree to which incoming information is, or can be, structured (p. 222)

peg-word technique: a mnemonic technique that involves taking each item to be remembered and relating it to a peg word with an interactive image (p. 246)

picture-superiority effect: the finding that concepts are more likely to be remembered if they are presented as pictures rather than words (p. 224)

primacy effect: the finding that items at the beginning of a list are remembered better than items presented in the middle of the list (p. 210)

priming: the benefit in performance from having previously seen a word (p. 236)

procedural memory: the nonconscious forms of memory, such as priming and the learning of skills and habits (p. 239)

prospective memory: the ability to remember the activities and plans one has to perform in the future (p. 248)

recall: an explicit memory test in which participants must retrieve information given relatively little information (p. 217)

recency effect: the finding that items presented at the end of a list are remembered better than items presented in the middle of the list (p. 210)

recognition: an explicit memory test in which participants must discriminate items previously presented from new items (p. 217)

rehearsal: mental practice (p. 216)

remember-know paradigm: a recognition task requiring participants to indicate whether they truly remember (i.e., consciously recollect) that an event occurred or whether they simply know that it did (p. 243)

repetition: the presentation of an item more than once (p. 215)

retrieval: the processes that lead to the reactivation of a memory (p. 213)

retrieval cues: reminders; information that assists in the reactivation of stored information (p. 226)

retrieval failure: forgetting that occurs due to a lack of appropriate retrieval cues (p. 226)

retrospective memory: memory for past events (p. 248)

self-reference effect: material that is related to the self tends to be well-remembered (p. 223)

semantic memory: the knowledge of information about the world that does not include contextual elements (p. 211)

serial position effect: the finding that memory for words in a list depends on their relative position (p. 210)

spacing effect: the advantage of distributed repetitions over massed repetitions (p. 215)

storage: the retention of a memory representation (p. 213)

testing effect: the finding that periodic retrieval of information is an effective means of improving long-term memory for that information (p. 232)

transfer-appropriate processing: the degree to which the processing performed at encoding maps onto the processes required at retrieval (p. 220)

unconscious plagiarism: wrongly taking credit for an idea when in reality one is implicitly remembering an idea from another source (p. 235)

von Restorff phenomenon: the finding that information that stands out from its context tends to be well-remembered (p. 223)

word-fragment completion: an implicit memory test in which fragmented words are presented for completion (p. 236)

word-stem completion: an implicit memory test requiring participants to complete a three-letter stem with the first word that comes to mind (p. 236)

7

Memory Distortions

After clocking out, John, the checker at the grocery store, and his coworkers, Bart and Yolanda, head out to the parking lot. "Whew," Bart groans, "That was intense. People always think they need to stock up on milk and bread the first time they see a snowflake."

"Yeah! But I might have done the same thing if I wasn't going home this weekend," responds John.

"Going home?! We were supposed to study together this weekend," Yolanda protests.

"I said we MIGHT be able to study together this weekend."

"I remember exactly what you said. You said that we'd DEFINITELY get together and study this weekend," Yolanda insists.

"How can you remember *exactly* what I said?" John responds defensively.

"Well how do you know *you* didn't say that?"

"Because I distinctly remember phrasing it in a very specific way so it wouldn't be taken wrong. I said, 'I'll definitely try and work it so we can get together and study this weekend.' Obviously, that worked really well." John is becoming sarcastic.

Bart enters the fray. "It's not a big deal. Who knows who said what and how?" He tries to change the subject. "I've got a great idea. Let's go bowling for a study break tonight."

John gives Bart an irritated look.

"What?" Bart inquires.

"Bowling?" John asks pointedly.

"Yeah. Don't you wanna go?"

"I brought up bowling as a study break last weekend, and you thought the idea was ridiculous."

"Really? Well, I guess ideas are better when I come up with them."

Their bickering is interrupted by a shout—"STOP THAT MAN!!!!"

They all whip around. Racing by is a young purse snatcher, being chased futilely by a couple of puffing middle-agers who soon give up the chase.

"Did you see him?" they pant.

"Not too well," Yolanda offers "I was so startled, all I saw was a blur."

"I was scared to death. All I saw was the gun." Bart shivers.

"Gun? I didn't see a gun," John disagrees. "He was carrying the purse he took, but that's it."

"I'm sure he had a gun," Bart insists.

"Oh Bart, stop shooting off your mouth." John tries to lighten things up with a pun.

"Real funny, John."

"Here come the campus police. Keep those memories fresh!"

"Hi, I'm Alex. I work for the campus police. Tell me what you saw." Alex listens, pen in hand, as the witnesses tell their stories. He wants them to hurry up so he can get to his family reunion, which is due to start in a few hours.

One of the joys of having two memory researchers in the house is the fact that we each think our memories are better than the other's, which sets the stage for what we fondly call "memory fights," much like the one you just read about. Both Yolanda and John are absolutely convinced that their version of the conversation is the correct one, but they both can't be right. Memory fights highlight a fundamental principle of memory: it's not perfect; in fact, sometimes it's far from it. How we remember a person, place, or event depends on a host of factors, many of which we discussed in Chapter 6. Memory is not a simple process of rote retrieval or replay; rather, it's largely a matter of reconstruction. We remember (or reconstruct) past events with the help of fragmentary information, our own expectations and biases, and sometimes those of others. As implied by a line in the opening scenario ("Alexander listens, pen in hand, as the witnesses tell their stories"), remembering is the reconstruction of a story—a pretty good reconstruction in some cases, perhaps, but still a reconstruction.

Stop *and* **Think!**   ## RECONSTRUCTING (AND DISTORTING?)

After you've been out with at least two friends (i.e., studying, going to dinner, going to a party), engage them in a conversation about what happened. Ask a range of questions, such as the following:

- What happened, in chronological order?
- Who was wearing what?
- Who said what?
- What were the context-specific details (i.e., where and how were you all sitting, etc.)?
- What were any distinctive events that occurred?

Then answer these questions:

- How complete and clear were memories?
- How confident did the rememberers seem about their recollections?
- How were the recollections of your friends similar? How were they different?
- Did you start any "memory fights"?

The material in this chapter may seem a bit hard to accept, perhaps even a little threatening. It's hard for us to acknowledge that something that seems so real and tangible—our own personal history—is actually a rather fragile reconstruction that is subject to a host of distortions. These so-called **memory distortions** have become a hot topic in memory research.

The Sins of Memory

Memory researcher Daniel Schacter puts an interesting spin on the processes by which memory fails, calling them the "seven sins of memory," which evokes an image of the biblical "seven deadly sins." Although the sins of memory may not be deadly, they certainly are frustrating. And as you'll see in our discussions of eyewitness memory and so-called recovered memories of child abuse, these "sins" can have tremendous ramifications. According to Schacter, the sins of memory include **transience,** or the loss of information from memory with the passage of time; **absentmindedness,** which refers to problems with the interface between attention and long-term memory; and **blocking,** which is a failure in retrieval of information stored in long-term memory. Schacter classifies transience, absentmindedness, and blocking as *sins of omission*—failures to bring something to mind. Two sins of omission have already been discussed: absentmindedness—the culprit responsible for action slips (Chapter 4)—and transience—forgetting (Chapter 6). Blocking will be discussed in the context of knowledge retrieval from semantic memory (Chapter 9).

The remaining four sins of memory are *sins of commission;* all of them involve the presence of unwanted or inaccurate memories (Schacter, 2001). **Misattribution** refers to a memory that is ascribed to the wrong source; you thought one of your friends said something when actually another friend did. **Suggestibility** occurs when someone is led to a false recollection, perhaps through leading questions or suggestions of others. The memory sin of **bias** refers to the influence of who we are—our beliefs, expectations, and desires—on what we remember. Finally, **persistence** refers to the continued (but unwanted) automatic retrieval of memories that we'd just as soon forget. This sin will be discussed in Chapter 8 (autobiographical memory). In this chapter, we focus on the three other sins of commission—misattribution, suggestibility, and bias.

Stop *and* **Think!**   ## CONFESSING YOUR SINS

Attempt to spot the seven sins of memory, as discussed by Schacter (2001). You could do this in one of two contexts:

1. As you're going through this chapter, identify the sins (a) as sins of omission or commission and (b) as one of the specific types discussed by Schacter.
2. Keep a journal of memory errors. Once you become aware of a memory failure, log it as either a sin of omission or commission and then as one of Schacter's seven sins. Take note of when you are likely to fall victim to each of these sins and if any patterns emerge.

A classic early investigation of reconstructive memory processes was conducted by Carmichael, Hogan, and Walters (1932). These investigators presented participants with ambiguous sketches, each of which could sensibly be interpreted as one of two objects. In Figure 7.1, the first sketch could be interpreted as a broom or a rifle; the second as barbells or eyeglasses; the third as the numeral 4 or 7. The twist was that participants were given different labels for the presented objects. Half of the participants were told that the pictures were of a broom, barbells, and the number 4; the other half were given the alternative labels—gun, eyeglasses, and the number 7. Later, memory was tested; participants were to draw the figures they had seen. The results revealed that the label had a striking effect on what was remembered. In spite of the fact that all participants had seen identical sketches, their retrieval sketches were quite different, depending on the label they had received. Gone were the ambiguous-looking sketches that could be interpreted in one of two ways. Participants' sketches depicted completely unambiguous renditions of the objects they had seen, renditions that were consistent with the encoded label. Participants who were given the label "broom" sketched a broom; those who were given the label "gun" sketched a gun. The label biased the way the object was encoded and, as result, the way the memory was reconstructed.

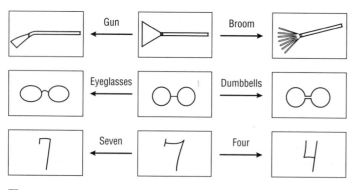

An application of Carmichael and colleagues' results isn't hard to come by. Take the "memory fights" we just mentioned. Quite often, people disagree about some sequence of events because they have different labels (i.e., a biased view) for what happened or what was said. In the case of our opening scenario, John is truly confounded by Yolanda's interpretation of what he said. It's likely that when she heard it, she may have labeled what he said as "We'll study together this weekend." John, on the other hand, probably labeled what he said more in terms of "if I can work

Figure 7.1 Figures presented by Carmichael et al. (1932), along with participants' reproductions, given different labels for the items.
From Carmichael, L., Hogan, H. P., & Walters, A. A. (1932). An experimental psychology of the effect of language on the reproduction of visually perceived form. *Journal of Experimental Psychology, 15,* 73–86.

it out." When retrieval of the comment occurs later, each has a different label for the comment and consequently the memories differ. This (along with the results of the Carmichael study) is a clear example of the memory sin of bias (Schacter, 2001)—that is, when expectations and beliefs exert an undue influence on what is remembered.

Stop *and* **Think!**

DRAWING FROM MEMORY

Try out the Carmichael and Hogan (1932) study on some acquaintances. Present each item on the list below. But for half of your participants, present the picture with the left-hand label. For the other half, present the same pictures but with the right-hand label. After the list has been presented, have them free recall the list in picture form. (It would be best if you could delay the test for as long as possible—at least 5 to 10 minutes, or days if possible).

Verbal Labels	Stimulus Figures	Verbal Labels
curtains in a window		diamond in a rectangle
seven		four
ship's wheel		sun
hourglass		table
kidney bean		canoe
pine tree		trowel
gun		broom
two		eight

Take a look at the pictures sketched by your participants.

- How far did they deviate from the originals?
- Did the deviation reflect the bias implicit in the picture labels?

STOP *and* REVIEW!

1. True or false? Memory is not susceptible to distortion.
2. In general, what is a memory sin of omission? List the different sins of omission.
3. Explain and list the sins of commission.
4. True or false? Labeling an event in a certain way affects how that memory is retrieved.

➤ Memory is a reconstructive process that is subject to a host of distortions.

➤ The memory sins of omission refer to errors in which information is absent or forgotten. These include blocking, transience, and absentmindedness.

➤ The memory sins of commission refer to the presence of unwanted or inaccurate memories. These include misattribution, suggestibility, bias, and persistence.

➤ The label that is applied to an event or object biases the way it is remembered.

Eyewitness Memory

Although the early work of Carmichael and colleagues (1932) served (in part) as a foundation for later work on the reconstructive nature of memory, the results lay relatively fallow due to the tremendous influence of behaviorism. The fragility of eyewitness memory was empirically investigated by some early psychologists, such as Hugo Munsterberg (often cited as one of the forefathers of applied psychology), but as behaviorism held sway, research on the fallibility of memory in this domain ebbed. As the "cognitive revolution" took firm hold, things began to change, as researchers began to discover the vagaries of eyewitness memory and the consequent implications. Consider cases of wrongful conviction, which are increasingly coming to light, given advances in DNA technology. Wells and Bradfield (1998) report that of the known cases in which people were wrongfully convicted by juries (and were later exonerated), mistaken eyewitness identification accounts for more of these wrongful convictions than all other causes combined. So it would seem that the concern over the accuracy of eyewitnesses' recollection is clearly well-justified. Let's examine some of the factors that affect it.

Encoding, Retrieval, and Eyewitness Recollection

Countless investigations have been conducted to determine exactly which factors affect the accuracy of eyewitness recollection. One helpful way to organize the findings from this work is by using the tried-and-true distinction between encoding and retrieval introduced in Chapter 6. You'll recall that *encoding* refers to the processes by which information is acquired and stored—that is, the processes through which a memory representation is formed. *Retrieval* refers to the collection of processes that allow us to retrieve the memory representation, or perhaps more correctly, to *reconstruct* it. As stated in Chapter 6, distinguishing between encoding and retrieval factors is largely a matter of descriptive convenience; you can't really discuss one without considering the other. But for descriptive ease, we'll examine factors that are more intimately tied with encoding and storage, followed by those that are more likely to exert an influence on retrieval.

Encoding and Storage Factors.   A number of factors influence eyewitness memory by affecting how the event is initially encoded or by affecting (or infecting, as it turns out) the memory while it's in storage. Let's examine some of these variables.

Perceptual Factors.   There are a number of factors that influence the accuracy of reports of a witnessed event. The more obvious factors include the quality of the viewing conditions—light levels, angle of view, distance from the event. The players in our opening story didn't have much of a chance or much of a viewing angle from which to view the crime. Also, none of them really got a chance to look directly at the criminal, which limited their recall; someone who looks at and rehearses the face of a criminal is more likely to remember it than someone who doesn't.

Emotion and Stress.   Our encoding of an event is also influenced by the emotional arousal and stress that are often a powerful component of a witnessed event. In the story that opens this chapter, there is a question about the accuracy of Bart's memory; he mentions how frightened he was and that he noticed only the gun—a memory which is disputed. One way in which the effects of stress can manifest themselves is through a phenomenon termed **weapon focus.** The presence of a weapon can serve to focus one's attention quite narrowly, resulting in a lack of peripheral detail in the memory representation, although the central detail—the weapon—is remembered quite well (Cutler, Penrod, & Martens, 1987; Kramer, Buckhout, & Eugenio, 1989). In a review of the literature on the effects of emotional stress on eyewitness memory, Christiansen (1992) arrives at a conclusion consistent with this finding. Emotional stress narrows attention such that central details are processed more fully, at the expense of peripheral ones. Emotional events also tend to be elaborated on later (i.e., as we "tell the story"), further benefitting memory for central details.

What would you remember if you were a witness?

Cross-Racial Identification.   One of the more intriguing factors that can influence eyewitness accuracy involves an interaction between the race of the observer and the race of the observed. Research on face recognition demonstrates that people are better at recognizing faces of their own race relative to faces of those of other races (Bothwell, Brigham, & Malpass, 1989; Shapiro & Penrod, 1986). Although the effect of race has not been extensively studied in the context of eyewitness memory, some evidence indicates that race can be a factor in eyewitness identifications (e.g., Lindsay, Ross, Smith, & Flanagan, 1999; Shapiro & Penrod, 1986).

Unconscious Transference. Sometimes previous exposure to someone, either through a photo array in a police station or through a chance encounter, can make that person seem familiar at a later point, sometimes with near-tragic consequences. In her book *Witness for the Defense,* Loftus (1991) relates the story of Howard Haupt, who was charged with the kidnapping and murder of a child in Las Vegas. The crimes had occurred near a hotel where Haupt had been a guest. Several witnesses saw a man luring the boy from the hotel's video arcade and walking with him through the hotel. Haupt was wrongly identified as that man. Two explanations for this possible misidentification are possible. One is a retrieval factor, which we will discuss shortly; the other is an encoding factor. Let's discuss this second factor—**unconscious transference**—which occurs when witnesses fail to distinguish between a target person (i.e., a criminal) and another person encountered at a different time whose face is also familiar (Loftus, 1976). This may have been at play in the Haupt case; witnesses did see Howard Haupt at the hotel where the crime took place. The witnesses may have seen his face as well as the kidnapper's face and assumed that the two people were one and the same. Therefore, when presented with his face at a later point in time, they identified Haupt as the kidnapper. (Due, in part, to Loftus's testimony assailing the reliability of the eyewitness identifications, Haupt was acquitted of the charges.)

In a study by Ross and colleagues (Ross, Ceci, Dunning, and Toglia, 1994, experiment 1), participants watched a film of teachers interacting with students. At the end of the film, a female teacher, on a break, enters a cafeteria and is subsequently robbed by a male assailant. All participants saw the same film, with one exception. In the transference condition, participants saw a male bystander reading a book to children several minutes before the robbery. Participants in the control condition did not see this bystander. After viewing the film, participants were shown a lineup of five individuals—the bystander and four unfamiliar foils; participants were asked whether the assailant was in the lineup and, if so, to identify him. The results from experiment 1 are presented in Table 7.1a. Participants in the transference condition were almost three times more likely than control participants to identify the bystander as the assailant. In addition, control participants were almost twice as likely as transference participants to indicate that the assailant was not in the lineup.

Ross and colleagues contend that participants in the transference condition believed that the

Table 7.1a   Results of the Ross et al. (1994) Study

Condition	Experiment 1 Percentage of Participants Choosing:		Experiment 2 Percentage of Participants Choosing:	
	Bystander	Not in lineup	Bystander	Not in Lineup
Transference	60.9	33.7	25.0	57.5
Control	21.9	64.4	21.9	64.4

From Ross, D. R., Ceci, S. J., Dunning, D., & Toglia, M. P. (1994). Unconscious transference and mistaken identity: When a witness misidentifies a familiar with an innocent person. *Journal of Applied Psychology, 79,* 918–930. Copyright 1994 by American Psychological Association. Reprinted by permission.

Table 7.1b Response Bias View

	Percentage Choosing Correct Alternative	Percentage Choosing Each Alternative, if Guessing		Total
		Correct Alternative	Wrong Alternative	
Nonmisled	50	25	25	75% correct
Misled	50	0	50	50% correct

From Ross, D. R., Ceci, S. J., Dunning, D., & Toglia, M. P. (1994). Unconscious transference and mistaken identity: When a witness misidentifies a familiar with an innocent person. *Journal of Applied Psychology, 79,* 918–930. Copyright 1994 by American Psychological Association. Reprinted by permission.

assailant and the bystander were the same person seen at two different times. This assumption was supported by the fact that 66% of the transference participants indicated that the assailant was seen in a context other than the cafeteria, and of those participants, 95% indicated that he was seen reading a book to children (the bystander's activity). In contrast, only 4.1% of control participants indicated that the assailant had been seen in a context other than the cafeteria. This seems to confirm that unconscious transference results from an inability to keep two memories separate from each other, resulting in a sort of "merged memory" in which the reading bystander and the assailant become one and the same. This is an example of the memory sin of misattribution—ascribing a memory to the wrong source (Schacter, 2001).

In experiment 2, Ross and colleagues directly tested this idea by telling transference participants immediately before viewing the lineup that the assailant and the bystander were two different people. This instruction eliminated the unconscious transference effect. As you can see in Table 7.1b, the results of experiment 2 indicate that transference and control participants did not differ significantly in the percentage who indicated the bystander was the culprit or in the percentage who indicated the assailant was not in the lineup. Furthermore, the number of transference participants who misidentified the bystander as the assailant was fewer in experiment 2 than in experiment 1. Therefore, it is possible to distinguish the two memories at the time of retrieval. However, the information needed for this distinction is not available in a real-world situation, and the likelihood of misidentifying an innocent bystander exists

The Misinformation Effect. Research on eyewitness memory has revealed what has been termed a **misinformation effect**—the finding that misleading information presented between the encoding of an event and its subsequent recall influences witnesses' memory. This corresponds to two of the memory sins discussed earlier. First, it reflects suggestibility; sometimes our recollections are unduly influenced by the prompting or expectations of others. Second, it's often an instance of misattribution, as witnesses get confused and misattribute misinformation to the original event. By the way, this effect is also an example of a type of interference that we discussed in Chapter 4—retroactive interference. You'll recall that retroactive interference occurs when later information interferes with the ability to retain previously encoded information. This is precisely what happens in the misinformation effect. The misleading information works backward in time to distort memory of the original event. In fact, in our opening story, John may come to remember that the situation he viewed involved a gun, although he didn't seem to have any memory of it at the time of the crime.

A study by Loftus, Miller, and Burns (1978) clearly demonstrates the misinformation effect. In the first phase of the study, participants viewed a series of color slides depicting an auto accident. For half of the participants, one of the slides depicted a car at a stop sign; for the other half, it was a yield sign. In a second phase of the experiment, 20 questions were asked about the slide sequence. Some participants were asked "Did another car pass the red Datsun when it stopped at the yield sign?" and others were asked "Did another car pass the red Datsun when it stopped at the stop sign?" So half the participants were misled, and half were given consistent information. A short time later, participants were given pairs of slides and were asked to pick the one that came from the original series. Participants who were given consistent information in the questionnaire chose correctly 75% of the time; those who were misled by the questionnaire chose correctly only 40% of the time. The researchers concluded that the misleading information altered participants' version of the events, leading to errant event recall.

Stop *and* Think!   IMPLANT SOME MISINFORMATION

Be careful with this demonstration. See if you can implant a piece of misinformation. You'll want to take advantage of some of the memory principles you've read about. Pick an event that happened a while ago and one that you think your friends might be a little fuzzy on. Try and convince them of some detail that wasn't the case. (This, of course, assumes that you have a fairly good memory of the event in question!)

- Were you successful in your attempt?
- Why were you or why weren't you?
- What was it about the original event (and/or the misinformation) that made it particularly malleable or nonmalleable?

What Happens to the Original Memory? What is the underlying reason for such misreporting? Has the misleading information irrevocably altered the memory representation for the original event? Or is the errant memory report simply due to confusion on the part of these study participants over whether they should report the information from the event, the information from the questionnaire, or both? This theoretical issue has been the focus of much debate. The *memory impairment view* contends that the original memory is inalterably affected by the presentation of misleading postevent information. This is the view favored by Loftus, who believes that the new memory replaces the memory that existed prior to the misinformation.

One study that seems to support the memory impairment view is rooted in a theory about recognition memory. Recognition memory involves a conscious component whereby we effortfully and consciously recall an event along with the supporting context. Perhaps less obvious is a nonconscious component, which can be conceived of as a feeling of familiarity or fluency with information you've encountered previously. This "gut feeling" that you've experienced this situation before may occur in the absence (or presence) of any conscious recollection.

To tease apart these conscious and nonconscious components of memory and further delineate the specifics of the misinformation effect, Lindsay (1990) employed a *process-dissociation* procedure (e.g., Jacoby, 1991). In his study, Lindsay presented participants with a filmed event, followed by the introduction of misleading postevent information. Participants were told explicitly that the postevent information did not contain any correct details about the original event. Therefore, it could be assumed that if they thought of this information later and remembered that it had been presented after the actual event, they would be able to dismiss it as incorrect.

Lindsay manipulated the ease with which participants would be able to access the postevent information. Some (in the easier condition) were given the misleading postevent information days after the original event, in an environment that differed from the original event, and immediately before the memory test. Under these conditions, it was believed that postevent information would be easily rejected. Other participants (in the more difficult condition) were given the misleading postevent information right after the actual event and under similar viewing conditions. In addition, the memory test was delayed for two days. Importantly, before the memory test, participants were told emphatically that postevent information was not to be recalled.

The results revealed different influences of misleading postevent information in the two conditions. In the easier condition, participants rarely if ever reported postevent information; they had no trouble discriminating between the original event and subsequent information. However, recall in the more difficult condition was a different story. In spite of explicit and emphatic instructions to not report postevent information, these participants often recalled it anyway. This indicates a deleterious and nonconscious influence of postevent information on memory. If participants had consciously recollected the information as postevent, they wouldn't have reported it. Instead, they recalled it as part of the original event, just as the memory impairment view would predict.

Not all believe that misinformation impairs the original memory. An alternative account is termed the *response bias view.* Some researchers (e.g., McCloskey & Zaragoza, 1985; Zaragoza, McCloskey, & Jamis, 1987) contend that the presentation of misinformation after an event leads to a response bias on the part of the rememberer rather than a genuine distortion of the memory for the original event. Let's reconsider the stop-sign/yield-sign experiment conducted by Loftus, Miller, and Burns (1978). According to the response bias view, a subtle factor in the characteristics of the misinformation and the memory test affects guessing on the two-choice recognition test (i.e., stop sign or yield sign), making it look like misled participants had a worse memory for the event.

The argument is a bit involved, so read carefully and use Table 7.1b (p. 261) to assist you. Let's assume that approximately 50% of the participants will remember the event and make the correct choice. The other 50% are forced to guess between a stop sign and a yield sign. In the nonmisled condition, about half of these participants (approximately 25%) will guess correctly, meaning that about 75% of the nonmisled participants will get the right answer. However, in the misled condition, the participants will not be guessing randomly; they'll be biased to choose the misinformation to which they were exposed (approximately all 50% will guess incorrectly), leaving 50% of the misled participants to get the right an-swer. The bottom line is that the group given misinformation may show less accurate mem-ory, but it's not because their memory for the original event is any worse; it's because they have another alternative that seems familiar. If this response tendency is removed from the situation, then there will be no memory disadvantage for the misled participants.

To test the response bias view, McCloskey and Zaragoza (1985) presented participants with an event that involved a man using a hammer. Subsequently, half of the participants were presented with some misinformation that mentioned a screwdriver rather than a hammer; the other half was not given any misleading information. The twist in this study was a change in the memory test; McCloskey and Zaragoza employed a modified recog-nition test. Instead of pitting "hammer" against "screwdriver," which would lead to a re-sponse bias in the misled group, they offered "hammer" and "wrench" as the choices. As in the previous situation, 50% in both conditions should remember the hammer and make the correct choice. The other 50% are forced to guess between a hammer and a wrench. But in this type of recognition test, there is no response bias present in the misled condition—there is no particular bias to pick "wrench" (it has never been presented). According to the memory impairment view, the misled participants should still be more likely than the non-misled participants to falsely recognize "wrench," because the original memory for "ham-mer" has been impaired. However, according to the response bias view, both the misled and nonmisled participants who do not remember "hammer" should be equally likely to falsely recognize "wrench"—both will be guessing. The finding was consistent with the re-sponse bias view: performance did not differ between participants who had been misled and those who hadn't.

The controversy over what actually happens to the original memory representation remains. Although there is support for both views, it's difficult to show definitively whether or not the originally encoded memory is impaired or whether it is less likely to be reported because of a response bias (Watkins, 1990). It may be that either could be the case, given different circumstances. In addition, the eyewitnesses in the Loftus (1979) study weren't really so wrong; they remembered an accident involving two cars and the general dynamics of the crash. Is it really important whether the person was at a stop or a yield sign? Do triv-ial details like that matter?

As Loftus (1979, 1991) notes, these details are anything but trivial, and they matter tremendously. A jury's perception of a defendant's guilt or innocence could turn on such a detail. If a witness remembers a mustache or a weapon where there was none, the wrong person may find themselves on the wrong side of prison bars. Although the fate of the orig-inally encoded information may be important in evaluating different theories of how we encode and retrieve witnessed events, it seems relatively unimportant in a forensic setting; all that really matters in a police station or courtroom is that a person often misreports what they saw. Whether that's because the memory representation is fundamentally dif-ferent or because they're biased to respond in a certain way is almost a moot point. Either way, they misreport.

Retrieval Factors.   Eyewitness accuracy is not just a product of how events are encoded and stored. The way in which memory is queried also determines what will be remem-bered or, at least, what people are willing to report. Let's examine some of these factors.

Lineups.   Attempting to recall a witnessed event can be likened to a recall test. Little or nothing in the way of cues is presented, and the person must provide an accurate summary of what they witnessed. Attempting to identify which of several people committed a crime can be likened to a recognition test. When presented with a lineup of people (via either a photo array or a live presentation), a variety of factors can affect whether a choice is made and whether that choice is accurate. In other words, eyewitness identification is influenced by the specifics of the retrieval environment.

Let's consider the four possible outcomes in a lineup situation. The first is an *identification failure*—the culprit (the person who actually committed the crime) is in the lineup but the witness does not identify anyone in the lineup as the culprit. This is clearly a negative outcome, because the criminal goes back on the street. The second is a *correct rejection*—the culprit is not in the lineup, and the witness correctly states that the culprit is not there. The third is a *correct identification*—the culprit is in the lineup, and the witness correctly identifies the person. The fourth is an *incorrect identification*—a person other than the culprit is chosen from the lineup. This outcome is doubly negative and highly undesirable; the real criminal is still free, and the wrong person is accused of the crime.

The goal of a lineup is not to nab *someone;* the goal is to identify the person responsible for the crime. Put in the terms just discussed, lineups ought to be constructed in such a way as to maximize correct identifications and correct rejections and to minimize identification failures and incorrect identifications. Over the past two decades, a tremendous amount has been learned about the proper procedures for conducting lineups. These procedures are typically aimed at maximizing correct identifications (hence minimizing identification failures) and minimizing incorrect identifications (hence maximizing correct rejections).

Photo Bias. Brown, Deffenbacher, and Sturgill (1977) conducted a study demonstrating **photo bias**—the increase in probability that a person will be recognized as the culprit due to previous exposure (e.g., a lineup or photo array). They had participants view a photo array of individuals labeled "criminals" for 25 seconds each; the participants were told that later they might be required to identify the individuals from mugshots or in lineups. After viewing the criminals, participants were exposed to mugshot pictures. Some of the mugshots were of the original criminals, and some were not. A week later, lineups were staged, and participants had to determine whether each included one of the original "criminals." There was a strong influence of mugshots on the incorrect selection of noncriminals. Witnesses were more than twice as likely to incorrectly identify noncriminals who were included in the mugshots than noncriminals not viewed in the mugshots (20% versus 8%). Obviously, presentation of the mugshot photos led participants to have vague familiarity with the faces that was then wrongly attributed to the original "crime."

Let's reconsider the Haupt case and its relationship to the phenomenon of photo bias. There is one fact that we left out when we told the story. At first, witnesses saw Haupt's picture in a photo array, yet he was never chosen as the culprit (Loftus, 1991). Subsequently, each witness was taken to Haupt's place of work; he was viewed in isolation and hence was the only choice. In this context, he was identified by several witnesses as the man seen walking with the boy at the hotel months earlier. The problem with this identification should be obvious; witnesses had seen Haupt in the photo array, and therefore he was a familiar face. Their later recognition of him may have resulted from the misattribution of this familiarity; they decided that because he was familiar, he must have been the person walking with the victim. This argument is particularly compelling when you consider that no one identified him as the kidnapper in the original photo array.

Functional Size. One way to assess the fairness of a lineup is to evaluate its **functional size** (Loftus, 1979; Cutler & Penrod, 1995). Imagine a lineup in which the suspect is 20 years old and rather seedy looking and the other five members are 30-something professionals in suits. Of course, the seedy individual will stick out like a guilty thumb. In this case, the lineup size is not really six; it's one. The functional size of a lineup is a reflection of the probability that any one person might be selected just based on how they look. To assess functional size, Wells and colleagues (1979) propose that one needs to look at non-witnesses to the crime and who they choose from the lineup. If you think about it, someone who did not witness the crime should be equally likely to choose any of the people in the lineup as the culprit; the nonwitness is simply guessing.

In order to determine functional size, a simple formula is used: divide the number of nonwitnesses to a crime by the number of those nonwitnesses who choose the suspect. If there are four nonwitnesses and all of them pick the same suspect, the functional size of the lineup is one (4/4). This indicates an unfair lineup, because the same person is being chosen every time by individuals who didn't even witness the crime! The disproportionate rate at which the suspect was chosen could only have been based on the suspect's appearance, because a nonwitness has no other information on which to make the decision. To be a fair lineup, the functional size ought to be the same as the actual number of people in the lineup (4/1). All other things being equal, all members of the lineup should have an equal likelihood of being chosen.

Lineup Presentation Procedures. The example just described seems to be an extreme case of a biased lineup. Surely things aren't this unfair in practice? Well . . . consider the procedure known as a **show-up;** a show-up is basically a lineup of one. Often, when police have someone in custody, they will simply have a witness look at that person and make a judgment as to whether they are the culprit. Clearly, this type of "lineup" is incredibly biased. The witness knows that the police wouldn't present this person unless it was fairly certain that they're "the one." Also, the pressure to make the judgment in this situation is even more intense than in the more standard lineup. This was a problem in the Haupt case; the situation in which Haupt was identified as the culprit was a show-up—the witnesses were brought to his place of employment.

A more subtle factor in lineup fairness relates to the manner in which the lineup alternatives are presented. A **simultaneous lineup** is what most people picture: lineup members are presented at the same time, and the witness must choose one. A **sequential lineup** presentation is the rarer case; lineup members are presented one at a time, and the witness must decide whether each of the lineup members is or is not the culprit. Investigations of both modes of presentation have indicated that sequential lineups are superior (Wells, 1993). Sequential lineups tend to maximize correct identifications (choosing the culprit when the culprit is in the lineup) and minimize incorrect identifications (choosing someone from the lineup who is not the culprit).

According to Wells (1993), sequential lineups are preferable to simultaneous ones due to the different strategies that the two invoke. Simultaneous lineups encourage witnesses to use a *relative judgment strategy* in which witnesses evaluate which of the lineup members most resembles the culprit they have in mind. Wells contends that this strategy encourages witnesses to pick someone. Sequential lineups, on the other hand, encourage an *absolute judgment strategy* in which witnesses are more likely to assess each individual in isolation, asking themselves, "Is this the one?" In addition to differences in judgment strategy employed, witnesses in a sequential lineup scenario are unaware of how many people are in the lineup; they never know if one more person might be coming and therefore will experience less pressure to pick someone. Also apparent are the effects that instructions can have on witnesses' choices or on their tendency to choose. Wells notes that when faced with a lineup, witnesses feel compelled to choose, increasing the chances of an incorrect identification. To combat this tendency, Wells suggests that witnesses be advised that the culprit may or may not be in the lineup.

Finally, research indicates that the fairness of a lineup is also determined by how the distractors (i.e., the nonsuspects) are selected. Wells, Rydell, and Seelau (1993) compared lineups in which the distractors matched the appearance of the suspect to lineups in which the distractors matched a witness description of the culprit. Matching distractors in terms of suspect appearance has the potential to inadvertently provide information that may not have been noticed by witnesses, altering their memory for the culprit (e.g., "Gee, all of these people have a big nose; I didn't really notice, but I guess my mugger must have had a big nose."). In contrast, matching to a witness description of the culprit may allow for the exoneration of a nonculprit who has a noticeable feature that was not part of the description (e.g., "Well, I know it can't be that guy, because that guy has kind of a big nose; my mugger didn't have a big nose."). Consistent with this analysis, Wells and colleagues (1993) found that when lineup distractors were matched in terms of a culprit's description, rather than the suspect's appearance, the correct identification rate increased and the incorrect identification rate decreased.

Hypnosis. A popular assumption about memory is that everything is stored, and given the right retrieval prompt or method, a memory will be "unlocked" and related accurately. You've already been presented with a good deal of evidence that this is simply not the case. A corollary to this common assumption is a belief that hypnosis can be used during retrieval as a way to reach and replay memories that are proving difficult to access. In spite of this common belief, research on hypnosis provides no conclusive evidence that it reliably enhances memory (Smith, 1983). Hypnosis may lead to an increase in the amount of information reported, but this increase is evident in both correct detail and fabricated detail (termed **confabulation**). The heightened suggestibility associated with hypnosis makes the rememberer more willing to label something as a memory; it also makes one highly susceptible to the suggestions of others. Orne and colleagues (Orne, Soskis, Dinges, & Orne, 1984) note several deleterious consequences of this suggestibility. First, requests for further information may be met with compliance, even if the witness doesn't have anything else to report. Second, the suggestions to which the witness does respond may well become incorporated in their memory for the event (i.e., the misinformation effect). Third, hypnosis often involves instructions to imagine the target event. As you'll read later, the simple act of imagining how events may have occurred can lead a person to be less certain regarding whether they actually did (e.g., Hyman & Pentland, 1996). And fourth, information of which the witness would typically be unsure is reported with increased confidence.

This last consequence can be particularly harmful when we consider the impact of confidence on juries. Witnesses who are extremely confident—who swear that this is the way it

Juries tend to be swayed by confident eyewitnesses.

happened—are especially compelling. But this begs an important question: Is confidence a reliable indicator of memory accuracy? Here we revisit the concept of metacognition: Are people good judges of what they know? A good deal of research demonstrates that the correlation between confidence and memory accuracy is rather weak. A review of the literature by Wells and Murray (1984) reveals the correlation to be only about 0.07. Clearly, the assuredness with which a witness proclaims "I'm sure that's the one who did it!" should be eyed with caution. Unfortunately, jurors are not always cautious in considering the testimony of eyewitnesses. Research reveals that juries tend to overbelieve witnesses, particularly confident ones (Cutler & Penrod, 1995). This overbelief is even more disturbing in light of another finding: eyewitness confidence is malleable. When eyewitnesses are given confirmatory feedback about their memory reports or eyewitness identification (e.g., "Yes, other people identified that person as well"), they become more confident about what they're reporting (e.g., Wells, Ferguson, & Lindsay, 1981; Wells & Bradfield, 1998).

As it turns out, however, the relationship between confidence and accuracy is quite complex. Certain variables moderate their relationship. It seems that sometimes confidence can be a reliable indicator of accuracy. According to the **optimality hypothesis** (Deffenbacher, 1980) the relationship between confidence and accuracy is stronger to the degree that the encoding, storage, and retrieval of the event in question occurred under optimal conditions. For example, if viewing conditions were poor (e.g., dim lighting, poor viewing angle), then witnesses' confidence is not a good indicator of their memory accuracy; however, under better conditions (good lighting, clear view of the events), confidence is a reasonably good indicator of accuracy. There is a fair amount of support for the optimality hypothesis (e.g., Brigham, 1990; Cutler & Penrod, 1989). Given this hypothesis, Bart's assertion in the opening story that he's sure he saw a gun should carry little or no weight, particularly given that his view of the situation was a brief, poorly positioned glimpse.

Back to the issue of hypnosis. Although hypnosis may lead to increased recall under some circumstances, this increased recall comes with a price—more erroneous detail, misplaced confidence, and perhaps permanent misinformation effects. Therefore, its use should be minimized, and any memory evidence gathered through its use should be closely scrutinized.

The Cognitive Interview.   It's apparent that the reports and identifications offered by eyewitnesses can be distorted by a number of untoward influences. Concern over these influences led a group of researchers to develop the **cognitive interview technique** (Fisher & Geiselman, 1992). The cognitive interview has four primary features. First, there is an attempt to make the witness comfortable (e.g., by engaging in some relaxing and ice-breaking conversation at the beginning of the interview). Second, the witness is queried with *open-ended questions* (e.g., "Tell me what happened.") that elicit answers with multiple pieces of information rather than with *closed-ended questions* (e.g., "Where did the culprit put the money?") that elicit one specific piece of information and abbreviated answers. These latter types of questions are typical of police interviews. Third, the cognitive interview takes advantage of what we know about memory by implementing mnemonic instructions that can facilitate memory. For example, witnesses are encouraged to mentally reinstate the context of the encoded event and to try to recall the event from different perspectives and in different orders, using as many different retrieval pathways as possible (e.g., Anderson & Pichert, 1978). Both of these techniques take advantage of that tried-and-true principle from Chapter 6— encoding specificity (Tulving & Thomson, 1973). A fourth feature of the cognitive interview is allowing witnesses some freedom in exactly how they describe events (e.g., using sketches).

In many ways, the cognitive interview is like a hypnotic interview, but without the dangers of creating highly suggestible witnesses and misplaced confidence. For this reason, the cognitive interview has become the preferred technique (e.g., Kebbel & Wagstaff, 1998; Wells, Malpass, Lindsay, Fisher, Turtle, & Fulero, 2000) and has met with good success. Compared to a standard police interview, the cognitive interview elicits anywhere from 35 to 75% more information, with no increase in incorrect responses (e.g., Kohnken, Milne, Memon, & Bull, 1999).

An Applied Triumph

You may be amazed at the amount of information about eyewitness memory that's been amassed over the last 25 years, and what we've presented here is but a small snippet. You may also be wondering whether these research findings have had any systematic impact within the criminal justice system. In 1999, the U.S. Justice Department issued the first national guide for the collection and preservation of eyewitness evidence. As noted by Wells and colleagues (2000), psychological research (along with DNA-based exonerations and media pressure) played a large role in demonstrating the need for these guidelines and also provided the scientific foundation for their content. These guidelines (available for anyone to peruse) make many recommendations, some of which are listed in Figure 7.2. These guidelines seek to minimize leading

---

To enhance accuracy of eyewitness memory, law enforcement officials should:

- Establish rapport with the witness
- Encourage the witness to volunteer information but not prompt the witnesss
- Ask open-ended questions but not ask leading questions
- Caution the witness against guessing
- Select the lineup fillers so that they fit the witness's description of the perpetrator
- Instruct witness that perpetrator may or may not be in lineup
- Avoid giving feedback to the witness after the lineup
- Use sequential, rather than simultaneous, lineups

Figure 7.2   Guidelines for the preservation of eyewitness memory.

Adapted from Wells, G. L., Malpass, R. S., Lindsay, R. C. L., Fisher, R. P., Turtle, J. W., & Fulero, S. M. (2000). From the lab to the police station: A successful application of eyewitness research. *American Psychologist, 55,* 581–598.

eyewitnesses in their attempts to recall events and to ensure that lineup procedures maximize the probability of correct identifications while minimizing the probability of incorrect identifications.

Stop and Think!   ## AVOIDING (MEMORY) SIN

Go to the following Website (http://www.ncjrs.org/pdffiles1/nij/178240.pdf) and take a look at the new guidelines that psychologists helped put together. The guidelines are titled "Eyewitness Evidence: A Guide for Law Enforcement." Go through the guide and identify the contributions of experimental psychologists and how they help to remedy some of the memory distortion problems discussed in this chapter.

RECURRING RESEARCH THEME
Cognition and Individual Differences

Children's Suggestibility

A fair amount of research on the topic of memory suggestibility and distortion has investigated these effects in children (e.g., Ceci & Bruck, 1993; Bruck & Ceci, 1997).

The reliability of children's memories is of great concern when one considers the role that a child's recollection can play in investigations of child abuse. More often than not, the only people who know of the abuse are the perpetrator(s) and the victim(s). Given that the child is likely to be the only party who will cooperate with authorities in such investigations, the question of memory suggestibility is one of great importance. How accurate are children's memories for daily events and for traumatic events? Are children more suggestible than adults? How can we tell when a child is relating accurate information from memory?

These questions have come to the fore of cognitive developmental research as the 1980s and 1990s saw a number of high-profile cases in which allegations of child sexual abuse were made at a number of day-care centers across the country (e.g., the Little Rascals day-care center in North Carolina and the McMartin preschool in California). The allegations of abuse were based largely on the reports of children, often in response to direct questioning of parents and other authorities. Based on the records of these cases, there is good reason to believe that many of the allegations may have been false, produced through pressure, suggestive questioning, and the suggestible nature of the child witnesses. Given the potential dangers of relying on child witnesses in cases such as these, researchers redoubled their efforts to determine the factors that affect a child's recollections, and the 1980s and 1990s witnessed a tremendous amount of progress in this area.

Bruck and Ceci (1999) reviewed some of the critical findings from studies of child suggestibility. One significant finding relates to **interviewer bias;** research evidence indicates that the accuracy of children's reports can be unduly influenced by interviewer beliefs about an event. Children seem to follow the lead of the interviewer and give biased reports of events (e.g, Thompson, Clarke-Stewart, & LePore, 1997). Also, the style of questioning influences reporting accuracy. Children tend to be more accurate in answering open-ended questions (i.e., "Tell me what happened") than more leading closed-ended questions ("Tell me how you bumped your head") (Peterson & Bell, 1996). Sound familiar? The cognitive interview technique we just discussed also advocates the use of open-ended questioning, which leads to better memory in adults; it's not surprising that the same principle applies to children's recall.

Some believe that the pressures of reporting personal and embarrassing events such as sexual abuse may make the use of anatomically detailed dolls an effective interviewing aid. This reasoning seems sound; the use of such dolls might make children more comfortable and allow them to overcome language and memory problems. Unfortunately, research indicates that the use of anatomically detailed dolls only creates more problems in reporting, particularly with younger children (Bruck, Ceci, & Francoeur, 2000). Dolls seem to be particularly suggestive if the interviewer has predisposed notions of abuse having occurred and asks the child to demonstrate the abuse using the doll. Bruck, Ceci, Francoeur, and Renick (1995) interviewed three- and four-year-old children who had undergone a medical examination; for some of the children, this included a routine genital exam. After the exam, children were given a doll and asked "Show me how the doctor touched your genitals." Disturbingly, many of the children who had not been touched in the genital area nonetheless demonstrated such touching with the doll, and those who had been touched demonstrated extensive touching that had never taken place. Taken together, these findings reveal a host of suggestive influences on a child's memory. Importantly, Bruck and Ceci (1999) point out that children can be accurate reporters of events if interviewed with caution and without suggestive techniques.

STOP *and* REVIEW!

1. Identify the encoding and storage factors that affect the accuracy of eyewitness testimony.
2. Relate the memory impairment view and the response bias view to the explanation of the misinformation effect.
3. True or false? In order to maximize correct identifications and minimize incorrect identifications, sequential lineups are more effective than simultaneous lineups.
4. Explain the relationship between confidence and memory accuracy.

➤ Eyewitness testimony is fallible and is affected by many factors that operate at encoding and storage. These factors include perceptual factors such as the quality of viewing conditions and level of attention. Also, it's more difficult to identify a face of another race. Emotional stress can narrow the focus of attention and lead to decreased recall of details. Exposure to misinformation increases the chances of misremembering.

➤ The response bias view attributes the misinformation effect to the fact that participants are biased to respond with misinformation because of its familiarity. However, the original memory may be intact. The memory impairment view contends that the memory for the original event is altered by misinformation.

➤ A number of retrieval factors influence eyewitness memory, including the structure of line-ups. Exposure to photos increases the likelihood of making an incorrect choice from a lineup. For a lineup to be fair, each person must have an equal chance of being chosen by a nonwitness. Sequential lineups lead to greater accuracy in correctly identifying a culprit than simultaneous lineups.

➤ Other retrieval factors include hypnosis, which can increase recall but at the expense of in-creased confabulation and misplaced confidence. Confidence is not a very reliable indica-tor of memory accuracy; it's a better predictor if viewing conditions are optimal. The cognitive interview technique implements principles of memory to enhance witness recall and minimize inaccuracy.

Illusory Memories

Research investigating the vagaries of eyewitness testimony leaves little doubt about the fragile nature of our reconstructions of previous events. It doesn't take much to tweak your memory for an event so that you remember that you saw a Sprite can instead of a Coke can. Although this may seem somewhat disconcerting, maybe it's not surprising. But what may come as a surprise is the ease with which we can create a memory out of thin air. Sometimes—more often than you might think—people can remember something that flat out did not happen. An ever-growing body of evidence studying the phenomenon of **illusory memory** (or **memory illusions** or **false memories**) has generally taken one of two basic tacks: one is a laboratory paradigm employing the basic list-learning approach discussed in Chapter 6. The other, partly in response to concerns of ecological validity, attempts to determine whether illusory memories can occur for everyday events like getting lost at a shopping mall.

The Laboratory Approach

Much of the recent focus on memory illusions stems from an investigation conducted by Roediger and McDermott (1995). These investigators scoured the periodical stacks in the library and then blew the dust off of a 1959 study by Deese, the subject of which was "particular verbal intrusions in list recall"—in other words, remembering words that had not occurred (i.e., intrusions) in presented lists. Participants saw lists of related words like *doze, rest,* and *snore* that all related to a theme word—in this case, *sleep*. But the theme word was never presented. In spite of this, it was often remembered by participants. Does this effect sound familiar? In our discussion of prototypes in Chapter 5, we reviewed a study by Posner, Goldsmith, and Welton (1967) that bears a striking resemblance to the Deese study. In the Posner study, participants were presented with dot patterns that were statistically generated distortions of a prototype. The parallel in the Deese study was that words related to a particular theme. In the study by Posner and colleagues, the prototype itself was never presented, just as the theme word was never presented in the Deese study. In both studies, participants tended to confidently confirm that they had seen the never-presented item. In the

Rough	Sleep	Slow	Soft
smooth	bed	fast	hard
bumpy	rest	lethargic	light
road	awake	stop	pillow
tough	tired	listless	plush
sandpaper	dream	snail	loud
jagged	wake	cautious	cotton
ready	snooze	delay	fur
coarse	blanket	traffic	touch
uneven	doze	turtle	fluffy
riders	slumber	hesitant	feather
rugged	snore	speed	furry
sand	nap	quick	downy
boards	peace	sluggish	kitten
ground	yawn	wait	skin
gravel	drowsy	molasses	tender

Figure 7.3   Themed lists used in the illusory memory study of Roediger and McDermott (1995).
From Roediger, H. L., & McDermott, K. B. (1995). Creating false memories: Remembering words not presented in lists. *Journal of Experimental Psychology: Learning, Memory, and Cognition, 21*, 803–814. Copyright 1995 by the American Psychological Association. Reprinted by permission.

Posner and colleagues study, this was the prototype dot pattern; in the Deese study, it was the never-presented theme word.

Roediger and McDermott (1995) replicated and extended the Deese study in an attempt to illuminate the nature of illusory memories. They adapted the Deese procedure in order to investigate false recognition as well as false recall. In experiment 2, all participants were presented with a series of 15-word themed lists (a sample of the lists is presented in Figure 7.3), followed by an immediate test of recall. After all lists had been presented, participants were given a recognition test that included the presented items and, more important, the nonpresented theme words for each of the lists. The recall and recognition results are presented in Figure 7.4. As you can see, illusory memories were quite common; the theme word was falsely recalled nearly half the time. Even more striking are the recognition results (the first two bars on the second graph); the theme word was falsely recognized at a level equivalent to correct recognition!

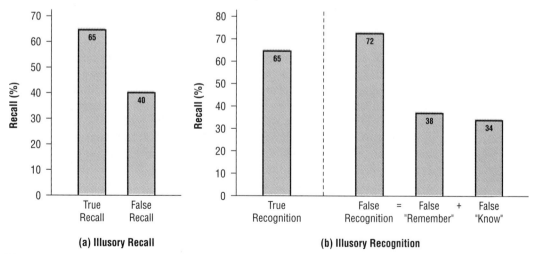

(a) Illusory Recall   **(b) Illusory Recognition**

Figure 7.4   Results from Roediger and McDermott (1995). Note the striking levels of illusory recall. Even more surprising are the false recognition rates, which are equal to true recognition! In addition, many of these illusory recognition experiences seem to have involved recollective remembering.
From Roediger, H. L., & McDermott, K. B. (1995). Creating false memories: Remembering words not presented in lists. *Journal of Experimental Psychology: Learning, Memory, and Cognition, 21*, 803–814. Copyright 1995 by the American Psychological Association. Reprinted by permission.

Stop *and* Think!

ILLUSORY MEMORIES

Recruit some of your friends and give them the following lists (taken from Roediger & McDermott, 1995). You can either read the lists (without reading the theme word, of course) or present each of the items on a separate index card. After you've presented each of the lists, have your participants recall all of the items. Take note of how often they recalled the themed word (i.e., how many illusory memories occurred). Also note how the number of theme word intrusions compares with other types of intrusions.

Rough	*Sleep*
smooth	bed
bumpy	rest
road	awake
tough	tired
sandpaper	dream
jagged	wake
ready	snooze
coarse	blanket
uneven	doze
riders	slumber
rugged	snore
sand	nap
boards	peace
ground	yawn
gravel	drowsy

Roediger and McDermott (1995) were also interested in investigating the *metamemory* accompanying these false memories—that is, a person's phenomenological experience when recognizing a word that has not occurred. To do this they used the remember-know judgment procedure discussed in Chapter 6. Recall that in this procedure, participants are given an extra judgment task if they recognize an item as previously shown. After this decision, they must judge whether they remembered the occurrence of the item (complete with contextual details) or simply knew that the item occurred (but could recall no details of its presentation). Look again at Figure 7.4b (the last two bars). Roediger and McDermott found that false recognition often was not simply a case of misattributed familiarity of the theme word. On more than half of the trials, participants remembered (i.e., consciously recollected) that the word had occurred, when it actually had not. In other words, they had created a fairly detailed memory of the word's occurrence.

The Everyday Memory Approach

False recall and recognition is not limited to remembering a single word after presentation of its associates. Recently, researchers have been able to induce participants into falsely remembering a set of complex events, as detailed, in some cases, as an authentic memory. One of the first investigations to demonstrate such wholesale false remembering was conducted

Have you ever been lost in a shopping mall? Are you sure?

by Loftus and colleagues (e.g., Loftus and Pickrell, 1995). These investigators set out to determine whether they could induce participants to completely fabricate a memory. The participants were misled a bit; the study was ostensibly an investigation of childhood memories. With the help of a family member, the investigators discovered three actual experiences for which the participants were likely to have genuine memories. The twist was that a fabricated experience (getting lost in a shopping mall) was added. The participants were interviewed about all four events (three authentic, one not) and asked to write about the events in as much detail as they could remember. They then were interviewed twice about each of the events over the subsequent two weeks. During these interviews, family members "played along" with the researchers, attempting to draw out details about each of the events.

Most of the time, participants correctly reported that they recalled nothing about the fabricated event. But a significant proportion (25%) of the 24 participants generated a false memory. Participants' confidence in these memories and their level of detail wasn't quite as high as it was for memories of authentic events, but still, the memories were pretty convincing. How could an event that didn't happen become a fairly detailed and confidently held memory? Loftus, Feldman, and Dashiell (1995) offer some possibilities. Perhaps, unbeknownst to the family members, the person really had been lost, and the memory was authentic. A more likely possibility is that prompting and probing led participants to (implicitly) use a "getting lost" schema in imagining what it must have been like. Combining this schematic information with specific information about known locations (e.g., a local mall) could lead to a fairly detailed, but false, memory episode.

Critical Events Presented to Participants

1. Got in trouble for calling 911
2. Had to go to the emergency room late at night
3. Found a $10 bill in a parking lot
4. Won a stuffed animal at a carnival game
5. Gave someone a haircut
6. Had a lifeguard pull you out of the water
7. Got stuck in a tree and had to have someone help you down
8. Broke a window with your hand

Figure 7.5   Have any of these events happened to you? Are you sure?

From Garry, M., Manning, C. G., Loftus, E. F., & Sherman, S. J. (1996). Imagination inflation: Imagining a childhood event inflates confidence that it occurred. *Psychonomic Bulletin and Review, 3*, 208–214. Reprinted by permission of the Psychonomic Society, Inc.

Imagination Inflation.   The research demonstrating the ease with which a false memory can be implanted speaks to the power of imagination in creating false memories. As we pointed out in our earlier discussion of hypnosis, it turns out that simply imagining that an event occurred increases the likelihood of someone remembering that it really did occur. This phenomenon has been termed **imagination inflation:** the finding that mental simulation of an event leads to an increase in belief that the event may have actually occurred.

One of the first studies to demonstrate this phenomenon was conducted by Garry, Manning, Loftus, and Sherman (1996). These investigators employed a three-stage procedure to demonstrate the memorial power of imagination. First, participants were presented with events and were asked to rate the likelihood that these events had happened to them as children (see Figure 7.5). Two weeks later, participants were asked to imagine that some of the low likelihood events had really happened and to supply some detail about how the event might have played itself out. Finally, in a clever twist designed to get participants to rate again the childhood events, the experimenters acted panicked and explained to the participants that they had lost their original ratings. This allowed for a comparison of estimated event likelihood both pre- and postimagination. This comparison yielded strong evidence of imagination inflation. When participants rated the events for a second time, their ratings of event likelihood went up (i.e., inflated), but only for the imagined events.

Imagination inflation is a subtle effect; imagining how a fictional event could have happened makes one a little less certain that it didn't happen. This effect demonstrates that simply imagining an event is enough to plant the seed of a memory. One interpretation of the findings is that when participants encountered the event in the second rating session, the ones they had imagined seemed more familiar. However, this familiarity was misattributed to the possibility of a remote childhood memory rather than to the imagination session. In other words, participants failed to pin down the source of the familiarity. As you're about to see, failure to ascertain correctly the source of an event memory lies at the heart of memory distortion.

RECURRING RESEARCH THEME

Cognition and Neuroscience

Distinguishing between True and False Memories

Given that research into memory illusions is quite a hot topic, you shouldn't be surprised that it's been wedded to another hot topic—cognitive neuroscience. Fabiani, Stadler, and Wessels (2000) provide some intriguing evidence that while our behavior and judgment may be fooled by the presentation of a new but highly familiar item, our brain isn't. Apparently, brain activity during true and false recognition reveals some telltale differences. Real experiences seem to leave a "sensory signature" that can be used to differentiate between true and false memories.

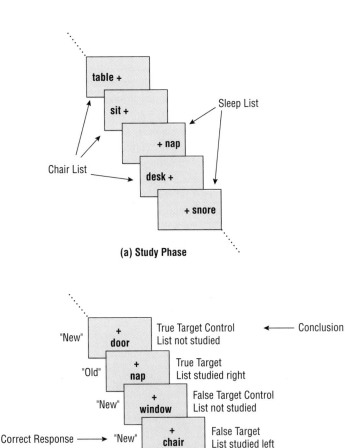

(a) Study Phase

(b) Test Phase

Figure 7.6 An overview of the procedure used by Fabiani et al. (2000). In the study phase, items from a given associative list were presented to the left or right of fixation (i.e., were processed primarily by the right or left hemisphere, respectively). In a recognition phase, words were displayed in the center of the display for recognition, and ERP responses were recorded.

From Fabiani, M., Stadler, M. A., & Wessels, F. (2000). True but not false memories produce a sensory signature in human lateralized brain potentials. *Journal of Cognitive Neuroscience, 12,* 941–949. Reprinted by permission of MIT Press.

Fabiani and colleagues began with the assumption (as do other cognitive neuroscientists) that retrieval of information from memory involves the reactivation of the sensory information that was present at encoding. Because false memories are not associated with a sensory event (they didn't occur), this reactivation cannot occur. Therefore, differences in brain activity between true and false memories should be evident in regions of the brain associated with the sensory experience of encoding the event. Previous research by Gratton, Corballis, and Jain (1997) revealed a potential way to pick up on these differences. This study showed that when a stimulus was encoded predominantly by one hemisphere of the brain, the ERP (event-related potential) response evoked by the stimulus during recognition was larger on that same side of the brain. In other words, if the word was predominantly encoded by the left hemisphere at study, then a stronger ERP response occurred in the left hemisphere during recognition.

Fabiani and colleagues applied this reasoning to true and false recognition and the ERP responses associated with each. A sketch of their procedure is provided in Figure 7.6. In the study phase, list items from the laboratory-based illusory memory paradigm were presented to participants. All words from a given associative list (e.g., the *sleep* list) were presented to the left or right of a fixation point (which meant they were processed primarily by the right or left hemisphere, respectively). The encoding phase (the "study phase") was followed by a recognition phase (the "test phase") in which words were displayed in the center of the display and ERP responses were recorded. Participants were to judge whether each item was old or new. The recognition list included words presented earlier, the theme words, and unrelated control words that had not been presented earlier.

As is typically the case in investigations of illusory memory, participants demonstrated high levels of false recognition; theme words were called "old" as frequently as were presented items. More important, the ERP responses differentiated between true and false recognition. ERP responses for the recognition of words that had actually been presented were lateralized: a greater ERP response occurred in the hemisphere that had encoded the word than in the hemisphere that did not encode it. No such differentiation was found in the ERP responses associated with false recognition. In these cases, the pattern of ERP responses was the same in both hemispheres. Fabiani and colleagues conclude that although people often can't distinguish between true and false memories in terms of conscious decisions (i.e., a recognition judgment), brain activity does yield some telltale signs that do allow for this discrimination.

STOP *and* REVIEW!

1. True or false? Although false memories were implanted in the Roediger and McDermott (1995) study, the participants didn't truly remember the "false" words; they were simply guessing that these words had occurred.
2. Is it possible to implant a false memory of anything other than a simple word? Explain.
3. Fabiani, Stadler, and Wessels (2000) used _____ to distinguish between true and false memories.
   a. CT scan
   b. PET scan
   c. the ERP response
   d. fMRI

➤ Memory illusions involve the creation of a memory for an event that did not happen. Using a list-learning paradigm, Roediger and McDermott (1995) found high levels of false recall and false recognition. False recognition was often associated with a sense of conscious recollection.

➤ Studies of everyday memory also indicate the prevalence of memory illusions. False memories for entire events (e.g., getting lost in a shopping mall) can be implanted and are recalled in convincing detail. In addition, simply imagining an event makes one more likely to assent to the idea that the event may have really occurred.

➤ Neurocognitive research indicates that it is possible to discriminate between true and false memories by using brain activity as an index. Using the ERP response, Fabiani, Stadler, and Wessels (2000) revealed that at retrieval, true memories include a distinctive sensory signature that false memories do not.

Sources of Memory Error

Before you began reading this chapter, the matter of retrieving a memory may have seemed relatively straightforward. But by now, it's become apparent that remembering is actually an elaborate orchestration of several processes, all of which must play themselves out successfully in order for memory to be accurate.

A Constructive Memory Framework

Dodson and Schacter (2001b) map out five stages necessary for the accurate encoding and retrieval of a memory—termed a *constructive memory framework*. Two of these processes characterize the encoding of an event. First, a *feature-binding process* occurs: all of the components of the encoded event—including the sights, the sounds, the people and what they said—must all somehow cohere into a unitized memory representation. Failure to bind the elements of an episode because of stress, emotion, lack of attention, or some other factor will result in disembodied memory fragments "floating around." Because of the disembodied nature of these fragments, their source is unclear. Second, the bound episodes must be kept separate from one another (*pattern separation*); otherwise, you'll confuse the sources of events. For example, if you repeatedly engage in the same activities or interact with the same friends at the same place, memory for these episodes will be difficult to separate; there are not enough unique features to differentiate the memories. Eventually, you may have just a memory of what generally happens when you and your friends go to your favorite hangout rather than a detailed memory of each occasion.

Three of the processes in the constructive memory framework operate at retrieval. Retrieval requires the use of a cue to get to the right memory—a process termed *focusing* (Norman & Schacter, 1996). A general retrieval cue like "hanging out with friends in the student union" wouldn't be very useful, because it fails to focus the memory search onto a unique episode. Something more distinctive about a particular episode (i.e., "the time the server spilled a cup of coffee on you") would better focus the memory search and hence serve as a more useful cue. The next process, called *pattern completion*, involves the successful reconstruction of the product from this focused search. But retrieval doesn't end here. After a pattern has been completed, a decision must be made. This stage, labeled *criterion setting*, involves discriminating true experiences from imagined experiences (i.e., "Did this really happen, or did I just imagine it?").

In order to decide whether a memory is the product of encoding an actual event or an imagined event, people rely on a number of factors, such as whether the memory includes perceptual detail or semantic vividness—in other words, how fully fleshed out the memory is. The more perceptually salient the memory is, the more likely it will be judged a true memory rather than an imagined memory. Criterion setting as the source of memory errors is evident in the effects of hypnosis on memory. The effects of hypnosis occur at retrieval, as the rememberer lowers the criterion for labeling a memory as valid. In hypnosis, criterion setting is influenced by the highly suggestible state of the rememberer.

Source Monitoring and Misattribution

The five stages in the constructive memory framework highlight the importance of keeping memories differentiated from one another. Johnson (1988) characterizes **source monitoring** (the process of correctly identifying the source of remembered information) as a series of decisions. First, we must engage in **reality monitoring**—attributing the experienced memory to either a perceived external event or an internally generated event (i.e., event or imagination). If the memory is attributed to an externally perceived event, the source of the event must be determined ("Did I hear this in class? On the news? From a friend?). The inability to distinguish between the sources of event memories is termed **source confusion** and represents a failure of the source-monitoring process. Some researchers (e.g., Johnson, Nolde, & Leonardis, 1996) go so far as to suggest that all memory errors (except for errors of omission) stem from source confusion. Indeed, confusion over the source of memories has been a recurrent theme in this chapter. Another way of putting it is that we often *misattribute* our memories to incorrect sources.

Source Confusion and Eyewitness Memory.   Many, if not most, of the problems in eyewitness memory are instances of source confusion. This source confusion occurs at both encoding and retrieval. Let's reexamine two encoding factors—the misinformation effect and unconscious transference—in light of the notion of source confusion. After exposure to misinformation, witnesses fail to distinguish the source of the misinformation and the source of the actual memory, blending them into one representation. The same blending process occurs in unconscious transference; a bystander and a culprit are assumed to be the same person due to a failure to remember the source of the encounters. Source confusion also occurs at retrieval with photo bias; rather than recognizing that the suspect's familiarity derives from having encountered the face earlier in a photo array, we confuse the source of the encounter and misattribute the familiarity, claiming that the person seen in the photo array is the culprit.

Source Confusion and Illusory Memories.   The illusory memories induced in laboratory experiments indicate a failure in the reality-monitoring phase of the source-monitoring process. Participants fail to distinguish the internally generated target word (e.g., *sleep*) from the externally derived perceptual events (seeing the words *doze, rest, snore,* etc.). As Roediger and McDermott (1995) note, this failure is somewhat surprising, given that the illusory memories and the true memories differ in terms of the perceptual information they offer. The representations underlying illusory memories offer little or nothing in the way of perceptual characteristics, and so should be accurately labeled as internally generated and hence false. But source confusion remains, and illusory memories occur.

Imagination inflation provides another example of source memory confusion. As we noted in our discussion of the Garry and colleagues (1996) study, participants became a little less sure about the nonoccurrence of a fictional event. This may have been because imagined events seem to share many of the characteristics of remote memories (Johnson, Foley, Suengas, & Raye, 1988). Both are fairly diffuse, making it difficult to distinguish between them (Garry et al., 1996) to arrive at the correct reality-monitoring decision. This

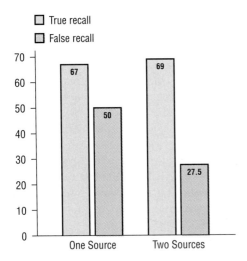

Reducing False Recall with Source Monitoring

Figure 7.7 Results from the Hicks and Marsh study (1999). When participants were sensitized to the source of the encoded event by having to encode the event in two different ways, false memories were reduced.

From Hicks, M., & Marsh, J. (1999). Attempts to reduce the incidence of false recall with source monitoring. *Journal of Experimental Psychology: Learning, Memory, and Cognition, 25,* 1195–1209. Copyright 1999 by the American Psychological Society. Reprinted by permission.

problem in reality monitoring made participants more willing to entertain the possibility that the fictional event was real.

Enhancing Source Monitoring.   If source confusion is at the root of illusory memories, then enhancing source monitoring should serve to reduce them. This was the basic idea underlying a study by Hicks and Marsh (1999). They reasoned that if the source of the memories was a salient aspect of the encoding episode, then the memory representations would have complete and distinctive information regarding source. In this context a potentially false memory would be scrutinized more closely because it would lack this distinctive source information and consequently would be less likely to be judged a true memory.

In order to make source information more salient, the investigators had participants encode themed lists in one of two ways. In the two-source condition, half of the words in each list were spoken by the experimenter, while the other half were visually presented and followed by participant generation. (Participants were to rearrange two letters: frgo—frog.) The source information in this condition was very distinct; one source was auditory and relatively passive (listening), while the other was visual and relatively active (generating). Therefore, false recall was expected to be low. In the one-source condition, the items on each list were read by the experimenter. Therefore, false recall was expected to be high due to the lack of distinctive source information. The results of the study are presented in Figure 7.7. As you can see, the level of false recall was quite high in the one-source condition. But in the two-source condition, false recall was reduced by nearly half. Sensitizing participants to source by making it a salient dimension at encoding made it easier to use source information at retrieval. As a result, memories for nonpresented words were scrutinized more closely, and a lack of source information was interpreted as evidence that the item did not occur.

The Distinctiveness Heuristic.   In the same spirit, Dodson and Schacter (2001b) propose that false memories can be reduced by using what they term a **distinctiveness heuristic.** Basically, this is a retrieval strategy that's based on metamemory—people's knowledge of what a real memory should be like. If memories lack certain distinctive information that a rememberer assumes the memory ought to have, then the event is judged as new. This heuristic would come into play at the final stage of the Dodson and Schacter (2001a) constructive memory framework—criterion setting, or the process whereby we assess whether there's enough evidence of actual occurrence to label an event a memory. In our opening scenario, John uses the distinctiveness heuristic in making a deliberate attempt to remember exactly what he was saying to Yolanda about studying together. At retrieval, he remembers quite vividly what he said because of this distinctive encoding.

The reduction in false remembering shown by Hicks and Marsh (1999) is consistent with this view. When participants had distinctive information related to source (two-source condition), false remembering was reduced. Also, Dodson and Schacter (2000a) provide additional evidence, comparing illusory remembering in conditions where participants said words aloud or when they simply listened to the words. False remembering was less pronounced in the "say aloud" condition. According to the investigators, participants in the "say aloud" condition had a higher criterion for judging an event as old at retrieval, relative to those who simply heard the words. Participants expected to remember having said the words, and if this information was not part of the memory, the event was judged to be new. Although the distinctiveness heuristic may be effective in reducing illusory recall, it is far from being a panacea; as you've read, even illusory memories can include vivid detail that would lead one to judge the event as real.

Social Influences and Constructive Remembering

Studies of illusory memories and imagination inflation involve compliance; participants are asked to imagine events that occurred, complete with the requisite detail. In some studies, family members are recruited to help "sell" the story. These conclusions point to another source of memory errors—the social context in which remembering occurs. Although this may seem self-evident to the layperson who has had plenty of experience reminiscing with friends, memory research has just recently begun to reflect the fact that remembering (and misremembering) is quite often a social enterprise (e.g., Weldon, 2000).

Roediger, Meade, and Bergman (2001) found evidence for what they term the **social contagion effect.** The basic idea is that our memories can be "infected" by the memories of others. In this study, pairs of participants were presented with household scenes (e.g., a kitchen). In the collaborative recall condition, members of the pair took turns recalling items from the scene. One participant was actually a confederate of the experimenter and deliberately engaged in false recall of several items. After the joint recall session, the non-confederate participant was tested alone and asked to recall as accurately as possible all of the items they had seen across all of the scenes. In the control condition, the participants never participated in the collaborative recall; they recalled the items in isolation

The results of the isolated recall provide clear evidence of infection; false recall was nearly four times greater in the collaborative recall condition relative to a control condition. Additionally, the social contagion effect was stronger when the confederate falsely remembered items that were consistent with the presented scenes (e.g., a hair dryer in a bathroom) than when they were inconsistent (e.g., toaster in a bathroom). The finding fits well with the idea that providing distinctive source information reduces illusory memories. Think about it: Wouldn't you be likely to remember something as strange as a toaster in a bathroom? If participants were unable to access this distinctive information, then the item would be correctly rejected as new.

Roediger and colleagues also utilized the process dissociation procedure described previously in Chapter 6. Recall the general idea: recognition memory involves a conscious component and a nonconscious component. These researchers found that the majority of falsely remembered words were associated with a feeling of familiarity (a nonconscious component) rather an actual recollection of the word being presented (a conscious component). This indicates that participants could not recall source information; if they had, they would have rightfully attributed the familiarity of the recognized item to the fact that the confederate had brought it up.

RECURRING RESEARCH THEME
Cognition and Consciousness

Unconscious Plagiarism

In Chapter 6, we discussed the notion of unconscious plagiarism—where someone comes up with an idea or suggestion only to find out that it was one they had heard earlier. It seems that unwittingly, we sometimes claim someone else's idea as our own. We discussed this as an example of implicit memory—where a previous encounter with some event is reflected in a nonconscious way. Unconscious plagiarism also serves as an excellent example of a source monitoring failure. Although an idea seems familiar, we fail to attribute this familiarity to the correct source—namely, having heard the idea before. In our opening story, John is incredulous when he hears Bart suggest bowling, because John had suggested bowling earlier, to Bart's deaf ears. But not completely deaf, as it turns out. Bart "remembers" the idea later but loses the source, attributing it to his own thought process.

An investigation by Marsh, Landau, and Hicks (1997) investigated the role of source monitoring in unconscious plagiarism. Experiment 1 served as a basic demonstration of unconscious plagiarism in the context of idea generation. In this experiment, participants in groups of around 20 were asked for ideas regarding how to solve problems (e.g., "How can the number of traffic accidents be reduced?"). Participants volunteered their answers by raising their hands until 15 solutions had been generated. Then participants were required to generate on their own two completely novel solutions to the problems. This occurred either immediately or one week after the group session. Unconscious plagiarism would be indicated by the propensity to generate ideas that had come out of the group session, and indeed, this did occur in both conditions. However, this plagiarism was much more pronounced in the one-week delay condition than in the immediate delay condition. This makes sense: as an event recedes into the past, our grasp on it becomes more tenuous; one of the features we lose may be the source of the memory. Therefore, a familiar idea for which we cannot determine the source has the potential to be mislabeled as our own.

In addition to having participants generate novel ideas, some participants were given a recognition test in which participants were asked to determine the source of each of the ideas that had been generated throughout the experiment. They were presented with new ideas, ideas that had been generated by their comrades and ideas they had generated. In contrast to the idea-generation task, this recognition of the source showed little such bias. Ideas generated by others were recognized as one's own less than 1% of the time. So while generation of ideas indicated plagiarism, asking about where these ideas had come from did not. This indicates that while information about the source may be available during cognitive processing, people don't always make good use of it.

The results of subsequent experiments supported the idea that unconscious plagiarism during idea generation is the result of a failure to monitor the source carefully during the generation task. In experiment 2, the investigators attempted to reduce unconscious plagiarism by instructing participants to consider the source actively during the final generation task. Under these conditions, the incidence of unconscious plagiarism was greatly reduced. A control group not specifically instructed to consider the source plagiarized at a rate similar to that in experiment 1. In experiment 3, the investigators attempted to increase unconscious plagiarism by making it especially difficult to monitor the source during final generation. To do this, they added time pressure to the mix: participants had to generate their novel solutions as quickly as possible. Consistent with the authors' hypothesis, this manipulation led to greatly increased levels of plagiarism during idea generation. The requirement to produce an idea quickly prevented participants from taking the time and making the effort to consider the source of their ideas closely.

So it seems that failure to monitor the source of the idea effectively leads to unconscious plagiarism—but why? Marsh, Landau, and Hicks (1999) offer the following analysis. During final generation, ideas come to mind, and we implicitly assess how familiar we are with them and how fluently they are processed. The fluency of an idea that pops to mind first may be misattributed to current thinking rather than to the previous encounter with the idea. More deliberate consideration of the source prevents this type of error. Less deliberate consideration of the source exacerbates it.

STOP *and* REVIEW!

1. Identify the five stages in the constructive memory framework.
2. Explain the stages involved in source monitoring.
3. True or false? The misattribution of source information is purported to be responsible for memory errors of commission.
4. True or false? The social contagion effect refers to the fact that memories are immune to distortion from social influences.

➤ A constructive memory framework proposes that five stages are necessary for accurate memory reconstruction: feature binding, pattern separation, focusing, pattern completion, and criterion setting.

➤ Also important to memory reconstruction is the process of source monitoring, which involves correctly identifying the source of remembered information. Source monitoring involves a reality-monitoring decision. If attributed to an external event, then the source of the event must be determined.

➤ Failure of the source-monitoring process results in source confusion. The consequent misattribution of source information is the primary cause of memory errors of commission and is responsible for many errors in eyewitness memory and memory illusions. These errors can be avoided by making the source of the event a salient aspect of the encoding situation. The distinctiveness heuristic assumes that if a memory lacks the distinctive information a rememberer assumes the memory ought to have, then the event is judged as new.

> ➤ The social contagion effect refers to the fact that memories can be affected/infected by others.

The Recovered Memory Controversy

The issue of the accuracy and inaccuracy of memory lies at the heart of a fierce debate that raged throughout the 1990s, and still provokes strong feelings today, although the deep divide may be closing a bit. At the center of the controversy lies the question of repressed, and subsequently recovered, memories that typically involve childhood sexual abuse. The early 1990s saw a rapidly growing number of these cases. These claims, coupled with research demonstrating the reconstructive nature of memory, has caused grave concern in the psychological community regarding the validity of **recovered memories.** The recovery of a *repressed memory* has the potential to completely devastate a family; that this devastation would occur as the result of a recovered memory that is false seems particularly tragic. In response to the increasing number of recovered memory cases, experimental and clinical researchers have intensified their investigations into the nature of illusory memories and the nature of memory for trauma.

Repression

The notion of **repression** stems from Sigmund Freud's psychoanalytic approach to personality and psychotherapy. You're probably familiar with Freud's claims; the most relevant for present purposes is Freud's contention that traumatic memories are submerged in the unconscious. Although these repressed feelings and memories are unavailable to consciousness in any direct way, they do manifest themselves, most notably through problems in adjustment and behavior. Freud's notion of repression has become the centerpiece for some approaches to psychotherapy; these approaches champion the liberation of repressed memories as the road to recovery.

Some confusion exists regarding exactly what is meant by repression. Freud himself wasn't consistent in his application of the term. As Lindsay (1998) notes, scholars have differed widely, and sometimes wildly, about the specific meaning of repression. At one extreme (the *special mechanism view*), the term can be used to refer to a special mechanism, unlike any memory mechanism we've discussed to this point, whereby memories for traumatic events are encapsulated in a more or less complete and accurate form. At some later point, the memories return. Less extreme versions of this view might allow for some forgetting and error in the repressed memory but would retain the notion of a specialized mechanism whereby a memory is repressed, stored, and recovered.

Most memory researchers are skeptical of the special mechanism view, and for good reason. As Roediger and Bergman (1998) note, several elements of it fly in the face of over a century of experimental research on the basic workings of memory. Therefore, memory researchers are likely to adopt another quite different view of repression. According to what might be termed the *ordinary forgetting view* (Lindsay, 1998), memory for trauma is nothing special; we forget traumatic events according to the same rules whereby we forget joyous or run-of-the-mill events. For example, an individual who has experienced a traumatic event may choose not to think about it; after a substantial period of time in which the memory is unrehearsed, the memory becomes less retrievable. And any memory, even if it is rehearsed, is subject to the ravages of time and interference. Most memory researchers adopt some version of this ordinary forgetting view and attempt to account for repressed memories in these terms.

To avoid the Freudian associations with the term *repression,* a number of alternatives have been proposed, *recovered memories* being the most common. But this term has its own problems, as noted by Lindsay (1998); most take it to mean "repressed and then recovered memories." Also, the very words *recovered memory* imply that the memory is an accurate one, when it's evident that this is not always the case. Lindsay proposes the term *recovered memory experience* to emphasize that the subjective experience of the remem-berer is the phenomenon that needs to be analyzed.

As Schooler (1994) points out, resolving the controversy over the validity of recovered memory experiences requires an answer to two basic questions: First, is it possible to completely forget and subsequently recover memories for traumatic events? Second, can false memories for traumatic experiences be fabricated?

Can We Completely Forget and Recover Traumatic Events?   At the center of recovered memory claims is the idea that traumatic events are often forgotten. Several researchers who have gathered retrospective reports of abuse victims (e.g., Briere & Conte, 1993; Herman & Schatzow, 1987) report that clients often go through extended periods in which the abuse is forgotten. However, as Schooler (1994) and others note, this research is rife with problems in interpretation. First, the events cannot be definitively corroborated; neither can it be ascertained exactly how the respondents interpreted the questions. Also, the fact that abuse experiences were forgotten for a period of time does not necessarily mean that they were completely inaccessible.

Williams (1994) took a more direct route to corroborating cases of lost traumatic memories, finding individuals who had been admitted 17 years earlier to sexual abuse clinics and interviewing them about their current knowledge of the experience. Of the 129 women she managed to interview, a substantial portion (38%) had no memory of the incident for which they were admitted. Although this finding does provide more compelling evidence for the forgetting of sex-related trauma than do the retrospective reports discussed above, it is subject to some interpretational limitations of its own. The majority of those who reported forgetting did recall other episodes of abuse; so the particular episode that was the subject of the research may simply have been confused with others (recall that a common cause of memory failure is source confusion). But compellingly, removing these individuals left 12% who reported that they were never sexually abused when they actually were.

So substantial forgetting of traumatic events can happen, but this seems to be the exception rather than the rule. A great deal of research indicates that children often have quite intact memories for a variety of nonsexual traumas, such as kidnapping (Terr, 1979), sniper attack (Pynoos & Nader, 1989), and emergency room treatment (Howe, Courage, & Peterson, 1994). Findings that reveal relatively intact memories for these events stand in stark contrast to claims of massive repression of childhood sexual abuse. But, on the other hand, there are some informative differences between the traumas listed above and sexual abuse. As Schooler (1994) points out, the traumas listed above all relate to single instances that could be discussed with relatively little embarrassment. Neither of these typically characterize childhood sexual abuse. And in fact, one study that does approximate some elements of sexual abuse in its involvement of an embarrassing and painful event (urinary tract catheterization) does lend some support to the notion that such events might be more subject to forgetting (Goodman, Quas, Batterman-Faunce, Riddlesberger, & Kuhn, 1994).

In addition, some theorists contend that the encoding and storage of particularly traumatic events may differ in important ways from the encoding and storage of more mundane events (e.g., Spiegel, 1994; van der Kolk, 1994), although the mechanisms have not yet been well-specified. Basically, these views contend that the storage of particularly traumatic events can be fragmented; the elements of these memories remain unintegrated. Remember the constructive memory framework, which states that in order for a memory to be accurately retrieved, the components of the encoded event must be bound together. Stress and emotion, like that associated with a traumatic event, could interrupt this feature-binding process. Therefore, recall would be difficult and should (and does) occur in the form of nonverbal fragments—as images, sights, or sounds. But these accounts fail to explain how such fragmented memories could serve as the basis for an integrated, detailed memory (Roediger & Bergman, 1998).

Physiological evidence seems to support the idea that encoding of stressful events is different than that of nonstressful events. Specifically, stressful events produce a complex pattern of effects on explicit memory (discussed in Chapter 6). Explicit recall involves brain structures in and around the medial temporal lobe, including the amygdala and the hippocampus (Nadel & Jacobs, 1998). Each area is responsible for different aspects of explicit memory. In addition, each area is affected in a characteristic manner by stressful events, with concomitant effects on explicit memory for those events. Nadel and Jacobs (1998) provide a useful synthesis of the evidence, spelling out the role of each set of structures in forming memories of stressful events. The amygdala seems to be essential for remembering emotionally charged events. The hippocampus seems to be the structure responsible for "putting it all together," allowing for the consolidation of each element of the memory into a coherent episode (i.e., the feature-binding process).

Stress has complex and varying effects on these brain structures. For example, high levels of stress enhance the functioning of the amygdala but disrupt the functioning of the hippocampus. Jacobs and Nadel (1998) suggest that the differential effects of stress on these structures account for some of the oddities of memories for trauma. For example, victims sometimes fail to recall the context of the event but can vividly recall how they felt (the emotions surrounding the event). Because the stress has enhanced the functioning of the amygdala and interfered with the functioning of the hippocampus, memory for the stressful event demonstrates a predictable pattern of strength and weakness: memory in the form of feelings or mood states is enhanced, while memory in the form of a coherent episode is poor.

So the issue may be one of poor encoding rather than forgetting. Therefore, caution should be taken when considering the issue of "recovery"; because the elements of the memory are not fully integrated at encoding, there is no coherent representation to retrieve.

Therefore (literally), the memory has to be "pieced together." As Nadel and Jacobs (1998) point out, the narratives that are woven around these memory fragments are likely to be a joint product of several sources, including real emotion fragments from the experience as well as inferences, guesses, and suggestions from other sources—all of which may well feed the memory distortion processes we have discussed in this chapter.

Stop *and* Think!

RECOVERING POSITIVE AND NEGATIVE MEMORIES

Reflect on your memories for positive and negative events from your life:

- Do you seem to have more of one than the other?
- Do you remember these events in detail?
- Do positive and negative memories differ in the level of detail?
- Are there any memories that you've "recovered" recently—in other words, events that you hadn't thought of for a very long time but have recently "popped back into mind"?
- What are these memories like?
- Are they detailed or fragmented?
- Are the memories for positive, negative, or emotionally neutral events?

Corroborated Cases of Recovered Memories.   Much of the evidence for the reality of recovered memories is anecdotal and based on uncorroborated case studies. However, there are a number of corroborated cases that lend some valuable insight into the conditions associated with valid memory recovery. Schooler, Bendiksen, and Ambadar (1997) outline four such cases and note several themes that the memory recoveries seemed to have in common. First, the cues present in the recovery situation corresponded to elements of the originally encoded experience (consistent with the encoding specificity principle discussed in Chapter 6); that is, the memories were triggered by a retrieval cue that reinstated some aspect(s) of the encoded experience. Another aspect of recovery was that it tended to occur very suddenly and was accompanied by extreme shock and emotion. Finally, if the memory was not always forgotten (i.e., it had been previously reported to others), there was evidence that the experience was interpreted differently at the time of "recovery" than it had been previously. In two of the corroborated cases, the rememberers were shocked to find out they had previously related the abuse incident to their husbands. That is, they believed they were completely unaware of the memory, but corroborating evidence demonstrated that they were aware of it. Schooler and colleagues label this a "forgot-it-all-along effect," suggesting that because the recovered memory "packs such a punch," the rememberer assumes that it must have been completely forgotten. Recall that a feeling of familiarity is interpreted as evidence that an event is "old." In this case the stunning lack of familiarity is taken as evidence that the event had never been remembered, when perhaps it had.

Can False Memories for Traumatic Events Be Created?   This is a tough question to answer directly. It would be unethical to attempt to implant false memories of traumatic events such as sexual abuse. But it is quite evident that we can be fairly easily convinced that something happened when it really didn't. Clearly, under any circumstances, mem-

Some fear that the therapeutic setting has the potential to increase memory suggestibility.

ory is a reconstructive enterprise. This is especially the case in the highly suggestive context that characterizes some therapeutic techniques.

Memory Work and Suggestive Influences in Therapy. The research we've discussed on false memories has led to great concern about the risk of false memory creation in the therapeutic context, where some of the factors conducive to false remembering can be present. First, the therapeutic context itself is suggestive, as the client will tend to trust the expertise of the therapist and be open to therapeutic suggestion. In addition to the general suggestibility of this context, some therapeutic approaches involve what is sometimes termed *memory work*—elaborate attempts to retrieve memories using methods that include repeated imagining, hypnosis, and group attempts to retrieve memories. As you've read, imagining (Hyman & Pentland, 1996; Goff & Roediger, 1998), hypnosis (Orne, Soskis, Dinges, & Orne, 1984), and social conformity pressures (Roediger, Meade, & Bergman, 2001) are three factors that heighten the likelihood of forming illusory memories.

By no means is anyone suggesting that these suggestive techniques are used by all therapists. But given the devastating potential of a false memory of childhood abuse, any usage of these techniques may be too much. So how commonly are they used? A number of studies have surveyed clinical practitioners to ascertain their beliefs and practices. For example, Poole, Lindsay, Memon, and Bull (1995) surveyed a random sample of licensed clinicians in the United States and Britain about their beliefs and practices. A majority of the therapists (over 70%) reported using at least one memory-recovery technique (i.e., imagining, hypnosis, dream interpretation), and approximately 25% of those therapists used a combination of such techniques along with suggestions that placed an emphasis on the importance of recovering memories (i.e., telling clients that memory recovery was necessary for therapy to be effective).

These figures seem to indicate widespread use of memory-recovery techniques. However, a criticism of the Poole and colleagues (1995) study is that the survey did not distinguish between techniques used with clients who always remembered their abuse and those who had no previous memories of abuse. Surely, the techniques are more dangerous with the second group than the first group. A survey by Polusny and Follette (1996) asked clinicians to report which memory recovery techniques they used with clients who reported no memories of abuse but whom the clinician strongly suspected were abused. Suggestive techniques (e.g., hypnosis) were cited by 20% to 35% of the therapists, depending on the particular technique. So it seems that a substantial minority of therapists do employ techniques that enhance the likelihood of false remembering when they suspect child sexual abuse. However, Courtois (1997) points out that the survey also revealed that very few respondents indicate childhood sexual abuse as a focus of their therapy; so these techniques would come into play relatively infrequently. Still, there are potential dangers in using these techniques when they do come into play.

Self-Help Books and Checklists. Suggestive influences also exist outside of the therapeutic context. Skeptics of recovered memory have expressed considerable concern about self-help books designed to aid in the recovery of childhood sexual abuse. These books include highly suggestive statements. For example, in *The Courage to Heal* (Bass & Davis, 1988), the authors state

> If you are unable to remember any specific instances . . . but still have a feeling that some-thing abusive happened to you, it probably did. . . . If you think you were abused, and your life shows the symptoms, then you were. (p. 21)

and offer advice for recovering memories, such as

> If you don't remember what happened to you, write about what you do remember. Re-create the context in which the abuse happened even if you don't remember the specifics of the abuse yet. . . . Often when women think they don't remember, they actually remember quite a lot. (p. 83)

In addition to these sorts of suggestive statements and advice, many recovery books include checklists of symptoms that allegedly serve as indicators of previous abuse; how-ever, these checklists are not derived or validated in any systematic manner, and the "symp-toms" are so vague and nonspecific that they could apply to anyone. For example, Bass and Davis suggest that affirmative answers to the following questions may be suggestive of pre-vious abuse:

> Do you feel different from other people? . . . Do you have trouble feeling motivated? . . . Do you feel you have to be perfect? . . . Do you have trouble expressing your feelings? . . . Do you find that your relationships just don't work out? . . . Do you find yourself clinging to the people you care about? (p. 35)

Coupling this list with such assertions as "If you think you were abused and your life shows the symptoms, then you were" has tremendous suggestive potential (Kihlstrom, 1998). These books undoubtedly offer great comfort to those who vividly remember and suffer the effects of childhood sexual abuse. But with a reader who has no memories but is be-ginning to explore the possibility, such suggestions pose a serious risk of eliciting a false memory.

Stop *and* Think!   ## SCRUTINIZING SELF-HELP

Take a trip to the local bookstore and peruse some of the books in the self-help/recovery sec-tions. You could also surf the Internet and look for Websites devoted to these issues.

- Do these books and Websites feature general symptoms checklists?
- Do they discuss any memory-recovery techniques that may lead to memory distortion?
- Are any caveats about these techniques mentioned?

- Do they specifically mention the issue of false memories?
- How do they deal with the possibility?

Converging Evidence of False Recovered Memories.   Although there is no direct experimental evidence of false trauma memories being implanted, there are several converging lines of evidence that suggest that this does occur (Schacter, Norman, & Koutstaal, 1997). First, many clinical practitioners have reported clients recovering memories of satanic ritual abuse (e.g., Wakefield & Underwager, 1994); however, these instances are never corroborated, and extensive investigations by law authorities continually fail to find evidence of satanic abuse (e.g., Nathan & Snedeker, 1995). Recovering memories of other experiences involving highly unlikely events (e.g., being abducted by aliens) would also seem to be evidence for memory implantation (Schacter, Norman, & Koutstaal, 1997). The reality of false memory implantation is also suggested by the existence of significant numbers of *retractors*—individuals who recover memories of abuse but later recant their reports (e.g., Nelson & Simpson, 1994).

Finally, the research we've discussed throughout this chapter constitutes a third line of evidence that memories can be implanted. Consider the range of events for which memories have been implanted or judgments of possible memories inflated: being lost in a mall (Loftus & Pickrell, 1995), spilling a punch bowl at a wedding reception (Hyman & Pentland, 1996), and being hospitalized overnight (Hyman, Husband, & Billings, 1995). Although these false memory experiences are certainly not on a par with sexual abuse, to dismiss their significance completely would seem reckless (Lindsay, 1998).

What Constitutes Valid Evidence?   One reason that common ground has been so difficult to reach in the debate over recovered memories relates to the fundamental differences over what constitutes good evidence. The databases that clinicians and memory researchers rely on to make their arguments are quite different. Clinicians base much of their argument for the validity of recovered memories on their interactions with clients and other evidence in the form of case studies and interviews. But because these sources of data are descriptive and thus subject to various self-report biases, experimental psychologists are reluctant to draw definitive conclusions from them. But the database emphasized by memory researchers—the extensive data demonstrating our propensity toward illusory memories—leaves many clinicians unmoved. They point out that illusory memories are, in large part, laboratory contrivances that don't generalize to the real-world issue of how it is that we store and retrieve memories for trauma.

Finding a Middle Ground

As you can see, it's pretty clear from the preceding discussion that the answer to both of Schooler's (1994) questions is yes. Entire episodes of one's life can be completely forgotten for a period of time; further, there is evidence that such forgetting may be more severe for more painful and/or embarrassing circumstances. Also, there seem to be a significant number of recovered memory experiences that can be corroborated. On the other hand, it is just as clear that memories for entire events can be created, particularly in circumstances that involve imagining, hypnosis, and/or conformity pressures—all of which can be present in the therapeutic setting.

Given the affirmative answers to these questions, the issue becomes one of discrimination: How can we tell when a recovered memory experience is valid (i.e., the event really happened) and when it is not? Memory researchers tend to be most skeptical of memories that emerge from therapeutic interactions involving suggestive memory techniques, particularly when the client entered therapy for nonspecific reasons not related to sexual abuse. Recall that the corroborated cases reported by Schooler, Bendiksen, and Ambadar (1997) involved sudden remembering, cued by an event that shared characteristics of the original abuse.

The APA's Position on Recovered Memory.   In the midst of the controversy over the validity of recovered memory experiences, the American Psychological Association appointed a special working group to review the scientific literature on memory and abuse experiences and to identify future research and training needs relevant to evaluating recovered memory experiences. The working group was composed of prominent researchers and clinicians who represented a range of views on the reality of recovered memory experiences. The five conclusions reached by the group (APA, 1996) serve as a worthwhile summary of where the field stands on this matter:

- Controversies regarding adult recollections should not be allowed to obscure the fact that childhood sexual abuse is a complex and pervasive problem in America that has historically gone unacknowledged.
- Most people who were sexually abused as children remember all or part of what happened to them.
- It is possible for memories of abuse that have been forgotten for a long time to be remembered.
- It is also possible to construct convincing pseudomemories for events that never occurred.
- There are gaps in our knowledge about the processes that lead to accurate and inaccurate recollections of childhood abuse.

S T O P *and* R E V I E W !

1. True or false? Most memory researchers adopt the "ordinary forgetting view" regarding the failure to remember traumatic events.
2. How is the encoding of stressful events different from the encoding of nonstressful events?
3. Discuss the common themes found in corroborated cases of recovered memories.
4. Discuss the evidence that indicates false memories of traumatic events can be implanted.
5. Why has it been difficult to establish the criteria for what constitutes true or false recovered memories?

➤ The existence of repressed and subsequently recovered memories has been an issue of much debate. Some believe that there is a special mechanism responsible for the forgetting of traumatic events; most memory researchers adhere to the "ordinary forgetting view"—traumatic events are forgotten according to the same rules whereby any event may be forgotten. Forgetting childhood sexual abuse is the exception rather than the rule.

➤ Some research does indicate that the encoding of stressful events is different from that of nonstressful events. Memory in the form of feelings and images is enhanced; however, memory in the form of a coherent episode is poor. Therefore the "recovery" of such memories is reconstructive in nature and subject to the negative influences discussed throughout this chapter.

➤ Corroborated cases of recovered memories indicate that valid memories tend to appear suddenly and in a context that reinstates some aspect of the abuse situation. Valid memory recovery also tends to be accompanied by great surprise and emotion.

➤ Evidence suggests that it is possible to implant false memories of traumatic events. One piece of evidence is the existence of retractors (individuals who recover memories of abuse but later recant their reports). Self-help books and therapeutic approaches that focus on memory recovery can provide a suggestive environment that may lead to the creation of memories of childhood sexual abuse.

➤ Current concern is focused on distinguishing between true and false memories of abuse. Common ground between clinicians and experimental researchers has been difficult to reach because of differing definitions about what constitutes good evidence. Memory researchers tend to value well-controlled basic studies of memory and are less persuaded by descriptive evidence, such as case studies. Clinical researchers tend to show a complementary bias.

GLOSSARY

absentmindedness: a lack of attention resulting in long-term memory distortion (p. 255)

bias: the influence of our beliefs, expectations, and desires on what we remember (p. 255)

blocking: a failure in retrieval of information stored in long-term memory (p. 255)

cognitive interview technique: an interview procedure that incorporates practices known to maximize the chances of complete and accurate memory (p. 269)

confabulation: the introduction of inaccurate detail to memories (p. 267)

distinctiveness heuristic: a rule of thumb used to determine whether a retrieved memory is real; the remember assesses whether enough detailed infor-

mation is present in the memory to deem it true (p. 281)

functional size: a reflection of the probability that any one person might be selected based solely on how they look; a fair lineup has a functional size equivalent to the number of people in the lineup (p. 266)

illusory memory (memory illusions or false memories): the remembering of events that never occurred (p. 272)

imagination inflation: the finding that mental simulation of an event leads to an increase in belief that the event may have actually occurred (p. 276)

interviewer bias: the beliefs and expectations of someone querying the memory of another individual, which can lead to errant memory reports (p. 271)

memory distortions: errors in remembering (p. 255)

misattribution: ascribing a memory to the wrong source (p. 255)

misinformation effect: the influence on the witness's memory of misleading information presented between the encoding of an event and its subsequent recall (p. 261)

optimality hypothesis: the idea that the relationship between confidence and accuracy is stronger to the degree that the encoding, storage, and retrieval of the event were optimal (p. 268)

persistence: the continued (but unwanted) automatic retrieval of memories that we'd prefer to forget (p. 255)

photo bias: the increase in probability that a person will be recognized as the culprit due to previous exposure (e.g., a lineup or photo array) (p. 265)

reality monitoring: a decision regarding whether a memory corresponds to either a perceived external event or an internally generated event (p. 280)

recovered memories: the return of memories that have previously been forgotten (p. 285)

repression: the Freudian notion that anxiety-provoking thoughts and memories are blocked from consciousness (p. 285)

sequential lineup: a lineup in which the witness must choose from lineup members presented one at a time (p. 266)

show-up: a lineup of one (p. 266)

simultaneous lineup: a lineup in which the witness must choose from lineup members presented at the same time (p. 266)

social contagion effect: the finding that a person's recall in a collaborative setting can be affected by the recall of others (p. 282)

source confusion: the inability to distinguish between the sources of event memories (p. 280)

source monitoring: the process of correctly identifying the source of remembered information (p. 280)

suggestibility: the malleability of memory to the leading questions or the suggestions of others (p. 255)

transience: the loss of information from memory with the passage of time (p. 255)

unconscious transference: what happens when witnesses fail to distinguish between a target person (i.e., a criminal) and another person encountered at a different time whose face is also familiar (p. 260)

weapon focus: the tendency for the presence of a weapon to focus attention narrowly, resulting in a lack of peripheral detail in the memory representation (p. 259)

8

Remembering the Personal Past

Alexander wraps up his interviews with John, Bart, and Yolanda in time to arrive as his family reunion only a half hour late. He joins his sister Eleanor, who is talking to a group of relatives

"I'll never forget that day when Alexander, Zach, and I went to the zoo. First, we stopped to get gas, and Zach went in to get a Coke. He'd been complaining about being thirsty all the way there . . . blah blah blah . . . "

Boy, how does she do that? Alexander muses. Eleanor always goes into such painstaking detail. I'm lucky if I can remember what happened yesterday.

She continues. "Do you remember, Mitchell? It was the day after Princess Diana's death, and you were too tired to go, after staying up all night watching the news."

"Yeah, I remember. Di's death was a real shock. I heard about it on a news update that broke into a bad TV movie. I just sat there, just kind of stunned, and stayed up all night watching the news updates about it. I was so tired the next day."

Thinking of the zoo pulls Alexander into his own private world. It recalls to him the summer he worked at the zoo's concession stand. He had so much fun working with his girlfriend Heather, especially their first kiss behind the ice cream machine! He can still smell the baking waffle cones.

I guess there would be no point in relating that memory. It really isn't relevant, Alexander thinks disappointedly. He snaps back into the present.

Eleanor is still talking about the zoo. " . . . and then the lion woke up. Boy, I've loved the zoo ever since I first went there when I was 2."

How does she remember that far back, Alexander marvels. I can't remember anything earlier than when I was 5. I don't have a good enough memory for these family reunions. Think I'll check out what's happening in the kitchen.

Boy, that smell takes me back to when I was a little boy! Alexander reminisces.

"Hey, Aunt Martha . . . how's that bread doing?"

"Oh hi, Alexander! I don't think this yeast is working," Aunt Martha says worriedly.

How can she possibly know that? Alexander wonders.

Everyday Memory

When we tell people that we teach psychology, this information elicits knowing glances or furrowed brows, or worse yet, comments like "Ohhhh . . . going to analyze me, huh?" We quickly inform these new acquaintances that no, we don't really care about their problems (in a clinical sense, at least); we do memory research. This triggers an entirely different (and at times, equally frustrating) set of questions and comments, such as "Why do I have such a terrible memory for my childhood?" or "I'll never forget what I was doing when I heard that Princess Diana was killed" or "Why do I remember things differently than my spouse?" Why should we, as memory researchers, find these questions about memory frustrating? Because, until fairly recently, we haven't had very good answers to these questions. These questions are partially answered by material discussed in Chapters 6 and 7. But there is something unique about these questions, something that goes unaddressed by the material presented in Chapters 6 and 7. These questions refer to one's personal experience and use of memory in an everyday context. As such, they aren't fully addressed by much of the memory research discussed thus far.

Neisser's Challenge: Ecological Validity and Memory Research

As you've no doubt noticed, cognitive psychology research is quite elegant: every confounding variable is anticipated and controlled, and each aspect of responding is carefully and precisely measured. To put it in terms of a concept introduced in Chapter 2, the *internal validity* of cognitive research is nothing short of impressive. Cognitive psychology no doubt owes to behaviorism a debt of gratitude on this score; behaviorist challenges to the notion of scientifically analyzing mental processes (as defined by structuralists and functionalists) meant that any new approach to the study of cognition would have to live up to extremely high methodological standards. Cognitive psychology has more than answered the challenge.

But while saluting the incredible progress cognitive psychology has made in establishing an empirical base, many would say it has come at a cost. Often, the *ecological validity* of cognitive psychology research has fallen well short of impressive. There exists a natural tension between the internal validity and the ecological validity of any research enterprise. You trade off one to get more of the other; more controlled is less natural, and vice versa. Take memory, for example; a great deal of the research in the first three decades of experimental work on memory fit a pretty standard pattern. Word lists carefully constructed to control for the effects of various extraneous variables were presented under precisely controlled conditions, and participant memory was tested with a number of standard laboratory memory tasks, like free recall or recognition. But one might argue that the number of words you can recall from a list of 48 concrete and abstract words presented for four seconds each doesn't tell you that much about why you can't remember events from your life that occurred before age 3. The emphasis in memory research (and cognition research in general) has always been on internal validity, often at the expense of ecological validity

In an important address to cognitive psychologists in 1977, Ulric Neisser delivered a blistering critique of the memory research that had accumulated in the first quarter century of cognition research, a critique that was directed at the emphasis on internal validity. According to Neisser (1978), "If X is an interesting or socially significant aspect of memory, then psychologists have hardly ever studied X" (p. 4). These were fighting words, to say the least. Neisser was basically saying that the first 30 years of memory research had been boring and trivial. Neisser went even further, claiming that although firm empirical generalizations about memory had indeed been made, most of these generalizations "are so obvious that every 10-year-old child knows them anyway." Extremely harsh words, perhaps, but many cognitive psychologists took them to heart. Since Neisser's address, there has been a veritable explosion of research on what might be considered "everyday" memory. The explosion is evident in the chart in Figure 8.1, which plots the combined number of citations found in the psychology research database PsychINFO, using the search terms "everyday memory" and "autobiographical memory." Up until 1983, slightly more than a dozen psychology writings were directed at issues of everyday memory, all but one occurring after Neisser's call to arms. Since 1983, there have been over one thousand

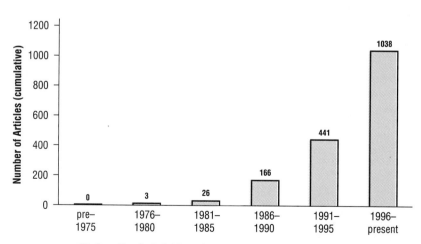

Figure 8.1
Number of psychology articles found in the PsychINFO database, using "everyday memory" or "autobiographical memory" as search terms. Note the dramatic increase in research citations for these topics over the past 20 years.

Citations That Include "Everyday Memory" or "Autobiographical Memory" investigations of these phenomena. The fact that you're reading an entire chapter devoted to everyday memory is another testament to this incredible trend; most cognitive psychology textbooks devote only subsections of chapters to everyday memory topics like childhood amnesia and flashbulb memory.

Everyday Memory Research: Bankrupt?   Not everyone jumped on Neisser's bandwagon. In an influential countercritique, Banaji and Crowder (1989) decried what they termed the "bankruptcy of everyday memory," objecting strongly to most of Neisser's claims. They drew an analogy between the psychologist who conducts well-controlled basic laboratory research on memory and the chemist who does controlled experimentation on the properties of yeast in order to establish why bread dough rises. In their view, the precisely controlled experimentation of the chemist is a more sensible approach and is more likely to yield meaningful results than "loitering in professional bakeries and taking careful notes" (p. 1187). They add that memory psychologists should not be embarrassed or frustrated when faced with questions that can't really be answered by basic research. "What other science," they ask, "has established that its students should decide on the importance of questions by checking first with Aunt Martha?" (p. 1187). Banaji and Crowder argue that in everyday memory contexts (such as attempting to remember events from one's life), the uncontrolled factors are so numerous that generalizability of the results is limited, not increased. Banaji and Crowder assert that the emphasis on internal validity in investigations of memory is entirely appropriate and is likely to be the road to truly generalizable principles of memory function.

Striking a Middle Ground.   Following Banaji and Crowder's (1989) critique, a number of researchers came to the defense of everyday memory research (e.g., Conway, 1991) and/or emphasized the value of both laboratory and everyday approaches (e.g., Loftus, 1991; Tulving, 1991). Tulving (1991) makes the important point that memory research is not a "zero-sum game" (i.e., someone must win, and someone must lose); forsaking everyday memory research for a basic laboratory approach, or vice versa, would be "throwing the baby out with the bath water." Both approaches can be quite valid and generalizable, and both approaches should be employed to discover the principles of memory function.

Since the opening salvos of the everyday memory debate, the dust has settled, and to no one's surprise, both laboratory and everyday approaches to the study of memory are still standing. And both approaches are probably the richer for the exchange. Laboratory psychologists are more sensitive to issues of external validity, and everyday researchers are more sensitive to issues of precision and control. In this chapter, we'll review some of the discoveries that have been made by researchers investigating issues of everyday memory, so you'll be well-informed in your conversations with "Aunt Martha" at your family reunions!

STOP and REVIEW!

1. True or false? Traditional memory research is high in ecological validity.
2. Discuss Neisser's criticism of traditional memory research.

3. Which of the following accurately describes the current state of research in memory?
   a. Everyday approaches are the sole focus of memory research.
   b. Laboratory-based approaches are the sole focus of memory research.
   c. Both everyday approaches and laboratory-based approaches are used in memory research.
   d. Memory researchers are concerned with internal, but not ecological, validity.

➤ Traditional laboratory-based memory research is high in internal validity (experimental control), but quite low in ecological validity (generalizability to the real world). There is a tension between internal validity and ecological validity. You must trade off one to get more of the other.

➤ Neisser delivered a critique of the laboratory-based approach to memory research, claiming it was boring, noninformative, and not very generalizable to everyday life. In answer to his challenge, recent years have witnessed an astounding increase in the number of studies devoted to everyday memory.

➤ Not everyone agreed with Neisser's critique, arguing that controlled laboratory-based memory research is more likely to yield meaningful and generalizable results than everyday memory research. Others argued that both approaches to memory research are valuable. Currently, both types of research programs are actively pursued.

Autobiographical Memory
Basic Issues and Methodology

The most popular topic of investigation within the realm of everyday memory has no doubt been autobiographical memory (AM), or memory for the experiences that comprise a person's life story, or *autobiography*. It's somewhat surprising that it took cognitive psychology so long to mine this important area of research. A person's past history is at the core of their identity. It shouldn't surprise you to learn, then, that autobiographical memories are as varied as the people who produce them. Given this level of complexity and individual variation, perhaps it isn't so surprising that it took cognitive psychology so long to explore this area. As you'll see, a host of variables affect the form and quality of autobiographical memories, including emotion, developmental stage, and the gender or cultural background of the rememberer.

Memories versus Facts

On reviewing some of the early research on autobiographical memory, Conway (1990) provides a useful distinction between an **autobiographical memory** and an **autobiographical fact** (see also Brewer, 1986); the characteristics of each are presented in Table 8.1. For your authors, an example of an autobiographical memory would be the events that took place on our wedding day. An example of an autobiographical fact would be the knowledge that we have three cats. Both of these are autobiographical in the sense that they

Table 8.1 **Characteristics of Autobiographical Memories and Autobiographical Facts**

	Autobiographical Memories	Autobiographical Facts
Experience of remembering	Always present	Rarely present
Personal interpretation	Frequent	Rare
Truthfulness	Variable	High
Context-specific sensory attributes	Always present	Rarely present
Self-reference	High	High
Duration of memory	Years	Years

From Conway, M. A. (1990). *Cognitive models of memory.* Cambridge, MA: MIT Press. Reprinted by permission.

are part of our life story, but they are very different from each other. Both autobiographical memories and facts are high in self-reference; they are both closely related to our personal identity; and they both will likely last for years—we're not likely to forget our wedding day or the fact that we own three cats.

But that's where the similarities between autobiographical memories and facts end. Autobiographical memories feature an experience of remembering. When either of us thinks of our wedding day, a sort of "reliving" experience occurs: we can see, hear, and feel the sights, sounds, and emotions that occurred on that day. No such reliving experience occurs when we think of the fact that we have three cats. It's just something we know about our lives. Another difference is that autobiographical memories quite often feature an interpretation on the part of the remember. We each have our own interpretation of and reaction to the events of our wedding day. However, we have no personal spin on the fact that we own three cats; we just do. Related to this difference is the notion of veridicality: Are autobiographical memories and facts "true"? Consistent with the idea that autobiographical memories are often subject to interpretation, it should come as no surprise that their "truth" can be quite variable. After all, as you learned in Chapter 7, our memories don't function as videotape recorders. Autobiographical facts fare much better on the dimension of truth; the facts that you know about your life are more or less "true," unless you're suffering some sort of psychopathological break with reality.

Let's consider the distinction between autobiographical memories and facts in light of another well-worn memory distinction: Tulving's distinction between *episodic* and *semantic* memories (discussed in Chapter 6). Recall that episodic memories are memories for personally experienced events that can be tied to a specific time and place, while semantic memories refer to knowledge or information about the world that is not tied to any specific contextual information like time or place. Autobiographical memories would be considered episodic memories in that they are essentially relived personal experiences rich in contextual detail. Autobiographical facts would be considered semantic memories in that they refer to simple, context-free knowledge of one's own personal world.

An autobiographical memory (our wedding day) and an autobiographical fact (we have three cats).

Linton (1975), in a self-study of her own memory, found that some memories undergo a transition from specific episodic memories (i.e., autobiographical memories) to a more generic semantic memories (i.e., autobiographical facts). For example, think about your memories about college. When you started college, no doubt every day was remembered as its own distinct event (autobiographical memory) for about a week or so, after which you began to form more general semantic memories about the types of things that happen in college (autobiographical facts). This transition from specific event memories to more general representations of repeated events is a common theme in much of the work on autobiographical memory. You'll read more about these sorts of general knowledge representations in Chapter 9. Our discussion in this chapter will focus primarily on autobiographical memories rather than autobiographical facts.

Stop and Think!

PERSONAL FACTS AND MEMORIES

In Chapter 6, you generated both episodic and semantic memories and compared their characteristics. Try this same exercise, but this time for autobiographical memories and autobiographical facts:

- Come up with an example of an autobiographical memory and an autobiographical fact.
- Examine Table 8.1, which summarizes the key distinctions between these two types of memory.

- Assess the distinction between these types of memory by analyzing your examples. For each example, evaluate whether or not it fits each of the characteristics listed.
- Note how autobiographical memories and autobiographical facts are distinct.

Methods of Investigation

Traditional studies of memory like the ones discussed in Chapter 6 are, in many ways, quite different from the ones we'll be discussing in this chapter. Typically, in these traditional sorts of studies, some type of material is presented during an encoding phase; then at some later point in time, memory for this information is tested, and the completeness and accuracy of the memory are assessed. Autobiographical memory research differs in significant ways from this model. First, no event is presented; the memories being assessed are for events that have happened, sometimes long ago and always out of the control of the experimenter. Second, accuracy of autobiographical memory can be difficult to assess. Who holds the right answer about what happened in the past? Even attempts to corroborate memories by talking to other people who experienced the same event are subject to that person's interpretations, biases, and just plain old forgetting.

Because there is no real way to control the events being remembered or to judge the accuracy of those memories, autobiographical memory researchers focus on aspects that can be assessed, such as the age of the recalled memories, their vividness and detail, their emotional intensity, and how these characteristics differ systematically across different groups of people (men and women, young and old, East Asian and European). And, in spite of the difficulties involved, a number of studies have been successful in evaluating the accuracy of autobiographical memories.

A number of methods have been developed to investigate recall of life episodes. Some require the recall of specific events or well-defined periods from one's life. Targeted event recall can allow for some assessment of memory accuracy. Often, corroborating information about the target event exists, either through the public record (in the case of memory for news events) or through family members (in the case of memory for major life events). However, evaluation of memory accuracy is limited by the completeness and accuracy of the corroborating source—be it public accounts or your Aunt Martha.

Most autobiographical memories recalled by the use of the technique of targeted event recall would be things that stood out in a person's life. The **diary technique** allows for a broader range of memories to be sampled—both the mundane and the distinctive. In this technique, the participant keeps a running record of events that occur in daily life; in other words, an event diary is kept and, at some point, is used to query memory. In addition, the diary technique allows for firmer conclusions about memory accuracy. The remembered events can be verified as having occurred because they were recorded and dated as they occurred (or immediately after). Therefore, diary studies have been the primary vehicle for understanding the processes by which we date our autobiographical memories or place them correctly in time.

Another technique for eliciting autobiographical memories involves a sampling procedure similar to the cued recall test you read about in Chapter 6. In the cue word technique, participants are presented with many word cues. They are asked to retrieve an autobiographical memory associated with each word and to write a short description of it and date the event. The use of this technique allows the researcher to assess something we're about to discuss in great detail: the autobiographical memory retention function—the distribution of personal episodic memories across the lifespan.

STOP *and* REVIEW!

1. Explain the difference between an autobiographical memory and an autobiographical fact.
2. True or false? Memory for events makes a transition from autobiographical facts to autobiographical memories.
3. Briefly describe the diary technique for investigating autobiographical memory.
4. Describe the cue word technique for investigating autobiographical memory.

➤ An autobiographical memory (a type of episodic memory) refers to memory for personal life experiences. An autobiographical fact (a type of semantic memory) refers to a piece of general knowledge about oneself.

➤ Memory for events seems to undergo a transition from episodic to semantic. Initially, experiences are recalled as distinct episodes. With a great deal of repetition, memory for these events becomes general knowledge (autobiographical memories become autobiographical facts).

➤ A number of methods are used in the study of autobiographical memory. Targeted event recall asks specific questions about a particular event or period from one's life. The diary technique requires the participant to record a number of events each day for a span of time, and memory for these events is tested later.

➤ In the cue word technique, word cues are presented, and participants must recall an autobiographical memory in response to each. This technique allows researchers to assess the autobiographical memory retention function—the distribution of personal episode memories across the lifespan.

The Autobiographical Memory Retention Function

Rubin, Wetzler, and Nebes (1986) conducted an extensive study attempting to investigate the shape of the memory function across the entire lifespan. Their analysis included participants ranging in age from 18 to 76. The complete memory function is presented in Figure 8.2. What you see plotted is the number of memories recalled from each period of life. Note the peaks and valleys of this retention function. These researchers observed that these patterns are indicative of three basic phenomena. First, there are very few memories from the early years of life and almost none before the age of about 3—a phenomenon typically termed **childhood amnesia.** Second, there is a disproportionately greater number of memories from ages 10 to 30—a phenomenon termed the **reminiscence bump.**

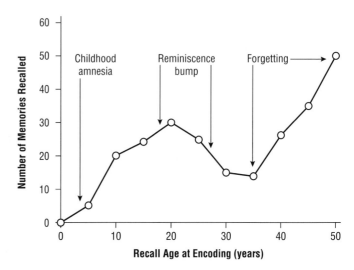

Figure 8.2 Autobiographical memories retrieved as a function of life period.

From Anderson, S. J., & Conway, M. A. (1997). Representations of autobiographical memories. In M. A. Conway (Ed.), *Cognitive models of memory* (pp. 217–246). Cambridge, MA: MIT Press. Reprinted with permission.

Third (and only evident for the older participants), there is a standard forgetting curve for information that occurs in the last 20 years. Most of the information recalled by older adults is for events that have happened recently. The specifics of this retention function have occupied autobiographical memory researchers' attention over the past 15 years and will be discussed in much of this chapter.

Stop and Think!   CUING YOUR PAST

For each of the following, try and recall a specific autobiographical memory. For each one you recall, write a brief (less than 10-word) description:

bananas
lake
grass
bubble
toast

For each of the memories you've generated, take note of

- whether it's an autobiographical fact or an autobiographical memory
- how old you were when the event occurred
- whether your memory is positive or negative emotionally

Plot the five memories you recalled as a function of your age at time of the memory and evaluate them in terms of the autobiographical retention function. Were the following key components of this function evident?

- lack of early childhood memories (childhood amnesia)
- many recent memories and fewer earlier memories (forgetting function)
- more memories between ages 10 and 30 (reminiscence bump)

Childhood Amnesia

Look again at the first part of the retention function shown in Figure 8.2—memories for events from the first decade of life. What you see is a precipitous drop in the number of memories reported before the age of 10 and a complete lack of any memories at all before the age of 2 or 3. The paucity of memories from the first few years of life has been termed childhood amnesia (or, less commonly, infantile amnesia). This finding has been recorded by many researchers, using a variety of methods. We should make note of the terminology we'll be using in this section. Researchers often speak of "the emergence (or development of) autobiographical memory" or "the offset of childhood amnesia." These two phrases can be considered synonymous; they describe exactly the same process. As the amnesia of childhood is lifted, autobiographical memory emerges. We'll be using both of these phrases in our discussion.

Investigating memories for early childhood presents a formidable methodological challenge. One big problem is that there is no way to check on the accuracy of what is reported. In other words, in studies where participants attempt to remember events from their childhood, there are no guarantees that participants are truly remembering the events. Think of the big events you may remember from your childhood. Can you determine if these memories are real or not? Perhaps what you're remembering is someone else's description of the event or the pictures you've seen since. In our opening story, Eleanor's recollection of having gone to the zoo at age 2 could well be a partial product of stories or pictures of that particular trip. This is especially likely, since her memory seems to be a bit earlier than the traditional "cutoff" for childhood memories.

Stop *and* Think!

CHILDHOOD AMNESIA

Think back to the earliest memory you can retrieve from your life. Once you've retrieved this memory, note the following things about it:

- How old were you when the event occurred?
- Is the memory general (an autobiographical fact) or specific (an autobiographical memory)?
- How vivid is the memory?
- Is the memory emotionally positive or emotionally negative?
- To what degree do you think the memory has been influenced by later rehearsals (retellings, pictures, etc.)?
- Can anyone corroborate your memory?
- If so, does their recollection match yours?

To avoid some of the pitfalls of faulty and subjective autobiographical recall, one research strategy involves asking participants about salient events from their childhood that can be corroborated. For example, Usher and Neisser (1993) asked participants to recall a number of critical events from their childhood that were documented and that could be checked with relatives and records. The events included birth of a sibling, a family move, the death of a family member, and a hospitalization. In addition, they were asked how frequently and recently they had rehearsed (i.e., thought about) the event and whether they had been exposed to pictures of it. Memory was tested with a set of questions asking basic information about each of the events.

The results are summarized in Figure 8.3. The figure plots recall scores for each of the events as a function of the age when it was experienced. The typical retention pattern for early childhood events was obtained: relatively poor memory before the age of 5. In addition, the offset of childhood amnesia occurred at different times, depending on the particular event. Memories for the birth of a sibling and hospitalization went further back than memories for a death or a family move. Hospitalization may be well-remembered because it is such a distinctive, involving, and frightening event—a combination that makes the event unforgettable (Usher & Neisser, 1993). The birth of a sibling may be memorable because it becomes the first installment of a story that will be told again and again—in other words, the story receives a great deal of rehearsal. This explanation provides a preview of one explanation for autobiographical memory development you'll be reading about shortly—an account that cites language development as a major factor.

You might imagine that there would be a relatively straightforward relationship between rehearsal of these salient events (in the form of family stories, photographs, imaginings, etc.) and their later recall. Not so; the relationship is actually quite complex. The effect of rehearsal depended on the child's age at the time of the experience. If the child was 3 years old or younger at the time of the event, family stories and photographs actually led to fewer memories than if the child was 4 or 5; in this case, family stories and photographs tended to make the memories stronger. Usher and Neisser suggest that a 2- or 3-year-old's memory may be relatively fragile and that their memories may be easily confused with stories and photographs. (Remember the idea of source confusion presented in Chapter 7.) The more of these that are present, the more obscured the actual memory becomes. But since a 4- or 5-year-old's memory may be less tenuous, these rehearsals are probably beneficial.

Figure 8.3 Results from Usher and Neisser (1993). Childhood amnesia is evident, but the precise pattern of recall differs with the nature of the event in question.

From Usher, J. A., & Neisser, U. (1993). Childhood amnesia and the beginnings of memory for four early life events. *Journal of Experimental Psychology: General, 122,* 155–165. Copyright 1993 by the American Psychological Association. Reprinted with permission.

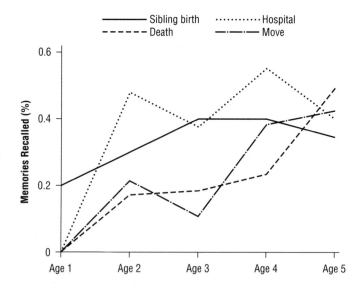

Explanations for the Offset of Childhood Amnesia.   At some level, the very existence of childhood amnesia is baffling. Many important and exciting things are happening during our first couple of years of life. Why is it that we can't retain any of it? When do we start "writing our life stories" cognitively? A number of factors have been implicated in the emergence of autobiographical memory. Some accounts emphasize neurological development, attempting to map the development of brain subsystems to the development of autobiographical memory. Other accounts take a more psychological tack, attempting to explain the development of autobiographical memory as a function of the development of language, or alternatively, as a manifestation of the development of a "self."

The Brain and Autobiographical Memory Development.   One possible source of the memory deficits that characterize childhood amnesia is the immaturity of the developing infant brain. Perhaps the neurological structures that subserve the complex processing that leads to autobiographical memories are not fully developed; hence, early memories are not formed. In young organisms, the hippocampal areas of the forebrain, critical for the formation of new long-term memories, are underdeveloped (Nadel & Zola-Morgan, 1984; Squire 1987). Also, the prefrontal cortex undergoes rapid development at around age 1, with a coincident improvement in the proficiency with which certain cognitive tasks are performed (e.g., Diamond & Doar, 1989). The development of a capacity for autobiographical memory would be limited to the extent that it is subserved by these brain areas.

This physiological approach to explaining childhood amnesia also seems to fit with some findings on people who have suffered damage to the hippocampus. As discussed in Chapter 6, patients who have suffered such damage often show a dissociation in memory abilities. They are unable to effectively store (or perhaps retrieve) events that been recently experienced, yet they show preserved ability to learn, and they retain many perceptual and cognitive skills (e.g., Squire & Zola-Morgan, 1988). This view contends that memory is not one thing but actually several different subsystems. (You'll remember this argument from Chapter 6 regarding the corresponding distinction between declarative and procedural memory.) So how might this apply to childhood amnesia? An early suggestion (Bachevalier & Mishkin, 1984; Schacter & Moscovitch, 1984) was that infant memory may obey a similar dissociation. Basically, infants have an early-developing procedural system that allows them to succeed on relatively simple memory tasks—like forming associations between events and remembering how to perform tasks such as walking, talking, eating, and so on—and a later-developing (declarative) system that serves as the basis for more complex memories. This later-developing system serves as the basis for autobiographical memories.

Social-Cognitive Development.   Even if this distinction were correct (and many believe it to be, at best, oversimplified), it would only explain childhood amnesia for events that occur extremely early in life. As we've seen, childhood amnesia extends to ages 3 or 4. Neurological underdevelopment wouldn't be able to explain childhood amnesia for those events that occur relatively late in toddlerhood. Complicating the picture even more is that children themselves do not show childhood amnesia. In other words, little kids (ages 2 to 3) can remember things that happened when they were even littler kids (e.g., ages 1 to 2) (Fivush, Gray, & Fromhoff, 1987). Think about it—a three-year-old can relate something that happened when they were 18 months old, but when 20 years old, their retrieval of this event is extremely unlikely. The fact that they could retrieve it when they were three years old suggests that the basic brain "machinery" is in place, which casts doubt on a purely neurological account of childhood amnesia.

Development of Language. One of the more popular accounts for childhood amnesia cites developing language skills as the critical factor in the emergence of autobiographical memory. In one of the earlier accounts of the emergence of autobiographical memory, Pillemer and White (1989) suggest that autobiographical memory develops pretty much in lock step with the development of language. In other words, children begin to remember events from their lives as soon as they are capable of describing these events with language. It makes sense, then, that the emergence of autobiographical memory would mirror the highlights in language development. Children make the most dramatic linguistic strides between ages 2 to 4 (at least in terms of verbal expression), so this is when they start verbally recounting their experiences; in other words, this is when they start developing autobiographical memory.

The importance of language in autobiographical memory has been found in a number of studies demonstrating consistent differences in *narrative style*—the way that families reminisce about, or narrate, past events (Fivush, 1991; Reese & Fivush, 1993). When conversing with their daughters, parents tend to adopt what is termed an *elaborative style;* this consists of long and richly detailed discussions of past events. When conversing with their sons, parents are more likely to adopt what is termed a *pragmatic style.* A pragmatic style of reminiscing is more succinct and contains less detail and elaboration. The style of reminiscing influences the quality of childhood memories; children of elaborative parents have better elaborated accounts of past events than do children of pragmatic parents. Given that this difference between elaborative and pragmatic styles is linked to the sex of a child, it's not surprising that Davis (1999) found evidence for female superiority in autobiographical recall. This difference in narrative style could underlie one's ability to relate past events in great detail, as Eleanor was doing in the story that opens this chapter.

Nelson (1993) also cites language as the critical factor in the development of autobiographical memory. Her *social interaction view* claims that autobiographical memory emerges as parents begin to engage in memory talk with their children. Parents play an active role in guiding and shaping a child's view of "what happened." They serve as "play-by-play announcers," pointing out what was important, how it happened, and why it happened. As events are discussed and recounted, the child begins to build a generic event memory for events that are often repeated (e.g., trips to the zoo) and also, with more unique events, begins to build the autobiographical memory system.

Development of a Cognitive Self. Not all believe that language is the critical variable in the emergence of autobiographical memory. Howe and Courage (1993, 1997) believe that while language is critical to the expression of stored experiences, it is not the same thing as the stored experiences. In other words, the symbols used to express what happened yesterday are just that—symbols. Just because an 18-month-old child doesn't have the linguistic skill to tell the story of what happened yesterday doesn't mean they don't have a sophisticated notion of what happened yesterday. Language is the most powerful means for

One's development of a sense of self plays an important role in autobiographical memory.

expressing experience, but it doesn't determine whether the event is remembered. So what is the critical factor in the offset of childhood amnesia?

According to Howe and Courage, it is the development of the sense of self. A *sense of self* (or self-concept) refers to one's knowledge that one is a person with unique and recognizable characteristics, and that one thinks and knows things about the world and can serve as a causal agent. This developing sense of self becomes an important organizer of autobiographical experiences. Since autobiographical memory is basically the knowledge of oneself and one's experience, it makes sense that children don't really demonstrate autobiographical memory until they have a sense of themselves as independent entities. Howe and Courage view language as the mechanism by which autobiographical memories are "let out," not the basis for their development.

So where does this leave us? There is no doubt that the emergence of autobiographical memory involves a complex interplay between the developing brain, the use of language, and the child's developing sense of who they are (or indeed, that they are someone). But because research has revealed an apparent sophistication of infant memory, the answer to the offset of childhood amnesia would seem to lie someplace other than with the brain.

RECURRING RESEARCH THEME
Cognition and Individual Differences

Cross-Cultural and Sex Differences in Childhood Amnesia

Given that the offset of childhood amnesia seems to depend on social (development of self) and cognitive (development of language) factors, the diversity of people's experiences in relation to these two factors should affect this offset. A study by Mac-Donald, Uesiliana, and Hayne (2000) investigated whether differences in early narrative style and interaction might influence the offset of childhood amnesia. This study compared New Zealanders of varying cultural origins: native New Zealanders, New Zealanders of European descent, and New Zealanders of Asian descent. Native New Zealanders (the Maori) have a particularly strong sense of cultural identity and place a strong emphasis on oral tradition, passing down richly descriptive accounts of the past. Based on this characteristic of the Maori people, the researchers hypothesized that the estimated offset of childhood amnesia would occur at a relatively young age. And, given the relatively sparse narrative style of Asian parents and children, the authors expected to find a relatively late offset of childhood amnesia for participants of Asian origin, with participants of European origin somewhere in between.

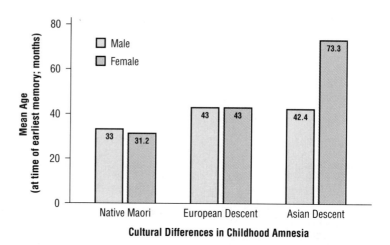

Figure 8.4 Results from MacDonald, Uesiliana, and Hayne (2000) demonstrating offset of childhood amnesia as a function of culture and age.

From MacDonald, S., Uesiliana, K., & Hayne, H. (2000). Cross-cultural and gender differences in childhood amnesia. *Memory, 8*, 365–376. Copyright 2000. Reprinted by permission of Psychology Press, Ltd.

The procedure they employed was simple; participants were asked simply to recount and date their earliest personal recollection.

The results are presented in Figure 8.4; as you can see, differences in earliest recollections fit the predictions nicely. As predicted, the age of the earliest reported memories was oldest for the Maori New Zealanders; in other words, they recalled events from earlier in their development than the other two groups. Asian participants reported significantly later recollections; particularly striking is that this finding was localized in women of Asian descent. This sex difference had not been found in an earlier study of Korean children (Han, Leichtman, & Wang, 1998), suggesting variation within Asian cultures themselves. (The Asian students in the MacDonald and others' study were primarily Chinese.)

Why did women of Asian descent show such strikingly late personal recollections? MacDonald and colleagues speculate that the long history of socialization differences between men and women in China, a culture that favors men economically and socially, has led to a greater emphasis on the personal experiences and accomplishments of men. As a result, Chinese men have a better developed sense of self than do Chinese women. In light of Howe and Courage's (1997) account of childhood amnesia, it's not surprising that this difference in development and elaboration of the self would lead to differences in the development of autobiographical recall and the offset of childhood amnesia.

The Reminiscence Bump

What an odd title for a section! It sounds like a new dance that cognitive psychologists are doing. But actually, the reminiscence bump refers to another distinctive aspect of the retention function people show for the memories from their lives. Namely, people recall a disproportionately greater number of memories for events that occur between the ages of 10 and 30 (see Figure 8.2, p. 304). Can you think of why this might be the case? Many of the events that occur in this period are "firsts," and many would be considered life milestones: first kiss, first date, first job, first year of college . . . the list goes on. These events serve as signposts in the stories of our lives. They're salient, distinctive, and important, so it's no wonder that they're well-remembered.

This explanation sounds pretty reasonable until you consider some findings from a study by Rubin, Rahhal, and Poon (1998). These researchers reviewed evidence that demonstrates a reminiscence bump not only for personally experienced events (i.e., autobiographical memories), but also for autobiographical facts like the things that people prefer (like movies, books, and music) as well as the events that people think are important or significant historically (like World War II or President Kennedy's assassination). For example, in a study by Holbrook and Schindler (1989), participants across a wide range of ages were asked to rate how much they enjoyed excerpts from songs that had been popular at different times from the 1930s to the 1980s. People showed a marked preference for songs that were popular when they were between the ages of 10 to 30. In a similar study, Larsen (1996) had older adults (average age 68) recall a particularly memorable reading experience. Books that were particularly memorable tended to be read between the ages of 10 and 40. Schulster (1996) reported a similar effect for memorable films.

Not only do personal preferences seem to exhibit this "bump," but so do general semantic memories; things we learn in early adulthood are remembered best. Rubin, Rahhal, and Poon (1998) gave participants multiple-choice tests of their general knowledge for information learned at different times throughout their lifespan. These included questions about the Academy Awards, the World Series, and current events. As you can see in Figure 8.5, the reminiscence bump was evident. People knew much more about events

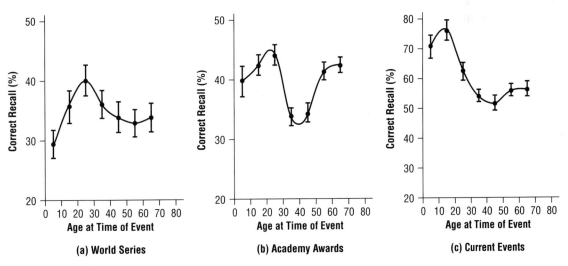

(a) World Series   **(b) Academy Awards**   **(c) Current Events**

Figure 8.5 Results from Rubin, Rahall, and Poon (1998) demonstrating that the autobiographical retention function characterizes semantic knowledge as well as memory for life episodes.

From Rubin, D. C., Rahhal, T. A., & Poon, L. W. (1998). Things learned in early adulthood are remembered best. *Memory and Cognition, 26,* 3–19. Reprinted by permission of the Psychonomic Society, Inc.

that had happened in their early adulthood than during any other period. (Recent events were also remembered fairly well, as you can see.)

These authors suggest a variety of explanations, any or all of which could play a role. First, it may be that the memory mechanisms described in Chapter 6 favor the retrieval of events from early adulthood because of their importance and distinctiveness. According to this view, these events are thought of (i.e., rehearsed) often due to their importance and are not subject to much interference because of their distinctiveness. A second account might claim that because our cognitive abilities and brain function are at their peak in early adulthood, things experienced during this period would be remembered best. A third explanation lies in the notion of identity formation. As you know from experience, the period from adolescence to early adulthood is a critical time for the formation of an individual's identity (Erickson, 1950). So events that occur during this critical period will be the most defining ones, the ones that are most often recounted and incorporated into one's life story.

A recent review by Habermas and Bluck (2000) fits nicely with this third view. The article, cleverly titled "Getting a Life: The Emergence of the Life Story in Adolescence," points out that the cognitive tools a person needs to *construct* a coherent life story, as well as the social and motivational reasons one needs to *have* a life story, both develop during adolescence. So in some ways, early adulthood is the beginning of the life story. It's no wonder, then, that both personally experienced events and general knowledge learned during this time are so memorable. This analysis provides an interesting parallel to the *cognitive self* explanation for the offset of childhood amnesia. Just as childhood events are encoded more memorably when we've developed a sense *that* we are, later life events are encoded more memorably when we've developed a sense of exactly *who* we are.

Forgetting

Let's go back to our favorite figure—the retention function for autobiographical memory across the lifespan (Figure 8.2, p. 304). We've already discussed two of the three components that characterize this function—childhood amnesia and the reminiscence bump. The third characteristic of this function is forgetting—as we might expect, given what we know about memory. For the period immediately preceding recall, there is a pretty standard forgetting curve: recent events are remembered fairly well, but recall falls off pretty quickly for events that aren't as recent. Wagenaar (1986) found that memory dropped from nearly 75% correct to less than 33% correct over a four-year period. You'll note that this is the same pattern of forgetting found in countless studies of memory, beginning with Ebbinghaus's classic self-study (discussed in Chapter 1).

It's not too difficult to come up with some general reasons for autobiographical memory forgetting. As you've seen in Chapter 6, the causes of forgetting are many. Probably the most common cause of autobiographical forgetting is a simple lack of rehearsal; if events are not thought about or discussed (i.e., rehearsed), the corresponding memory representation will be, at best, transient and, at worst, nonexistent. There is also an incredible potential for interference between autobiographical episodes; one need only think of all of the events that have occurred over the past month and how hard it is to retrieve one in the face of the others; most events don't really stand out. This relates to another likely cause of AM forgetting; many of the daily events in which we partake are routine; every day, we get up, eat breakfast, go to work or school, and so on. When events are this regular and routine, they blend together. Recall what happens when events are repeated, as noted by Linton (1975): repeated episodes lose their individualized character, transitioning from autobiographical (episodic) memories to autobiographical facts (personalized semantic memories).

Odors and the Autobiographical Memory Retention Function

When we discuss autobiographical memories in class or with friends, the question of whether odors as especially strong memory cues invariably arises. Everyone has had the experience of a vivid memory leaping into consciousness in the presence of a distinctive odor, like Aunt Martha's baking bread in the opening story. The most famous example of this is a literary one, from Marcel Proust's *Swann's Way* (1922/1960):

> I raised to my lips a spoonful of the tea in which I had soaked a morsel of the cake. No sooner had the warm liquid, and the crumbs with it, touched my palate than a shudder ran through my whole body, and I stopped, intent upon the extraordinary changes that were taking place. . . . I was conscious that it was connected with the taste of tea and cake, but that it infinitely transcended those savours. (p. 58)

What Proust experienced was the apparent power of odors to elicit memories that are especially old and vivid; this has been termed the **Proust phenomenon** (Chu & Downes, 2000). Proust's anecdote provides a powerful description of the power of olfactory cues. But anecdotes are poor evidence, and experimental evidence for this phenomenon is mixed. A study by Rubin, Groth, and Goldsmith (1984) compared word cues and odor cues for autobiographical memory recall. Contrary to Proust's anecdotal evidence, there was no difference in the age or vividness of the memories recalled with olfactory cues relative to those recalled with nonolfactory cues. A later study by Chu and Downes (2000) tested older adults; the researchers reasoned that this population would yield a fairer test of age differences in odor-cued memory distributions. Their results, presented in Figure 8.6, reveal an intriguing interaction. Memories cued by verbal labels demonstrated the typical reminiscence bump beginning in adolescence. Memories evoked by odor cues, however, were most likely to be recalled before age 10; so, indeed, these odor-cued memories were reliably older.

While this later study supports the idea that odors are more likely to cue older autobiographical memories, the correspondence of odor cues and vividness and emotionality of memories awaits further research. In a follow-up to their earlier study, Chu and Downes (2002) did find that odor-cued memories tended to be much richer in detail relative to word-cued memories.

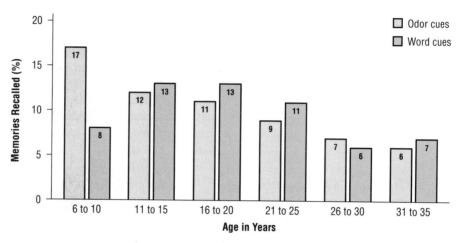

Proportion of Memories for Different Life Periods

Figure 8.6 Recall as a function of odor and word cues. Odor cues tended to lead to more remote memories.

From Chu, S., & Downes, J. J. (2000). Long live Proust: The odour-cued autobiographical memory bump. *Cognition*, 75, B41. Copyright 2000, Elsevier Science (USA). Reprinted by permission.

Stop *and* Think!

WHAT'S THAT SMELL?

Do some personal introspection about odors and memories and answer the following questions:

- Are there any smells that cue particularly strong memories for you?
- What are these smells, and what are the accompanying memories?
- Are these memories especially vivid?
- Are the memories from especially early in life?
- Do any of the memories share a common theme?

If you're having trouble coming up with odor-cued memories, try to think of memories you associate with these odors:

- a hospital or nursing home
- fresh-baked cookies
- bread baking
- perfume
- gasoline

STOP *and* REVIEW!

1. List and briefly describe the three basic components of the autobiographical memory function.

2. Define childhood amnesia and list three possible factors that allow for the emergence of autobiographical memory.

3. The reminiscence bump refers to a disproportionately large number of memories from this life period:

   a. ages 0 to 10

   b. ages 10 to 30

   c. ages 30 to 50

   d. ages 50 to 70

   e. adolescence

4. True or false? Memories elicited by odor cues tend to be more vivid and detailed than those elicited by other cues.

➤ Autobiographical memories retrieved throughout the lifespan follow a predictable pattern. First, there is a forgetting function, as many memories are retrieved from the last several years before the age of recall. Second, there are a disproportionate number of memories recalled from between the ages of 10 and 30 (the reminiscence bump), and third, relatively few memories are recalled from early childhood, and none before the age of about 3.

➤ The lack of memories before the age of about 3 is termed childhood amnesia. Possible reasons for the lack of early memories and the eventual emergence of autobiographical memory include a lack of maturity of the brain before age 1. The most important factors in the emergence of autobiographical memory seem to be the large strides in language development and development of the self-concept that occur at around age 2.

➤ The preponderance of memories from between the ages of 10 and 30 is called the reminiscence bump and probably results in part from the distinctiveness of the events occurring within that particular time period. Because these events are important in forming one's identity, they receive a good deal of rehearsal.

➤ There is some evidence that odors serve as especially potent cues for autobiographical memories. The memories elicited by odors tend to be detailed and vivid and are likely to be for remote events.

Factors Affecting Retrieval of Autobiographical Memories

There is little doubt that much autobiographical memory forgetting is the result of retrieval failure; information about our experiences is available to be retrieved, but we need the right cue to access it (recall the availability/accessibility distinction discussed in Chapter 6). Everyone has had the experience of having "forgotten" memories come flooding back when you revisit some location, event, or person. These experiences are likely to occur in situations like the family reunion that Alexander attends in this chapter's opening story. Going to a relative's house where you used to spend a good deal of time and talking to those you used to see can be strong retrieval cues. This phenomenon is basically the autobiographical memory version of the context reinstatement effect we talked about in Chapter 6. The representations of autobiographical memories are no doubt richly detailed and elaborated; these elaborations can serve to make the memory easier to access at retrieval, should the retrieval environment reactivate some of these elaborations.

Encoding Specificity in Autobiographical Memory

Context reinstatement is an example of the powerful memory principle (discussed in Chapter 6) termed *encoding specificity.* According to this principle, memory will be successful to the degree that the cues present at retrieval match the way the event was encoded. Marian and Neisser (2000) developed an intriguing test of this idea for autobiographical memory. Their research participants were bilingual individuals who were fluent in Russian and English. Each was a student at a U.S. university and had immigrated from Russia around a decade earlier. So their autobiographical memories included events that occurred when they lived in Russia and events that had occurred since their arrival in the United States.

Marian and Neisser's method was disarmingly simple. They interviewed each participant, using the cue-word method described earlier to elicit autobiographical memories. Here's the catch: half of the cue words were presented in Russian, and half of the cue words were presented in English. Can you see where this is going? Marian and Neisser (in line with the encoding specificity principle) hypothesized that autobiographical memories would be especially accessible if the language of retrieval matched the language of encoding. So when participants were interviewed and presented with cue words in Russian, they should recall more "Russian memories" (defined as an event in which the only language used by anyone involved was Russian). The parallel prediction was made for the English interview and cue condition. The results, presented in Figure 8.7a, confirm the prediction neatly.

Marian and Neisser explain their result by noting the inherently linguistic nature of autobiographical memories (discussed earlier in the context of the offset of childhood amnesia). Memories are not only expressed through language, but also include language as a fundamental feature of the encoded event. When this salient feature is presented again at retrieval, the entire memory representation is more likely to become active.

If you're particularly interested in experimental design, a thought may have occurred to you as you read about this study. The retrieval procedure used by Marian and Neisser involved the entire interview, which was conducted either in Russian or English. In addition, the cue words were presented in the corresponding language (e.g., in the Russian interview, Russian cue words were presented). This raises an interesting question: What was more important in producing the language-dependent recall—the Russian (or English) cue words or the ambience (or feeling) created by the Russian (or English) interview?

This question was tested in a second study in which Marian and Neisser separated the effects of cue word and interview ambience by adding two conditions to the mix. In addition to conditions in which they interviewed and cued in the same language, they added conditions in which the interviewing was done in one language while cues were presented in the other. For instance, the interaction with the participants might occur entirely in Russian except for the presentation of the cue words, which would occur in English. By adding these conditions, Marian and Neisser hoped to determine which aspect of the retrieval environment was more critical for recall.

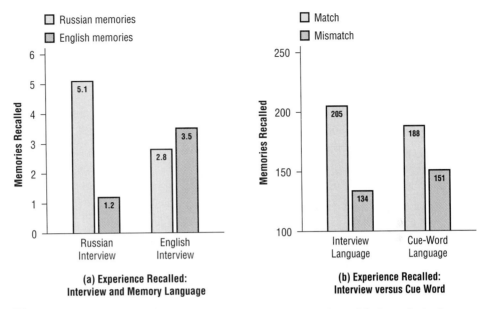

Figure 8.7 Results from Marian and Neisser (2000). Chart (a) shows that, given a particular interview language, more memories encoded in that language were recalled. Chart (b) shows that the match between interview language and memory language was a stronger determinant of memory than was the match between the cue-word language and memory language.

From Marian, V., & Neisser, U. (2000). Language-dependent recall of autobiographical memories. *Journal of Experimental Psychology: General, 129,* 361–368. Copyright 2000 by the American Psychological Association. Reprinted by permission.

The results are presented in the Figure 8.7b. This figure presents the number of autobiographical memories recalled by participants as a function of whether the language of the recalled memory matched or didn't match the language of the cue word, and whether the language of the recalled memory matched or didn't match the language of the interview. As you can see, a mismatch of either type led to lower levels of recall, but the effect of the interview (ambient) language seems to be the more important factor. Marian and Neisser explain this result by appealing to the notion of a *language mode.* As they point out, using a certain language doesn't just involve saying specific words; it involves a more general way of thinking that is specific to that language. This *state of mind* is distinctive and will likely serve as an effective cue if present at retrieval (i.e., facilitates the *focusing stage* of the constructive memory framework discussed in Chapter 7). The Marian and Neisser (2000) study reveals that retrieval of life experiences obeys a tried-and-true principle of memory—the encoding specificity principle. But other than the general cue that context provides, what other guides do we have for autobiographical memory retrieval? How are autobiographical memories organized and accessed? As you've seen, our memories for past events are far from perfect; autobiographical memory represents a proficient storyteller much more than it does some type of errorless recording and playback system.

Retrieval Cues for Autobiographical Memory

We've seen that the principle of encoding specificity applies to the retrieval of autobiographical memories. What other cues serve as useful triggers for autobiographical memories? Suppose your authors wanted to recall an episode from a visit to Toronto in the summer of 2001. Given the following set of W questions (what? when? where? who?) used in a study by Wagenaar (1986), which do you think would serve as the best cues for memory retrieval?

- What comprised the memory (our visit to Niagara falls)
- When the event occurred (June 25, 2001)
- Where it occurred (at a restaurant)
- Who was involved (Greg and Bridget)

Well, *what* do you think? "What" served as the best memory cue. The "when" cue was the least helpful. So the cue "our trip to Niagara Falls" will lead to quicker and better recall of that particular event than will "June 25, 2001."

These results are consistent with those found in a diary study by Brewer (1988). He found that location ("where") and time ("when") were poor cues for retrieval, but actions ("what") were good cues for retrieval. Once again, this makes sense; in trying to remind a friend of an incident at a restaurant, it would be more effective to say "Remember the time you won $150 playing pull tabs" than "remember that time at Ol' Mexico?" This sec-

What did *you* do on June 25, 2001?

ond cue will be relatively ineffective, particularly if going to Ol' Mexico is a repeated event. This result seems to indicate that the repetition of events leads to poor episodic memories (i.e., autobiographical memories), which replicates the result found in Linton's (1975) self-study indicating that event repetitions lead to a transition from specific episodic memories (i.e., autobiographical memories) to more general semantic memories (i.e., autobiographical facts).

A Constructivist Model of Autobiographical Memory Organization and Retrieval

These findings that "what" is very powerful in the retrieval of autobiographical memories suggests that autobiographical memories may be organized (at least in part) in terms of clusters of similar events. In line with this general idea, Conway (1991, 1997; see also Barsalou, 1988) developed a **constructivist model of autobiographical memory,** which proposes that rather than being retrieved as whole episodes, autobiographical memories are reconstructed from an autobiographical knowledge base. According to Conway (1997), autobiographical memories are personal interpretations of life events, not truthful records of these events. Let's take a closer look at this theory.

Levels of Knowledge in Autobiographical Memories.   Based on research investigating the effect of various sorts of cues on the speed and ease of access to autobiographical memory (Conway & Bekerian, 1987; Anderson & Conway, 1993), Conway proposes that people possess an *autobiographical knowledge base* that is organized hierarchically, with three distinct layers of knowledge (see Figure 8.8). The first layer is *lifetime periods,* substantial slices of our lifetime that are characterized by specific goals, plans, or themes (e.g., the authors' years in graduate school at Purdue). Also, within a given lifetime period,

We tend to remember memories in terms of certain lifetime periods—for instance, your authors remember their years at Purdue.

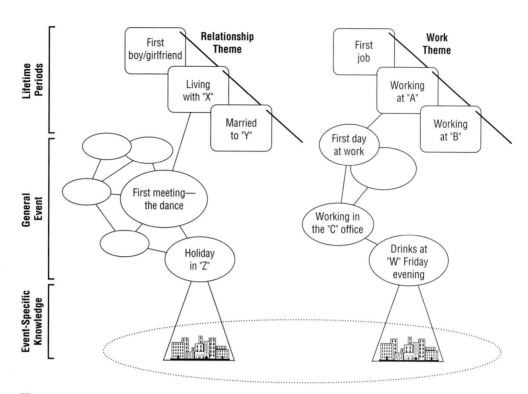

Figure 8.8 Conway's hierarchical model of autobiographical memory retrieval. (See the text for explanation.)

From Conway, M. A. (1990). *Autobiographical memory: An introduction.* Buckingham, UK: Open University Press. Reprinted by permission.

autobiographical knowledge is organized into different thematic categories, such as academic experiences and relationships. The second layer of knowledge is *general events,* a more specific representation of particular events that occurred over the weeks and months that make up each lifetime period. For example, Greg remembers all the times he shot pool at Locomotives, a local dive in West Lafayette, Indiana (and Bridget remembers watching him!). Knowledge at the general-event level can be used to access information at the third level of storage, *event-specific knowledge.* At this level are sensory-perceptual details that can be used to construct a specific memory. For example, we remember the particular Friday afternoon happy hour when we met each other for the first time over a pitcher of Old Milwaukee Light (how romantic!). This type of cognitive organization should sound familiar. Recall the idea of levels of categorization (superordinate level, basic level, and subordinate level) discussed in Chapter 5? It seems that autobiographical memories are organized in much the same way.

According to this model, autobiographical remembering involves a process of retrieval from the autobiographical memory knowledge base that proceeds from general to specific levels. The construction of an autobiographical memory takes place "on the spot." Cognitively, this means that we use working-memory processes to generate a memory that is consistent with current *task demands* and goals. In the opening story, Alexander begins with a cue (zoo), which leads to the retrieval of a lifetime period (the summer he worked at the zoo concession stand), which leads to the retrieval of general events (working with his girlfriend Heather), which leads to an event-specific knowledge (their first kiss behind the ice cream machine). An interesting implication of this constructive model of autobiographical memory is that it's possible (even likely) that someone would remember the same event differently on two different occasions.

RECURRING RESEARCH THEME
Cognition and Neuroscience

PET Scanning Autobiographical Memories

Given the relative newness of research on autobiographical memory, it's not surprising that not much neuroscientific work exists on the topic. But some recent work by Conway and colleagues (Conway, Pleydell-Pearce, & Whitecross, 2001; Conway & Pleydell-Pearce, 2001; Conway et al., 1999) has cast some light on the brain processes underlying the construction of an autobiographical memory.

Conway and colleagues (1999) elaborate on the model of autobiographical memory construction derived above and attempt to relate the processes in their constructive model to cortical areas in the brain. Previous research on brain activity during episodic memory retrieval revealed a number of consistent findings. One you may remember from Chapter 6; recall HERA (hemispheric encoding/retrieval asymmetry) model proposed by Nyberg, Cabeza, and Tulving (1996). These researchers found that the retrieval processes used during memory tasks, such as free and cued recall, involved extensive right-hemisphere activation and relatively little left-hemisphere activation (in contrast to encoding, which revealed the opposite pattern).

Conway and colleagues (1999) were interested in any possible differences between the rote type recall of episodic memories that characterizes a laboratory memory task and the constructive recall that characterizes autobiographical memory. They had participants perform two different memory tasks while they were being PET scanned. One was a standard paired-associate task in which participants memorized word pairs and were asked to recall the second member of the pair, given the first. The other task was to generate specific autobiographical memories in response to presented cue words. To verify that they had indeed generated a memory, participants gave a one-word description to the experimenter.

The scanning results featured some interesting surprises. Markedly different patterns of activation characterized the paired-associate and autobiographical-memory-generation tasks. Activity during the paired-associate test mirrored earlier findings of Nyberg and others (1996): increased activation in the right hemisphere, particularly temporal and prefrontal regions. However, activity during autobiographical memory generation featured prominent and intense activation in the left hemisphere, particularly in the frontal regions. Conway and Turk (1999) consider this left-hemisphere activation a "distinguishing feature" of autobiographical memory recall and propose that it reflects the operation of a self-memory system located in the left frontal areas. Converging evidence for this suggestion comes from brain-imaging studies of the self-reference effect (discussed in Chapter 6), which have revealed extensive left-hemisphere activation (Craik et al., 1999).

This constructivist model fits nicely with a number of findings from investigations of autobiographical memory. First, a study by Barsalou (1988) had participants generate specific memories of what they had done over their summer vacation. In spite of instructions to be specific, over 60% of the memories generated by participants were general memories, like "I read a lot" or "We went to the beach." This suggests that rather than directly accessing specific memories, people sample from general knowledge of the period—specifically, the intermediate level (Conway, 1997). It's interesting to note that this is precisely the same level at which people tend to access categories; instead of thinking of "animals" (superordinate level) or "a fat Tabby who loves Pounce treats" (subordinate level), we think "cat" (basic, or intermediate, level). Second, Conway and Bekerian (1987) found that recalling from a given lifetime period led to substantial priming effects in recalling other events from that same period, which would be expected if life events were categorized in this manner. Third, retrieval of autobiographical memories is typically a slow and effortful reconstruction rather than a rapid retrieval of facts. For example, it will take you longer to reconstruct what you did last June than it will to retrieve the colors of the rainbow or the 12 months of the year. Finally, the model's proposal that autobiographical memories are constructed "on the fly," and therefore can vary depending on the retrieval circumstances, is consistent with the fact that autobiographical memories can be variable across multiple recalls.

Stop *and* **Think!**

RECONSTRUCTING AUTOBIOGRAPHICAL MEMORIES

Try and remember any event that relates to

- summer vacations
- Christmas
- final exams

Take special note of the reconstruction process that you go through:

- Does this process match the autobiographical retrieval process as outlined by Conway?
- Was this reconstructive process rapid or slow?
- Do your memories seem to be hierarchically organized?

Try and fit the elements of your memory within the framework laid out in Figure 8.8.

RECURRING RESEARCH THEME

Cognition and Consciousness

Involuntary Retrieval of Autobiographical Memories

The research described in this chapter has dealt almost exclusively with effortful and conscious retrieval of autobiographical memories—cases in which people actively seek to reconstruct a memory from their past. But that's not always the way autobiographical memories are retrieved; quite often, memories enter consciousness without any effort or deliberate search. In fact, these unconsciously cued memories comprise a fair number of the autobiographical memories that we experience on a daily basis (e.g., Brewin, Christodoulides, & Hutchinson, 1996). But these memories have not been the subject of much investigation, for reasons that may be apparent: involuntary memories are just that—involuntary; therefore, neither the rememberer nor the experimenter can exert control over their appearance. This makes them difficult to study in a systematic manner. They have, however, long been of interest in a clinical setting; those who suffer from posttraumatic stress disorder often experience intrusive, frightening, involuntary recollections (Christiansen, 1992).

Berntsen (1996, 1998) performed a series of investigations to compare the characteristics of voluntary and involuntary memories. To study involuntary autobiographical memories, Berntsen (1996) had participants record two involuntary memories a day in a diary. Then, in a follow-up study (Berntsen, 1998), cue words derived from the previously collected diaries were used (with a different sample of participants) to elicit voluntary autobiographical memories. Berntsen compared voluntary and involuntary memories on a number of key variables: level of specificity, emotional intensity, amount of rehearsal, and event recency.

The investigation revealed differences between involuntary and voluntary memories. Perhaps the most striking was the level of specificity of the memories; nearly 90% of the involuntary memories were of specific events. The number of specific memories voluntarily recalled in response to cues was just over 60%, replicating the findings from Barsalou (1988), who found that voluntary memories were likely to be general-event memories. Voluntary memories were more likely to be generic descriptions of events (i.e., from the intermediate level of the autobiographical knowledge base, as described above). Involuntary memories tended to have received less frequent rehearsals relative to voluntary memories. In addition, involuntary memories were more likely to show a **Pollyanna effect,** with a predominance of positive memories recalled. Finally, involuntary memories tended to be of more recent origin than voluntary memories, contrary to popular folklore (e.g., Salaman, 1970).

Based on what seem to be fairly salient differences between involuntary and voluntary memories, particularly in their level of specificity and the way in which they're retrieved, Berntsen (1998) proposes that there may be two different systems for autobiographical memory retrieval. The hierarchical autobiographical knowledge base described above is the system used in voluntary searches of autobiographical memory and is likely to yield general (intermediate-level) autobiographical memories. A second system might serve as the basis for the spontaneous retrieval of highly specific and unique episodes, which are cued by particular situations. So according to this (speculative) view, involuntary memories are not reconstructed; they are more or less directly retrieved as episodes. Whether this added complexity in the proposed processes involved in autobiographical memory retrieval is warranted awaits further empirical test.

Stop and Think!

WHAT POPS INTO YOUR HEAD?

For the next week or so, keep a running diary of memories that just seem to "pop into your head" for no apparent reason (that is, involuntary memories). Jot a short description of each memory. After you've accumulated a number of these memories, evaluate them to determine if they show the same characteristics revealed in Berntsen's (1996) study.

- Do the involuntary memories tend to be recent?
- Do your involuntary memories tend to be positive?
- Do your involuntary memories tend to be specific rather than general?

STOP *and* REVIEW!

1. Discuss the role of the encoding specificity principle in autobiographical memory.
2. The most effective cue for retrieving an episode appears to be which of these "W's"?
   a. what happened
   b. where something happened
   c. when something happened
   d. who was present
3. Name the three levels of the autobiographical memory database, according to the constructivist model.

➤ A good deal of autobiographical memory forgetting is probably due to retrieval failure. Some evidence supports the notion that reinstating encoding context aids in the retrieval of autobiographical memories. Marian and Neisser (2000) found that participants in a bilingual memory interview tended to recall autobiographical episodes that matched the language of the interview.

➤ Aside from context, the best cues for autobiographical memories tend to be hints about what happened in a specific episode, rather than where or when it happened or with whom.

➤ According to the constructivist view of autobiographical memories, autobiographical remembering is a reconstructive process based on three different levels of knowledge (lifetime periods, general events, and event-specific knowledge). Neuroscientific evidence regarding the construction of autobiographical memories reveals a progression from left-frontal activation to right-hemisphere temporal and parietal activation.

Emotion and Autobiographical Memory

Of all the influences on our life's memories, perhaps none is so evident as emotion. Many of the events we remember are emotionally charged: your first kiss; hearing a startling piece of news, good or bad; the time you won the spelling bee (actually, we both came in second—sniff); your favorite team winning the World Series or your college winning the NCAA basketball championship. The impact of emotion on autobiographical memories has been a focal point of investigation and, as we'll see, a source of some controversy. A number of studies have attempted to determine how we remember autobiographical experiences associated with particular emotions. In one early study, Robinson (1980) used the cuing technique, asking people to retrieve memories in response to emotion-word prompts such as *angry*. The study revealed that emotional experiences were associated with shorter retrieval times than nonemotional experiences, implying that emotional events enjoy heightened accessibility in memory. Let's now turn to discussion of autobiographical memories that are among the most accessible ones you have.

Flashbulb Memories

No doubt one of the most interesting and well-documented forms of emotional memory is **flashbulb memory**—a detailed, vivid, and confidently held memory for the circumstances surrounding when you heard some startling bit of news. Our parents will never forget what they were doing when they heard the news of John F. Kennedy's assassination; we'll never forget what we were doing when we heard about (or saw) the explosion of the space shuttle *Challenger*. And none of us will ever forget what we were doing when we heard that two airliners had hit and toppled the World Trade Center towers. Memories for when you heard the news of a surprising event are striking in their degree of detail and vividness, and therefore we'd swear to their accuracy. Indeed, the term *flashbulb* implies that the events are brief in duration, surprising, and lead to photograph-quality memories. As you'll see, there is some truth to these assertions.

Almost everyone will remember vividly the circumstances in which they heard about the tragic events of September 11, 2001.

Flashbulb Account A

"When I first heard about the explosion I was sitting in my freshman dorm room with my roommate and we were watching TV. It came on a news flash and we were both totally shocked. I was really upset and I went upstairs to talk to a friend of mine and then I called my parents."

Flashbulb Account B

"I was in my religion class and some people walked in and started talking about [it]. I didn't know any details except that it had exploded and the schoolteacher's students had all been watching which I thought was so sad. Then after class I went to my room and watched the TV program talking about it and I got all the details from that."

Figure 8.9

Two sample accounts of the *Challenger* explosion (from Neisser and Harsch, 1992).

From Neisser, U., & Harsch, N. (1992). Phantom flashbulbs: False recollections of hearing the news about *Challenger*. In E. Winograd & U. Neisser (Eds.), *Affect and accuracy in recall: Studies of "flashbulb" memories* (pp. 9–31). New York: Cambridge University Press. Reprinted by permission of Cambridge University Press.

Characteristics of Flashbulbs.   The defining research on flashbulb memories was reported by Brown and Kulik (1977). They asked adults to report their memory for when they heard about the assassinations of John F. Kennedy, Martin Luther King, Jr., and Malcolm X, among others. One of the most striking things to emerge from their investigation was the consistency in the types of information reported about these memories. The flashbulb memories that people reported tended to include five categories of information: *location* (where they heard), *activity* (what they were doing), *source* (who told them), *emotion* (how they felt emotionally when they heard), and *aftermath* (what they did next). You'll note that Alexander's flashbulb memory of Princess Diana's death fits each of these characteristics. Figure 8.9 presents two accounts of the space shuttle *Challenger* explosion taken from participants in an investigation by Neisser and Harsch (1992). Note that each account includes each of the five components of a flashbulb memory.

Stop *and* Think!   ## IS IT A FLASHBULB?

Try and retrieve a flashbulb memory. Once you have, see whether it includes the components that typically characterize these memories:

who told you
where you heard
what you were doing when you heard
how you felt
what you did next

Then answer these questions:

- Is this memory personally relevant to you in any way?
- What factors do you think have led to its vividness?

What Produces a Flashbulb?   What accounts for the seeming clarity, accuracy, and vividness of these memories? Early in the investigation of flashbulb memories, Brown and Kulik (1977) proposed that any event that was particularly surprising and consequential (such as the assassination of a leader) receives prioritized processing in the brain, almost as if the memory of the event was "seared in" by a special brain mechanism. This account is typically termed "Now Print!" Such a mechanism would have high adaptive value; an organism that can remember consequential past events is more likely to adapt to changing conditions. Brown and Kulik also proposed that the more consequential the event, the more rehearsal it receives. People think about the event frequently and relate it to others, which leads the memory to be more detailed.

This mechanism leads to one of the central questions about flashbulb memories—their accuracy. Subjectively, flashbulb memories seem so clear, but how accurate are they? And how do flashbulb memories hold up over time? Research has provided mixed results. Early returns indicated that such memories were highly accurate; Pillemer (1984) found that participants' memories for the 1982 assassination attempt on former president Ronald Reagan included many accurate details two months after the event and that seven months later they had lost very little of that detail. But a number of studies of people's recollections for hearing about the space shuttle *Challenger* explosion gave researchers some pause. Mc-Closkey, Wible, and Cohen (1988) found that these recollections were not astoundingly accurate; only a little over half of the accounts were consistent across two tests given one week and nine months later.

One of the most striking examples of inconsistency was provided by Neisser and Harsch (1992). Look back at the accounts of the space shuttle *Challenger* explosion in Figure 8.9. We mentioned that these were two different accounts, but we left out the interesting fact that these accounts are from the same person. Neisser and Harsch found evidence for what they termed *phantom flashbulbs.* The day following the tragedy, the researchers gave a questionnaire to participants regarding the circumstances under which they first heard the news (account B). Two and a half years later, participants were once again given this questionnaire (account A). Much to Neisser and Harsch's surprise, there were many serious errors in reporting (although many accounts were correct as well). Even showing the participants their original (day-after) recall protocols failed to bring the memories back! And even when interviewed six months after this point in time, these erroneous accounts remained consistent.

What mechanisms account for such striking inconsistencies and misplaced confidence? One trend in the misremembrances was a phenomenon termed *TV priority* (Neisser & Harsch, 1992): many of the mistaken recollections were associated with having heard about the event on television. The researchers suggest that these mistakes likely arose in several ways. Participants no doubt watched a good deal of follow-up news reports on the tragedy; the image of the space shuttle going up in flames was widely and repeatedly broadcast; indeed, one still sees it occasionally replayed today. Perhaps most interesting of all, Neisser and Harsch propose that people have a schema for hearing about disaster news, a schema that includes having watched TV coverage. For example, how many of you heard about the World Trade Center attack on TV? Given the prominence of TV in our culture, this is the avenue by which we most frequently hear about disasters. Therefore, it isn't surprising that a later reconstruction of how one heard a piece of news would include a memory of having seen it on TV. Another type of error observed was the *time slice error*—participants vividly recalled an occasion on which they heard about the event. And indeed, this was an instance of hearing about the event, but it wasn't the first instance. So participants remembered the wrong "slice" of time. To use a term from Chapter 7, this is a failure in source monitoring (failing to correctly attribute the source of a memory).

So it seems that the evidence is mixed regarding the accuracy and durability of flash-bulb memories. A number of studies (e.g., Christiansen, 1989; Pillemer, 1984) have found these memories to be more accurate than the typical memory, while other studies (e.g., Bohannon & Symons, 1992; Neisser & Harsch, 1992) have found a fair amount of distortion in these memories. A study by Schmolck, Buffalo, and Squire (2000) pinpointed one possible source of the discrepant findings. The authors noted that studies that found more distortion typically featured a longer delay between the event and recollection; studies with shorter delays demonstrated less distortion and better overall recollection. They tested this observation by investigating students' flashbulb memories for the O. J. Simpson trial verdict. These quick-thinking researchers, who knew a flashbulb memory when they encoded one, tested students three days after the verdict was announced, and then again 15 months or 32 months later. Their results (see Figure 8.10) indicated a powerful interaction of delay with both accuracy and distortion. At the 15-month delay, 38% of the recollections showed no real distortions, with only 11% containing significant distortions. However, at the 32-month delay, only 20% of the recollections were without distortions, and nearly half included major distortions. In accordance with what you read in Chapter 7 about false memories, even flashbulb memories can show significant distortions, given a long retention interval.

What were you doing when O.J. Simpson was declared not guilty?

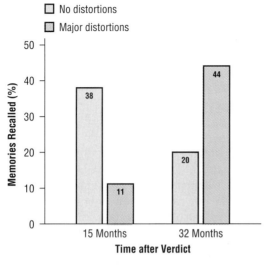

Accuracy and Distortion in Flashbulb Memories

Figure 8.10 Results from Schmolck, Buffalo, and Squire (2000). Major distortions in flashbulb memories for the O. J. Simpson trial verdict announcement were much more likely at the long retention interval.

From Schmolck, H., Buffalo, L. R., & Squire, L. R. (2000). Memory distortions develop over time: Recollections of the O. J. Simpson trial verdict after 15 and 32 months. *Psychological Science, 11,* 39–45. Copyright 2000 by Blackwell, Inc. Reprinted by permission.

Based on studies like these, the current view on the formation of flashbulb memories is that for the most part, flashbulb memories can be accounted for by appealing to some of the well-known factors that have been shown to influence memory in countless laboratory studies: degree of rehearsal, distinctiveness, and salience or personal relevance. Each of these factors leads to well-formed memories of any event. But Schooler and Eich (2000) suggest that while these usual memory mechanisms can account for the formation of flashbulbs, the operation of these basic mechanisms is somehow supplemented and/or intensified by emotion. The nature of emotion's effect is still unclear; it may alter the initial encoding of the event, or it may enhance the likelihood that the event is rehearsed on a later occasion.

It is also important to note that even if flashbulbs are phenomenologically "special" in their seeming vividness and detail, they are not special in one respect. They involve the same reconstructive memory processes, and hence the distortion, that characterize any other memory. But even in the face of significant distortion, the degree of vividness and clarity that characterizes flashbulb memories does seem to distinguish them from other episodic memories. So in answer to the question "Are flashbulbs a special type of memory?" most memory researchers would probably answer "Yeah, sort of." Or perhaps with a little more attention to grammar, they'd say "Flashbulb memories are 'special, but not so special'" (Christiansen, 1989).

Effects of Mood on Remembered Events

A second area of investigation that lies at the crossroads of emotion and memory is the relationship between mood and the types of memories people recall. If we're in a sad mood, do we recall sad experiences? Might such a link be at the root of psychological disorders like depression?

Mood Dependence.   A great deal of the research on the interplay between mood and memory has focused on one phenomenon. **Mood-dependent memory** refers to the finding that retrieval of a previously encoded event is enhanced when the mood experienced at retrieval matches the mood that was present at encoding. Sound familiar? It should; the principle of mood dependency is conceptually quite similar to Tulving's encoding specificity principle, discussed in Chapter 6. This phenomenon would seem to have some important ramifications for mood disorders. If one is depressed, does this lead to enhanced retrieval of negative autobiographical memories? And does this inclination, in turn, deepen depression?

Depression and Autobiographical Memory Recall.   The interplay between mood and memory has important implications for the treatment of depression. As we've seen, people often tend to recall events that are congruent with their current mood; as you might expect, people suffering from depression are likely to retrieve negative memories. Indeed, this is the case for both traditional laboratory materials, such as words and stories, and for autobiographical experiences (e.g., Williams & Scott, 1988). The bias is also evident in speed of retrieval; depressives are faster at retrieving negative events from memory and slower at retrieving positive events, relative to nondepressed controls. This *preferential treatment* for negative experiences can both worsen depression and impair one's attempt to overcome it. (See Blaney, 1986, for a review of the relationship between affect and memory.)

Another possible reason for this dominance of negative autobiographical recall, and for its continuing hold on those suffering from depressive disorders, is a tendency to be overly general in autobiographical recall (Williams, 1996). For example, if asked to recall an academic failure from college, a nondepressed individual may recall that they really struggled on their midterm in biology. In contrast, in response to the same prompt, a depressed individual might remember that last semester was a complete disaster. Stated in terms of the constructionist model of autobiographical memory, depressives recall events from the higher (more general) level of the autobiographical knowledge hierarchy.

Research indicates that the relative inability of depressed individuals to be specific in remembering past events leads to a number of memory deficits. For instance, lack of specificity in their remembering has been linked to their inability to solve present problems (Evans, Williams, O'Loughlin, & Howells, 1992). This makes sense; if people are unable to remember previous problems, along with the specifics of how the situations were resolved, then current problems will be more difficult to master. Lack of specificity in autobiographical memory also affects our perceptions of the future. Williams, Ellis, Tyers, Healy, Rose, and MacLeod (1996) found that suicidally depressed patients' lack of specificity about the past was associated with an inability to imagine future events. Based on this, depressed individuals will have trouble imagining in any specific and concrete way how things might get better in the future. This deficit in future problem solving makes depression that much harder to overcome.

S T O P *and* R E V I E W !

1. What is a flashbulb memory?
2. What are the five types of information typically included in a flashbulb memory?
3. Name two characteristics of autobiographical recall and how they relate to depression.

> Emotion has a number of powerful influences on autobiographical memory and is thought to play an important role in flashbulb memories, which are detailed, vivid, and confidently held memories for the circumstances surrounding when you heard some startling bit of news.

> Flashbulb memories tend to include information about who told you about the event, where you were, what you were doing, how you felt, and what you did after you heard. These memories tend to be vivid and confidently held. But despite their vividness, these memories are subject to forgetting, as is evident in phantom flashbulbs.

> Mood dependence refers to the fact that recall is better when retrieval mood matches encoding mood. Mood dependence seems to play an important role in depression. Due to their mood state, depressed individuals tend to recall a disproportionate number of negative memories. In addition, memories of depressed individuals tend to be overly general, which may affect their future thinking and problem solving.

Conclusion: Functions of Autobiographical Memory

What is the importance of autobiographical memory? What are its functions? Bruce (1989) distinguishes between two senses of the word *function*. One sense is that of *adaptive significance:* Why would some set of memory processes have evolved in a particular way? Is there something adaptive about having strikingly vivid memories of newsworthy events, as in the case of flashbulb memories? Bruce also refers to another sense of function—*real-world usefulness:* What good is this type of memory to our daily living? Pillemer (1992, 1998) offers some compelling answers to these questions. According to his view, autobiographical memories serve three important functions: communicative, emotional, and directive.

Communicative Function

Autobiographical memory serves a *communicative function*. A significant part of the conversations we have with others involves telling them personal stories relevant to the topic at hand. Specific autobiographical memories are especially powerful in this regard. Relating details of personally experienced events makes our communications seem more truthful and believable and tends to make them more persuasive (Pillemer, 1992). Relating detailed autobiographical memories also allows us to connect emotionally with others in an intimate and immediate way. What would provoke a stronger reaction in you—a friend telling you that they came from a tough background, or the same friend telling you that her parents had divorced when she was 4, she had battled and overcome cancer when she was 10, and she was suspended in high school for underage drinking? Clearly, more detailed and personal memories offer you a greater sense of intimacy and a stronger connection with your friend. You will likely also feel empathetic and relate a similarly detailed and personal story of your own.

Emotional Function

According to Pillemer (1998), autobiographical memory also serves an important emotional function in that it helps us organize, reflect on, and think through important life events. Most approaches to psychotherapy place a good deal of emphasis on the connection between one's personal memories and psychological functioning. As you read earlier, the inability of many depressives to recall the specifics of memories deters their ability to solve current problems and to imagine a better future. According to some (e.g., Herman, 1992), recounting one's personal memories of trauma in detail is critical for recovery. But it's also important to note that the vivid reliving of trauma is not always associated with positive consequences, as in the case of posttraumatic stress disorder.

Directive Function

Finally, Pillemer (1998) notes what he terms the directive functions of autobiographical memory. Remembering personally experienced events in detail can help direct future behavior. For example, there may be important events from your life where you really "learned your lesson"—when you mistakenly trusted someone, when you failed to plan ahead, when you were needlessly worried about something. Recollecting events of this sort can serve to change future behavior. Pillemer relates an especially relevant example, the recollection of an English major in college that was critical in shaping her career aspirations:

> My first Shakespeare class . . . would have to rank as one of my most influential experiences, since it started me on the life I'm following now (graduate school in Elizabethan literature). But the memory I have from that class is very small and tight. . . . I remember the first day best. I was fascinated by the easy way [the professor] roamed through Shakespeare, by just the amount of knowledge that he had. He seemed to know everything. In fact, after class, I asked him if he could identify a quote I had found about fencing, "Keep up your bright swords, for the new dew will rust them." Immediately, he said "Othello, Act 1, Scene 2, I believe." Which turned out to be exactly right. I wanted to know a body of literature that well. I'm still working on it. (Pillemer et al., 1996, p. 330)

Clearly, this student's memory of this specific encounter with her English professor served an important directive function.

One final point about the functions of memory outlined by Pillemer (1998): none of these functions is completely dependent on memory accuracy. In other words, for autobiographical memory to serve us in communication, in emotional adjustment, and in life direction, it isn't always critical that we remember events correctly. As Pillemer states, "From a functionalist perspective, it is permissible and often valuable to view personal event memory as a belief system rather than a mechanistic entity filled with traces that are objectively true or false." In other words, autobiographical memory serves us well, even if it's far from 100% accurate.

STOP *and* REVIEW!

1. What are the two main questions asked about the function of autobiographical memory?
2. Explain the communicative function of autobiographical memory.
3. True or false? The emotional functions of autobiographical memory help us organize important life events.
4. Learning a life lesson is an example of autobiographical memory's
   a. directive function.
   b. emotional function.
   c. communicative function.
5. Is autobiographical memory's function dependent on autobiographical memory accuracy?

➤ The notion of the functions of autobiographical memory relates to two questions: What is autobiographical memory's adaptive significance? What uses does it serve in day-to-day life?

➤ The communicative function of autobiographical memory allows for emotional connection with others and affords our communications with them more credibility and believability.

➤ The emotional function of autobiographical memory helps us organize, reflect on, and think through important life events.

➤ The directive function of autobiographical memory relates to the ways in which personal recollection can serve as life lessons, helping to direct our lives in certain ways.

➤ The functions of autobiographical memory don't really depend on memory accuracy.

GLOSSARY

autobiographical fact: the general (context-free) knowledge about oneself and one's personal history (p. 299)

autobiographical memory: the memory for the specific experiences that comprise a person's life story (p. 299)

childhood amnesia: the inability to recall events from one's life that occurred before the ages of 3 or 4 (p. 303)

constructivist model of autobiographical memory: a view that proposes that rather than being retrieved as whole episodes, autobiographical memories are reconstructed from an autobiographical knowledge base (p. 319)

diary technique: a method for investigating autobiographical memory in which the participant keeps a running record of events that occur in daily life (p. 302)

flashbulb memory: a detailed, vivid, and confidently held memory for the circumstances surrounding when you heard some startling bit of news (p. 325)

mood-dependent memory: the finding that retrieval of a previously encoded event is enhanced when the mood experienced at retrieval matches the mood present at encoding (p. 330)

Pollyanna effect: the tendency to recall positive autobiographical memories more easily than negative ones (p. 323)

Proust phenomenon: the apparent power of odors to elicit memories that are especially old and vivid (p. 313)

reminiscence bump: the disproportionately greater number of life memories that can be recalled from the ages of 10 to 30 (p. 303)

9

Knowledge Representation and Retrieval

Eleanor offers to take Mitchell and Zach home after the reunion. She turns on the radio. Yay—the Beatles! She starts singing and swaying to the music—"It's been a long day's night, and I been sleeping like a dog."

"Those aren't the words, you know. It's sleeping like a log or working like a dog," Zach comments.

"Well, close enough. Say, who was the guy who was gonna be the Beatles drummer but got dumped at the last minute when they hired Ringo?"

"I have no idea."

"I think his name started with P . . . Paul . . . No, that's Paul McCartney. His last name was short . . . buh . . . B something. Darn it! It's on the tip of my tongue."

"Whatever," Zach responds disinterestedly.

Mitchell decides to change the subject. "Is a robin a bird?"

"Of course it is," Eleanor answers without hesitation.

"How about a penguin. Is that a bird?"

Eleanor pauses. "Ummm, yes? Why are you asking these questions?"

"No reason. Just curious what you think."

"Oh?"

"So are you ready for the final?" Zach asks, still wondering whether a penguin is really a bird.

"You know, I don't think it's going to be so bad. The tests have all been cumulative. I've been through all the material several times. I feel like I know it," responds Mitchell.

"Good! I hope eventually I feel as ready as you sound. El, when you get to this next intersection, you're going to want to turn left; then at the four-way stop, you'll turn right. The house is up about a block on the left, right next to the coffee shop . . ."

"Pete Best! That's his name!" Eleanor interrupts triumphantly.

The preceding three chapters have dealt primarily with the phenomena of episodic memory—our recollection of previous events, complete with contextual details. Indeed, this is memory as we experience it day to day. However, conscious recollection of previous events is only a portion of the long-term memory picture. In fact, one could make the argument that most remembering doesn't involve the conscious recollection of episodes. Consider everyday tasks like getting up, dressing, driving to school, and fixing dinner. You could conceivably accomplish all of these without recalling previous events or episodes from your past. But you could not accomplish any of these tasks without procedural memory (memory for how to do things, discussed in Chapter 6) or remembering (i.e., knowing) what a toothbrush, shower, car, or hamburger is. The database of general knowledge that enables our successful interaction with the world around us is termed **semantic memory**. In contrast to episodic memory, semantic memory is typically devoid of any context; you don't recollect the first time you heard about or used a toothbrush or a car; you just know what they are. You might think of semantic memory as a mental dictionary in which you look up (i.e., retrieve) concepts during cognitive processing. In addition, semantic memory serves as a mental encyclopedia that houses important facts, historical information, and the like.

You'll remember the distinction we made in Chapter 6 between episodic and semantic memory and the idea that not all researchers agree that they represent two different memory systems. Some have suggested variations on the episodic-semantic distinction that underline the commonalities between the two. Tulving (1983) suggests that semantic memory consists of facts about the world as well as facts from our daily lives (i.e., that we own three cats). As we pointed out in our discussion of autobiographical memory (Chapter 8), it's likely that episodic memories become semantic ones. In other words, as the facts and events from our daily lives are repeated, they lose contextual detail and become more like general facts about the world (i.e., semantic memories).

Cognitive psychologists have investigated a number of important issues regarding semantic memory, or what is sometimes termed simply knowledge: How is knowledge organized? How is knowledge retrieved? What is the best way to describe how knowledge is represented—in terms of lists of features, networks of facts, or some other representational mode? Do we have multiple forms of representation—for example, both a verbal representation of the word *robin* as well as an imaginal mode of representation that allows us to visualize a robin?

The material we'll discuss in this chapter is a bit different from the ground already covered. You may have noticed that we've tried to emphasize cognitive processes within applied settings—the everyday situations you "think your way through." The findings and phenomena we'll be discussing in this chapter are decidedly nonapplied and the issues that are addressed by these findings are, for the most part, theoretical. The fact that in the vignette Eleanor answers the question "Is a robin a bird?" more quickly than "Is a penguin a bird?" doesn't have any particular ramifications for her everyday life. In fact, she wonders why Mitchell even asks the question. But differences in how we categorize things with similar characteristics is quite informative, giving us an idea of how our knowledge is organized and accessed.

Representing and Retrieving Categorical Knowledge

The topics we'll discuss in this section should ring a bell. You'll recall that in Chapter 5, we discussed the idea of concepts and categories and their basic structure and representation. Here, we will discuss how information about these categories may be accessed and retrieved. In addition, we'll discuss how specific items from categories are compared and contrasted with one another.

Basic Methodology

A **category verification task** can be used to determine how we access categorical knowledge. In this task, participants are asked to verify or deny simple statements like "A car is a vehicle" or "A tiger is a bird" as quickly as possible. Just like Eleanor in our opening vignette, we tend to verify that "a robin is a bird" more quickly than "a penguin is a bird." A **feature verification task** is used to assess how the features of categories are stored and accessed. For example, we tend to verify that "a cat has pointy ears" faster than "a cat has skin." As you might suspect, accuracy is not really of concern in these studies. In general, these questions are relatively easy, and people almost never make mistakes unless they're trying to answer too quickly (recall the speed-accuracy trade-off discussed in Chapter 2). Speed is the more informative dependent variable in studies of category and feature verification; for example, we tend to verify that "a robin is a bird" more quickly than "a penguin is a bird." The fact that this is a consistent difference tells us something about how knowledge is organized. In some way, *robin* is more tightly connected with the more general concept "bird" than *penguin* is. In addition, the fact that we tend to verify "a cat has pointy ears" faster than "a cat has skin" tells us something about the proximity of these features to the concept "cat." Let's take a look at some general theoretical notions that have been suggested to account for the way we relate and retrieve stored information.

The Hierarchical Network Model

Semantic network approaches propose that knowledge is stored in the form of associative networks in which concepts are represented by nodes. Other nodes connected with the

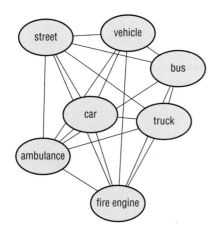

Figure 9.1 A simple semantic network.

primary concept node relate to concepts or features of a given concept. Consider the example presented in Figure 9.1. As you can see, similar concepts are "close to" one another, as are a given concept's features. It's important to note that when using these models, the phrases "close to" and "nearby" are used in a colloquial sense; that is, the concept "vehicle" is figuratively close to the concept "car." Another important clarification: this type of model is not the same as (indeed, it's quite different than) the neural network approaches to knowledge and cognition that we've discussed elsewhere. The networks we're about to discuss are not based on brain structure, as are neural networks (although the two approaches could be considered kindred theoretical spirits). In neural network models, the representations (nodes) correspond to neurons, and the connections between the nodes correspond to the complex interconnections between neurons that form neural networks. In the neural network approach, these nodes and links are unlabeled—that is, there is no neuron that corresponds to the concept "robin," and no neural connection that connects this concept to the concept "bird."

Semantic network models are only a generally descriptive metaphor; their network architecture is simply a matter of convenience and ease of description. The nodes in semantic network models do correspond to specific concepts (i.e., "tree"), and the links between these nodes do correspond to relationships between concepts (i.e., "tree" is connected to "leaves"). These types of labeled networks provide a convenient way to describe and represent simple concepts. Knowledge retrieval is described within the framework offered by these models as a process of traversing the nodes by "gliding" along the associative links.

As we just noted, the neural network and semantic network approaches are similar in at least one basic way. Both architectures rely on the concept of excitatory connections between representations as a way of explaining knowledge activation and retrieval. As you'll see, semantic network models posit **spreading activation,** a process whereby the activation of one node spreads to other, related nodes. Neural network models posit a similar mechanism whereby activation of one node can lead to the activation (or inhibition) of other nodes. So the two approaches are not without similarity.

Collins and Quillian (1969, 1970) proposed the first semantic network model, the **hierarchical network model.** The model's name highlights the major structural assumption of the model—that concepts are organized hierarchically, with specific concepts nested within more general ones. This should sound familiar; we discussed these levels of categorization in Chapter 5. Figure 9.2 provides a graphic depiction of the model. As you can see, three levels are represented (corresponding to the levels of categorization discussed in Chapter 5). Nodes at the superordinate level represent the most general concepts (i.e., "animal"); nodes at the basic level represent more specific categorical subsets (e.g., "dog"); nodes at the subordinate level represent even more specific concepts (e.g., "chihuahua"). Attached to each of these *concept nodes* are particular features of the concepts (e.g., has pointy ears, is yippy, likes Taco Bell), termed *feature nodes.* So how does the model work? Verification of statements about category membership (e.g., "A dog is an animal") activates

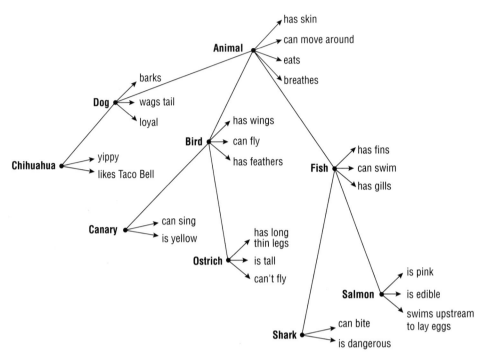

Figure 9.2 A hierarchical knowledge network.

From Collins, A. M., & Quillian, M. R. (1969). Retrieval time from semantic memory. *Journal of Verbal Learning and Verbal Behavior, 8,* 240–247. Copyright 1969, Elsevier Science (USA). Reprinted by permission.

the node corresponding to the concept "dog"; from there, a spread of activation moves to linked concepts and features in the network. The activation of the basic-level concept "dog" will eventually get to the associated superordinate-level concept "animal," leading to an affirmative response.

The Category Size Effect.   These network dynamics lead to a straightforward prediction: it should take longer to traverse the links from a subordinate-level concept (i.e., "chihuahua") to a superordinate-level concept (i.e., "animal") than to do the same from a subordinate-level concept to a basic-level concept (i.e., "dog"). This prediction, as it turns out, is a pretty consistent finding termed the **category size effect.** As you can see in the bottom line of Figure 9.3, people are quicker to verify a concept as a member of a smaller category ("dog") than they are to verify the concept as a member of a larger category ("animal") The hierarchical model neatly accounts for this effect.

Stop *and* Think!   **TESTING THE CATEGORY SIZE EFFECT**

Recruit a couple of willing participants, and present them with the following sentence verification task.

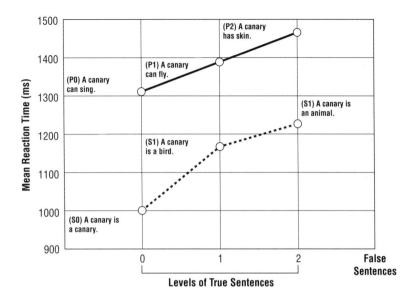

Figure 9.3 Early findings from studies of category verification, demonstrating a category size effect along with verification findings consistent with the assumption of cognitive economy.

From Collins, A. M., & Quillian, M. R. (1970). Does category size affect reaction time? *Journal of Verbal Learning and Verbal Behavior, 9,* 432–438. Copyright 1969, Elsevier Science (USA). Reprinted by permission.

1. Give them the items from each list below (test each list separately).
2. Have them respond "true" or "false" to each statement as quickly as possible.
3. Record the time it takes them to complete each of the lists.

List 1	List 2
A bird is an animal.	A robin is a bird.
A canary is a living thing.	A cactus is a plant.
A cactus is a tool.	A canary is a dog.
A tiger is a vehicle.	A vehicle is a living thing.
A poodle is a dog.	A banjo is a musical instrument.
A bat is a living thing.	A cat is a vehicle.
A chair is a living thing.	A tree is a living thing.
A banjo is an animal.	A piano is an animal.

List 1 involves traversing a total of 14 category levels across all of the items, while list 2 involves traversing a total of only 8—one per item.

- Did list 1 take a longer time to complete than list 2?
- Did your participants demonstrate the category size effect?

Cognitive Economy.   Another feature of the hierarchical network model is a certain "thriftiness" in the way information is stored, a characteristic that Conrad (1972) terms **cognitive economy.** Cognitive economy means that the feature information of a concept is stored in the highest possible level of representation. Take the concept "cat" and the feature "has skin"; according to the principle of cognitive economy, the "has skin" feature is stored nonredundantly and at the highest possible place in the network. In other words, "has skin" will be stored at the level of "animal," and verification of the statement "A cat has skin" will require traversal from the basic level ("cat") to the superordinate level ("animal"). This feature of the model makes good sense; it does seem absurd to assume that the feature "has skin" would be stored with every single animal in the network. It makes more sense to assume economical storage. Collins and Quillian (1969) found support for their assumption by comparing feature verification reaction times (RTs) for statements that required participants to traverse 0, 1, or 2 levels in the hierarchical network (see the top line in Figure 9.3). The RT findings perfectly paralleled the findings from category verification. The more distant the feature was from the target concept, the longer it took to verify the target-feature relationship.

The idea of cognitive economy also describes the first assumption of the model that we discussed—the hierarchical organization of subordinate-, basic-, and superordinate-level categories that predicts the category size effect. The links between these concept levels are organized economically; rather than have three links between the concepts "salmon," "fish," and "animal" ("salmon-fish," "salmon-animal," and "fish-animal"), only two links are necessary ("salmon" to "fish" and "fish" to "animal"). The fact that a salmon is an animal can be inferred from this more economical system of links.

Problems for the Hierarchical Network Model.   Alas, although the early research returns provided some support for the existence of hierarchically organized knowledge networks, problems began to arise.

Falsification RTs.   One weakness relates to a question that may have occurred to you. Up to this point, we've only considered cases where statements are true. What happens in the case of false statements, like "A bird meows"? It turns out that RTs for false statements parallel those of true statements. However, the explanation for this result isn't as clear. It seems silly to assume that "does not meow" would be stored as a feature of "bird" (particularly in light of the cognitive economy principle).

Collins and Quillian (1969) proposed several accounts of falsification RTs. According to the *contradiction hypothesis,* false responses require that a contradiction be found between the information in the hierarchical knowledge network and what the statement claims. So the statement "A canary is green" would lead to a search of memory that would turn up the fact that canaries are yellow, and the presented statement would be rejected. This hypothesis leads to exactly the same prediction for falsifications as for verifications: the more distance that must be transversed in the network, the longer it should take to find a contradiction. For example, the statement "A bird meows" requires movement from the basic-level concept node to a feature node at the same level. This should lead to a quicker falsification time than for "A canary meows," because in this case, the knowledge search would need to move from the subordinate-level concept node to a basic-level feature node. Unfortunately, the results of the study by Collins and Quillian contradicted their prediction: the RT increase was negligibly small and in the opposite direction! That is, it took a longer time to reject "A bird meows" than it did to reject "A canary meows." Collins and Quillian provide some alternative accounts of falsification processes, but they are quite complex and don't account all that well for the data. So falsification results continue to be a bit of a problem for the hierarchical model (Chang, 1986).

The Reverse Category Size Effect.   The cornerstone finding of a category size effect turns out to depend on how stimuli are constructed. Rips, Shoben, and Smith (1973) found evidence of a *reverse category size effect.* They compared two conditions in which the hierarchical category structures were slightly different. The first condition was the traditional category structure (e.g., "collie"–"dog"–"animal"). The other condition used a less traditional category structure (e.g., "dog"–"mammal"–"animal"). According to the hierarchical network model, the verification of category membership should take the longest as you move from the smaller to larger categories, regardless of condition. However, the researchers found an interesting interaction: a category size effect was found for the traditional category structure, but the nontraditional category condition yielded a reversal of the effect (e.g., "A dog is a mammal" was verified more slowly than "A dog is an animal"). Clearly, this finding is problematic for the hierarchical network model. Can you think of what may have led to this violation of the hierarchical network model's prediction? Although mammal may be a smaller category than animal, it is not as familiar. Less familiar concepts lead to slower verification. This leads us to another finding that proves even more problematic for the hierarchical network model.

The Typicality Effect.   Another standard finding from studies of categorical knowledge representation, the typicality effect, seems to pound an empirical nail in the coffin of the hierarchical network approach. The **typicality effect** refers to the finding that speed in verifying category membership depends on how typical the instance of the category is. For example people are quicker to verify that "A robin is a bird" relative to "A penguin is a bird," because "robin" is a more typical or familiar example of the category. Put in terms of a concept from Chapter 5, the category membership of prototypes is verified more quickly than that of nonprototypes. Why is this finding problematic for the hierarchical network model? Because the model says nothing about certain category members having prominence or primacy over others. Canaries, robins, owls, egrets, and flamingos are all birds, and all should be verified as such with equal ease. But, in reality, certain category members serve as better examples than others and are retrieved more easily.

The Feature Comparison Model

Semantic networks may provide a sensible approach to modeling how we access and retrieve categorical information, but there are other possible architectures. Based on some of the problems encountered by the hierarchical network model, Smith, Shoben, and Rips (1974) proposed a **feature comparison model** that was decidedly different. Rather than a complex interrelated network of concepts, knowledge consists of a set of descriptions, or what might be termed *feature lists.* So, concepts are not nodes in a network but are sets of semantic features that reflect the meaning of the concept.

Which of these is a "better" bird?

Representation and Information Retrieval.   Another important assumption of the model is a distinction between two types of features. **Defining features** are those that are essential to the meaning of the conccpt. **Characteristic features** are those that are not essential; sometimes, these are termed accidental features. Smith, Shoben, and Rips (1974) propose that the features of any given concept can be classified along a continuum from defining to characteristic. For example, defining features for the concept "bird" might be that it has wings and two legs; characteristic features might be that a particular bird might be brownish in color or may be kept as a pet. When we make categorization decisions, defining features are given more weight; when it comes right down to it, these are the features that are the concept.

The feature comparison model proposes that information retrieval in response to a categorization query is either a one- or two-stage process, depending on the nature of the target concepts. Take a look at a sketch of the model presented in Figure 9.4. When a query is presented, the feature lists (both defining and characteristic) corresponding to the two concepts are retrieved, and an overall comparison is made. If this rough comparison yields a great deal of overlap ("A canary is a bird") or almost no overlap ("A canary is a fish"), this will elicit a *quick true response* or *quick false response,* respectively. These types of decisions are made relatively quickly, because a one-stage rough comparison of features yields enough evidence for the decision.

How about the case in which less typical instances of a category are presented, as in the case of "A penguin is a bird"? In this case, the stage 1 comparison will yield some overlapping features but also many nonoverlapping features. In cases where feature lists yield a moderate amount of overlap, a second decision stage is necessary. In the stage 2 comparison, only the defining features are compared: When it comes right down to it, is a pen-

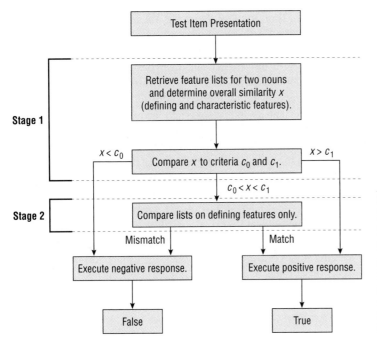

Test Item Presentation

Retrieve feature lists for two nouns and determine overall similarity x (defining and characteristic features).

Stage 1

$x < c_0$ Compare x to criteria c_0 and c_1. $x > c_1$

$c_0 < x < c_1$

Stage 2

Compare lists on defining features only.

Mismatch   Match

Execute negative response.   Execute positive response.

False   True

Figure 9.4 Steps involved in category/feature verification, according to the feature comparison model.

From Smith, E. E., Shoben, E. J., Rips L. J. (1974). Structure and process in semantic memory: A featural model for semantic decisions. *Psychological Review, 81,* 214–241. Copyright 1974 by the American Psychological Association. Reprinted by permission.

guin a bird? This comparison will yield a match, and the statement will be confirmed. But because of the additional processing stage, judging these less typical category instances takes more time.

The astute reader (this means you) may have noticed that the last two paragraphs redescribe the typicality effect—and, indeed, one of the major accomplishments of the feature comparison model is that it easily accounts for this effect. Typical instances of a category are verified more quickly because they overlap more with the general category concept. Another strength of this model is that it explains what is sometimes termed the **false relatedness effect,** an effect that can not be easily explained by the hierarchical network model. Falsification RTs take longer when two concepts are somewhat related (i.e., "A robin is a tree") than when the two concepts are not at all related (i.e., "A robin is a brick"). According to the feature comparison model, the brick-robin comparison would yield no overlapping features, leading to a quick falsification. The tree-robin comparison would yield some overlapping features (i.e., living thing) and thus would lead to slower falsification RTs. Implicit in the preceding points is another strength of the feature list model: it provides a more elegant account of falsification RT data (Smith, Shoben, & Rips, 1974).

Problems for the Feature Comparison Model.   In spite of its successes, the feature comparison model (in its simpler forms) runs into a number of significant problems. For one thing, it doesn't really account for the category size effect. Consider the comparison between "A penguin is a bird" (small category) and "A penguin is an animal" (large category).

Verification of the second is longer than the first. However, the feature list model makes the opposite (and wrong) prediction. For both queries, a stage 2 analysis is likely: both penguin-bird and penguin-animal are likely to lead to moderate feature overlap. In stage 2, only defining features are compared, and smaller categories have more defining features than larger ones. Therefore, smaller categories would be associated with longer reaction times, which is exactly the opposite of what happens. In addition, the model doesn't really provide a mechanism whereby feature statements (i.e., "A canary is yellow") are verified or falsified. It would seem that assessing such statements would involve comparing the feature list for the concepts "canary" and "yellow things," which doesn't seem very plausible. The only feature on the list for "yellow things" would be "it's yellow."

Another problem with the model is its reliance on the distinction between defining and characteristic features. As we noted in our discussion of the classical view of concepts in Chapter 5, it's quite difficult to specify which features of a concept are truly essential. Smith, Shoben, and Rips (1974) do propose that this variable is a continuum rather than a dichotomy, but it's still not clear where defining features leave off and characteristic features start. Also, the processing stages outlined in the model (see Figure 9.4) implicitly assume a dichotomy between these types of features; a stage 2 decision requires that the comparison be between defining features.

Evaluation: Hierarchical Network or Feature Comparison?   It's difficult to evaluate which of these two approaches is more successful. Indeed, as Chang (1986) points out, the findings that support one approach turn out to be the Achilles' heel for the other. The hierarchical network model predicts category size effects but cannot account for effects of typicality; conversely, the feature comparison model can easily account for the effects of typicality but has trouble handling category size effects. More recent data haven't done much to resolve the issue. But one thing is for certain: the architecture espoused by the hierarchical network model—that of an associative network—has become part and parcel of several influential accounts of knowledge representation and cognitive processes in general.

The Spreading Activation Model

In response to some of the difficulties encountered by the hierarchical network model (in particular the typicality effect), Collins and Loftus (1975) propose an extensive revision, termed the **spreading activation model** (although the original hierarchical model also proposed a spread of activation). This theory makes a number of assumptions about the representation of categorical knowledge in addition to the central assumption that concept nodes are linked in an associative network. But unlike the original Collins and Quillian (1969) model, associations are not strictly hierarchical. In fact, the links that connect concepts represent a wide variety of relationships. As you can see in the network pictured in Figure 9.5, the relationships include category membership (violet to flower), property to concept (red to sunrise) relation, and more subtle relationships, like those between street-ambulance and house-fire.

Collins and Loftus (1975) propose a number of processing assumptions. When a given concept is presented, the corresponding node is activated, and the activation spreads out

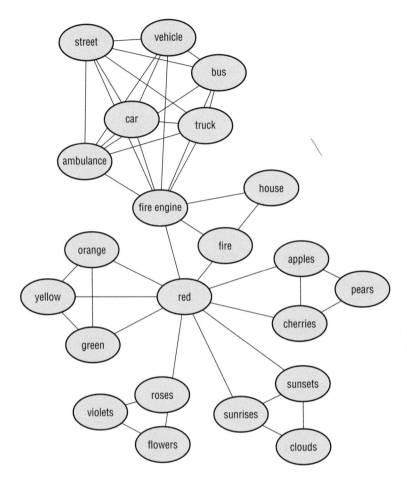

Figure 9.5 A sample of a knowledge network according to the Collins and Loftus spreading activation model.

From Collins, A. M., & Loftus, E. F. (1975). A spreading-activation theory of semantic processing. *Psychological Review, 82*, 407–428. Copyright 1975 by the American Psychological Association. Reprinted by permission.

to other concepts in the network. The strength of activation decreases as a function of time, distance, and the number of concepts activated: the more concepts that are activated, the less activation any one concept receives. Finally, the activation that reaches any concept node is summed up, and if the activation passes some threshold value, that concept will be activated.

Priming.   To discuss the assumptions of the spreading activation model, we'll now introduce another popular methodology—the **lexical decision task,** which involves deciding whether or not a presented letter string (i.e., BRUF) is a word. Once again, speed, not accuracy, is the variable of primary interest. Using this task, researchers have found evidence of priming in semantic memory. As you read in Chapter 6, priming refers to a benefit in memory performance due to previous exposure to some item. To investigate priming in semantic memory (termed *semantic priming*), a word (typically termed the *prime*) is presented before the letter string (typically termed the *target*). The prime is either related or unrelated to the target. **Semantic priming** refers to the benefit in lexical decision (a speedup in RT) that occurs as a function of the prime. For example, people identify that the target *robin* is a word faster if it is preceded by the prime *bird* than when the target is presented alone or by an unrelated prime (e.g., *weapon*).

The spreading activation model provides a straightforward account of semantic priming. Priming will result when a concept like "cherry" is activated beyond a threshold level. So consider what happens in the network when a prime (e.g., *red*) is presented. Presentation of the word *red* activates that concept, and the activation spreads out from there; concepts receiving activation would no doubt include "orange," "fire," and, of course, "cherry." The activation gives these concepts a "head start" toward the threshold that needs to be reached for identification. So when the word *cherry* is actually presented, the responder is almost ready (primed and ready, as it were) to verify it as a word.

RECURRING RESEARCH THEME
Cognition and Consciousness

Conscious and Nonconscious Factors in Semantic Priming

One of the assumptions about spreading activation is that it occurs automatically. Recall the characteristics of an automatic process (discussed in Chapter 4): automatic processes occur without intention, are not subject to conscious control, and consume little in the way of mental resources. Conversely, controlled processing is intentional, deliberate, and takes mental effort. In a classic study, Neely (1977) sought to tease apart the automatic and controlled components of semantic priming within semantic networks.

Neely's procedure utilized a lexical decision task in which a word prime preceded a target. Within this context, Neely manipulated **stimulus onset asynchrony (SOA),** the time lag between presentation of the prime and presentation of the target. Given that spreading activation takes time, you might imagine that some SOAs would be too short for it to occur, preventing semantic priming. Conversely, if SOA is long, spreading activation will fade, and some type of conscious preparation will need to take over. Think about it: if you get the word *bird* and then sit there for three seconds, you're going to be plenty ready for the appearance the target of *robin.* Any semantic priming you get will not be the result of simple spreading activation. So effects that occur at short SOAs would be reflective of automatic spreading activation; effects that occur at long SOAs would be reflective of a conscious strategy. Neely added a twist to the traditional semantic priming procedure. Participants received the primes *body* or *building,* but when they saw the prime *body,* they would actually receive the name of a building part on most trials. Therefore, on receiving this prime, they should shift their attention accordingly. The converse would be true when they saw the prime *building;* most of the time, this would be followed by a body part. Primes were separated from targets by durations ranging from quite short (250 milliseconds) to quite long (2,000 milliseconds).

Some interesting predictions can be derived from Neely's procedure and the assumption of automatic spreading activation. Consider the body-building part condition; when presented with the prime *body,* automatic spreading activation will lead to temporarily increased availability for words like *heart, leg,* and so on. But there will be no automatic spreading activation for building parts like *door* or *window;* these are distant from one another in the semantic network. But given a long enough pause between the prime *body* and the target *building part,* participants might shift their attention to expect a building part. So, *body* could be an effective prime for a building part if participants have time to shift their attention. The more time they have, the more semantic priming there will be.

Even more intriguing predictions can be derived for trials in which participants received targets that were unexpected. Recall that *body* indicated that a building part was going to be presented on most trials. On some trials, Neely threw participants a curve, presenting them with an unexpected target; instead of getting a building part, they actually got a body part, like *arm.* These trials led to a unique prediction. At short SOAs, it doesn't really matter what participants expect, because spreading activation is nonconscious and will result in semantic priming for related items but not for unrelated items (i.e., *body* will prime the response to *arm*). But at the long SOAs, spreading activation is done, and strategy takes over as participants wait for the category not designated by the prime. When they get a related word, rather than being aided by the prime, they should be hampered by it (i.e., *body* will inhibit the response to *arm*).

The results are presented in Figure 9.6. This graph presents the results for two of the critical conditions in Neely's study. The solid line is from the unexpected-related target condition. These are trials in which the participants were told to shift their category expectation when they

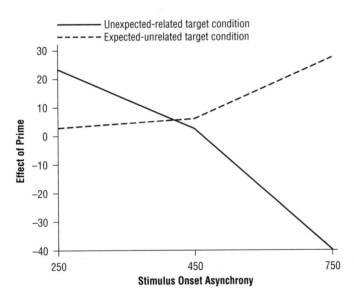

Expectancy and Spreading Activation on Priming

Figure 9.6 Results from Neely's (1977) study. At short SOAs, unexpected primes have a facilitatory effect due to automatic spreading activation; at longer SOAs, primes have an inhibitory effect.

From Neely, J. S. (1977). Semantic priming and retrieval from lexical memory. Roles of inhibitionless spreading activation and limited-capacity attention. *Journal of Experimental Psychology: General, 106,* 226–254. Copyright 1977 by the American Psychological Association. Reprinted by permission.

saw the prime (e.g., if you see a body part, expect a building part), but then unexpectedly were given a word that actually was semantically related to the prime. The dotted line is from the expected-unrelated target condition. These are trials in which the participants were told to shift their category expectation when they saw the prime (e.g., if you see a body part, expect a building part) and, as they expected, given a word that actually was semantically unrelated to the prime. The means are laid out in terms of whether the primes in each of these two conditions led to facilitation or inhibition in deciding about the target word. These facilitation and inhibition scores were computed by comparing RTs in these prime conditions to conditions where the string xxxxx was presented as a prime. If a prime led to faster RTs than xxxxx, then there is facilitation; if slower, then there is inhibition.

As you can see, this is a beautifully elegant, if extremely complex, design. The results confirmed Neely's suspicions about the role of automatic spreading activation and strategic control in priming. Let's examine the graph. In the expected-unrelated target condition, the prime *body* facilitated the building part target but only at long SOAs. The expectation of a building part target, given a body part as a prime, is a conscious and strategic process that takes time to develop. So the body parts did not prime responses to the building parts, except at longer SOAs. Now let's look at the unexpected-related target condition. Here we see precisely the opposite pattern. At short SOAs participants couldn't help but be facilitated by a body part prime preceding a body part target (e.g., *arm*) because of automatic spreading activation. But if more time was allowed for the strategic expectation to be implemented (seeing a body part and expecting a building part), then automatic spreading activation is gone, and the clash between the expectation and the presentation of a related word actually inhibits responding. Neely's results seemed to demonstrate the automatic and nonconscious nature of spreading activation and also that strategic and conscious processes play an important role in the activation of semantic networks.

However, later research (Stolz and Besner, 1999) indicates that this presumably automatic spreading activation is subject to attentional control. Priming can be prevented if a secondary task is sufficiently demanding to tie up attentional resources. Stolz and Besner (1999) conclude that spreading activation is not automatic, as originally proposed by Collins and Loftus (1975). However, Stolz and Besner make an important distinction between automatic and nonconscious processing:

> Consciousness need not result in control of processing, and control need not imply consciousness, contrary to the long-standing claim in the psychological literature that there is a strong dependency between consciousness and control (and non-consciousness and lack of control). (p. 64)

In other words, consciousness doesn't necessarily imply control, and nonconsciousness does not necessarily imply lack of control. Spreading activation could be both under strategic control and also be nonconscious.

STOP *and* REVIEW!

1. True or false? The primary dependent variable in category and feature verification tasks is reaction time.
2. The hierarchical network model can explain which of the following?
   a. falsification RTs
   b. typicality effect
   c. category size effect
   d. false relatedness effect
3. What are are the strengths and weaknesses of the feature comparison model?
4. True or false? The spreading activation model is organized in a strictly hierarchical manner.

➤ Semantic memory can be defined as our database of general knowledge about the world. Category and feature verification tasks are used to assess how categories and their features are stored and accessed. Reaction time is the primary dependent variable of interest.

> The hierarchical network model assumes an associative network of concepts and features that are organized hierarchically and economically. This model predicts the category size effect but runs into trouble with falsification RTs, reverse category size effects, false relatedness effects, and typicality effects.

> The feature comparison model represents concepts as sets of defining and characteristic features. It proposes a two-stage decision for the verification of category statements. The strengths of this model (explanations for the typicality effect, the false relatedness effect, and falsification RTs) are undermined by its weaknesses (inability to explain the category size effect and no mechanism for feature verification).

> The spreading activation model is a nonhierarchial network model that represents categorical knowledge in an associative network of nodes representing various relationships. The model proposes spreading activation that decreases with time, distance, and total activation. The model is supported by semantic priming found in lexical decision tasks. Some evidence indicates that priming is nonconscious and/or automatic.

Representing and Retrieving Propositions

As you'll read in the next two chapters, knowledge retrieval is at the heart of language use. We need to be able to select the appropriate concepts during language production and decipher the concepts we receive during language comprehension. Although the models proposed to explain the representation of categorical knowledge are fairly successful in providing a simple model of knowledge retrieval, they are clearly limited by their simplicity. This simplicity has allowed for clear tests of basic assumptions and has generated a great deal of fundamental data that has formed the basis for other theories of knowledge representation. However, language isn't this simple. The range of the conversation taking place among Eleanor, Zach, and Mitchell in the opening scenario demonstrates that everyday access to and use of language extends well beyond verification of simple statements.

Anderson (1974, 1982) proposes a different type of network model of general knowledge centered not on simple noun concepts but on propositions. A **proposition** is the smallest unit of knowledge that can stand alone and be declared true or false. More specifically, it's a mental representation of the relationship among people, objects, actions, and events—as Kosslyn (1994) puts it, "a mental sentence." But propositions aren't really words themselves; as McNamara (1994) notes, "they are best thought of as ideas that can be put into words." They're the abstract representations underlying what we think and say. For example, "The sky is blue" is a simple statement of the relationship between the sky and one of its well-known properties and as such will be stored in semantic memory. A more complex idea such as "The sky was blue, so Greg and Bridget bought some food and went

A complex scene that can be represented as simple propositions.

for a picnic by lake number 8,679" (in our home state of Minnesota, the "land of 10,000 lakes") would be stored in terms of its component propositions.

According to Anderson (1976), knowledge is represented in the form of **propositional networks,** which are constructed from the facts and relationships we learn and experience. Figure 9.7 depicts a propositional network that corresponds to knowledge of those legendary adversaries, dogs, cats, and mice. You'll note that this network is similar but more complex than those proposed earlier. There are nodes that correspond to the major players within this knowledge scenario (i.e., dogs, cats, and mice) as well as links that connect these nodes and specify the nature of the relationship between the concepts (dogs bark at cats, cats chase mice, etc.).

Stop *and*
Think!

SEMANTIC NETWORKS

Consider the following concepts:

dog   birthday   ocean   clothing   vegetable

For each concept:

1. Come up with a "minisemantic network" by generating the first five or six associated concepts that come to mind and connecting them via arrows.

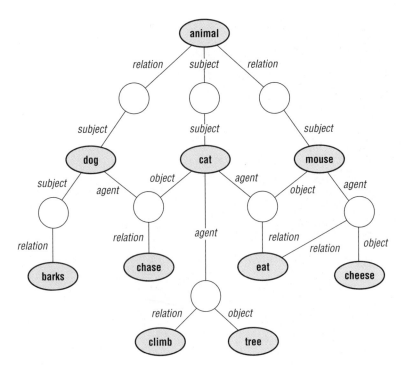

Figure 9.7
Dog/cat/mouse network.

From McNamara, T. P. (1994). Knowledge representation. In R. L. Sternberg (Ed.), *Thinking and problem solving* (pp. 81–117). New York: Academic Press. Reprinted by permission.

2. Look at the relationships that hold among the given concept and all the ones you generated.
- Are the generated concepts properties of the given concept?
- Are they properties of other members of the same category?
- Or are the relationships more complex, as might be described by the propositional network theories?

Mediated Priming

One phenomenon that supports the propositional network view is called **mediated priming.** Given that it is a network approach, the propositional view predicts that concepts prime other concepts in the network and that the amount of priming depends on the degree of their separation. So two concepts that share a proposition, like "mouse" and "cheese," will prime each other. The concepts of "cat" and "cheese" will show less priming because they are more distantly related; they're separated by a proposition: "Cats chase mice" and "Mice like cheese." Even less priming will be observed between "dog" and "cheese," because yet another proposition separates these concepts: "Dogs chase cats," "Cats chase mice," and "Mice like cheese."

This phenomenon has been observed in a number of studies (e.g., Balota & Larch, 1986; McNamara & Altarriba, 1988). McNamara (1992) investigated the relationship between distance in a propositional network and speed of information access. Distance was

Are dogs related to cheese?

defined as the number of associations that separate a prime and a target in memory. For instance, consider these primes and targets: *mane* and *lion, lion* and *tiger,* and *tiger* and *stripes.* Based on these connections, one might expect to find mediated priming of *mane* on *stripes.* But because activation weakens as it spreads, the mediated priming effect will be weaker than the classic priming effect demonstrated by Neely (1977) and many others. Also as the number of mediators increases, spreading activation will fade, and priming will fail to occur.

To test the limits of spreading activation and investigate the phenomenon of mediated priming, McNamara (1992; McNamara & Altarriba, 1988) needed information about associative relationships in memory. To gather this basic information, participants were given single words and asked to generate associates. From these responses, associative chains were constructed (e.g., dog–cat–mouse–cheese) such that successive pairs were directly associated (e.g., dog-cat), but nonsuccessive pairs (e.g., dog-mouse) were not. This ensures that any priming effect is due to the mediation of some intervening concept rather than a direct link. After construction of these chains, priming in lexical decision tasks was assessed. Participants received prime-target pairs that differed in distance. Consistent with the predictions derived from the propositional networks generated by participants, the amount of priming was a systematic function of the distance between concepts. The demonstration that one concept can prime an ostensibly unrelated one provides strong evidence for the spread of activation through a propositional network.

The Fan Effect

Another phenomenon that supports the idea of a propositional network is termed the *fan effect*. The **fan effect** refers to the finding that as more and more facts are learned about some concept, the ability to quickly and easily retrieve any one of those facts decreases, almost as if our knowledge representation resources have been spread too thin. Anderson (1974) investigated the fan effect in a series of studies in which participants learned sets of (experimenter-generated) "facts" expressed as simple propositions like those listed in Figure 9.8. Participants studied a set of facts about people in locations; the number of people and locations ranged from one to three. After memorizing the set of facts, participants were required to make rapid recognition decisions about presented facts. During this recognition phase, facts presented earlier (termed *targets*) were mixed with facts that included names and locations from the first phase but in novel combinations (termed *foils*). Each target sentence and foil sentence varied in the number of facts that had been associated with its respective person and location.

Sound a bit confusing? It is. But look at the sample materials in Figure 9.8. Take the target sentence "A hippie is in the park." (Yes, that's right . . . a "hippie"; keep in mind the experiment was done in 1974.) This sentence was presented during the first phase and again during the recognition phase. If you take a look, both the person word *hippie* and the location word *park* appear in three other target sentences. Now look at the target sentence "A debutante is in the bank"; the person word and the location word appear only once. Based on the propositional network model and its assumption of spreading activation, Anderson (1974) predicted and found a fan effect. The more propositions (i.e., facts) to which a person or location belongs, the longer it will take to recognize or reject a sentence that contains those persons/locations. That is, because the concepts "hippie" and "park" are each connected to three facts, they will take longer to recognize than "debutante" and "bank," which are connected to only one fact each. Simply put, the more facts you know about something, the more difficult it is to retrieve any one of those facts. Anderson's explanation for this phenomenon is based on the concept of competition between propositions and their respective components (Anderson, 1974; Anderson & Reder, 1999). Different pieces of knowledge compete for limited capacity; the more that compete, the less activation that any one gets, an account termed *response competition*.

Response competition is not the only mechanism that can explain difficulties in retrieving knowledge from propositional networks. Some

The *hippie* is in the *park*.
The captain is in the church.
The fireman is in the cave.
The *debutante* is in the *bank*.
The captain is in the **park**.
The fireman is in the church.
The **hippie** is in the cave.
The fireman is in the **park**.
The **hippie** is in the church.

Figure 9.8 Example propositions like those from Anderson's (1974) study of the fan effect.

From Anderson, J. R. (1974). Retrieval of propositional information from long-term memory. *Cognitive Psychology, 6,* 451–474. Copyright 1974, Elsevier Science (USA). Reprinted by permission.

they

A hippie and a debutante.

researchers (e.g., Anderson & Bell, 2001) propose an additional mechanism termed *response inhibition.* According to this view, when we attempt to retrieve a piece of knowledge, other knowledge is activated as well. This ancillary activation inhibits the retrieval of the information that we want (Anderson, Bjork, & Bjork, 1994). Simply put, the process of retrieving a piece of information can serve to inhibit the ability to retrieve other pieces of information. In the case of the fan effect, retrieving a fact (i.e., the hippie is in the park) actively suppresses other facts about the hippie and other facts about the park. This inhibition makes the concepts more difficult to retrieve on subsequent attempts.

STOP *and* REVIEW!

1. A propositional network model seems necessary because
   a. the hierarchical network model cannot explain typicality effect.
   b. the feature comparison model cannot explain the category size effect.
   c. previous networks were too complex, and parsimony was needed.
   d. networks involving nouns and features are too simple to account for language use.
2. True or false? A propositional network consists of concepts and links that specify the relationship between two concepts.

3. True or false? The fan effect can only be explained by invoking the idea of response competition.

➤ The models for the representation of categorical knowledge provide a simple account of knowledge retrieval but are limited by their simplicity. Language use involves more than the simple retrieval of noun concepts. Therefore, the propositional network models propose that knowledge is represented in terms of propositions rather than nouns and features.

➤ A propositional network consists of nodes that correspond to major concepts within a knowledge scenario; links that connect these nodes specify the nature of the relationship between the concepts.

➤ Mediated priming and the fan effect support propositional models. The inhibition observed in the fan effect can be attributed to response competition or response inhibition

Representing and Retrieving Other Types of Knowledge

Our semantic memory doesn't consist simply of noun concepts and their corresponding features or of abstract statements of relationships espoused by the propositional network approach. Semantic memory also includes information about people we've encountered throughout our lives (like their names and faces), what we've learned through our years of formal education (did you realize you're in the 15th grade or so?), our knowledge of facts and the trivia that relate to our interests and hobbies—the list goes on.

These particular categories of knowledge have not received nearly as much theoretical and empirical attention as have simple noun concepts like "bird." This is primarily due

How do we represent knowledge of everyday concepts, like books or music?

to the relative uniformity in people's representations and definitions of simple concepts; this uniformity allows for experimental manipulation and control. Control is much more difficult in investigations of knowledge that is likely to differ widely between individuals. Although everyone knows what a book is, Bridget is one of the few people who can list all of the thrillers written by Mary Higgins Clark. These sorts of detail comprise a great deal of our knowledge.

We are faced once again with the notion of *ecological validity*—the study of cognition in its everyday forms. The empirical study of autobiographical memory (discussed in Chapter 8) was one answer to Neisser's (1977) call to arms for more ecologically valid research within the domain of episodic memory. In this section, we'll examine some of the answers from the domain of semantic memory.

Knowledge Learned through Formal Instruction

Much of the knowledge you carry around in your head is information you learned in school. A number of researchers—most notably Bahrick and associates (Bahrick, 1984, 2000; Bahrick, Hall, & Berger, 1996; Bahrick & Hall, 1991)—have investigated the characteristics and dynamics of this sort of knowledge. Such research presents significant methodological challenges. Since the researcher is interested in the long-term maintenance of knowledge over time, time becomes an important variable. As you know, the retention interval (the amount of time that passes between encoding and retrieval) has been one of the classic variables in memory research since the pioneering work of Ebbinghaus (discussed in Chapter 1). But in contrast to traditional work on episodic memory, research on the maintenance of semantic memory requires the assessment of retention after intervals of years. To assess changes over this span of time requires a choice between a longitudinal approach and a cross-sectional approach. A **longitudinal approach** involves following the same group of participants over a span of time and recording the measure of interest at

Do you remember what you learned in school?

regular intervals throughout that span. A **cross-sectional approach** involves collecting all measures at the same time but collecting from groups that differ in age. By comparing the performance of these groups, one can assess the differences found among age groups and make inferences about changes over time.

It turns out that the major disadvantage of the longitudinal approach is the major advantage of the cross-sectional approach, and vice versa. Longitudinal designs place the researcher in the relatively unfeasible situation of having to follow a group of participants for years; this requirement is fraught with perils, most noteworthy of which are participants dropping out, and having to wait years for the data. Also, the data take years to collect. While cross-sectional designs are much more feasible (the data can be collected in a relatively short span of time), they have a serious problem of their own. When groups of individuals of differing ages are compared, more than just their age varies; they also have different backgrounds and different experiences, all of which may obscure the age-related changes that are the focus of study. (Recall our discussion of confounding variables in Chapter 2.) Longitudinal designs don't have this problem; since the same group of participants is being tested at all times, changes over time can be more confidently attributed to age-related changes. In practice, cross-sectional designs are much more common because of their notable practical advantages. But the use of these designs does create a host of methodological issues; the researcher must be aware of any preexperimental differences among the participants.

Foreign Language Vocabulary. Systematic research on the retention of information learned in school pretty much began with Bahrick's cross-sectional investigations of how we retain foreign language vocabulary. In these classic studies (Bahrick, 1979, 1984), the participants were individuals who had learned Spanish in either high school or college from one to 50 years earlier. Participants were administered various tests to assess their knowledge of Spanish, including reading comprehension, vocabulary recall and recognition, and grammar. A background questionnaire was also included to take stock of any important differences among participants other than age. These factors included the level of original language training, grades received, and the amount of rehearsal since the language was originally learned (i.e., continuing to read, write, or speak Spanish).

A sample of Bahrick's findings for recall of a Spanish word, given its English equivalent as a cue, is presented in Figure 9.9. A number of things are apparent at first glance. There's a pretty standard forgetting curve; information is lost early in the retention interval, but this loss levels off later. But even after 25 years or more, participants still retained a fair amount of information. More important, however, this long-term retention was dependent on the degree of initial learning. Those with only a year of Spanish forgot everything relatively quickly. And not surprisingly, the people with more training showed better overall retention.

Permastore. Based on his findings, Bahrick (1984) proposes what might be considered a subcategory of long-term memory, which he terms *permastore.* **Permastore** is the store of knowledge that has been learned so thoroughly (i.e., overlearned), that its storage is essentially permanent; we won't forget it. It is important to note that this definition seems to indicate that permastore is a location in memory, but as you know, memories are

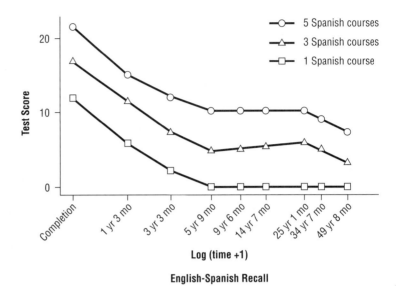

Figure 9.9 Knowledge of Spanish learned in high school over the lifespan.

From Bahrick, H. P. (1984). Semantic memory content in permastore. Fifty years of memory for Spanish learned in school. *Journal of Experimental Psychology: General,* *113,* 1–26. Copyright 1984 by the American Psychological Association. Reprinted by permission.

not stored in given locations in the brain. The concept of different memory stores is a holdover from information-processing terminology and is descriptive only.

Given the results from the recall of Spanish study, Bahrick proposes that the amount of information in permastore varies with a number of factors, including the level of initial learning, the grades received, and the way in which memory is tested. Surprisingly, it seems that a large amount of information can reside in permastore even if it receives a minimal amount of subsequent rehearsal after initial learning. Most of Bahrick's participants engaged in very little rehearsal during the retention interval; in spite of this, large amounts of information were available for retrieval 25 years or more later. One other intriguing note about permastore; based on some more subtle aspects of his data, Bahrick (1984) contends that the transition of information to permastore is discrete rather than continuous. Information is not encoded semipermanently; it's either in permastore, or it's not. (And if it's not, it will be lost from long-term memory unless it receives additional learning trials.)

Math.   In a later investigation, Bahrick and Hall (1991) investigated the retention of material from high school algebra. Participants in the study had all taken algebra, but only some of them had subsequently enrolled in college-level mathematics. As in the earlier studies (e.g., Bahrick, 1984), Bahrick and Hall took stock of important factors such as level of performance in high school algebra, subsequent rehearsals of the material, and scores on the Scholastic Aptitude Test (SAT). The results of this study were intriguing; although factors like SAT scores and grades did relate to overall levels of performance, they were relatively unimportant in predicting the maintenance of knowledge over time. The only really good predictor of knowledge maintenance was the time period over which the material was initially learned. Material learned over the course of a longer period persisted for decades; the same material learned over a shorter period of time vanished relatively quickly (Bahrick & Hall, 1991).

Cognitive Psychology.   Appropriately enough, one investigation of information learned through formal instruction focuses on the very class you're currently enjoying—cognitive psychology! Conway, Cohen, and Stanhope (1991) examined retention of knowledge acquired in a cognitive psychology class taught over the course of one year at the Open University (located in England). The cognitive psychology course was highly structured, allowing for a systematic assessment of retention for different sorts of information, such as basic research methods, researcher names, theoretical concepts, and empirical findings. In addition to testing retention, the researchers also assessed participant confidence regarding what they had learned.

The findings (some of which are presented in Figure 9.10) reveal the classic forgetting curve: a great deal of forgetting occurs in the period immediately following completion of the course. As you might expect, the speed of forgetting is greater when retention is measured with recall relative to when it's tested with recognition (consistent with the findings from episodic memory presented in Chapter 6). You're much more likely to recognize the names and concepts you're learning in class than you are to recall them. Conway and colleagues also observed more rapid forgetting of names than of facts, a testament to the difficulty of retaining names. Names serve as a sort of arbitrary, disconnected label for a person; they don't really have semantic associates and thus are particularly difficult to

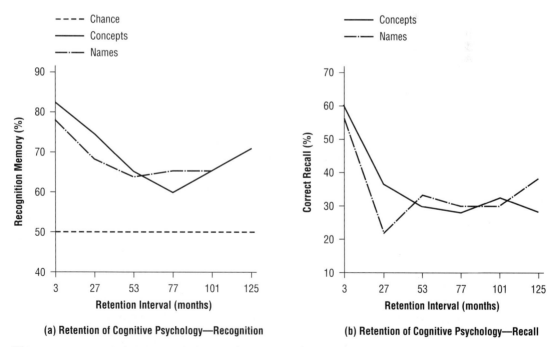

(a) Retention of Cognitive Psychology—Recognition   **(b) Retention of Cognitive Psychology—Recall**

Figure 9.10 Retention of knowledge learned in a cognitive psychology class.

From Conway, M. A., Cohen, G., & Stanhope, N. (1991). On the very long-term retention of knowledge acquired through formal education: Twelve years of cognitive psychology. *Journal of Experimental Psychology: General, 120,* 395–409. Copyright 1991 by the American Psychological Association. Reprinted by permission.

retain. This rapid forgetting for names is unfortunate, but take heart! As you can see, re-tention of names and concepts stays well above chance for over 10 years, demonstrating that much of the material qualified as permastore. We'll have more to say about the re-trieval of names shortly.

Particularly compelling to the authors was the sturdiness of what participants had learned about research methods. Retention of knowledge about general research methods showed no decline over the retention interval! Conway and colleagues offer a couple of rea-sons for the persistence of these particular concepts. First, the cognitive psychology course in question was a methods course, leading to more exposure to, and hands-on practice with, research methods. In addition, because research methods are covered in a number of psychology courses, they enjoy the benefit of spaced repetition. It's informative, at this point, to make a connection between the persistence of information learned about re-search methods and the Ebbinghausian notion of savings in relearning. You'll recall (from Chapter 1) that savings refers to the benefit we gain from having learned material previ-ously. It's much easier to learn something in a second and third encounter, particularly if those encounters are sufficiently spaced out.

The confidence ratings collected by the researchers revealed some intriguing patterns. Recall from our previous discussion of distortions in eyewitness memory (Chapter 7) that confidence is not always a very good indicator of memory accuracy. This weak relation-ship characterized knowledge of cognitive psychology as well; there was only a weak rela-tionship between confidence and accuracy on the knowledge test. Also intriguing was the relationship between the grade achieved in the course and confidence; people who ob-tained top grades in the course were no more confident in their knowledge than were stu-dents who obtained lower grades in the course (all received at least a passing grade). Also, confidence ratings fell throughout the retention interval, reflecting participant under-standing that memory tends to decline with an increasing retention interval—another ex-ample of metamemory.

The fact that a good deal of knowledge was reported by participants even in the ab-sence of much confidence suggests that much of what they retained could be classified as implicit memory (Conway, Cohen, & Stanhope, 1991). You'll recall from Chapter 6 that implicit memory is reflected in changes in performance not accompanied by conscious recollection. In this study, participants didn't consciously recollect the knowledge they were expressing on the test; if they had consciously recollected their knowledge, they would have been more confident in their performance on the test. The fact that they performed fairly well even in the absence of confidence suggests that they weren't really basing their answers on conscious recollection.

Educational Implications.   Research on the retention of knowledge learned through for-mal instruction has some serious implications for how information should be taught and retaught and provides a further demonstration of a powerful encoding principle discussed in Chapter 6. Recall the notion of spaced repetitions: repeating material at spaced inter-vals over a period of time leads to better retention than learning the same information through closely spaced repetitions over a shorter interval. The evidence just discussed demonstrates the benefits of spaced practice but on a much grander scale. The most im-portant factor in later retention seems to be the level of original learning and, more important, the length of time over which it takes place. Material that is repeatedly retrieved is better remembered than material that is not (even if the latter material was learned extremely well).

These conclusions have important educational implications. One aim of education is to instill knowledge; wouldn't it be nice if that knowledge were to remain in long-term memory rather than being forgotten the day after a test is taken? Based on the results from studies of knowledge maintenance, Bahrick (2000; Bahrick & Hall, 1991) offers some recommendations (some of which you may not like!). For example, let's consider the unpopular cumulative final. Bahrick's research indicates that you will have a better chance of retaining course-related information if the professor asks you to repeatedly rehearse the information over the course of the entire semester in preparation for a cumulative final. That's why, in the chapter opening story, Mitchell feels pretty confident about his upcoming final; his professor has had the class relearn and retrieve the same concepts over the semester; as a result, Mitchell knows the material better.

People's Names

As experts in memory, the most common complaint we hear from family and friends is an inability to remember names. Retrieving names is the final stage of a process we discussed in Chapter 5—face recognition. Since we've already discussed the recognition of faces, in this brief section we turn specifically to the issue of name representation and retrieval and why names prove especially difficult to remember. Although a detailed examination is beyond the scope of our present discussion, suffice it to say that people's names do indeed seem to be represented and retrieved in a manner distinct from the retrieval of other information.

Hanley and Cowell (1988) conducted a study that highlighted the special difficulty in retrieving people's names. Participants were presented with familiar faces and asked to recognize them as familiar, provide biographical information about them, and, finally, name them. The pattern of errors was quite revealing; in many instances, people could recognize that a face was familiar but couldn't provide any biographical information about the person or name the person. Other times, participants could recognize the face as familiar and provide some biographical information but could not name the person. And, revealingly, the converse was almost never true; it was almost never the case that the name was retrieved in the absence of any other information about the person.

These results indicate a gradient of difficulty in the processes of person recognition, with the most difficult task being name retrieval. Young, Ellis, and Flude (1988) provided converging evidence for the notion of a difficulty gradient using a reaction time (RT) task. The RT for recognizing a face as familiar is reliably faster than the RT for retrieving biographical information about the person; and this RT is faster than the RT for retrieving the name. Based on this evidence, some propose that the retrieval of names and the retrieval of biographical information comprise different processes and stages within a person-recognition system.

Two theories have been offered to explain why the retrieval of a person's name is more difficult than the retrieval of other information about that person. The Bruce and Young (1986) model proposes a serial process for accessing information about a person. First, a face must activate a face recognition unit (FRU)—a stored representation of that face in memory. If activated, the person is recognized as familiar. Next, the FRU must activate the person identity node (PIN), which stores biographical information about the person. If activated, this biographical information becomes available. Next, the PIN must activate the terminal node, which stores the name of the person. This model accounts for the finding that names are retrieved slower than other information about a person; name retrieval is the last node activated in the system. It can also explain why a name is sometimes not remembered, while other information about the person is; information about the person must be retrieved before the name can be retrieved. Therefore, a name will never be activated in the absence of information retrieval about the person.

Another model, the *interactive activation and competition (IAC) model* (Burton & Bruce, 1992), assumes that there are separate FRUs (stored representations of faces), PINs (which in this model are multimodal general representations of people), and semantic information units (SIUs). An SIU contains both biographical information and names. There is no separate representation for names. In addition, the activation and retrieval process is parallel, not serial. So the face of David Letterman will simultaneously activate his PIN, his FRU, and his SIU. His SIU will include "talk show host," "lived in Indiana," and the name "David Letterman." "Talk show host" will also be linked to the Jay Leno PIN and "lived in Indiana" will also be linked to the Larry Bird PIN. But the name "David Letterman" will be linked only to the David Letterman PIN (see Figure 9.11).

Superior access to biographical information like "talk show host" and "lived in Indiana" relative to the name "David Letterman" can be explained by a faster buildup of activation for his biographical information relative to his name. For example, when we encounter the funniest man in late-night TV, activation spreads from the David Letterman PIN to "talk show host" and "lived in Indiana" back to the David Letterman PIN, but also to the Jay Leno PIN and the Larry Bird PIN, respectively. The David Letterman PIN and the Jay Leno PIN will reactivate "talk show host," and the David Letterman PIN and the Larry Bird PIN will reactivate "lived in Indiana." But the name "David Letterman" only receives activation from the David Letterman PIN specifically. So over time, nodes that refer to more general pieces of biographical information (e.g., "lives in Indiana" and "talk show host") will receive more activation than the person's name, which is completely unique and corresponds only to that person. Due to this faster buildup of activation, biographical information will be in a state of higher activation than will a specific name and hence will be more retrievable. The empirical jury is still out on whether the parallel or serial model of name retrieval provides a better account of the data.

Songs

Given its omnipresence in our daily lives, it's surprising that we don't know more about the processes involved in remembering songs. Knowing the lyrics to songs is truly a prodigious feat of semantic memory. Think of your favorite musical artist and then recall everything you know by and about them. Chances are, it's a vast amount of information. In Greg's case, his favorite group is the Beatles, and his knowledge of their songs is extensive. What accounts for the fact that he can sing any lyric from any of their hundreds of songs? How are these songs stored in Greg's memory, and what allows for their rapid and easy retrieval?

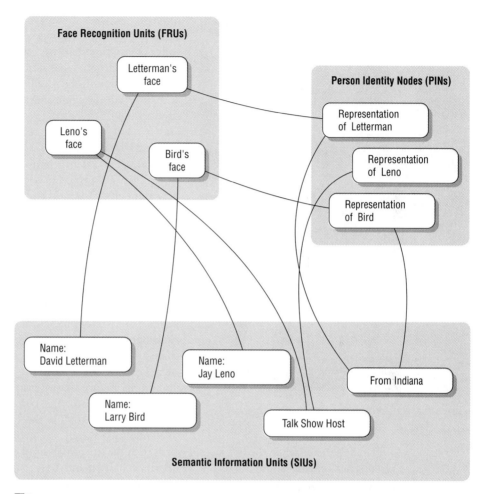

Figure 9.11 A portion of the knowledge network representing names and faces, according to the interactive activation and competition (IAC) model. Face recognition units (FRUs) code a particular face and are responsible for recognition. Semantic information units (SIUs) code semantic information associated with a face. Person identity nodes (PINs) are multimodal (general) representations of a person. Naming a person requires activation of the name information located with the SIU. (See the text for further explanation.)

Adapted from Burton, A. M., & Bruce, V. (1993). Naming faces and naming names: Exploring an interactive activation model of person recognition memory. *Memory, 1,* 457–480.

Not too many studies have investigated memory for music, but there are some notable exceptions. Coincidentally, one of them is cleverly titled "Memorabeatlia," and as you may expect, it examines memory for songs and lyrics using Beatles tunes. Hyman and Rubin (1990) were interested in discovering the cuing relationship between song titles and song lyrics and the variables that dictate knowledge of melodies and lyrics. One obvious

Whose song lyrics do you know perfectly?

difference between memory for words and stories and memory for songs is that memory for songs is exact (verbatim); memory for words and stories is not. What accounts for the absolute precision in the recall of songs? Hyman and Rubin addressed this question by analyzing cued recall of Beatles song lyrics, noting which lines of a song tended to be recalled particularly well and which lines served as the best cues for song titles. Participants performed one of two straightforward tasks: (1) lyric recall, in which they were given the title and the first line for sixty-four Beatles songs and were asked to write as many of the lyrics as they could for each, or (2) cued recall, in which they were given one line from a Beatles song and asked to write the title, first line, and one other line from the song.

So what factors were related to knowing any given line from a song? The recall data revealed a number of predictors. A line was more likely to be recalled to the degree that it was repeated, shared words with the title, and occurred early in the song (more evidence of the ubiquitous nature of the primacy effect discussed in Chapter 6). The cuing data revealed one major predictor for the recall of a song title: not surprisingly, song titles were most likely to be recalled when the line shared words with the title. Analysis of errors in the recall of lyrics revealed some interesting regularities. Participants were rather poor at remembering lines; only about 20% of lines were recalled correctly. However, when a line was recalled, it was recalled verbatim. And even though most lines couldn't be remembered verbatim, the mistakes in recall preserved information from the correct lyric. Specifically, though participants inaccurately recalled lyrics, they still tended to preserve the meaning, rhyming, and rhythm of the correct line, as Eleanor did in the opening story of this chapter. Hyman and Rubin (1990) concluded that the organization of semantic memory is not solely based on meaning; the physical structure of information is also important.

This finding also relates to the issue of how melody and lyrics are represented in memory. The fact that misrecalled lyrics maintain the rhythm of the melody provides some evidence that the two may be represented as a unit. You may have found this to be true when you think about your knowledge of music. To remember lyrics, you may need to hum the accompanying melody to yourself. The notion that melody-lyric integration underlies our knowledge of music is consistent with the results of a study by Serafine, Crowder, and Repp (1984). These researchers presented participants with excerpts from 24 folk songs and later tested their recognition of the songs. The important finding was that melodies were better recognized when they were accompanied by their respective lyrics relative to when they were presented alone. The same pattern held for lyrics; they were better recognized when accompanied by their respective melody than when they were presented alone. Although this study investigated memory for songs with an episodic memory task, the results, which indicated that songs are stored as a blend of melody and text, may speak to their long-term representation in semantic memory as well.

Stop *and* **Think!** ### LYRIC KNOWLEDGE

If you're a music fan, try and generate the lyrics to some of your favorite songs. You might try and do this under a few different conditions:

1. Try and recall the lyrics.
2. Try and recall the lyrics while mentally playing the melody.
3. Try and recall the lyrics as you're listening to the song.

Reflect on the differences between 1, 2, and 3. Look at your pattern of errors.

- Were there any differences between them in terms of ease of recall?
- Did they fit with the findings discussed in the chapter?
- Did the patterns of errors differ between the conditions?

STOP *and* REVIEW!

1. Identify the two approaches used to study knowledge learned through formal education.
2. Transition to permastore
   a. is more likely if learning occurs over a short period of time.
   b. depends on the level of initial learning.
   c. depends on the type of material being learned.
   d. is more likely if the material is in a foreign language than in math.
3. Identify the gradient of difficulty in person recognition.
4. True or false? Research on the memory for songs indicates that the melody and lyrics are retrieved as separate units

➤ For reasons of ecological validity, research on semantic memory has expanded into areas of real-world knowledge. One prominent area of research is memory for material learned in school. These investigations involve the use of longitudinal and cross-sectional research designs.

➤ Study of knowledge learned through formal education (foreign language vocabulary, math, and cognitive psychology) has suggested a type of long-term memory termed permastore. Information becomes permastore in an all-or-none manner, and whether it does depends on the level of initial learning and the length of time over which learning takes place (spaced repetitions over a long period of time being best).

➤ Studies on memory for names indicate that names are particularly difficult to retrieve. There is a gradient of difficulty in person-recognition tasks. Recognizing a face as familiar is least difficult, while name retrieval is most difficult. Researchers have proposed models of name retrieval that emphasize either serial or parallel processing of person information.

> ➤ People are rather poor at remembering lines from songs; lines that are recalled are usually recalled verbatim. Also, inaccurately recalled lyrics tend to preserve meaning, rhyming, and rhythm, indicating that semantic memory organization is sensitive to meaning and the physical structure of information. Research also indicates that the melody and lyrics are stored together and retrieved as one unit.

Forgetting in Semantic Memory

In Chapters 6, 7, and 8, we discussed many of the ways in which episodic memory—our memory for events—goes awry. As you've no doubt experienced while taking a test, semantic memory can also go awry; the inability to retrieve information in semantic memory is a frustratingly common reality. Sometimes, we can't retrieve information simply because it isn't there; we never learned it in the first place. A more interesting and revealing situation is when knowledge is indeed represented in semantic memory but retrieval is somehow blocked.

Is his name on the tip of your tongue?

The Tip-of-the-Tongue Phenomenon

Quick—name the person pictured in the photo. Chances are this question might bring about an experience that cognitive psychologists have labeled (fittingly enough) tip-of-the-tongue phenomenon (Brown & McNeill, 1966). **Tip-of-the-tongue (TOT) phenomenon** occurs when we're fairly certain that we know a piece of information but, when queried, we can't come up with it; the answer is "on the tip of the tongue." Given stronger retrieval cues—for example, when offered the choices Kelsey Grammar, Liam Neeson, and David Hyde Pierce—you may come up with the answer (David Hyde Pierce). The retrieval blocks that underlie the tip-of-the-tongue experience are a primary reason many students prefer multiple-choice questions (like those above) rather than fill-in-the-blank questions (like the initial request to identify the person in the picture). Fill-in-the-blank questions leave no room for retrieval failure, while multiple-choice questions provide the answer that may be on the tip of your tongue. Retrieval blocks are another demonstration of the fundamental distinction between availability and accessibility that we discussed in Chapter 6. Failure to offer a piece of knowledge doesn't mean that the knowledge isn't there; it may be available in your general knowledge store but temporarily inaccessible, given the retrieval cues. Unfortunately, having an answer on the tip of the tongue doesn't get you partial credit.

Tip-of-the-tongue experiences are intriguing to researchers because they provide a rare window into the process of knowledge retrieval. Brown (1991) likens the TOT experience to "slow-motion photography" of the retrieval process. However, TOT experiences are difficult to investigate empirically because they occur spontaneously and are hard to control. Researchers generally take one of two tacks. One is to have participants keep a running diary of these experiences, noting their characteristics. The other is to try and induce TOTs by asking general-knowledge questions that are in a midrange of difficulty and seize on the ones that produce the TOT state. Another methodological note: studies have investigated TOTs using both episodic and semantic memory tasks. Because most everyday TOT experiences involve retrieval from semantic memory, we'll stick to those in the our discussion.

Characteristics of TOTs.   How often do TOTs occur? In a review of the literature, Brown (1991) reports that, although the estimates range across different studies, naturally occurring TOT experiences occur a few times a week, on average. In laboratory studies, TOTs are induced on about 10 to 20% of the questions asked by experimenters. Some evidence, most of it anecdotal, suggests that TOTs may be more likely to occur under conditions of stress (e.g., Brown, 1991; Cohen & Faulkner, 1986). In a similar vein, Brown and McNeill (1966) report that emotional agitation is a notable correlate of TOTs, as it is for Eleanor, when she can't think of the name of would-be Beatles drummer Pete Best.

You probably know from your own TOT experiences that your consciousness is often bombarded by (wrong) alternatives. And these alternatives aren't random; they are related to the target word. Investigations of the specific characteristics of these wrong alternatives have yielded some intriguing regularities. Quite often (anywhere from 50 to 75% of the time), people successfully guess the first letter of the target (e.g., Brown & McNeill, 1966; Koriat & Lieblich, 1974). This is what happened with Eleanor in the opening scenario. Interestingly, the final letter position is also frequently recalled at a level higher than chance. This provides an intriguing parallel to the serial position effect discussed in Chapter 6— another instance of how the salience of primacy and recency affects cognitive processing. Research indicates that during TOT states, people often think of words that are similar in sound or meaning to the desired word (Cohen & Faulkner, 1986; Reason, 1984). In addition, the syllabic structure of wrong alternatives is similar to the desired one (Lovelace, 1987). These regularities in the orthographic (physical) structure of wrong alternatives provide a hint that the organization of semantic memory is, in some part, based on the physical structure of words (Collins & Loftus, 1975). Note that a similar conclusion was reached based on investigations of memory for songs.

Stop and Think!   **PLACING INFORMATION ON THE TIP OF THE TONGUE**

This exercise will give you some idea of how TOT research is conducted. Recruit a couple of friends and try to induce TOTs by asking them some trivia questions. (You can make these questions up based on what you know or get some questions from a trivia game you may have handy.)

1. Read each question, and give participants 5 or 10 seconds to answer it.
2. For each question they can't answer, ask them if the answer is on the tip of their tongue.
3. If it is, ask them to verbalize any possibilities that come to mind and record these.
4. Note whether the possibilities generated seem to resemble the actual answer in terms of sound and/or meaning.

What types of information are likely to lead to TOTs? It turns out that proper names are quite often the culprit. More specifically, a number of diary studies indicate that attempts at retrieving people's names are the most common producer of TOT states (Burke, MacKay, Worthley, & Wade, 1991; Gruneberg, Smith, & Winfrow, 1973). Blocks are common for both the names of acquaintances and for the names of famous figures. The reason that proper names prompt TOTs more than other stimuli is unclear. It could be a matter of the salience of the TOT experience; as Brown (1991) notes, we're less likely to notice and remember instances when we block on a "normal" word during conversation than when we block on a name. When we block on a "normal" word, we can fairly quickly insert another alternative. Therefore, we are not likely to notice or remember the incident. The same is not true when we block on a name; we can't simply insert the name Krista when we are talking about Molly. This inability may make the incident more distinct and hence more memorable.

Resolving TOTs.   Say the answer is on the tip of your tongue; how likely are you to spit it out? The probability may seem frustratingly low when you encounter a TOT during an exam. However, research indicates that about 33 to 50% of the time, people come up with the correct answer within a couple of minutes (e.g., Sharp, 1989; Yarmey, 1973); and although the estimates range quite a bit, the majority of TOTs seem to be resolved after a delay of minutes or days.

Another question of interest to researchers is the nature of the cognitive processing that precedes TOT resolution. Is the answer obtained after an active and effortful search process, or is it more likely that the answer spontaneously "pops up" in the absence of any conscious retrieval effort, as it did in the opening story when Eleanor recalled the name Pete Best? Some studies (e.g., Burke et al., 1991; Reason & Lucas, 1984) report that answers "pop up" anywhere from 25 to 50% of the time. Norman and Bobrow (1979) propose that spontaneous solutions occur because of nonconscious processes that continue toward the resolution of a TOT even when it isn't currently in consciousness. (You'll read about a similar phenomenon in Chapter 12 called incubation.) However, to trigger these processes, an initial period of sustained conscious effort (e.g., generating possibilities) is necessary. It is also possible that a TOT may resolve during an effortful memory search through a cue from some environmental stimulus or by looking up the answer.

Stop *and* Think!

DEAR DIARY . . . I HAD A TOT EXPERIENCE TODAY

Now you'll be using the other method for analyzing TOTs—a running diary. Keep track of when you experience TOTs, and take note of these questions:

- What type of information tends to be the subject of the TOT?

- What is your state of mind before and during your experience of your TOT?
- What are the characteristics of any wrong alternatives you generate while in the TOT state?
- How does the TOT resolve—via a pop up or deliberate effort?
- How long does it take to resolve?

What Causes TOTs?   What are the characteristics of retrieval that would lead one to experience a TOT? Two types of accounts are generally proposed (summarized by Brown, 1991); one account cites *incomplete activation* as the source of TOTs. According to this view, words that induce TOTs have been partially activated but not enough to bring them into consciousness. This results in a retrieval process whereby we try to construct an idea of what the concept must be (Reed, 1974). The most salient aspects of the concept—the general meaning, strong associates, the first letter—are characteristics that only need partial activation to enter consciousness. Based on constructive processing that proceeds from these associates, the TOT can be resolved. So basically, TOTs are the result of a memory search process that has been dramatically slowed (Brown, 1991).

Alternatively, another account for TOTs characterizes them in terms of a memory search that has taken a wrong turn and hit a dead end, or at least a detour. According to the *blocking view,* when a memory search brings us to the wrong location (an incorrect answer), the wrongly activated concept becomes a competitor and serves to block the retrieval of the desired one. This blocking can be quite strong, because the competing concept shares semantic and/or structural similarity with the target word. This view seems to have some intuitive validity and fits well with the notion of response inhibition as an explanation for the fan effect we discussed earlier. Recall that according to this account, retrieving one fact about a concept in a proposition actively suppresses the ability to retrieve other facts about the same concept. The one glaring problem with the blocking explanation is that during many TOTs, there is no alternative word that presents itself. It's unclear what's doing the blocking in these cases.

Jones and Langford (1987) compared the incomplete activation and blocking views in a deceptively simple study. Intending to induce TOTs, they presented definitions of words along with word hints that varied in terms of their relationship to the intended target. The word hints were similar phonologically (sound), semantically (meaning), in both ways, or neither way. According to the incomplete activation view, these words should help retrieval, because they increase activation of related concepts, enhancing the chances that target word activation will exceed the threshold level and trigger retrieval. But according to the blocking view, these words should do just the opposite; they serve as dead-ends, sidetracking the search process. Participants should end up endlessly retrieving the hint words at the expense of the targets. The results supported the blocking view; phonologically related word hints increased the number of TOTs, indicating that processing these words inhibited, or blocked, retrieval of the target. The semantic relatedness of the hints had no effect. This underscores the phonological nature of TOTs and suggests that generating similar-sounding words when in a TOT state may actually delay its resolution.

Feeling of Knowing.   Research on the TOT experience has provided important insights on metacognition, our knowledge of our own cognitive processing. One of the trademark characteristics of the TOT state is what has been termed a *feeling-of-knowing;* we feel quite confident that we know the information. Is this feeling accurate? When researchers collect feeling-of-knowing judgments from someone experiencing a TOT, they can test metacognitive accuracy by having participants attempt to pick out the answer, given some choices. If feelings of knowing are accurate, people should be able to pick out the answer at a level above chance; this is indeed the case. When people report that they would recognize an answer that is currently on the tip of their tongue, it turns out that the answer really is available the majority of the time (see Nelson, 1984, for a review).

There are two theories offered to explain feeling-of-knowing judgments. According to the *target retrievability hypothesis* (Koriat, 1991), when information cannot be consciously retrieved, the resulting feeling of knowing is based on the partial retrieval of that information. Alternatively, the *cue familiarity hypothesis* (Metcalfe, Schwartz, & Joaquin, 1993) states that a feeling-of-knowing judgment is due not to partial access of unrecalled information but to the familiarity of the cue; the more familiar the cue, the higher the feeling-of-knowing judgment. There is support for both of these accounts, so a definitive conclusion has not been reached. However, regardless of their source, feeling-of-knowing judgments seem to be good predictors of the ability to recognize unrecallable information.

RECURRING RESEARCH THEME
Cognition and Individual Differences

Age Differences in the TOT Experience

In Chapter 6, we discussed some memory differences between older and younger adults. One such difference is that older adults have more difficulty with tasks to the degree that they require self-initiated retrieval. For example, free recall is more likely than recognition to reveal age-related deficits, because in free recall almost no retrieval support is given. Rememberers are left pretty much to their own devices in attempting to drive retrieval. This isn't the case in recognition, in which the answer is actually presented and need only be recognized.

How do these facts of retrieval relate to tip-of-the-tongue phenomenon? Situations that give rise to TOTs are best likened to recall; a question is posed, and a person must retrieve the answer. Given the age deficits observed in free recall, it shouldn't surprise you to learn that there are also age-related differences in the TOT experience. Elderly adults are more likely to experience TOTs relative to younger adults. In fact, Burke, Mackay, Worthley, and Wade (1991) found that middle-aged adults reported significantly more TOT experiences than younger adults (1.4 per week versus 1.0 per week), while the oldest group reported still more, 1.7 per week. Burke and colleagues also found that TOTs take longer to resolve in older participants and that active strategies like generating possible answers are more characteristic of younger participants. Older participants were more likely to experience spontaneous "pop-ups" of the answer.

Burke and colleagues propose two possible explanations for the higher incidence of TOTs in older adults. First, it appears that TOT experiences are especially likely for pieces of information that have not been activated for long periods of time. According to the *inactive trace hypothesis,* older adults, by virtue of their age, have more such pieces of information stored in semantic memory and will experience more TOTs. Another factor cited by Burke and colleagues is an age-related deficit in the efficiency of the connections between semantic representations and phonological representations. In other words, our ability to translate what we know into spoken form declines with age. As a result, there are more instances in which knowledge is activated but naming is blocked (Burke, Mackay, Worthley, and Wade, 1991). This interpretation is supported by the relative lack of alternatives generated by older adults while in a TOT state.

The idea that increased TOTs in older adults result from decreased efficiency in the connections between semantic representations and phonological representations is termed the *transmission deficit hypothesis.* This hypothesis received further support from the results of an investigation by Rastle and Burke (1996). In this study, the investigators were able to lessen the number of TOT experiences by having participants engage in prior processing of the words. In an initial phase, participants were required to pronounce each of 45 words presented visually. After this phase, an ostensibly unrelated general-knowledge test was presented. Half of these questions had answers that had been pronounced in the earlier phase. It turned out that the prior processing that occurred in phase 1 reduced TOTs by 50% for both older and younger adults, supporting the transmission deficit idea. Recent production of a word sensitizes the connection between phonological and semantic representations, thereby increasing the probability that a phonological label can be accessed, given the activation of semantic information.

STOP *and* REVIEW !

1. Define the TOT state. What type of information is most likely to lead to a TOT state?
2. Distinguish between the incomplete activation and blocking views of TOT states.
3. True or false? The feeling-of-knowing judgment that accompanies a TOT state is usually in error.

➤ The tip-of-the-tongue (TOT) phenomenon occurs when information cannot be retrieved from semantic memory, yet there is a strong sense that one knows the information. TOT states occur fairly regularly and are often accompanied by fragmentary information about the desired information, such as the initial letter. TOT states occur most commonly for names.

➤ Most TOTs are eventually resolved, either through an effortful search or a spontaneous "pop-up" of the answer. The incomplete activation view of TOTs is that the desired information is activated but below some level critical for retrieval. The blocking view contends that other (wrong) alternatives become activated, inhibiting the activation of the desired concept.

➤ Typically, TOT states are accompanied by a strong feeling of knowing, a metacognitive judgment that one does know the desired information. Feeling-of-knowing judgments are usually valid and may arise due to partial retrieval of information or due to the familiarity of the information that cues the TOT state.

Analog Representation

All of the topics discussed thus far have focused on information that is verbal in nature: the information is represented by letters and words. All of the experiments assessing the retrieval and maintenance of this knowledge were conducted using verbal stimuli and verbal responses. However, there's another major body of research and theory that examines knowledge representation of a different form. Rather than answering the question "Does a robin have wings?" simply imagine a robin. Are you bringing to mind a visual image? A good deal of research evidence points to the prominence of imaginal forms of representation; these are sometimes referred to as *analog representations,* because the nature of the imaginal representation corresponds to (i.e., is analogous to) the real-world object. In other words, the robin you just visualized corresponds in some fundamental ways to an actual robin.

The Study of Visual Imagery

The question of whether *imaginal representations* exist and whether they serve any important information-processing purpose has been a center of controversy since the inception of cognitive psychology. In fact, this question dates back to psychology's forebears in philosophy. A number of philosophical questions about mental images have been at the center of this debate: Does mental imagery exist? Do we regularly think in the form of mental images? Do mental images serve a purpose, or are they simply by-products of nonimaginal thinking? We should note here that our discussion will focus on visual imagery, given that it's the most investigated and arguably the most salient. However, there certainly are other forms of mental imagery; it's not difficult to mentally conjure up your favorite song and "hear" it or to imagine the feel of a cool breeze or the smell of bread being baked.

Just like all aspects of cognition, the experience of a visual image is impossible to observe directly; people can't project the images they experience onto a screen. To make mental images "visible," cognitive researchers have developed some creative methods.

Mental Rotation.   Shepard and Metzler (1971) developed a method that has served as one of the blueprints for empirically investigating the properties of visual images, and they performed a watershed investigation of the properties of visual images. The task they developed is termed the **mental rotation task.** Take a look at Figure 9.12: the pairs of figures are similar, but they differ along an axis of rotation. The figures on the right have been rotated 45 degrees relative to the ones on the left. If asked whether the two figures are the same or different (except for the degree of rotation), how would you make the decision? Shepard and Metzler speculated that a process of mental rotation (using imagery to manipulate one image to match the orientation of the other) underlies this decision and that the decision would take a measurable amount of time.

They presented participants with a series of pairs like those in Figure 9.12; for each pair, a simple "same" or "different" judgment was required. The members of the figure pairs differed from each other by varying degrees of rotation, from zero degrees (same orientation) to 180 degrees (mirror image). The results, presented in Figure 9.13, are about

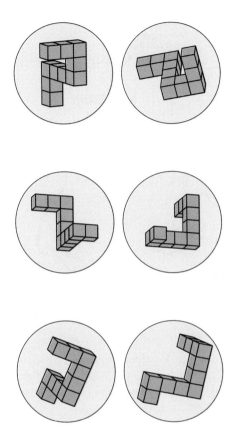

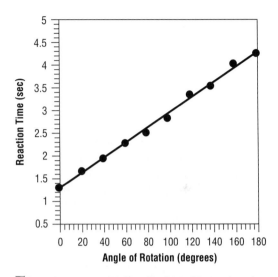

Figure 9.12 Stimuli used by Shepard and Metzler (1971) in their study of mental rotation.

as perfect as you'll ever see. As the degree of rotation increased, so did RT for the same-different judgment. Not only that, the increase was incredibly consistent across varying degrees of rotation, almost as if each degree of rotation added a constant amount of time to the decision process. Shepard and Metzler interpreted their results as evidence that the task was accomplished by mentally rotating one of the figures until its orientation matched the other. Then the rotated figure (a visual image) was compared to the standard figure, which was still physically visible. Some support for this interpretation comes from the participants in the study, who reported that they accomplished the task by mentally rotating the image. While this is introspective evidence and far from conclusive, it does provide converging evidence for Shepard and Metzler's interpretation.

This classic investigation served to define much of imagery research. Researchers scrambled to replicate and extend Shepard and Metzler's results. And replicate they did; the basic pattern of results was repeated across a wide variety of materials, including rotations in three-dimensional planes (Shepard & Metzler, 1971), polygons (Cooper, 1975), and body parts (Cooper & Shepard, 1975; Parsons, 1987).

A different approach to investigating the properties of visual images and whether they function as analogs to visual perception was undertaken by Kosslyn and colleagues in a

Figure 9.14 Fictional island shown to participants in the Kosslyn, Ball, and Reiser (1978) study. Subjects in the study first memorized this map, including the various landmarks (the hut, the well, the patch of grass, and so on). Subjects then formed a mental image of this map for the scanning procedure.

From Kosslyn, S. M., Ball, T. M., & Reiser, B. J. (1978). Visual images preserve metric spatial information: Evidence from studies of image scanning. *Journal of Experimental Psychology: Human Perception and Performance, 4,* 47–60. Copyright 1978 by the American Psychological Association. Reprinted by permission.

series of investigations that have spanned two decades (e.g., Kosslyn, Murphy, Bernesderfer, & Feinstein, 1977; Kosslyn, Reiser, Farah, & Fliegel, 1983; Kosslyn, Chabris, Marsolek, & Koenig, 1992). Throughout this span, Kosslyn has employed a variety of clever tasks to further illuminate how we process and use visual images.

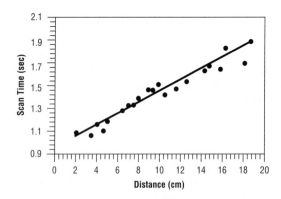

Figure 9.15 Image-scanning data reported by Kosslyn et al. (1978). Note the steady increase in scanning time as a function of distance scanned.

From, Kosslyn, S. M., Ball, T. M., & Reiser, B. J. (1978). Visual images preserve metric spatial information: Evidence from studies of image scanning. *Journal of Experimental Psychology: Human Perception and Performance, 4,* 47–60. Copyright 1978 by the American Psychological Association. Reprinted by permission.

Image Scanning. In a classic investigation of imagery processes, Kosslyn, Ball, and Reiser (1978) sought to determine whether we scan mental images in the same way we might scan a picture that's physically present in front of us. Participants in their study were presented with the map pictured in Figure 9.14, depicting a fictitious island (could it be Gilligan's?). They were instructed to memorize it along with some of its designated features. After committing the map to memory, they performed an *image-scanning task.* They were asked to form a visual image of the map and focus on a particular location (e.g., the hut). Then they were presented a location that either was or was not on the map. Their task was to scan from the original location to the named location (if this location was on the map) and press a button when they got there. Figure 9.15 presents the scanning time for all possible pairings of the seven locations on the map. What you see is strikingly similar to the mental rotation results: a near linear increase in RT with increasing map distance. Once again, it seems that visual images are analogous to their physical counterparts; mental maps seem to retain the spatial relationships that characterize their physical analogs.

Stop *and* Think!

MENTAL TRAVEL ACROSS CAMPUS

This mental scanning demonstration will take a little bit of advance preparation. Sit down with a campus map and find pairs of locations on the map that represent a range of distances (i.e., two locations that are relatively close or relatively far, and some that are a moderate distance from one another). Once you've got these pairs set, recruit a few friends for a mental map-scanning study. You'll need some sort of stopwatch to record response times.

1. Have them form a mental image of campus (perhaps even giving them the map at first to "fix" the image).
2. Then ask them to imagine a dot starting at one location and ending at the second location in the pair.
3. When they "arrive" at the second location, they should say "stop," and you should record the scanning time.

Then answer the following questions:

- Did you find the predicted relationship between the distance to be scanned and response time?
- Did participants have any trouble performing the task?
- Did they feel that they were using a visual image to accomplish it?
- Did participants have any sense of what you were doing and why?
- Do you think there was any sort of expectancy bias at work?

Methodological Problems?   Some (Richman, Mitchell, & Reznick, 1979; Pylyshyn, 1981) have argued that the results of image-scanning studies are not the result of using imagery but are the result of **task demands**—people's tacit knowledge regarding the behavior of objects in space. Because people know that it takes time to travel across any kind of space, this knowledge implicitly (and possibly unconsciously) guides their responding. For longer distances, they respond more slowly; for shorter distances, more quickly. Kosslyn (1994) cites a number of studies that undermine this explanation (Finke & Pinker, 1982, 1983: Pinker, Choate, & Finke, 1984) but agrees that people do have control over some of the processes involved in image scanning (e.g., speed of scanning) but not others (e.g., the effects of scanning over variable distances). According to Kosslyn, this issue has never been successfully resolved, because it is difficult to determine definitively whether or not knowledge and expectations unconsciously dictate behavior in imagery experiments. As a result, researchers have moved onto empirical questions that are more tractable.

Image Inspection.   Another task used by Kosslyn to investigate the properties of visual images is an *image inspection task,* which involves the inspection of mental images in order to pick out details. In this type of experiment, participants are asked to imagine a rabbit

Figure 9.16

Figures used by Kosslyn (1975) in his study of image comparison and perception of image detail.

From Kosslyn, S. M. (1975). Information representation in visual images. *Cognitive Psychology, 7,* 341–370. Copyright 1975, Elsevier Science (USA). Reprinted by permission.

(a)

(b)

either next to an image of an elephant or next to an image of a fly. Why these odd pairings? Kosslyn speculated that this would affect the size of the rabbit image. In the first condition, the rabbit would be relatively small, and details would be difficult to pick up in the image, as in Figure 9.16a. By contrast, in the second condition (Figure 9.16b), the rabbit would be relatively large, and details would be easier to pick up in the image.

In the Kosslyn (1975) study, after participants imagined the "target animal" (e.g., rabbit) next to the "context animal" (e.g., fly or elephant), they were then presented a property (e.g., whiskers) and were asked to determine as quickly as possible whether the target animal possessed the property. They were told to determine this by searching for the property within their visual image. The results were clear-cut: when target animals were imagined next to a large context animal, participants' response time was longer than when the target animal was imagined next to a smaller context animal. Once again, the findings indicated that visual images are analogous to pictures; scrutinizing the details of a small image is relatively difficult, just as scrutinizing the details of a matchbook-sized picture would be.

The Imagery Debate

The results from studies of mental rotation, image scanning, and image inspection would, on the face of it, seem to provide fairly compelling evidence that we are indeed capable of visual imagery and that imagery is a useful mode of processing that functions in a matter analogous to actual visual perception. However, this contention is controversial. Let's consider each side of this debate in more detail.

The Functional Equivalence View.   The way we manipulate, scan, and form images seems to mirror the way we manipulate, scan, and draw real pictures. In other words, images serve as depictions, or analogs, of actual physical objects and layouts. Visual images retain the characteristics of the scenes or layouts they depict. This view of the similarity between visual images and actual percepts has been termed the **functional equivalence view**—that is, images and transformations of images are functionally equivalent to percepts of real physical objects and their transformations (Finke & Shepard, 1986). According to this view, in the opening story, Eleanor has a mental representation of Zach's verbal directions that is analogous to a map sketched on a piece of paper. Eleanor's mental scanning and manipulation of her mental map is analogous to the inspection and rotation she might engage in if she were holding a map in her hands.

Cooper and Lang (1996) reviewed several versions of the functional equivalence view. Weaker versions of this view contend that there are parallels between the processes involved in visual imagery and visual perception—that is, there are some notable similarities between them. Moderate versions (e.g., Kosslyn, 1981) argue for a much closer correspondence between visual images and perceived objects. According to this moderate view, the processes whereby we construct, manipulate, and scan mental images are closely analogous to, rather than loosely associated with, the way we would draw or construct, manipulate, and inspect perceived objects. This moderate view is consistent with the results from studies of mental rotation, scanning, and inspection just discussed.

The strongest version of the functional equivalence view holds that images and percepts are generated by the same underlying mechanisms as visual perception. In Chapter 4, you read about the visuo-spatial sketchpad component of working memory. According to strong version of the functional equivalence view of imagery, the operation of this sketchpad is akin to the operation of vision. Evidence supporting this view comes from studies of selective interference. You may recall from Chapter 4 the study by Brooks (1967) in which participants were to imagine a block letter F and, while holding it in mind, perform a conjoint task that was either visual or auditory. The findings demonstrated selective interference: holding a visual image in mind interfered with the performance of the visual task but did not interfere with the performance of the auditory task. This selective pattern of interference suggests that imagining and perceiving share similar mechanisms.

The Propositionalist View.   Although the findings from studies of imagery seem quite persuasive on their face, some (e.g., Pylyshyn, 1973, 1981; Anderson, 1978) contend that it is unnecessary to postulate analog representations to account for these findings. In other words, one need not refer to the existence and operation of visual images to explain the results from studies of mental rotation and scanning. These researchers espouse what has typically been termed the *propositionalist view,* asserting that we need only postulate one type of knowledge representation—propositions—to account for cognitive processing in all situations, including those that ostensibly involve visual imagery. Thinking in terms of these "mental sentences"—statements of the relationships between objects—would yield results like those obtained in studies of visual imagery. In the opening story, Eleanor may have an experience of a visual image that corresponds to the directions she's being given, but she is not using this mental image to accomplish anything. Her images are *epiphenomenal,* a by-product of thinking about the propositional relationships embedded in Zach's instructions. So for the sake of parsimony, or theoretical thriftiness, propositional theorists postulate that propositions are the only mode of representation and processing. But you'll recall that the evidence for the processing of visual images is pretty compelling. What explanations for these phenomena have been offered by the propositional theorists?

Let's look at the mental scanning studies. Propositional theorists (e.g., Pylyshyn, 1981) argue that participants memorize the spatial relationships between objects. These spatial relationships are represented in terms of linked propositions: objects far apart in the space would be far apart in the list of propositions, and objects close together in the space would be close together in the list. Consequently, systematic increases in reaction time reflect the amount of time needed to move through the list of propositions: the more propositions, the longer the reaction time.

Resolving the Debate.   To an extent, the questions of whether visual images are truly visual and whether they serve a purpose in representation and processing remain philosophical ones that can't be definitively answered by empirical data. Whatever the result, a propositional theorist could always argue that only knowledge of concepts and the relations between them (i.e., propositions) are used for processing. Yes, people experience visual imagery, and yes, they think they're using images to answer questions. But ultimately, decisions and judgments are based solely on propositional knowledge. However, a growing body of evidence from cognitive neuroscience suggests that this assertion may lack support.

RECURRING RESEARCH THEME
Cognition and Neuroscience

Brain Mechanisms in Visual Imagery and Perception

One of the strongest claims of the functional equivalence view is that visual imagery involves the same neural substrates as does visual perception. If visual imagery truly relies on an analog representational system, it wouldn't be surprising to find these commonalities. The majority of studies do find evidence that occipital areas—the brain areas responsible for vision—are active during visual imagery. D'Esposito, Detre, Aguirre, Stallcup, Alsop, Tippet, and Farah (1997) were interested in which hemisphere serves as the locus of processing during visual imagery.

The procedure employed by D'Esposito and colleagues was straightforward; participants were presented with words naming concrete referents (e.g., *giraffe*), and were to generate a mental image. To isolate visual image generation, the task was made as simple as possible. Participants generated images from memory, and their eyes were closed to eliminate externally derived visual stimulation. In this way, any activity in the visual areas of the brain could be attributed to imagery.

Regional brain activity was assessed through the use of fMRI. Brain images of those who formed visual images were compared with those of a control group of participants, who were treated identically to the visual imagery group except for the instructions to form images of the presented words. To minimize the possibility of spontaneous image generation, the control group was presented with abstract words that didn't lend themselves to visual imagery. The results indicated that visual imagery is indeed a function of the visual association cortex and that visual image processing is asymmetrical, with a locus in the left hemisphere (see also Behrmann, 2000). The fact that the neural substrate underlying image generation is similar to that underlying visual perception provides strong evidence for an analog code and for the suggestion that the processing of this analog code has some of the same characteristics as the processing of a visible stimulus.

Although the propositional view may be parsimonious in its proposal of only one mode of processing, it lacks parsimony in its account of some results from studies of mental imagery, most significantly mental rotation. It's difficult to imagine that arrangements of cubes, polygons, and letters (some of the stimuli from studies of mental rotation) are encoded solely in terms of propositional relationships and that mental rotation RTs are a product of some proposition comparison process. It becomes even more difficult when one considers the striking regularity of the relationship between the degree of rotation and decision time. It actually seems much more parsimonious to assume that we manipulate an analogous representation to arrive at an answer (although this assumption does entail an additional mode of representation). And given results from studies of the neurological substrates of visual imagery and their similarity to those of visual perception, the case that visual imagery is a distinct and important mode of representation has become even stronger.

STOP *and* REVIEW!

1. Describe the results found in studies using mental rotation tasks.
2. True or false? Some have argued that image-scanning results may be an outgrowth of task demands.
3. True or false? Neuroscientific studies support the propositionalist view more than the functional equivalence view.

➤ A good deal of evidence suggests that an imaginal form of representation exists in addition to verbal representations. Research with mental rotation tasks has found that the greater the degree of rotation between two figures, the longer it takes to determine if the figures are the same or different.

➤ Research using image-scanning tasks has found that the farther apart two objects are in an imaginal representation, the longer it takes to scan from one to the other. Some have argued that these results may have resulted from task demands, but the issue has never been conclusively resolved. Research with image inspection tasks has found that the smaller the visual image, the harder it is to identify features of that image.

➤ According to the functional equivalence view, processes underlying visual imagery are similar to those underlying visual perception; images are analogs of actual physical objects. Propositional theorists claim that the processes can be explained in terms of propositional knowledge. A definitive empirical answer to the debate has been difficult to achieve. Neuroscientific studies of imagery lend support to the functional equivalence view.

GLOSSARY

category size effect: the finding that it takes longer to verify or deny membership in a large category than it does to verify or deny membership in a small category (p. 338)

category verification task: a task used to assess semantic memory structure in which participants are asked to verify or deny statements about category membership (p. 336)

characteristic features: those characteristics that are often present but not essential to the identity of a concept (p. 342)

cognitive economy: the idea that feature information in semantic networks is stored nonredundantly at the highest possible level of representation in the network (p. 340)

cross-sectional approach: a research design that involves assessing developmental changes by simultaneously comparing the performance of groups that differ in age (p. 357)

defining features: those characteristics that are essential to the identity of a concept (p. 342)

false relatedness effect: the finding that falsification RTs take longer when two concepts are somewhat related than when the two concepts are not at all related (p. 343)

fan effect: the finding that as more and more facts are learned about some concept, the ability to quickly and easily retrieve any single one of those facts decreases (p. 353)

feature comparison model: a model positing that a concept is represented as a set of descriptions, or "feature lists" (p. 341)

feature verification task: a task used to assess semantic memory structure in which participants are asked to verify or deny statements about the features of concepts (p. 336)

functional equivalence view: the view that mental images share properties with their physical analogs and are accessed and manipulated in a similar way (p. 376)

hierarchical network model: a model positing that concepts are organized hierarchically, with specific concepts nested within more general ones (p. 337)

lexical decision task: the process of deciding whether or not a presented letter string (i.e., BRUF) is a word (p. 345)

longitudinal approach: a research design that involves assessing developmental changes by following the same group of participants over some span of time (p. 356)

mediated priming: the finding that the amount of priming between two concepts in a semantic or propositional network will depend on the degree of their separation (p. 351)

mental rotation task: a task that involves judging whether two presented figures match in orientation (p. 372)

permastore: the store of knowledge that has been learned so thoroughly that its storage is essentially permanent (p. 357)

proposition: the smallest unit of knowledge that can stand alone and be declared true or false (p. 349)

propositional network: networks of propositions constructed from the facts and relationships we learn and experience (p. 350)

semantic memory: the database of general knowledge that enables our successful interaction with the world around us (p. 335)

semantic priming: the benefit in lexical decision (a speedup in RT) that occurs as a function of receiving a semantically related prime (p. 345)

spreading activation: the spread of excitation to related concepts that occurs when a given concept is activated in semantic memory (p. 337)

spreading activation model: a nonhierarchical network model that posits links of varying types among related concepts in semantic memory and assumes spread of activation during knowledge retrieval (p. 344)

stimulus onset asynchrony (SOA): the time lag, in a semantic priming task, between presentation of the prime and presentation of the target (p. 346)

task demands: the features of the task that lead participants to form expectations about what should and should not occur, thus biasing their responding (p. 375)

tip-of-the-tongue (TOT) phenomenon: a block in retrieval accompanied by a strong feeling of knowing (p. 366)

typicality effect: the speed in verifying category membership is faster for typical members of a category relative to less typical members (p. 341)

10

Language: General Principles and Speech Processing

After Eleanor drops Zach off, he heads to the coffee shop; he can use a strong cup of coffee before he starts studying. As he walks up to the counter, he recognizes Colleen from his cognitive psychology class. "Hey, how's it going?" Zach asks.

"Great!" Colleen chirps.

"Say, didn't I see your picture in the school newspaper? Why were you in there?"

"Oh, I won the Miss Teen America contest last weekend."

"Wow! I didn't know you did those pageants."

"I don't like to make a big deal of it, I guess. What can I get you?"

"Large coffee, with a depth charge of espresso."

"Here you go. Long night of studying coming up?" As she hands him the coffee, it spills on the counter.

"Oh, my gooshness!" Colleen exclaims.

Gooshness? Zach thinks. That's funny. She averaged "gosh" and "goodness." "Serving coffee probably wasn't your talent at the pageant, huh?" he jokes.

Colleen smiles. "Sorry about that. I guess I'm just stressed about my physics final."

Zach thinks wistfully that Colleen's smile is enough to win a talent contest. "Don't worry about spilling the coffee or your final; I'm sure you'll pull it off."

Colleen looks confused. "Did you say something about insuring bullets?"

"No, **I'm sure** you'll **pull it** off!" Zach laughs.

"I hope so. Oh, look at the bayy-beee!"

"The what?!? Oh, the baby." It's Colleen's older sister Emily with Colleen's brand-new baby nephew. "Oh yeah, he's really cute." Zach says, even though he doesn't really mean it.

"What's yoour naaame, cyooo-tee? Aren't you preh-shuss?" Colleen coos sweetly.

I wish she'd talk to me like that, Zach thinks as he leaves.

What Is Language?

Perhaps our most impressive and important cognitive achievement as human beings is language—the intricate symphony of representations and processes that allows us to communicate our thoughts to others. Indeed, Pinker (1994b) esteems language as "the jewel in the crown of cognition." Like the proverbial jewel, language is in many ways the culmination of all of our cognitive processes; in fact, it quite often serves as the means through which cognitive processes are revealed. And, like a jewel, language is arguably the most beautifully complex and valuable aspect of cognition. Where would we be without the ability to tell others what we know, think, and understand or without the ability to comprehend this information when expressed by others? Indeed, comparing language to a jewel in a crown, like Zach's reference to a "depth charge" of espresso, demonstrates the flexibility of language—the ability to express ourselves literally or metaphorically.

The ease with which we acquire and use language is amazing, considering what is involved. We take our language ability for granted, rarely giving it a second thought. In the next two chapters, we'll take a closer look at some of the basic features of language. We'll also examine a number of the "instruments" in the "symphony"—the basic cognitive processes that we've discussed in earlier chapters, such as pattern recognition, working memory, and knowledge representation, all of which are critical to language.

Words and Rules

First, let's define what we mean by a language and then consider how various communication systems do and do not fit the definition. We'll begin with a relatively simple definition. **Language** can be defined as a set of symbols and principles for the combination of these symbols that allow for communication and comprehension. Linguist Stephen Pinker (1999) sums it up neatly in the title of his book on language: *Words _and_ Rules* (emphasis added). Your ability to read and understand this textbook is based entirely on your knowledge of the words you're reading as well as your (mostly implicit) understanding of the rules that dictate how they may be combined.

One obvious characteristic of language is that everything to which we refer is symbolized by a word. This is a simple fact, but stunning, when you consider the tens of thousands of these symbols that you know and the relative ease and speed with which you retrieve them; naming an everyday object takes well under one second. All the words a person knows comprises their *mental lexicon,* or mental dictionary. Your mental lexicon is a significant part of semantic memory, the general knowledge store that we introduced in Chapter 6 and examined in detail in Chapter 9. Each representation in the mental lexicon is thought to include more than just a representation of word meaning. It includes other information that we know about a word, such as its sound, its written form, and the roles it can take on in a sentence (e.g., noun, verb, etc.). We'll be returning to the mental lexicon at several points in our subsequent discussion.

Obviously, language doesn't consist simply of all the words we know thrown together in whatever grouping we please. If we were to say "walked me in cat front of the just," you would probably wonder whether we should be coauthoring a textbook. But if we were to simply rearrange these words—"the cat just walked in front of me"—you would have no confusion. Along with the words we use to represent objects, ideas, and actions are rules that govern how these symbols may be combined. The term commonly used to describe these rules is **grammar.** Although grammar is often used to describe the arrangement of words in sentences and words in paragraphs, it's actually a more general term referring to the rules for combining any unit of language, be it a sound, word, or sentence.

Design Features of Language

One framework that has proven useful in capturing some of the major characteristics of language was proposed by Hockett (1960), who delineated a number of **design features** shared by many (in some cases, all) languages. A complete list of these characteristics is presented in Table 10.1. In scanning the list, you might find that some of the design features seem to be more at the core of what language is. Think back to the distinction we made in Chapter 5 between characteristic features and defining features of a concept. This distinction can be loosely applied here. Certain design features of language seem to be more defining—that is, they seem to be central to what language truly is (Harley, 1995). Let's consider a few of these design features.

Language is not simply a group of sounds or marks on a piece of paper. These sounds and marks mean something. This aspect of language is termed **semanticity**—that is, the symbols of language refer to meaningful aspects of the real world. In addition, the symbols of language exhibit **arbitrariness**—that is, they (typically) in no way represent the concepts to which they refer. There's no reason that these particular shapes—C–A–T—should be used to denote a little four-legged furry thing that says "meow." This little furry thing could have just as easily been called a froog. Although this arbitrariness makes learning the symbols of language a formidable task, it also affords language tremendous power: theoretically, any symbol can be used to represent anything. Although arbitrariness is the general rule, there are exceptions. You may have noticed one such exception in the above sentence—*meow.* This word actually does bear some resemblance to the real-world features it represents. Also, some languages (American Sign Language, for one) do include symbols with a close correspondence to the named concept or feature.

Table 10.1 **Design Features of Human Languages**

Design Feature	Description
Vocal-auditory channel	Auditory reception of voice message
Rapid fading	Disappearance of message over time
Broadcast transmission and directional reception	Hearing of message by anyone within earshot; locating by direction
Interchangeability	Reproduction of linguistic message by the receiver
Total feedback	Complete understanding of what has just been said
Specialization	Communication is only purpose of speech transmission
Semanticity	Specific meanings of language sounds
Arbitrariness	Little or no connection between linguistic symbols and what they represent
Discreteness	Language symbols are categorical, not continuous
Displacement	Communication of ideas that are remote in space and time
Productivity	Understanding by listener of unique information
Traditional transmission	Teaching and learning of "detailed conventions" of language
Reflectiveness	Thinking about and communication about language
Prevarication	Deceptive use of language
Duality of patterning	Combining the same limited number of linguistic symbols (i.e., simple sounds and letters) in different ways (e.g., cat, act, tack)

Adapted from Hockett, C. F. (1960). The origins of speech. *Scientific American, 203,* 89–96.

Language has the power to transport us beyond the present place and moment. We can talk about what we're going to do tomorrow or what we did yesterday as easily as we can talk about things in the present. In other words, language allows for **displacement** in time. Colleen demonstrates this characteristic when she informs Zach that she won the pageant last weekend. Language also allows for displacement of another sort—the creation of alternate realities through deception. In other words, we can lie. This design feature is termed **prevarication,** as exhibited by Zach's insincere comment about Colleen's new nephew. The flexibility of language is also evident in the design feature of **reflectiveness.** Language allows us to communicate about the very topic of language; in other words, we can use language to reflect on language, which is what we're doing in this chapter and what Zach did in his private conjecture about Colleen's speech error (gooshness).

Perhaps the most important design feature is **productivity.** From the vast array of symbols (words) available and rules for their combination, an infinite array of new messages can be formed. It's sort of mind boggling when you consider that virtually every statement you utter is new; you've never said it exactly that way before. This versatility is the product of a productive system of words and rules.

Stop *and* Think!

LOOKING AT LINGUISTIC UNIVERSALS

Take a look at the design features of language listed in Table 10.1.

1. Pick out the ones you feel are most important to and/or most defining of human language and think about why they are.

2. Of these, pick one or two that are the most important.
3. Look at the ones you consider less important and think about why they are.

Animal Language?

One philosophical and empirical question that has fueled much debate is whether non-human species are capable of language. There is no question that they are capable of communication—the exchange of information through some type of signal. Even the lowly insect is capable of basic information exchange. Von Frisch (1967) demonstrated that honeybees produce a complex dance that signals the location of nectar to other members of the hive. Many other species engage in various sorts of communication. For example, vervet monkeys use a variety of calls to warn other vervets of specific predatory dangers, such as the presence of snakes or eagles. These calls elicit specific predator-appropriate avoidance behaviors (Demers, 1988).

So nonhuman species can communicate, but is this communication considered language? Your intuition is probably that it isn't, and most researchers would agree. Let's consider these nonhuman communication systems in relation to the design features of a language. Semanticity is present to some extent. The dances of the honeybee and the warning cries of the vervet monkey might be considered "words" of a sort, because they do mean something (e.g., "an eagle is approaching"). Also, animal language is not completely arbitrary. For example, the vervet warning sign for "an eagle approaching" includes looking up, which does relate to the content of the message. Animal language systems are rigid and don't allow for change, so displacement (e.g., "an eagle will approach tomorrow") isn't possible. Animal communication systems do not have the numerous symbols and rule systems that allow for endless novel combinations (productivity). The rigidity of animal language systems prevents prevarication—the deliberate misrepresentation of information

Are they using language?

(e.g., a wiseacre vervet issuing a snake warning when there is no danger)—as well as the ability to reflect on the communication system itself. Clearly, the built-in communication systems of honeybees, vervet monkeys, and the like fall well short of the design features that are at the heart of human language. Some research into the possibility of animal language has been directed at finding out whether nonhumans have the capability to learn and use systems of words and rules.

Language Training Projects.   Over the past 30 years, a substantial number of language training projects have been conducted with a range of nonhuman species in order to determine whether language is or is not a uniquely human faculty. These projects have investigated the representational and communicative abilities of common chimpanzees (e.g., Gardner & Gardner, 1975; Premack, 1970; Premack & Premack, 1983; Terrace, Petitto, Sanders, & Bever, 1979), pygmy chimpanzees (Rumbaugh, 1977; Savage-Rumbaugh, Rumbaugh, & Boysen, 1980), sea lions (Gisiner & Schusterman, 1992), bottlenosed dolphins (Herman, Kuczaj, & Holder, 1993), and African grey parrots (Pepperberg, 1999a,b).

The criteria applied to assess whether other species exhibit language essentially boil down to the two components of language described earlier: words and rules. First, do apes, parrots, and other animals learn to associate labels with objects in the world? Second, can these animals take the symbols they've learned and spontaneously combine them in unique and novel ways using rules? You do this every time you open your mouth or sit down at the word processor to type something. Are nonhumans capable of this novel gen-

Are they using language?

eration? In a recent review of language training projects, Savage-Rumbaugh and Brakke (1996) provide a useful scheme for considering the successes of these training projects and the extent to which these successes might be labeled language. Their review addresses three different points critical to the answer—namely, applying words to concepts, responding appropriately to commands, and using language in a social context.

Labeling: Is It Word Learning?   Let's take a look at whether nonhuman species are capable of mastering this first simple component of language: Can they learn to apply words to concepts? Almost all language training projects involve teaching the animal students labels for salient objects in their environment. For example, the Premacks (e.g., Premack & Premack, 1983) taught their chimpanzee, Sarah, to associate a set of plastic chips with objects in her environment. She was trained extensively on these "words" and was required to place the chips on a magnetized board in response to questions. Sarah was quite successful in learning and producing symbols in the appropriate context.

Similar (and quite astounding) successes have been reported by Pepperberg in her studies of African grey parrots, most notably her parrot Alex (Pepperberg, 1999a,b). In the training model, one trainer (trainer A) asks another (trainer B) to name an object (e.g., key). After trainer B does so successfully, trainer A asks Alex to do so. This procedure is repeated, with trainers A and B occasionally changing roles and with Alex being encouraged to participate. Another interesting aspect to the procedure is Alex's reward. Rather than getting some type of treat, Alex is simply given the thing he named to grasp in his beak for a moment. The criterion for learning is 80% accuracy in naming an object or one of its properties. Using this method, Alex has learned dozens of symbols, including object words (e.g., paper and rock), color words, and numbers.

These results are quite impressive, but do they demonstrate linguistic ability? Savage-Rumbaugh and Brakke (1996) aren't convinced. Both Sarah and Alex succeeded in associating labels with objects, to be sure, but it's not clear whether the labels are truly *referential*. Think of how humans use words. If I tell you that I'm going to the library to get a book to read, the word *book* refers to the same (or very similar) concept in our respective heads. Note that I'm not holding up a book and saying "book." In the naming studies described above, the labels are not used in a referential manner. An object is simply held up, and the chimp or parrot gives a label that they've associated with it. There's no evidence that the label *is* the thing.

Language as Learning to Do as You Are Told.   Savage-Rumbaugh and Brakke (1996) discuss a second possible manifestation of language that has been observed in language training studies: appropriate responses to commands issued in some sort of artificial language. These research projects help to get at the second component of language—rules. Appropriate responses to requests or commands generated from the rules of a language would indicate a capacity for grammar. Interestingly, sea mammals have been the subject of some of these studies—namely, the sea lions Rockie and Gertie (e.g., Schusterman & Krieger, 1988) and the bottlenosed dolphins Ake and Phoenix (e.g., Herman, Richards, & Wolz, 1984). These studies have investigated whether these animals can respond appropriately to symbolic relations such as "fetch the hoop to the frisbee" or "surfboard basket tailtouch." Although the ability to respond to these sorts of commands seems a bit more languagelike than simply labeling objects, Savage-Rumbaugh and Brakke note that when compared to the language of children, these instances of communication fall short of language. The only reason the dolphins engaged in these interactions was to get a fish. Outside of this context, they would have no reason to engage in the communication. In stark contrast, a child uses language in a much more intentional and deliberate way. If a child plays a new game and enjoys it, they are able to refer to the game later in a request to play it again. No such capacity is evident in these sea mammals. Savage-Rumbaugh and Brakke do note that the animals may be capable of more, but given the limits of the testing situation, their abilities fall well short of linguistic expression.

Language as Engaging in Social Routines.   Language involves the use of words and rules in spontaneous interactions with others. By its very nature, language is social; it involves intentional and referential communication between at least two people. To assess the ability of nonhumans to apply the words and rules of a language in this context, a number of researchers have conducted what Savage-Rumbaugh and Brakke (1996) refer to as *cross-fostering studies* (e.g., Gardner & Gardner, 1975; Terrace et al., 1979). In these studies, selected signs from American Sign Language (ASL) were taught to chimpanzees within the context of daily interactions. Communication occurred throughout the day, and the experimenters treated the chimpanzees' gesturing as intentional even if it wasn't, just as adults do with young children. Eventually, the chimpanzees (most notably the star pupil Washoe) started to produce symbols, just as small children start to produce words.

So was Washoe learning language? In spite of the surface similarities between this training situation and a child learning language, there were some critical differences. To help the chimps learn the signs, the experimenters shaped their hands into the appropriate signs until the chimps "got it." Once the sign was learned, the chimps had to give it in order to gain access to certain desired activities (e.g., food or tickle games). Here, the signs served the same function as the labels learned by dolphins and sea lions: the signs are simply responses made to achieve a particular end. The animals aren't really communicating any type of idea or intention; their utterances seem limited to requests and are never used referentially (Savage-Rumbaugh & Brekke, 1996). So once again, we have evidence for successful labeling and manipulation of symbols but not for truly linguistic capabilities.

Kanzi and the Bonobos.   Although many, if not most, researchers would agree that the results discussed thus far fall well short of human language, some striking results have been found in investigations of the linguistic abilities of the pygmy chimpanzee, or bonobo. Kanzi is perhaps the most famous student in this breed, which has undergone extensive investigation by Savage-Rumbaugh and colleagues. Bonobos are more similar to humans (in terms of their social and sexual interactions) than are common chimpanzees (like Sarah and Washoe). Savage-Rumbaugh suspected this similarity might indicate a similarity in the development of communicative behavior.

The work of Savage-Rumbaugh and colleagues with Kanzi is noteworthy in a number of respects. First is the manner in which Kanzi learned; initially his learning was spontaneous. Trainers were teaching Kanzi's mother, Matata, to use a system of symbols, termed *lexigrams* (see Figure 10.1). When Matata was separated from Kanzi for breeding purposes, the researchers were surprised to learn that he had picked up many of the lexigraphic signs.

Figure 10.1 Lexigraphic symbols used in the bonobo language studies of Savage-Rumbaugh and colleagues.
Courtesy of Language Research Center, Georgia State University.

In subsequent investigations, the focus came squarely on Kanzi and his ability to learn and manipulate these lexigraphic symbols.

Kanzi's learning was fast and spontaneous. It wasn't necessary to explicitly train him in the lexigraphic language. He learned simply through constant interaction and interchange with caretakers about the events and routines of each day. As they spoke, the caretakers would point to whatever symbols happened to be relevant. In addition to speaking and referring to lexigraphic symbols, caretakers also used informal gestures and a smattering of ASL signs. Another noteworthy difference in the study of Kanzi was that the human communication system was combined with Kanzi's physical environment. Rather than raising Kanzi as a human child and attempting to engage him in humanlike conversation about objects and activities chosen by humans (as had been done with Sarah and Washoe), the communication system was allowed to evolve during Kanzi's everyday adventures in his 55-acre playground. Finally, the work with Kanzi was noteworthy in the sheer volume of data recorded by the researchers. Using automated, rigorous, and consistent data-recording methods, Savage-Rumbaugh and colleagues amassed a corpus of over 13,000 utterances generated by Kanzi over a four-month period.

A painstaking analysis of the utterances generated by Kanzi indicated that he was quite capable of generating novel combinations of symbols. And these combinations weren't just random strings of symbols and gestures. It was clear that Kanzi made a distinction between types of words (nouns and verbs, basically) and was able to place these types in the appropriate slots of an utterance. Even more impressive, the analysis also indicated that Kanzi made up his own grammatical rules and used them consistently, a sign of the productivity that characterizes human language. In sum, work with Kanzi has yielded the most impressive evidence to date of languagelike abilities in nonhumans. First, the language was learned spontaneously, in the absence of formal instruction, just as it is with human children. Second, the symbols used seem truly referential in nature. Third, the symbols were combined in a novel and rule-governed manner. And importantly, these utterances were not initiated by external events in the immediate context.

Evaluation.   Some, the prominent linguists Noam Chomsky and Steven Pinker among them, remain unconvinced by the demonstrations offered in the preceding studies. As impressive and surprising as these abilities may be, they are not language. As you'll read later, this nativistic view of language holds that nonhuman animals are simply not equipped neurologically to learn a complex system of language; language is based in specific brain structures that have evolved only in humans. But still, there is heated debate. Opponents of Chomsky's view (e.g., Greenfield & Savage-Rumbaugh, 1990), who refer to it as "creationist," point out that given the (99%) genetic similarity between humans and other primates, it would be surprising if there wasn't some degree of similarity in their linguistic abilities. (But this is an oversimplification; see Pinker, 1994a, for a rejoinder to this genetic claim.) Kako (1999), in a recent review of the work with Alex, Ake and Phoenix, and the bonobos, notes that there is considerable evidence of word and rule use and that the question of language abilities in animals merits further investigation.

Is Language Modular?

Chomsky's contention that human language is a unique, species-specific ability relates to a general philosophical issue regarding the nature of language. Some theorists, including Chomsky (e.g., Chomsky, 1975) believe language to be modular in function. The **modular view** holds that language is made up of a unique set of abilities and capacities that cannot be reduced to or explained solely in terms of other cognitive processes. According to this view, language is special. Correlaries to the modularity view are that language is species specific (only humans possess the module) and innate (the module is present from birth). The *nonmodular view* contends that language perception, production, and comprehension are the joint product of the cognitive processes we've been discussing throughout the text. The debate is largely a philosophical one; no experiment can provide a definitive answer to the question. Nevertheless, it is an argument that bears importantly on many aspects of language, as you'll see throughout our discussion.

R E C U R R I N G   R E S E A R C H   T H E M E

Cognition and Neuroscience

Modularity of Lyrics and Tunes

As noted above, the language-as-modular argument contends that the cognitive operations underlying language are unique to language. Not everyone buys the modularity argument; many believe similar processes are involved in the processing of language and other abilities, such as music. Some of the research that bears on this conclusion has been done using event-related potentials (ERPs). You'll recall that ERPs are derived from electroencephalographs (EEGs), which assess the gross electrical activity of the brain. One finding from ERP research on the processes of language is an N400 wave, termed the *N400* because it's characterized by a negative-voltage brain wave that peaks about 400 milliseconds after the onset of a word (Gazzaniga, Ivry, & Mangun, 1998). The N400 is particularly sensitive to the semantic dimension (i.e., the meaning) of language (Kutas & Hillyard, 1970); a particularly strong N400 occurs after the presentation of a semantically incongruous word ("He spread the warm bread with *socks*"). There is a musical "cousin" to the N400 wave: the P600—a positive-voltage brain wave that peaks around 600 milliseconds after the presentation of a musically incongruous ("wrong") note.

Besson, Faita, Peretz, Bonnel, and Requin (1998) were interested in what happens when semantic incongruity (the wrong words) meets musical incongruity (the wrong notes). In their investigation (cleverly titled "Singing in the Brain"—get it?), they presented opera excerpts to professional musicians from the Marseilles (France) opera under three different conditions: (1) the passage had the correct words throughout but ended on an incongruous word; (2) the passage had the correct notes throughout but ended with an incongruous note; and (3) the passage ended with both an incongruous musical note and an incongruous word. They were interested in whether the ERPs produced in response to the semantic incongruity would be affected by the musical context, and vice versa.

The nonmodular view suggests that the processing of the semantic (lyrics) and musical (notes) aspects of vocal music is affected by each other. Consequently, the associated N400 response (to semantic incongruity) and P600 (to musical incongruity) brain waves should deviate from the normal shape observed when each is presented in isolation. On the other hand, the modular view would suggest that these aspects of vocal music are processed independently of one another, so there should be no interaction apparent in the brain processing of lyrics and musical notes. As a result, the standard N400 and P600 brain waves should be observed.

The simple effects replicated those of earlier studies. Incongruous words, even in the context of music, led to an N400 response; incongruous notes, even when attached to words, led to the standard P600 response. Most relevant to the question of modularity is the finding that when a passage featured both types of incongruity, the resulting brain response was not some "average" of the N400 and P600 responses. Instead, the response to this "double violation" was a standard N400 and a standard P600, indicating that the processing underlying each violation was separate. Thus, the on-line cortical processing of music and words seems to be at least partially independent, suggesting to the authors that "the exquisite unity of vocal music" (Risset, 1991, p. 497) arises, in part, from separate processing centers, as the modular view would predict.

Linguistics and Psycholinguistics

Cognitive psychologists certainly do not have a corner on the investigation of language. Cognition researchers investigate what would be termed *psycholinguistics*—the psychological processes involved in using language, as reflected in processes as varied as speech perception to conversing politely. Psycholinguists are also interested in exactly how we execute our language abilities, or *linguistic performance.*

Psycholinguistics is related to another field known simply as *linguistics.* Linguists would not be particularly interested in the exact mechanisms by which speech is perceived or misperceived, nor would they be interested in the social dynamics involved in maintaining a friendly conversational flow. These are psychological questions and issues of precisely how language plays itself out. Linguists would be interested in language in its pure form—the rules that define it and our knowledge of those rules. This (relatively) pure knowledge of language and its rules is termed *linguistic competence.* In the following discussion, we will be concerned primarily with psycholinguistics and the cognitive processes that combine to allow for our seamless ability to speak, read, write, and understand.

Language: Levels of Analysis

As you may have already gathered, language is a topic that encompasses all of the cognitive processes we've discussed thus far in some way or another. Presenting a representative sample of this research is, quite frankly, a daunting task. Fortunately, the very nature of language provides a ready-made organizational rubric—its hierarchical structure—that we'll use to survey the field. Language can be analyzed on a number of different levels, each of which features its own set of methodologies, empirical findings, and theoretical issues.

At a molecular level, language involves the analysis of the small bits of information that we know as letters and speech sounds. The next level in the hierarchy is made up of words: How are words represented and accessed in semantic memory during language comprehension and production? Next, one must consider the syntactic and semantic rules that nonconsciously guide our ability to form sentences. In this chapter we will traverse this hierarchy in the context of spoken language. Then we'll turn to written language in Chapter 11.

STOP *and* REVIEW!

1. The most fundamental design feature of language is
   a. prevarication
   b. semanticity
   c. arbitrariness
   d. productivity
2. Comment on whether animals are capable of language.
3. Distinguish between the modular and nonmodular views of language.
4. True or false? Linguists are primarily interested in assessing linguistic performance.

➤ Language can be defined as a communication system that employs words and rules. True languages share important design features such as semanticity, displacement, arbitrariness, and prevarication. The most fundamental design feature is productivity, the fact that the words and rules of language can be combined in an infinite variety of ways.

➤ A good deal of research has addressed whether animals are capable of learning human language systems. This research has revealed that a variety of species (including seals, dolphins, parrots, and chimpanzees) are capable of using symbols to refer to concepts. Whether they can combine these symbols in novel ways based on a system of rules is unclear, but some studies (particularly with the bonobo chimpanzees) do indicate the rudiments of this ability.

➤ The modular view contends that language involves mechanisms that are devoted exclusively to language. The nonmodular view contends that language is accomplished through the combination and integration of other cognitive processes like perception and working memory. No specialized set of language mechanisms is necessary.

➤ Psycholinguists study the psychological processes involved in understanding and producing language, also termed linguistic performance. Linguists are interested in language itself, including its structure and proper usage. This aspect of language is termed linguistic competence. Language can be analyzed by taking stock of its hierarchical structure.

Phonology: The Basic Elements of Spoken Language

We now begin our trek up the language hierarchy for spoken language. **Phonology** refers to the analysis of basic speech sounds. Understanding spoken language is an exercise in auditory perception and pattern recognition. First, sounds must be registered in the auditory system (perception); subsequently, these sounds must activate representations of the corresponding concepts in semantic memory (pattern recognition).

A great deal of research has investigated the basic components of speech and how they are perceived, as well as how a given string of speech sounds is identified as a word. Recall the distinction between bottom-up processing and top-down processing discussed in Chapter 3. Bottom-up processing refers to the identification of a pattern based on the component data. But as you'll see, speech perception and recognition involve more than just the compilation of speech data. Understanding speech involves extensive top-down processing whereby we use everything but the data to aid in pattern recognition. Speech signals are quite often unclear or imperfect; therefore, we must rely on surrounding information or previous knowledge to disambiguate the signal.

The Components of Speech: Phones and Phonemes

Let's take a look at the "data" that comprise spoken language. Given that most of us have more experience working with visual language processing (processing written letters) than we do in analyzing basic speech sounds, let's start with a visual analogy. Consider the visual identification of the letter *a*. It always has the same component features (more or less) in approximately the same arrangement, regardless of the particular word in which it is embedded. But the sound /a/ (/ / indicate the sound, apart from spelling) in a spoken word has different component features depending on the context. For example, the /a/ sound in *cat* is different when a person from the East Coast, the Deep South, or England says it. Each of these people speaks with a different accent, so the /a/ sound is not the same. How can that be? In order to understand this, we have to look at the actual physical sounds that make up the words.

The acoustic structure of a speech signal can be viewed with the use of a *sound spectrograph* that, when presented with a speech signal, yields a *sound spectrogram.* The spectrogram plots what are basically bursts of energy (sound waves of differing frequency) that result from speech. Sample sound spectrograms for several different words are presented in Figure 10.2. The vertical axis represents frequency, and the horizontal axis represents time. Intensity of the auditory signal is represented by the darkness of the frequency bands. The particular physical stimulus elicited by speech is different, depending on factors such as rate, stress, intonation, accent, and surrounding sounds.

Because some variations in the speech signal are due to purely physical properties of the speech waveform, the smallest unit that we need to identify must be defined by the acoustic properties of a sound. This segment of speech is called a **phone.** For example, the *o* in *boat* spoken by a Minnesotan is physically different from the *o* in *boat* spoken by a New Yorker. The two sounds are phonetically different from each other; they represent two different phones. However, such phonetic (physical sound) differences do not change the meaning of a word: an *o* is an *o* no matter who says it. Therefore, we need another term—**phoneme**—to refer to categories of speech sounds that are clearly different and that change the meaning of a spoken signal. For example, the phonemes /b/ and /p/ yield quite different concepts when combined with the segment *-ig.* The phonemes of American English are listed in Table 10.2. These phonemes can be categorized as consonants or vowels. It's important to note that the number of phonemes in a word doesn't necessarily correspond with

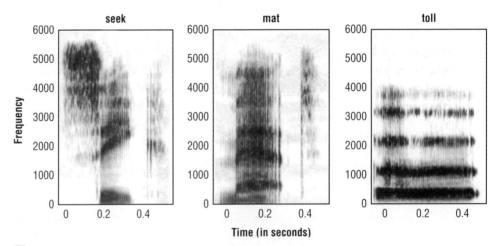

Figure 10.2 Sound spectrograms for several different words.

From Denes, P. D., & Pinson, E. N. (1993). *The speech chain.* New York: Freeman. Copyright 1993 by W. H. Freeman and Company. Reprinted by permission.

Table 10.2   The Basic Sounds of English

Vowels	Consonants	
ee as in h*ea*t	*t* as in *t*ee	*s* as in *s*ee
i as in h*i*t	*p* as in *p*ea	*sh* as in *sh*ell
e as in h*ea*d	*k* as in *k*ey	*h* as in *h*e
ae as in h*a*d	*b* as in *b*ee	*v* as in *v*iew
ah as in f*a*ther	*d* as in *d*awn	*th* as in *th*en
aw as in c*a*ll	*g* as in *g*o	*z* as in *z*oo
u as in p*u*t	*m* as in *m*e	*zh* as in gara*g*e
oo as in c*oo*l	*n* as in *n*o	*l* as in *l*aw
o as in t*o*n	*ng* as in si*ng*	*r* as in *r*ed
uh as in th*e*	*f* as in *f*ee	*y* as in *y*ou
er as in b*ir*d	Θ as in *th*in	*w* as in *w*e
oi as in t*oi*l		
au as in sh*ou*t		
ei as in t*a*ke		
ou as in t*o*ne		
ai as in m*i*ght		

From Denes, P. D., & Pinson, E. N. (1993). *The speech chain.* New York: Freeman. Reprinted by permission.

the number of letters. Some phonemes are represented by a pair of letters (e.g., /ou/). Try to identify the number of phonemes in the word *boat.* Is it four? Or three? Remember that phonemes are sounds, and sounds don't necessarily correspond one to one with letters. Boat has three phonemes: /b/, /oa/, and /t/.

Producing Phonemes. Speech sounds are products of the vocal tract and can be described in terms of the movement of the structures within it (see Figure 10.3). Differences among speech sounds result from differences in the way that airflow is or is not obstructed. Vowel phonemes involve a continuous flow of air through the vocal tract. Consonant phonemes involve some type of obstruction of the airflow. (Take note of this difference between vowels and consonants by making a few sounds of each type.)

Different vowel phonemes are the product of differences in the position of the tongue—the front, middle, or back of the mouth. Say some different vowels and see how the placement of your tongue varies as you pronounce each one.

Consonant phonemes differ along three dimensions (see Table 10.3). First, they differ in their **place of articulation,** which basically refers to the part(s) of the vocal tract used to make the sound (i.e., where the sound is made). For example /p/ is termed bilabial, because it is articulated at the lips; /th/ is termed dental, because it is articulated with the teeth. (Test this yourself—it's fun!) Consonant phonemes also differ in their **manner of articulation,** which refers to exactly how the airflow is obstructed. For example, *stop consonants* (e.g., /t/) involve a complete disruption of airflow, whereas *fricatives* (e.g., /f/) involve only a partial disruption. Finally, consonant phonemes differ in voicing. **Voicing** relates to what the vocal cords do when the airflow disruption stops. If the vocal cords vibrate at this point, the phoneme is termed voiced. If the vocal cords vibrate after the disruption stops, it's termed voiceless. Voicing is a little difficult to grasp, but this demonstration might help. Put one hand in front of your lips and one hand on your throat (over your vocal cords). Now (really) slowly pronounce the /b/ sound. Notice how your hand feels a puff of air at the same time your vocal cords vibrate; /b/ is a voiced consonant. Now slowly pronounce (exaggerate how slowly you pronounce it) the /p/ sound. Notice how your hand feels the puff of air before your vocal cords vibrate; /p/ is a voiceless consonant.

Stop *and* Think!   **WHAT'S YOUR MOUTH DOING?**

Take a look at the list of phonemes in Table 10.2 and the diagram of the vocal tract in Figure 10.3.

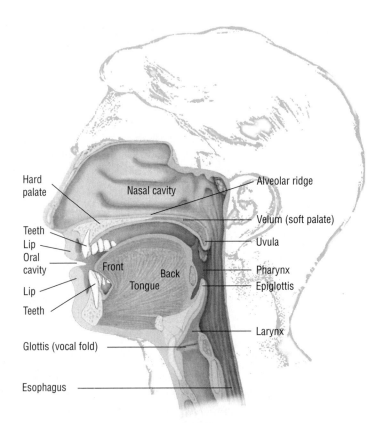

Figure 10.3 The vocal tract.

From Glucksberg, S., & Danks, J. H. (1975). *Experimental psycholinguistics: An introduction.* Hillsdale, NJ: Erlbaum. Reprinted by permission of Lawrence Erlbaum Associates.

Table 10.3 **English Consonants and Their Production**

Manner of Articulation		Place of Articulation						
		Bilabial	Labiodental	Dental	Alveolar	Palatal	Velar	Glottal
Stops	voiceless	p (*pat*)			t (*tack*)		k (*cat*)	
	voiced	b (*bat*)			d (*dig*)		g (*get*)	
Fricatives	voiceless		f (*fat*)	Θ (*thin*)	s (*sat*)	š (*fish*)		h (*hat*)
	voiced		v (*vat*)	ð (*then*)	z (*zap*)	ž (*azure*)		
Affricatives	voiceless					č (*church*)		
	voiced					ǰ (*judge*)		
Nasals		m (*mat*)			n (*nat*)		ŋ (*sing*)	
Liquids					l (*late*)	r (*rate*)		
Glides		w (*win*)				y (*yet*)		

From Glucksberg, S., & Danks, J. H. (1975). *Experimental psycholinguistics: An introduction.* Hillsdale, NJ: Erlbaum. Reprinted by permission of Lawrence Erlbaum Associates. Reprinted by permission.

1. Do a little self-study of how the vocal tract produces these phonemes.
2. Sample some of the phonemes from Table 10.2, enunciating them carefully.
3. Take careful note of what every element of the vocal tract is doing (teeth, tongue, throat, vocal cords, etc.).

Perceiving Phonemes.   How are speech sounds perceived and successfully combined during the process of word recognition? Speech perception is quite a difficult task. Speech sounds are present only briefly and, as we just noted, can vary widely from speaker to speaker. They differ in what are termed **suprasegmental factors**—aspects of the speech signal such as rate, stress, and intonation—over and above the actual phonemes. In addition to differences produced by suprasegmental factors, any given phoneme within a word is affected by surrounding phonemes. The *a* in *cat* sounds different than the *a* in *hand,* because the *a*'s are surrounded by different phonemes. This poses a significant problem for the perceptual system. How do we perceive a given phoneme as the same when uttered by different speakers or in two different contexts?

Invariance.   The fact that a given phoneme sounds different depending on neighboring phonemes is termed **coarticulation;** phonemes are, to some extent, articulated together (see Figure 10.4). In spite of this, we perceive more-or-less identical /a/ sounds in the words *cat* and *hand.* In other words, the perception of phonemes is *invariant* across different contexts. Although coarticulation does make it a bit of a challenge to perceive phonemes as invariant, it does aid word recognition by hinting at what sounds are coming next. As Harley (1995) points out, the fact that the phoneme /b/ in *ball* and *bull* is articulated differently provides information about what is coming next, thereby facilitating recognition of later phonemes.

Categorical Perception.   The invariance in perceiving phonemes in spite of their different acoustic properties is the result of a fundamental characteristic of speech perception termed *categorical perception.* **Categorical perception** refers to our tendency to perceive phonemes in a relatively broad (i.e., categorical) fashion; we don't discriminate between subtle shadings in the way a particular phoneme sounds. This would seem to solve the problems associated with coarticulation. Each phoneme represents a distinct category; any particular variation of one of these phonemes is still placed firmly into the appropriate category. Consider a classic demonstration of this phenomenon by Liberman, Harris, Hoffman, and Griffith (1957). These researchers used a speech synthesizer to produce and present speech sounds that differed

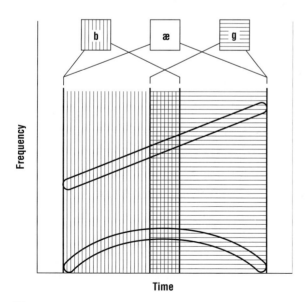

Figure 10.4 Coarticulation—the sound of each phoneme is influenced by surrounding phonemes.

along a continuum of place of articulation (*b–d–g*). In spite of the continuous variation in the speech signals presented, participants did not classify the sounds continuously. Rather, they placed the sounds into three distinct categories, corresponding to the phonemes /b/, /d/, and /g/. They didn't hear *b*-ish *g*'s or *g*-ish *d*'s. Although these results indicate that we may sort widely varied speech sounds into a much smaller number of simple phoneme categories, more recent work has cast some doubt on the phenomenon. We'll discuss this evidence a bit later.

Theories.   How do we solve the problem of invariance? How is it that we are able to perceive a phoneme in pretty much the same way in spite of striking differences in the physical signal it produces? Given the complexities involved in the perception of speech and the relative ease with which we accomplish it, some theorists believe that speech perception is "special," involving mechanisms that are devoted to nothing but speech perception. Does this type of argument sound familiar? It's exactly the type of argument that's offered for language being modular. Here we revisit the issue of modularity within the context of speech: Is there a speech perception module? To what degree is speech perception a special ability or just another instance of auditory perception?

Speech Is Special. A modular approach to speech perception, the **motor theory of speech perception**, proposed by Liberman and colleagues (e.g., Liberman, Cooper, Shankweiler, & Studdert-Kennedy, 1967), posits a close link between the mechanisms we use to articulate speech and our perception of speech. Basically, implicit knowledge about how speech sounds are articulated aids in the perception of those same sounds when we hear them. For example, we have implicit knowledge about coarticulation and how it confuses the mapping from acoustic signal to the phonemes intended by the speaker; this tacit knowledge of articulation allows us to decipher the spoken message (Miller, 1990). This approach is sometimes termed the motor theory, because it contends that the basic representations we use for speech perception are the articulatory gestures we use to produce the sounds when we speak. In other words, speech perception and speech production rely on the same specialized representations (Liberman & Whalen, 2000). Two other important principles follow. First, because only humans possess the mechanisms necessary for speech, only humans are capable of understanding speech. Second, speech perception is innate; infants are born equipped with the representations that allow for speech perception and production.

The argument that speech perception involves a specialized module is consistent with a number of observations, most of which relate to the ease of speech perception in spite of a supposed lack of correspondence between the physical speech signal and the patterns that need to be identified from within it (i.e., phonemes). Recall the problem of coarticulation and the consequent need for categorical perception. The phoneme /a/ always has different phonetic features, depending on the context in which it's embedded, so there's really nothing for the perceptual system to "grab hold" of in order to identify it. Therefore, speech perception must rely on a special mechanism—categorical perception. Recall that categorical perception refers to our supposed tendency to hear phonemes categorically. Put another way, we fail to make distinctions between phonemes that are indeed physically different. Categorical perception is an important aid to speech perception, given the variability of a phoneme in different contexts. It is also unique in comparison to other forms of perception, which demonstrates that we are able to make relatively fine discriminations, not just categorical ones. Thus, speech perception seems to be special.

Another argument for a specialized speech processor is the breathtaking speed apparently necessary for the perception of speech. Phonemes occur at a rate of around 10 to 20 per second. Our normal perceptual mechanisms are simply not capable of making so many discriminations in such a short period of time. To decode these rapid-fire speech stimuli, a special mechanism is needed.

Speech as Auditory Perception. A nonmodular approach to speech perception contends that speech perception is just another exercise in auditory perception and pattern recognition. The basic mechanisms that accomplish these tasks are the same ones we use to decode speech. No special mechanism is necessary (e.g., Massaro, 1994). And because other species have auditory systems similar to our own, the ability to perceive speech sounds should not be unique to humans. An example of this approach is the **auditory theory of speech perception** (Miller, 1990).

In support of the auditory theory of speech perception, Massaro (1994) systematically counters each of the arguments outlined above for the special status of speech perception. Recall the argument that there are really no discernible physical features that define a given phoneme, because phonemes differ so widely with context. Massaro points out that this is only a problem for speech perception if the basic unit of perception is a phoneme, and there is good reason to believe that this isn't the case. If the perceptual units of analysis for speech are syllables (which may involve as many as three or four phonemes in combination), then the problem of invariance is not nearly as much of a problem. This also deflates another argument for the speech-is-special theory: the unmanageable speed of speech input. If the basic unit of speech perception is a cluster of phonemes, then we wouldn't need to process 10 to 20 units per second; it would be more like 5 to 10 units, which is more within range of normal perceptual abilities.

Massaro also takes issue with the assumption that we perceive speech sounds categorically, contending that this assumption is simply wrong. As it turns out, categorical perception is more evident with consonants than with vowels (Repp, 1984). Also, research on how we perceive and recognize speech sounds has revealed that although people have the experience of categorical perception, they are actually capable of more fine-grained distinctions than previously thought. This relates to a distinction we made in Chapter 3. Recall our discussion of consciousness and the effects of subliminal primes on responding. You'll recall that although people reported not seeing subliminal primes, their forced-choice responses indicated that they had processed the prime. The same thing happens in speech perception. People report not hearing differences between phoneme categories, but a more fine-grained analysis of processing reveals that they can make subtle distinctions (Massaro, 1994). According to Massaro, what appears to be categorical perception is actually an artifact of the way speech perception was tested and interpreted in early research. (This rather subtle argument lies beyond the scope of coverage here; see Massaro, 1994, pp. 225–230, for a detailed discussion.)

Finally, the speech-as-special argument contends that the speech perception module exists only for humans, since the module is linked directly to the ability to speak. But some research indicates that nonhumans can perceive speech. For example, Kleunder, Diehl, and Killeen (1987) found that quail (of all things!) were able to distinguish among different phonemic categories. So aspects of the auditory (speech) signal itself must provide information that allows for successful perception.

In spite of strong counterarguments, the speech-as-special view is still alive and well. In a review of the controversy, Liberman and Whalen (2000) argue persuasively for the speech perception module, pointing out a number of characteristics of speech processing that aren't addressed by the auditory perception account. One rather compelling argument is what Mattingly and Liberman (1987) term the *requirement for parity:* those involved in any communication exchange must have knowledge of what "counts" as part of the communication system and what doesn't. Consider an example discussed by Liberman and Whalen. A sniff and the phoneme /b/ are both auditory percepts, but clearly only the latter is a speech signal. How do the speaker and the listener both know this? How did one category of auditory percepts (phonemes like /b/) achieve phonological significance whereas others (e.g., sniffs) did not? The auditory perception view doesn't really provide an answer. But in the speech-as-special view, phoneme perception is unique and directly tied to phoneme production; our knowledge of what counts as speech is built into the system.

RECURRING RESEARCH THEME

Cognition and Individual Differences

Perception of Click Consonants

A ubiquitous finding in investigations of language and brain processing is the language specialization of the left hemisphere. A left-hemisphere advantage in phoneme perception is most obvious in the perception of consonant phonemes (e.g., Zattore, Evans, Meyer, & Gjedde, 1992); this advantage is present from early infancy (Best, Hoffman, & Glanville, 1982). Best and Avery (1999) conducted a study of consonant perception and brain lateralization that addressed some of the fundamental theoretical issues sketched above. More specifically, they investigated (1) to what degree the mechanisms for speech perception are innate or shaped through experience, and (2) to what degree these mechanisms are general (as suggested by the auditory theory) or specialized for speech (as suggested by the motor theory).

Best and Avery studied the brain lateralization associated with the perception of "click consonants" in English and Zulu speakers. The Zulu language is one of several African languages that features click consonants, which are "produced by creating a small area of suction in the mouth and releasing abruptly at the tongue (e.g., tsk sound) or the lips (e.g., kiss sound)" (Best & Avery, 1999, p. 65). These clicks have linguistic significance for Zulu speakers but are heard as nonspeech sounds by English speakers. These clicks also allow for a test of the two views of speech perception: speech perception as a general mechanism versus speech perception as

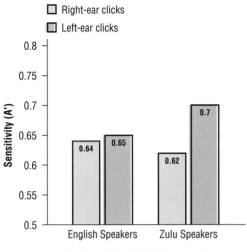

Sensitivity to Click Consonants

Figure 10.5 Results from Best and Avery (1999). Zulu speakers were more sensitive than were English speakers to click consonants, but only for clicks presented to the right ear (i.e., the left hemisphere).

From Best, C. T. & Avery, R. A. (1999). Left-hemisphere advantage for click consonants is determined by linguistic significance and experience. *Psychological Science, 10,* 65–70. Copyright 1999 by Blackwell, Inc. Reprinted by permission.

a specialized module. Why? Because although they're perceived as nonlanguage sounds by English speakers, clicks have the acoustic properties of speech to which a generalized mechanism (localized in the left hemisphere) should be sensitive. But if speech perception is a linguistically based special ability that is fine-tuned by experience, one might expect that only the left hemispheres of Zulu speakers would show increased sensitivity to click consonants.

Best and Avery investigated left-hemisphere specialization for click consonants within a dichotic-listening paradigm (discussed in Chapter 4). Participants were instructed to attend to one ear but heard clicks in both ears. Because of the contralaterality of brain function, clicks presented to the right ear would be processed primarily by the left hemisphere, while clicks presented to the left ear would be processed primarily by the right hemisphere. After being presented with clicks in each ear, participants were presented with four "probe" clicks. Their task was to indicate whether the set of probe clicks included the click they had heard in the attended ear. If the left hemisphere is involved in the processing of click consonants, then the right ear should show higher sensitivity than the left ear.

The results are presented in Figure 10.5. As you can see, the sensitivity to click consonants varied with the native tongue. English speakers demonstrated no difference in sensitivity to these consonants between the right and left ears (and hence between the brain's hemispheres). In contrast, Zulu speakers showed a right-ear (i.e., left-hemisphere) advantage in the perception of click consonants, suggesting specialized brain processes in the left hemisphere that are fine-tuned by experience in perceiving and producing these clicks during everyday language use. These results suggest that the processes of speech perception differ in important ways from simple auditory perception, as the motor theory of speech perception suggests.

The Role of Context.   At the beginning of this section, we discussed the issues of bottom-up processing and top-down processing. Thus far, we have been discussing primarily bottom-up processing—the identification of a pattern based on information that is part of the pattern (i.e., data in the form of speech sounds). But as we noted, speech perception also involves top-down processing—the use of context and/or previous knowledge to disambiguate a messy signal. A particularly compelling demonstration of the role of context comes from a classic study by Warren (1970) in which participants were presented with one of these four sentences.

1. It was found that the *eel was on the axle.
2. It was found that the *eel was on the shoe.
3. It was found that the *eel was on the orange.
4. It was found that the *eel was on the table.

The presented sentences were completely identical except for the last word in the sentence. A coughing sound was spliced into the tape (at the point where the asterisk is) for each sentence. You can probably anticipate the result; participants restored the missing phoneme, but exactly which phoneme depended on the particular semantic context. This finding has been dubbed the **phonemic restoration effect** and serves as a testament to the importance of top-down processing—the role that previous knowledge and context play in processing and identification.

Phoneme Boundaries.   The set of phonemes that define a given language shows tremendous variation cross-linguistically. Some languages have phonemes and phonemic boundaries that are nonexistent in others. For example, native speakers of Japanese have trouble discerning between the phonemic segments /l/ and /r/, because in Japanese, these two belong to the same underlying category. The development of language-specific phoneme boundaries occurs early in infancy; some evidence indicates that phonemic tuning is already under way as early as six months of age (Kuhl, Williams, Lacerda, Stevens, & Lindblom, 1992). And not only do infants seem to "tune in" to phonemic differences that are relevant to their language, they also seem to "tune out" differences that are not relevant (Bates, Devescovi, & Wulfeck, 2001). That is, there seems to be a process of suppression in speech perception that eliminates nonnative phoneme contrasts from the perceptual repertoire. Some speculate that this *learned inhibition,* as Bates and colleagues (2001) term it, may be part of the reason that adults can't seem to learn a second language without an accent (McClelland, Thomas, McCandliss, & Fiez, 1999).

Motherese.   The fact that infants tune in phoneme-relevant distinctions and tune out phoneme-irrelevant distinctions prompts an important question. How are infants able to make out the basic sounds that form the basis for language? Deciphering the basic sound elements of a language is one of the many bewildering perceptual tasks faced by infants. Intuitively, it seems obvious that they gain this knowledge from experience—by listening to adult speakers of their respective languages. In our opening story, Colleen's speech to her new nephew is exaggerated, drawn out, and delivered in a sweet and deliberate voice. The manner in which speech is delivered to infants has been dubbed **motherese,** and it seems to substantially aid infants' speech processing. Research shows that across cultures adult speech to infants is higher-pitched, has exaggerated "ups" and "downs" in pitch, and has a slower cadence (Fernald & Simon, 1984). Also, infants show a marked preference for this type of speech relative to normal adult speech (Fernald, 1985). In our opening story, Zach also likes Colleen's slow, sweet speech, albeit for different reasons.

Motherese aids in the perception of individual phonemes by exaggerating their critical features. This contrasts with typical adult speech, which has poorly formed and articulated consonant and vowel phonemes. Kuhl and colleagues (1992) assessed natural language input of mothers to children in the United States, Russia, and Sweden and found that in all spoken languages, vowel sounds are more (in the authors' words) "acoustically extreme" and "stretched out." The modifications that adults lend to the speech signal provide useful information about basic speech sounds that are exploited by the infant's rapidly developing perceptual system (Kuhl et al., 1992).

Stop and Think!

MOTHERESE

This exercise requires access to a baby, perhaps a niece or nephew, or your own (although it would be much easier to observe someone else engaging in motherese). Eavesdrop on the way the adult caregiver talks to the infant, noting specific characteristics of the speech.

- How do these characteristics compare to the adult's normal mode of speech?
- How are phonemes exaggerated?
- Which seem to be more exaggerated?
- Are word boundaries emphasized?

STOP and REVIEW!

1. Describe the difference in how vowel and consonant phonemes are produced.
2. What is categorical perception, and how does it relate to invariance in our perception of speech sounds?
3. What is the basic idea behind the auditory theory of speech perception?
4. True or false? Infants are able to tune out phonemic differences not relevant to their native language.

➤ Vowel phonemes involve a continuous flow of air through the vocal tract and are the product of differences in the position of the tongue. Consonant phonemes involve some type of obstruction of airflow in the vocal tract and are produced by varying three dimensions: place of articulation, manner of articulation, and voicing.

➤ Coarticulation refers to the fact that the nature of phoneme transmission varies depending on neighboring phonemes. The invariance in perceiving phonemes, in spite of their different acoustic properties, is the result of categorical perception—our tendency to not discriminate between subtle shadings in the way a particular phoneme sounds.

➤ According to the motor theory of speech perception, the same mechanisms and representations underlie speech production and speech perception. According to the auditory theory, speech perception is the product of "regular" auditory perceptual processes. Perception of language-specific phonemes (such as click consonants) is consistent with the existence of a special mechanism. Top-down processing plays an important role in speech perception.

➤ Motherese refers to the exaggerated, musical way adults communicate with infants that aids infant processing of speech. The development of language-specific phoneme boundaries occurs early in infancy. Infants tune in to phonemic differences relevant to their language and tune out differences that are not relevant.

From Sounds to Words

Perceiving and producing individual phonemes is necessary, but certainly not sufficient, to allow for the production and comprehension of spoken communication. Sounds must be combined into meaningful units—words. One of the most amazing things about language is the incredible speed with which we access information about words. In the previous sentence you read nineteen words and were able to access enough about their meanings to understand them and their relation to one another to comprehend the idea of the sentence, all in a matter of about five seconds.

The Mental Lexicon

What are the processes that account for the fast and efficient retrieval of word information from semantic memory, our storehouse of general knowledge? Researchers commonly use the term **mental lexicon** to refer to our mental dictionary. The mental lexicon is really just another way of referring to the general knowledge represented in semantic memory (Chapter 9), albeit with a more linguistic bent. The process by which a concept is activated within the lexicon is termed **lexical access.** What factors influence our access to and recognition of words?

Factors Affecting Lexical Access.   One factor that affects lexical access is word frequency, which refers to how commonly a word occurs in day-to-day linguistic encounters. High-frequency words (e.g., *house*) are more easily and quickly accessed than low-frequency words (e.g., *bungalow*). In a divided-attention study that investigated lexical access, Foss (1969) had participants perform a phoneme-monitoring task. They were to listen for a target phoneme (e.g., /g/) while attempting to comprehend a speech passage. The target phonemes immediately followed either low-frequency or high-frequency words within the passage. Detection times for the target phonemes were longer when the phonemes followed low-frequency words relative to when they followed high-frequency words. Foss concluded that phoneme detection was slower in this condition due to the increased mental effort required for access to low-frequency words.

Another factor that affects lexical access is *lexical ambiguity,* which occurs when a word with two possible meanings (e.g., *bank*) is encountered. This raises several interesting questions with regard to lexical access. Do ambiguous words have two separate representations in semantic memory? Are both representations activated when the word is encountered or only the one relevant to the particular context? An early study by Foss (1970) suggested that the first scenario is the case. The study used a phoneme-monitoring task; participants listened for target phonemes, which appeared immediately after words with only one possible meaning or words with two possible meanings. Foss found that participants were slower in detecting phonemes that followed ambiguous words, ostensibly because the ongoing disambiguation of the word delayed the detection of the subsequent phoneme. This suggests that all meanings of ambiguous words are activated, at least temporarily; context then leads to disambiguation of the word. Later research has muddled the picture a bit, revealing quite a complex relationship between the particular nature of the ambiguous word and the nature of the disambiguating context.

The Bilingual Lexicon.   Bilinguals, individuals fluent in two (or more) languages, make an interesting case for questions of lexical access. How are concepts represented in the memory of bilingual individuals? To put it in concrete terms, when a Spanish-English bilingual sees a cat, how many representations are activated? The answer to the question of whether a single concept is stored as one general representation or as two distinct and language-specific representations seems to be "both." Some findings indicate equivalent performance regardless of the language in which concepts are presented. For example, in an investigation of bilingual semantic memory, Caramazza and Brones (1980) had Spanish-English bilinguals decide whether a presented word (e.g., *gun*) was a member of a more general category (e.g., "weapon"). In this study, it didn't matter whether or not the language of the presented word matched the language of the presented category name. This suggests that a general representation of the concept is being activated. This general activation facilitates the form of that concept in either language. However, Kirsner and his colleagues (Kirsner, Smith, Lockhart, King, & Jain, 1984; Cristofanini, Kirsner, & Milech, 1989) found that priming in a lexical decision task is not as strong when cross-language equivalents are used as primes relative to when a word is repeated in the same language. In other words, *miedo* (Spanish for "fear") is not as good a prime for *fear* as the word itself; *fear-fear* leads to faster RTs than *miedo-fear*. Note that there should be no difference between these conditions if both *fear* and *miedo* lead to the activation of one general (language-nonspecific) representation.

Currently, researchers are likely to adopt a hybrid view. If words are concrete (*dog*), high in frequency (*book*), or cross-linguistic cognates of one another (i.e., they have similar phonological properties in both languages, like *flauta* and *flute*), they tend to be accessed via a common representation. Conversely, words representing concepts that are abstract (*fear*), low in frequency (*unicorn*), or noncognates (*mesa* and *table*) tend to be accessed via separate representations for each language.

Morphology

Just as there are rules for combining the sounds of a language (the rules of phonology), there are rules for manipulating and changing phonemes to produce different words and word forms. This aspect of language is termed **morphology.** A **morpheme** is the smallest unit of language that carries meaning; it may refer to a single word (e.g., *tree*) or to a prefix or suffix that changes the precise meaning of the word (e.g., the *s* in *trees*). Word morphemes are termed **free morphemes,** because they may stand alone; prefix or suffix morphemes are termed **bound morphemes,** because they must accompany (i.e., they must be bound to) a free morpheme in order to stand alone. Let's consider the word *unprepared*. How many morphemes does this word have? It has three: *un* (bound morpheme; negates the verb); *prepare* (free morpheme); and *ed* (bound morpheme; indicates past tense).

"Morphing" Words: Two Systems?   What happens when we add morphemes to words? How does *mouse* become *mice*? How do we go from a *word* to a bunch of *words*? In the latter case, we have an example of a regular transformation (add *-s* to make something plural); in the former, an irregular transformation (*mouse* to *mice*). Pinker (1990, 1991) proposes that making these transformations relies on two separate systems. First, for regular forms, we have a system of rules that are implemented to make the appropriate transformations.

Second, for irregular forms we have an associative system whereby regular-irregular pairs (*mouse-mice*) are simply committed to memory and used to retrieve each other.

What's the evidence for two systems rather than one? Pinker (1991) notes a number of dissociations that support the existence of two systems for morphing words. One interesting dissociation occurs in children as they learn the words and rules of language. At about age 3 or so, children begin to make mistakes termed **overregularization**: the child extends a grammatical rule too far, treating an irregular form as regular (e.g., adding *-ed* to *go* to come up with a past tense *goed*). Funny thing is, before this point, children tend to use correct irregular forms (i.e., they use *went*, not *goed*). As children begin to apply the rules of language (e.g., add *-ed* to indicate that an action took place in the past), they start making mistakes that they've never made before. As the child gets older, they get better at discerning when the rule applies and when it doesn't, adding *-ed* (or not) accordingly. This rather odd sequence—from doing it right, to doing it wrong, and back to doing it right—suggests that two systems are at play and occasionally in conflict (Pinker, 1991).

Word Boundaries

As you read in the section on phonology, the fact that individual sounds in a word run together poses a significant problem for the speech perception system. The same problem arises when we need to segment these sounds into words. Identification is not a simple matter of identifying the blank spaces in the acoustic signal. Take a look at the spectrograph in Figure 10.6. You'll notice a pretty weak relationship between the breaks in the speech signal and the breaks between the words themselves. In other words, the "data" of the acoustic signal provide limited information regarding word boundaries. But you know from personal experience that understanding the component words of an utterance is (phenomenologically) a trivial matter. Given this, how is it that we are able to segment words? Once again, an interaction of bottom-up and top-down processes is at work.

It turns out that there are clues in the data themselves; evidence indicates that we are able to use factors such as the stress patterns of words and the rhythms of speech to distinguish among the words of a spoken sentence. One idea, termed the *metrical segmentation strategy* (Cutler & Carter, 1987), proposes that the segmentation of words is dependent on the phonology of the particular language. For example, in English, the important (content) words in a sentence are much more likely to start with what is called a strong syllable (one that contains a nonreduced vowel sound—a short or long vowel sound like the initial vowel sounds in *eagle, candor, bacon*) and end with a weak syllable (a "schwa" sound, like "uh"— the second vowel sounds in each of the aforementioned words). Based on this, our perceptual systems are "tuned" to detect word boundaries when a strong syllable is encountered (Vroomen, van Zon, & de Gelder, 1996). In line with this idea, Cutler and Butterfield (1992) found that listeners showed strong tendencies to mistakenly insert word boundaries before strong syllables and mistakenly delete word boundaries before weak syllables.

Implicit Learning of Word Boundaries.   Some fascinating research by Saffran and colleagues (e.g., Saffran, Aslin, and Newport, 1996) suggests that statistical regularities present in speech sequences can be exploited to discern word boundaries. Some syllable combinations are more likely to appear within a word, while other syllable combinations are more likely to appear between words than within them. For example, in the phrase

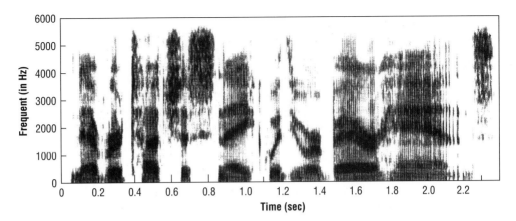

Figure 10.6 Speech spectrogram for a spoken sentence, "Never touch a snake with your bare hands." Note the lack of discernible boundaries.

From Liberman, A. M. (1970). The grammars of speech and language. *Cognitive Psychology, 1,* 301–323. Copyright 1970, Elsevier Science (USA). Reprinted by permission.

"pretty baby," the syllables *pre* and *ty* are more likely to occur within a word than *ty* and *ba*. Therefore, after constant exposure to speech, word boundaries will tend to be placed between *ty* and *ba* rather than between *pre* and *ty*. And, surprisingly, it seems that exposure need not be all that constant; infants are powerful little statisticians who pick up on these sorts of statistical properties of the speech signal quite easily.

Saffran, Aslin, and Newport (1996) presented infants for a period of two minutes with a continuous speech stream composed of four different three-syllable nonsense words strung together in random order. The infants heard something like *bidaku/padoti/golabu/bidaku* (slashes inserted to indicate experimenter-defined words). The stream was presented continuously, with no breaks whatsoever. The only cues to the experimenter-defined words were the differences in transitional probabilities between pairs of syllables within and between words. Some syllable pairs (*da* and *ku*) were more likely to occur within rather than between the experimenter-defined words, and some syllable pairs (*ku* and *pa*) were more likely to occur between rather than within the experimenter-defined words.

To find out whether the infants had learned the experimenter-defined "words" after this brief two-minute exposure, they were presented with two different types of test trials: (1) the previously defined "words" extracted from the two-minute stream the infants listened to, or (2) new experimenter-defined words containing the same syllables but in new combinations. Infants could control their listening time by staring or not staring at a blinking light. If the infant stared at the light, the same sequence was continually presented. If the infant stopped staring at the light, a new sequence was presented.

Let's take a few minutes to describe this method. Infants prefer novelty and will alter their behavior to gain access to novel events. So if the infants had picked up on the experimenter-defined "words" during the initial two-minute sequence, they should then prefer to listen to some other sequence during the test phase—that is, stimuli of type 2. If, on the other hand, they had not picked up on the experimenter-defined "words" and had essentially been listening to a string of syllables for two minutes, they should show no difference in preference for test stimuli of type 1 and 2. Both are simply strings of the syllables they had heard earlier and are equally boring. Infants' listening times indicated a preference for novelty—that is, they preferred to listen to the test sequences of type 2—the same syllables, but in new combinations. This indicates that they recognized the test sequences of type 1 as sequences they had heard before. During the two-minute encoding sequence, these infants had extracted the experimenter-defined "words!"

Saffran, Aslin, and Newport underline how striking this finding is. Infants were able to pick up on word boundaries after only two minutes of exposure to a speech signal that basically had no cues—no pauses, no intonation, no variations in contour . . . nothing. And, if anything, the procedure of this study underestimates the power of infants in a real-world context, where other cues (e.g., motherese) are there to aid in the detection of word boundaries. This ability to pick up on word boundaries effortlessly and automatically serves as a tremendously powerful tool in language acquisition.

Stop *and* Think!

FINDING PROBABILISTIC CONSTRAINTS

Look at any paragraph or two from this (or any other) chapter.

1. Analyze the syllable boundaries that occur within words.
2. Compare these boundaries to the ones that occur between words.
3. Note any systematic differences in these two types of syllable transitions.

Mondegreens.   Even with these sorts of cues, the perception of word boundaries remains a challenging perceptual task; misheard word boundaries have been dubbed **mondegreens.** In the opening scenario, Colleen's "slip of the ear" ("insuring bullets") is a case in point. Song lyrics are fertile ground for mondegreens. (How many times have you heard someone say "I can't understand the lyrics"?) We are not used to hearing language set to music; in some cases, it's almost like listening to a foreign language. One well-known musical mondegreen involves the butchering of a Jimi Hendrix classic in which one line of the song is heard as " 'Scuse me while I kiss this guy." When the "data" for bottom-up processing are distorted or ambiguous (as they often are in sung lyrics), we apply our knowledge of words and make our best guess (which is often wrong). Top-down processing is playing a prominent role in the present example; "kissing a guy" fits with our previous knowledge a little better than "kissing the sky." Top-down processing could quite often lead to the successful resolution of ambiguous lyrics in a couple of ways. First, extensive experience with a given artist or type of music is likely to "fine-tune" our ability to process the "acoustic signals" produced. Second, knowing what someone is singing about—be it love, money, or the weather—is likely to aid recognition and segmentation. Colleen's mondegreen in the opening scenario seems a bit less plausible when you consider the powerful influence of top-down processing.

The importance of top-down processing in on-line speech processing is evident in another circumstance. Have you ever traveled abroad and been amazed at the speed with which people speak? In reality, this is most likely a misperception; the natives aren't speaking any more quickly than you do in your native tongue. But your lack of familiarity with the language (i.e., your inability to top-down process) prevents you from effectively parsing it into words; it's almost as if you're hearing a raw speech signal.

Stop *and* **Think!**   ANNA LIZING MISS HURD LYRICS

Monitor your conversations in the coming weeks for mondegreens, or misheard speech.

1. Interview some friends to see if they have any examples of misheard song lyrics.
2. Look at the misheard speech and/or song lyrics, and evaluate ways in which boundaries were misheard.
3. Analyze the failures of bottom-up processing and the role of top-down processing involved in mishearing the speech signal.

STOP *and* REVIEW!

1. True or false? Low-frequency words are more easily and quickly accessed from the mental lexicon.
2. What is the difference between a free and a bound morpheme?
3. According to the metrical segmentation strategy,
   a. we use stress patterns to facilitate finding word boundaries.
   b. we use the statistical regularities in the sound sequences between and within words to find word boundaries.
   c. word segmentation depends on the phonology of the language.
   d. word segmentation depends on rhythm of the speech signal.
4. What is a mondegreen?

➤ In regard to the mental lexicon, high-frequency and nonambiguous words are more easily accessed than low-frequency and ambiguous words. When an ambiguous word is encountered, both meanings are temporarily activated; context leads to disambiguation. Bilinguals seem to have lexicons corresponding to each language.

➤ Morphology refers to an analysis of the meaningful units of language. A morpheme is the smallest unit of language that carries meaning and may refer to a single word (free morpheme) or a prefix or suffix (bound morphemes). The combination of morphemes may rely on two separate systems—one for regular forms and one for irregular forms.

➤ Identification of word boundaries is a perceptual challenge, due to the weak relationship between breaks in the speech signal and breaks between words. Stress patterns of words and the rhythms of speech aid in this identification. The metrical segmentation strategy proposes that word segmentation is dependent on the phonology of the particular language. Word boundaries can also be identified via statistical regularities in the speech streams.

➤ The ambiguity of speech sequences leads to mondegreens (misheard word boundaries). When the speech signal is distorted or ambiguous, we apply our knowledge of words and make our best guess, which is often wrong. The importance of top-down processing is also observed when we have difficulty parsing words in a foreign language because of a lack of familiarity.

Syntax and Semantics
Putting Words Together

We've discussed the basic components of language—sounds and words—and although individual words are the stuff out of which language is made, we have still said very little about language. Our mental lexicon includes more information than simple information about word sound and meaning. Consider this rather bizarre sentence: "Odorless fragrant clouds jump colorfully." Information represented in the mental lexicon allows you to assess this sentence quickly as nonsense. Something can't be odorless and fragrant, and clouds don't jump, and jumping doesn't occur colorfully. Still, this sentence isn't completely off, is it? It seems to sound like (or read like) a normal sentence in terms of structure.

Information about the possible roles that words can play in sentences is also included in the mental lexicon. For example, the lexical entry for the word *jump* would include the fact that it can be a noun (taking a jump into the pool) or a verb (jumping into the pool). Furthermore, what allows us to understand that "Greg threw the ball to Bridget "and "The ball was thrown to Bridget by Greg" are conveying exactly the same meaning? How do we immediately judge the word sequence "Bridget ball Greg the to threw" as jibberish? The essence of language lies not in individual words, but in the combinations of particular words that we assemble to convey some particular meaning. The term **syntax** refers to the set of rules that specify legal combinations of words within a given language. **Semantics** refers to the rules governing the effective transmission of meaning.

Transformational Grammar

Let's take a closer look at one of the defining characteristics of language—the system of rules that allows one to take a finite set of symbols and produce an infinite array of sentences. You may remember from Chapter 1 that it was linguist Noam Chomsky's revolutionary ideas about the mental representation of rules for language that provided what may have been the most devastating blow to the behaviorist account of complex behavior. Chomsky argued convincingly that the breathtaking variety and creativity demonstrated by speakers of any language could not be accounted for by the simple mechanisms of imitation, positive reinforcement, and stimulus-response chaining. To Chomsky, it was inconceivable that such a simple, highly constrained mechanism could be at the root of language, with its infinite flexibility, novelty, and creativity. To account for the powerful design features of language, there must be a complex system of rules that allows for virtually infinite combinations of the symbols of language. Another piece of "thought evidence" for this view is that children say things that adults never say (e.g., "Look at the mouses") and make mistakes in grammar that adults never make (e.g., "I goed to the bathroom"). For Chomsky, this implies that they are applying stored rules (rules that are represented physiologically from birth) to the symbols of language.

Syntactic rules are at the heart of Chomsky's linguistic theory. According to Chomsky, we are born with an implicit sensitivity to sentence structure and the rules of syntax. When this implicit sensitivity is engaged by spoken language, it begins to develop rapidly in the absence of any formal "teaching." Chomsky's approach to how we engage in language is termed **transformational grammar.** Although the theory is not generally considered a complete model of language, it revolutionized the way language was viewed when it was first proposed and pretty much single-handedly established the field of psycholinguistics. At the heart of Chomsky's approach to language is the notion that language is based on rules. These rules apply to syntactic structure of sentences, and we have implicit knowledge of these rules.

A central component in any rule-based (i.e., grammar-based) description of language is the notion of *phrase structure.* Intuitively, it is usually a pretty simple matter to break a sentence down into its component phrases, termed **constituents.** Consider how you would break up the following sentence: "The engaging professor entertained the class." (No doubt this sentence describes your usual experiences in class!) Chances are you'd break the sentence into two major phrases, or constituents—a noun phrase ("The engaging professor") and a verb phrase ("entertained the class"). Each of these constituents can in turn be broken down into still smaller parts. The noun phrase consists of an article (*the*), an adjective (*engaging*), and a noun (*professor*); the verb phrase consists of a verb (*entertained*) and an object phrase (*the class*). Why the painstaking analysis of this sentence? We want to demonstrate the notion of phrase structure and to make it clear that we all have some intuitive notion of phrase structure rules—the rules that define the fundamental components of a sentence, the types of words that typically comprise these components, and how these words may be arranged.

Stop and Think!

CONSIDERING CONSTITUENTS

In order to realize the "psychological reality" of how we perceive sentences in terms of constituents,

1. Go to any of the story installments that begin each chapter.
2. Pick out a few sample sentences.
3. Break the sentences into their constituents.

The idea that we use phrase structure rules to generate and comprehend sentences seems plausible, but before long this concept runs into problems. Consider the following sentence: "The shooting of the hunters was terrible." If you examine the sentence for a moment, you'll notice that the meaning is ambiguous. Does it mean that the hunters couldn't hit the broad side of a barn? Or could it be that somebody shot the hunters? Breaking the sentence down into its constituents doesn't help: "The shooting of the hunters" . . . "was terrible." The ambiguity remains. So a theory of grammar based only on phrase structure rules seems to lack something.

Surface Structure and Deep Structure. Based on the inadequacy of phrase structure in describing how a sentence like this can be formulated or understood, Chomsky had the critical insight that sentences must exist at two levels—both as an idea and as a concrete representation of that idea. He termed these deep structure and surface structure, respectively. The **deep structure** of a sentence conveys its meaning. The **surface structure** of a sentence is the particular phrase ordering used to convey that meaning. The sentence "The shooting of the hunters was terrible" is an example of *deep-structure ambiguity*; in spite of the single surface structure, the sentence has two possible deep structures.

Two other scenarios make it apparent that phrase structure rules are insufficient for describing an understanding of language. Consider these sentences:

The professor is easy to please.
The professor is eager to please.

Although neither of these are necessarily true of any of your professors, note that describing the sentences in terms of phrase structure doesn't differentiate between them. Once again, the distinction between surface structure and deep structure is critical; while the phrase structures are nearly identical, the deep structures are quite different. Finally, consider these two sentences:

The professor graded the tests.
The tests were graded by the professor.

In this case, phrase structure rules make the sentences seem radically different; the noun phrase in one is the verb phrase in the other, and vice versa. But it's easy to see that these sentences are expressing identical ideas. In Chomsky's terms, these sentences have different surface structures but identical deep structures. According to the theory of transformational grammar, we use the rules of phrase structure to generate the underlying idea, or deep structure, of the sentence. Then, *transformational rules* are applied to the deep structure to generate a surface structure that conveys the intended meaning.

Psychological Reality of Transformational Grammar.   Chomsky's (1965) theory of transformational grammar, and the distinction between surface and deep structure, generated a tremendous amount of research, much of it dedicated to exploring the *psychological reality* of transformational grammar, or what actually happens when we comprehend language. Many researchers have assumed that the comprehension of language is basically a process that starts with the surface structure of a sentence and ends with the realization of the deep structure. The complementary assumption is that the expression of language proceeds in an opposite direction—from an intended deep structure to a corresponding surface structure.

These two assumptions lead to an easily testable prediction. The longer the "distance" from surface structure to deep structure (i.e., the more transformations that are required), the more psychologically complex the sentence should seem and the more difficult it should be to comprehend. This idea was dubbed the *derivational theory of complexity.* The early returns on this theory were promising; consider the following pair of sentences:

The opera singer sings too loudly.
The opera singer does not sing too loudly.

This pair of sentences involves a transformation from affirmative to negative; such sentences are more difficult to comprehend. Consider this pair of sentences:

The band recorded another lame album.
Another lame album was recorded by the band.

This pair of sentences requires a transformation from active to passive; such sentences are more difficult to comprehend.

However, not all results supported the idea of derivational complexity. Consider these two sentences:

The test was aced by Susan.
The test was aced.

The second sentence is more derivationally complex than the first, as it involves a deletion transformation (i.e., "by Susan" must be deleted from the first sentence to create the second sentence). Yet research comparing the comprehension of sentences like the second yields no differences in comprehension difficulty (Carroll, 1994). So it seems that the psychological reality of transformational grammar can be called into question. Supporters argue that the theory is one of linguistic competence rather than linguistic performance. That is, the ideas suggested by transformational grammar describe our knowledge of language, not necessarily how this knowledge is executed on a moment-to-moment basis.

Evaluation. Although some of the specific predictions made by Chomsky's theory were not always supported, his notion that a productive system of rules was at the heart of language use was extremely important and served as the starting point for just about every other theoretical approach to language. Chomsky himself has proposed numerous revisions to his own theory (e.g., Chomsky, 1975, 1986), with several important principles remaining more or less constant. In all iterations of his approach to language remain the ideas that language acquisition and use are based on a system of rules (sometimes termed a *universal grammar*) that is innate and species specific. Chomsky's approach to language is a classic modular approach: language is a unique and specialized ability, the acquisition and use of which are not likely to be explained by appealing to general cognitive processes.

The Constraint-Based Approach

Chomsky's theory (at least many of the assumptions underlying it) remained the dominant force in psycholinguistic research for years. His assumptions that language is nonlearnable and depends on rules that are with us from birth have been considered practically sacrosanct. But a serious challenge to this view has been mounted by a recent approach that suggests that the structural aspects of language may be learnable. You'll recall that Chomsky argued that a simple associationistic account could not possibly explain the rapid development and astounding creativity of language. The notion that language is learned is highly improbable, due to what Chomsky termed "the poverty of the stimulus." How can children possibly learn language? Children hear grammatical and ungrammatical sentences that aren't labeled as grammatical and ungrammatical; what they hear is widely variable; and they don't get any sort of negative evidence—that is, what is not allowable, given the structure of the language. So basically, with almost no direction, children learn language and learn it rapidly. Given that the learning environment provides no help (i.e.. is an impoverished stimulus) language cannot possibly be learned based solely on environmental input (although certainly environmental input is critical).

Well, it turns out that the stimulus for language learning may not be so impoverished after all. An up-and-coming approach has reintroduced the notion that language may indeed be learnable, based simply on the incoming data. The challenge to Chomsky's approach comes not from a return to a behavioristic approach but from the neural network approach to cognition. And the associations that may account for the learning and use of language are not the stimulus-response associations postulated by the behaviorists, but the associations of neural networks distributed throughout the human brain. The same neural networks that carry out perceiving, recognizing, and remembering are also responsible for learning and implementing linguistic knowledge about sentence structure and word meaning. A special modular system need not be proposed to explain language learning and use (i.e., a nonmodular approach to language may suffice).

Recall the connectionist approach to cognition we discussed in Chapter 1. According to this approach, knowledge is embodied in distributed networks of excitatory and inhibitory connections between neuronlike units in the brain. These networks "learn" (i.e., are modified) through experience. Network connections are built up, solidified, and modified as we experience the world day to day. According to the **constraint-based approach** to language (e.g., Seidenberg, 1997), the gradual development and fine-tuning of neural networks during early linguistic experience play an important role in the rapid learning of language as well as in the cross-cultural consistency in the rate of language development.

Language is full of the probabilistic constraints that can be discovered by neural networks and exploited during the process of language learning. To get a better handle on the constraint-based approach, think back to the speech perception research that demonstrated infants' ability to compute word boundaries. With as little as two minutes of exposure to speech, infants could use the probability of syllable pairs occurring within and between experimenter-defined words to distinguish experimenter-defined words from similar ones in which the syllables were rearranged. The same type of probabilistic constraints are present within sentences. Consider the following examples (from Seidenberg, 1997):

1. The plane left for the East Coast.
2. The plane left for the reporter was missing.
3. The note left for the reporter was missing.

What constraints are available for the processing of these sentences? It turns out there are several. First, the meaning of *plane* as a vehicle is much more likely than its other meanings. Also, the word *left* is used more often in the active form (as in sentence 1) than in the passive form (as in sentences 2 and 3). Also, the phrase "the plane left" imposes constraints on interpreting the relationships between the words; *plane* could not possibly be a modifier of *left,* so "the plane left" cannot be a noun phrase. Another constraint is apparent in comparing sentences 2 and 3: sentence 3 is easier to comprehend, because it is much more plausible for a note to be left than it is for a plane to be left. In sentence 2, both senses of "the plane left" need to be considered, causing a temporary "hiccup" in comprehension. Constraints like these can be easily and rapidly learned by a neural network through repeated experience with linguistic strings (i.e., sentences). Combine this idea with the recent findings regarding infants' stunning abilities to do a probability analysis on a string of speech sounds in the space of two minutes and you have the beginnings of a compelling argument for how language might be learned in the absence of any special grammar-learning module.

Not everyone is persuaded by the constraint-based approach. Pinker (1996) notes that while probabilistic constraints might allow infants to learn how syllables combine to form words, this does not generalize to learning how words combine to form sentences. Words comprise a finite set of items, all of which can be deciphered and committed to memory. Sentences do not comprise a finite set of possibilities; they're an open-class (i.e., theoretically limitless) set and cannot all be committed to memory. Also, grammar doesn't just sequence words; it combines words hierarchically and relates them to a meaning. So learning how syllables are sequenced and learning how words are sequenced are different "computational" problems. What works for deciphering words won't work for comprehending and producing sentences on the fly.

It's also important to note that in many ways, the debate over whether language is learned or innate oversimplifies matters. There is no doubt that the acquisition of language involves both sorts of mechanisms. As Pinker (1996) notes,

> The contrast . . . between "learning" and "innate factors" is a poor basis for explaining a process as complex as language acquisition. All parts of human psychology depend on experience, and learning always requires innate neural machinery to do the learning. Only by analyzing what exactly is learned and what kinds of mechanisms are capable of learning it can we make sense of the interesting data. (p. 1852)

STOP *and* REVIEW!

1. Define and distinguish between syntax and semantics.
2. True or false? Surface structure refers to the meaning of a sentence.
3. What's the main idea behind the constraint-based approach to grammar?

➤ Synax refers to the rules we observe in combining words to form sentences, while semantics refers to the rules that dictate the effective communication of meaning. Syntax forms the basis for Chomsky's theory of transformational grammar, which proposes that comprehension and production of language involve transformations between two levels of sentence representation—meaning and physical structure.

➤ The phrase structure of a sentence refers to the way in which phrases combine to form sentences. Analysis of phrase structure is inadequate in explaining how we use language. Instead, Chomsky proposes that sentences are represented by both a surface structure (the words and phrases that form the sentence) and a deep structure (the intended meaning of the sentence). The brain mechanisms underlying transformational grammar are innate and unique to humans.

➤ The constraint-based view challenges Chomsky's contention that language is innate and to some extent preprogrammed. According to the constraint-based approach, some aspects of language structure may be learnable based on repeated experience with the typical syntactic structures of a given language. Experience with the constraints of language fine-tunes neural networks, eventually making them sensitive to a wide variety of sentence structures.

Sentence Planning and Production

Whereas volumes of research have been produced on the topics of speech perception and how syntactic and semantic factors influence comprehension, comparatively little research has been done on the processes underlying speech production. What are the processes involved in producing syntactically correct and semantically appropriate chains of speech?

Can you imagine why there might be such a discrepancy in the amount of research on the production, as opposed to the perception, of language? The reason is, in large part, methodological. It's much easier to control what someone experiences than it is to control what someone talks about or says. What someone reads or listens to can be controlled by an experimenter in a laboratory, and their reaction to it can be straightforwardly assessed in terms of accuracy. However, what someone says is a spontaneous and generative product of what they're thinking, and it's difficult to control this spontaneity and generativity. Indeed, even if you could manage to control it, you would no longer be studying true language production.

Stages in Language Production

In spite of the methodological difficulties inherent in the investigation of speech production, researchers have begun to get a better handle on the processes involved. One useful framework for research on language production was proposed by Levelt (1989). This framework can be characterized as an information-processing approach, in that it proposes four sequential steps in the production of language. The first step is *conceptualizing* what we want to say; the next step is *planning,* in which we formulate what is termed a *linguistic plan*— basically, organizing our thoughts in terms of language. The third step is *articulating* the linguistic plan. Finally, language production involves a process of *self-monitoring,* in which we keep track of what we're saying and whether the message and tone are as intended. We should note here that this section will deal primarily with the *mechanics,* or basic processes, involved in the planning and production of speech. However, there is another large body of research on language production, which investigates speech in its social context—in other words, conversation. We'll be discussing conversation a little bit later.

Conceptualizing.   As you can imagine, some of the four processes proposed by Levelt (1989) are easier to investigate than others. Not much research has been conducted on the conceptualization stage; this makes sense, for the reasons discussed above. There is no objective way to find out how ideas come together in anticipation of speech. Many believe that there is a sort of "mentalese"—a representational system distinct from language— from which linguistic expression proceeds, but there is little agreement on its form (Carroll, 1994). It seems obvious that this first stage of speaking exists, but it's hard to say much about it. Most research on language production has been done on the latter three stages.

Planning and Articulating.   Most of the research on language production has dealt with the processes by which we devise our linguistic plans and articulate them in speech. You might think that getting a handle on how people devise a linguistic plan would be nearly as difficult as figuring out how they conceptualize their thoughts. This is a challenge, but there is a rich source of data available that has served as the primary database for research and theory. This batadase—oops!—database—is slips of the tongue.

Slips of the Tongue.   You may do it several times a day: you get tongue-tied, you put the right word in the wrong slot of the sentence—in other words, you commit what psycholinguists term **slips of the tongue.** Slips of the tongue provide a valuable window into the processes involved in language production. They're also a close cousin of the action slips we discussed in Chapter 4. In fact, slips of the tongue are a type of action slip that we did not discuss, leaving it for discussion in this chapter

Types of Slips. Systematic research into naturally occurring slips of the tongue has identified eight basic categories. Table 10.4 provides examples of each category, taken from the students in our cognitive psychology classes. A **shift** occurs when one speech segment disappears from its appropriate location and appears somewhere else: "He was dunk in prublic." (The phoneme /r/ disappears from *drunk* and appears in *public.*) An **exchange** occurs when two segments change places (both segments disappear from their appropriate location): "Do you want water in your lemon?" (The words *lemon* and *water* switch places.) An **anticipation** occurs when a later segment replaces an earlier segment but does not disappear from its appropriate location. "Twitch on the television." (The later phoneme /t/ replaces the earlier phoneme /s/.) The opposite of an anticipation is a **perseveration,** in which an earlier segment replaces a later segment but does not disappear from its appropriate location: "I haven't deleted the diles yet." (The early phoneme /d/ replaces the later phoneme /f/.) A **deletion** refers to leaving something out: "I have to wind the tape." (The morpheme *re* is deleted from *rewind*). An **addition** refers to inserting something: "He is homoslexual." (The phoneme /l/ is added to *homosexual.*) A **substitution** occurs when an intruder replaces an intended segment: "Lets play some TV." (The word *play* replaces the word *watch.*) Finally, a **blend** occurs when two words combine into one, apparently because they are both being considered for selection. Colleen's exclamation "Oh, my gooshness" represents a blend of *gosh* and *goodness.*

In looking at the samples of each type of error given in Table 10.4, you might notice that they can occur at any linguistic level, be it a sound (phoneme), a morpheme (e.g., suffixes or prefixes), or a word. And if an utterance contains a slip of the tongue, it tends to be at only one linguistic level; you typically wouldn't switch two phonemes and switch two words within the same utterance.

In addition to noting these eight categories of error that occur with some regularity, Garrett (1975) and

Table 10.4 Categories of Speech Errors, with Examples

Type of Error	Example
Shift	He was dunk in prublic (drunk in public).
Exchange	Do you want water in your lemon (lemon in your water)?
Anticipation	Twitch on the television (switch on the television).
Perseveration	I haven't deleted the diles yet (deleted the files yet).
Addition	He is homoslexual (homosexual).
Deletion	Before I take the tape back I need to wind it (rewind it).
Substitution	Let's play some TV (watch some TV).
Blend	Oh, my gooshness (gosh/goodness).

Adapted from Carroll, D. W. (1994). *Psychology of language* (2nd ed.). Pacific Grove, CA: Brooks/Cole.

Fromkin (1973) note several additional consistencies in slips of the tongue. Elements within an utterance that interact

- tend to come from similar positions within a word (switching the initial segments of two words rather than switching the end of one word with the beginning of another)
- tend to be similar to one another (e.g., consonants switched with consonants)
- receive the same sort of stress (i.e., emphasis, or accent) they would have had had they not interacted
- seem to be based on phonological, rather than semantic, similarity (e.g., saying "Sesame Street crackers" instead of "sesame seed crackers")

Slips of the tongues also seem to obey the rules of phonology: even when sounds are switched, the resulting errant "word" sounds like a word. For example, what slip would you expect from a combination of *slippery* and *slick?* If you said *slickery,* you're right; neither *slickpery* nor *slipkery* fit in with English phonology and would not be the type of error we'd make.

Theoretical Accounts. A number of explanations for slips of the tongue have been proposed. These accounts are based in the proposed processes by which speech is produced (i.e., linguistic planning). One major dimension along which these accounts differ is whether the planning and articulation of speech involve serial (step-by-step) or parallel (simultaneous) processes and whether these processes interact with one another. Serial accounts of linguistic planning have been proposed by Fromkin (1973) and Garrett (1988, 1992); their general structure is presented in Figure 10.7. Basically, these models propose a number of substages within the broader stages of linguistic planning. Basically, once we conceptualize what we want to say, we then determine the stress patterns and syntactic structure for our utterance. Then content words and free morphemes are retrieved. (These are the words that convey the meaning of the sentence.) Next, bound morphemes (prefixes and suffixes) are added, followed by the addition of function words and overt articulation.

Stage 1—conceptualization, determination of stress patterns, determination of syntactical structure

Stage 2—content words and free morphemes added

| | *student* | *prepare* | | | *test* |

Stage 3—bound morphemes added

| | students | prepar*ed* | | | test |

Stage 4—function words added

| *The* | students | prepared | *for* | *the* | test |

Stage 5—overt articulation

Figure 10.7 Serial speech production accounts for the articulation of the idea of "students preparing for a test in the past."

One important assumption of these models is that the linguistic planning stages are independent of one another. Consistent with this assumption, many slips seem to occur only at one level of planning. Consider this classic slip of the tongue reported by Fromkin(1973): "a weekend for maniacs." The intended phrase was "a maniac for weekends." There are several interesting things about this error. First, the stress pattern of the sentence remained the same, as if that was determined separately. The content words *weekend* and *maniac* switched places, but the *s* morpheme was left stranded at the end of the sentence rather than moving with the word *maniac;* this suggests that the suffix *s* was added separately from the content word *weekend.* Also, and perhaps most interesting, the sound generated for the stranded morpheme *s* fits the new context. An *s* at the end of weekends is a /z/ sound, but the *s* at the end of maniac is a "hissing" /s/ sound. When *weekend* and *maniac* switch places, the /s/ sound is adjusted to match its new context; this phenomenon is termed *accommodation.* Accommodation suggests that sounds are assembled after (and independently of) assembly of the words in the sentence.

Other accounts (Dell's parallel activation model) of linguistic planning propose parallel processing: processors for the production of speech exist at a number of distinct levels (as just proposed), but these processors are capable of operating simultaneously (e.g., MacKay, 1987; Dell, 1986; Dell, Chang, & Griffin, 1999). These models propose that words in the lexicon are represented at four different levels—in terms of their sound (phonology), morphology, syntactic roles, and meaning. Processing units at each of these levels work in parallel, and may excite or inhibit processing within the same level as well as at other levels.

Let's take a look at how these models would explain another phenomenon noted with slips of the tongue—a lexical bias effect. Read the following sequences of phrases out loud (first one sequence, then the other) and quickly (from Carroll, 1994):

Sequence A	Sequence B
ball doze	big dolt
bash door	bang doll
bean deck	best dump
bell dark	bark dog
darn bore	dart board

Some studies have used tasks like this to induce speech slips in the laboratory. In this example, a bias induced by the phonological similarity of each of the first four phrases (/b/ followed by /d/) sometimes causes a slip on the fifth phrase (switching the /d/ and /b/ phonemes). Did you make an error in sequence A and/or B? It turns out that errors are much more likely for sequences like A, demonstrating the *lexical bias effect.* Induced speech errors that result in words (*barn dore*) are more likely than those that result in nonwords (*bart doard*). Dell's parallel activation model has a ready explanation of the lexical bias effect. This theory assumes that true words would have morphological representations, but nonwords would not. Activation of these representations would excite the corresponding processors at the phoneme level, making errors more likely. This error-inducing feedback would only be present for words, however, making it less likely that errors would result in nonwords.

R E C U R R I N G   R E S E A R C H   T H E M E
Cognition and Consciousness

Slips of the Tongue: Unconscious Motivation?

The study of slips of the tongue has a long and distinguished history within the discipline of psychology. No less than Sigmund Freud, the founder of psychoanalysis himself, investigated such slips of the tongue; they even bear his name—the so-called Freudian slip. Freud's view of these errors was decidedly different than those just described. Freud's interpretation of these sorts of errors was not in terms of the cognitive processes that lead up to the errors, but in terms of what Freud viewed as the *unconscious motivation* for these errors. For Freud, slips of the tongue were a window into a person's fears, anxieties, or wishes. The person who goes into Dairy Queen and orders ice cream topped with "Reese's penis" (instead of Reese's Pieces—true story!) has done more than made a word error. According to Freud, this slip *means* something; it reflects something about unconscious motivation (although for this particular example, we dare not go any further).

Is there any truth to Freud's claim? It seems unlikely that every slip of the tongue we make has a hidden meaning. But could unconscious thoughts play a role in slips of the tongue? You might imagine that addressing this question by noting naturally occurring errors (as the studies discussed previously have primarily done) would yield a biased sample of errors and leave many questions unanswered. When someone commits a slip, it's anybody's guess as to why it occurred. However, if you can set up a situation in which slips are under experimental control, you have a more reliable way of assessing their causes.

Motley (1985) reports an intriguing series of studies assessing the Freudian account of slips of the tongue. Motley and Baars (1979) used a laboratory procedure that induced participants to make slips, more specifically *spoonerisms*—simple switches between the initial sounds of nearby words (e.g., saying "fluit fries" instead of "fruit flies"). Motley and Baars had participants read two-word phrases (like "fruit fly") silently; every so often, a buzzer sounded. On these occasions, participants were to read the presented pair out loud; of course, these trials were the ones of interest. Just to make errors a little more likely, the researchers preceded these spoken trials with a series of phrases that "primed the pump," so to speak (see the demonstration for the lexical ambiguity effect above). For example, to make the error "fluit fries" more likely to occur, the immediately preceding trials would be similar (e.g., "flag fright").

So where does hidden motivation come in? To engage participants in a given motivational frame, Motley and Baars (1979) varied the context in which the study was conducted. They preoccupied one group of participants with shock-related anxiety; these participants were hooked up to (bogus) electrodes and told that they would be receiving an occasional electric shock during the procedure (although they never did). Another group was preoccupied with what might be called (for want of a better phrase) sexual anxieties; they were tested by "an attractive and provocatively dressed woman" (p. 118). A control condition was tested using an identical procedure but with neither environmental manipulation. The word pairs presented to participants, when rearranged, referred to either shock-related (e.g., the pair *worst cottage* was presented, so the likely error was *cursed wattage)* or sex-related concerns (e.g., the pair *share boulders* was presented, with the likely error being *bare shoulders*—no, we're not kidding).

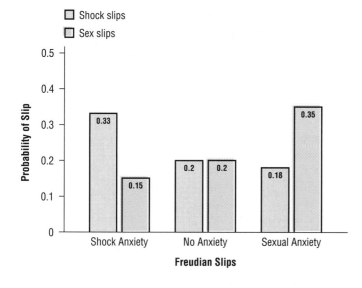

Figure 10.8 Results from Motley and Baars (1985) suggesting that motivational factors can play a role in slips of the tongue. The slips elicited tended to be consistent with the experimenter-induced motivation. From Motley, M. T. (1985). Slips of the tongue. *Scientific American, 253,* 116–127. Reprinted by permission.

The results were consistent with the Freudian view of slips of the tongue. As you can see in Figure 10.8, participants who were anxious about possible shocks were more likely to make shock-related errors; participants (all men by the way) who were anxious about sexual material were more likely to make sex-related errors. This humorous finding in no way discounts or qualifies what we've said about slips, the regularities they feature, and the possible underlying mechanisms. It simply adds another dimension to their explanation; in some cases, it seems that slips of the tongue can be made more likely by contextual variables, like what is currently occupying one's mind. But certainly many (probably most) speech errors are more innocent, resulting from the misassemblage of linguistic units.

Stop *and* Think!

FRIDIAN SLEUPS

Over the next few weeks, monitor your own and others' conversations for speech errors.

1. Take note of what type they are (following the classification scheme provided in Table 10.4, p. 417).
2. Note when they seem to occur.
3. Record whether any of them seem "motivated" in the Freudian sense.
4. Indicate the level at which the slip occurred (phoneme, morpheme, word).
5. For the serial account of linguistic planning, indicate the stage at which the slip occurred.

Self-Monitoring. The final stage in Levelt's (1989) conceptualization of speech production is self-monitoring. Self-monitoring refers to the processes whereby we keep track of what we're saying and change it on line if necessary. It's unclear whether we actually edit what we say before we say it, but the fact that we edit what we have already said is not in doubt (Carroll, 1994). Often we engage in *self-repair*—we stop ourselves and correct what we've just said. Levelt (1983) noted that self-repairs have a consistent structure. First, we interrupt ourselves when we detect an error. Second, we issue what might be termed an *editing expression,* like "um," "oh, wait," or "sorry." Finally, we "repair" what we've just said by saying such things as "er . . . I mean."

Conversation

Our final topic of discussion involves yet another dimension of speech processing. Recall that linguistic analysis can be conducted at a number of levels, including phonology, syntax, and semantics. When we consider the real-world contexts in which language is used, another factor is added to the mix; this factor is termed **pragmatics.** Pragmatics refers to the practical knowledge we need to use language effectively.

Conversational Structure.   It is readily apparent (although seldom really noticed) that conversations have a fairly stable structure. If you consider the typical conversation in which you engage, you can probably come up with most of the notable characteristics that have been revealed by empirical research (e.g., Jaffe & Feldstein, 1970; Sacks, Schegloff, & Jefferson, 1974). First, conversations usually start with one of a number of standard greetings (Schegloff, 1972)—like Zach's rather unoriginal "Hey, how's it going?"—in spite of the fact there are an infinite number of things that could be said. (Try opening a conversation with something other than a standard remark and observe the ensuing confusion.)

These stock openers elicit stock answers most of the time (e.g., "pretty good!" or "not much!"). In fact, if the stock answer isn't given (e.g., Q: "What's up?" A: "Well, I've really been having a tough time lately"), there is a conversational "bump in the road." Another standard feature of conversations is **turn taking**—the speakers alternate in what might be described as ABABAB fashion; conversational overlap is exceedingly rare. However, you might also notice that individual styles of turn taking vary widely. Some folks take long turns, while others tend to take shorter ones. Some (e.g., Jaffe & Feldstein, 1970) have suggested that the length of a turn is a fairly stable characteristic within a given individual's conversational interactions.

A number of pretty standard signals indicate a change in turn—a head nod, a glance, a questioning tone. Sacks, Shegloff, and Jefferson (1974) propose three principles that (implicitly) guide turn taking in conversations. The current speaker may choose the next speaker by directing a comment or question to a particular person. If this doesn't happen, then it is acceptable for any person to step into the conversational "gap." Or the original speaker may simply continue talking. These authors suggest that turn-taking principles are ordered in terms of priority. The first is the most important, and the last is the least important. For example, if someone directs a question to you in conversation and another person starts talking (i.e., initiates a turn), this would be conversationally inappropriate. The predictable rhythm of conversation, and the unwritten rules that seem to guide this rhythm, is an important source of conversational coherence. Violation of these rhythms leads to confusion, frustration, and misunderstanding.

Conversation not only obeys some basic structural principles, but there also seem to be unwritten rules that speakers follow when conversing. One might characterize these rules as comprising a sort of contract between speakers. Grice (1975) spells out a number of characteristics that seem to define this contract. These "maxims," as they're termed, all support one overriding principle: cooperation. The four maxims are:

Quantity: Say as much as you need to, but not more.

Quality: Don't say things that you believe to be false; don't say things for which you lack evidence.

Relation: Be relevant to the topic at hand.

Manner: Be clear; avoid obscurity and ambiguity.

For an appreciation of how important these maxims are to our daily interactions, think of people you know who regularly violate them and how others react to these people.

Stop *and* Think!

BE A CONVERSATIONAL PAIN

This one's a little chancy (but fun!). To see how important the Gricean maxims of conversation are, deliberately violate them in the course of some conversation.

1. Say too much, not enough, or fail to cooperate in some way.
2. Observe the effects on the conversation.
3. Be sure to "debrief" your fellow conversationalists!

A simpler alternative to this is to think of all the people you regularly converse with:

- Which of them violates the Gricean maxims?
- What impact do these violations have on their conversations?

Gender and Conversation.   Based on your own experience, you probably know that conversations can be as varied as the people who are having them. Much research has investigated the factors that lead to this variation in conversation; a good deal of evidence points to differences in the ways that women and men use language and in the ways that they converse (Tannen, 1993). Pioneering work on these differences was done by Lakoff (1975), who enumerated a number of differences in the ways that women and men use language. (It's important to note that Lakoff's work, while influential, was more of a sociological study based largely on informal observation.)

One difference noted by Lakoff (1975) is that women tend to be more polite than men. One indicator of this difference is that women tend to use more indirect requests, in which the meaning communicated does not match the explicitly stated meaning of the request. For example, technically, the answer to the question "Do you know what time it is?" is "Yes" or "No," not "3:15." In spite of this, everyone expects the answer to this question to be a specific time. Indirect speech acts and indirect requests are considered to be polite ways of speaking and requesting and are more characteristic of women's speech. Lakoff notes a number of other characteristics of women's language. Women tend to employ more tag questions and hedges in conversation. Tag questions are questions placed at the end of a statement, as in "It's hot out today, *isn't it?*" Hedges are qualifiers, like "kind of" or "could be." In the opening scenario, Colleen hedges a bit in discussing her success in the

CHECK YOUR E-MAIL HERE

How do you portray yourself when you introduce yourself via e-mail?

pageant. Another oft-observed difference in male and female conversational interaction is the incidence of interruption; male conversations tend to feature more interruption than female conversations. When males and females talk to each other, males are more likely to interrupt (Zimmerman & West, 1975).

Although most would agree that there are significant differences in the ways that women and men converse, not everyone would agree about what these differences indicate. Some claim that differences in conversational style reflect the relative differences in power between women and men and that conversational differences are but one manifestation of deeply rooted cultural differences. Others contend that the conversational differences simply reflect differences in ways of interacting rather than the social position of women relative to men.

Some evidence indicates that gender differences in conversing may not be as prominent as previously believed and that conversation may be as much a function of the situation in which it takes place as it is a function of speaker gender. Thomson, Murachver, and Green (2001) note that speakers will change their language style so that it converges with the style of the person(s) they are speaking with. In other words, men talk more like women when they talk to women, and vice versa. You may have observed this in your own experience; your talk molds itself to your conversational partner.

Thomson and colleagues investigated this notion in a thoroughly modern arena of discourse—electronic mail (e-mail). In their study, each participant communicated via e-mail with two different "net pals," one of whom was ostensibly a woman, the other a man. In reality (and unbeknownst to the participant) each net pal was actually the researcher, writing from a script and using either female-style or male-style language. The results were surprising, given previous evidence regarding gender differences in conversational interaction. The nature of what was said (and how it was said) did not differ with the gender of the participant; it differed with the (supposed) gender of the net pal. When female and male participants thought they were e-mailing a woman, they conversed more like women; when they thought they were e-mailing a man, they conversed more like men. The researchers conclude that "male" and "female" styles of conversing are not so much a static characteristic of individuals but rather emerge in certain conversational contexts. In the opening story, it's evident that Zach is talking to Colleen in a much different manner than he'd talk to his buddies on the soccer team.

Stop and Think!   ## INNOCENT EAVESDROPPING

Either in your daily conversations with friends, or by nonobtrusively observing the conversations of others, see if you can notice any differences in the ways women and men converse. Try to observe women and men in both same-sex and mixed-sex groups.

- What, if any, differences did you notice?

The study by Thomson, Murachver, and Green (2001) suggests that we present ourselves differently in electronic conversation depending on whether we're addressing a woman or a man. Look back over some of your e-mails to different friends.

- Do you see any evidence of a difference?
- If so, what seem to be the differences?

STOP and REVIEW!

1. Name and briefly describe the four stages in language production.
2. True or false? Slips of the tongue are an example of the conceptualization stage of language production.
3. Explain the sequence of stages in the serial account of speech production.
4. Identify the elements of the standard structure of conversations.

➤ The four stages in language production are conceptualizing (determining what it is we want to say), planning (organizing our thoughts in terms of language), articulating (executing the linguistic plan), and self-monitoring (keeping track of content and tone).

➤ Slips of the tongue offer insight into planning and articulation of speech. Slips of the tongue include shifts, exchanges, anticipations, perseverations, deletions, additions, substitutions, and blends. Slips can occur at any linguistic level—phoneme, morpheme, or word. Interactive speech elements tend to come from similar positions in a word and receive the same sort of stress. Errors often seem to be based primarily on phonological similarity. Research indicates that slips of the tongue can be motivated (i.e., as in Freudian slips).

➤ A serial account of linquistic planning proposes that after conceptualizing, we determine the syntactic structure for the utterance. Free morphemes are retrieved, followed by bound morphemes and function words. Then we assemble the appropriate phonological segments and articulate them. Parallel processing accounts propose that words in the lexicon are represented at each linguistic level (phonology, morphology, syntactic, and semantic) and work in parallel, exciting or inhibiting processing within that level. Slips of the tongue can be explained by both accounts of linguistic planning.

➤ Pragmatics refers to the practical knowledge we need to use language effectively, particularly in conversations. Conversations typically have a standard structure that includes a greeting, turn taking, and little overlap. Conversation seems to be guided by unwritten rules that are based on the principle of cooperation.

GLOSSARY

addition: a speech error in which an inappropriate segment is inserted into an utterance (p. 417)

anticipation: a speech error in which a later segment replaces an earlier segment but does not disappear from its appropriate location (p. 417)

arbitrariness: the lack of an inherent relationship between the symbols of language and what they represent (p. 383)

auditory theory of speech perception: the idea that the basic mechanisms that accomplish auditory perception are the same ones we use to decode speech (p. 399)

blend: a speech error in which two words combine into one, apparently because they are both being considered for selection (p. 417)

bound morphemes: morphemes that need to be used in conjunction with a free morpheme (i.e., prefixes and suffixes) (p. 405)

categorical perception: our tendency to perceive phonemes in a relatively broad (i.e., categorical) fashion (p. 397)

coarticulation: the overlap in the acoustic signal produced by consecutive phonemes; phonemes are articulated together to some extent (p. 397)

constituents: the component phrases of a sentence (p. 411)

constraint-based approach: the idea that language is learned through gradual development and fine-tuning of neural networks during early linguistic experience, picking up on probabilistic constraints of language (p. 414)

deep structure: the idea being expressed by a given phrase structure (p. 412)

deletion: a speech error in which a segment is left out of an utterance (p. 417)

design features: the characteristics that communication systems share (p. 383)

displacement: the ability language allows us for communication about things not in the present moment (p. 384)

exchange: a speech error in which two speech segments within an utterance change places (p. 417)

free morphemes: morphemes that can stand alone (p. 405)

grammar: the rules that govern how the symbols of a language may be combined. (p. 383)

language: a set of symbols and rules for the combination of these symbols that allow for communication and comprehension among individuals (p. 382)

lexical access: the process by which a concept is activated within the mental lexicon (p. 404)

manner of articulation: the nature of how airflow is obstructed in producing a speech sound (p. 395)

mental lexicon: our general knowledge system of words and their characteristics (p. 404)

modular view: the view that some cognitive processes (e.g., language) are accomplished by a set of structures and/or processes devoted exclusively to that process and to nothing else (p. 390)

mondegreens: misheard word boundaries (p. 408)

morpheme: the smallest unit of language that carries meaning (p. 405)

morphology: the aspect of language that deals with manipulating and changing phonemes to produce different words and word forms (p. 405)

motherese: the melodic and exaggerated manner in which adults speak to infants, which seems to aid in the development of their speech perception abilities (p. 402)

motor theory of speech perception: the idea that a common set of representations underlies speech perception and speech production and that implicit knowledge about how speech sounds are articulated aids in the perception of the sounds (p. 398)

overregularization: the overapplication of a morphological rule, such as adding -*ed* to an irregular verb (p. 406)

perseveration: a speech error in which an earlier segment replaces a later segment but does not disappear from its appropriate location (p. 417)

phone: the smallest unit of speech that is discriminable in terms of its acoustic properties (p. 394)

phoneme: the categories of speech sounds that are clearly different and that change the meaning of a spoken signal (p. 394)

phonemic restoration effect: the tendency for our perceptual system to "fill in" missing speech sounds (p. 402)

phonology: the aspect of language that deals with the analysis of basic speech sounds (p. 393)

place of articulation: the part(s) of the vocal tract used to make a speech sound (p. 395)

pragmatics: the practical knowledge we need to use language effectively (p. 422)

prevarication: the ability language allows us for misrepresentation and deception (p. 384)

productivity: the fact that words and rules for their combination allow for an infinite array of new messages to be formed (p. 384)

reflectiveness: the ability language allows us for reflecting on language itself (p. 384)

semanticity: the fact that symbols of language refer to meaningful aspects of the real world (p. 383)

semantics: the rules governing the effective transmission of meaning (p. 410)

shift: a speech error in which one speech segment disappears from its appropriate location and appears somewhere else (p. 417)

slips of the tongue: speech errors (p. 417)

substitution: a speech error in which an intruder replaces an intended segment in an utterance (p. 417)

suprasegmental factors: the aspects of the speech signal—such as rate, stress, and intonation—over and above the actual phonemes (p. 397)

surface structure: the phrase structure used to express an idea (p. 412)

syntax: the set of rules that specify legal combinations of words within a given language (p. 410)

transformational grammar: Chomsky's view that language is based on a set of innate syntactic rules that allow for movement between ideas and the structures we use to communicate those ideas (p. 411)

turn taking: the predictable alternation between speakers in a conversation (p. 422)

voicing: what the vocal cords do when the airflow disruption stops (p. 395)

11

Language: Processing the Written Word

After her shift at the coffee shop, Colleen pours herself a complimentary mocha and then heads to the library for some serious study. She pulls out her intro physics book. A little light reading, she muses wryly. She lasts about 10 minutes before throwing the book down and picking up the latest Mary Higgins Clark novel. She can't wait to see who committed the murder. She thought she had it figured out, but . . .

Her not-so-studious silence is broken . . . "Hey."

She looks up; it's Donna.

"Hi, Donna."

"Are you ready? I hear it's going to be really hard."

"What is?" Colleen asks, tired and a little confused.

"The physics test."

"Oh, yeah, I'd be surprised if it's not. Unfortunately, I'm sure the prof won't ask who the murderer is," Colleen jokes, holding up what she's really reading.

Donna laughs. "I've just been staring at a computer monitor for 45 minutes, waiting for some mysterious force to move my fingers toward the keyboard."

"Ah, the ol' writer's block, huh?"

"Yeah, it's so frustrating."

"Well, I bet you made some progress by just thinking about it," Colleen says encouragingly.

"Maybe, but it sure doesn't feel like it."

"Hang in there . . . I suppose I should get back to my reading"

"OK . . . enjoy your novel!"

Colleen chuckles. "Actually, I meant my physics reading."

"Oh," Donna laughs. "Maybe you'll find out at the end that Isaac Newton did it."

In the last chapter we scaled the language hierarchy in the context of spoken communication. This chapter will make the same journey, but in the context of written communication. You're engaging in it right now. Let's take a closer look at the processes going on in written communication.

Reading

Just as speech perception involves the formulation of meaning from an inherently meaningless stimulus—air displacement in the form of sound waves—reading involves the formulation of meaning from little squiggles of different shapes, sizes, and spacings on a sheet of paper or similar medium. It's truly a wonder that we so quickly and effortlessly afford such a stimulus meaning. In the last four or five decades, a legion of researchers have amassed a great deal of information about the processes involved in reading and what happens when they go astray.

Top-Down and Bottom-Up Processes in Reading

Reading is basically an (albeit intricate) exercise in pattern recognition. A pattern of stimulation is encoded in the visual system, and a corresponding representation is activated in

What processes are taking place during reading?

semantic memory. A theme you've encountered throughout the text is the fact that our mental processes involve a mix of bottom-up processing (building "up," starting with the sense data we take in) and top-down processing (working "down" from expectations and previous knowledge). Reading is no different; printed letters and words serve as the data that drive processing. But much of the processing in reading is driven by material not on the printed page—namely, our expectations and knowledge about what we're reading. Theoretical accounts of reading processes place varying degrees of emphasis on each, but there is no doubt that both are important.

Eye Movements

The processing of information during reading starts at the point where the eyes take in the printed page. This being the case, the movements of the eyes across the printed page have been a primary focus of reading research. As you'll see, the consistencies in the speed and pattern of our eyes' trek through a written passage, along with the variables that influence these consistencies, can reveal much about the underlying mental processes.

Methodology.   It may strike you that eye movements must be a difficult thing to measure. After all, you can't gather much information from just staring at someone's eyes as they read. (Try it—you're likely to get a whap across the head!) But the ever-resourceful cognitive researchers have developed techniques for tracking eye movements. One method involves shining an (invisible) infrared light beam onto the eye, which is then reflected back from the cornea or retina to a sensor. The method is relatively noninvasive; readers are free to do as they please—to reread, slow down, speed up—as the eye-movement tracking continues. However, we say "relatively" noninvasive because participants do have to subject themselves to some minor contortions. So that eye movements can be distinguished from head movements, the head has to be held in place; also, although we typically look down to read, the eye-movement setup typically requires looking straight ahead. In spite of this, there doesn't seem to be any appreciable difference in reading comprehension between a normal and on experimental reading situation (Tinker, 1939).

Saccades and Fixations.   If you think about how your eyes must move as you scan across a page of this book, you may think that your eyes scan smoothly across the page from left to right, then back again. This impression is mistaken. Your eyes actually move in a series of stops, pauses, and starts, termed *saccades* and *fixations*. **Saccades** are the discrete movements that our eyes make from one point to another when we're reading, taking in a visual scene, or searching for an object (Rayner, 1998); they occur continually. The saccades we make during reading are typically six to eight letters in length and take about 20 milliseconds. During saccades, we seem to take in little or no visual information, a phenomenon termed **saccadic suppression** (Matin, 1974); indeed, eye movements occur with such velocity that if we did take in information, it would probably register as a blur. It's not completely clear whether or not cognitive processing is suppressed during saccades; the empirical jury is still out on this issue.

In between saccades are **fixations,** in which the eyes pause briefly to take in information. Fixations typically last anywhere from 200 to 300 milliseconds. The length depends

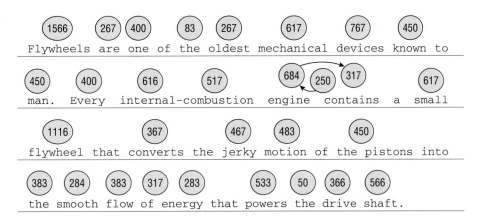

Figure 11.1 Length of eye fixations on words in a passage of text.

From Just, M. A., & Carpenter, P. A. (1987). *The psychology of reading and language comprehension*. Boston: Allyn and Bacon. Copyright 1987 by Pearson Education. Reprinted by permission of the publisher.

on the nature of the reading task, be it silent reading, reading aloud, or reading music. Consecutive fixations in the same spot are sometimes labeled **gazes;** the summed duration of these gazes, (i.e., **gaze duration**) is another dependent variable in the study of reading. The pattern of fixations, gazes, and saccades can be seen in Figure 11.1, which presents eye-fixation data, along with the text that was being read (from Rayner & Pollatsek, 1989). You'll note a number of interesting characteristics of eye fixations and eye movements. First, some words are fixated twice and some not at all. Notice how content words, like *devices* and *combustion,* receive more gaze time than do function words like *and* and *that;* sometimes, these function words are not fixated at all. About 80% of content words and only 40% of function words are fixated. Also, the more unfamiliar a word (e.g., *flywheel*), the longer the fixation. Overall, approximately 65% of the words in a given text are fixated; this proportion varies with content and with the characteristics of the reader. It is important to note that fixation is not a necessity for identification. We'll return to this question shortly in our discussion of perceptual span.

Word Skipping.   What leads a reader to skip certain words? One factor is how predictable a word is based on the context; words that are highly constrained (i.e., the word is about the only one that would make sense, given the context) are more likely to be skipped than words that are less constrained (Balota, Pollatsek, & Rayner, 1985). In addition, high-frequency words are more likely to be skipped than low-frequency words (Rayner & Well, 1996). The variable that most strongly determines whether a word will be skipped is word length (Brysbaert & Vitu, 1998). Short words (e.g., *an, the*) are much more likely to be skipped, relative to longer words (e.g., *flywheels, devices*). This makes sense; shorter, more predictable words don't carry very much of the meaning in text, so spending too much time on them would be inefficient.

READING FROM THE TOP DOWN

Have two of your friends read this passage:

> In the previous chapter, we sketched some of the basics of language, such as its basic definition, major components, and fundamentals of speech perception. Although language is first and foremost a spoken medium, it takes only a moment's thought to consider its many different expressions. After all, we're not talking to you about cognitive psychology; we've written this text, and you're reading it— and not only that, but understanding it. After you learn about cognitive psychology, we're sure that you'll be so excited by it that you'll engage your classmates in conversation about it.

Tell one of your friends to count the number of *f*'s in this passage. Have the other count the number of *m*'s. There are 11 of each, but the *f*'s tend to be in shorter, more predictable words that are likely to be skipped during reading. See if your friends' letter counting fits this pattern.

Regressive Saccades.   You'll also notice that on occasion, the eyes move backward; these backward movements are termed **regressive saccades,** and they constitute about 10 to 15% of all saccades. These occur when a reader makes too long a saccade and has to backtrack, or if a word is particularly difficult to decipher. Regressive saccades may even occur within a word (Rayner, 1998). Good and poor readers differ in the "quality" of their regressive eye saccades. Good readers are better at regressing back to exactly where they encountered a problem; in contrast, poor readers must do more backtracking in order to zero in on where they had a problem (Murray & Kennedy, 1988). Based on the poorly placed eye movements of poor readers, you might be tempted to jump to the conclusion that poor reading is caused by inefficiency of eye movements. Indeed, this is what many reading specialists believed to be the case decades ago. As a result, many programs were designed to train eye movements in the hope of improving reading. Unfortunately, later research showed that inefficient eye saccades and fixation patterns were a symptom, rather than the cause, of poor reading. As a result, these programs proved to be unsuccessful (Tinker, 1958).

Perceptual Span.   You may have noticed that when you read, your eyes basically "look ahead." The amount of text that the eyes can cover effectively to the right of any given fixation is termed **perceptual span.** For the English alphabet, perceptual span is about three characters to the left and 15 or so characters to the right of any given fixation (McConkie & Rayner, 1976). Interestingly, the characteristics of the perceptual span differ depending on the writing system (i.e., the orthography) of the language in question. For Hebrew, which is read from right to left, the perceptual span is a mirror image of English; three characters to the right and about 15 to the left of fixation. Another interesting fact about the perceptual span is that it differs with the difficulty of the material. In our opening story, Colleen's span for reading her physics text is quite likely shorter than her span for reading lighter material, like her mystery novel.

How are we influenced by what falls slightly out of fixation but within the perceptual span? Such information is termed *parafoveal* (because it falls outside of the fovea—the point of central focus). Evidence indicates that parafoveal information aids in lexical access; in other words, getting the first few letters of the next word aids the word recognition process. Parafoveal information also allows the reader to detect word length and where word boundaries are (a decidedly easier task than deciphering word boundaries in spoken language!) so the reader knows where to look next (e.g., Rayner & Morris, 1992). The detection of word length allows for the identification and skipping of short function words (Blanchard, Pollatsek, & Rayner, 1989), which makes reading the fast and efficient process that it is in most circumstances.

Speed Reading?

A discussion of reading wouldn't be complete without some mention of the popular notion of speed reading. You've probably heard the claims and maybe taken the courses. Is there anything to it? What is speed reading, and does it work? The claims of speed-reading proponents smack of late-night infomercial hokum. The results from controlled studies of speed reading do little to dispel this general impression.

The Claims. The claims that speed reading can double your reading speed and improve your comprehension sound pretty fantastic. One method we found on the Internet even made the preposterous claim that you could increase your reading speed to 25,000 words per minute! So what are the magic methods that supposedly lead to these breathtaking results? Is there any possible truth to the claims? The short answer is no. But we'll give you the long answer. (But it won't be so long if it only takes you 30 seconds to read the next couple of pages!)

According to those who champion the speed-reading methods, the typical reading speed of 250 to 350 words per minute can be increased to thousands of words per minute by applying some relatively simple mechanical techniques. One claim is that the brain does not process things to maximal efficiency; it "wastes time" with too many saccades. (This is similar to the baseless claim that we use only 10% of our brain, as discussed in Chapter 2.) Also, the inner speech that typically accompanies reading is claimed to be an unnecessary "drag" on the system. So the goals of speed reading are to increase the information taken in during each eye fixation (thus cutting down on the number of movements) and to eliminate inner speech. Some evidence suggests that speed readers are indeed reading very differently than normal readers. Studies by Thomas (1962) and McLaughlin (1969) found that speed readers fixate for about the same length of time as normal readers, but they fixate only once per line. Even stranger, the speed readers in these studies read down the left-hand page and up the right-hand page! That is, they read the right-hand page in the reverse order. Needless to say, understanding of the passage wasn't so great with this method.

Empirical Tests. Rigorous empirical tests of speed reading are few and far between. Much of the "evidence" is anecdotal, or based on self-report testimonials; as you know, anecdotes make poor evidence. And even the anecdotes aren't completely supportive of speed-reading effectiveness (Carver, 1971). The methodologically sound research that has been done fails to support the fantastic claims. According to Just and Carpenter (1987), many studies of speed reading fail to measure what was learned from the material read, others use tests with easy multiple-choice questions, and still others fail to test an appropriate control group.

Probably the most thorough (and methodologically sound) study of speed reading was conducted by Just, Carpenter, and Masson (1982). In their study, speed readers were compared with two control groups: normal readers and normal readers who were instructed to "skim." Figure 11.2 shows a sample of the eye fixations made by each type of reader. The readers were tested for their understanding of the general idea of the passage, as well as for their memory of details. The results demonstrated that all readers did fairly well on the general information questions. However, on the detailed information questions, normal readers performed better.

Speed readers seem to show the reading equivalent of a speed-accuracy trade-off. You may recall from Chapter 2 that reaction time (RT) and accuracy often trade off in performance situations; if people are trying to be especially fast, their accuracy is likely to suffer. The same is true of speed reading; if someone blazes through a reading passage, then their accuracy (in terms of memory for detail) is likely to suffer. You've probably experienced this yourself when you've tried skimming a book. Although you may have gone through the "mechanics" of reading some of the material, you may feel like you haven't read it at all. Why? Because the essence of reading is not perceptual processing; the essence of reading is understanding or comprehension.

STOP *and* REVIEW!

1. Which of the following is *false* about saccades?
   a. They are six to eight letters in length.
   b. No visual information is taken in during them.
   c. Saccades last between 100 and 150 milliseconds.
   d. Between saccades, the eye fixates on the passage.
2. Identify the types of words that receive long and short gaze times.
3. Describe the pattern of regressive saccades in good and poor readers.
4. Describe the characteristics of perceptual span.
5. True or false? There is good empirical evidence supporting the value of speed reading.

➤ When we read, our eyes move across the page in a series of jumps and pauses termed saccades and fixations. Saccades are six to eight letters in length and take about 20 milliseconds. During saccades, little or no visual information is taken in (saccadic suppression). During fixations, we take in text information. Fixations typically last anywhere from 200 to 300 milliseconds, depending on the type of material or goal of the reading task.

➤ Content words receive more gaze time than do function words. The more unfamiliar the word, the longer the fixation. Highly constrained words, high-frequency words, and short words are most likely to be skipped.

➤ Saccades can be regressive. Good readers are better at regressing back to exactly where they encountered a problem; poor readers' eye movements are inefficient. However, this is a symptom of poor reading rather than the cause.

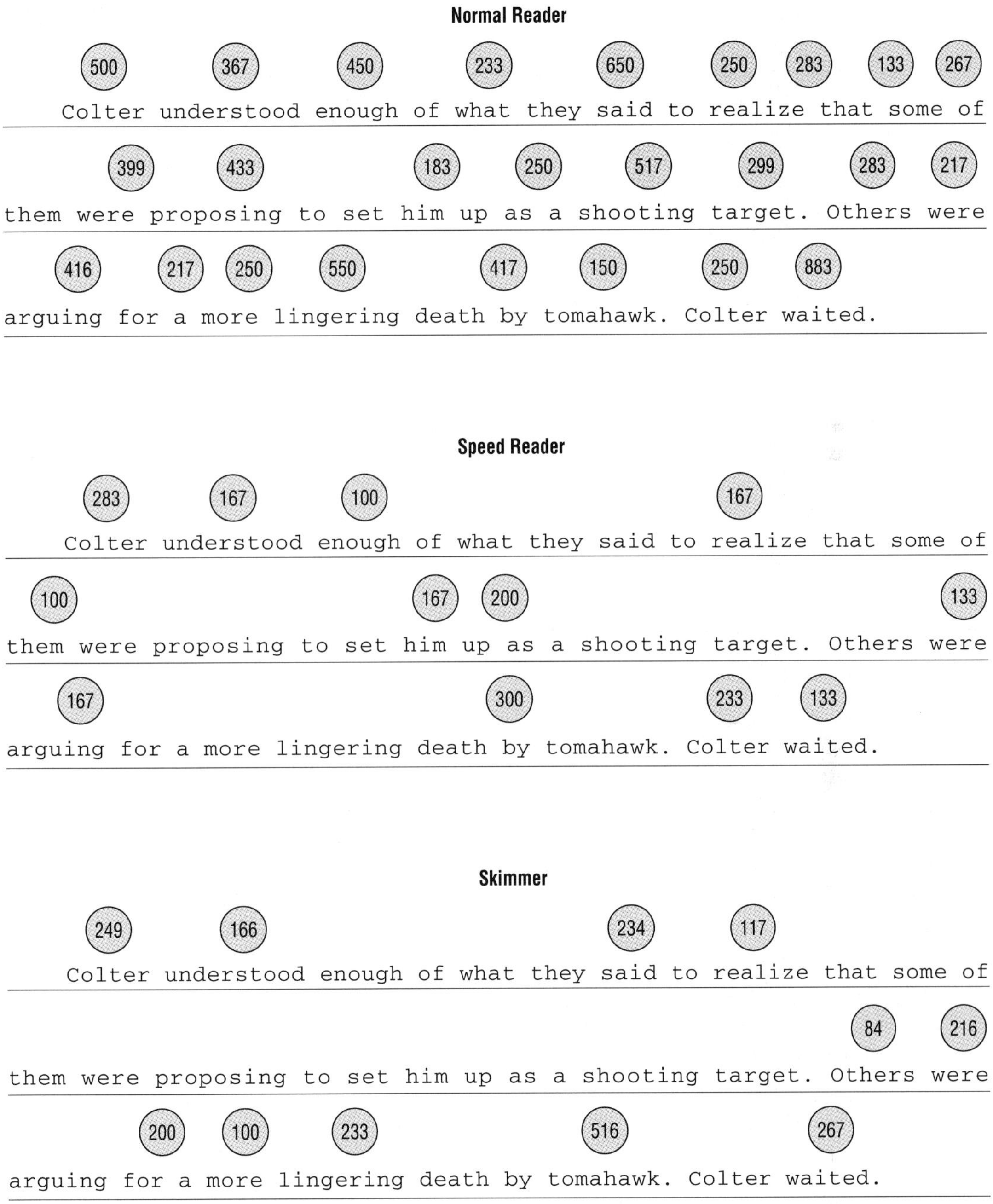

Normal Reader

(500) (367) (450) (233) (650) (250) (283) (133) (267)

Colter understood enough of what they said to realize that some of

(399) (433) (183) (250) (517) (299) (283) (217)

them were proposing to set him up as a shooting target. Others were

(416) (217) (250) (550) (417) (150) (250) (883)

arguing for a more lingering death by tomahawk. Colter waited.

Speed Reader

(283) (167) (100) (167)

Colter understood enough of what they said to realize that some of

(100) (167) (200) (133)

them were proposing to set him up as a shooting target. Others were

(167) (300) (233) (133)

arguing for a more lingering death by tomahawk. Colter waited.

Skimmer

(249) (166) (234) (117)

Colter understood enough of what they said to realize that some of

(84) (216)

them were proposing to set him up as a shooting target. Others were

(200) (100) (233) (516) (267)

arguing for a more lingering death by tomahawk. Colter waited.

Figure 11.2 Eye fixations of normal readers, speed readers, and skimmers.

From Just, M. A., & Carpenter, P. A. (1987). *The psychology of reading and language comprehension.* Boston: Allyn and Bacon. Copyright 1987 by Pearson Education. Reprinted by permission of the publisher.

> ➤ Perceptual span is about three characters to the left and 15 or so characters to the right of any given fixation for the English alphabet. Perceptual span is shorter the more difficult the material. Parafoveal information aids in lexical access and allows for the detection of word length and the spotting of word boundaries.

> ➤ In spite of strong claims, there is little evidence that speed reading is effective. Speed readers do fairly well in their understanding of the general idea of a passage but fail to grasp the details. This same pattern characterizes readers who "skim" rather than read.

Word Recognition

Now that you have a basic understanding of the mechanics of reading, let's take a step up in the language hierarchy. In the previous chapter, this involved moving from sounds to spoken words; here, we move from letters to written words. It's obvious that the look of a written word—its **orthography**—is an important factor in its visual recognition. The view that orthography provides the major route to word recognition is termed the **direct-access view.** Words are recognized by using the written label to access the appropriate semantic memory representation directly. Labeling this as the "direct" view implies that there must also be an "indirect" view. Indeed there is. The **indirect-access** (or **phonological**) **view** of word recognition proposes that word recognition goes through the phonological representation of the word prior to the word's identification. In other words, visual recognition of the word *apple* as a sweet red thing you pick off trees in the fall involves the activation of the word's sound. This view might remind you of the motor theory of speech perception we discussed in Chapter 10—the view that the recognition of speech is aided by one's own knowledge and experience with the articulation of speech. Although it may seem a bit counterintuitive, the indirect-access view has a good deal of support. It seems that even when we are silently looking at a printed word, the "road to recognition" seems to go through its phonological characteristics. And as you'll see, reading instruction that follows this road is much more successful than instruction that doesn't.

Stop and Think!   RECONSIDERING READING

Carefully read a randomly chosen passage from this text and observe whatever difficulties you might have.

- What is the source of the difficulties?
- How did your reading processes attempt to deal with these difficulties (i.e., did you backtrack, etc.)?
- As you were reading, was there any evidence that you used the auditory route to word recognition (i.e., sounding words out)?

Read a passage from the story at the beginning of one of the chapters. Did you have fewer problems with this? Have a friend read a passage from the text and a passage from the story at the beginning of one of the chapters. (Be sure the passages are of the same length.) Which passage did they read more quickly?

The ever-resourceful cognitive psychologists have come up with a novel way to investigate the issue of direct versus indirect access—by analyzing the visual recognition of homophones. Homophones are word pairs with the same component sounds but different spellings and different meanings (e.g., *reed* and *read*). A study by Van Orden (1987) took advantage of the ambiguity of homophones to provide a test of phonologically mediated (indirect) access to semantic memory during word recognition. In this study (experiment 1), participants were presented with a category-verification task; a category name (e.g., *flower*) was followed by one of three types of stimuli: a member of the category (e.g., *tulip*), a homophone of a member of the category (e.g., *rows,* which is a "phonological replica" of *rose*), or a word orthographically similar to a member of the category (e.g., *robs,* which has orthography similar to *rose*). The task was to indicate if the word was a member of the category as quickly as possible. If access is direct, then *rows* and *robs* should both cause problems, because they're visually similar to *rose.* If identifying a word involves activation of a phonological code, however, then *rows* should activate two meanings (a line and a flower), because there are two meanings attached to the sound /roz/. Therefore, there should be a good deal of misclassification of *rows* and other homophones as being members of the stated category (flower). In line with this prediction, participants made categorization mistakes nearly 20% of the time for homophones but only 3% of the time for orthographically similar words; it's almost like homophones are "pseudomembers" of a category. This suggests strongly that word recognition involves access to sound.

Even more compelling evidence comes from research employing pseudohomophones. A pseudohomophone is a made-up word that sounds like a real word (e.g., *brane* for *brain*). Luo, Johnson, and Gallo (1998) tested whether pseudohomophones might show effects of semantic relatedness. In other words, would *chare* (mistakenly) be viewed as related to *table* because it sounds identical to *chair?* If access to the mental lexicon is direct (i.e., not phonologically mediated), then you might expect that the pair *table-chare* would be easily classified as unrelated. If such access is mediated by phonology, however, then it is likely that such pairs would lead to more errors and/or a slower RT in judgments of semantic relatedness. The results are presented in Figure 11.3; as you can see, pseudohomophones led to more errors and slower RTs, suggesting that access to the mental lexicon involves phonological information.

Many researchers favor what is typically termed a **dual-route view** of word recognition, proposing that word recognition can proceed by either a direct (visual label only) route or an indirect (visual label plus phonological representation) route. Some of the strongest evidence for such a dual-route model comes from the study of dyslexia, a condition characterized by problems in visual word recognition.

Dyslexia

You're no doubt familiar with the term **dyslexia,** which is a condition that involves severe reading difficulties (among them difficulties in word recognition). It's important to note that dyslexia is not simply poor reading. The difficulty of poor readers is often rooted in largely noncognitive factors like emotion or motivation. Dyslexic readers show difficulty in reading in the absence of these problems. Also, dyslexics score in the normal range on traditional measures of intelligence.

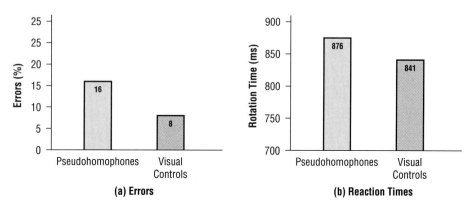

Figure 11.3 Results from Luo, Johnson, and Gallo (1998). When used in relatedness judgments (e.g., chare-table), pseudohomophones led to more errors and longer reaction times, suggesting a phonological route in visual word recognition.

From Luo, C. R., Johnson, R. A., & Gallo, D. A. (1998). Automatic activation of phonological information in reading: Evidence from the semantic relatedness decision task. *Memory and Cognition, 26,* 833–843. Reprinted by permission of the Psychonomic Society, Inc.

Varieties of Dyslexia.   Dyslexia is typically classified as acquired or developmental. In **acquired dyslexia,** language difficulties arise from some type of brain damage. Alternatively, **developmental dyslexia** refers to language difficulties not associated with any obvious brain damage. Although the etiology of acquired and developmental dyslexia is different, the behavioral manifestation—problems in word identification—is similar. Therefore, in the following discussion we will focus on the specific behavioral manifestations in different types of dyslexia rather than on their etiology.

Surface Dyslexia.   People with **surface dyslexia** must rely almost completely on the indirect-access (phonological) route to word recognition, literally "sounding out" words as they encounter them. As a result, they have particular difficulty with words that have irregular pronunciations. For example, the words *steak* or *break* would be pronounced as *steek* or *breek,* because the /ee/ pronunciation of *ea* is the more regular one. However, surface dyslexics are capable of pronouncing some irregular words correctly, so it seems that the phonological route is not the only route available. For example, if a dyslexic pronounces the irregular word *hearth* correctly, they obviously aren't sounding it out. In spite of this, it does appear that the indirect-access route to word identification is the one predominantly used by this type of dyslexic.

Phonological Dyslexia.   **Phonological dyslexia** is quite unusual, and it's a bit surprising that it was even discovered; it probably wouldn't have been unless psychologists looked for it (Ellis, 1984). Phonological dyslexics have a selective inability to read pseudowords (i.e., fake words) like *bleer.* Interestingly, they have little or no trouble with familiar words, regular or irregular. Therefore, it seems that phonological dyslexics have trouble with the indirect-access route to word recognition. The fact that they are unable to sound out a pseudoword is an indication that they are unable to sound out words in general and consequently must rely on the direct-access (nonphonological) route to word recognition. Indeed, the mere existence of phonological dyslexia is often marshaled as evidence that there must be a direct route. If the only way to successfully read a word label is to access its phonological representation, then phonological dyslexics should have tremendous difficulty reading. But as we just pointed out, they don't.

Deep Dyslexia.   People with **deep dyslexia** exhibit some of the difficulties seen in surface and phonological dyslexia—namely, some problems in reading both words and nonwords. However, the most striking aspect of deep dyslexia is a deficit in semantics (the meaning of language); that is, deep dyslexics exhibit semantic errors in reading. For instance, they may read *daughter* as *sister*. They also have an easier time reading words with concrete and imageable referents (e.g., *truck*) relative to words that are more abstract (e.g., *love*). In addition, function words, like *below*, present a problem; often, deep dyslexics will randomly substitute another function word, like *into*. Ellis (1984) suggests that the semantic aspect of the mental lexicon is impaired in some way. Others (e.g., Patterson & Besner, 1984) suggest that left-hemisphere reading processes are completely disrupted so that word recognition must rely on the limited linguistic capacities of the right hemisphere.

Evaluation.   In general, the most common source of the problems observed in dyslexia concerns single-word encoding. More specifically, dyslexics seem to have difficulty taking a visually presented word, decoding it, and retrieving the corresponding sounds—a process that has been termed *phonological assembly*. Put simply, they have trouble processing the correspondence between orthography (the look of a word) and phonology (the sound of a word). However, the extent of this problem varies with the nature of the dyslexia, providing support for the dual-route view of word recognition. Due to these difficulties in phonological assembly, dyslexics tend to be poor spellers; the nature of their misspellings is informative. Just and Carpenter (1987) found that the spelling errors of dyslexics tend to be phonetically unacceptable ones. A phonetically acceptable misspelling would be *lurn* instead of *learn,* because it retains the letter-to-pronunciation correspondence. The misspellings of normal readers tend to be phonetically acceptable. By contrast, dyslexic misspellings are more likely to be unacceptable (e.g., *insules* instead of *insult*).

These problems in individual word recognition have detrimental effects on the reading of dyslexics. Just and Carpenter (1987) enumerate several of the deficits that are observed in dyslexics. Their observations of a sample of dyslexic readers revealed a number of striking deficiencies when compared to nondyslexic readers. First, dyslexic readers tended to read more slowly and with more pronunciation errors than nondyslexic readers; also, their comprehension was poorer than nondyslexic readers. Figure 11.4 provides an example of the difficulties encountered by dyslexic readers; as you can see in (a),

(no response)
_____ Toscanini called them the "best boys' choir in the world." They

sang   *commadors...I don't know*
have sung to kings and commoners, capitalists and comrades. With the

            young
freshness of youth yet all the professionalism of mature musicians, they

            hands   *where it be where it be the inter*
put their hearts and souls into every note, whether it be the interlacing

harmonics   *Gos...I don't know*   *they infarences of*
harmonies of a Gastoldi madrigal or the infectious three-quarter-time of

    Scores
a Strauss waltz.

    Through the performance, through the performer
_____ Though the performers are young–from 10 to 14–their choir is

                18, 1498 where Hangsinvar...
ancient. It was formed in 1498, when Hapsburg Emperor Maximilian I

                            the...I don't know
collected a group of eight boys to sing in his chapel, the Hopburgkapelle,

    Virginia's imprissit imperial
in the heart of Vienna's imperial palace.

(a)

Figure 11.4 Reading patterns in a dyslexic. Panel a depicts a dyslexic's vocalization during reading, and panel b shows eye movements while reading.

From Just, M. A., & Carpenter, P. A. (1987). *The psychology of reading and language comprehension.* Boston: Allyn and Bacon. Copyright 1987 by Pearson Education. Reprinted by permission of the publisher.

this particular reader had great difficulty pronouncing specific words, indicative of a problem in converting printed text to phonological output. Problems with specific words can also be seen in this reader's saccades while reading aloud. As you can see in (b), the gaze durations were very long, particularly for words that were eventually mispronounced, and there were many regressive saccades. This pattern is also observed in the silent reading of dyslexics. Just and Carpenter note that these difficulties are especially noteworthy in light of the fact that this particular reader was an academically strong engineering student.

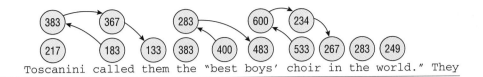

Toscanini called them the "best boys' choir in the world." They

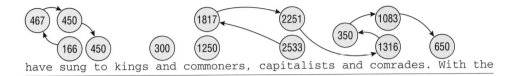

have sung to kings and commoners, capitalists and comrades. With the

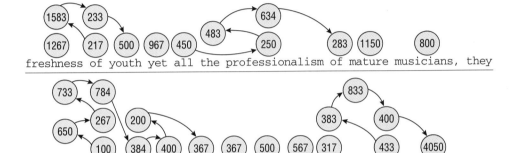

freshness of youth yet all the professionalism of mature musicians, they

put their hearts and souls into every note, whether it be the interlacing

(b)

Figure 11.4 (continued)

Cognition and Neuroscience

Left-Hemisphere Connectivity and Dyslexia

Due to the numerous ways in which dyslexia can manifest itself, pinning down its causes has proven to be a difficult task. Recent research on the neural correlates of dyslexia has revealed abnormalities in the left-hemisphere systems that underlie certain language functions, most notably the processes that allow for the mapping of visual representations (printed words) into phonological ones. Take a look at the brain areas indicated in Figure 11.5; these areas and the connections between them form a network that turns out to be an important neural substrate for reading. The critical areas include the lingual gyrus, an important center for orthographic (i.e., written word form) processing; the superior temporal gyrus, an important center for accessing lexical representations of words; and the angular gyrus, which is believed to serve as a mediator between these areas, relating the output from the orthographic processing to the lexical representation. In a normal brain, these areas are functionally connected and work together to allow reading.

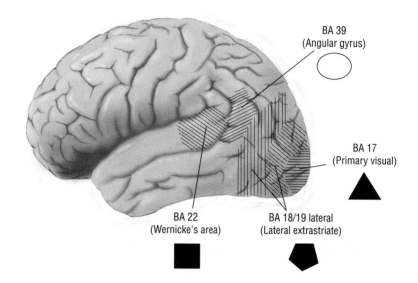

Figure 11.5 The left-hemisphere reading network investigated by Pugh et al. (2000) in their study of dyslexics.

From Pugh, K. R., Mencl, W. E., Shaywitz, B. A., Shaywitz, S. E., Fulbright, R. K., Constable, R. T., Skudlarski, P., Marchione, K. E., Jenner, A. R., Fletcher, J. M., Liberman, A. M., Shankweiler, D. P., Katz, L., Lacadie, C., Gore, J. C. (2000). The angular gyrus in developmental dyslexia: Task-specific differences in functional connectivity within posterior cortex. *Psychological Science 11*, 51–56. Copyright 2000 by Blackwell, Inc. Reprinted by permission.

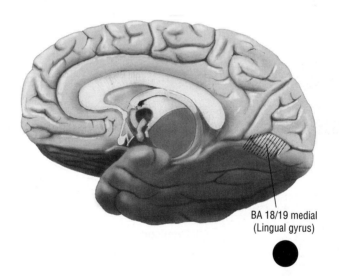

But the dyslexic brain is not normal; evidence indicates that dyslexic brains have suffered a breakdown in the connectivity of these three areas. Horwitz, Rumsey, and Donohue (1998) PET scanned brains of dyslexic and nondyslexic individuals while engaged in word and non-word reading tasks. The brain scans of dyslexics revealed a relatively weak correlation between activity in the left angular gyrus and activity in the other two temporal areas; the areas were not working in concert. In contrast, brain scans of nondyslexics indicated a strong correlation between these three areas. This lack of a relationship in dyslexics and the strength of the relationship in nondyslexics indicates that the joint activity of these three areas is an important neural substrate of word identification.

Pugh and colleagues (2000) sought to delineate more clearly the relationship between the operation of this network and the word-identification deficits that define dyslexia. They wanted to find out whether this breakdown in connectivity was part of a global deficit that would be reflected on many cognitive tasks (both linguistic and nonlinguistic) or whether the breakdown in connectivity was a purely linguistic phenomenon.

To determine whether the problems in this network underlie global or linguistic-specific deficits, these researchers compared dyslexics and nondyslexics on five different cognitive/perceptual tasks and used functional magnetic resonance imaging (fMRI) to take stock of the activity of the left hemisphere. All conditions involved the presentation of a pair of stimuli for which participants were to respond "same" or "different." In a baseline (nonlinguistic) condition, two lines were presented for a same-different judgment (i.e., "Are the lines the same or different lengths?"). Two other tasks involved the materials of language (letters and letter sequences) but did not involve linguistic processing. In one of these tasks, participants were to compare the case alternation of two letter strings (e.g., *SjSj* and *Sjsj*); in the other, they were to determine whether two presented letters (e.g., *E* and *T*) rhymed. Although these tasks do require "the stuff" of language (i.e., letters), they don't require the phonological assembly of sounds that occurs when we read an entire word. Finally, two of the tasks did require phonological assembly; in one, participants had to decide whether or not two presented nonwords (e.g., *BOFE* and *TAFE*) rhymed. In the other, participants made a semantic judgment, assessing whether two presented words (e.g., *rose* and *daisy*) were members of the same category. This task required phonological assembly and access to the meaning of the word in the mental lexicon.

Pugh and colleagues weren't as interested in speed or accuracy as they were in comparing the brain activity of dyslexics and nondyslexics. More specifically, they were interested in the degree to which the angular gyrus and the temporal areas (the network described above) were concurrently activated during each of the tasks. The variety of tasks allowed the researchers to assess whether the problems in left-hemisphere functional connectivity are associated with global or linguistic-specific effects. Global effects would be indicated by weak correlations between the critical brain areas on all of the tasks described above. Linguistic-specific deficits would be manifested by weak correlations only during the language tasks requiring phonological assembly—the nonword rhyming task and the category task.

The results revealed markedly different patterns of activation between dyslexics and nondyslexics; and importantly, these differences were observed only on the language tasks requiring phonological assembly. In nondyslexics, there was a strong relationship between activity in the angular gyrus and temporal areas, particularly on the language tasks. By contrast, dyslexics showed no association in the activity of these areas on the language tasks. This striking difference suggests that the operation of this left-hemisphere network is a critical neural substrate for word recognition—more specifically, phonological assembly. The requirement to put together a string of sounds is the critical difference between the language and nonlanguage tasks. Only when this phonological assembly was required did dyslexics show a breakdown in connectivity between the important language-processing areas. Pugh and colleagues (2000) explain their findings by suggesting that dyslexics have a basic left-hemisphere weakness in phonological representation that limits their ability to build phonological representations of printed words. An interesting sidelight to the left-hemisphere findings were those from the (comparably less linguistic) right hemisphere. Here, dyslexics showed normal connectivity between the critical areas. This, along with earlier evidence cited by these researchers, suggests that perhaps the right hemisphere performs some compensatory language processing in the face of left-hemisphere deficits.

How Should Reading Be Taught?

As you've seen, cognitive researchers have amassed a wealth of data on the processes that underlie word recognition. So of course, their research findings provide a critical database that can be used to address an important educational question: What's the best method for teaching children to read? Educators have wrestled with this question for decades, and a clear answer emerges from research on reading. Before we give away the answer, let's review the reading techniques that have been used. The **whole-word approach** involves the rote learning of words, which children eventually learn to recognize on a quick glance. Basically, children are taught to apprehend whole words at a time; you can think of this as a top-down approach. The bottom-up alternative to this approach is termed the **phonics approach,** which involves sounding words out by noting the correspondence between the component letters and their sounds. This technique runs into problems when there is an irregular mapping of letters to sounds (which happens quite often in English).

Because of these problems with the phonics approach, some espouse a **whole-language approach.** This approach is in the spirit of the whole-word approach but is even broader in its application of top-down elements. In this approach, young readers are given engaging things to read on their own and are encouraged to guess at new or unfamiliar words by using illustrations, context, and story line. They are also encouraged to make up their own stories. Basically, the aim of the whole-language approach is to make reading and reading instruction fun. The approach is almost antiphonics. According to the whole-language approach, the mechanics of sound-to-letter mappings should not be taught explicitly, and a child should not be corrected when they mispronounce a word, because they will eventually arrive at the correct usage and pronunciation of the words on their own.

In a recent review of these three methods for reading instruction, Rayner, Foorman, Perfetti, Pesetsky, and Seidenberg (2001) provide ample evidence for a clear winner . . . the phonics approach. As you read earlier, a great deal of research indicates that reading involves access to the phonological representations of words. Rayner and colleagues point out that this is the case even for highly skilled readers. Therefore, it appears that learning letter-to-sound correspondences is vitally important to reading instruction. The evidence supporting this assertion is overwhelming; recent reviews of the evidence by the National Reading Panel and the National Research Council clearly demonstrate the superiority of the phonics approach over the other two approaches in producing higher reading achievement. Rayner and colleagues (2002) note that the whole-word and whole-language approaches are not without their merit and suggest that elements from these techniques might be effectively combined with the phonics approach. But phonics must be the foundation, as these authors emphasize:

> Reading must be grounded in a firm understanding of the connections between letters and sounds. Instructors should recognize the ample evidence that youngsters who are directly taught phonics become better at reading, spelling and comprehension than those who must pick up all the confusing rules of English on their own. Educators who deny this reality are neglecting decades of research. They are also neglecting the needs of their students. (p. 91)

STOP and REVIEW!

1. Distinguish between the direct-access view and indirect-access view to word recognition.
2. True or false? *Dyslexia* is basically another term for poor reading.
3. The source of most of the problems observed in dyslexia is
   a. regressive saccades
   b. inability to use the direct-access route to word recognition
   c. problems in reading familiar words
   d. difficulty in phonological assembly
4. What does neurological research indicate about the origins of dyslexia?
5. Should children be taught to read by sounding out words or by trying to figure out words based on pictures and story lines? Explain.

➤ The direct-access view proposes that words are recognized by direct access to the semantic memory representation of the word. The indirect-access (or phonological) view proposes that recognition requires activation of a word's phonological representation. Many favor a dual-route view, which proposes that word recognition can proceed either directly or indirectly.

➤ Word recognition processes can be informed by examining the set of disorders collectively termed *dyslexia*. Dyslexia is not synonymous with poor reading; it is characterized by specific deficits in visual word recognition. People with surface dyslexia rely completely on the indirect-access route to recognition. People with phonological dyslexia have a selective inability to read pseudowords. People with deep dyslexia have difficulty with semantic aspects of reading.

➤ The most common source of the problems observed in dyslexia is difficulty in phonological assembly, the extent of which varies depending on the type of dyslexia. Problems in phonological assembly lead to slow reading, pronunciation errors when reading aloud, poor comprehension, long gaze durations (especially for words eventually mispronounced), and many regressive saccades.

➤ Neurological research indicates that dyslexia is partially the result of a breakdown in connectivity in left-hemisphere language networks. The right hemisphere seems to perform some compensatory language processing in the face of left-hemisphere deficits.

➤ Research on teaching reading indicates that the phonics approach (teaching letter-to-sound correspondences) is more effective than either the whole-word or whole-language approach.

Sentence-Level Processing

Consider the following sentence: "The crowd booed the referee after his terrible call." It's clear that when we read, we implicitly understand not only the meaning of the individual words in the sentence, but also the structure of the sentence: the subject (the crowd), the object (the referee), and the connecting verb (booed). We understand each of these components and their interaction—the "who is doing what to whom," if you will. How do we arrive at this understanding? You no doubt have the intuition that it depends on a number of different factors: we must (1) successfully recognize each word in the sentence, (2) discern the grammatical structure of the sentence, and (3) form a representation of the meaning expressed by the sentence. In other words, sentence comprehension involves analysis at the word (discussed in the previous section), syntactic, and semantic levels.

Sentence Parsing

The identification of the component elements of a sentence and their grammatical relation to one another—a process termed **parsing**—is vital for language. Consider a brief excerpt from our opening story.

> She lasts about 10 minutes before throwing the book down and picking up the latest Mary Higgins Clark novel. She can't wait to see who committed the murder.

Although you know that Mary Higgins Clark is a person, you mindlessly (but appropriately) interpret her name here as a modifier for *novel,* and as part of the noun phrase "Mary Higgins Clark novel." Due to this immediate and accurate parsing, you don't even consider the possibility that the *she* in the following sentence could refer to Mary Higgins Clark. You instinctively know it refers to Colleen.

Parsing usually occurs so seamlessly that you don't even notice you're doing it. How is it accomplished? How are the components of a sentence recognized and combined? Does the syntactic (i.e., structural) analysis of a sentence have to finish before we compute the meaning of a sentence, or is meaning computed along with syntax?

The Importance of Syntax.   According to some views of sentence parsing, syntax is central. Put in terms of a concept we introduced in Chapter 10, we parse sentences according to their phrase structure. Word order (i.e., surface structure) helps the reader determine the phrase structure and thus serves the primary role in sentence comprehension. For example, sentences with a noun-verb-noun (i.e., subject-verb-object, or SVO) phrase structure are quite common in English, so the tacit assumption of a reader would be that sentences fit this general structure; this assumption helps guide parsing.

The Garden-Path Approach.   One approach to parsing is termed the **garden-path approach** (e.g., Frazier & Rayner, 1982), because it assumes that the reader follows a simple, word-by-word path through the sentence, attempting to fit each word within the assumed syntactic structure. Consider this sentence: "The professor argued the student's position passionately." If we (as English speakers) parse this sentence according to the garden-path approach, we will assume that it fits a standard SVO (subject-verb-object) structure. You might imagine a representation of this sentence that includes two major "nodes" corresponding to each of the sentence constituents: the noun phrase ("the professor") and the verb phrase ("argued the student's case passionately").

		Noun phrase	*Verb phrase*
Noun phrase	*Verb*	*Noun phrase*	*Adverb*
The professor	argued	the student's position	passionately.

According to the garden-path approach, as we read we assume the simplest syntactic structure and then revise this assumption if it proves to be wrong. For example, when we read the sentence above, we make the simplest possible assumption about its syntax; we assume that the phrase "the student's position" is the object of the just-encountered word *argued.* This type of simplifying assumption makes sense when one considers the limited capacity and time pressures faced by the human information processor.

Let's get a little more specific. The garden-path approach assumes that we use two different heuristics, or rules of thumb, to parse a sentence. One heuristic is termed *minimal attachment.* This principle is that one does not assume that the syntax of the sentence is more complicated than it probably is. For instance, we could assume that the phrase "the student's position" starts a whole new sentence embedded within the main sentence. However, we do not make this assumption. Another way to look at it is that as readers, we are parsimonious (i.e., minimal) about assuming new phrases. A second heuristic that converges on this interpretation of the sentence is the principle of *late closure.* According to this principle, we try and attach each word that we encounter to the phrase that's currently being processed. In this case, "the student's position" is assumed to be part of the verb phrase.

If our syntactic analysis proceeds down the garden path as just described, then we should have a problem with this sentence: "The professor argued the student's position was indefensible." Did you stumble over this sentence? Initially, it seems that the professor is arguing the student's position, but when the word *was* is encountered, the interpretation of the sentence must change. The professor is arguing against the student's position. This is termed a **garden-path sentence.**

Garden-path sentences provide strong evidence for the garden-path model of parsing proposed by Frazier and Rayner (1982). According to this model, when this sentence is read, "the student's position" will be placed within the verb phrase that starts with the word *argued,* because of the principles of minimal attachment and late closure. However, when the word *was* is encountered, this interpretation is rendered invalid; at this point, a new syntactic interpretation is constructed. Studies of on-line reading behavior confirm the difficulty readers have when they encounter garden-path sentences; these sentences are associated with longer reading times, longer fixations, and more regressive saccades (Frazier & Rayner, 1982). The difficulty in processing garden-path sentences seems quite general; even blind readers of Braille show regressive movements to cope with the ambiguity these sentences create (Mousty & Bertelsen, 1992). The difficulty encountered in garden-path sentences supports the notion that our initial attempts at parsing are based on the principles of minimal attachment and late closure and confirms our (quite sensible) bias to read sentences as subject-verb-object. (This bias is not shared by many other languages, which use other sentence structures such as subject-object-verb; see Bates, Devescovi, and Wulveck, 2001).

Stop *and* Think!   ## SKIPPING UP THE GARDEN PATH

Badly worded headlines provide amusing examples of being led up the garden path. Consider the following examples.

Prostitutes Appeal to Pope
College Graduates Blind Senior Citizen
Complaints about NBA Refs Growing Ugly

Find some examples of garden-path sentences from newspapers or Internet sites. (There are, no doubt, Websites explicitly devoted to these unfortunate headlines.) Analyze what you found by considering the following questions:

- How much effort did it take to "get" each interpretation of the headline/sentence?
- Which interpretation did you arrive at first?
- Was it easy to come up with the alternative?
- Was it difficult to figure out both interpretations?
- What parts of headlines/sentences (i.e., parts of speech) seem to be the most sensitive to misinterpretation?
- How did your general knowledge help you to disambiguate the headline/sentence?

The Importance of Semantics.   The difficulty we encounter when presented with ambiguous language stimuli like garden-path sentences makes a second aspect of sentence processing evident. Obviously, understanding the standard SVO syntactic structure that serves as the basis for so much of our communication in the English language is not enough for language understanding and production. If it was, you'd come up with sentences like "The hen polished the dictionary." As we said earlier, semantics refers to the manner in which we convey and understand the meaning of language. Most of the theorizing we discussed in Chapter 10 (in particular, Chomsky's approach) relegated semantics to a secondary role, while certainly not denying the importance of semantic factors in language.

One approach that highlights the importance of meaning is termed the **case-grammar approach** (Fillmore, 1968). This approach contends that sentences are parsed through the assignment of words to various **case roles.** Case roles specify who (or what) is doing what to whom (or what) (tortured syntax indeed!). Consider the following example: "Jim shot the ball through the hoop." Rather than parsing the sentence into syntactic components like noun phrase and verb phrase, the case-grammar approach assumes that the sentence is understood by parsing it into the roles played by each word in the sentence. In the sample sentence above, Jim serves the case role of agent, the basketball serves the case role of patient, and the hoop serves the case role of goal. Understanding and producing sentences is an exercise in decomposing and composing the case-role assignments, rather than the syntactic-role assignments, for the words in the sentence.

Sentence Comprehension

The importance of both syntax and semantics in sentence parsing and understanding is a given. Psycholinguistic researchers are interested in the specifics of the interplay between syntax and semantics. Does one have primary importance? Does one affect the other, or do semantic and syntactic analyses proceed independently of each other? Do these analyses occur in parallel or serially?

According to what might be termed the **autonomous view,** the analyses of syntax and semantics proceed independently (i.e., autonomously) of each other and the processing is serial. Sentence comprehension involves (in this precise order) computing the syntactic structure of the sentence followed by building a representation of the meaning being expressed in the sentence. The garden-path approach discussed above is an example of this type of approach. This view has the flavor of the information-processing approach, with its serial view of cognitive processes. An **interactionist view** of sentence comprehension proposes the same component processes but suggests that syntactic and semantic analyses occur in parallel (i.e., simultaneously). Furthermore, these processes depend on each other. This view has more of a connectionist flavor, in that it emphasizes parallel processing of different language modules. The autonomous and interactionist views highlight two separate but related issues. First, do syntactic and semantic processing proceed in parallel or serially? Second, do syntactic and semantic processing proceed independently of each other, or do they interact?

Independent or Dependent Modules?   One source of evidence that syntax and semantics comprise distinct language modules are dissociations in performance between these two aspects of language. As you've seen in a number of places throughout the text, evidence that two processes may be based on fundamentally different mechanisms is provided by dissociations—instances in which one cognitive process is impacted by some variable while another is not or when the process is affected in the opposite fashion. This logic has been used to argue for the independence of syntactic and semantic processing in speech. The most commonly cited dissociation is between two types of aphasia: Broca's aphasia and Wernicke's aphasia. **Broca's aphasia,** associated with frontal lobe brain damage, tends to involve a breakdown of structure; speech is telegraphic and incorrectly structured. However, use of content words (i.e., nouns and verbs) is less affected. So there seems to be a loss in syntactic ability but a preserved semantic ability. **Wernicke's aphasia,** which is associated with temporal lobe brain damage, tends to involve a breakdown of semantic aspects of language. Wernicke's aphasics speak in intact sentence structures but with a distorted choice of content words. So there seems to be a loss of semantic ability with preserved syntactic ability. This dissociation is consistent with the view that syntactic and semantic processing are based on separate independent systems; if they were based on the same system, damage to one would mean damage to the other.

Serial or Parallel?   Earlier, we discussed the garden-path approach to sentence parsing, which assumes that we follow one syntactic interpretation of a sentence until that interpretation leads up the wrong path, in which case we regroup and reinterpret. The garden-path approach is consistent with the autonomous view; sentence parsing is ultimately guided by syntactic structure. Semantic (i.e., meaning-based) factors do not exert their effect until later stages of sentence comprehension. In other words, syntactic analysis is primary, and semantic analysis is, in some respects, secondary. If this is true, then syntactic analysis should proceed unaffected by meaning. However, if you think about it, the difficulty encountered in the processing of garden-path sentences could be viewed as either a syntactic or a semantic influence on parsing. After all, the juncture in the sentence that creates problems involves a change in meaning as well as a change in phrase structure. If there is an influence of semantic factors, then we might expect that the meaning of a sentence would influence whether or not the garden-path effect occurs.

A study addressing this general question was done by Pickering and Traxler (1998). They hypothesized that if semantic factors influence syntactic ones, then the difficulty induced by a garden-path sentence should be more severe when the initial interpretation makes sense than when it doesn't. In other words, silly sentences shouldn't be as likely to induce a garden-path effect. Consider these two sentences:

> As the woman edited the magazine amused all the reporters.
> As the woman sailed the magazine amused all the reporters.

Both of these are identical in terms of syntax, and both are garden-path sentences. According to the garden-path principles of late closure and minimal attachment, the phrase "the magazine" should be placed with the verb in each sentence, leading to difficulties in comprehension for both.

But there is a critical difference between the initial parts of these two sentences: one is plausible ("As the woman edited the magazine"), and one is not plausible ("As the woman sailed the magazine"). Does this semantic difference in these syntactically identical sentences impact comprehension of the sentence? Pickering and Traxler (1998) had participants read garden-path sentences that were either plausible or implausible to investigate the possibility of semantic effects in comprehension. Their results demonstrated stronger garden-path effects for plausible sentences. The semantic plausibility of the sentence induced more of a "commitment" from readers; once a particular semantic interpretation was made, encountering a syntactic change that caused the interpretation to be wrong created more problems in comprehending the sentence. If the sentence was not semantically plausible, the correct syntactic decision was usually made, reducing the difficulty normally seen with garden-path sentences. Interestingly, implausible sentences did produce some garden-path effects, indicating the importance of syntactic factors.

The cognitive struggle in which we seem to engage when faced with the syntactic ambiguity of garden-path sentences can be compared to what happens when we're faced with lexical ambiguity (i.e., a word with two different meanings). You'll recall (from Chapter 10) that, somewhat surprisingly, all interpretations of a word are considered (however briefly) before context finally leads to the selection of the appropriate interpretation. The same general pattern seems to apply to garden-path sentences, at least to some degree; multiple interpretations are considered, and context biases one of them. This finding seems to support the interactionist view that syntactic and semantic analyses occur in parallel.

Working Memory and Parsing.   It should come as no surprise that the on-line processing of sentences is influenced by moment-to-moment demands on attention. Research demonstrates that the strength of garden-path effects depends on working-memory capacity. Just and Carpenter (1992) compared participants with high and low working-memory capacity in their comprehension of garden-path sentences. As you read earlier, a garden-path sentence like "The evidence examined by the lawyer shocked the jury" is less likely to lead to interpretation difficulties because the verb *examined* can't plausibly go along with "the evidence" (i.e., evidence is an inanimate object so it could not examine something). However, Just and Carpenter found that comprehension depended on capacity. Readers with high capacity were more likely than those with lower capacity to use the status of the noun *evidence* to disambiguate the remainder of the sentence. So difficulties in interpreting garden-path sentences may arise from capacity limitations rather than from the serial processing of syntax and semantics. So debate goes on (with apologies to Sonny and Cher), providing fertile ground for further research.

Evaluation.   It appears that the results of studies on the independence-of-modules issue and on the type-of-processing issue leave us in a theoretical quandary. The former studies support the autonomous view, but the latter studies support the interactionist view. So which is right? No clear answer has been reached, but Harley (1995) indicates that, on balance, the bulk of the evidence seems to favor the autonomous view (independent, serial processing). Early stages of sentence processing seem to be guided by syntax, by way of the principles of late closure and minimal attachment. Later stages seem to involve the evaluation of the analysis performed to that point. At this later stage, semantic information plays a more prominent role in comprehension. And, as the research on the role of working memory demonstrates, the precise operation of syntactic and semantic processes no doubt depends on a given reader's capacity.

RECURRING RESEARCH THEME
Cognition and Individual Differences

Cross-Linguistic Differences in Cues for Sentence Comprehension

Almost all of the research discussed in these two chapters on language is based on research with native English readers who read, what else. . . . English! As Bates, Devescovi, and Wulfeck (2001) note, this is an unfortunate state of affairs. To some extent, psycholinguistics involves the search for universal principles of language processing. Obviously, if psycholinguistic research is dominated by studies using English, the results are severely limited in their generalizability. This is especially true when one considers the vast differences that exist between the languages of the world with regard to what MacWhinney and Bates (1989) term the *cue validity of grammatical structures* in comprehending sentences. In other words, how do particular combinations of words tip off a reader to the meaning of a sentence? As we noted earlier, in English, word order is an extremely powerful cue. Consider these words: *cow chased horse.* Given their rigid adherence to the subject-verb-object sentence structure, English speakers would almost universally interpret this word combination as meaning that the cow (the subject) chased (verb) the horse (object), even though the idea expressed seems a bit strange. But the validity of this particular word ordering as a cue is by no means universal.

In an exhaustive analysis of the cue validity of various languages, MacWhinney and Bates compared native speakers from over a dozen different language backgrounds in order to assess the hierarchy of cues used to comprehend sentences. More specifically, they were interested in cross-linguistic differences in which sentence cues were used for actor assignment. In our cow example above, the cow is the actor (to English speakers, at least). What other cues can affect actor assignment, and how do these differ between languages? To assess this, MacWhinney and Bates report a series of studies that employed a "Who did it?" task (Bates, Devescovi, & Wulfeck, 2001) under different presentation conditions. Simple sentences—like "The cow chased the horse" or "The rock kissed the cow"—were used to find out how speakers of various languages would determine who did the chasing and the kissing.

Two conditions employed in these studies varied the syntactic (whether the verb agreed with the first noun or second noun) and the semantic relationship between the two nouns (e.g., animate-animate, inanimate-animate, animate-inanimate). The investigators were interested in determining which cues would win out in determining "who did what to whom." The results yielded some intriguing differences. As expected, English speakers rigidly followed word order as a cue, asserting that the cow did the chasing and the rock did the kissing. However, for the latter sentence ("The rock kissed the cow"), animacy overruled word order for most other languages. (Rocks are inanimate objects, therefore they can't kiss. Therefore, the cow must have kissed the rock.) When word order was pitted against verb agreement, as in "The cows is chasing the horse," English speakers once again relied on word order rather than agreement, ascribing the action to the cow. Speakers of more richly inflected languages (languages that feature numerous permutations of a given word based on its number, gender, tense, or grammatical relations to other words) tended to favor agreement over word order. Since *horse* and *is* are both singular forms, they belong together. To sum up: the evidence on cross-linguistic differences in sentence comprehension supports the conclusion that speakers of a given language demonstrate processing biases that reflect the structure and the statistical biases present within their own language (Bates, Devescovi, & Wulfeck, 2001).

STOP *and* REVIEW!

1. What is the basic idea behind the garden-path approach to sentence parsing?
2. True or false? The case-grammar approach stresses the importance of syntax in parsing sentences.
3. According to the autonomous view,
   a. semantic and syntactic processing are not important in sentence parsing
   b. semantic and syntactic processing are independent of each other
   c. semantic and syntactic processing occur in parallel
   d. semantic processing has been shown to be the most accurate view of sentence parsing

➤ Some approaches to sentence comprehension place primary emphasis on syntax. According to the garden-path approach, we parse sentences according to syntactic rules and test one interpretation at a time. Difficulty in the processing of garden-path sentences is consistent with this approach. Garden-path sentences are associated with longer reading times, longer fixations, and more regressive saccades.

➤ Some approaches to sentence comprehension stress the importance of semantics. One example of this is the case-grammar approach. According to this approach, sentences are parsed by the assignment of words to various case roles that reflect the role of the concept within the given sentence.

➤ According to the autonomous view, syntactic and semantic processing are independent and operate serially, with syntactic processing occurring before a semantic analysis. According to the interactionist view, syntactic and semantic processing are in constant interaction and occur simultaneously. Working memory capacity appears to be an important determinant of whether we operate in an autonomous or interactionist mode.

Discourse Comprehension

All of the research we've discussed up to this point has a serious limitation: it's based primarily on how people process single sentences in isolation. But you almost never read single sentences in isolation; you read a flow of connected discourse. Simply put, **discourse** refers to linguistic output longer than a sentence. How does a reader understand a chain of sentences and paragraphs while keeping in mind and understanding the major themes? Research on the topic of *discourse comprehension* constitutes another major emphasis within the field of psycholinguistics.

Levels of Representation

When we read connected discourse, we obviously have some mental representation of it. Our representation of discourse exists at a number of different levels. Psychological work on discourse representation has concentrated on three of these levels, as suggested by van Dijk and Kintsch (1983). First, discourse may be represented as a **surface code,** which refers to its precise wording. Our representation of discourse does not include the surface code, except for the last few words read (more on this later). Discourse may also be represented as a **textbase,** which refers to the major facts and themes (i.e., the "stripped-down" meaning) of the discourse. Finally, our representation of discourse is thought to include a **situation model.** The situation model for a selection of discourse refers to the "world" it creates; this model is created from a combination of the places, settings, people, and events in the discourse and the background knowledge possessed by the reader. We'll discuss the van Dijk and Kintsch model in a bit more detail later, but these three levels of discourse representation provide a useful framework for thinking about some of the issues.

Structure and Coherence

Comprehension of connected discourse depends on much more than the content of the individual sentences. Consider this story:

> The play wasn't very good. Greg bought a Tyrannosaurus rex and some batteries. The mall was crowded. Bridget wondered about the airplane. Greg's feet were tired. Greg and Bridget ate dinner. Anne told Bridget to come over around 1:00. Greg relaxed and watched some college football. Jim had no problem putting it together.

Did you follow that? Probably not; it's a pretty poor description of what we did one weekend (sounds like an exciting life, doesn't it?), and it's not very easy to follow. The events aren't in any apparent order, and there's no connection between the individual ideas expressed in each sentence. This lack of connection is a lack of what is typically termed **local structure**—the explicit and/or implicit connections between individual sentences. Discourse that has some local structure is much easier to understand and remember. Now consider this passage.

> If the balloons popped, the sound wouldn't be able to carry far, since everything would be too far away from the correct floor. A closed window would also prevent the sound from carrying, since most buildings tend to be well-insulated. Since the whole operation depends on the steady flow of electricity, a break in the middle of the wire would also cause problems. Of course, the fellow could shout, but the human voice is not loud enough to carry that far. An additional problem is that a string could break on the instrument. Then there could be no accompaniment to the message. It is clear that the best situation would involve less distance. Then there would be fewer potential problems. With face-to-face contact, the least number of things could go wrong.

Here, the individual sentences seem to hang together better; there does seem to be some local structure. But still, the passage is difficult to get a handle on, this time because it lacks a broader context, or what is termed global structure. **Global structure** refers to the general knowledge that we bring to bear on what we're reading. The lack of context for this passage prevents it from enjoying any global structure. As is the case with the first passage, we're not likely to understand or remember much about it unless, perhaps, we see a picture that provides some idea of what's going on (see Figure 11.6).

Both local and global structure relate to a more general principle—**coherence.** Connected discourse should hang together, or cohere, both in terms of a sentence-to-sentence flow and in terms of broader themes. Global structure leads to global coherence; local structure leads to local coherence. What is it about the structure of connected discourse and our processing of it that produces coherence, thus benefitting understanding and memory?

Anaphoric Reference.   One important source of coherence in discourse is anaphoric reference. **Anaphoric reference** occurs when a current expression refers to something encountered earlier in the text. For example:

> Greg was anxious to get to the music store to buy the latest CD by *his* favorite group. He figured that *it* was likely to sell out the first day *it* was on sale. He left for the store; the traffic was terrible, and it took him 30 minutes to get *there.*

In this sentence, *his* refers back to Greg, *it* refers back to the CD (twice, in fact), and *there* refers to the music store's location. The referring expression is called an **anaphor,** and the

Figure 11.6 Does this help you interpret the passage?

From Bransford, J. D., & Johnson, M. K. (1972). Contextual prerequisites for understanding: Some investigations of comprehension and recall. *Journal of Verbal Learning and Verbal Behavior, 11,* 717–726. Reprinted by permission of Lawrence Erlbaum Associates.

corresponding events are termed **antecedents.** Although it doesn't seem to require much thought to make these connections, the connections are vital for a text to maintain coherence. When you encounter an anaphoric reference in discourse, you must make the connection back to the antecedent. Based on this, you may be able to intuit one variable that puts a strain on anaphoric reference (and thus works against coherence)—the amount of separation between the anaphor and its antecedent. If *he* refers to a person five or six sentences back, the connection is not likely to be made, and the text will lose coherence.

The effects of delay on the ability to make anaphoric reference makes one fact of comprehension apparent: comprehension is critically dependent on working memory. You'll recall that working memory is the "mental workbench" that we use for the processing of information currently in conscious awareness. As such, it plays an important role as we integrate the elements of what we're reading with what we've just read, as well as with our general knowledge. In the case of anaphoric reference, the reader must retain in working memory the major players in the discourse (mainly subjects and objects of sentences) and integrate these with the subsequent anaphora. The more distant the connection between ideas in the text and their corresponding anaphora, the greater the strain on working memory. Indeed, in an extensive meta-analytic review, Daneman and Merikle (1996) found that working-memory span (discussed in Chapter 4) serves as a good predictor of text comprehension.

A number of factors influence the accessibility of the antecedents that need to be retrieved when anaphora are encountered. An antecedent is retrieved more easily if it occurs frequently throughout a text (Crawley, 1986), if it has occurred recently (von Eckardt & Potter, 1985), or if it has received first mention (i.e., whether the antecedent was one of the first concepts mentioned in a text; Gernsbacher, 1989). The latter two findings provide an interesting parallel to the effects of primacy and recency in working memory (discussed in Chapter 4). You'll recall that words occurring early and late in a list are the easiest to recall.

Stop *and* Think!

ANALYZING ANAPHOR

Once again, flip to one of the stories that begin the chapters. As you read over it, take note of all of the anaphoric references made.

- Do the anaphora help maintain the coherence of the text?
- Are there any anaphora that are unclear?
- Do the anaphora help to maintain global coherence, local coherence, or both?

Given and New Information.   Another factor that allows us to maintain coherence as we read or listen to discourse is termed the **given-new contract** (Clark and Haviland, 1977). The given-new contract refers to an implicit "agreement" between a writer and a reader (or between a speaker and a listener). This implicit agreement means that all discourse includes information that is assumed to be known by the reader (termed **given information**—you could think of it as background information) and information that is assumed to be unknown (termed **new information**). For example, consider the following sentence: "My cognitive psychology professor gives really challenging exams." When you read this sentence, the given information is what you already assume—that your cognitive psychology professor gives exams. The new information is what you probably didn't know—that these exams are really challenging. Clark and Haviland (1977) propose three components in following the given-new contract. First, a reader must determine what information in a sentence is given and what is new; next, the reader must figure out what the given information refers back to earlier in the text. Finally, the new information must also be linked to that part of the text.

The implicit agreement to use given information and supplement it with new information is present in all forms of discourse, including spoken. In our story, Colleen is a little confused when Donna says simply "I hear it's going to be really hard" because Donna has only provided the new information without the context of the given information. Consequently, Colleen's comprehension suffers.

Inferences.   In a given piece of discourse, not everything is explicitly stated: "After the storm, the sun came out, and the leprechaun started searching for the gold." If you remember that sentence from Chapter 1, we're really impressed! We repeat it here to demonstrate how easily inferences are made during reading. Chances are your processing of this sentence went well beyond the explicitly stated facts. You may have "read between the lines" and inferred that the leprechaun will be in search of a rainbow and that the gold he finds will be in a pot. These facts are not explicitly stated, but chances are good they would be part of your representation of the sentence. **Inferences** are conclusions drawn by a reader that are not explicitly stated in the discourse. Our ability to combine the information in the text with our world knowledge provides another important source of coherence for the reader. At least one prominent example is apparent in the conversational context of the opening story. Based on Donna's remark about staring at a blank screen, Colleen rightly infers that she's suffering from writer's block.

A classic study by Kintsch (1974) demonstrates that inferences, just like explicit statements, are part of the text representation. In this study, readers were presented with texts that included information about events that were either explicitly stated or simply implied. For example,

1. A carelessly discarded burning cigarette started a fire.
   The fire destroyed many acres of virgin forest.

2. A burning cigarette was carelessly discarded.
   The fire destroyed many acres of virgin forest.

In version 1, the fact that the cigarette started a fire is explicitly stated; in version 2, this fact is only implied. After reading the text containing the target sentence, participants were given a sentence-verification task in which they were to confirm or deny the truth of certain sentences based on what they read. Some of the sentences were explicitly stated (e.g., "The fire destroyed many acres of virgin forest") and some were implied (e.g., "A cigarette started a fire"). Reaction time to make this decision was recorded. The sentence-verification task was used to see if the implied information was inferred and had become part of the discourse representation. Kintsch also varied the delay between when the passage was read and when the sentence-verification task occurred. Some participants were tested immediately; others, after 15 minutes had passed.

Take a look at the results depicted in Figure 11.7. As you can see, a fairly striking interaction was found. When the sentence-verification task was given immediately after the text was read, participants were quicker to verify the explicitly presented facts than they were to verify the facts that had simply been implied. But something interesting happened after a short delay: in this condition, there was no difference in verification time between explicitly stated facts and implied facts. Apparently, information resulting from an

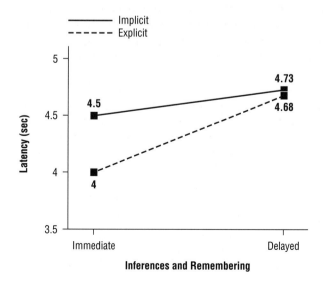

Figure 11.7 Results from Kintsch's (1974) study of inferences in reading. After a brief delay, implied facts (ostensibly inferred by the participants) are verified as quickly as are explicitly stated facts.

From Kintsch, W. (1974). *The representation of meaning in memory.* Hillsdale, NJ: Erlbaum. Reprinted by permission of Lawrence Erlbaum Associates.

inference becomes (after a short delay) just as prominent in the discourse representation as explicitly stated facts.

Types of Inferences.   Psychologists make a distinction between bridging inferences and elaborative inferences. A **bridging inference** is a relation constructed to connect two sentences or ideas that are not connected explicitly. Consider the following sentences:

> Hank was learning to be a better dancer.
> The instructor was very patient.

Although it isn't explicitly stated, we assume that "the instructor" is a dance instructor teaching Hank. Our inference serves as a "bridge" that connects the second sentence to the first. Bridging inferences are also called **backward inferences;** they allow us to connect material currently being encountered backward to earlier material. Bridging inferences add a great deal of coherence to a text. Consider a case where a bridging inference is unlikely:

> Hank was learning to be a better dancer.
> The pilot was very patient.

These two sentences don't cohere at all; our previous knowledge doesn't support an inference between "pilots" and "learning to be a better dancer." Our ability to use previous knowledge to bridge gaps in written text is critical for our ability to maintain a coherent representation.

An important type of bridging inference is a **causal inference,** in which readers figure out what must have prompted an event about which they have just read. Consider the following passage:

> As Keisha rode her bike at breakneck speed, a squirrel ran out in the road. Seconds later, Keisha found herself and her bike lying in a ditch at the side of the road.

There is little doubt that you now have the idea that Keisha wrecked her bike trying to avoid the squirrel that ran out in the road. If so, you made a causal inference; nothing in the sentence explicitly states that this is what happened, but it's hard not to make the inference. You'll note that this inference works backward in time, from Keisha lying in a ditch back to what must have happened immediately before.

Elaborative inferences involve adding extra information to one's representation of a text; the information is useful, but not necessary for coherence (Singer, 1990). For example, if you read the sentence "Hank was learning to be a better dancer," you might infer that he was taking dance lessons—a sensible assumption, but not explicitly stated. Elaborative inferences are also termed **forward inferences,** because in making them, we move beyond (or forward from) the text. The distinction between bridging and elaborative inferences seems to be a valuable one, as indicated in a study by Singer (1980). In this study, participants read one of the following three passages. The first explicitly states a piece of information; the second requires a bridging inference; the third is one in which an elaborative inference could be made.

1. The pitcher threw the ball to first base. The runner was halfway to second. (explicit)
2. The pitcher threw to first base. The ball sailed into right field. (bridging inference: *ball*)

3. The pitcher threw to first base. The runner was halfway to second. (elaborative inference: *ball*)

Note that for passage 2, an inference tying *ball* back to *throw* must be made to maintain coherence. A bridging inference is not necessary for coherence in the case of passage 3. However, an elaborative inference is possible.

After reading passages 1, 2, or 3, participants were to verify as quickly as possible if a sentence was true based on the following sentence.

4. The pitcher threw a ball.

The results are presented in Figure 11.8. As you can see, sentence 4 was verified most quickly in conditions 1 and 2. This finding makes sense for passage 1, since it explicitly mentions the ball. But it's surprising for passage 2, which doesn't. In fact, making the bridging inference in passage 2 seems to be just as good as having it be explicit, which basically replicates Kintsch's (1974) findings. Singer concludes that the bridging inference is made at encoding, and becomes part of the representation. Participants who saw passage 3 took significantly longer to verify sentence 4. This indicates that the inference was not made until they had actually read the question—that is, at retrieval rather than at encoding. The inference required in passage 3 is an elaborative inference. It is not necessary for coherence and so is not made at encoding.

A particularly compelling demonstration of making an elaborative inference comes from a classic study by Sulin and Dooling (1974). They presented participants with passages such as the following:

Gerald Martin strove to undermine the existing government to satisfy his political ambitions. Many of the people of his country supported his efforts. Current political problems made it relatively easy for Martin to take over. Certain groups remained loyal to the old government and gave Martin trouble. He confronted these groups directly and so silenced them. He

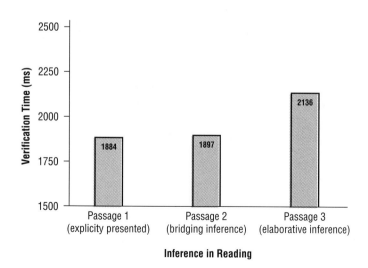

Figure 11.8 Results from Singer's (1980) study of inferences. A sentence that led to a bridging inference was as effective as explicitly presenting the same information, as indicated by the verification times.

From Singer, M. (1980). The role of case-filling inferences in the coherence of brief passages. *Discourse Processes, 3,* 185–201. Reprinted by permission of Lawrence Erlbaum Associates.

became a ruthless, uncontrollable dictator. The ultimate effect of his rule was the downfall of his country. (p. 256)

Some of the participants read the passage exactly as above; others read it with the name Adolph Hitler substituted for Gerald Martin. Can you see where this is going? Participants who read this paragraph, using the name of Adolph Hitler, went beyond the information presented and made elaborative inferences. For example, these participants were likely to remember that a statement about hatred of Jews had occurred in the passage, when it actually had not. Participants made elaborative inferences based on their knowledge of Hitler; these inferences, although sensible, were inaccurate. The sensible inferences that we make while reading are at the root of many of the memory distortions we discussed in Chapter 7.

When Are Inferences Made?   One of the central questions in research on inferences concerns how often they are made and with what degree of effort. Do we make inferences whenever we have the chance, or are they made more selectively and only under certain circumstances? Related to this question is the issue of attention's role. Is forming inferences an automatic, effortless process that occurs in the absence of any conscious strategy? Or is forming inferences a strategic and effortful process?

According to what might be termed the *constructivist view* of text processing, we are constantly making inferences whenever we can, combining our knowledge with the information in the text to form a rather elaborate working model of the text. Text comprehension is characterized as an intelligent and strategic search for meaning (e.g., Graesser, Singer, & Trabasso, 1994). We actively seek to build a relationship between the various elements in the text (the actors, their actions, and other events). Whenever an inference is offered by the elements of a text, that inference is drawn.

The constructivist view contends that the formation of inferences is an active, searching process. In contrast, the *minimalist view,* championed primarily by McKoon and Ratcliff (1992), contends that making inferences is an automatic, memory-driven process that is engaged only under a minimal number of circumstances. Our "default setting" in reading is not to constantly search for and make all of the inferences that are possible. McKoon and Ratcliff make use of the distinction between local and global coherence and claim that inferences are made primarily to maintain local coherence. Therefore, we infer to connect segments of the text that occur in close proximity. We do not regularly make inferences to connect remote ideas. A second circumstance under which inferences are drawn is when information is very familiar or readily available in long-term memory.

McKoon and Ratcliff acknowledge that many inferences are made as a result of motivated strategies on the part of the reader. In other words, the reader who is motivated and has specific goals and strategies in mind will look for connections and find them. Bridget's experience with reading Mary Higgins Clark mystery novels reflects this type of motivation. According to Bridget, the joy of reading a mystery novel is trying to figure out "whodunit." In order to do this, she is motivated to make connections between what she is currently reading and information that was presented earlier in the book—just as Colleen, in the opening story, probably does. As for whether inferences are constantly and automatically made on line, this occurs only in the limited set of circumstances outlined above.

STOP *and* REVIEW !

1. Identify the three levels of discourse representation.
2. What is anaphoric reference?
3. "The movie I decided to rent last night was *Star Wars*." What is the new information?
   a. that a movie was rented
   b. that a movie was rented last night
   c. that I decided to rent a movie
   d. that the movie I rented was *Star Wars*
4. True or false? Elaborative references are needed for coherence.
5. When do we make inferences, according to the constructivist view and the minimalist view?

➤ Discourse refers to linguistic output longer than a sentence and can be represented at three different levels, termed a *surface code,* a *textbase,* and a *situation model.* Coherence is important for discourse comprehension at both a sentence-to-sentence (local) and entire-passage (global) level.

➤ One source of coherence is anaphoric reference, which is when current information makes reference to earlier information. The amount of separation between the anaphor and its antecedent affects coherence. The ability to make anaphoric reference depends on working memory. Frequency of occurrence and first mention influence antecedent accessibility.

➤ Coherence is also aided by the given-new contract, an implicit understanding that new information is being presented in the context of common background (i.e., given) information.

➤ Inferences involve going beyond the information provided in a text. Bridging inferences involve drawing conclusions that tie new material back to older material and are important for maintaining coherence. Elaborative inferences involve drawing conclusions that add to the detail of a text representation but are not necessary for coherence.

➤ According to the constructivist view of inferences, we constantly and automatically draw inferences as we read a text. According to the minimalist view of inferences, inferences are made primarily to preserve local coherence.

Discourse Memory and Representation

Now that we've discussed some of the processes involved in the initial reading and coding of discourse, let's turn to the processes whereby we store it for the long term. You'll note some parallels between the findings and models that we'll discuss and the some of the findings and theories that we discussed in the context of episodic memory (Chapters 6 through 8) and semantic memory (Chapter 9).

Memory for Discourse

Much of the work on discourse comprehension has focused on our memory for connected discourse. As you know from the chapter on memory distortions (Chapter 7), memory is perhaps better characterized as a storyteller rather than as some sort of recording device. Much of the work supporting this conclusion comes from research on memory for discourse. In fact, what may be the most-cited study of memory distortion was actually a study on discourse memory. Consider the following story:

> One night two young men from Egulac went down to the river to hunt seals, and while they were there, it became foggy and calm. Then they heard war-cries, and they thought: "Maybe this is a war-party." They escaped to the shore and hid behind a log. Now canoes came up, and they heard the noise of the paddles, and saw one canoe coming up to them, There were five men in the canoe, and they said:
>
> "What do you think? We wish to take you along. We are going up the river to make war on the people."
>
> One of the young men said: "I have no arrows."
>
> "Arrows are in the canoe," they said.
>
> "I will not go along. I might be killed. My relatives do not know where I have gone. But you," he said, "may go with them."
>
> So one of the young men went, but the other returned home.
>
> And the warriors went on up the river to a town on the other side of Kalama. The people came down to the water, and they began to fight, and many were killed. But presently the young man heard one of the warriors say, "Quick, let us go home: that Indian has been hit." Now he thought: "Oh, they are ghosts." He did not feel sick, but they said he had been shot.
>
> So the canoes went back to Egulac, and the young man went ashore to his house, and made a fire. And he told everybody and said: "Behold I accompanied the ghosts, and we went to fight. Many of our fellows were killed, and many of those who attacked us were killed. They said I was hit, and I did not feel sick."
>
> He told it all, and then he became quiet. When the sun rose he fell down. Something black came out of his mouth. His face became contorted. The people jumped up and cried. He was dead.

Kind of leaves you scratching your head, doesn't it? The story is one that we alluded to in Chapter 1—you'll recall Sir Frederick Bartlett and his classic research on memory. One theme of his research was the reconstructive nature of story memory, and one of his most famous stories was the one you just read, titled "War of the Ghosts." Now that it's been a few seconds since you read it, close your book and try to recall it in as much detail as you can.

Stop *and* Think!   **WAR OF THE INFERENCES**

Go back to your recall of the "War of the Ghosts" story. (Or if you haven't read it and tested your recall of it, do so now.)

1. Try to come up with all of the inferences you made while reading this text.
2. Look at your recall of the story and determine whether any inferences you must have made are apparent in your recall protocol.

Gist versus Verbatim Memory.   You probably found the story pretty difficult to recall, and maybe impossible to recall word for word. So did Bartlett's (1932) participants. De-

Two Indians were out fishing for seals in the Bay of Manapan, when along came five other Indians in a war canoe. They were going fighting.

"Come with us," said the five to the two, "and fight."

"I cannot come," was the answer of the one, "for I have an old mother at home who is dependent on me." The other said he could not come, because he had no arms. "That is no difficulty," the others replied, "for we have plenty in the canoe with us"; so he got into the canoe and went with them.

In a fight soon afterwards this Indian received a mortal wound. Finding that his hour was coming, he cried out that he was about to die. "Nonsense," said one of the others, "you will not die." But he did.

Figure 11.9

One sample recall from Bartlett's (1932) study. Compare it with the original story.

From Bartlett, F. (1932). *Remembering: A study in experimental and social psychology.* New York: Macmillan.

tails that were hard to fathom or that didn't make much sense would be omitted or distorted to be more consistent with participant knowledge. Sensible details that weren't part of the original story were sometimes added. A sample recall of the "War of the Ghosts" passage is given in Figure 11.9. Compare it with your own recall and see if you made the same mistakes as Barlett's participants did approximately 70 years ago. We'll return to Bartlett's study a little later when we discuss models of discourse representation.

Your experience, along with the findings of Bartlett, reflects one of the most time-worn distinctions in discourse memory: gist memory versus verbatim memory. **Gist memory** refers to the basic ideas or main points of a piece of discourse (in Chomskian terms, the deep structure); **verbatim memory** refers to exact wording (in Chomskian terms, the surface structure). Consistent with the picture of memory that emerged in Chapter 7 (where we discussed memory distortions), we're much better at gist recall than we are at verbatim recall. Although we do remember many things verbatim (e.g., songs, poems, prayers), these are the exceptions rather than the rule. Virtually everything we read or hear is almost immediately distilled into its essence, or gist.

The speed with which this occurs was revealed in a classic study by Sachs (1967). She presented participants with a passage about the invention of the telescope:

There is an interesting story about the telescope. In Holland, a man named Lippershey was an eyeglass maker. One day his children were playing with some lenses. They discovered that things seemed very close if two lenses were about a foot apart. Lippershey began experiments and his "spyglass" attracted much attention. *He sent a letter about it to Galileo, the great Italian scientist* (T1). Galileo at once realized the importance of the discovery and set out to build an instrument of his own. He used an old organ pipe with one lens curved out and the other curved in. On the first clear night he pointed the glass towards the sky. He was amazed to find the empty dark spaces filled with brightly gleaming stars! (T2). Night after night Galileo climbed to a high tower, sweeping the sky with his telescope. One night he saw Jupiter, and to his great surprise discovered with it three bright stars, two to the east and one to the west. On the next night, however, all were to the west. A few nights later there were four little stars (T3).

At one of three different points in the passage (marked T1, T2, and T3 above), Sachs assessed readers' memory for the italicized sentence. She did so with a recognition test in

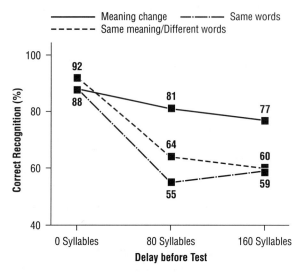

Transition from Verbatim to Gist Memory

Figure 11.10 Results from Sachs's (1967) study of verbatim and gist memory. As more time passed between reading and test, participants were less likely to remember the exact wording of the sentence but still were quite likely to remember the gist of the sentence.

From Sachs, J. (1967). Recognition memory for syntactic and semantic aspects of connected discourse. *Perception and Psychophysics, 2,* 437–442. Reprinted by permission of the Psychonomic Society, Inc.

which she gave one of three types of sentences: the word-for-word target sentence; a transformed version of the sentence that retained the meaning (e.g., "A letter was sent about it to Galileo, the great Italian scientist"); or a sentence that retained some of the words but changed the meaning (e.g., "Galileo, the great Italian scientist, sent him a letter about it"). Participants were to determine whether the test sentence was identical to a sentence from the passage.

The results, presented in Figure 11.10, provide a demonstration of the transition from verbatim to gist memory. (The graph shows the number of correct responses on a recognition test; a correct response could be yes or no, depending on the type of sentence presented.) At T1, immediately after the presentation of the target sentence, participants showed near-perfect discrimination, saying yes to the sentence containing the same words, or no to the sentence that maintained the same meaning but used different words. When recognition of the target sentence was tested later in the passage (at T2 and T3), performance dropped sharply in the conditions where participants had to notice a change in the surface structure (verbatim form) of the sentence. Because the test sentence retained the meaning of the target sentence, the two were difficult to discriminate. But look at the condition where the test sentence changed the meaning of the original sentence; here, participants were not fooled—they realized it was different. This classic finding provides an elegant demonstration of how readers quickly collapse the surface structure of what they read while retaining the deep structure.

Models of Discourse Comprehension

Reading and remembering a selection of discourse require that we form some internal representation. What is the nature of this representation? A number of proposals have been offered to describe how discourse is represented.

Schemas.   One of the most ubiquitous explanations for how we come to understand and remember discourse is based on the notion of schemata, or schemas. Based on his participants' sketchy yet sensible recall of "War of the Ghosts," Bartlett (1932) proposed that recall was based on some generalized form of knowledge representation. A *schema* refers to the general knowledge we possess about some person, place, or event. Schemas make new information easy to assimilate, understand, and remember. For example, your notions about war (guns, fighting, killing) and ghosts (mysterious, magical) may well have guided your encoding and retrieval of "War of the Ghosts."

Four processes are thought to underlie the use of schemas in understanding discourse (Alba & Hasher, 1983). First, the important parts of the incoming message need to be selected and attended. The second stage of schema use is the abstraction of meaning from what we're reading and a disposal of the verbatim details. This process was highlighted in the gist versus verbatim memory study conducted by Sachs (1967). Third, the appropriate schema needs to be activated; recall the "balloon" passage discussed in the section on discourse comprehension. This passage was nearly impossible to understand, because the general knowledge you needed to understand it was inactive. But once you saw the picture depicting the situation, the meaning became clear. Finally, the information taken in and the information activated to comprehend it must be integrated into a single unified representation.

Scripts. A special type of schema is a **script**, which is a generalized knowledge representation of routine activities. Scripts include information about the typical objects, situations, and activities encountered in conjunction with certain activities. Schank and Abelson (1977) propose that the information represented in scripts is essential to our understanding of discourse. Scripts do seem to be psychologically "real." Bower, Black, and Turner (1979) had participants list activities commonly associated with certain situations, such as going to a restaurant or attending a lecture. Their responses showed a striking level of consistency. Just as people tend to mention "apple" when you ask them to give an example of fruit, they tend to say "take notes" when asked for things that happen at a lecture. Scripts have many of the same characteristics as concepts (discussed in Chapter 5), such as prototypical members and graded structure.

According to Schank and Abelson's (1977) original conceptualization of scripts, elements of a story that are irrelevant to the major theme or purpose of a script will not be well-encoded or remembered. Also distracting events—ones that are salient, but not consistent with the theme of a script—should be particularly well-encoded and well-remembered because of their distinctiveness. In accordance with these hypotheses, Bower and colleagues found that participants were unlikely to recall script-irrelevant details (e.g., the color of the waiter's shoes) but were very likely to recall distracting and salient events that stood out from the scripts (e.g., the waiter spilling water on the restaurant guests).

Research also indicates that the use of scripts is an important element in the coherent representation of text. Walker and Yekovich (1987) found that central elements of scripts (such as "taking notes" for attending a lecture) were comprehended faster than were more peripheral elements (such as "falling asleep"), even if the central elements had not been explicitly presented. In other words, when we encounter a script-typical concept, it's much easier to find the antecedent and make the bridging inference that's necessary for coherence.

Although there is no doubt that the notions of schemas and scripts have been an important driving force in research on discourse representation, they have been found wanting by many. The concepts are quite general and vague and really serve more as simple descriptions of the characteristics of discourse comprehension and memory rather than as explanations. Schema- and script-based theories don't provide very precise accounts of how we make inferences or how we connect anaphors to their antecedents.

Stop *and* Think!   **YOU CAN BE A SCRIPTWRITER! (NO, NOT THE HOLLYWOOD KIND)**

Enlist a few friends as subjects and ask them to generate the first five elements that come to mind when they think of the following situations:

going home for the holidays
first day of (college) classes
going to a movie with friends
finals week
graduation

Look over the responses provided, and tally them up.

- What degree of commonality was there in the responses?
- Do these activities seem to have fairly consistent "scripts"?

Story Grammars.   Some researchers (e.g., Mandler, 1987; Rumelhart, 1975; Thorndyke, 1977) took the notion of sentence grammar and applied it to how we encode and understand longer pieces of discourse. Just as sentences have standard elements (e.g., subject, object, etc.), so do stories. Stories have settings, plots, themes, and resolutions; these elements comprise what is termed a **story grammar.** You might think of a story grammar as a schema that represents the developments typically encountered as we read a story (Carroll, 1994). The story-grammar approach to comprehension proposes that we understand stories by parsing them into their components, much like we do sentences. Our representation of discourse consists of episodes that correspond to the important elements of a story (e.g., the beginning, some important development, and a conclusion). The notion that we remember discourse as a series of story-grammar-based episodes has received some empirical support. Episodes seem to be important defining units in our representations of stories. Recall of episodes in a story tends to be all or none, almost as if each episode were encoded as one "chunk" of information (e.g., Glenn, 1978). Also, the length of one episode doesn't seem to affect the ability to remember another episode, suggesting that they're processed as partially independent "chunks."

Although the story-grammar approach has enjoyed some success, it suffers from the same lack of definition that characterizes the schema-based approach. In contrast to the well-defined syntactic components of a sentence (e.g., nouns, verbs, etc.), it's not easy to state definitively what the corresponding components are for stories. Similarly, the notion of an episode is not easy to define precisely. Story grammars and schemas serve as useful descriptions of some of the processes of discourse comprehension but fall short of providing a comprehensive explanation of how we comprehend text.

Propositions: The Construction-Integration Model.   Perhaps the most influential theory of discourse comprehension was proposed by Kintsch and van Dijk (1978) and later revised by Kintsch (1988, 1998). The basic idea underlying the theory is that the major ideas from discourse are encoded and represented as propositions (true or false statements about the relationships between events)—the same kind of propositions we discussed in Chapter 9. Propositional networks (also discussed in Chapter 9) represent the relationships between propositions. According to the Kintsch and van Dijk model, we encode text as a series of propositions. Propositions are expressed primarily in terms of *arguments* and *predicates*. The argument is usually the focus of the proposition, or what the proposition is about. The predicate is the information given about the argument. Some sentences might consist of a single proposition:

> The dog ran.
> Argument: dog   Predicate: run

Or, as is more often the case, a sentence may contain a series of two or more propositions:

> The frightened dog ran from the massive cat.

There are several relationships expressed in this sentence and hence a number of propositions.

> Argument: dog   Predicate: run
> Argument: dog   Predicate: frightened
> Argument: cat   Predicate: massive

Breaking a complex sentence into a series of propositions essentially boils down to a "rewrite" in terms of simple sentences, such as:

> The dog ran.
> The dog was frightened.
> (The dog ran) away from a cat.
> The cat was massive.

Another important point about the propositional encoding of text is that the encoding is hierarchical, with the most important propositions (representing the major theme or events of a text) at the top of the hierarchy and more tangential propositions (representing relatively unimportant details from the text) at the bottom. According to the Kintsch and van Dijk model (and later versions of it—e.g., Kintsch 1988, 1998), as we read discourse, we construct a network of hierarchically related propositions and integrate this network with our world knowledge. The model has been dubbed the **construction-integration model** of comprehension.

The notion of working memory plays an important role in this conceptualization of comprehension. Because of the well-known limits on working memory, we are limited in our ability to consider propositions concurrently as we are reading. Typically, we encode discourse in "cycles" of 6 to 12 propositions. (Note the connection to the "magical number" 7 ± 2 that describes immediate memory span for unrelated items we discussed in Chapter 4.) Given this selectivity, what determines the contents of working memory? The propositions most likely to be held in working memory at any given point are those that are high up in the hierarchy (i.e., the most important, or central, propositions) and those that have occurred recently. When propositions overlap (i.e., working memory load is low), processing of text is relatively easy, because all of the propositions are in working memory concurrently. More stress is placed on the limited capacity of working memory when a proposition does not overlap with its current contents. In these cases, we must search for an earlier antecedent and perhaps make a bridging inference to a distant point in the text; comprehension is more difficult as a result.

A number of research findings support the basic tenets of this approach. For example, Kintsch and Keenan (1973) estimated the time taken to read a passage and found a strong relationship between this measure and the number of propositions in the text. This is to be expected if we encode texts in terms of propositions; working-memory limits would be felt more severely (and reading would slow) as the number of propositions increased. The notion of a propositional hierarchy is also supported by a **levels effect** in discourse memory. This refers to the oft-replicated finding that information from higher levels of a text-representation hierarchy are more likely to be recalled than information from lower levels (e.g., McKoon, 1977; van Dijk & Kintsch, 1983).

The propositional network model has a distinctly bottom-up flavor. According to the propositional approach, we build a text representation based on the data in the text. In contrast, schema-based theories propose that we come to a representation of the text "from the top down," by imposing schematic knowledge on the incoming information. It is important to note, however, the importance of world knowledge in both approaches.

Structure-Building Framework.   A relatively straightforward, yet compelling view of text comprehension has been proposed by Gernsbacher (1991, 1997). She terms her approach the structure-building framework. According to the **structure-building framework,** comprehension is all about building **structures,** or coherent mental representations of the information in the text. Three subprocesses comprise structure building. The first process is termed *laying a foundation* and occurs whenever a new topic is introduced. The fact that readers tend to slow down when taking in the first sentence of a paragraph, even if that sentence isn't the topic sentence, suggests that readers are laying a foundation for later material. This foundation-laying process is driven by what Gernsbacher terms *first mention.* A host of studies have demonstrated that the first participant mentioned in a sentence or passage of text is easier to access later than participants mentioned later. Consider this sentence:

The student asked the professor a question

Verifying that the phrase "the student" occurs in the sentence turns out to be faster than if the actors in the sentence are reversed to read "The professor asked the student a question." In the former case, "the student" serves as the foundation for the representation of that particular sentence. This finding, termed the **advantage of first mention,** holds true for both spoken and written comprehension (e.g., McDonald & MacWhinney, 1995), and also cross-linguistically (e.g., Carreiras, Gernsbacher, & Villa, 1995; Sun, 1997).

The advantage of first mention seems to conflict with another well-established finding in text comprehension, the **advantage of clause recency.** The later a clause is in a sentence, the easier it is to recall (e.g., von Eckardt & Potter, 1985). On closer examination, the two don't really conflict; the advantage of first mention occurs if memory is tested after a bit of a delay. The advantage of clause recency occurs if memory is tested immediately. The idea of first mention and clause recency is another example of the notions of primacy and recency discussed in Chapter 4.

The second process in structure building is *mapping*. Once a foundation has been laid, the comprehender maps on subsequent information. Mapping involves using world knowledge and linguistic knowledge to relate new information to information already encoded. In other words, cues that provide for coherence of a text (e.g., anaphoric reference and inferencing) are used in the process of mapping. If the incoming material is unrelated to the current foundation, then a new structure is begun, and a new foundation laid. This is the third process in the structure-building framework—*shifting*. Shifting also occurs when an overt cue—such as "on the other hand," or "later that same day"—is encountered. The existence of this process is indicated by the finding that cues to a new story episode (i.e., a change in scene) slow down comprehension (Gernsbacher, 1989).

Consider how you might have used these three processes in representing the events of the opening story. First, you've got Colleen studying as a foundation. You map immediately subsequent information onto this foundation, including inferences and anaphoric reference. She's bored with the material, she'd rather be reading something else, and she starts to do so. Then you shifted and started laying a new foundation as a new character, Donna, was introduced. Now Colleen's conversation with Donna becomes the active structure, and so on.

To help accomplish the subprocesses involved in structure building, Gernsbacher (1991, 1997) proposes two general mechanisms: suppression and enhancement. These mechanisms are not unique to language; they're also used in other domains of cognition. *Suppression* involves (in Gernsbacher's words) a "fine-tuning" of the activation of a word's meanings. Recall our discussion of lexical ambiguity in Chapter 10. Evidence indicates that multiple meanings of a word are activated simultaneously, yet the inappropriate ones are quickly weeded out (fine-tuned) and inhibited. This process is guided by suppression. *Enhancement* is the converse of suppression and involves processes that increase the accessibility of information in memory. For example, given the semantic and syntactic constraints of a given sentence, certain concepts become enhanced and more accessible to comprehension and production.

The structure-building approach is an intuitively appealing framework, and it provides an extremely useful basis for analyzing broad aspects of text comprehension. In addition, some of its more specific assumptions have received good empirical support. Later research has attempted to extend the model by investigating individual differences in structure building as well as its neurological substrates (e.g., Robertson et al., 2000).

Stop *and* Think!　　## STRUCTURE BUILDING

As you read, the processes of text comprehension go on with little or no explicit notice. A little reflection might make them more apparent. As you did in the Stop and Think! Analyzing Anaphor, turn back to one installment of the story that begins each chapter and reread it. But this time, try and take note of the processes that comprise structure building.

laying a foundation
mapping
shifting

In reading the text passage that you choose, note the following:

- When do you tend to start a new foundation?

- What factors allow you to map information onto the foundation?
- What factors cause you to shift from one foundation to another?

Metacomprehension

Before we leave the section on discourse, let's look at one final issue—one that's critical to your performance as a student. When you close this book and put it aside for the night (if you can . . . it is a page turner, isn't it?), how will you be able to judge how well you know it? In other words, do you know if you know it? The term **metacomprehension** is used to describe our knowledge about what we do and don't understand from a text we've read. The news isn't good; people have pretty poor metacomprehension skills. Maki (1998) reports that across an extensive series of studies, the correlation between what participants thought they knew from short texts and what they actually did know averaged a meager 0.27. So people aren't very good judges of their own comprehension. The implications for mastering class material are a bit disturbing; feeling like you "really know this stuff" doesn't tell you whether you actually do. Some recent results provide a glimmer of hope. Rawson, Dunlosky, and Thiede (2000) found that simply rereading a text improved metacomprehension accuracy. So if you read and reread your text materials, chances are your metacomprehension is a better predictor than indicated by Maki's findings. Still, Rawson, Dunlosky, and Thiede found the correlation to be only 0.60—a moderate correlation but far from perfect. So beware of overconfidence. Read, reread, and re-reread.

RECURRING RESEARCH THEME
Cognition and Consciousness

Priming of Associations in Text Rereading

In Chapter 6, we went into some detail about implicit memory—remembering events in the absence of conscious awareness. Implicit memory is often reflected in measures of priming—the benefit in performance one enjoys due to a previous encounter with an event. Given that reading often involves later rereading, you might expect that this rereading would reveal a benefit due to the initial encounters with the material. Indeed, there is an increase in speed when we reread material. Incidentally, you may have made a connection to Ebbinghaus's memory research discussed in Chapter 1. Ebbinghaus's measure of memory was savings—the reduction in the number of trials it took to learn a list of words because of prior exposure to the list. When we reread text, savings is indicated by an increase in speed with no loss (perhaps even a gain) in comprehension.

Monti and colleagues (1997) were interested in investigating the possible sources of priming in text rereading. They note four possibilities, two of which involve the global meaning of the text, two of which do not. First, a rereading benefit may derive from the repetition of the global meaning of the text. If it is assumed that people construct a mental representation of the text, then already having a model in place will facilitate the reading of the text on a second pass. A second possible source of rereading benefit is the associations formed between consecutive words. If pairs of consecutive words are associated during reading, the pairs will be read faster the second time around. The third possible source of priming in rereading is individual word repetition; each time a word is encountered, it is processed more quickly. The cumulative effect of this individual word repetition priming is to decrease reading time. Finally, rereading may be faster because of a simple practice effect: the more you read, the faster you get. It doesn't matter whether it's the same words or the same combinations of words.

The study by Monti and colleagues investigated these possibilities using a participant variable; they studied young adults, older adults, and older adults with Alzheimer's disease. A good deal of previous evidence had indicated dissociations between implicit and explicit memory in older adults and Alzheimer's patients. Specifically, while explicit memory is impaired in older adults and quite severely impaired in Alzheimer's patients, performance on a variety of tasks indicates that implicit memory is intact. Extending this to the domain of text processing, Monti and colleagues were interested in whether this preserved implicit memory would extend to the rereading of text and, if so, which of the four sources of priming would turn out to be important.

To find out, the researchers presented a text for reading and rereading in a number of different conditions. In one condition, participants read the same piece of text three times. Rereading in this condition would benefit from all four sources of priming. The global context, word pairs, and individual words could all potentially produce priming, and in addition, a general reading practice effect would be at work. In a second condition, the words of the text were rearranged to disrupt the global structure of the text; however, word pairs were left intact. In this condition, all sources of priming were potentially in play except for priming from the text's global structure. In a third condition, both the global structure and word pairs were disrupted, leaving only the repetition of individual words as a possible source of priming.

The results are presented in Figure 11.11. The separate lines within each panel represent the reading time for the three different participant groups across each of three reading trials. The influence of each priming source is evident from the improvement in reading time from trial 1 to trial 3. One finding of interest is that all groups showed significant improvement over trials; rereading was faster, even for Alzheimer's patients. This fits with the finding of preserved implicit memory in this population. You'll also notice that overall, older adults and Alzheimer's patients were slower readers.

How about the main question regarding the source of priming in text rereading? Monti and colleagues concluded that global structure plays little or no role. Notice that the improvement across trials was no better in the normal text condition than it was in the conditions where the words were rearranged to disrupt the global structure. Thus, global structure doesn't seem to underlie the priming that occurs when we reread text. Between-word associations do lead to an improvement in reading speed. Take a look at the middle panel (same-random, in which word pairs remained intact). Here, the increase in reading speed was just as great as for the condition where the entire text was intact, indicating that between-word associations are an important source of priming in rereading. The far right panel (different-random) shows that even when words were completely scrambled, there was still some small improvement from trials 1 to 3. From this, the researchers concluded that rereading also benefits from the repetition of individual words. Finally, in a second experiment, the investigators demonstrated that some improvement in speed of rereading occurred due to a simple practice effect: reading improves from trial to trial even if none of the material is the same.

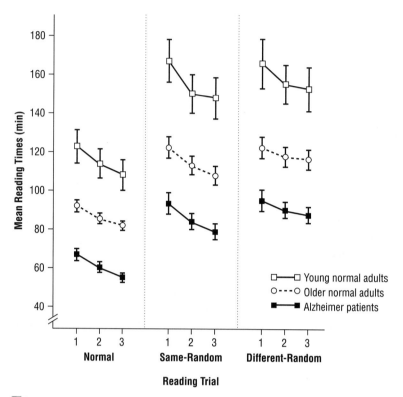

Young normal adults
Older normal adults
Alzheimer patients

Figure 11.11 Results from the Monti et al. (1997) study of priming in text rereading. Note the increase in speed seen when we reread a text, a manifestation of implicit memory. This improvement is apparent in both older adults and Alzheimer's patients.

From Monti, L. A., Gabrieli, J. D. E., Wilson, R. S., Beckett, L. A., Grinnell, E., Lange, K. L., & Reminger, S. L. (1997). Sources of priming in text rereading: Intact implicit memory for new associations in older adults and in patients with Alzheimer's disease. *Psychology and Aging, 12,* 536–547. Copyright 1997 by the American Psychological Association. Reprinted by permission.

In sum, the increase in speed seen when we reread a text can be considered a manifestation of implicit memory and is intact in older adults and Alzheimer's patients. The sources of this priming effect seem to be the associations between words and the repetition of the individual words themselves, along with a general practice effect.

STOP *and* REVIEW!

1. True or false? Gist memory for discourse is much better than verbatim memory.
2. What is a story grammar? How does this view of comprehension relate to the notion of syntax?

3. Which of the following models is supported by a levels effect in discourse memory?
   a. story grammar
   b. construction-integration model
   c. structure-building framework
   d. schemas/scripts
4. List and briefly describe the three processes in discourse representation proposed by the structure-building framework.
5. Identify how metacomprehension skills can be improved.

➤ Memory for the gist of a text tends to be quite good, while memory for verbatim details is quite poor. The transition from a verbatim to gist representation occurs fairly rapidly as a passage is encoded.

➤ The notion of schemas/scripts provides a useful descriptive model of discourse comprehension. Generalized knowledge structures about everyday objects and activities allow for efficient encoding of major ideas from discourse. According to the story-grammar approach, discourse is understood by appealing to "discourse syntax," analogous to sentence syntax.

➤ According to the construction-integration approach, we represent discourse in terms of propositions, or relations between objects and events. Consistent with this view, comprehension of discourse is closely related to the number of propositions in a text. The account is also supported by a levels effect, the finding that higher-level propositions are easier to recall than lower-level ones.

➤ According to the structure-building approach, the representation of discourse involves laying a foundation for new ideas, mapping on subsequent information, and shifting to a new foundation on a change in topic. This approach is supported by the strong influence of first mention and clause recentcy in text comprehension.

➤ Metacomprehension, our knowledge about what we understand from a text we've read, is typically lacking. People aren't good judges of their own comprehension. Rereading texts seems to aid in metacomprehension. Rereading is also associated with increases in speed that are even observed in Alzheimer's patients, an example of preserved implicit memory.

Writing

Having discussed comprehension at the discourse level, you should be able to call on your text comprehension prowess to guess what this next section will be about. If so, *write* a note telling yourself how bright you are.

For all of the voluminous investigations devoted to the processes of language described up to this point, there is comparatively little on an aspect of language that is central to your status as a student (and that is, perhaps, even a thorn in your side)—writing. In fact, many if not most textbooks on cognition don't cover writing at all. Why the lack of attention? A few reasons pop to mind: first, as discussed in Chapter 10, it's much easier to control what people comprehend than it is to control what they produce. Second, writing is an instance of language production that plays itself out over an extended period of time. Think about how you write. Writing is likely to involve processes that extend over days, weeks, even years (as in the case of this textbook)! This makes it a tough empirical nut to crack.

Still, language production in the form of writing is an important window into language, in particular, and cognition, in general. In fact, invoking a concept that you learned about in Chapter 5, Kellogg (1994) considers writing to be a *prototype* of the thinking process. He gives several justifications for this lofty characterization. First, quality writing requires quality thinking. Take it from us (and your instructors)—a poorly written paper indicates that you don't really comprehend the material very well. In addition, Kellogg points out that writing is a tool for thinking; writing about something forces you to find out what you know and don't know about a topic. A final reason that writing might be considered prototypical thinking is that writing involves a great deal of cognitive effort and self-reflection (i.e., metacognition).

Kellogg provides an overview of the writing process. As you read through the upcoming section about the processes involved in writing, you can understand his contention that writing is quintessential thinking. It also appears to be the quintessential use of all of the language processes we've discussed up to this point. You may also be struck by the similarity between writing as language production and the models of speech production discussed in the Chapter 10: both approaches emphasize stages of initial idea generation and formulation (*conceptualizing* in speech and *collecting* in writing), processes whereby ideas are initially produced (*planning and articulating* in speech and *planning and organizing* in writing), and processes of evaluation (*self-monitoring* in speech and *reviewing* in writing).

Collecting and Planning

The initial stage of writing, *collecting,* involves gathering information, be it through books, magazines, newspapers, lectures. And collecting the information isn't enough; the writer must comprehend the information and translate it into mental representations that form the basis for later thinking and writing (Kellogg, 1994). *Planning* describes the processes whereby we figure out how to best reach our goal as a writer, whether it be to entertain, make someone laugh, or get at least a B. During the process of writing, you may find yourself staring straight ahead, not really "doing" anything. These are moments when, Kellogg asserts, planning is taking place. You might also plan by sketching, doodling, or making notes to yourself. Writing an outline is one common device used during the planning process. So Colleen's encouraging remarks to Donna in the opening story have some basis; even when it seems like no progress is made, progress is probably being made.

Translating and Reviewing

Processes of *translation* involve what Chomsky would characterize as a transformation from deep structure (the ideas) to surface structure (the written expression of the ideas). The writer needs to lay down the ideas while implementing correct syntactic and semantic form and following pragmatic rules of expression. Finally, reviewing processes provide for a check on the success of the first three processes (Kellogg, 1994). Has the writer accomplished the goal, and if not, what revisions are necessary to do so?

The processes involved in writing.

Unique to writing (as opposed to generating a spoken sentence) are particular demands of the task environment. Writing takes place under conditions that are sure to affect the nature of the product. According to Kellogg (1994), these factors include the reason for writing, the topic, the intended audience, the deadline, the availability of informational resources, the availability of technology supports (i.e., a word processor), and whether or not you're working with someone else. Each of these factors impacts the product.

Stop and Think!   WRESTLING WITH WRITING

Pick a writing assignment that needs to be completed in the next few weeks and do a bit of introspection on how you approach the project. Try and classify each step in the development of your written project in terms of the stages laid out by Kellogg (1994):

collecting
planning
translating
reviewing

- What specific activities do you engage in during each of these processes?
- Which of these processes takes the most time?
- Which of these stages proves to be the most demanding or difficult?
- Do you give any of the stages "short shrift"?
- Which of the stages are most crucial for producing a satisfactory product?

STOP and REVIEW!

1. Identify the aspects of writing that make it a prototype of thinking.
2. Identify the processes involved in writing.
3. The demands of the task environment include
   a. the intended audience.
   b. the availability of informational resources.
   c. whether or not you're working with someone else.
   d. your ability to use technology.

➤ Writing is a prototype of the thinking process: quality writing requires quality thinking; writing forces you to find out what you know and don't know; writing involves cognitive effort and self-reflection.

➤ The writing process involves collecting, planning, translating, and reviewing.

➤ Unique to writing are the particular demands of the task environment, which include the reason for writing, the topic, the intended audience, the deadline, the availability of informational resources, the availability of technology supports, and whether or not you're working with someone else. Each of these factors impacts the product.

GLOSSARY

acquired dyslexia: dyslexia arising from some type of brain damage (p. 438)

advantage of clause recency: the finding that the later a clause is in a sentence, the easier it is to recall (p. 468)

advantage of first mention: the finding that the first item mentioned in a sentence or passage of text is easier to access than items mentioned later (p. 468)

anaphor: the referring expression in anaphoric reference (p. 454)

anaphoric reference: when a current expression refers to something encountered earlier in the text. (p. 454)

antecedents: the events to which anaphors refer (p. 455)

autonomous view: the idea that the analyses of syntax and semantics proceed independently and in a serial manner (p. 449)

bridging inference (or **backward inference**): a relation constructed to connect two sentences or ideas that are not connected explicitly (p. 458)

Broca's aphasia: a language disorder that tends to feature syntactic difficulties in language production (p. 449)

case-grammar approach: an approach to sentence comprehension emphasizing the assignment of words to various semantic case roles (p. 448)

case roles: specify who is doing what to whom (p. 448)

causal inference: a backward inference whereby someone draws a conclusion about the cause of an event (p. 458)

coherence: the degree to which parts of a text hang together (p. 454)

construction-integration model: a propositional network model of text comprehension that posits that we construct a network of hierarchically related propositions and integrate this network with our world knowledge (p. 467)

deep dyslexia: dyslexia characterized by semantic errors in reading (p. 439)

developmental dyslexia: dyslexia not associated with any obvious brain damage (p. 438)

direct-access view: the view that orthography provides the major route to word recognition (p. 436)

discourse: linguistic output longer than a sentence (p. 453)

dual-route view: the idea that word recognition can proceed by either direct (visual label only) or indirect (visual label plus phonological representation) routes (p. 437)

dyslexia: a condition involving severe reading difficulties, often including difficulties in word recognition (p. 437)

elaborative inferences (or **forward inferences**): the conclusions drawn while reading that are useful but not necessary for coherence (p. 458)

fixations: the brief pauses in eye movements during which the eye takes in information (p. 430)

garden-path approach: a theory of sentence processing that assumes that readers follow a simple, word-by-word path through the sentence, testing one syntactic structure until it's proven wrong (p. 446)

garden-path sentence: a sentence in which the initial interpretation proves to be incorrect (p. 447)

gaze duration: the summed duration of fixations (p. 431)

gazes: consecutive fixations in the same location (p. 431)

gist memory: the memory for the general idea of a text (p. 463)

given information: information known by the reader (p. 456)

given-new contract: implicit "agreement" whereby discourse is assumed to include information already known by the reader (i.e., given information) and information that is assumed to be unknown (i.e., new information) (p. 456)

global structure: the general knowledge we bring to bear on what we're reading (p. 454)

indirect-access (or **phonological**) **view:** the view that word recognition goes through the phonological representation of the word prior to the word's identification (p. 436)

inferences: conclusions drawn by a reader that are not explicitly stated in the discourse (p. 456)

interactionist view: the idea that the analyses of syntax and semantics proceed in parallel and interact (p. 449)

levels effect: the finding that information from higher levels of a text-representation hierarchy are more likely to be recalled than information from lower levels (p. 468)

local structure: the explicit and/or implicit connections between individual sentences (p. 454)

metacomprehension: our knowledge about what we do and don't understand from a text we've read (p. 470)

new information: information previously unknown to the reader (p. 456)

orthography: the physical structure of a written word (p. 436)

parsing: the identification of the component elements of a sentence and their grammatical relation to one another (p. 446)

perceptual span: the amount of text that the eyes can cover effectively to the right of any given fixation (p. 432)

phonics approach: an approach to teaching reading that emphasizes the mapping of sounds to letters (p. 444)

phonological dyslexia: dyslexia associated with a selective inability to read pseudowords (p. 438)

regressive saccades: backward eye movements (p. 432)

saccades: the discrete movements that our eyes make from one point to another when we're reading, taking in a visual scene or searching for an object (p. 430)

saccadic suppression: the fact that, during saccades, we take in little or no information (p. 430)

script: a generalized knowledge representation of a routine activity (p. 465)

situation model: the "world" created by a piece of discourse—a combination of the places, settings, people, and events in the discourse and the background knowledge possessed by the reader (p. 453)

story grammar: a schema that represents the developments typically encountered as we read a story (p. 466)

structure-building framework: the view that text comprehension involves successive building of structures (p. 468)

structures: coherent mental representations of the information in the text (p. 468)

surface code: the precise wording of a passage of discourse (p. 453)

surface dyslexia: dyslexia associated with difficulty with words that have irregular pronunciations (p. 438)

textbase: the major facts and themes of the discourse (p. 453)

whole-language approach: an approach to teaching reading that emphasizes the role of story content and context (and deemphasizes the role of phonics) (p. 444)

whole-word approach: an approach to teaching reading that emphasizes the wholistic apprehension of complete words (p. 444)

verbatim memory: the memory for the exact wording of a text (p. 463)

Wernicke's aphasia: a language disorder that tends to feature semantic difficulties in language production (p. 449)

12

Problem Solving

Donna goes back to her computer station at the back of the library and stares at the computer screen, but nothing comes to her. She sits back in her chair and sighs. The semester seemed really manageable back in September—three psychology classes and a physics class. Only two of the classes require final term papers. What could be easier? Now, on December 5, she glumly wonders if surgery might not be easier.

I can't do this anymore. When am I going to realize I can't do this all-night thing? she asks herself. Trying to avoid studying, she looks at the list of things she has to get done the next day: study for a couple of hours at the library, get gas, pick up some groceries, get a prescription filled, come home, get Fatcat to the vet, be back home by 5:00 and class at 7:00.

She calculates: Let's see, I want to be home by 5:00. That means I have to be out of the vet's by 4:45; I'd better leave myself an hour to get that done, so everything else has to be done by 3:30 or so. And if you add those two other errands, I have to be out of school by 1:00 to get everything done by 5:00. She gives up on writing for the night and heads home.

She wakes up early the next day and, bleary-eyed, makes it through the morning's classes as best she can, banging her head on the desk only once in the six times she falls asleep. Her next class is not until evening, so she decides to take a short nap in the library and then begin her errands.

For the most part, everything proceeds according to plan, with one big exception—the always enjoyable task of getting Fatcat into his carrier. It takes 15 minutes and six cat treats, but finally, he is in. Fatcat puts on his usual performance while in the box—meowing, scratching, pawing—in a vain attempt to ride shotgun.

She makes it home by 5:00, just in time to flick on *The Simpsons*. Afterward, she drifts in and out of another much-needed nap. Suddenly, an idea hits her. *Maybe I can get an extension on the paper—better yet, maybe I can get an extension for the whole class. The professor's a pretty nice guy—he'll probably go for it.* Happy hopeful thoughts fill her head as she dozes off.

Donna has a problem: procrastination and a set of challenging classes have put her in a tough spot. There are only two weeks left in the semester, and she has a lot to do—write two major research papers and study for three final exams. Oh, and we can't forget that she works 30 hours a week and needs to maintain a B average in order to keep her scholarship. Grappling with this complex scenario involves the processes a cognitive psychologist would term *problem solving*.

What Is a Problem?

A **problem** consists of several basic components: an **initial state** (the situation at the beginning of the problem), a **goal state** (the solution to the problem), a set of *rules* (or constraints) that must be followed, and usually, a set of *obstacles* that must be overcome. In the present example, the initial state is Donna, in a panic, staring at a blank computer screen, trying to get a start on her first paper. The goal state is two finished research papers and sterling performance (OK, B-level performance) on three finals, which will result in a happy trip home for semester break. The rules and obstacles are numerous. The research paper topics are difficult, and many of the sources she has found are not in the school's library. She only has two weeks to finish everything. She's working at Walmart, and they just asked her to work extra hours because of the Christmas rush . . . shall we go on? *Problem solving* seems a most apt term.

Well-Defined and Ill-Defined Problems

The problems we face every day, from the morning crossword puzzle to retrieving keys from a locked car, can be classified along a continuum from well-defined to ill-defined. **Well-defined problems** are clear and structured; the initial state, goal state, and constraints are all understood, and once you reach a solution, it's easily assessed. Solving an anagram (unscrambling letters to form a word) is an extremely well-defined problem. Consider the name Vince Goti—one of the characters in our ongoing saga. (You met him in Chapter 1 when he decided to take the day off.) Can you rearrange the letters in his name to form a word? The initial state of this problem is the set of scrambled letters; the goal state is a word; the constraints are to use only the letters provided. Once you arrive at a solution, it's clear whether you're right or wrong. (Did you get it? It's cognitive—aren't we clever?!) In contrast to well-defined problems, an **ill-defined problem** is fuzzy and abstract. One of the term papers Donna has to write is a good example of an ill-defined problem. She's not quite sure where she's starting, where she needs to get to, or what the constraints are. The topic is up to her, the length is up to her, and she's not 100% sure "what the professor wants." In addition, once she's come up with a solution, she's really not sure if it's a good one. She may think the paper is good, but she's not the one grading it. Needless to say, ill-defined problems tend to present more of a challenge to the solver.

Routine and Nonroutine Problems

Problems also vary in terms of how familiar we are with the procedures they involve. A **routine problem** is one that can be solved by applying well-practiced procedures. Consider the task of writing a psychology research paper. For a senior psychology major, this may be a fairly routine problem, consisting of individual tasks that have been performed many times: identifying a topic, searching the library, and organizing the paper. But a first-time psychology student, taking their first course in research methods, would likely find this problem decidedly nonroutine, having never identified a research topic, searched research literature, or organized a research paper. As you might expect, people tend to find more challenge in a **nonroutine problem.**

Consider the relation between how routine a problem is and whether the problem is well- or ill-defined. You might imagine that as the procedures involved in solving problems become more routine, people have an easier time giving the problem some definition. Let's turn back to psychology students. For the senior psychology major, four years of psychology classes have made the procedures involved in writing a research paper increasingly routine. As a result, the student has an easier time conceptualizing and proceeding with the assignment (i.e., the problem is more well-defined). For our beginning student, all of the subtasks involved in writing a research paper are nonroutine. So, this student will have a more difficult time *defining the problem* (i.e., the problem is more ill-defined).

Problem-Solving Research: Some Methodological Challenges

Of all of the cognitive processes discussed throughout this text, problem solving may be the most complex. In many ways, problem solving is the culmination of all of the processes that make up our cognitive arsenal. Completing the assignments faced by Donna requires perception (to take in the problem information), pattern recognition (to recognize words in the paper guidelines and on the final exams), attention and working memory (to hold the information in conscious awareness when necessary), language (to understand the exam items), and decision processes (to decide how to prioritize what has to be done).

As a result of this complexity, problem solving often occurs over a much longer time interval than many of the cognitive processes discussed in the text (such as naming a word

---

One Saturday night at a local country dance, 40 people, 20 men and 20 women showed up to dance. The dance was a "contra dance," in which men and women face each other in lines. From 8:00 to 10:00 P.M. there were 20 heterosexual couples (consisting of one man and one woman each; i.e., two women or two men cannot dance together) dancing on the floor. At 10:00 P.M., however, 2 women left, leaving 38 people to dance. Could the dance caller make arrangements so that the remaining people could all dance together at the same time in 19 heterosexual couples? The dance caller must remain a caller only and cannot take a partner. Answer yes or no, and give the reasoning behind your answer.

Figure 12.1   Can you solve this problem?

From Gick, M. L., & McGarry, S. J. (1992). Learning from mistakes. Inducing analogous solution failures to a source problem produces later successes in analogical transfer. *Journal of Experimental Psychology: Learning, Memory and Cognition, 18,* 623–639. Copyright 1992 by the American Psychological Association. Reprinted by permission.

or remembering a string of digits). The time required to solve a problem presents a challenge to researchers. Often, participants can only be presented with one problem within a reasonable time frame (which precludes the study of many everyday problems!). Therefore, assessing problem solving in terms of accuracy rate (as is the practice in many other domains of cognitive psychology) provides a rather gross estimate of problem-solving proficiency. Measuring solution times provides some useful information but doesn't shed much light on the nature of the processing that occurs during problem solving. Take the country dance problem presented in Figure 12.1; it may take someone a few moments to solve this problem, and the solution is either yes or no, with a brief justification. In reality, almost everyone solves this problem (the correct answer is no), and they would solve it fairly quickly. But the fact that 95% of people solve a given problem in an average of 30 seconds tells us nothing about exactly how the problem was solved.

Verbal Protocols.   In order to gain a window into the processes of problem solving, researchers have made extensive use of verbal protocols. **Verbal protocols** are reports generated by problem solvers as they "think out loud" during the solution process. Verbal protocols might be considered a close cousin of the introspective technique employed in the early days of psychology by the structuralists (discussed in Chapter 1). Recall that the structuralists attempted to gain insight into the components of conscious experience by asking people to introspect and report on a variety of perceptual experiences. Whereas structuralist introspections provided rather static descriptions of the contents of awareness for relatively short and discrete periods of time, verbal protocols attempt to give a more dynamic view of cognitive processing as it occurs over a longer span of time.

As is the case with introspective reports of any type, verbal protocols have a number of potentially serious limitations. First, not everyone has the verbal ability required to reflect accurately on what they're thinking. Second, there is no way to assess the accuracy of a verbal report; indeed, it may be that the most important processes cannot be verbalized at all. Finally, the mere act of thinking out loud may interfere with or change the very nature of the thought processes being described. In the years since introspection was reintroduced as a legitimate means of gathering data about thought processes, debate has raged over its validity. Some (e.g., Nisbett & Wilson, 1977) argue that the interpretational difficulties associated with verbal protocols render them essentially useless as a means of analyzing higher thought processes. Others (e.g., Ericsson & Simon, 1980, 1984) have demonstrated that in most cases, verbalizing cognitive processing has a minimal influence on performance. In spite of their potential problems, verbal protocols have proven valuable to problem-solving researchers, and no doubt their use will continue.

Stop *and* Think!   **THINKING OUT LOUD**

Pick out some everyday problem (like choosing the courses you have to take next semester, or planning out a birthday party) and spend about 15 minutes on solving it. Here's the catch: Think out loud while you're doing it:

1. Collect your own verbal protocol (you might use a tape recorder to record your observations).
2. Observe the sorts of processes your mind seems to go through as you're "talking it out."
3. Reflect on your own protocol and how it demonstrates problem-solving principles.

The Varied Nature of Problems.   The complexity of problem solving presents another challenge to researchers. The term *problem* can apply to a breathtakingly diverse set of circumstances, from solving math problems to writing a term paper to figuring out an alternative route home during rush-hour traffic. Getting problem solving into the cognitive psychology laboratory can be a challenging task indeed. In most studies, researchers use fairly short, discrete, circumscribed sorts of problems—much like the brain teasers and puzzles you see in newspapers, magazines, and puzzle books. This makes the investigation of problem solving more tractable. It is assumed that the basic processes used for these sorts of problems are the same ones we employ when we face complex problems.

Mayer (1992) provides some order to the diversity by distinguishing between five sorts of problems. **Transformation problems** present the solver with a goal state; the solver must find the proper strategies, or "moves," that will eventually transform the initial state into the goal state. **Arrangement problems** involve presentation of all the necessary elements to solve the problem; the solver must figure out how the elements are to be arranged. In **induction problems,** the solver is given a series of exemplars or instances and must figure out the pattern or rule that relates the instances. In **deduction problems,** premises or conditions are given, and the solver must determine whether a conclusion fits these premises. Actually, deduction and induction are forms of everyday reasoning and will be discussed in more depth in Chapter 13. Finally, **divergent problems** require the solver to generate as many solutions as possible to a given problem. It's important to note that many of the complex problems we face every day are actually sets of problems that may involve aspects of any or all of these five problem types. Now that you have read about each of these problem types, examine the problems presented in Figure 12.2. Try to determine the type of problem that each represents.

1. Tower of Hanoi Problem

   The rings must be rearranged so that the pyramid on the far left peg ends up on the far right peg. The following constraints must be observed:

   A larger ring can never be above a smaller one.
   Only one ring can be moved at a time

2. "KIGVIN"
   Rearrange the letters to form another word.

3. Think of as many uses for a brick as you can.

4. "All professors are caring people" and "All caring people are good";
   would you accept the conclusion that "All professors are good"?

5. Take a look at the following number sequence:
   8, 5, 4, 1, 7, 6, 10, 0
   What is the next number in the sequence?

Figure 12.2 Some sample problems from studies of problem solving. Can you identify each type?

1. Transformation 2. Arrangement 3. Divergent 4. Deduction 5. Induction

STOP *and* REVIEW!

1. Which of these problems is the most well-defined?
   a. writing a paper
   b. working a crossword puzzle
   c. figuring out a college major
   d. searching for a house to rent
2. What are verbal protocols, and why are they employed in problem-solving research?
3. True or false? Solving an anagram is an example of a transformation problem.
4. How many ways can a food processor be used to make dinner preparation faster? What type of problem is this?

➤ A problem consists of an initial state (the situation at the beginning of the problem), a goal state (the solution to the problem), a set of rules (or constraints) to follow, and a set of obstacles that must be overcome.

➤ Problems range from well-defined (clear and structured, solution easily assessed) to ill-defined (fuzzy and abstract, solution not easily assessed.) Problems also vary along a continuum from routine (involving well-practiced procedures) to nonroutine (involving less familiar procedures).

> Revealing the nature of problem-solving processes presents a methodological challenge to researchers, due to the time and complexity involved. Reaction time and accuracy are limited in the information they provide about problem solving. Therefore problem-solving researchers often use verbal protocols—verbal reports generated by problem solvers during solution.

> Problem types include transformation problems (solvers must transform the initial state into the goal), arrangement problems (solvers must figure out how presented problem elements are to be arranged), induction (solvers must figure out the rule that relates presented examples), deduction (premises are given and solvers must determine if a conclusion follows), and divergent problems (solvers generate as many solutions as possible to a given problem).

Approaches to the Study of Problem Solving

The study of problem solving has a surprisingly rich and varied history. Believe it or not, some of the earliest work on problem solving was conducted with a veritable menagerie of animal subjects, including rats, cats, monkeys, and those titans of cognition, goldfish (Dewsbury, 2000). In many ways, the evolution of problem-solving research mirrors the evolution of cognitive psychology in general, as outlined in Chapter 1. The key players in the debate over the processes underlying problem solving have been behaviorists, Gestalt psychologists, and information-processing psychologists.

Thorndike and the Behaviorists: Problem Solving as Associative Learning

One of the first systematic studies of problem solving was conducted by E. L. Thorndike in the late 1800s. Thorndike was interested in the basic processes involved in learning. His subjects were cats, which he placed in a predicament that cats most definitely do not enjoy. He put cats in what he termed "puzzle boxes." Basically, these were home-made enclosures; this posed a problem for his feline subjects, because cats hate being enclosed. Phrased in terms of the problem components, the initial state was being in an enclosed space; the goal state was to be outside of the enclosure (just like Fatcat wants to be, in our opening story). The constraint was basically the enclosure itself and the fact that its construction prevented escape. Thorndike was interested in whether the ability to solve this confinement problem would appear suddenly, as an insight, or gradually, through a process of trial and error.

Take a look at Figure 12.3, which shows the puzzle box along with the solution times for a sample cat, graphed over a series of trials. The cats basically learned through trial and error. When first placed in the box, the cats behaved more or less randomly—meowing, scratching, and pawing in a vain attempt to escape their predicament. But as you can see in the figure, over the course of many trials, they eventually figured out how to escape, finally learning the response well enough to quickly escape whenever placed in the situation.

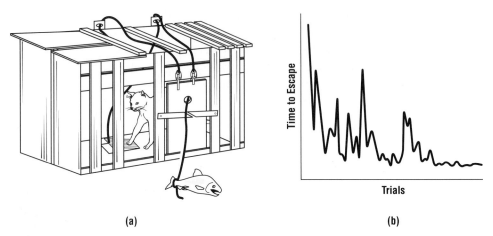

Figure 12.3 A rendition of Thorndike's puzzle box and idealized response data showing trial-and-error learning.

Thorndike described this learning process with what he termed the **law of effect.** According to the law of effect, if a response leads to a satisfying outcome, the connection between the response and the situation in which it took place (in this case, the puzzle box) will be strengthened. If a response leads to a nonsatisfying outcome, this connection will be weakened. Over the course of many experiences in the box, consider what happens. Ineffective responses like crying and scratching will weaken and disappear, while more effective responses that get the cat closer to escape will increase. So eventually, the cat will engage only in those effective responses and quickly exit the box. Behaviorists believe that contrary to what you might think intuitively, problem solving is essentially a "mindless" process whereby learned responses automatically play themselves out. As you might recall from Chapter 1, this stimulus-response account is preferred by behaviorists as an account for all varieties of behavior, not just problem solving.

Kohler and the Gestalt Psychologists: Problem Solving as Insight

Gestalt psychologists have a radically different (and decidedly more cognitive) view of problem solving. Recall from Chapter 1 the basic tenets of the Gestalt approach: the mind has an inherent tendency to organize incoming information, and these organizational processes are the defining feature of cognition. So, rather than a mindless playing out of associations that gradually build up over time, problem solving involves a restructuring or reorganization of problem elements that results in a sudden realization of the solution.

Consider the work of the pioneering Gestalt psychologist Wolfgang Kohler, who conducted extensive investigations of problem solving in apes (Kohler, 1925). In one task, an ape was put in a pen with some crates, and something desirable (like a banana) was suspended from the ceiling, just out of reach. The solution to this problem was to drag the crates over and use them as steps to reach the banana. What interested Kohler was the manner in which apes seemed to be solving this problem (and other ones like it). Contrary to the gradual trial-and-error process observed by Thorndike, Kohler noticed that apes sat for a while as if they were pondering the problem; then all of a sudden they would jump up, push the crates to the appropriate spot, stack them, and fetch their treat. What led to this sudden solution? For Gestalt psychologists, problem solving involves a process of restructuring whereby problem elements are suddenly reorganized and seen in a new way. The sudden and successful restructuring of problem elements is termed **insight,** and this is a major focus of the Gestalt approach.

Contrasting the Behaviorist and Gestalt Views.   The Gestalt approach characterizes problem solving as a process of apprehending relationships between problem elements, and failures in problem solving as failures to correctly or completely encode these relationships. This view contrasts sharply with the behaviorist characterization of problem solving as the mindless execution of a well-learned response. A behaviorist would have explained the apes' behavior as a series of simple responses learned through association. Over the course of many experiences in acquiring food that was difficult to attain, the apes formed a dominant response of stacking and standing on objects in order to do so, much as Thorndike's cats learned appropriate escape responses after many trials of confinement.

Both the behaviorist and Gestalt approaches to problem solving are compelling in some ways but deficient in others. The appeal of the behaviorist approach is its precision and simplicity. Many seemingly complex behaviors can be characterized as sets of simple responses that are based on a straightforward association mechanism. But as discussed in Chapter 1, the behaviorists are limited in what they could explain via a simple stimulus-response (S-R) association mechanism. This analysis seems to apply fairly well to the behavior of Thorndike's cats but fails to explain more novel and creative behavior. The Gestalt approach has the converse set of strengths and limitations. To its credit, it attempts to explain novel and creative behavior in terms of mental representations, but to its detriment, it is imprecise and vague. Gestalt psychologists have never provided really satisfactory (i.e., testable) definitions for concepts like "insight" and "restructuring of problem elements."

Let's finish our evaluation of these two approaches by applying them to Donna's problem. She has to fit writing two research papers and studying for three final exams into the space of two weeks. It's hard to imagine her solution to this problem as the triggering of a series of associations that have been built up through experience. Behavior in this situation is much too complex and unpredictable to be adequately explained in such simple terms. But it's also hard to imagine that Donna sits in her room and then all of a sudden, in a burst of insight, exclaims, "I know exactly how to successfully write two papers and ace three exams!" It seems like what's needed is a view that has the precision of behaviorism but that also allows for novel and creative solutions to problems. In the 1950s, the information-processing approach emerged as the dominant paradigm for explaining problem solving.

Newell, Simon, and the Cognitive Psychologists: Problem Solving as Information Processing

You'll recall from Chapter 1 that one of the major factors in the emergence of cognitive psychology was the development of the computer, which served notice that intelligent behavior (of a sort) was not the exclusive province of human beings. Early cognitive psychologists (e.g. Newell, Shaw, & Simon, 1958) felt that computer programs might serve as useful tools for modeling human problem solving. Just as a computer solves problems by executing programs using information stored in some type of database, humans solve problems by applying mental processes to representations in memory. So, if you design a computer program that can solve a reasoning problem, you've essentially proposed a possible theory for how humans do the same.

The General Problem Solver.   Newell and Simon (1972) originated the conceptualization of problem solving as a step-by-step progression from an initial state to a goal state. They did so within the framework of a computer program termed the **General Problem Solver (GPS),** which they proposed as a general model of human problem solving—one that can be applied to any problem. Basically, the GPS approach to problem solving attempts to minimize the "distance" between an initial state and a goal state by breaking the problem down into a series of subgoals. This **subgoal analysis** is accomplished through the application of **operators,** which is basically a fancy word for problem-solving techniques. These techniques are applied (at a microlevel) to reduce the difference between the current state and the current subgoal state and (at a macrolevel) to reduce the difference between the initial state and the final goal state. Figure 12.4 lists a possible set of subgoals for Donna's end-of-semester problem. Another important aspect of GPS is the notion of problem space. **Problem space** basically refers to the problem solver's mental representation of the initial state, the goal state, all possible intermediate (subgoal) states, and the operators that can be applied to reach these subgoals. Hence, the problem-solving process is essentially an excursion through problem space.

We'll be referring back to certain aspects of this conceptualization of problem solving later, but for now, note the features that define GPS as an information-processing model. First, information in the external world (e.g., the problem information) is transformed into an internal (mental) representation. Then, in a sequential fashion, various mental operations are applied to this representation to transform it into other representations that are closer and closer to the goal state. This general information-processing framework has served as the model for modern problem-solving research. Given this, it should come as no surprise that problem solving is usually characterized as a steplike progression

---

Subgoal 1

Study for cognitive psych exam (read the book, outline notes, meet with study group)

Subgoal 2

Study for physics exam (read the book, meet with prof to discuss unclear points, highlight important passages in reading)

Subgoal 3

Finalize paper topic for psychology (check with prof about topic, go to library, see if there are enough relevant resources)

Figure 12.4   A set of subgoals that one might attempt to reach for the end-of-semester problem (along with nested subgoals).

Wallas	Bransford & Franks	Polya
Preparation	Identify the problem.	Understand the problem.
Incubation	Define the problem correctly.	Devise a plan.
Illumination	Explore your options.	Carry out the plan.
Verification	Act on the chosen strategy. Look back and evaluate.	

Table 12.1 A Sampling of the Stages Involved in Problem Solving

through a series of stages. Table 12.1 lists three such characterizations by different researchers (e.g., Bransford & Stein, 1993; Polya, 1957; Wallas, 1926). From these, a pretty standard picture emerges. Problem solving involves an initial phase in which the problem is defined and a representation formed. Then, the problem solver embarks on a process of generating and testing possible solutions.

STOP *and* REVIEW!

1. Which of these concepts would a behaviorist *not* make reference to in explaining problem solving?
   a. responses
   b. behavior
   c. insight
   d. learning
2. True or false? Insight involves the restructuring of problem elements.
3. What is the the information-processing approach to problem solving?

➤ Behaviorists view problem solving as a learning process that can be described in terms of the law of effect. That is, if a response leads to a satisfying outcome, the connection between the response and the situation will be strengthened; if a response leads to a non-satisfying outcome, this connection will be weakened. Problem solving is viewed as the formation of increasingly complex chains of stimulus-response connections.

➤ Gestalt psychologists view problem solving as a process whereby the elements of a problem must be restructured. Often, problem restructuring results in a sudden insight regarding problem solution.

➤ The information-processing approach views problem solving as a stagelike progression from starting state to goal state. One of the first attempts to model this process was within the framework of a computer program termed General Problem Solver. GPS posits problem solving as successive reductions in "distance" between an initial state and a goal state by breaking a problem down into a series of subgoals (subgoal analysis)—in other words, as an excursion through problem space.

Problem Representation

As stated above, problem solving involves a process of converting presented information into some type of internal mental representation. Within the framework of GPS, **problem representation** involves correctly specifying the problem space—in other words, correctly identifying the initial state as well as the operators that may be applied within the constraints of the problem. The process of problem representation may seem automatic or trivial in some respects, but it is a critical component of successful problem solving. And the ways in which problems can be represented are as varied as problems themselves. Let's look at a few examples. As you read each one, try and solve it, taking note of the particular manner in which you represent the problem.

1. Once there was a monk who lived in a monastery at the foot of a mountain. Every year, the monk made a pilgrimage to the top of a mountain to fast and pray. He would start out on the mountain path at 6 A.M., climbing and resting as the spirit struck him, but making sure that he reached the shrine at exactly 6 P.M. that evening. He then prayed and fasted all night. At exactly 6 A.M. the next day, he began to descend the mountain path, resting here and there along the way, but making sure that he reached his monastery by 6 P.M. of that day. Prove that there must be a spot along the path that the monk will pass at exactly the same time on the two days.

2. A man bought a white horse for $60 and then sold it for $70. Then he bought it back for $80 and sold it for $90. What was his net gain (or net loss) in the horse business?

Clearly, these two problems would lead the problem solver to form different problem representations. The problem about the monk (based on Duncker, 1945) leads the problem solver to form a visual representation of the monk ascending and descending the mountain. The horse-trading problem leads the problem solver to form an arithmetic representation, since the solver must add and subtract the appropriate numbers to come up with a solution. Not only will these problems lead to different representations, but the ability to solve the problems depends critically on the exact nature of the representation. Take the monk problem: one possible representation is to form two separate visualizations—one of the monk ascending and another of him descending. A much more effective representation is to imagine these two excursions superimposed; it immediately becomes apparent that there must be a point of intersection. This point would be the critical spot in the path (see Figure 12.5).

The horse-trading problem was used in a study by Maier and Burke (1967), who found that less than 40% of participants could successfully solve it. Did you? The answer

Figure 12.5 The monk problem proves to be much more manageable when represented appropriately. Visualization makes it apparent that the ascent up the mountain and the descent down the mountain must intersect at some point.

is $20. The key to an easy solution, once again, is problem representation. Consider this similar problem:

> A man bought a white horse for $60 and then sold it for $70. Then he bought a black horse for $80 and sold it for $90. What was his net gain (or net loss) in the horse business?

This problem seems similar to problem 2 above. But it's not just similar; it's pretty much identical. When presented this way, as two separate transactions involving different horses instead of a continuous pair of transactions involving the same horse, everyone gets the solution. Clearly, the manner in which the problem solver mentally "sets up" the problem has powerful implications for whether it is solved.

R E C U R R I N G   R E S E A R C H   T H E M E
Cognition and Individual Differences

Stereotype Threat Can Hinder Problem Representation

"Here's a math word problem." Does this statement make the hair on the back of your neck stand up? Most of us have been plagued by word problems throughout our school years. In order to solve these problems you must represent the problem in proper mathematical form. This, as we all know, seems an impossible task at times. Consider this comment from a fellow sufferer: "I have no idea how to set up a formula for this. I really don't know what to do with this one."

This person obviously is having difficulty with problem representation. What factors contribute to such difficulty? Limitations in mathematical knowledge and/or ability, you might be thinking. Does it change your view to know that this comment comes from a female problem solver? Aha, you may think, that's it—women aren't very good at math, right? Well, yes, according to a common cultural stereotype, though the real story is infinitely more complex than that. A woman's belief in this stereotype can interfere with her ability to devise a strategy to represent a mathematical problem properly and, consequently, her ability to solve it. Surprisingly (and troublingly), the comment above came from a woman with a strong mathematical background who participated in a study on the effects of stereotype threat on mathematical problem solving.

Quinn and Spencer (2001) were interested in why women who have strong math skills underperform in comparison to their male peers. They believed that the answer resides in the interaction between the cultural stereotype about women's math ability and the testing situation. This interaction creates **stereotype threat.** Stereotype threat occurs when a member of a negatively stereotyped group feels that the stereotype might be used to judge their behavior, thus resulting in a negative judgment that will propagate the stereotype. Take the woman who made the above comment, reflecting her difficulty or frustration when confronting a math problem. She may feel that the difficulty she's having will be used by others to validate and perpetuate the stereotype that women aren't good at math. The anxiety created by this apprehension may interfere with her ability to accurately represent the problem, and her performance will suffer, not because as a woman she is inherently inferior in math, but because of a self-fulfilling prophecy driven by this stereotype.

In order to test this idea, Quinn and Spencer (2001) had men and women solve either math word problems or numeric/algebraic equivalents of the word problems. A sample problem is presented in Figure 12.6. The mathematical knowledge necessary to answer these problems

Word problem: A sporting goods store sold 64 Frisbees in one week, some for $3.00 and the rest for $4.00 each. If receipts from Frisbee sales for the week totaled $204, what is the fewest number of $4.00 Frisbees that could have been sold?

Numeric/algebraic equivalent: $3(64 - x) + 4(x) = 204$

$x =$

(a) 24   (b) 12   (c) 8   (d) 4   (e) 2

Figure 12.6   Sample problem used by Quinn and Spencer (2001) in both word and numeric/algebraic form.

From Quinn, D. M., & Spencer, S. J. (2001). The interference of stereotype threat with women's generation of mathematical problem-solving strategies. *Journal of Social Issues, 57,* 55–71. Copyright 2001 by Blackwell, Inc. Reprinted by permission.

was equivalent in both conditions; however, the word problem condition required participants to transform the problem into its proper mathematical representation. The results are presented in the top panel of Table 12.2. Men outperformed women on word problems only; on the more straightforward numeric/algebraic problems, men and women did not differ. Apparently, women had the mathematical ability to solve the problem but ran into interference in conditions that required an involved stage of problem representation. Quinn and Spencer assumed this interference was produced by stereotype threat.

In order to test this assumption, the authors manipulated the level of stereotype threat in the situation. Participants in a low-stereotype-threat condition were told that the test had been shown previously to be gender fair, yielding equivalent performance between men and women. Participants in the high-threat conditions were not given this information. The results are presented in the middle panel of Table 12.2. In the high-stereotype-threat condition, men outperformed women; in the low-stereotype-threat condition, there were no sex-related differences.

In order to determine if the deficits found were really due to difficulties in problem representation, participants in the second experiment were recorded while solving the problems. (Remember the verbal protocol procedure we discussed earlier?) The number of problems in which participants could not determine a strategy (i.e., proper problem representation) to solve the problem (i.e., a "failure rate") was assessed. The results are presented in the bottom panel of Table 12.2. In the high-stereotype-threat condition, females had higher failure rates than males. In the low-threat condition, these failure rates were equivalent. It appears that when stereotype threat is reduced, women

Table 12.2   **Results from Quinn and Spencer (2001)**

		Problem Type	
Correct Solutions (%)		**Word**	**Numeric**
Gender	Female	8	38
	Male	20	40

		Stereotype Threat	
Correct Solutions (%)		**High**	**Low**
Gender	Female	26	39
	Male	45	34

		Stereotype Threat	
Failures (%)		**High**	**Low**
Gender	Female	14	4
	Male	2	9

Note: stereotype threat is associated with a lower likelihood of problem solution.

From Quinn, D. M., & Spencer, S. J. (2001). The interference of stereotype threat with women's generation of mathematical problem-solving strategies. *Journal of Social Issues, 57,* 55–71. Copyright 2001 by Blackwell, Inc. Reprinted by permission.

perform equally as well as men, quite possibly because an obstacle to successful problem representation has been removed.

While the gap between male and female performance on math may be closing (Cole, 1997), the cultural stereotype about women's inferior math skills remains, and women must battle it continually. This battle is hard enough to win in the classroom, but under stressful standardized testing situations like the Graduate Record Exam (GRE), the effects of this stereotype may be even more damaging. As Quinn and Spencer (2001) conclude, if teachers and educators were sensitive to

> the subtle ways they may shape math situations for girls and women, then we believe even greater changes could be made in women's attitudes toward math and their math performance . . . [and] one day break the ugly cycle of the stereotype leading to poor performance and the poor performance in turn feeding the stereotype. (p. 69)

Rigidity in Representation

The initial representation of a problem is critical in its eventual solution. Failure in representation might result from a number of factors: the problem elements may not have received sufficient attention; the problem elements may not have been understood; or previous experience with similar problems may have led you to encode the problem elements in a rigid manner. Let's consider the following induction problem previously presented in Figure 12.2.

Take a look at the following number sequence: 8, 5, 4, 1, 7, 6, 10, 0. Now, attempt to figure out the rule that generated the sequence. This challenging problem is not what it seems to be. In an attempt to identify some pattern in these differences, you no doubt attempted to calculate the difference between each consecutive pair of numbers in this way: "Let's see, 8 and 5 differ by 3, 5 and 4 differ by 1, 4 and 1 differ by 3 . . . " If you followed this line of reasoning, you could add and subtract all day and still not come up with the correct solution. The key to the problem lies in viewing the numbers as words rather than numerical values. Does this hint help? The numbers in the sequence are arranged alphabetically. However, given that in your experience, most number sequences are arranged numerically, not alphabetically, you no doubt struggled quite a bit with this problem.

Mental Set.   This tendency to rely on habits and procedures used in the past is termed **mental set.** A mental set can interfere with your ability to solve everyday problems. An anecdote from our life provides an (embarrassing for Bridget) example of mental set. We drove to a restaurant for dinner, and Bridget was delayed in exiting the car because she was looking for something in her purse. Greg, unaware of this, locked the door with the remote control. After finding what she needed, Bridget attempted to unlock the car with her automatic lock control, but with no success. So she sat there, unable to figure out how to get out of the car. After letting her wait long enough to maximize his own amusement, Greg pointed to the lock and motioned for her to lift it. Bridget had used the automatic locking control so regularly that it had become the only option in her mind—reflecting her mental set.

Mental set tends to affect the representation phase of problem solving, as past experience leads to an inappropriate representation of the problem. For Bridget, her past experience with the car led her to represent the problem of unlocking the car in only one way (with the automatic lock control). In the number sequence problem, your tendency to view digits numerically instead of in terms of verbal labels most likely prevented you from solving the problem. Consider if the problem had been presented in this way: eight, five, four, one, seven, six, ten, zero. Chances are, the correct solution may have come to you more easily. As we can see, people seem to make unnecessary assumptions or follow habits acquired through past experience that impede the problem-solving process.

Perhaps the best-known research paradigm for investigating mental set is the water jar problems developed by Luchins (1942). These problems require that the solver measure certain (goal) amounts of liquid by filling and emptying jars of various volumes (see Figure 12.7). For example, suppose jar A holds 10 units, jar B holds 35 units, and jar C holds 4 units. If you are given a goal amount of 17 units, you could reach this goal using the following steps: fill jar B; then, fill jar A from jar B; this leaves 25 units in jar B. Then, fill jar C twice from jar B; this will leave 17 units in B. In one condition, Luchins presented one group with five problems that could all be solved with this formula (B-A-2C). In the other condition, another group was given five problems that did not have the B-A-2C solution. Both groups received the same sixth problem in which jar A holds 23 units, jar B holds 49 units, and jar C holds 3 units. The goal is to measure out 20 units. In this situation, solvers who had seen the B-A-2C rule five times continued to apply it, even though it was unnecessarily difficult; this problem could be solved with a simple A-C. Solvers with

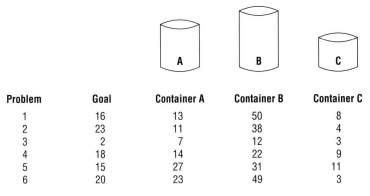

Problem	Goal	Container A	Container B	Container C
1	16	13	50	8
2	23	11	38	4
3	2	7	12	3
4	18	14	22	9
5	15	27	31	11
6	20	23	49	3

Figure 12.7 The Luchins water jar problems. Using the specified volumes of containers A, B, and C, the task is to measure out the goal amount. For example, in problem 1, you would fill up A, pour from A into B twice, and pour from A into C once. This would leave the desired amount in container A. How would you arrive at the remaining goal amounts?

From Luchins, A. M. (1942). Mechanization in problem solving—the effect of Einstellung. *Psychological Monographs, 54,* 95.

no previous experience with the B-A-2C solution saw this solution immediately. The conclusion: previous experience with a particular approach to problems can blind the solver to other alternatives.

Functional Fixedness.   Take a look at one of the classics of problem-solving research presented in Figure 12.8—Duncker's candle problem. This problem provides a nice example of a close cousin of mental set termed **functional fixedness.** Functional fixedness refers to people's tendency to view objects in a narrow, fixed sense—that is, in terms of the typical functions of the object. In his classic experiment, Duncker presented participants with a number of objects, including the following critical materials: some matches, tacks, two small boxes, and two candles. The problem was to attach the candles to the wall and light them.

In order to influence the solvers' problem representations, Duncker presented the materials in one of three conditions. In the functional fixedness condition, the boxes were each filled with one of the three critical materials: candles, matches, and tacks. In the first control condition, the boxes sat empty, alongside the other materials. In a second control condition, the boxes contained materials not critical to the solution, like buttons. The correct solution is to tack the boxes to the wall and use them as candleholders, placing a candle in each box, which can then be safely lit. The key to solving this problem is to view the boxes as boxes, not as boxes of matches, tacks, or candles. Note that this is an issue of problem representation. In the first control condition, all of the subjects successfully solved the problem. But in the first and second control conditions (in which the boxes were narrowly perceived as containers for the objects they were holding), less than one-third of the participants successfully solved the problem.

Stop *and* Think!   **MENTAL RUTS**

Try and think of times when you were absolutely stuck on some type of problem.

1. Describe the circumstances.
2. Note how you were able to overcome whatever obstacle(s) blocked your way.
3. Classify your examples as (1) mental set or (2) functional fixedness.

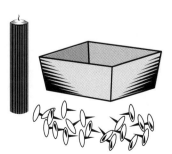

Figure 12.8 Two conditions of Duncker's candle problem. How would you attach the candle to the wall so that it burns properly?

From Duncker, K. (1945). On problem solving. *Psychological Monographs, 58,* 1–112.

Thinking of things in the same old way is not always a bad thing. As noted by Bransford and Stein (1993), most situations in life require that we think conventionally as opposed to nonconventionally. Conventional, everyday thinking (because it tends to rely on processes that have become automatic, as discussed in Chapter 4) tends to be quicker and requires less conscious effort, allowing us to do other things at the same time. The best-case scenario for effective problem solving may be to balance conventional and nonconventional thinking, sticking with the basics unless the circumstances demand a more creative solution.

STOP *and* REVIEW!

1. Which of the following is not involved in problem representation?
   a. correctly identifying the initial state
   b. correctly identifying the operators
   c. correctly identifying the subgoals
   d. correctly identifying the constraints of the problem
2. Define mental set and functional fixedness.
3. True or false? Thinking of things in "the same old way" is always detrimental to the problem-solving process.

➤ Problem representation involves correctly identifying the initial state as well as the operators that may be applied within the constraints of the problem. The initial problem representation is critical in the eventual solution to a problem. Failure to represent a problem correctly is likely to hinder finding a solution.

➤ Rigidity in the representation phase can be seen in cases of mental set (the tendency to rely on habits and procedures used in the past) and functional fixedness (the tendency to view objects in terms of the typical functions of the object). Problem representation can also be hindered by social and personal factors, such as stereotype threat.

➤ Thinking of things in a typical way is often advantageous. Such automatic processing tends to be quick and efficient. Effective problem solving involves a balance of conventional and nonconventional thinking.

Problem Solution

Once a problem has been successfully transformed from externally presented information into an internal representation, the next phase of the problem-solving process involves searching for, testing, and evaluating problem solutions. Within the context of Newell and Simon's (1972) information-processing approach, problem solution amounts to traveling through the problem space. Two general approaches to this excursion are through algorithms or heuristics; each approach has different implications for exactly how the problem space is traversed.

Algorithms

An **algorithm** is basically a set of rules that can be applied systematically to solve certain sorts of problems. A mathematical formula is a good example of an algorithm. Suppose I were to tell you that the two shorter sides of a right triangle had lengths of 3" and 4". You could easily apply a well-known algorithm (the Pythagorean theorem) to calculate the length of the hypotenuse (5"). Algorithms are very powerful problem-solving techniques; applied correctly, an algorithm will always lead to the correct solution, if one exists. But it's not a perfect world; algorithms are seldom if ever used to solve problems on a day-to-day basis.

For human problem solvers, algorithms are often unfeasible, for a couple of reasons. The Pythagorean theorem is easy enough to apply, but consider a more difficult problem. Suppose someone asked you to solve the word anagram *kigvin* (an arrangement problem previously presented in Figure 12.2). You could solve this problem algorithmically by systematically working through every possible letter combination, but you would have to consider hundreds of possibilities. Think of it in terms of problem space; obviously, hundreds of possible sequences comprise this extremely large problem space. The exhaustive nature of algorithms makes them overly tedious and quite impractical, at least for humans. On the other hand, computers are well-suited to algorithmic problem solving because they are well-suited for what algorithms require: speed, power, and reliable application. A second factor that limits the usefulness of algorithms is that there simply aren't any for most of the problems we face on a daily basis. Alas, life is not a right triangle. There is no algorithm for deciding on a college major or a career, for figuring out how to complete two papers and study for three finals over the space of two weeks, or for deciding how to be happy in life. These very complex and ill-defined problems demand a more flexible, dynamic approach.

Heuristics

Given the strengths (flexibility) and limitations (computing power) of the human problem solver, along with the fact that most problems are ill-defined and have relatively large problem spaces, heuristic problem solving is much more effective. **Heuristics** are general

Heuristics come in handy when playing games.

strategies or rules of thumb that can be applied to various problems. Heuristics serve as "shortcuts" through problem space. Take another look at the anagram *kigvin*. Immediately, you reject certain possibilities because of your morphological knowledge of the English language. For example, no English words start with *gk* or *vg* or *ikn,* so these would not be explicitly considered. While the algorithmic approach entails the consideration of every possible solution, the strength of the heuristic approach is that the trip through problem space is faster; the solutions come more quickly. But unlike algorithms, heuristics do not guarantee a correct solution. (By the way, the solution is *viking.*)

Specific heuristics exist for specific problem domains. One of our favorite card games is euchre, the object of which is to win tricks by playing high, or trump, cards. When dealt a hand in euchre (or any card game, for that matter), you certainly can't consider every possible play of the cards in preparation for your bid (although it seems like some people do!). Instead, you do a quick heuristic evaluation of your hand. If you have at least two cards that are pretty certain to win a trick, then a bid is a good risk. In addition to the heuristics that apply to specific situations, there are a number of general-purpose heuristics that can be applied to a wide array of problems.

Stop *and* Think!   ## YOUR OWN HEURISTICS

Consider the personal problem solving you do everyday.

- Are there any everyday problems for which you use algorithms?
- What types of problems do these tend to be?

You no doubt use heuristics a great deal.

1. Generate a list of strategies, or shortcuts, you use to solve everyday problems.
2. List the heuristics you use in your favorite game or sport to make it more likely you'll succeed.

Working Backward.   One effective strategy for solving some problems is to focus on the goal state and work backward in order to map out the steps that would get you there. This is exactly the strategy that Donna took in our opening story. She started with her goal (home by 5:00) and worked backward in time to figure out when each errand needed to be finished. **Working backward** aids problem solving by imposing constraints on what may be a difficult-to-define problem.

Means-End Analysis.   The General Problem Solver developed by Newell and Simon utilizes the heuristic known as means-end analysis. **Means-end analysis** involves breaking a problem down into smaller subgoals, where accomplishing each subgoal moves the solver closer to the final goal—the problem's solution. As the term *means-end analysis* implies, the solver systematically attempts to devise means to get to each of the subgoals' ends. Means-end analysis can be an effective way to solve a transformation problem, which involves moving from the initial state to the goal state through a series of transformations. For example, Donna's problem of two papers and three final exams isn't going to be solved overnight. It's only going to be manageable if she breaks it up into a series of subgoals and systematically accomplishes each. As she does, she will slowly but surely reach her goal.

Stop *and* Think! ## MAKING BIG PROBLEMS INTO LITTLE ONES

As you read, one pretty effective problem-solving heuristic is means-end analysis, which essentially amounts to breaking a problem down into smaller parts. Consider these everyday problems:

finding a job
finding an apartment
planning a spring break trip
raising a child
planning a wedding
deciding what to do on the weekend

For each of these problems,

1. Try to break the general goal down into a series of subgoals.
2. See if you can break these subgoals down into still smaller subgoals.

Analogies. Before you read on, take a look at the mutilated checkerboard problem described in Figure 12.9 and try to come up with a solution. Did you solve it? Chances are, you didn't; this is a fairly difficult problem. Did the problem ring any bells? Remind you of anything else in the chapter? It turns out that this problem is analogous to the country dance problem discussed earlier and presented in Figure 12.1. As in that problem, the key to the solution lies in realizing that it is going to be impossible to pair off each of the black-and-white combinations of the checkerboard if two squares of the same color are removed, just as it is impossible to form man-woman dance partnerings if there is not an equal number of men and women.

The connection between these problems is an example of an analogic relationship. **Analogies**—using problems that have already been solved as aids for representing and solving the problem currently being faced—is potentially one of the most powerful heuristics. Have you ever said, "Hey, this is just like the time when . . . "? If so, you've been thinking in terms of an analogy. The use of analogies in problem solving has been investigated extensively by problem-solving researchers (much more than any of the other heuristics), and the news isn't too good. Research indicates that problem solvers are unlikely to use analogies to aid in problem solving unless they are practically "hit over the head" with the connections between problems. This is why you may not have realized the connection between the mutilated checkerboard and country dance problems. But, as you'll see, there are conditions that encourage the successful application of analogies.

You are given a checkerboard and 32 dominoes. Each domino covers adjacent squares on the board. Thus, 32 dominoes can cover all 64 squares of the checkerboard. Now suppose two squares are cut off at diagonally opposite corners of the board. If possible, show how you would place 31 dominoes on the board so that all 62 of the remaining squares are covered. If you think it is impossible, give a proof of why.

Figure 12.9 The mutilated checkerboard problem.

From Wickelgren, W. A. (1974). *How to solve problems.* New York: Freeman. Copyright 1974 by W. H. Freeman and Company. Reprinted by permission.

Suppose you are a doctor faced with a patient who has a malignant tumor in his stomach. It is impossible to operate on the tumor, but unless the tumor is destroyed, the patient will die. There is a kind of ray that can be used to destroy the tumor. If the rays reach the tumor all at once at a sufficiently high intensity, the tumor will be destroyed. Unfortunately, at this intensity, the healthy tissue that the rays pass through on the way to the tumor will also be destroyed. At lower intensities, the rays are harmless to healthy tissue, but they will not affect the tumor either. What type of procedure might be used to destroy the tumor with the rays and at the same time avoid destroying the healthy tissue?

Figure 12.10   The radiation problem.

From Duncker, K. (1945). On problem solving. *Psychological Monographs, 58*, 1–112.

Duncker (the problem-solving pioneer who developed the candle problem) developed what has become known as the radiation problem, presented in Figure 12.10. Can you solve it? The correct solution is to aim many radiation beams (at sufficiently weak intensity to avoid damage) at the tumor from different angles. Hence, the tumor receives the summed energy of the radiation (and is destroyed), while the surrounding tissue is unharmed. In a classic series of studies, Gick and Holyoak (1980, 1983) utilized the radiation problem developed by Duncker (1945) to investigate whether an analogous problem might help solvers succeed at finding a solution to it.

In their initial series of investigations on whether analogies might aid in problem solving, Gick and Holyoak (1980) presented participants with one of several stories analogous to the radiation problem. For example, in the commander problem, a military commander is trying to capture the military headquarters of an opposing force. The headquarters are located on an island connected to the surrounding area by several bridges. A bridge can only accommodate a few tanks, which will not be enough for a successful attack. Therefore, the military commander conducts the attack by sending a few tanks across each bridge; this results in enough tanks arriving at the island for a successful attack. After looking over this initial story (the *source problem*) under the guise of a story-comprehension task, participants were given the radiation problem (the *target problem*). Some participants were given only the target problem; in this condition, 10% came up with the convergence solution. Some participants were instructed to memorize the source problem and then tried to solve the target problem. In this condition, 30% of participants came up with the convergence solution. A comparison of these two conditions indicates that 20% of participants spontaneously noticed the analogous relationship and used it.

In a follow-up series of investigations, Gick and Holyoak (1983) set out to determine the conditions under which analogical transfer would occur. They attempted to get solvers to notice and use analogies under three different conditions. In the analogy-plus-general-principle condition, participants received an analogous problem plus an extra passage that basically stated the underlying principle (or, in Gick and Holyoak's terms, the underlying *schema*)—namely, that simultaneously applying small forces from different locations is as effective as applying one large force from the same location. In the analogy-plus-diagram condition, participants received an analogous problem plus a diagram (multiple arrows converging on one location) that sketched out the underlying schema. Alternatively, in the analogy-plus-another-analogous-problem condition, the participants received two analogous problems and were asked to find the relationship between them. Which of these three conditions (if any) do you think would be most likely to lead to the transfer of the analogy?

Figure 12.11 summarizes the results from experiments that tested these different conditions. Each pair of bars represents a comparison between one of the three conditions dis-

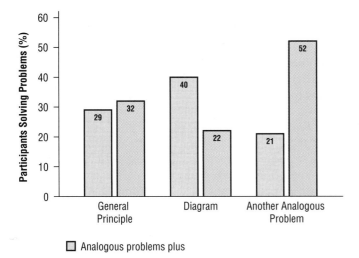

Figure 12.11 Results from Gick and Holyoak (1983). Analogous transfer only occurred when participants were presented with two analogous problems and were required to map out their relation. (See the text for further discussion of the study.)

From Gick, M. L., & Holyoak, K. J. (1983). Schema induction and analogical transfer. *Cognitive Psychology, 15,* 1–38. Copyright 1983, Elsevier Science (USA). Reprinted by permission.

cussed above to an analogy-alone condition in which the participants just received one analogous problem. As you can see, only one of the analogy hints was successful. Providing a diagram (analogy-plus-diagram condition) or a statement of the general principle underlying the problem (analogy-plus-general-principle condition) did not help participants to spontaneously recognize and use the analogy. However, when subjects read and related two analogous stories (analogy-plus-another-analogous-problem condition), they were able to use the knowledge in the new problem. Gick and Holyoak explain that in this condition, solvers were able to map the connections between the two different problems. This mapping process is a defining feature of analogical reasoning and a critical determinant of whether an analogous problem is going to be an aid. Gick and Holyoak term this mapping process *schema induction.* A schema (discussed in Chapters 7 and 9) is a mental representation of facts and procedures that apply to a specific object or situation. In this context, a schema is a mental representation of the underlying principles that multiple problems share. Once this schema is formed, the problem solver can make use of it in solving analogous problems.

Let's examine the steps that are necessary for analogies to succeed as problem-solving techniques. Some researchers (e.g., Novick & Holyoak, 1991) summarize the role of analogy by describing three processes that might be termed *noticing, mapping,* and *schema development.* First, the problem solver must *notice* that a relationship exists between the two problems in question. Next, the solver must be able to *map* the key elements of the two problems (e.g., that the tumor in the radiation problem can be represented as the military headquarters in the commander problem). Finally, the solver must arrive at a general *schema* underlying the problems that will allow for the solution of the target problem (i.e., the convergence schema).

A good deal of research (e.g., Holyoak & Koh, 1987; Ross, 1987) reveals that the first stage, where a relationship must be noticed, is a major culprit in failures of analogical problem solving. Why is this the case? It's basically a failure of memory; the problem currently being faced fails to trigger the memory of other problems that may be helpful. A hint to specifically use the related problem (which serves as a retrieval cue) leads the solver to use the previous problem. But in most everyday cases of problem solving, there's no one to provide hints about other analogous problems. So what factors promote the spontaneous recognition and retrieval of a related problem? One answer to this question relates to the types of features the two problem situations may or may not share.

Surface versus Structural Features.   Our ability to notice, map, and develop schemata depends on the particular *type of similarity*. Researchers generally distinguish between the *surface features* and the *structural features* of problems (e.g., Gentner 1989). **Surface features** are the specific elements of the problem. If two problems share surface similarity, this means that the parts of the problems look pretty similar. A fiasco that occurred while printing the first draft of this very chapter serves as a good example. One of our printers (the newer one) decided to start munching paper as it printed, and it shut down. As we flailed around, looking for the printer manual to get instructions on clearing a paper jam from the new printer, we realized (via analogy) that this printer probably would work like our old printer. Paper jams on our old printer get cleared by opening up the back of the printer. Sure enough, the same principle applied to the new printer. The two problems shared surface features, the relationship was noticed, and the problem was solved.

Structural features are the underlying relationships among the surface features of the two problems. If two problems are structurally similar, they may look quite different on the surface but have underlying similarities in terms of relationships. Does this sound familiar? Remember the distinction we made in Chapter 10 between surface structure and deep structure? Two sentences could have different surface structures (i.e., look similar) but have the same deep structures (i.e., mean the same thing). For example, "The dog chased the cat" and "The cat was chased by the dog" have different structures but the same meaning.

Think about the radiation and commander problems. These problems are completely different in terms of their surface features: military attack versus cancer. Yet in terms of structural features, they are pretty much the same. Both require the use of many smaller forces applied simultaneously from different directions. In spite of the fundamental (structural) similarity between the radiation and commander problems, their dissimilarity on the surface is likely to prevent your making a connection between the two. Simply put, in many circumstances, structural similarity is not enough to cue your memory regarding previous problems; the reminder must be more obvious.

Even though a good deal of research indicates that people aren't too good at picking up on analogies unless the relationship is pretty obvious (Gick & Holyoak, 1980, 1983; Hayes & Simon, 1977), a couple of studies give reason for hope. Needham and Begg (1991) invoke the notion of transfer-appropriate processing (described in Chapter 6) to explain some failures of analogical transfer. The transfer-appropriate-processing principle basically states that we're more likely to remember something if the processing that is required at retrieval matches the processing used at encoding. Needham and Begg note that previous research often featured a mismatch of retrieval and encoding processing. At encoding, the person encounters a story (the source problem) and typically is asked to process it in some meaningful way, such as summarizing or answering story-comprehension questions (not a solution-finding process). According to Needham and Begg, these procedures don't transfer very well to a (retrieval) situation that requires a solution-finding process (i.e., solving the target problem). Therefore, it's no wonder that solvers fail to notice the analogy.

Needham and Begg tested their idea by varying the instructions presented with the source problems. Some participants received memory-oriented instructions; they were told that they would be reading some stories that they should try to remember. Others received solution-finding instructions; they were told that they should try to figure out why the solution to each of the story problems was correct (these were the same stories read by the memory-oriented participants). The results fit perfectly with the transfer-appropriate-processing prediction. Those who received problem-oriented instructions with the source problems successfully solved more of the analogous target problems than participants who received memory-oriented instructions (90% versus 69%). Overall, the results indicate that people are likely to notice connections between problems and problem situations to the extent that they receive similar sorts of processing.

An interesting finding from Needham and Begg's study was that although most solution-finding processors were able to apply the source problems to target problems, most (80%) were not able to remember the solutions of the source problems. This may seem counterintuitive to you, but Needham and Begg assert that this finding follows directly from the transfer-appropriate-processing framework. In the problem-oriented condition, participants are preparing to solve problems, not memorize solutions. At retrieval, if asked to solve problems, they do well, because the encoding task is appropriate for the requirements of the retrieval task. However, if asked to recall the solutions, they do poorly, because the problem-solving encoding task is not appropriate for the requirements of a pure memory retrieval task.

A study by Blanchette and Dunbar (2000) provides yet another hopeful assessment of analogy use. As you've read, people often fail to pick up on analogies unless there is surface similarity. But the seeming ineffectiveness of structural similarity for analogy use is deceiving; some research suggests that it might be (at least in part) an artifact of the cognitive psychology laboratory. Several studies of real-world problem solving indicate that the analogies people use are based on structural features, not surface ones (e.g., Dunbar 1995). In their study, Blanchette and Dunbar had participants produce their own analogies to various target problems and the characteristics of these generated analogies were evaluated. The results indicated that when analogies were produced by participants, the analogies shared structural similarity, rather than surface similarity, with the target problem. This finding indicates that people in everyday circumstances may actually be more sensitive to structural similarity than suggested by earlier research.

STOP *and* REVIEW!

1. An algorithm would be most suitable for solving which of these problems?
   a. writing a paper
   b. buying a car
   c. planning a party
   d. balancing your checkbook

2. True or false? Heuristics are more practically useful than algorithms.

3. What is an analogy? How might it aid problem solving?

4. True or false? Most errors made in using analogies occur in the schema-development stage.

5. What type of similarity is more likely to lead to analogical transfer?

➤ Algorithms involve the systematic and exhaustive application of rules for specific types of problems. Algorithms guarantee a solution if correctly applied. For human problem solvers, algorithms are limited in their usefulness, because their exhaustive nature makes their use tedious. Also, algorithms do not exist for most everyday problems.

➤ Heuristics are rules of thumb. They're generally preferable to algorithms because they tend to be more efficient. Heuristics include working backward, means-end analysis (breaking a problem down into smaller subgoals), and the use of analogies (the application of previous solution procedures to current problems).

➤ Analogies are a heuristic strategy of using an already-solved problem to represent and solve a current problem. Research indicates that people often fail to make the critical connections between analogous problems spontaneously.

➤ The steps necessary for analogies to succeed as a problem-solving technique are *noticing* that a relationship exists, *mapping* the problem elements, and *schema development,* detecting a general principle underlying the problems. Many failures in analogical problem solving occur in the noticing stage.

➤ Making the connection between two analogous problems is more likely if two analogous problems share surface features (the problem elements) than if they share only structural features (the underlying relationships). However, in everyday situations, people may actually be more sensitive to structural similarity than laboratory research would indicate.

Experts: Masters of Representation and Solution

A good deal of research in the area of problem solving has been devoted to the notion of **expertise,** which can be defined as exceptional knowledge and/or performance in some specific problem domain. For some time, it was commonly believed that the exceptional performance of an expert reflected some innate capacity or talent. Since the advent of cognitive psychology in the 1950s, this view has given way to what might be termed an information-processing account of expertise (Ericsson & Charness, 1994). Rather than viewing expert performance as the product of innate capacities, many researchers now view it as an outgrowth of learning and repetition over the course of years that produces an extensive body of knowledge and an extremely well-learned set of skills. One estimate is that expertise involves approximately 10 years of continuous exposure to a given domain, comprising thousands of hours of practice (Ericsson and Charness, 1994).

Table 12.3 **The Many Areas of Expertise Investigated by Problem-Solving Researchers**

chess	gymnastics
computer programming	figure skating
medical diagnosis	basketball
bridge	ballet
othello	algebra
baseball	musical notation
field hockey	maps
football	soap opera knowledge
serving tables	soccer

For the past 50 years, researchers have investigated differences in the cognitive processing of experts and novices. Table 12.3 provides a list of some of the areas in which researchers have investigated expert performance (based on Vicente & Wang, 1998). To some extent, experts might be considered *skilled memorizers* (Deakin & Allard, 1991); in fact, one popular framework for explaining expertise effects in problem solving is termed *skilled-memory theory* (Ericsson & Polson, 1988). According to this framework, there are a number of fundamental differences between experts and novices, all to the advantage of experts. First, the semantic networks that we talked about in Chapter 9 are much more richly elaborated in experts. Second, experts have quicker and more direct access to long-term memory. Third, information is more easily encoded into long-term memory by experts, and the speed of this encoding improves with practice. It is critical to note here that these memory skills seem to be specific to the domain in which they were acquired in the first place; there's no reason to believe that a waiter who's exceptionally good at remembering drink orders is going to be exceptionally good at remembering chessboard configurations (although there is some evidence that there can be transfer of expertise; see Kimball & Holyoak, 2000, for a brief review).

Stop and Think!   **ANALYZING YOUR EXPERTISE**

Table 12.3 lists over a dozen areas of expertise that have been investigated by cognitive researchers. Below are some of the advantages that experts have over novices:

richer semantic networks
faster retrieval from memory
faster encoding into memory

Consider some area of "personal expertise"; it can be anything—a game you're good at, a skill you've developed at work, athletic performance.

1. Reflect on how your expertise demonstrates these characteristics.
2. Compare your performance in your domain with that of a novice.

Expert Advantages

As stated previously, the core of problem solving is memory—the long-term memory that allows for the storage of domain-related general knowledge and specific episodes and the working memory that allows for quick and efficient on-line processing of problem information. A groundbreaking investigation of expert memory was conducted by DeGroot (1946/1978), who investigated memory in chess players of varying skill levels by presenting them with brief glimpses of meaningful board positions and then having them reconstruct the boards. Perhaps not surprisingly, recall differed as a function of expertise, with the best players recalling the boards almost perfectly.

Another classic study by Chase and Simon (1973) replicated DeGroot's findings but included an encoding condition in which the chess pieces were randomly rearranged to find out whether the advantage enjoyed by experts was a general one (good working memory overall) or a specific one (exceptionally good working memory for chess game configurations they'd seen before). Interestingly, while expert chess players remembered game configurations better than novices, they demonstrated no superiority in memory for random board configurations. Chase and Simon explained the superiority in the former condition by appealing to the notion of chunking in working memory (discussed in Chapter 4). According to this account, experts can instantly recognize game board configurations based on their extensive knowledge and experience base. As a result, they can easily and quickly chunk pieces, and these chunks become increasingly larger and more complex; each of the 7 ± 2 (the magical number) chunks in memory contains more information.

Later evidence has demonstrated that the superior memory exhibited by the experts in these studies is not an exclusive function of working memory, because it doesn't seem subject to many of the limits you read about in Chapter 4. For example, Charness (1976) found that expert memory for chess positions was not diminished by delay, even with an interfering task. Also, Gobet and Simon (1996) found that chess masters who quickly glimpsed several game boards were able to process more chunks than the typical view of working memory would allow. Ericsson and Kintsch (1995) propose the idea of **long-term working memory** to explain expert advantages in on-line processing. Basically, this theory states that experts can bypass the limits of working memory by using the information in working memory to directly access LTM; in essence working memory serves as a retrieval cue for information in LTM.

In Chapter 4, we talked about a long-distance runner (S. F.) with a prodigious digit span that reached nearly 80 items. He accomplished this feat by associating the digits being presented with running times. So the sequence 24857 might be encoded as "2:48 and 57 seconds," a very decent marathon time. Now in LTM, this information would be fairly easily retrieved because "decent marathon time" would be a good retrieval cue. Developing these sorts of retrieval cues takes years and years of practice.

Aside from the general advantages in the power and efficiency of memory within their domain area, expert problem solvers also use general strategies that differ from those of novices. For example, Chi, Feltovich, and Glaser (1981) found that experts tend to search problem space in a forward fashion, reasoning from givens toward the goal. Novices, on the other hand, tend to think about the goal and reason backward about the steps that will lead there. Also, experts are much better at picking up on structural features of problems, whereas novices are more likely to focus on surface features. Given what you've learned about analogy, you've probably inferred (correctly) that experts are more likely to recognize analogous problems or situations when faced with a new one (within their area of expertise).

Expert Disadvantages: Costs of Expertise

Although experts enjoy tremendous advantages in processing (primarily within their own domain), there is what might be considered a "downside" to expertise. For example, in the

Chase and Simon (1973) study, novices were actually a little better at recall of randomly arranged chess pieces. Also, some studies of medical expertise (e.g., Patel & Medley-Mark, 1985) have revealed that those at an intermediate level of knowledge (e.g., residents in a teaching hospital) actually remember more information about specific patient cases than do experts (e.g., experienced physicians); this has been termed the **intermediate effect.** Finally, Voss, Vesonder, and Spilich (1980) found that baseball experts were worse than novices in recall of baseball-irrelevant details from a baseball story. Taken together, these findings indicate that while experts may be able to encode important information by relating it to richly elaborated schemata, this can come at the expense of attention to (and subsequent retrieval of) detail information.

An investigation by Wiley (1998) suggests that expertise itself may actually function as a type of mental set. In her experiment, Wiley wanted to find out whether expertise might prevent solvers from coming up with creative solutions to problems, due to the tendency to think of things in an automatic, expertise-driven fashion. She employed the Remote Associates Test (RAT), in which solvers look at three apparently unrelated words and generate one word that ties the triplet together. For example, if presented with *apple, family, house* the remote associate is *tree* (apple *tree*, family *tree*, and *tree*house). The ability to make the connection between the three terms and come up with the remote associate is taken as a sign of creativity.

Wiley tested experts and novices in baseball, presenting them with RAT items. On all trials, the first word (e.g., *plate*) formed a baseball phrase (home plate). The remote associate (*home*) was further supported by the second word (e.g., *broken*—broken home). However, the third word presented was the critical one. On baseball-consistent trials, the third word presented (e.g., *rest*) was also consistent with the baseball interpretation of the remote associate (rest home). This was not the case on baseball-misleading trials; to the contrary, although a baseball-related word seemed likely given the first two words, the third word rendered the baseball-related term incorrect (e.g., *plate, broken, shot—glass*).

Can you see where this experiment is going? Wiley suspected that baseball experts would be likely to start thinking *baseball*, as soon as they saw the word *plate*, the result being that they would be stumped if the final word didn't match the word they had generated. The results supported her hypothesis. As you can see in Figure 12.12, performance of the expert subjects was very poor if they were misled; their ability to make creative connections was stifled by their tendency to think in terms of their area of expertise.

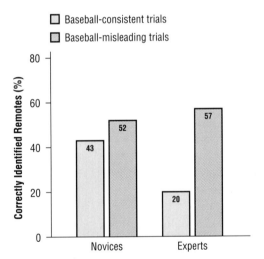

Figure 12.12 Results from Wiley's (1998) study of mental set. Baseball expertise inhibited creative problem solving, as measured by the ability to come up with remote associates.

From Wiley, J. (1998). Expertise as mental set: The effects of domain knowledge in creative problem solving. *Memory and Cognition, 26,* 716–730. Reprinted by permission of the Psychonomic Society, Inc.

S T O P *and* R E V I E W !

1. True or false? Expertise is a reflection of innate ability and skill.
2. Who remembers detail better?
   a. novices
   b. those with an intermediate level of knowledge
   c. experts
   d. no differences in the amount of detail remembered by these individuals
3. Explain the advantages and disadvantages of experts according to long-term working memory theory.
4. List some advantages and disadvantages that expert problem solvers have over novices.

➤ Expertise (exceptional knowledge and/or performance in some specific problem domain) is due to learning and repetition over years that produces an extensive body of knowledge and an extremely well-learned set of skills.

➤ Some studies show that those at an intermediate level of knowledge remember more information about specific cases than do experts—termed the intermediate effect.

➤ According to long-term working memory theory, knowledge networks are more richly elaborated in experts. Experts have quicker and more direct access to long-term memory, and information is more easily and quickly encoded into long-term memory by experts. However, experts' memory skills are limited to the domain of expertise.

➤ Experts seem able to bypass the limits of working memory by using WM information to access LTM directly. Processing advantages of experts come at the expense of memory for detail. The intermediate effect indicates that people with intermediate knowledge are better at detail retention. The tendency to think within an area of expertise can serve as a mental set.

Insight and Creativity

At the end of the last section, you read about a study in which experts were actually a bit impeded in problem solving due to their expertise. You shouldn't take the results of this study as evidence that expertise generally inhibits creativity; quite the contrary, the extensive knowledge and processing proficiency possessed by experts is important in their ability to find creative solutions. Let's take a closer look at the processes thought to underlie these mental breakthroughs.

Great thinkers have always been thinking about what constitutes great thinking. Still, most of the important questions remain unanswered. What is creativity? What are the processes that lead to creative products? And for that matter what are creative products? Can creativity be measured? Enhanced? Exhibited by anybody? In this section, we'll examine some of these questions more closely.

Based on an extensive analysis of several cases where great thinkers made significant breakthroughs, Wallas (1926) proposed that the processes leading up to a creative break-

through can be described in terms of four stages. In the first stage of *preparation,* the solver gathers information and makes initial attempts at problem solution. This initial stage corresponds roughly to the problem-representation phase of processing discussed earlier. Often, these attempts are stymied, leading to a period of *incubation,* which might be described as productive inactivity. You may have had the experience that when you were trying to solve a problem, putting it aside for a time seemed to allow for a breakthrough. We'll examine the empirical evidence for this experience later. After the incubation period, the problem solver arrives at a critical insight—an important realization or understanding that leads to what Wallas termed *illumination.* Ever see a cartoon where a lightbulb appears over a character's head? A solution to a problem has occurred suddenly, probably with a tangible "Aha!" feeling for the solver. In this chapter's story, Donna had an "Aha!" experience when she realized that she could do the whole class a favor by asking for an extension on the final paper. The final stage comprising creative thought is *verification,* in which the problem solver assesses whether the solution will actually work. (You'll have to wait for the final chapter to find out if Donna's solution did work.)

The Wallas framework provides a useful description of problem solving but is, by no means, an accepted theory. It was based on Wallas's introspections about the creative process and case studies on the introspections of creative individuals. Although too vague to really test, the theory has provided fodder for two of the more intriguing questions in problem-solving research. First, what is the nature of the ubiquitous experience we term *insight?* Do solutions to problems really appear out of nowhere? Second, if sudden breakthroughs in problem solving are a reality, can these be encouraged by a period of incubation?

Insight

One problem-solving phenomenon that has been a topic of extensive debate and investigation since the beginning of research on problem solving is the notion of insight. As we discussed earlier, *insight* involves the sudden realization of a problem's solution (or of a key idea necessary to the solution). The debate over the nature (or the very existence) of insight goes back to the Gestalt views of problem solving. Gestalt psychologists believe that the key to problem solution lies in a restructuring of the problem elements, which, if successful, leads to a sudden realization of the problem's solution. This sudden realization is insight. The notion of insight is controversial; many theorists believe that problem solving is an incremental process of getting closer and closer to a solution rather than a sudden realization. Another problem is that insight (until relatively recently) never has been clearly defined or experimentally demonstrated by Gestalt psychologists.

Even if insight is a reality, it would not apply to every problem. Many researchers make a distinction between noninsight and insight problems (which can be seen as loosely

Examples of Insight Problems

Water lilies double in area every 24 hours. At the beginning of summer, there is one water lily on the lake. It takes 60 days for the lake to become completely covered with water lilies. On which day is the lake half-covered?

A prisoner was attempting to escape from a tower. He found in his cell a rope which was half long enough to permit him to reach the ground safely. He divided the rope in half, and tied the two parts together and escaped. How could he have done this?

Examples of Noninsight Problems

Three people play a game in which one person loses and two people win each round. The one who loses must double the amount of money that each of the players has at that time. The three players agree to play three games. At the end of the three games, each player has lost one game, and each person has $8. What was the original stake of each player?

Next week I am going to have lunch with my friend, visit the new art gallery, go to the social security office, and have my teeth checked at the dentist. My friend cannot meet me on Wednesday; the social security office is closed weekends; the dentist has office hours only on Tuesday, Friday, and Saturday; the art gallery is closed Tuesday, Thursday, and weekends. What day can I do everything I planned?

Figure 12.13   Some examples of insight and noninsight problems used in the study by Metcalfe and Weibe (1987).

From Metcalfe, J., & Weibe, D. (1987). Intuition in insight and noninsight problem solving. *Memory and Cognition, 15,* 238–246. Reprinted by permission of the Psychonomic Society, Inc.

analogous to the earlier distinction between ill-defined and well-defined problems). **Non-insight problems** are those that are likely solved through incremental, or "grind out the solution," processes. They require analytical, step-by-step processing—like the problems in logic, arithmetic, chess, and the like. The transformation problem called the Tower of Hanoi (previously presented in Figure 12.2) is an example of a noninsight problem—no simple breakthrough is going to give you the answer. **Insight problems** are those in which the solution appears suddenly. Figure 12.13 presents a couple of these so-called insight problems, along with a couple noninsight problems.

Two of the key assumptions about insightful problem solving are (1) that it involves a mistaken assumption that, once removed, will clear the way to a successful solution of the problem, and (2) that the solver is hit with the solution suddenly, "out of the blue," and has what might be termed an "Aha!" experience. Let's take a look at some research that has addressed these fundamental assumptions.

Removal of a Mistaken Assumption?   Although the notion of insight was an integral part of much of the early work on problem solving, Weisberg and Alba (1981) observed that the concept remained vaguely defined and, in fact, had never been put to experimental test. This may have been due, in part, to the intuitive appeal of the idea. But intuitive appeal and common sense are poor bases for knowledge, so Weisberg and Alba embarked on an in-depth exploration of insight, focusing on the assumption that insight problems involve one key misassumption that, if removed, would lead to easy solution. They employed what is possibly the most thoroughly investigated insight problem, the nine-dot problem. The solver is asked to connect all the dots with four continuous lines without lifting the pencil from the paper, which is surprisingly difficult for most. The nine-dot problem and

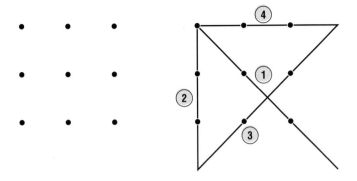

Figure 12.14 The nine-dot problem and solution.

From Weisberg, R. W., & Alba, J. W. (1981). An examination of the alleged role of "fixation" in the solution of several "insight" problems. *Journal of Experimental Psychology: General, 110,* 169–192. Copyright 1981 by the American Psychology Association. Reprinted by permission.

its solution are presented in Figure 12.14. The solution involves extending the lines beyond the boundary of the square defined by the nine dots. The mental set of staying within this boundary is the primary block that prevents successful solution. According to the notion of insight, removing this mental set should produce an easy solution.

Weisberg and Alba tested this idea in a series of deceptively simple experiments. They reasoned that if the inability to solve insight problems was truly an instance of blockage by one inappropriate assumption, removing the assumption should open the gates to almost instant solution. To test this hypothesis, they presented insight problems with or without hints. For example, some solvers faced with the nine-dot problem were told they would have to break the imaginary boundary created by the dots. Some solvers were given this hint, along with the first or the first and second lines that needed to be drawn. A control group was simply told to solve the puzzle. The results, presented in Figure 12.15, cast some doubt on the "all-or-nothing" view of insight. Solvers who were told to go outside the boundary were only slightly more likely to solve the problem. Even in the group given the first line, over one-third were unable to solve it. Clearly, this pattern does not fit the Gestalt prediction that nearly everyone would solve the problem once the block was

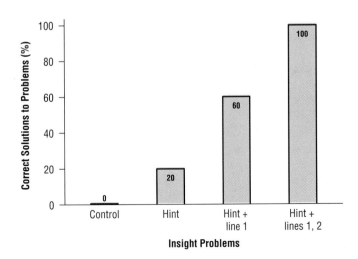

Figure 12.15 Results from Weisberg and Alba's (1981) study of insight in problem solving. Contrary to intuitive notions about insight, a hint did not lead to sudden and absolute realization of a problem's solution.

From Weisberg, R. W., & Alba, J. W. (1981). An examination of the alleged role of "fixation" in the solution of several "insight" problems. *Journal of Experimental Psychology: General, 110,* 169–192. Copyright 1981 by the American Psychological Association. Reprinted by permission.

removed. Based on the results of several experiments, Weisberg and Alba suggested that the term *insight* offers little more than a description of what a person experiences in solving some problems; it doesn't really specify how a problem is being solved. In addition, the notion of insight is circular: How do we know the problem was solved through insight? Because it was solved suddenly, with an "Aha!" experience. Why was there a sudden solution and an "Aha!" experience? Because the problem was solved through insight. There needs to be some way to define an insight problem without referring to the suddenness of the solution (see Weisberg, 1995, for some possibilities). We will discuss a possible resolution of this circularity in the following section.

The "Aha!" Experience.   Another defining feature of the insight experience is a sudden and tangible feeling of discovery, usually described as an "Aha!" experience. The issue of what someone is thinking as they think relates to metacognition. Metacognition refers to a person's knowledge of their own thought processes. In a series of clever experiments, Metcalfe (Metcalfe, 1986a; Metcalfe & Weibe, 1987) investigated the metacognition of problem solvers faced with different sorts of problems. Metcalfe and Weibe (1987) developed one of the more interesting dependent variables in cognitive psychology—*ratings of warmth* collected from problem solvers during their problem-solving attempts. You know the old "hot and cold" game when you're looking for something? If the hider tells you you're cold, you're nowhere near the hidden object; if you're hot, you're practically on top of it.

Metcalfe and Weibe adapted this game to problem solving by having subjects rate how warm they were with regard to the solution of a problem. Their reasoning was as follows: if insight involves sudden realization of the solution, solvers who are working on an insight problem should have no clue if they're close to a solution or not, and their warmth ratings should reflect this. They should report little warmth throughout the problem-solving interval until a solution finally appears. With a noninsight problem, however, the metacognition should be different: participants should realize that they're getting closer and closer to a solution, given the grind-it-out nature of a noninsight problem. To test their hypothesis, Metcalfe and Weibe (1987, experiment 2) presented participants with noninsight problems and insight problems like the ones previously presented in Figure 12.13. They were allowed four minutes for each problem, and within that interval, they were to rate their warmth every 15 seconds by making a mark on a scale. In addition to rating warmth, solvers were also asked to judge whether or not they would be able to solve each of the problems.

The results revealed some interesting differences in the metacognitive processes underlying solution of insight and noninsight problems. Simply put, metacognition was not nearly as good for the insight problems. Let's take a look at the warmth ratings. These were incremental for the noninsight problems, increasing gradually throughout the solution interval. Participants felt as if they were nearing a solution when they really were near a solution. For the insight problems, however, the warmth ratings didn't really increase at all throughout the solution interval until the problem was solved. So participants really had no idea if and when they were approaching a solution. The other metacognitive judgment ("Will I be able to solve this problem?") paralleled the warmth ratings. For the noninsight problems, participants were decent judges of whether they would be able to solve the problems. However, for the insight problems, participants were relatively poor judges of solution probability. They demonstrated overconfidence, underestimating how difficult the problems were.

The results from both metacognitive judgments indicate a fundamental difference between insight and noninsight problems. Participants' metacognitions about noninsight problems were more accurate and more predictive of actual performance. Metacognitions about insight problems tended to be unrelated to (or even negatively related to; see Metcalfe, 1987) the probability of eventual solution. Metcalfe and Weibe (1987) suggest that the processes underlying the solution of insight and noninsight problems may be fundamentally different and that the pattern of warmth ratings observed during a solution can be used as an indicator of whether a problem involves insight, thereby avoiding the circularity problem in defining insight.

In a critique of the metacognitive studies of insight, Weisberg (1992) lodges a number of objections to these conclusions. He acknowledges the subjective "Aha!" experience produced by some problems but points out that this does not necessarily mean that problems are solved suddenly, as the Gestalt position suggests. It may be that step-by-step processes are involved but that the solver is unaware of them.

RECURRING RESEARCH THEME
Cognition and Consciousness

Insight and Intuition

The issue of whether insight problem solving involves special, unconscious processes—like a sudden restructuring of problem elements or removal of some mistaken information—still stirs controversy in the field. Certainly, insight problems do seem unique phenomenologically—that is, in terms of the conscious experience that a problem solver has. Insight problem solving feels like an all-or-none process that occurs suddenly. But, as we just mentioned, an alternative conceptualization is that insight problem solving (like noninsight problem solving) is really more gradual, but the gradual progress is not open to conscious awareness.

This latter analysis of insight problem solving is supported by some fascinating research by Bowers, Regehr, Balthazard, and Parker (1990). These authors propose a two-stage model of insight (which they term *intuition*). In stage 1, the *guiding stage*, mnemonic networks relevant to the problem are activated, and this activation begins to spread. In essence, the problem solver is working on the problem unconsciously; the results of this unconscious processing may serve as a basis for a hunch or intuition regarding the solution. In stage 2 (the *integrative stage*), the buildup of activation reaches enough strength to break through into conscious awareness. This transition from stage 1 to stage 2 is insight.

Bowers and colleagues employed what they called *intuition tasks* (similar to an insight problem) to test this two-stage model of insight. One experiment used what the researchers termed the *dyads of triads* task, adapted from the Remote Associates Test you read about earlier. Participants were faced with two triads of words (e.g., *notch-flight-spin* and *clear-role-force*). For one of the triads, the words had a common associate; for the other one, no common associate existed. (In this example, words in the first triad all relate to *top;* words in the second triad have no common associate.) Participants were given 8 to 12 seconds to solve each triad; if they couldn't, they were asked to give a simple guess about which of the two triads was *coherent*—in other words, which of them was the one that could all be related to one word. They also rated their confidence in this judgment.

Let's relate the procedure to the two-stage model of insight and see what predictions the model generates. According to this view, when faced with the three words in a triad, unconscious processes immediately begin working on the problem (the guiding stage). Although solvers cannot report on these processes, evidence for the solution is building up unconsciously through spreading activation, which can serve as the basis for a hunch, or intuition, about the answer. This hunch should allow participants to succeed on the second task, picking which of the triads is coherent, even if they can't come up with the solution (i.e., even if they never reach the integrative stage).

The results provided support for the researchers' proposal. Participants were able to guess which triad was coherent at a rate well above chance, even when they couldn't come up with the solution. This suggests that incremental processes outside conscious awareness are at work on the problem, providing evidence for hunches or intuitions that are not open to the conscious awareness necessary for accurate metacognitive judgments. This may explain why Metcalfe (1986a,b; Metcalfe & Weibe, 1987) found that warmth judgments were poor indicators of whether solvers were close to an answer; they were getting closer to the solution, but they were not consciously aware of it. An appropriate analogy might be to liken the process to that of a sunrise (Wittgenstein, 1969): "our subjective experience is that the new day suddenly dawns, but the amount of light actually grows continuously over a fairly protracted period of time" (Siegler, 2000, p. 79). When solving problems, you may have the subjective experience that you arrived at the solution suddenly, when in reality you were (unconsciously) approaching that solution incrementally.

Does Incubation Lead to Insight?   One of the more controversial notions within the study of problem solving is **incubation,** or the idea that taking a break in problem solving leads to a quicker solution than does continuing effort. The idea is that the break allows for the elements of the problem to be reorganized or for unconscious processes to continue to work on the problem (perhaps as described above) and that this unconscious processing will not take place if conscious work on the problem continues. The anecdotal evidence for incubation is strong; everyday problem solvers, including scientists, artists, and writers, often observe that some critical realization or breakthrough occurs only after a period of frustration and setting the problem aside (Wallas, 1926). However, anecdotal evidence is viewed skeptically by scientists. As intuitive as it seems, this phenomenon has proven to be elusive quarry for problem-solving researchers, who, more often than not, have failed to find incubation effects (e.g., Dominowski & Jenrick, 1972; Olton, 1979; Olton & Johnson, 1976).

Smith (1995) suggests that incubation effects do occur, but only under specific circumstances—namely, when a problem is doable and when the solver is blocked in some way from the solution. The incubation period allows the interfering information to be forgotten, clearing the way for a solution. This effect was nicely demonstrated in a study

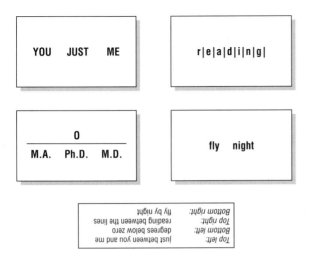

YOU   JUST   ME

r|e|a|d|i|n|g|

0
――――――――
M.A.   Ph.D.   M.D.

fly   night

Top left: just between you and me
Bottom left: degrees below zero
Top right: reading between the lines
Bottom right: fly by night

Figure 12.16 Sample rebus problems: Can you come up with the saying represented by each?

From Smith, S. M., & Blankenship, S. E. (1991). Incubation effects. *Bulletin of the Psychonomic Society, 27,* 311–314. Reprinted by permission of the Psychonomic Society, Inc.

by Smith and Blankenship (1989). In this study, participants attempted to solve rebus problems—basically, word puzzles in which pictures and words are used to indicate a common phrase. Some examples are given in Figure 12.16. In their experiment, Smith and Blankenship had participants solve these puzzles; for some, they provided a pair of misleading cue words. For example, in the fourth rebus problem presented in the figure, *fly* and *night* were presented as misleading cues; they're misleading because they suggest two compound words that are not correct solutions (i.e., *flypaper* and *overnight*). Then the researchers retested unsolved rebuses either immediately or after varying periods of incubation. After attempting to solve the rebus again, participants were asked to recall the cue word that went along with it originally. Consistent with Smith's (1995) analysis, longer break periods were associated with higher probabilities of solution. Memory for the misleading cues provides a possible explanation; memory for the misleading cues decreased as incubation time increased. Apparently, as the misleading cue was forgotten, the problem became more solvable.

Smith (1995) offers a contextual view of incubation, which is basically the encoding specificity in reverse. If you'll recall from Chapter 6, the *encoding specificity* principle states that retrieval will be effective to the degree that retrieval conditions match encoding conditions. The *contextual view* of incubation states that when problem solving is stymied, a solution will come more easily if there is a contextual change from the previous situation. Essentially, staying in the same situation continually reinstates the circumstances in which the failure to find a solution was first encountered, increasing the likelihood that the failure will continue. Changing the environment prevents this reinstatement, making success more likely. Smith provides some anecdotal support for this idea, noting that a number of famous cases of incubation followed by insight took place when the problem solver was in a completely different environment than usual. Donna's solution to her end-of-semester problem occurred not when she was staring at the computer, but when she was dozing in her chair. And it occurred long after she had originally thought about the problem.

The notion of insight has proven to be vague and difficult to define precisely, but by no means has it been relegated to the scrap heap of problem-solving research (far from it!). Much recent work has attempted to better specify the concept and to investigate with more precision the circumstances that are likely to lead to it. (See Sternberg and Davidson, 1995, for an entire volume devoted to the scientific investigation of insight.)

Creativity

When someone has an insight, demonstrating the ability to hurdle over the problem-solving obstacles that block us mere mortals, what do we say about them? It's quite likely that we would comment on their **creativity**. Creative individuals are able to think "outside the box"—to come up with new ideas, view old problems from a fresh perspective, and connect seemingly disparate problem situations. Several fundamental questions about creativity have been addressed by problem-solving researchers: What is creativity? What factors are related to creative solutions to problems? Can anyone be creative? Let's discuss some of the possible answers.

What Is Creativity?   Experts on creativity generally agree that creative solutions have two components—novelty and appropriateness (Lubart, 1994). Creative solutions are novel ones, different from previous solutions, and are usually unexpected. Yet surprise and originality alone do not make a problem solution creative. The solution must also satisfy the constraints of the problem at hand; it must fulfill a need and be sensible and useful (Lubart, 1994). Let's think back to Donna's (and possibly yours!) end-of-semester problem. One "solution" to the problem might be to fake one's death. That way, the assignments wouldn't need to be handed in, and the tests wouldn't need to be taken. Although it certainly fulfills the criterion of novelty, this solution is entirely inappropriate, failing to fit within the problem constraints. It would be considered aberrant rather than creative.

Factors Associated with Creativity.   In a review, Simonton (2000) presents a multidimensional perspective on creativity, noting that the topic cuts across a number of core disciplines in psychology. Obviously, *cognition* is involved, as creativity is the product of cognitive processes. Creativity is also influenced by a person's *personality* and style of thinking, and seems to follow a consistent pattern of *development* over the lifespan. Finally, creativity is (in part) a product of the intellectual and *social* environment in which a person works. Following is a view of creativity from each of these perspectives.

Cognition and Creativity.   Two contradictory ideas about cognitive processing in creativity have been proffered. One view asserts that creativity involves special processes and abilities, like the ability to quickly restructure problem information and connect seemingly remote possibilities. Conversely, another view contends that creative thinking is the product of garden-variety cognitive processing such as attention and memory. So which view is closer to the truth? One approach, dubbed the **creative cognition approach** by Smith, Ward, and Finke (1994), argues that the answer is probably that creative thinking can be the result of either type of process, or both. These researchers note that some famous discoveries, such as Kekule's discovery of the benzene ring (after he dreamt about snakes biting each others' tails), seem to have resulted from a special process similar to sudden restructuring or insight. On the other hand, some discoveries (e.g., Watson and Crick's discovery of DNA's structure) seem to have resulted from the more mundane, incremental processes of everyday cognition.

Another contradiction noted by Smith and colleagues is that although creativity obviously requires a great deal of old knowledge, it also requires that we do things in new ways. Indeed, Wiley's (1998) study on baseball experts making remote associations (a common measure of creativity) demonstrates that too much knowledge can actually hamper creativity. But all the same, you have no chance of exhibiting creativity in a given area if you know nothing about it. So where lies the "happy medium"? Schank and Cleary (1994) suggest that creativity involves the "intelligent misuse" of one's knowledge. According to this view, when people are faced with a situation where scripted knowledge doesn't really fit, they have to find a way to make it fit—hence the phrase "intelligent misuse" of knowledge. Given that many believe knowledge to be a critical component of creativity, it shouldn't surprise you to learn that creativity tends to be domain specific. Having a creative flair for writing stories does not mean that you'll demonstrate the same level of creativity in some other enterprise, such as photography (Smith, Ward & Finke, 1994).

Role of Individual Differences, Development, and Social Factors. So cognitive processing plays an important role in creativity. That being said, are there particular types of individuals who are more likely to successfully engage in creative thought? Simonton (2000) notes that the relationship between intelligence and creativity depends on the particular view of intelligence to which one subscribes. According to traditional, unidimensional views of intelligence, a certain level of intelligence is necessary to exhibit creativity, but beyond this minimal threshold, there seems to be little relationship between the two (Barron & Harrington, 1981). Multidimensional views, like Gardner's (1983) theory of multiple intelligences (i.e., the notion that there are seven or eight distinct and independent types of intelligence), propose forms of creativity specific to the various types of intelligence. According to Simonton, research into the relationship between personality and creativity has led to a fairly consistent profile of what might be termed the *creative personality.* The traits that creative individuals tend to exhibit include independence, nonconformity, a wide set of interests, openness to new experiences, flexibility, and risk taking.

Simonton also notes the developmental aspects of creativity, characterizing it as a constantly developing ability rather than a static attribute that some lucky folks are born with. According to Simonton's review (and perhaps counter to intuition), creativity is not always the product of a particularly comfortable environment. In fact, a person's potential to exhibit creativity seems dependent on having had a diverse set of life experiences, which then enhance an individual's ability to take fresh perspectives. Creative potential also depends on a person having faced sufficiently challenging life experiences, which helps develop the ability to persevere (Simonton, 1994). Such perseverance is important for creative problem solving, which, by definition, includes numerous obstacles.

Finally, creative behavior does not occur in a vacuum. Creative acts are also products of interpersonal, disciplinary, and sociocultural environments (Simonton, 2000). Research on creativity indicates a sensitivity to a number of interpersonal factors. For example, some evidence (e.g., Amabile, 1996) indicates that being evaluated by others can decrease creativity. The popular notion of **brainstorming** refers to the supposed creative benefit of generating ideas in groups. Unfortunately, research evidence fails to support a relationship between brainstorming and creativity. Still, the technique enjoys great popularity in corporate settings. Another social component of creativity is the disciplinary environment in which it takes place, in part because experts in a given area define what is deemed creative. Finally, creativity is partially dependent on the sociocultural milieu in which one's work is conducted. According to Simonton, cultural diversity enhances creativity; a civilization's creativity tends to thrive when it opens itself up to alien influences through immigration or foreign study.

Stop *and* **Think!**

WORKING BACKWARD TO DEFINE CREATIVITY

This exercise involves using a problem-solving strategy—working backward—to define a concept that has proven difficult to pin down: creativity.

1. Think of someone you think is really creative. (This could be a family member, friend, coworker or maybe be a well-known painter, musician, or author.)
2. Consider the factors that you think make them creative.
3. Compare these to the characteristics discussed in the text.

RECURRING RESEARCH THEME

Cognition and Neuroscience

Creativity and the Right Hemisphere

As you've seen in a number of places throughout the text, one of the major questions addressed by cognitive neuroscientists is the relative role of each brain hemisphere in accomplishing various cognitive tasks. As we noted in Chapter 2, the distinction between the left and right hemispheres is quite often overgeneralized in the popular press, with the left hemisphere labeled as the constrained "logical" hemisphere, and the right as the unfettered "creative" hemisphere. Although this is undoubtedly an oversimplification, recent evidence does suggest that the right hemisphere plays the more important role in creativity.

A series of investigations by Bowden and Beeman (1998) examines the role of the right hemisphere in creative thinking. Appropriately enough, the article is entitled "Getting the Right Idea." Bowden and Beeman begin with the assumption that insight problems involve more creative thought than noninsight problems, because insight problems require unusual interpretations and arrangements of problem elements. In other words, insight problems involve venturing into usually unexplored problem space.

Bowden and Beeman employed the Remote Associates Test (RAT). These researchers combined the logic of priming (which we discussed in many previous chapters) with the RAT to investigate the relative roles of the left and right hemispheres in making creative connections. Their logic was as follows: if the solution of an insight problem is associated to a greater degree with right-hemisphere activation, than solution-related concepts should show more priming when presented to the right hemisphere than to the left hemisphere. In their study, participants were presented with a word triad for 15 seconds. On all trials, the disappearance of the word triad was followed by the presentation of the solution word or a nonsolution word (a word that did not relate the three words together), which they were to pronounce as quickly as possible.

Critical to note here is exactly where the fourth word was presented. Sometimes it was presented left of fixation (i.e., to the right hemisphere), sometimes right of fixation (i.e., to the left hemisphere). The researchers reasoned that if the right hemisphere is more involved in creative problem solving, then pronunciation times should reveal more priming (i.e., faster pronunciation times for solution than nonsolution words) when presented to the right hemisphere. Why? Because the increased activation of the right hemisphere when solving (or attempting to solve) a problem should translate into an enhanced ability to say the solution word relative to the nonsolution word.

The results are shown in Figure 12.17a. What you see are priming scores. These scores were calculated by taking pronunciation times for nonsolution words (which basically boils down to basic word-naming RT) and subtracting the reaction times for solution words. Remember— these were the words on which participants had actively been working, so no doubt this "active work" served to speed up identification. The figure plots this speed-up in reaction time.

First, take a look at the solved problem condition; here you see a priming effect for both solved and unsolved problems, but the effect was greater for words presented to the right

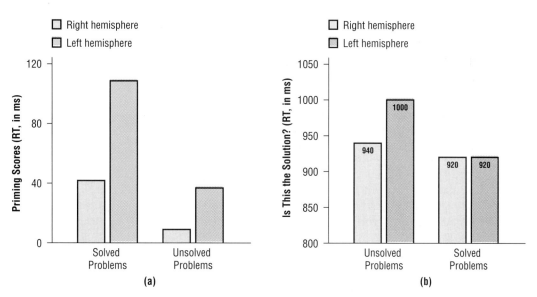

Figure 12.17 Results from Bowden and Beeman's (1998) study of hemispheric activation during insight problem solving. Note that RT priming for the identification of a solution was more prominent for problems processed primarily by the right hemisphere.

From Bowden, E. M., & Beeman, M. J. (1998). Getting the right idea: Semantic activation in the right hemisphere may help solve insight problems. *Psychological Science, 9,* 435–440. Copyright 1998 by Blackwell, Inc. Reprinted by permission.

hemisphere. This indicates that the activation of the solution word was greater in the right hemisphere; this greater activation led to greater priming in pronunciation. Now look at the unsolved problems, which offer an even more compelling picture. In this condition, participants looked at the three words but were unable to generate the solution word. In this situation a priming effect was found only for words presented to the right hemisphere (the small priming effect in the left hemisphere was not significantly greater than 0). This indicates that when a solution has not yet been consciously reached, the right hemisphere "knows what's coming" and is sped up in naming the solution word. The left hemisphere doesn't know what's coming and is not sped up.

In a follow-up study, Bowden and Beeman used exactly the same procedure but changed the required response. After presentation of the fourth word, participants had to make a simple yes-no response—yes if the word was the solution word, or no if it wasn't. The results are presented in Figure 12.17b. Not surprisingly, there was no difference between the right and left hemispheres for solved problems. Given that the solution had already been figured out, saying yes or no was trivially easy for either hemisphere. More interesting is the unsolved problem data. In this situation, participants were still engaged in solution processes. As you can see, the right hemisphere was much faster than the left hemisphere at classifying whether the presented word was the solution or not, indicating that only the right hemisphere was "aware" of the solution. Taken together, the results of the two studies suggest that activation of the right hemisphere is more strongly associated (relative to the left) with the (perhaps creative) processes involved in solving insight problems.

STOP *and* REVIEW!

1. The illumination phase of problem solving is synonymous with
   a. insight.
   b. incubation.
   c. problem representation.
   d. creativity.
2. True or false? A simple hint is enough to guarantee problem solution in the case of insight problems.
3. What is incubation?
4. Discuss the factors related to creativity.

➤ Wallas (1926) proposes a four-stage model of problem solving. In the preparation stage, the solver gathers information. This is followed by a period of incubation (productive inactivity), which leads to illumination or insight (sudden realization of a problem's solution). The solution is checked in a verification phase.

➤ Noninsight problems are solved through incremental processes; insight problems are those in which the solution appears suddenly. Research has cast some doubt on the assumption that insight involves an all-or-nothing breakthrough and shown that hints do not guarantee problem solution. Metacognitive research does verify that people can have an "Aha!" experience as they arrive at the solution to an insight problem.

➤ It is not clear whether a period of incubation (taking a break from problem solving) enhances problem solving, but a problem's solution can be preceded by unconscious activation of problem-related concepts, activation that is more evident in the right hemisphere. One view of incubation states that a contextual change from the solution-blocking situation increases the likelihood of finding a solution.

➤ Creative problem solving is viewed as the product of a number of disparate influences, the most important of which are the component cognitive processes. The creative cognition approach states that creativity is the product of both special processing and normal cognitive processing. Social, cultural, and individual difference variables also play an important role in creativity.

GLOSSARY

algorithm: a set of rules that can be applied systematically to solve certain sorts of problems (p. 496)

analogies: using problems that have already been solved as aids for representing and solving the problem currently being faced (p. 499)

arrangement problems: problems in which the solver must figure out how to put together the problem elements (p. 483)

brainstorming: the practice of generating ideas in a group setting, with no constraints on what can be suggested (p. 518)

creative cognition approach: the view that creative thinking involves both special and ordinary cognitive processing (p. 516)

creativity: the ability to come up with novel and appropriate solutions to problems (p. 516)

deduction problems: problems in which premises are given and the solver must determine whether a conclusion fits these premises (p. 483)

divergent problems: problems in which the solver must generate as many solutions as possible to a given problem (p. 483)

expertise: exceptional knowledge and/or performance in some specific problem domain (p. 504)

functional fixedness: people's tendency to view objects in a narrow, fixed sense; that is, in terms of the typical uses of the object (p. 495)

General Problem Solver (GPS): general computer model of problem solving that works by minimizing the "distance" between an initial state and a goal state by breaking a problem down into a series of subgoals (p. 488)

goal state: the solution to a problem (p. 480)

heuristics: general strategies, or "rules of thumb," that can be applied to various problems (p. 497)

ill-defined problem: a problem that is poorly structured; the initial state, goal state, and constraints are not well understood, and once you reach a solution, it's not easy to assess (p. 481)

incubation: the idea that taking a break in problem solving leads to a quicker solution than does continuing effort (p. 514)

induction problems: problems in which the solver is given a series of instances and must figure out the rule that relates the instances (p. 483)

initial state: the situation that exists at the beginning of the problem (p. 480)

insight: the sudden and successful restructuring of problem elements to reach a solution (p. 487)

insight problems: problems in which the solution appears suddenly (p. 510)

intermediate effect: the finding that those at an intermediate level of knowledge actually remember more information than do experts (p. 507)

law of effect: Thorndike's principle of associative learning that if a response leads to a satisfying outcome, the connection between the response and the situation in which it took place will be strengthened; if a response leads to a nonsatisfying outcome, this connection will be weakened (p. 486)

long-term working memory: the theory that experts bypass the limits of working memory by using the information in working memory to directly access long-term memory (p. 506)

means-end analysis: breaking a problem down into smaller subgoals, where accomplishing each subgoal moves the solver closer to the solution (p. 498)

mental set: the tendency to rely on habits and procedures used in the past (p. 493)

noninsight problems: problems that are likely to be solved through incremental processes (p. 510)

nonroutine problem: a problem that requires the application of unfamiliar procedures in order to reach a solution (p. 481)

operators: problem-solving techniques (p. 488)

problem: a situation in which we're faced with an initial state, a goal state, a set of rules that must be followed, and a set of obstacles that must be overcome (p. 480)

problem representation: the process of correctly identifying the initial state as well as the operators that may be applied within the constraints of the problem (p. 489)

problem space: the problem solver's mental representation of the initial state, goal states, all intermediate (subgoal) states, and the operators that can be applied to reach these subgoals (p. 488)

routine problem: a problem that can be solved by applying well-practiced procedures (p. 481)

stereotype threat: a situation that occurs when a member of a negatively stereotyped group feels that their behavior might fit the stereotype, thus perpetuating it (p. 491)

structural features: the underlying relationships among the elements of a problem (p. 502)

subgoal analysis: breaking a problem down into a series of subgoals (p. 488)

surface features: the specific elements of a problem (p. 502)

transformation problems: problems in which the solver must find the proper strategies, or "moves," that will eventually convert the initial state into the goal state (p. 483)

verbal protocols: reports generated by problem solvers as they "think out loud" during the solution process (p. 482)

well-defined problems: problems that are clear and structured and in which the initial state, goal state, and constraints are all understood (p. 480)

working backward: focusing on the goal state and working backward in order to map out the steps that would get you there (p. 498)

13

Reasoning, Judgment, and Decision Making

Well, here goes, Donna thinks. She strides up to the front of the room.

"You feeling better today, Professor Goti?"

"Yes, thank you," Vince says, a little guiltily. "What can I do for you?"

"Did you watch the games last weekend?"

"What games?"

"The NFL playoff games."

"No, I'm really not a big football fan."

"But you love baseball," Donna says quizzically.

"Yeah . . . but not football. Anyway, what do you need? There's a few things I have to look over quickly before we start class."

"Well . . . I was wondering . . ."

Vince knows what's coming.

". . . if maybe you would . . ."

Here it comes.

". . . extend the deadline for the final paper."

Vince sighs heavily inside. This is always such a tough call. His experience is that it only makes it tougher for students to extend deadlines. It's a license to procrastinate. He thinks hard. Also if I extend deadlines every time I'm asked, I'll become known as lenient. I'll use a little cognitive psychology, he muses.

"Well, if I extend the deadline, I'll probably add more to what you have to do. Or we can just stick with the assignment and deadline as is."

Donna furrows her brow and thinks for a minute. Add more to the assignment?! No thanks. I knew Professor Goti wouldn't just say yes.

"Well, I'll just try to get it done, I guess."

"That's probably best. See me if you need any help."

"Thanks, Professor G."

"You bet . . . oh, and Donna?"

"Yeah?"

"After the semester's over, remember to hang onto your textbooks. You never know when you might be able to use them again. Besides, you can only get about $5 back for an $80 text!"

Consider the following evaluations:

- If you don't manage your time effectively, then you aren't going to do well in your classes.
  My roommate is bombing all of his classes.
  He's not very good at time management.

- All my professors are cool.
  Cool people wouldn't get worked up about extending a paper deadline.
  So my professor shouldn't have a problem with giving the class an extra week.

- There's been a "pop" quiz every other Monday for two months.
  It's Sunday night, two weeks after the last quiz.
  I'd better get ready for a quiz tomorrow.

- Boy, that guy is sure a tall drink of water.
  He's at least 6' 6".
  He must be a basketball player.

- Should I buy that brand of new truck?
  The consumer magazines rave about it, but a friend of my brother's bought one, and it was a real lemon.
  I'd better not.

Complex Thinking
Reasoning, Judgment, and Decision Making

Each of these seemingly simple evaluations is actually quite complex at root. Each involves making certain assumptions and arriving at a conclusion. For some there is incomplete or missing information; others entail an educated guess. In other words, each scenario involves the processes we'll be discussing next: **reasoning, judgment,** and **decision making.** It's appropriate that a book about the processes of cognition ends with a chapter about complex thought processes that put all of the component parts of cognition together. Think about it. (Hopefully, after reading this text, you've grown fond of that phrase.) In each case, your attention is required to take in the information; pattern recognition helps you to identify the elements within each scenario; working memory allows you to consider the alternatives; long-term memory serves as the database from which you build your assumptions; and language allows you to express and process each of the assertions.

The chapter title—"Reasoning, Judgment, and Decision Making"—connotes that each of these elements depends on different processes and/or presents different challenges. The major difference seems to relate primarily to what each requires. Reasoning involves evaluation of a conclusion based solely on given information. Decision making and judgment require that one go beyond the information given. With judgment, you apply reasoning processes about given information, but you must use the given information to arrive at a conclusion (rather than simply evaluating a given conclusion). The pop quiz example involves judgment; you discern a pattern in particular events and form a conclusion (i.e., "Pop quizzes occur every two weeks"). Unlike in the first two examples, you must go beyond the information given.

Decision making involves an even further progression beyond the given information—to situations that involve uncertainty or risk. In decision making, you must evaluate given information, arrive at a judgment, and, based on this judgment, make a choice among several possible alternatives. This is "risky," because it involves a considerable amount of guesswork. Decision-making situations often provide limited information or require a degree of knowledge or computational skill that is well beyond the range of what humans can do. Take the car-buying scenario above; there's no possible way you can know every fact about every car, and there is no easy way to combine this information to arrive at the correct choice. Indeed, in this case, it's not even clear what the correct choice would be! So in cases of decision making, we stray well beyond the information given into uncertain territory.

Research Focus on Errors

As you'll see, the emphasis in research on reasoning, judgment, and decision making has been on the mistakes people make. In fact, after reading about all of the ways in which these processes go wrong, you may think that people are idiots. Quite the contrary; errors may be seen as the price we pay for quick and efficient processing. So why the emphasis on error? One reason, noted by Nobel Prize–winning psychologist Daniel Kahneman (1991), is informativeness. The conditions under which our thinking fails us reveal important aspects of cognitive processing. You've seen a number of examples of this throughout the text; theories of memory have been richly informed by the phenomena of memory distortion (Chapter 7); the nature of automaticity is revealed by our susceptibility to action slips (Chapter 4). Along the same lines, the patterns of error that are evident in reasoning, judgment, and decision making inform us about how these processes typically operate.

The fact that so much research focuses on error begs a question: How exactly do we know that a given chain of reasoning, judgment, or decision making is in error? What is the benchmark against which we compare people's thinking in order to evaluate whether the thinking was accurate or proper? This question relates to a distinction researchers make between two approaches to the study of reasoning, judgment, and decision making. One approach, termed a **normative approach,** describes how we *ought* to think in a given situation. As you'll see, we often fall short of this ideal, so researchers have developed what is termed a **descriptive approach.** This approach, as the label would imply, describes how we actually do think.

Let's consider an example that allows for a comparison of the approaches. Suppose a woman told you that she had 10 children—all boys. Suppose you were then asked to estimate the probability of her having a girl in her next pregnancy. What would be your answer? According to a normative analysis, your answer should be 50-50. But people often overestimate the probability of it being a girl. They look at the long run of boys, and because this seems so unusual and unlikely, they think that it is especially likely that the situation will "return to normal" (in other words, become half boys and half girls). One descriptive model of judgment claims that people use a principle termed *representativeness.* (We'll discuss this principle in more detail later; here, we'll keep it simple.) In this example, people will see 10 boys in a row as very nonrepresentative of what should happen in 10 pregnancies. For it to be representative, there should be as many boys as girls; therefore, a girl being born next will be seen as especially likely. Although this judgment violates the principles of basic probability (which serves as the normative model here), people often make it. As you'll see, normative models of reasoning, judgment, and decision making are not always a reasonable standard against which to compare human thought. People aren't calculators or statisticians, and they usually don't have all of the information they need to follow a normative model.

Rationality.   You're going to see throughout this chapter that people violate normative models of reasoning, judgment, and decision making. Does this mean that human beings are irrational? As we'll see, there is no one simple answer to this question. Adherence to or deviance from rational thought and behavior depend on a variety of factors, not to mention exactly how we define *rational.* Baron (1999) contends that rationality is not necessarily the same as accuracy (getting the "right" answer), and that irrationality is not necessarily the same as error (getting the "wrong" answer). By Baron's analysis, rationality involves choosing the methods that help one attain one's goals, whatever those may be. We can reason well but still have a decision work out badly; conversely, we can reason badly yet still luck into a good outcome.

STOP *and* REVIEW !

1. Distinguish between reasoning, judgment, and decision making.
2. Why does research in reasoning, judgment, and decision making emphasize error?
3. Explain the distinction between normative and descriptive approaches to the study of reasoning, judgment, and decision making.
4. Discuss what it means to be rational.

> Reasoning involves evaluating conclusions based on given information. Judgment involves the application of reasoning to arrive at a conclusion. Decision making involves the application of a judgment to choose among several possible alternatives.

> Research on thinking emphasizes error because analyzing the types of mistakes people make and when they make them can be quite informative with regard to typical cognitive processing.

> Normative models of reasoning, judgment, and decision making provide descriptions of how we ought to think, given objective standards of rationality. Descriptive models of decision making provide descriptions of how we do think in actual situations.

> Rationality depends on a variety of factors, including how we define *rational*. Baron (1999) proposes that rationality involves choosing methods that help attain one's goals.

Reasoning

Deductive Reasoning

Determining if a specific conclusion is valid based on general principles or assertions (i.e., **premises**) is termed **deductive reasoning.** Think about the way psychology experiments are often conducted. Let's say you want to do a study about memory encoding and retrieval. First, you would review the literature to examine the theories concerning the relationship between these two concepts. Then you find the encoding specificity principle, which states that retrieval is best when the conditions at retrieval match those at encoding; this is your *general premise.* From this general premise, you make a *specific prediction* (conclusion) about what should happen when you vary the mood of people at encoding and retrieval: people will retrieve more information if their mood during retrieval is the same as their mood at encoding. In this example, you went from a general principle (encoding specificity) and made a specific conclusion (about mood) based on that principle.

Deductive reasoning is like solving a well-defined problem (discussed in Chapter 12) in that deductive-reasoning problems involve a large degree of constraint, and the conclusion is easily assessed. It's also like a well-defined problem in that an algorithmic approach is appropriate for solution. Recall that algorithms are step-by-step, formulaic approaches to solving problems. As you'll see, algorithms exist for solving deductive-reasoning problems; if you have taken a course in logic, you've learned some of these techniques. Two forms of deductive reasoning have received a great deal of attention from cognitive researchers: syllogistic reasoning and conditional reasoning.

Syllogistic Reasoning.   The first type of deductive reasoning is called **syllogistic reasoning.** Consider the following *syllogism* (no doubt a familiar sight if you've had a logic course):

All students are bright.
All bright people complete assigned work on time.
Therefore, all students complete assigned work on time.

Syllogisms consist of two premises and a conclusion. The premises and conclusion may begin with a *universal quantifier* (all) or a *particular quantifier* (some). Also, the terms within a syllogism may be stated positively ("All A are B") or negatively ("All A are not B"). Syllogisms are either valid or invalid—that is, the conclusion either does or does not hold given the premises. There is an important difference between the validity of an argument and the truth value of an argument. When we speak of an argument being *valid,* we're just saying that the conclusion does follow from the premises. However (and this is important), it says nothing about whether the premises themselves are true. The truth value of an argument depends on both validity of the argument form and the truth of the premises. Consider this argument:

All professors are comedians.
All comedians are funny.
All professors are funny.

This argument is valid in form; the conclusion does follow from the premises. However, the truth (or soundness) of the argument also depends on the truth of the premises. You could take issue with either premise; if either premise is false, then the argument is not true (i.e., it is not sound).

Confused? You're not alone. People are quite often bedeviled by these sorts of reasoning problems, and consequently they make predictable errors. Try your hand at these (from Sternberg & Ben-Zeev, 2001):

1. All A are B.
   All C are B.
   Therefore, all A are C.
2. No oranges are apples.
   No lemons are oranges.
   Therefore, no apples are lemons.

Are these conclusions valid, based on their respective premises? No, they aren't, although many believe they are (Wilkins, 1928). What underlies these reasoning errors?

Atmosphere Effects.   One classic description of syllogistic reasoning errors is termed the **atmosphere effect** (Woodworth & Sells, 1935). According to this explanation, the quantifiers used in the premises combine to form an "atmosphere" within which the validity of the conclusion is assessed. For example, the premises in syllogism 1 create a "positive universal atmosphere" (stated positively and using universal quantifiers). This produces an erroneous tendency to claim that the universal and positive conclusion ("All A are C") is valid. A similar account would explain why people mistakenly think the conclusion in syllogism 2 is valid. The premises in this syllogism produce a "negative universal atmosphere" (stated negatively and using negative quantifiers), which produces the tendency to agree that the universal and negative conclusion ("No apples are lemons") is valid. What if the quantifiers are mixed (some and all) or the positive and negative statements are mixed? Consider this example:

All A are B.
Some C are not B.
Therefore, some C are not A.

In this case, the syllogism seems to take on a "particular and negative atmosphere." Therefore, the particular and negative conclusion ("Some C are not A") is likely to be accepted. (In this case, correctly, as this is a valid syllogism.)

Belief Bias.   Consider our early distinction between validity and truth value. Often, our beliefs about truth interfere with our ability to assess argument validity. Rather than evaluating the validity of the argument form, people can be swayed by the believability of the premises. Consider the following example:

> All intelligent beings are Simpsons fans.
> All dolphins are intelligent beings.
> Therefore, all dolphins are Simpsons fans.

You probably looked at this conclusion and thought "Dolphins can't be Simpsons fans" and therefore concluded that it was invalid. However, this is a perfectly valid conclusion, given the premises. The validity of a conclusion in no way depends on how nonsensical the premises sound. The tendency to allow belief to interfere with the evaluation of conclusions in syllogistic arguments has been termed **belief bias**. Consider another example:

> All smart people are reasonable.
> All Democrats are smart people.
> Therefore, all Democrats are reasonable.

If you are a Democrat you would probably be more likely to believe that this conclusion is valid, because it agrees with your prior beliefs. However, if you are a Republican you would probably believe the conclusion to be invalid, because it is contrary to your prior beliefs. Belief bias can have serious ramifications: we are prone to uncritically accept conclusions if we agree with them and uncritically reject conclusions if we disagree with them. Belief bias is one of a number of phenomena that you'll read about in this chapter where our knowledge and beliefs hinder, rather than facilitate, the processes of thought.

Stop *and* Think!   I LOVE LOGIC

Read the following syllogisms:

1. Some politicians are dishonest people.
   All dishonest people are untrustworthy.
   Some politicians are untrustworthy.

2. All college students are curious.
   All curious people read books.
   All college students read books.

3. No rock fans are priests.
   All priests are religious.
   No rock fans are religious.

4. Some lawyers are ambulance chasers.
   Some ambulance chasers are unethical.
   Some lawyers are unethical.

Now answer these questions:

- For which syllogisms was this determination difficult?
- Which were easier?
- Why?

Find some willing friends and see how well they reason. Ask them the questions above or try out some questions from the text to see if they demonstrate the biases you've been reading about.

1. valid 2. valid 3. invalid 4. invalid

RECURRING RESEARCH THEME

Cognition and Neuroscience

The Brain and Syllogistic Reasoning

Research mapping out the neurological correlates of performance on complex cognitive tasks, such as syllogistic reasoning, is in its relative infancy. In order to investigate the relative roles of the right and left hemispheres in syllogistic reasoning, Goel and colleagues (Goel, Gold, Kapur, & Houle, 1998) used two types of reasoning tasks: a "traditional" syllogism task and two types of relational reasoning tasks, one involving spatial premises and one involving nonspatial premises (see Figure 13.1). The pattern of cortical activation was compared to a baseline condition in which participants simply evaluated the semantic content of each task.

A predominance of left-hemisphere activation and an absence of right-hemisphere activation was found for all tasks. This finding supports previous studies indicating that reasoning is a left-hemisphere, language-based activity (Gazzaniga, 1985; Gazzaniga & Smiley, 1984). However, there was an interesting difference between the reasoning conditions: brain activation did not differ between the two relational conditions, but it did differ somewhat between the relational conditions and the syllogism condition. Subtracting the brain areas involved during relational reasoning from the brain areas activated during syllogistic reasoning revealed a number of areas uniquely activated for syllogisms. These included frontal and temporal areas associated with attention and working memory, suggesting that syllogisms are more demanding than relational-reasoning problems. The areas differentially activated also included temporal areas that have been linked to linguistic processing, suggesting that perhaps syllogistic reasoning involves heavier usage of the phonological component of working memory, the articulatory loop (discussed in Chapter 4).

Syllogism	Some officers are generals.
	No privates are generals.
	Some officers are not privates.
Spatial Relational	Officers are standing next to generals.
	Privates are standing behind generals.
	Privates are standing behind officers.
Nonspatial Relational	Officers are heavier than generals.
	Generals are heavier than privates.
	Privates are lighter than officers.

Figure 13.1   Sample syllogisms used by Goel et al. (1998).

From Goel, V., Gold, B., Kapur, S., & Houle, S. (1998). Neuroanatomical correlates of human reasoning. *Journal of Cognitive Neuroscience, 10,* 293–302. Reprinted by permission of MIT Press.

Conditional Reasoning: Minding Your *P's* and *Q's*.   The second form of deductive reasoning is called **conditional reasoning** (or if-then reasoning) and involves evaluating whether a particular conclusion is valid given that certain conditions (premises) hold. For example, consider the following premises 1 and 2 and the conclusion (3):

1. If someone likes Winnie-the Pooh, then they're a sensitive person.
2. Mary likes Winnie-the-Pooh.
3. Therefore, Mary is a sensitive person.

The *conditional statement* (1) provides the rule that is expressed in an *if-then* format: if P (some sort of antecedent condition), then Q (some sort of consequent condition).

So is statement 3 a valid conclusion, based on premises 1 and 2? Yes, given that sensitive people like Winnie-the-Pooh and given that Mary likes Winnie-the-Pooh, one can validly conclude that Mary is a sensitive person. Notice that the evaluation of a conclusion is in terms of validity, not truth. (See our earlier example about professors being funny!) It may not be true that people who like Winnie-the-Pooh are sensitive, but this is irrelevant to determining the validity of the conclusion. In conditional-reasoning tasks, like syllogistic-reasoning tasks, the goal is to determine only whether the conclusion can be derived logically from the premises.

Let's try another version of the reasoning problem. Once again, assess whether conclusion (3) is valid—that is, does it flow logically from premises 1 and 2?

1. If someone likes Winnie-the-Pooh, then they're a sensitive person.
2. Mary is a sensitive person.
3. Therefore, Mary likes Winnie-the-Pooh.

It seems, on the face of it, that the conclusion (3) is valid: Winnie-the-Pooh and sensitivity go together. But in reality, the conclusion is invalid. It could be that Mary is a sensitive person who couldn't care less about Winnie-the-Pooh. There are many reasons besides liking Winnie-the-Pooh that can indicate a person's sensitivity. People fall prey fairly easily to validating these sorts of erroneous conclusions. In actuality, conditional-reasoning conclusions can be evaluated quite easily if one applies a set of logical rules. Consider again the argument form of conditional-reasoning problems. Line 1 gives the if (antecedent)-then (consequent) contingency—that is, "If someone likes Winnie-the-Pooh, then they are a sensitive person." Line 2 either affirms or denies either the antecedent ("Mary does or does not like Winnie-the-Pooh") or the consequent ("Mary is or is not a sensitive person"). This creates four different argument forms, which are outlined in Figure 13.2.

Two of the forms have already been discussed. The first example is termed *affirming the antecedent*—"Mary likes Winnie-the-Pooh; therefore, Mary is a sensitive person." (In logic lingo, this argument form is termed *modus ponens.*) It is valid to conclude that Mary is a sensitive person, because the conditional statement gives us that rule: if a person likes Winnie-the-Pooh, then they're a sensitive person. It is stated that Mary likes Winnie-the-Pooh; therefore she must be a sensitive person. The second example we discussed above was (can you guess?) *affirming the consequent*—"Mary is a sensitive person; therefore, Mary likes Winnie-the-Pooh." As you saw, this is invalid; it does not necessarily follow that Mary likes Winnie-the-Pooh, given that she is a sensitive person. The conditional statement does not say anything about what sensitive people will like or will not like. It only tells what it means if a person likes Winnie-the-Pooh.

The other two argument forms involve denying each part of the conditional statement. *Denying the antecedent*—"Mary does not like Winnie-the-Pooh; therefore, Mary is not a sensitive person"—is invalid. If she does not like Winnie-the-Pooh, this does not necessarily

Condition statement:

If a person likes Winnie-the-Pooh, then they're a sensitive person.
(Antecedent)   *(Consequent)*

Four conditional-reasoning scenarios:

	Affirm	**Deny**
Antecedent	Mary likes Winnie-the-Pooh. Therefore, Mary is a sensitive person.	Mary does not like Winnie-the-Pooh. Therefore, Mary is not a sensitive person.
Consequent	Mary is a sensitive person. Therefore, Mary likes Winnie-the-Pooh.	Mary is not a sensitive person. Therefore, Mary does not like Winnie-the-Pooh.

Figure 13.2 Propositional calculus.

mean that she is not a sensitive person. There are many other correlates of sensitivity; liking Winnie-the-Pooh is just one of them. Finally, *denying the consequent*—"Mary is not sensitive; therefore, Mary does not like Winnie-the-Pooh"—is valid. (Logicians call this *modus tollens*.) If Mary is not sensitive, it is valid to conclude that she does not like Winnie-the-Pooh. According to the conditional statement, liking Winnie-the-Pooh means the person is sensitive. Given that we know that Mary is not sensitive, she must not like Winnie-the-Pooh.

As you might imagine, people run into a fair amount of difficulty when judging the validity of conclusions derived from if-then statements. No one walks around with a card in their pocket describing the valid and invalid argument forms. So what types of errors are common in these sorts of reasoning tasks? One tendency people have is to interpret the initial conditional statement as *biconditional*—thinking that "If *p*, then *q*" also means "If *q*, then *p*" (Wyer & Srull, 1989). In the problem above, people would tend to think that "If someone likes Winnie-the-Pooh, then they're a sensitive person" also means "If someone is a sensitive person, then they like Winnie-the-Pooh." But conditional statements don't work that way. By assuming that the if-then statement is biconditional, we are essentially assuming that *p* can be an antecedent or a consequent. If we affirm *p*, this only leads to a valid conclusion if *p* is an antecedent. If we make the biconditional assumption and assume *p* can also be the consequent, then affirming *p* leads to an invalid conclusion (see Figure 13.3).

Conditional statement:

If a person likes Winnie-the-Pooh (antecedent), then they're a sensitive person (consequent).

Affirm: Mary likes Winnie-the-Pooh.

Conclusion is valid, affirming the antecedent.

Biconditional assumption:

If a someone is a sensitive person (antecedent), then *they like Winnie-the-Pooh* (consequent).

Affirm: Mary likes Winnie-the-Pooh.

Conclusion is invalid, affirming the consequent.

Figure 13.3 Affirming the antecedent leads to a valid conclusion. However, affirming the consequent leads to an invalid conclusion and a common fallacy.

The opening story actually contains a couple of examples of conditional reasoning. Vince's musing "If I extend the deadline, I'll get a reputation for being lenient" is an if-then conditional statement. He decides not to extend the deadline, essentially denying the antecedent. But this is an invalid form, which means he won't necessarily avoid the label "lenient." Donna also engages in conditional reasoning when she ponders Vince's response "If the deadline is extended, he'll probably add more work." Mentally, Donna is no doubt affirming the antecedent and (validly) concluding that if she pushes for and receives the deadline extension, extra work will follow.

Stop *and* Think!

I LOVE LOGIC, THE SEQUEL

Try out the following conditional reasoning problems:

1. If I do really well on my GRE's, then I'll get into graduate school.
   I got into graduate school.
   Therefore, I did well on my GRE's.

2. If someone likes South Park, then they have a crude sense of humor.
   Joan likes South Park.
   Therefore, Joan has a crude sense of humor

3. If someone watches the Simpsons, they must be intelligent.
   Becky does not watch the Simpsons.
   Therefore, Becky is not intelligent.

4. If the tickets for the rock concert are under $50, then I will go to the concert.
   I did not go to the concert.
   Therefore, the tickets for the concert were not under $50.

Now answer these questions:

- Does each conclusion follow from its premises?
- Which are difficult?
- Which are easier?
- Why?
- What is the form of the argument (e.g., affirming the consequent)?

1. affirming the consequent (invalid)   2. affirming the antecedent (valid)
3. denying the antecedent (invalid)   4. denying the consequent (valid)

Wason's Selection Task. One of the most investigated conditional-reasoning tasks is the Wason Selection Task (WST). The classic version of this task is depicted in Figure 13.4a. The reasoner must decide which of the four cards needs to be turned over in order to determine whether the following if-then statement holds: if a card has a vowel on one side, then it must have an even number on the opposite side. Can you figure out which cards should be turned over? If you had a logic guide (as we mentioned earlier), you would realize that to test this conditional rule, you need to apply modus ponens and modus tollens. In other words, you would need to turn over the *E* card (affirming the antecedent, "if vowel"), and the 7 card (denying the consequent, "then even number"). However, people

If a card has a vowel on one side. then it must have an even number on the other side.

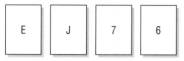

(a) Classic Version

If a person is under age 21, then they should be drinking a nonalcoholic beverage.

(b) Deontic Version

Figure 13.4 Two versions of the Wason Selection Task. Does one seem easier than the other?

From Wason, P. C., & Johnson-Laird, P. N. (1970). A conflict between selection and evaluating information in an inferential task. *British Journal of Psychology, 68,* 325–331. Copyright 1970, the British Journal of Psychology. Reprinted with kind permission of the British Psychological Society.

rarely choose this combination of cards; in fact, they choose these particular cards less than 10% of the time (Sternberg, 2001). The most common choices are to turn over the *E* and the 6 cards (nearly half choose 6, which amounts to the error of affirming the consequent) or only the *E* card. (About 33% choose this option.)

Why does this task pose such difficulty? One reason is the biconditional thinking discussed above: "If *p*, then *q*" is often misinterpreted to imply "If *q*, then *p*." As a result, the WST if-then statement is inappropriately interpreted as also meaning "If a card has an even number on one side, it must have a vowel on the other." Based on this invalid assumption, it seems that the 6 card must be turned over (applying the valid rule of affirming the antecedent). But the if-then statement is not biconditional. Turning over the 6 card demonstrates the error of affirming the consequent.

The selection tendencies revealed on the WST have been cited as evidence for a confirmatory bias in reasoning. **Confirmatory bias** refers to our tendency to seek out or notice evidence that is consistent with a particular hypothesis rather than evidence that would be inconsistent with the hypothesis. Once again, consider the selection task "If vowel, then even number." What would support, or help confirm, the validity of this rule? Answer: a vowel with an even number on the other side. What cards are most commonly turned? Answer: even numbers and vowels. If you'd thought in terms of disconfirmation—what should not be the case, given the rule—you'd have realized that odd numbers should never go with vowels. Thinking along these lines would more likely lead one to (correctly) turn over the *E* and 7 cards.

Deontic Versions of the WST. People don't perform poorly on all versions of the Wason Selection Task. Consider the deontic version in Figure 13.4b. In this case, the selection scenario is presented in a deontic context—that is, in terms of a social contract or a right (Griggs & Cox, 1982). The rule to be tested is "If a person is consuming alcohol, then the person must be at least 21 years old." Under these conditions, people are much more likely to turn over the correct cards—the age 17 card, and the beer card. A number of studies have demonstrated improved performance on the WST in such a context. Based on these findings, some (e.g., Cosmides, 1989) have gone so far as to suggest that **deontic reasoning** is a special form of thought that has evolved to allow people to reason about their own duties and social obligations—that is, the things they should or shouldn't do. The assertion that deontic reasoning is a specially evolved ability is controversial. Some (e.g., Almor & Sloman, 1996; Kirby 1994) have challenged it, showing that people can perform the selection task very well under conditions that do not involve some type of social contract.

Rules or Models?   Explanations for how we reason deductively generally fall into one of two camps. One view might be termed a "strict," or *rule-based account* of deductive reasoning (Rips, 1994). Basically, this view contends that people possess the representational equivalent of logic rules (basically, a mental version of the ones discussed earlier). These rules are then applied to the premises to determine if the conclusion is valid. A contrasting view is the *mental models view* of Johnson-Laird and colleagues (e.g., Bauer & Johnson-Laird, 1993). According to this approach, we first form a mental model based on the information in the premises and our own previous experience. Next, we search for a mental model in which the premises would be true but the stated conclusion would be false. If such a model is found, the conclusion is deemed invalid; if no such model is found, the conclusion is determined to be valid. Currently, the jury is still out regarding whether a rule-based account or a mental-models account provides a better explanation for deductive reasoning. It may well be that people rely on both sorts of processes (e.g., Smith, Langston, & Nisbett, 1992).

Inductive Reasoning

The flip side of the reasoning coin is **inductive reasoning.** Rather than working from general premises to arrive at a specific conclusions, we take the opposite tack, moving from specific pieces of data or information, and work toward a general conclusion. Think about theory development in psychology. Based on the results of specific empirical investigations, researchers will develop a general theory that explains each specific finding. Unlike deductive reasoning, where conclusions can be labeled valid or invalid with absolute certainty, inductive reasoning leads to uncertain conclusions that vary in their strength.

For an everyday example of inductive reasoning, consider the following:

Professor X gets upset when asked if she'll issue a paper extension.
Professor Y won't accept late papers.
Professor Z takes 20% off for each day a paper is late.

You might (correctly) induce from these specific pieces of data that professors find late papers unacceptable. Note the differences between this type of inductive reasoning and deductive reasoning. If this were a deductive-reasoning situation, you would be given the general principle—"Professors find late papers unacceptable"—and you would need to determine if the specific statements about professors X, Y, and Z follow from that general principle. In the above inductive-reasoning example, you are inferring the general principle ("Professors find late papers unacceptable") based on specific pieces of information about professors X, Y, and Z. Deductive reasoning moves from general to specific, while inductive reasoning moves from specific to general.

Bisanz, Bisanz, and Korpan (1994) describe some characteristics that seem to typify inductive reasoning. First, the product of inductive reasoning (the general principle) is not necessarily correct. Suppose you make the assumption that professors won't accept late papers or extend paper deadlines; you may miss an opportunity to get an extension. This characteristic of inductive reasoning provides a sharp contrast to deductive reasoning, in which the validity of a conclusion is inherent in the premises. Inductive arguments are evaluated in terms of their strength rather than their validity; in other words, how solid the conclusion is is based on the evidence. Second, as Rips (1990) points out, with inductive reasoning, there is a need for constraint on the conclusions reached. If there were none, you could come up with some pretty wild conclusions based on evidence. For example, given the pieces of evidence from professors X, Y, and Z, you could induce that people whose last names are letters of the alphabet don't like late papers. As you can see, constraint is needed in order to avoid unreasonable conclusions.

Confirmatory Bias Revisited.   Earlier we discussed Wason's Selection Task, which revealed people's tendency to seek out information consistent with a given hypothesis in deductive reasoning. The same effect can found for inductive reasoning. A classic study investigated the confirmatory bias within the context of social cognition—the information processing we perform about other people. Snyder and Swann (1978) had participants simulate the role of an interviewer whose task it was to discover whether an interviewee was extroverted (outgoing) or introverted (shy). The participants were given a suggested set of questions to ask the interviewee and were instructed to use the ones they thought would be the most diagnostic—in other words, the ones that would definitively determine whether the person was extroverted or not. Note how this situation involves inductive reasoning; the interviewers are to use the information derived from the answers to the questions to arrive at a general conclusion (i.e., that the person is extroverted). Rather than seeking out information that might be incongruent with what they were thinking, the interviewers tended to ask questions that were congruent with their hypothesis. If they expected an extrovert, then they asked questions that would reveal extroversion (e.g., "What are some reasons you like parties?"). Any answer would serve only to bolster the interviewer's already-held idea. Interviewers tended not to ask questions that would be inconsistent with extroversion and reveal contrary evidence.

Rule Based or Experience Based?   What mental structures and processes underlie inductive reasoning? Here there is a theoretical debate similar to the one found in deductive reasoning. Basically, researchers disagree over whether induction is based on formal, rule-driven processes or on more context-bound, experience-based heuristic processing. The rule-based view—termed the "strict," or *syntactic view* of inductive reasoning—states that inductive reasoning involves special processes and representations that operate in the abstract, outside of any real-life context. Conversely, the experience-based view, which Rips (1990) terms the *loose view,* contends that inductive reasoning is a little more "messy." According to this view, inductive reasoning involves updating the strengths of one's beliefs based on the recall of specific examples. In this view, inductive reasoning is strongly influenced by real-world context and does not involve special mental structures or built-in logic steps. Sloman (1996) proposes a likely scenario—that both types of processes, formal and loose, are involved in inductive reasoning.

The Omnipresence of Inductive Reasoning.   Inductive reasoning is pervasive; in some form, it underlies just about every other process we've talked about. The hallmark of cognition is to go beyond the information given to form a new conclusion. Let's reassess two of the cognitive processes we discussed in previous chapters through the lens of inductive reasoning.

Inductive Reasoning in Categorization.   The processes of categorization and concept formation are, by their very nature, inductive. As you learned in Chapters 5 and 9, forming a concept or category involves making a connection between specific instances that seem similar in some manner; in other words, concept formation and categorization involve deriving a general principle (i.e., a category) from specific examples (i.e., the members of the category).

Inductive reasoning provides another window through which to view the phenomenon known as the *typicality effect*—the finding that some members of a category are more readily identified as such. Rips (1974) extended these findings beyond simple judgments of category membership to inferences induced from the category members. Consider the following inductive arguments:

1. Robins are susceptible to disease A.
   Therefore, all birds are susceptible to disease A.
2. Turkeys are susceptible to disease B.
   Therefore, all birds are susceptible to disease B.

Participants rated argument 1 as more likely to be true, because robins are seen as more typical than turkeys. The typicality effect seems to carry over to reasoning about unknown properties; inferences from typical category members are "safer bets."

Another interesting phenomenon observed in inductive reasoning about categories might be termed a *diversity effect* (Rips, 1974). Which of the following inductive argument seems stronger?

1. Robins are susceptible to disease Y.
   Sparrows are susceptible to disease Y.
   Therefore, all birds are susceptible to disease Y.
2. Cardinals are susceptible to disease Z.
   Turkeys are susceptible to disease Z.
   Therefore, all birds are susceptible to disease Z.

In this case, people tend to rate the second argument as stronger, because cardinals and turkeys represent a more diverse set of birds relative to robins and sparrows. Because of this diversity, the conclusion seems more warranted and more likely to be true.

Inductive Reasoning in Problem Solving.   Another set of cognitive processes that depends critically on inductive reasoning is problem solving—more specifically, solving problems by analogy. As you learned in Chapter 12, analogies are a potentially powerful but underused tool; people often fail to make the necessary connections between problem situations. Making these connections involves the processes of inductive reasoning. Recall that in using analogies, people must recognize that two situations share superficial and/or structural characteristics and must use the connection between the two to come to a general solution that can be transferred to similar problems. So, specific problem situations are used to generate a general problem-solution procedure.

STOP *and* REVIEW!

1. True or false? If a syllogism is valid, the premises on which the conclusion is based are true.
2. Identify the two valid forms of a conditional-reasoning task.
3. True or false? Confirmatory bias is less likely to be seen in a deontic context.
4. Distinguish between the rule-based account and the mental models view of deductive reasoning.
5. True or false? Inductive reasoning could be described as moving from the specific to the general.

➤ Deductive reasoning involves determining whether a conclusion is valid based on premises. Syllogistic reasoning involves deciding whether two premises necessitate a conclusion. A valid syllogism is one in which the conclusion follows from the given premises. Validity does not refer to the truth of the premises. The atmosphere effect and belief bias interfere with judging the validity of a syllogism. Syllogistic reasoning seems to involve activity in the left frontal and temporal lobes.

➤ Conditional reasoning involves evaluating whether a particular conclusion is valid, given that certain conditions hold. A conditional statement fits the form "If p (antecedent), then q (consequent)." Affirming the antecedent and denying the consequent are valid forms; denying the antecedent and affirming the consequent are invalid forms.

➤ People often wrongly assume that conditional statements are biconditional (i.e., that "If p, then q" also means "If q, then p"). Confirmatory bias refers to our tendency to seek evidence that affirms our hypotheses; it is less likely to be shown in some applied contexts (i.e., a deontic reasoning situation based on social obligations).

➤ The rule-based account of reasoning contends that people possess the mental representational equivalent of logic rules. The mental models view contends that we base reasoning on models we build based on premises and our own previous experience.

➤ Inductive reasoning involves using specific information to arrive at a general conclusion. Confirmatory bias can lead to errors in inductive reasoning. Inductive reasoning may involve either (or both) rule-based or experience-based processing. Induction underlies a host of other cognitive processes, such as the use of analogy in problem solving, the formation of categories, and judgments about category membership.

Judgment

As you've seen, inductive reasoning involves arriving at general conclusions based on specific pieces of what might be called "data." Judgment is an extension of inductive reasoning. Hastie and Dawes (2001) define *judgment* as "the human ability to infer, estimate, and predict the character of unknown events" (p. 48). Judgment is much more a process of making educated guesses, based on (sometimes quite severely) limited information along with our previous knowledge, expectations, and beliefs. At the end of the story segment from the last chapter, you read that Donna had sized up her teacher as a "pretty nice guy." We make these sorts of judgments all the time. For example, when a friend tells you that there's this really interesting person they'd like to fix you up with, you're very likely to gather some initial data and arrive at a judgment. Your impression will be different if you find out that this person is a sculptor versus a business major. Right or wrong, this information is likely to lead you to strikingly different inferences (i.e., judgments) about this individual.

Much of the research on judgment has been conducted by social psychologists interested in how we perceive and think about other people. Indeed, much of the work in social cognition (the study of how we process information about other people) is concerned with the factors that underlie our judgments of others (such as our hypothetical sculptor or business student). Stereotypes—the positive or negative beliefs that we hold about members of certain groups—are largely based on the processes of judgment.

Even though judgments can be overly broad or outright wrong, it seems necessary that we make them. In almost every situation requiring a judgment, we usually don't have all of the information we need to arrive at an accurate conclusion. Even if we did, we do not possess the computational power required to successfully combine the information. So we take educated guesses. Does this sound familiar? It should, since it is similar to something you read about in Chapter 12—that is, our reliance on heuristics, or "rules of thumb," for solving certain types of problems. Heuristics serve as shortcuts across the problem space; with heuristics, one needn't consider every possible course of action to solve a problem. In the case of judgment, heuristics are rough assumptions we make that reduce the need for complete data and computational skill. As is the case with problem solving, judgment heuristics lighten the mental load considerably. But, as with problem solving, heuristics are no guarantee of a correct solution. In fact, because heuristics are based on our personal database and our own computational skills (or lack thereof), they can lead to systematic errors in judgment.

Basing Judgments on Memory: The Availability Heuristic

Try the demonstration in Table 13.1: scan the names and then come back to the reading. There were a total of 21 names. Try to estimate the number of first names that began with *J*, began with *C*, and began with *B*. Do you have your estimates? You may have guessed that there were more names that started with *J* than with the other letters. If you did, you fell victim to what is termed the availability heuristic. The **availability heuristic** indicates that we base our estimates of likelihood, or probability, on the ease with which we can think of examples. In this case, the names that begin with *J* are relatively well-known, while those names that begin with *C* or *B* are not. Therefore, *J* names seem more numerous because it is easier to remember famous rather than nonfamous names.

Consider why you would need such a heuristic in this situation. Given the characteristics of human attention and memory, it's simply not possible to memorize 21 names on

Table 13.1

Jimmy Stewart	James Thurber	Joyce Carol Oates
Bob Smitson	Carl Pavano	Chris Baines
Jack Kerouac	Beth Feynman	Jackie Robinson
Charlie Horton	Bobbi Castel	Cory Lidle
Cecil Patterson	Barbara Edison	Claude Shelet
Bill Arnold	Jennifer Aniston	Bruce Williamson
Charlene Tilton	Joan Crawford	Bess Severson

a brief glimpse. Therefore, you rely on a fairly sensible strategy: when asked about the names, you try and think of as many names as you can and see what letter these names start with. In other words, you turn to the information that is available in memory. The problem is, as you saw in detail in Chapter 7, memory is not always the most reliable database. When the availability heuristic is applied, systematic biases in memory can lead to systematic biases in judgment. Just because something seems like a common occurrence doesn't mean that it is. So availability in memory is not always the best basis for judgment; it is affected by a host of factors that can distort our judgment.

Biased Encoding.   The availability heuristic is based on the ease of retrieval from memory. But something may be easier to get out of memory because it is overrepresented in memory. Why might this occur? Consider the exercise you just did. Because the names that start with *J* are more familiar than the other names, you were much more likely to have encoded them successfully. So your memory retrieval is biased, because the information you've stored is biased.

Another study, conducted by Lichtenstein and colleagues (Lichtenstein, Slovic, Fischhoff, Layman, and Comb, 1978), on the cheery subject of causes of death provides another example. Before we talk about the study, try it yourself. Look at the causes-of-death pairs listed in Table 13.2. For each pair, decide which of the two causes results in more deaths. If you're like the participants in this study, you overestimated the frequency of some causes of death and underestimated others. For example, at the time this study was conducted, there were more deaths from stomach cancer than homicide, more from asthma than flood, more from stroke than motor vehicle accidents, and more from extreme cold than tornadoes. But the participants in the study tended to make the opposite estimates, overestimating the number of deaths caused by homicides, floods, auto accidents, and tornadoes and underestimating the number of deaths caused by stomach cancer, asthma, stroke, and extreme cold. When faced with this estimation task, the only possible way to do it is to sample memory for examples. In this case, however, you're likely to come up with a biased sample, because the first member of each cause-of-death pair (e.g., floods) is "front-page news." The very nature of such events is dramatic, and therefore deaths from such causes are more likely to be reported on the evening news and in magazines and newspapers. The second member of each pair (e.g., asthma) is undramatic. (When was the last time your newspaper reported someone dying of asthma?) The bias in reporting of these types of death leads to a biased knowledge base.

Your authors' personal experience in teaching in different geographic locales provides an example of the effects of a biased knowledge base. (Keep in mind that this example is anecdotal and subject to our own processes of memory distortion!) We began our teaching careers in Indiana, where tornadoes are probably the most serious weather hazard; in other words, they're front-page news. Hoosiers hear a great

Table 13.2

A.	Tornadoes	A.	Motor vehicle accidents
B.	Extreme cold	B.	Stroke
A.	Homicide	A.	Food poisoning
B.	Stomach cancer	B.	Smallpox vaccination
A.	All cancers	A.	Floods
B.	Heart disease	B.	Asthma

From Lichtenstein, S. (1978). Judged frequency of lethal events. *Journal of Experimental Psychology: Human Learning and Memory, 4,* 551–578. Copyright 1978 by the American Psychological Association. Reprinted by permission.

Which is the cause of more deaths?

deal about tornadoes and encode lots of information about the damage they wreak. We now teach in Minnesota, where the extreme cold is front-page news. Minnesotans are exposed to conditions of extreme cold for several months every year and so are likely to encode information about this hazard. In line with the experiential differences between our two populations of students, when we've asked students to compare tornadoes and extreme cold as causes of death, Indiana students were clearly biased to say "tornadoes." But since our move to Minnesota, we've heard more people claim "extreme cold" as the more common cause of death. Once again, the information that is encoded in memory exerts an influence on our judgments; differences or biases in encoding lead to differences or biases in judgment.

The media no doubt serves as one source of encoding-based availability biases. Vivid news reports of certain types of events lead us to overestimate their frequency and likelihood. For example, as Hastie and Dawes (2001) point out, when a former psychiatric patient commits a crime, the fact that they were formerly in treatment is often mentioned

Does vivid media coverage lead people to worry too much about certain events?

in the news report. But how often do we hear the negative case—"Harold Smith, who has never received psychiatric treatment, was arrested for murder today"? So being a former psychiatric patient and committing a crime are vividly connected. These biases in reporting can lead to biases in people's knowledge database. Many would contend that the media's vivid reporting is at the root of many public anxieties, such as the safety of drinking water, the likelihood of school shootings, or the chances of a plane crash. This is not to say that these issues are of no concern, but there is little doubt that vivid and intense reports may increase their prominence in memory in disproportion to the actual danger.

Biased Retrieval.   So the availability heuristic leads us astray when our memory contains a biased sample of information. Availability can also lead us astray if the sampling process itself is biased. Try the following demonstration, based on Tversky and Kahneman (1973), and estimate whether there are more of number 1 or number 2:

1. six-letter words that have the letter *n* as the fifth letter
2. words that fit the pattern __ __ __ *ing*

Participants in Tversky and Kahneman's study estimated that words of type 2 were much more likely than words of type 1. Can you see why this is a rather silly answer and why the answer must be type 1? The set of words defined by type 1 includes every single word that fits type 2—that is, words that fit type 2 are six letters long with the fifth letter being *n!* Therefore, there have to be more words that fit category 1. But making this judgment requires a person to sample memory, and people generate a biased sample because it's easier to think of words that end in *-ing* than it is to think of words that have *n* as the fifth letter. Note that the problem here is not one of encoding; the information stored in memory really does have more words with *n* as the fifth letter than words that fit the pattern _ _ _ *ing*. The problem here is one of retrieval; being asked to think of examples of words that end in -*ing* serves as a more precise, hence easier to use, retrieval cue.

Another instance of a retrieval-based bias in the use of the availability heuristic relates to recency. One of the most tried-and-true principles of memory research (going all the way back to Ebbinghaus's ubiquitous forgetting curve, discussed in Chapter 1) is that more recent events are easier to retrieve than more remote events. This is true for both immediate (working) memory and long-term memory. Therefore, the availability heuristic can lead us to overestimate the frequency of events because of their recency. Consider again the news reports of tragedies such as the hijackings on September 11, 2001. In addition to being selectively encoded into memory (as described above), these events also impact our judgment more when they've occurred recently and their aftermath is fresh in our minds. Therefore, people probably felt that the likelihood of being a victim of a terrorist attack was greater after than before the World Trade Center disaster. In reality, the probability may be less, because of the heightened security that resulted from that disaster.

RECURRING RESEARCH THEME
Cognition and Consciousness

Comparing Intuitive and Analytic Judgments

In a recent study, McMackin and Slovic (2000) were interested in discovering the best mode of operation for different types of judgments. What leads to better judgments—careful analysis, planning, and thought or more intuitive, nonconscious processes? You're probably thinking that each mode for making judgments is potentially good or bad, depending on the judgment that is to be made. In line with this general idea, McMackin and Slovic hypothesized that certain types of judgments would be better served by conscious, deliberate thought than by quicker, more intuitive processes. For other types of judgments, the opposite pattern would hold. They had participants perform two different tasks under two different judgment modes.

For one task (the more intuitive task), participants were shown ads and were asked to guess (or intuit) how well-liked these ads were by their fellow college students and to assign a corresponding rating to the ad. These ratings were then compared to actual ratings from a separate sample. The researchers expected that this task would benefit from a relatively quick, intuitive judgment. Since there is really no factual basis for this judgment, it won't help to think analytically and try to reason it out. In fact, a search for reasons for these judgments may lead to overthinking and second-guessing. For the second task, participants were given relatively obscure trivia questions like "How many cigarettes are consumed in the United States in a single year?" The researchers believed that because answers to these questions did have some factual basis, closer examination and analytic reasoning would lead to more reasonable estimates. Overly fast and nondeliberative processes would lead to less accurate responding.

To manipulate the amount of thought involved, each task was presented within one of two judgment modes. In the reasons condition, participants were asked to think analytically about their answers before giving them. In the corresponding control condition, participants were simply told to give an estimate. The results were exactly as predicted: having to think analytically about their judgments and describe the reasons behind them had opposite effects in the two conditions. Thinking analytically hindered participants' ability to accurately judge their fellow students' preferences for advertisements but improved accuracy on the trivia questions.

Stop and Think!

ASSESSING AVAILABILITY

Consider the following question: Do you think there are more letters in the English language that start with the letter *k* or that have *k* as the third letter? Now answer these questions:

- How did you arrive at your answer?
- Which of the judgment heuristics came into play?
- How might it have been biased?

Find two friends to be "research participants." Vary the conditions under which you give them this problem. For one of your "research participants," have them answer quickly. Tell the other to take as much time as needed to think about it. These two different conditions correspond to the ones investigated by McMackin and Slovic (2000).

- What would you expect under these two conditions?
- Why?

Illusory Correlations.   Everyone has heard claims or stories like the following:

I know a couple who had just given up trying to get pregnant, started to look into adoption, and then bam! They got pregnant!

Because of the vividness of some examples, like the above, people see relationships where none likely exist. To know if starting adoption proceedings really is associated with an increase in the chances of getting pregnant, one needs to know four different pieces of information: (1) how frequently people who can't conceive start adoption and get pregnant, (2) how frequently people who can't conceive start adoption and do not get pregnant, (3) how frequently people who can conceive start adoption and get pregnant, and (4) how frequently people who can conceive start adoption and do not get pregnant (see Table 13.3). All four pieces of data allow for an assessment of whether the circumstance (i.e., getting pregnant after starting adoption proceedings) occurs an inordinate number of times. Of course, people can't readily bring to mind all four pieces of information; they tend to rely on only the first piece, which

Table 13.3 Influence of Coincidental Events

Our tendency to notice distinctive coincidences causes us to be overly influenced by coincidental evidence.

	Gets Pregnant	Doesn't Get Pregnant
Start adoption proceedings	Distinctive coincidence	Nonevent
Don't start adoption proceedings	Nonevent	Nonevent

essentially boils down to noticing coincidences. When one notices primarily (or only) co-incidences, two events will seem to be linked even when they're not. This perception is termed **illusory correlation.**

One well-known example of an illusory correlation is the "*Sports Illustrated* jinx," which goes something like this: if someone appears on the cover of this well-known sports magazine, then they are doomed to suffer some calamity soon after—a season-ending injury, an awful performance slump, or personal problems. Of course, the correlation between appearing on the cover of *Sports Illustrated* and having some calamity befall is nonexistent; but people notice when such an appearance is followed by some bad event, and they don't notice other combinations of events, such as someone appearing on the cover and continuing to excel (e.g., Michael Jordan). This is also an example of the statistical principle termed *regression to the mean*. Sometimes an athlete performs below their average, sometimes above their average, but most of the time their performance hovers right around their average. (That's why it's called the average!) After performing far above or below their average, performance will tend to *regress toward the average*. Athletes only appear on the cover of *Sports Illustrated* when they perform well above average. So of course, their performance will tend to move back (i.e., regress) toward their mean level of performance.

It's important to note that (as with all of the judgment heuristics) the availability heuristic can be quite useful. If, based on thinking of examples from memory, you come to the conclusion that your professor is going to be a trifle annoyed (or worse) when you hand in a late paper, this is most likely an accurate judgment. In the chapter-opening story, Vince puts the availability heuristic to good use in reflecting on his experiences with extending paper deadlines and remembering that this typically got students into trouble. Use of the availability heuristic tends to get us into trouble only when there are especially memorable examples that seem to carry the weight of a thousand.

Basing Judgments on Similarity: The Representativeness Heuristic

We've all made judgments based on similarity. For example, we see an unusually tall person, say 6'8", and we make an assumption that anybody so tall must play basketball. But think about it. Most people, even tall people, don't play basketball. So why do we make such judgments? When trying to place a person in a particular category (e.g., basketball player), we have a tendency to base our judgment on the similarity between the person and the stereotype we hold about that category. In the opening vignette, Donna assumes that because Vince likes baseball, he probably likes football, too. Judgments like this rely on what is termed the **representativeness heuristic:** we assess the degree to which the object represents (is similar to) our basic idea (or stereotype) of that object. Donna holds a view of Vince as a sports fan and judges accordingly.

Ignoring Base Rates.   Let's consider a classic demonstration of this heuristic from a study by Kahneman and Tversky (1973, p. 241). Participants were given the following instructions:

A panel of psychologists have interviewed and administered personality tests to 30 engineers and 70 lawyers, all successful in their fields. On the basis of this information, thumbnail descriptions for each of these individuals have been written. For each description, please indicate the probability that the person described is an engineer, from 1 to 100.

Participants were then given the following description:

> Jack is a 45-year-old man. He is married and has 4 children. He is generally conservative, careful, and ambitious. He shows no interest in political and social issues and spends most of his time on his many hobbies, which include home carpentry, sailing, and mathematical puzzles.

Participants were required to rate the probability that Jack was an engineer. Probabilities would dictate that an engineer would be pulled from the 100 names about 30% of the time, because 30% is the proportion of engineers in this sample. This type of statistical information is termed *base rate*—the rate of occurrence of a particular category in the population or sample (i.e., how often a certain event tends to occur). Consider this example. The base rate of professional football players in the general population is quite low. The base rate of males in the general population is relatively high. If you select somebody out of the population at random, you're very unlikely to pick a professional football player. However, you're about 50% likely to pick a male. Now consider the engineer-lawyer problem above. Given that there are 30 engineers in the sample, the probability that a randomly drawn name is an engineer is 30/100, or 30%. Indeed, when participants were asked to estimate the probabilities without the personality description, this is the guess they made. But the description, which just happened to fit their stereotype of an engineer, overruled this base-rate information, leading participants to overestimate the probability (50%) that Jack was an engineer.

Racial profiling: A misapplication of the representativeness heuristic?

Use of the representativeness heuristic, and the concomitant tendency to ignore base rates, may relate to the use of the controversial practice known as racial profiling. Racial profiling involves the assumption that a certain type of criminal (i.e., a drug dealer) fits a certain profile; in many cases, the profile includes race as a prominent component. For example, in racial profiling, the "typical" or "average" drug dealer is often assumed to be young, black, and male. As is the case with the biased use of the representativeness heuristic (discussed above), use of the heuristic in this situation leads to judgment errors. Operating on the basis of this profile, police will be especially prone to detain and question individuals that fit, or represent, this profile. Just as we expect that 10 pregnancies should result in a mixture of boys and girls, so do we tend to expect criminals to fit a particular racial profile. Just as in the engineer-lawyer example, this expectation leads to biases in judgment and in subsequent behavior.

Table 13.4 **Profiling as an Instance of the Representativeness Heuristic**

Harris's (1999) observational study revealed that although African Americans comprise a small minority of drivers who are committing traffic violations, they comprise the majority of drivers who are actually pulled over.

		Caucasian	African American	Other Minorities
(a)	Drivers observed	4,314 (76%)	973 (17%)	241 (4%)
	Offenders observed	4,000 (74%)	938 (18%)	232 (4%)
		Caucasian	**African American**	**Other Minorities**
(b)	Drivers searched (out of 823)	162 (19.7%)	600 (73%)	61 (7.3%)

From Harris, D. A. (1999). *Driving while black: Racial profiling on our nation's highways.* ACLU Report. Washington, DC: ACLU. Reprinted by permission of the author and the American Civil Liberties Union.

Table 13.4 presents data from a study on traffic patterns conducted by Harris (1999). In this study, over 5,000 cars were observed on a state highway over the course of about two days, and the race of the driver was noted (this was possible in 97% of the cases). Also recorded was the number of drivers who were actually violating traffic laws at the time they were observed. Table 13.4a presents the number of drivers overall, as well as the number of violators, as a function of racial group. Note that the percentage of violators per racial group is a rough estimate of the base rate of individuals who could potentially be pulled over; as you can see 74% are white, and 18% are African American. Now look at Table 13.4b, which presents the number of motorists stopped in an 18-month period along the same stretch of highway. Over this time span, 823 motorists were stopped and searched. Just going by the base rate, you would expect that 609 (74%) of these motorists would be white. However, the traffic stops show that 600 (73%) of the motorists were African American. So although the base rate suggests that whites would be much more likely violators of traffic laws (and hence eligible to be stopped), actual behavior deviated strikingly from this baseline. The representativeness heuristic is strongly implicated as the culprit.

The Conjunction Fallacy.   Base rates aren't the only type of information people ignore when they make probability judgments. In their classic investigation of judgment heuristics, Tversky and Kahneman (1983, p. 299) presented the following problem to participants:

> Linda is 31 years old; she's single, outspoken, and very bright. She majored in philosophy. As a student, she was deeply consumed with issues of discrimination and social justice, and also participated in anti-nuclear demonstrations.

Based on this information about Linda, participants were asked to decide whether it was more likely that she was (1) a bank teller or (2) a bank teller who was active in the feminist movement. Which do you think? If you said 2, you'd agree with the vast majority of

Figure 13.5 Is it more likely that Linda is a bank teller or that she is a bank teller and a feminist?

Tversky and Kahneman's participants. (And somewhere, the math teacher who taught you about basic probability is crying.) If you think about it, there's no possible way that 2 could be more likely than 1, because 1 includes 2! If you think about the universe of bank tellers, you can imagine that some subset of them would consider themselves feminist bank tellers; so the chances of Linda being a feminist bank teller has to be smaller than (or at the very least the same as) the probability of her being a bank teller. Figure 13.5 makes this apparent.

Another way to look at it is that being a bank teller and a feminist is the conjunction of two events. The probability of a conjunction between two independent events is the probability of one multiplied by the probability of the other. Since probabilities are almost always less than one, conjunctions almost always have to be less likely than either event considered alone. For example, if the probability of event 1 is 0.5 and the probability of event 2 is 0.5, the probability of the conjunction of event 1 and event 2 is 0.25 (less than the 0.5 probability of either event in isolation). Failure to use this knowledge in the Linda problem is termed the **conjunction fallacy**. The conjunction fallacy is another compelling demonstration of the power of stereotypes. Because Linda fits the stereotype (i.e., is representative) of a liberal individual, we assume that she has to be a feminist, and we use this information as the basis for our judgment.

Misperception of Event Clusters.   When a given event has two different ways of working out, such as a coin flip, people tend to misconstrue what a random sequence should look like. That is, they tend to underestimate the number of streaks, or clusters of like events, that would occur in a truly random sequence. For example, look at the following two coin-flip sequences (where H is heads, and T is tails) and judge which is more likely:

H T H T T H T H H T H T

H H H H H H T T T T T T

If you think that the first sequence is a more likely outcome, you're incorrect—but not alone (Tversky & Kahneman, 1974). Each sequence has an equally low probability of occurring—namely $(\frac{1}{2})^{12}$. But because the first sequence represents how we picture the outcome of 12 coin flips, it's perceived as more likely. Runs of like events (six heads, then six tails) are perceived as extremely unlikely.

The Hot Hand.   The tendency to misperceive event clusters as indicating nonrandomness may underlie what sports fans term a "hot hand." This pet phrase of sports announcers refers to situations where it seems a player can do no wrong; for example, in basketball, a player has made six straight shots. While in the midst of these streaks, players are often said to be "in the zone" or "white hot." A study by Gilovich, Vallone, and Tversky (1983) suggests that the players' shots are nothing more than a random sequence dictated by the player's overall shooting percentage. These researchers were interested in whether

Is there such a thing as a "hot hand"?

there was any truth to the claim that players get "hot," and they investigated this by looking at the official shooting statistics of the 1983 Philadelphia 76ers (the only team to keep shot-by-shot records). If a hot-hand phenomenon exists, then the probability of making any particular shot should be higher, given that some number of immediately previous shots have been made. In other words, the probability of making any given shot should be higher, if the player is hot, and this "heat" carries over to subsequent shots. The study indicated that there was no relationship between making a basket and having made any number of previous baskets. A shooter is just as likely to make a shot after having missed the previous three baskets as they are if they'd made each shot. There was no support for the idea of a hot hand. So although clusters of events seem unlikely, they do arise, even within completely random sequences.

The Gambler's Fallacy. The representativeness heuristic, and its relation to the misperception of event clusters, also underlies what Kahneman and Tversky (1971) term the **gambler's fallacy.** This refers to the belief that after a run of bad luck (or a run of one certain type of outcome), that a change is "due" to occur. Because a run of events looks so unlikely, sometimes people believe that a return to normalcy is likely to occur. This misperception leads to people's prolonged stays at the blackjack table; if a you are on losing streak, you may feel that a winning streak has to be right around the corner. But in this situation, future events (i.e., better card hands) have nothing to do with whether you've won or lost previously. Nonetheless, people often overestimate the probability of winning after a losing streak and continue to play.

Basing Judgments on Initial Estimates: The Anchoring-and-Adjustment Heuristic

In many cases of judgment, people start with an idea, or standard, in mind. Say you were guessing how much money the average college student makes from working part time over the course of the school year. As we've seen, there's no way you can possibly know or calculate this value, so you do the next best thing: you use a rule of thumb to help educate your guess. If you are a working college student, you might recall that you earn $8.10 per

The gambler's fallacy: My luck *has* to turn soon.

hour and work 15 hours a week at your job. Based on this knowledge, you may estimate that the average working college student makes around $100 to $150 a week. Although the information from your own work experience is helpful to start the estimation process, it may exert too much influence, essentially "anchoring" your judgment. That is, our initial estimate or first impression tends to make us overly biased toward it. The heuristic involved in these judgments is termed **anchoring and adjustment.** We often make an initial estimate, based on knowledge or on presented information, and then make adjustments to that initial anchor to arrive at a final judgment. But just as an anchor holds a ship in place, your initial estimate can hold your guess in place, and you can fail to make sufficient adjustments. In the scenario, Vince's suggestion to Donna that her used textbook will fetch her about $5 will likely reduce Donna's expectation of what she might get for it.

Chapman and Bornstein (1996) investigated anchoring and adjustment in the context of personal-injury awards. In their study, participants read a (simulated) one-page discussion of a personal-injury suit involving a woman who developed ovarian cancer after taking birth-control pills. The only manipulation in the study (experiment 1) was the amount of money requested by the plaintiff for compensation—$100, $20,000, $5 million, and $1 billion. After reading the case with one of the four anchoring values, participants made a number of judgments, including compensatory damages and the likelihood that the defendant caused the plaintiff's injuries.

The results are described aptly by the title of the article: "The More You Ask For, the More You Get." The amount of compensatory damages awarded to the fictional plaintiff mirrored the anchor; the higher the anchor, the more money was awarded. Perhaps even more surprising was what the researchers termed a *cross-modality anchoring effect:* higher monetary anchors were not only associated with greater awards, but also with higher ratings of defendant blame. Although the procedure was quite different from an actual jury trial in important ways, there would still seem to be important ramifications of the anchoring-and-adjustment heuristic in this setting.

Stop *and* Think!   I HAVE NO IDEA . . .

Consider the following questions and decide whether the proposed estimate is greater than or less than the number designated. Come up with a quick answer, making your guess as precise as you can.

1. number of electoral votes belonging to Ohio for a presidential election—less than or more than 6?
   Your guess _____
2. number of times "Hello Dolly" was performed on Broadway—less than or more than 5,000?
   Your guess _____
3. number of men who have served as pope—less than or more than 100?
   Your guess _____
4. total area of the state of Utah, in square miles—less than or more than 100,000 square miles?
   Your guess _____
5. distance from Neptune to the sun—less than or more than 5 billion miles?
   Your guess _____

Compare your answer to the actual answers at end of this paragraph.

- How far off were you?
- Did the "anchor" presented in the question affect your answer?
- Did it make your guess too high or too low?
- What is you explanation for this?

1. 12   2. 2,844   3. 300   4. 36,420   5. 2.8 billion

The Spotlight Effect.   An interesting paper by Gilovich, Medvec, and Savitsky (2000) cites anchoring and adjustment as the underlying cause of what they term the *spotlight effect*. The **spotlight effect** refers to our tendency to believe that our actions and appearance are noticed by others more than they actually are—in other words, we believe that the "social spotlight" shines more brightly on us than it actually does. In three of their studies, these researchers had participants don a T-shirt that was embarrassing (Barry Manilow or Vanilla Ice) and then enter a room where other people were assembled and stay for a few minutes. Afterward, the participants were asked to estimate how many of the people assembled in the room had noticed their T-Shirt. The results clearly demonstrated the spotlight phenomenon: participants predicted that about twice as many people would notice their T-shirt as actually did. The result was even stronger in a later study, where participants were asked to wear a nonembarrassing (perhaps even cool) T-shirt of their choice (with Martin Luther King, Bob Marley, or Jerry Seinfeld); the result was the same: participants thought everyone would noticed their T-shirt, but few did.

So how is this an example of anchoring and adjustment? The researchers suspected that participants would be overly aware of and self-conscious about their T-shirts and that this intense self-awareness would serve as an anchor, leading to overestimates of how many

Inappropriately self-conscious?

other people noticed it. They tested this idea in a disarmingly simple manner. After participants estimated the number of people who had noticed their T-shirts, the experimenters asked participants if they had considered any other number. Their logic was simple. If participants' guesses were based on the very high anchor of one's own self-consciousness, then their initial estimate likely would be even higher than their final estimate. The results from these two experiments supported this anchoring-and-adjustment interpretation.

Biased Evaluation of Our Judgments

We've seen that people employ some pretty reasonable-sounding judgment heuristics in situations in which information, computational power, or both are lacking. We've also seen that people tend to overrely on heuristics, which sometimes leads to biased judgment. Sometimes we're not so great at estimating how much we know or when we knew it. We now turn to a couple of biases of this sort.

Hindsight Bias.   "I could have told you that was going to happen." Who hasn't heard (or offered) this little gem of wisdom? People always seem to have been sure that things would work out a certain way after they already have. This tendency is termed **hindsight bias** (and sometimes, quite descriptively, the I-knew-it-all-along effect). In the opening story, Donna shows this effect, thinking to herself "I knew Professor Goti wouldn't just say yes."

A good example of an everyday situation that may be powerfully influenced by the hindsight bias is civil litigation. Civil suits involve disputes in which a plaintiff claims that they are the victim of some type of harm caused by the defendant. The purpose of the suit is to determine whether the plaintiff is entitled to some type of monetary compensation. When a jury or judge has to make a determination about liability, they are required to judge whether the defendant could have foreseen what was going to happen and acted accordingly. But, as described above, people often fall victim to a hindsight bias. Therefore, they're likely to believe that "they knew it all along"—that they could have foreseen the events that led to the plaintiff's injury and therefore the defendant should have seen it coming, too.

A study by Hastie, Schkade, and Payne (1999) provides a dramatic demonstration of the hindsight bias in the context of a civil case with a plaintiff seeking punitive damages.

Was this accident foreseeable?

The scenario they used was based on an actual case of a California train derailment and a resulting toxic herbicide spill. The case was presented in two slightly different ways. In the foresight condition, participants were told that there was a potentially dangerous situation developing along mountainous railroad tracks in California and that the National Transportation Safety Board (NTSB) had deemed the situation unsafe and ordered the railroad to stop operations. Expert testimony supporting the NTSB finding was also presented. Participants were told that the railroad had appealed the NTSB order, and they were to evaluate whether the appeal should be upheld. In other words, participants had to demonstrate foresight, judging how likely it would be that an accident would occur.

In the hindsight condition, participants were given basically the same information, with one important addition: there had already been a train derailment with an associated toxic spill. Instead of ruling on an appeal of an NTSB order, participants were instructed to decide whether punitive damages against the railroad were in order. These participants were susceptible to hindsight bias; they knew that an accident had occurred and were basically asked whether the railroad should have seen it coming. The procedure required that all participants give an overall probability of an accident. The question in the foresight condition was: "Estimate the probability that a serious accident will happen." The question in the hindsight condition was: "*Ignoring what you now know,* what probability *would you have estimated* for a serious accident happening" (emphasis added). In addition to this overall judgment, participants in both conditions were asked to judge various elements of liability.

The results demonstrated a striking hindsight bias. The average probability estimate for the occurrence of an accident was 0.34 in foresight and 0.59 in hindsight; indeed, hindsight participants were fairly certain they could have predicted the accident. Judgment on the elements of liability are presented in Table 13.5. Hindsight participants rated the railroad company more harshly for each of these elements (except maliciousness, which was not statistically significant but was in the predicted direction). Notice that the exact same rating questions were presented to the foresight and hindsight participants. All questions related generally to the core issue of whether the company should have foreseen the accident. The hindsight participants were overwhelmingly more likely to say yes, based on knowledge they had gained after the fact.

Hastie, Schkade, and Payne (1999) contend that this type of hindsight bias is nearly inevitable when people are asked to reason about the causes and precursors to everyday events; this is pretty much what happens when juries or judges in civil trials consider punitive damages. To ameliorate the effects of hindsight bias, the authors offer a number of suggestions, including taking the question of punitive damages out of the hands of jurors and placing it in the hands of experts who might be less likely to fall victim to hindsight bias, given their extensive knowledge in the particular area.

Miscalibration of Confidence.   The fact that we overestimate the extent to which we knew something was going to happen demonstrates an insensitivity to what we knew and when we knew it. This general lack of sensitivity is also revealed by the finding that we have a general tendency to be overconfident (or, in some circumstances, underconfident) about what

---

Table 13.5 "They Should Have Seen It Coming"

Participants in a hindsight condition were much tougher on a defendant with regard to judgments on various elements of liability.

Judgments on Elements of Liability	Foresight Condition	Hindsight Condition
Defendant was (would be) reckless.	2.89	5.12
Risk was (is) foreseeable.	3.40	5.52
Defendant is (would be) liable for accident.	3.50	6.08
Defendant disregarded (is disregarding) grave risk.	3.36	5.59
Defendant was (is being) malicious.	1.80	2.12

Note: 1 = definitely "no"; 10 = definitely "yes."

From Hastie, R., Schkade, D. A., & Payne, J. W. (1999). Juror judgments in civil cases: Hindsight effects on judgments of liability for punitive damages. *Law and Human Behavior, 23,* 445–470. Reprinted by permission of Kluwer Academic/Plenum Publishers.

we know. In other words, we are not very good at calibrating our confidence. If confidence were perfectly calibrated to what we know, then our confidence would match our knowledge. If we were 50% sure about some set of facts, then we would get 50% of them correct. If we were 100% sure about another set of facts, then we would get all of them correct.

Many studies have investigated confidence calibration and revealed it to be "off" in a fairly systematic manner. For example, Fischhoff, Slovic, and Lichtenstein (1977) had people answer general-knowledge questions (e.g., "Is absinthe a type of liqueur or a type of precious stone?") and also rate their confidence that they had given a correct answer. If participants were completely guessing, their confidence rating should be 50%. Also, if confidence was well-calibrated, then the average confidence value should match the average percentage correct. The researchers found that participants tended to be overconfident; for questions about which they were 100% confident, they only managed to get some 75% or so correct. This **miscalibration of confidence** seems to be most serious in cases when we're extremely confident; it seems that people who are "absolutely sure" are the ones most likely to be wrong. It's important to note that although overconfidence is common, it is not always the rule. In cases where answers are rather easy to arrive at, we are actually a little underconfident. For instance, having taken a test that was fairly easy, you may be a little cautious in your estimation of how you did, perhaps to avoid "getting your hopes up." In this type of situation, people are a little too cautious in their estimates. (By the way, absinthe is a liqueur.)

Stop and Think! CONFIDENCE CALIBRATION

Your task here is to set a 90% confidence interval for each answer. In other words, your answer will be a range within which you're 90% sure the answer falls. Try to set your ranges so that they're not too narrow (overconfident) or too wide (underconfident) (from Russo and Schoemaker, 1989).

I am 90% confident the answer falls between:

1. Martin Luther King, Jr.'s, age at death   _____ and _____
2. length of the Nile River   _____ and _____
3. number of countries that belong to OPEC   _____ and _____
4. number of books in the Old Testament   _____ and _____
5. diameter of the moon in miles   _____ and _____
6. weight of an empty Boeing 747 (in pounds)   _____ and _____
7. year in which Mozart was born   _____ and _____
8. gestation period (days) for an Asian elephant   _____ and _____
9. air distance from London to Tokyo   _____ and _____
10. deepest (known) point in the ocean (in feet)   _____ and _____

If your confidence is well-calibrated to your accuracy, you should be correct on 90% or more of your intervals (answers on next page).

- Did you show good calibration of confidence?
- Was your range too narrow (overconfident)?
- Too wide (underconfident)?

• What is your explanation?

1. 39 years 2. 4,187 miles 3. 13 countries 4. 39 books 5. 2,160 miles
6. 390,000 lbs 7. 1756 8. 645 days 9. 5,959 miles 10. 36,198 feet

Plous (1993) notes the potentially grave consequences of overconfidence, citing a study by Bedau and Radelet (1987) on wrongful convictions for capital crimes. This study revealed 350 documented instances of innocent defendants being wrongfully convicted. Plous points out that this is an example of overconfidence. The standard of proof in a criminal trial is a volume of evidence that would suggest that a defendant is "guilty beyond a reasonable doubt." Obviously, the convictions of these innocent individuals were instances of overconfident juries that failed to find reasonable doubt when there was some to be found.

STOP *and* REVIEW!

1. Explain why we tend to use heuristics when making judgments.
2. True or false? An illusory correlation is likely to be made when the example is very vivid.
3. When people make judgments based on representativeness, they're basing judgments on
   a. recency in memory
   b. similarity
   c. their first impressions
   d. what they thought they knew before
4. The anchoring-and-adjustment heuristic can explain
   a. the spotlight effect
   b. hindsight bias
   c. the gambler's fallacy
   d. illusory correlation
5. True or false? We tend to be good judges of how much we know.

➤ The processes of judgment involve arriving at some conclusion about unknown events. Because of limits in capacity and information, we rely on heuristics, "shortcuts" that allow us to make quick judgments.

➤ The availability heuristic is the tendency to make judgments based on how easily an example can be brought to mind. Biases in the encoding and retrieval of events can lead to biased application of the availability heuristic. An illusory correlation is seeing a relationship between events when none exists due to the vividness of the example.

➤ With the representativeness heuristic, we make judgments based on how well an event or person fits our stereotype. This heuristic can lead to a tendency to violate basic principles of probability. People also tend to misperceive event clusters as nonrandom, leading to fallacious belief in a "hot hand" and the gambler's fallacy.

➤ The anchoring-and-adjustment heuristic occurs when a person makes an initial estimate and then fails to make sufficient adjustments to arrive at their final estimate. Anchoring and adjustment seems to underlie the spotlight effect.

> ➤ Judgments about our own judgments are also suspect. We tend to be poor judges of how much we know (miscalibration of confidence) or when we knew it (hindsight bias).

Decision Making

Despite the errors made in making judgments, they form an important part of the database for the process of decision making. For example, consider the following conversation:

Person A: If there's a good chance that Tom will be at the party, then I think we should go. What do you think the chances are he'll go?

Person B: Oh, I'm pretty sure he'll be there.

Person A: OK, then let's go.

In this situation, the decision (going to the party) is based on the judgment of another event happening (whether Tom will be there). But decision making goes beyond this judgment to include a choice between alternatives: Do you go to the party or stay home? The fact that decision making involves choice introduces another element to the thinking mix—that of risk, or uncertainty. When you choose among a number of alternatives, there is always a chance that your choice will be the wrong one.

RECURRING RESEARCH THEME
Cognition and Individual Differences

Cultural Differences in Decision-Making Overconfidence

The consequences in the above decision-making scenario are not dire. If Tom isn't at the party, you still might have a good time. But what if the decision were a bigger one? For example, suppose you had to decide on a contractor for an important building renovation and the contingent event was whether or not a particular company would come in on budget. The consequences of a faulty judgment in this situation could be serious. According to the *threshold approach to choice* (Clemen, 1991), if a decision (e.g., to choose a given contractor or not) depends on the likelihood of another event happening (e.g., to come in on budget), then the attractiveness of the option should increase as the probability of the other event increases. Once that probability reaches a minimal level of certainty, the alternative will be chosen. Given what you just learned about the relationship between confidence and judgment, you might anticipate that overconfidence will be at play in this situation: the minimal level of certainty may be reached too easily.

Is the minimal level of certainty likely to vary with culture? Would you be more concerned about overconfidence if the decision maker was American or Chinese? If you are like the participants in a study by Yates, Lee, and Shinotsuka (1996), you're probably thinking that the American would be more likely to fall victim to overconfidence. But you, like the study participants, are wrong. People from the Chinese culture show a greater overconfidence in their judgments than do Americans. What accounts for this difference?

Before addressing this question, the researchers wanted to be sure that the finding was reliable and practical. The difference in overconfidence had been demonstrated within the limited context of answering general-knowledge questions like "For which is the gestation period longer, (a) humans or (b) chimpanzees?" Using this type of question can assess whether overconfidence is present but it cannot assess the ramifications. In decision-making situations, there are ramifications of our judgments. Therefore, Yates and colleagues (Yates, Lee, Shinotsuka, Patalano, and Sieck, 1998) wanted to investigate whether overconfidence generalizes to the type of judgments needed to make practical decisions. In addition, these researchers wanted to determine if the greater overconfidence exhibited by Chinese participants would be found in a decision-making situation.

Participants from the United States and Taiwan were asked to take the role of a physician in a situation in which two new diseases that shared similar symptoms were discovered. They were instructed to examine a series of patient profiles, make a decision as to which disease the patient had, and rate their confidence in that judgment. They then received feedback concerning the accuracy of that diagnosis. The assumption was that over time, participants would learn which configuration of symptoms was diagnostic for each disease and this would affect their decision. Feedback was given in order to help participants calibrate their confidence.

The results indicated that all participants showed overconfidence; they were more confident in the accuracy of their decisions than was warranted by the actual measure of accuracy. This overconfidence effect was greater than that normally found with general-knowledge questions. Furthermore, Chinese participants showed more overconfidence than American participants, indicating that this cross-cultural difference in overconfidence in judgment generalizes to decision-making situations.

The authors suggest that cultural differences in approaches to cognitive tasks may be responsible for this difference. It is common in Chinese culture to emphasize the importance of memorization in the acquisition of knowledge. Given the prevalent belief that memory is veridical (i.e., it must be true) rather than reconstructive (i.e., it is subject to reconstructive processes, as you read about in Chapter 7), then cultures that rely on a memory strategy (in this case, memorization) would be more likely to show overconfidence. The authors conclude that "in situations where decisions are made using the logic underlying common Western ways of construing decision problems, ignoring the cultures of decision makers is risky" (p. 115).

Expected Utility: A Normative Approach

The study of simple choice and decision making has a long history. Economists have always been interested in the factors involved in choice and what type of model describes rational choice behavior. One of the most well-established theories of decision making is **expected utility theory.** Basically, this theory states that when faced with some type of uncertain choice, we make our decisions based on two factors—the expected utility of the outcomes and their respective probability. Utility refers to whatever end a person would like to achieve, be it happiness, money, or something else. Baron (1999) suggests that *good* might be a better word to use; utility refers to the amount of good that comes out of a decision (Broome, 1991). So basically, we weigh the good that might come out of each alternative against the costs of that alternative. We also assess the probability of each alternative occurring. Whichever alternative provides the best combination of "good" and "likelihood of turning out" will be the one we choose. Consider these choices:

Flip a coin; if it turns up heads, you get $40.

Roll the dice; if it comes up 4, you get $50.

Most people would probably choose the first option because it seems like a better combination of good and probability. You stand to get $10 less than if you chose the second option, but the probability of winning in the first option is much greater. This greater probability offsets the slight difference in monetary value.

Violations of Expected Utility.   Expected utility theory provides a normative description of decision making—that is, it lays out the ways human beings would choose among alternatives if they were perfectly rational decision makers. Given that expected utility theory provides a view of the ideal decision maker, it serves as a useful baseline against which actual decision making can be compared. So what should the ideal decision maker do and not do? Let's take a look at one of the normative predictions made by expected utility theory. According to the principle, our choices should show *invariance;* that is, a decision maker's choices should not depend on the way a choice is presented. (In other words, a preference should be invariant across different sorts of situations.) If I prefer choice A over choice B in situation 1, then I should prefer choice A over choice B in situation 14 (as long as A and B are identical in the two situations).

As you'll see, it's quite easy to get people to violate the assumption of invariance. People often do switch their preferences of one outcome over another, based only on how these outcomes are presented, thereby demonstrating *irrationality.* Consider the **preference reversals** shown in a classic series of studies by Lichtenstein and Slovic (1971, 1973). Their general procedure involved having participants look at two different gambles and decide (1) which gamble they would like to play and (2) how much the gamble was worth. Try this for yourself. Look at the choices in Figure 13.6. First, imagine which gamble you would choose; then for each pair, imagine that you "own" the gamble and are trying to sell it—How much will you charge? You would think that a rational person would be consistent. If they preferred one gamble over the other, they would also say it was worth more and set a higher price for it. (Is this what you did?) Lichtenstein and Slovic expected otherwise; they thought that the choice of which gamble to play would be influenced by the probability of winning, whereas the choice of the selling price for the gamble would depend on the potential dollar amount to be won. Think about why this preference reversal is irrational. If they think that one gamble should go

1.	80% chance to win $4.00	4.	10% chance to win $40.00
	20% chance to lose $.50		90% chance to lose $1.00
2.	95% chance to win $3.00	5.	50% chance to win $6.50
	5% chance to lose $2.00		50% chance to lose $1.00
3.	99% chance to win $4.00	6.	33% chance to win $16.00
	1% chance to lose $1.00		67% chance to lose $2.00

Figure 13.6   Sample choices in preference reversal experiments. For each of these pairs of gambles, (1) choose one of each pair of gambles, and then (2) imagine you "owned" each one and give it a selling price.

From Lichtenstein, S., & Slovic, P. (1971). Reversals of preference between bids and choices in gambling choices. *Journal of Experimental Psychology, 89,* 46–55. Copyright 1971 by the American Psychological Association. Reprinted by permission.

for a higher price than the other gamble, why didn't they choose it? And this result is not limited to questionnaires about theoretical choices given within a laboratory setting. Lichtenstein and Slovic (1973) found exactly the same results when they conducted the study in a Las Vegas casino (in which the sample included a number of card dealers!).

The preference-reversal phenomenon is only one of a number of phenomena that demonstrate the inadequacy of expected utility as a descriptive model of decision making. The expected-utility model fails to provide a good description of how we make choices in many circumstances because it assumes too much; humans rarely, if ever, have all of the information necessary to make a decision. Even if they did, they would lack the ability to combine and weigh the information accurately. Also, expected utility proposes that we base our decisions on expected consequences, but there is no real way to foresee consequences with any certainty. Expected utility is still one of the most common yardsticks by which the rationality of human decision making is measured, but psychologists have attempted to develop descriptive models of how we actually do make decisions in order to accommodate "irrationality."

Prospect Theory: A Descriptive Approach

One popular alternative to expected utility theory is Kahneman and Tversky's (1979) prospect theory. **Prospect theory** is a descriptive model of decision making; it attempts to describe how we make decisions and why our decisions violate the expected utility model. According to prospect theory, decisions are valued not based on the absolute value of the end result, as proposed by expected utility; instead, we value decisions based on the amount of gain or loss from what we have right now. Another important feature of the model is that it proposes that gains and losses are on different scales of value. Figure 13.7 plots the value that we place on gains and losses. Gains are to the right of center, and losses are to the left. Note that the value we attach to gains increases more slowly as a function of the size of the gain than does the (negative) value we place on losses, as a function of the size of the loss. Basically, we feel losses more acutely than we do gains; the psycholog-

Figure 13.7 Hypothetical value function proposed in prospect theory. Subjective value (vertical axis) is plotted against actual value (horizontal axis). Actual values to the right of center reflect gains, while actual values to the left of center reflect losses. Note the difference in rate of change for subjective value in the gain and loss domains. The same change in the loss domain is felt more acutely (reflected by a larger change in subjective value) than the same change in the gain domain.
From Kahneman, D., & Tversky, A. (1984) Choices, values, and frames. *American Psychologist, 39,* 341–350. Copyright 1984 by the American Psychologial Association. Reprinted by permission.

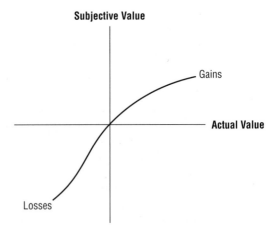

ical pain associated with losing $50 is greater than the psychological pleasure of gaining $50. Prospect theory predicts that people will be especially averse to loss and will show differences in preference depending on how alternatives are presented, or framed.

Framing.   Prospect theory predicts that our preferences will change whenever our reference point (i.e., what we have right now) changes. This means that decisions can be influenced by how information is presented. If information is presented in terms of a positive "gain frame" (emphasizing the certainty of what you have right now), we will be more likely to avoid risk (i.e., risk averse) and pick the surer bet. However, if the same information is presented in a negative "loss frame" (emphasizing what might be lost if a particular decision is made), we will be more likely to take a risk (i.e., risk prone) to avoid this loss. **Framing** is the term used to describe the effects of how a scenario is presented on our decisions.

Consider the results of a classic study by Tversky and Kahneman (1981, p. 453). Participants were presented with this scenario and two choices:

> Imagine the the U.S. is preparing for the outbreak of an unusual Asian disease, which is expected to kill 600 people. Two alternative programs for combating the disease have been proposed. Assume that the exact scientific estimate of the consequences of the program is as follows:
>
> If program A is adopted, 200 people will be saved.
>
> If program B is adopted, there is a $1/3$ probability that 600 people will be saved, and a $2/3$ probability that no one will be saved.

Other participants were presented with exactly the same problem but different choices:

> If program C is adopted, 400 people will die.
>
> If program D is adopted, there is a $1/3$ probability that nobody will die, and a $2/3$ probability that 600 people will die.

If you look closely, you'll note something a little peculiar: the choice between A and B is exactly the same as the choice between C and D, but they're worded differently. The first choice is presented in terms of what is to be gained, while the second is presented in terms of what is to be lost. Figure 13.8 shows the number of people who picked the non-risky (options A and C) and risky (options B and D) alternatives as a function of how the alternatives were presented. As you can see, when the alternatives were presented in a gain frame, people were *risk averse*—unwilling to take a risk and preferring the "sure" alternative. But when the exact same choices were reworded and presented in a loss frame, people were *risk prone*—much more willing to take a risk to avoid loss. In our gripping tale as the chapter opens, Vince tries to take advantage of risk aversion by offering a safe alternative (i.e., stick with the paper and deadline as is) compared to the risky one, in order to focus Donna on what she stands to lose if she pushes further for an extension.

You may wonder what this has to do with anything. Does this framing of alternatives have real-life implications? The answer is yes. Studies of medical decision making (McNeil, Pauker, Sox, & Tversky, 1986), decisions about health-related behaviors (Rothman & Salovey, 1997), and decisions about the continuation of romantic relationships (Boon & Griffin, 1996) have all shown influences of framing. So the effects of framing are seen in real-world contexts and seem to be wide ranging.

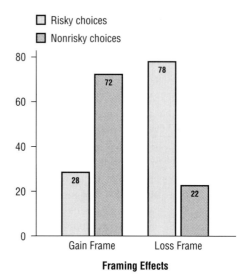

Figure 13.8 Note that when a choice is framed in terms of gains, a majority of participants make a nonrisky choice. Conversely, when the choice is framed in terms of loss, a majority of participants make a risky choice. From Tversky, A., & Kahneman, D. (1981). The framing of decisions and the psychology of choice. *Science, 211,* 453–458. Copyright 1981 by the American Psychological Association. Reprinted by permission.

Psychological Accounting.   The research on framing indicates that we make different choices depending on how the alternatives are worded, or framed. Kahneman and Tversky (1981, p. 457) demonstrate a similar effect in people's consideration of the outcomes of their decisions. According to the *psychological accounting principle,* people will make different decisions depending on how the outcome is felt or perceived. Consider the following scenarios:

1. Imagine that you have decided to see a play where admission is $10 a ticket. As you enter the theater, you discover that you have lost a $10 bill. Would you still pay $10 for a ticket to the play?
2. Imagine that you have decided to see a play where admission is $10 a ticket. As you enter the theater, you discover that you have lost the ticket. The seat was not marked, and the ticket cannot be recovered. Would you pay $10 for a ticket to the play?

In these scenarios, what is being manipulated is not the cost or benefit; it's the way that participants are likely to think about the extra $10 that needs to be spent. Kahneman and Tversky (1981) term this a difference in psychological accounting. In both scenarios, an extra 10 bucks needs to be shelled out. In which scenario does this seem more painful? In Kahneman and Tversky's study, participants were less willing to purchase a ticket in scenario 2. Why should this be? In this scenario, $10 has already been invested for the play, so spending another $10 seems an unattractive alternative. In scenario 1, we simply have lost $10, money that could have been spent for anything. So it seems that we are less averse to losing money from our general "psychological account" than we are from our "play account," which has already been tapped for the $10 play ticket. But this distinction is a little silly. In both scenarios, we're out $20, and we get to see a play; so there should be no difference in our willingness to spend 10 more dollars.

Sunk Costs.   Another interesting variation on the notion of psychological accounting relates to what has been termed the **sunk-cost effect.** This effect was demonstrated by Arkes and Blumer (1985). In one experiment, participants were to imagine that they had purchased tickets for two different ski trips: one ticket (for a ski trip to Wisconsin) cost $50, while the other ticket (for a ski trip to Michigan) cost $100. The scenario made it clear that the trip to Wisconsin was preferable because it would be more enjoyable. Then a complication arose: the two trips were on the same weekend, and the tickets were nonrefundable. Which trip would you choose to go on? Most participants chose the Michigan trip, even though the Wisconsin trip was touted as being more enjoyable. Why? Because, according to their "psychological accounting," not going to Michigan would waste more money. Keep in mind, however, that the costs were already "sunk." They were out $150 no matter what. But because more money was invested in the Michigan trip, participants felt that they had to follow through on this particular investment. When people have invested more time, effort, or money into a given situation, they feel more compelled to go ahead with it, sometimes "throwing good money after bad."

Stop *and* Think!   TV DINNERS

Read the following problem and make the choice yourself; then enlist a friend or two and see how they choose (from Arkes & Blumer, 1985):

> On your way home you buy a TV dinner on sale for $3 at a local grocery store. A few hours later, you decide it is time for dinner, so you get ready to put the TV dinner in the oven. Then you get an idea. You call up a friend to ask if he would like to come over for a quick TV dinner and then watch a good movie. Your friend says "Sure." So you go out to buy a second TV dinner. However, all of the on-sale TV dinners are gone. You therefore have to spend $5 (the regular price) for a TV dinner identical to the one you just bought for $3. You go home and put both dinners in the oven. When the two dinners are fully cooked, you get a call. Your friend is ill, and cannot come. You are not hungry enough to eat both dinners. You cannot freeze one. You must eat one and discard the other. Which one do you eat?

> Notice that there is no difference between the TV dinners in terms of their quality or the type of food; the only difference is that you spent more money on one of them.

- Did this make a difference in your decision?
- Did it make a difference to your friends?
- How do you explain this?

Epilogue

Let's return to a question we posed early in the chapter: Are we rational? Research's emphasis on error, noted at the beginning of the chapter, and much of the evidence from the research discussed throughout this chapter, may suggest we are not. But keep in mind that rational does not always mean accurate, and irrational doesn't always mean wrong. It is true that we don't follow the prescriptions of normative models of reasoning and decision making; instead, we rely on time- and energy-saving heuristics that lighten the mental load. Use of heuristics is rational, given the limitations on our abilities. However, when these heuristics are misapplied or used in an overly broad fashion, they can lead to irrational thinking.

S T O P *and* R E V I E W !

1. True or false? The fact that people show preference reversals cannot be explained by expected utility theory.
2. Which of these is *not* consistent with prospect theory?
   a. The framing effect.
   b. When a decision scenario is presented in terms of gain, we tend to be risk averse.
   c. When a decision scenario is presented in terms of loss, we tend to be risk prone.
   d. A gain is more psychologically powerful than a loss.
3. What is the sunk-cost effect?

➤ Decision making involves choosing among alternatives that have different costs, benefits, and consequences. Expected utility theory, a normative approach to decision making, contends choices are based on the attractiveness of consequences and the probability of the consequence. The outcome with the best combination is chosen. Choices should not vary with how choices are presented. Preference reversals indicate that they do.

➤ Prospect theory, a descriptive model, assumes that people make decisions based on what they have right now and that they interpret gains and losses on different scales, losses being more psychologically powerful than gains. This theory predicts the framing effect, whereby people are risk averse when faced with certain gains and risk prone when faced with certain losses.

➤ According to the psychological accounting principle, people make different decisions depending on how each outcome is felt The sunk-cost effect states that people overuse the resources already invested in a particular course of action as a decision criterion.

G L O S S A R Y

anchoring and adjustment: making an initial estimate based on knowledge or on presented information, and making adjustments to that initial anchor to arrive at a final judgment (p. 550)

atmosphere effect: quantifiers used in syllogistic reasoning premises combine to form an "atmosphere," within which the validity of the conclusion is assessed (p. 528)

availability heuristic: the basing of our estimates of likelihood, or probability, on the ease with which we can think of examples (p. 539)

belief bias: the tendency to allow belief to interfere with the evaluation of conclusions in syllogistic reasoning (p. 529)

conditional reasoning: a deductive reasoning task that involves evaluating whether a particular conclusion is valid given that certain conditions hold (p. 530)

confirmatory bias: our tendency to seek out or notice evidence that is consistent with a particular hypothesis rather than evidence that would be inconsistent with the hypothesis (p. 534)

conjunction fallacy: judging the joint probability of two events as more likely than just one, due to the representativeness heuristic (p. 548)

decision making: a process that involves evaluating given information, making a judgment, and based on these, making a choice among several possible alternatives (p. 525)

deductive reasoning: determining if a specific conclusion is valid based on general premises (p. 527)

deontic reasoning: reasoning about one's own duties and social obligations (p. 534)

descriptive approach: an approach to reasoning, judgment, and decision making that describes how we actually think (p. 526)

expected utility theory: the theory that states that when faced with uncertainty in choice, we make our decisions based on two factors—the expected utility of the outcomes and the respective probability of those outcomes (p. 558)

framing: the effect that how scenarios are presented affects our choice behavior (p. 561)

gambler's fallacy: the belief that after a run of one certain type of outcome, a change is "due" to occur (p. 549)

hindsight bias: the tendency to believe that we could have predicted the outcome of some chance event after the outcome has occurred (p. 552)

illusory correlation: when two events are vividly experienced together (i.e., a coincidence), they will seem to be linked even when they're not (p. 545)

inductive reasoning: reasoning in which we move from specific pieces of data or information toward a general conclusion (p. 535)

judgment: the application of reasoning processes about given information and the use of this information to arrive at a conclusion (p. 525)

miscalibration of confidence: the tendency to be overconfident (or underconfident) in our judgments and decisions (p. 555)

normative approach: an approach to reasoning, judgment, and decision making that describes how we ought to think in a given situation (p. 526)

preference reversals: switching our preferences of one outcome over another based only on how these outcomes are presented (p. 559)

premises: the general principles or assertions that form the basis for deductive reasoning (p. 527)

prospect theory: the idea that decisions are based on the amount of gain or loss from what we have right now (p. 560)

reasoning: the evaluation of a conclusion based solely on given information (p. 525)

representativeness heuristic: basing estimates of likelihood on the degree to which the object represents (is similar to) our basic idea (or stereotype) of that object (p. 545)

spotlight effect: the tendency to believe that our actions and appearance are noticed by others more than they actually are (p. 551)

sunk-cost effect: the tendency to continue investing in a given situation (even in the face of loss) after we have spent a good deal of time, effort, or money (p. 563)

syllogistic reasoning: determining whether a conclusion is valid given the truth of quantified (i.e., all, some, or none) premises (p. 527)

References

Alba, J. W., & Hasher, L. (1983). Is memory schematic? *Psychological Bulletin, 93,* 203–231.

Allen, G. A., Mahler, W. A., & Estes, W. K. (1969). Effects of recall tests on long-term retention of paired associates. *Journal of Verbal Learning and Verbal Behavior, 8,* 463–470.

Almor, A., & Sloman, S. A. (1996). Is deontic reasoning special? *Psychological Review, 103,* 174–180.

Amabile, T. M. (1996). *Creativity in context.* Boulder, CO: Westview Press.

American Psychological Association (APA), Working Group on Investigation of Memories of Childhood Abuse. (1996). *Final report.* Washington, DC: Author.

Anderson, J. R. (1974). Retrieval of propositional information from long-term memory. *Cognitive Psychology, 6,* 451–474.

Anderson, J. R. (1976). *Language, memory, and thought.* Hillsdale, NJ: Erlbaum.

Anderson, J. R. (1978). Arguments concerning representations for mental imagery. *Psychological Review, 86,* 395–406.

Anderson, J. R. (1982). Acquisition of cognitive skill. *Psychological Review, 89,* 369–406.

Anderson, J. R., & Bower, G. H. (1973). Human associative memory. Washington DC: Winston.

Anderson, J. R., & Reder, L. M. (1999). The fan effect: New results and new theories. *Journal of Experimental Psychology: General, 128,* 186–197.

Anderson, M. C., & Bell, T. (2001). Forgetting our facts: The role of inhibitory processes in the loss of propositional knowledge. *Journal of Experimental Psychology: General, 130,* 544–570.

Anderson, M. C., Bjork, R. A., & Bjork, E. L. (1994). Remembering can cause forgetting: Retrieval dynamics in long-term memory. *Journal of Experimental Psychology: Learning, Memory, & Cognition, 20,* 1063–1087.

Anderson, R. C., & Pichert, J. W. (1978). Recall of previously unrecallable information following a shift in perspective. *Journal of Verbal Learning and Verbal Behavior, 17,* 1–12.

Anderson, S. J., & Conway, M. A. (1993). Investigating the structure of autobiographical memories. *Journal of Experimental Psychology: Learning, Memory, and Cognition, 19,* 1178–1191.

Andersson, J., & Roennberg, J. (1996). Collaboration and memory: Effects of dyadic retrieval on different memory tasks. *Applied Cognitive Psychology, 10,* 171–181.

Arias, C., Curet, C. A., Moyano, H. F., Joekes, S. (1993). Echolocation: A study of auditory functioning in blind and sighted subjects. *Journal of Visual Impairment and Blindness, 87,* 73–77.

Arkes, H. R., & Blumer, C. (1985). The psychology of sunk cost. *Organizational Behavior and Human Decision Processes, 35,* 124–140.

Atkinson, R. C., & Shiffrin, R. M. (1968). Human memory: A proposed system and its control processes. In W. K. Spence and J. T. Spence (Eds.), *The psychology of learning and motivation,* Vol. 2: *Advances in learning and theory* (pp. 89–195). New York: Academic Press.

Awh, E., Jonides, J., Smith, E. E., Schumacher, E. H., Koeppe, R. A., & Katz, S. (1996). Dissociation of storage and rehearsal in verbal working memory: Evidence from positron emission tomography. *Psychological Science, 7,* 25–31.

Bachevalier, J., & Mishkin, M. (1984). An early and a late developing system for learning and retention in infant monkeys. *Behavioral Neuroscience, 98,* 70–77.

Baddeley, A. D. (1966). Short-term memory for word sequences as a function of acoustic, semantic, and formal similarity. *Quarterly Journal of Experimental Psychology, 18,* 362–365.

Baddeley, A. D. (1986). *Working memory.* Oxford: Oxford University Press.

Baddeley, A. D. (1993). Working memory or working attention? In A. Baddeley & L. Weiskrantz (Eds), *Attention: Selection, awareness, and control: A tribute to Donald Broadbent* (pp. 152–170). Gloucestershire, UK: Clarendon Press.

Baddeley, A. D. (2000). Short-term working memory. In E. Tulving & F. I. M. Craik (Eds.), *The Oxford handbook of memory* (pp. 77–92). New York: Oxford University Press.

Baddeley, A. D., Lewis, V., & Vallar, G. (1984). Exploring the articulatory loop. *Quarterly Journal of Experimental Psychology, 36,* 233–252.

Baddeley, A. D., Thompson, N., & Buchanan, M. (1975). Word length and the structure of short-term memory. *Journal of Verbal Learning and Verbal Behavior, 14,* 575–589.

Bahrick, H. P. (1979). Maintenance of knowledge: Questions about memory we forgot to ask. *Journal of Experimental Psychology: General, 108,* 296–308.

Bahrick, H. P. (1984). Semantic memory content in permastore: Fifty years of memory for Spanish learned in school. *Journal of Experimental Psychology: General, 113,* 1–29.

Bahrick, H. P. (2000). Long-term maintenance of knowledge. In E. Tulving and F. I. M. Craik (Eds.), *The Oxford handbook of memory* (pp. 347–362). New York: Academic Press.

Bahrick, H. P., & Hall, L. K. (1991). Lifetime maintenance of high school mathematics content. *Journal of Experimental Psychology: General, 120,* 20–33.

Bahrick, H. P., Hall, L. K., & Berger, S. A. (1996). Accuracy and distortion in memory for high school grades. *Psychological Science, 7,* 265–271.

Balch, W. R., Bowman, K., & Mohler, L. A. (1992). Music-dependent memory in immediate and delayed word recall. *Memory and Cognition, 20,* 21–28.

Balota, D. A., & Lorch, B. F. (1986). Depth of automatic spreading activation: Mediated priming effects in pronunciation but not in lexical decision. *Journal of Experimental Psychology: Learning, Memory, and Cognition, 12,* 336–345.

Balota, D. A., Pollatsek, A., & Rayner, K. (1985). The interaction of contextual constraints and parafoveal visual information in reading. *Cognitive Psychology, 17,* 364–390.

Banaji, M. R., & Crowder, R. G. (1989). The bankruptcy of everyday memory. *American Psychologist, 44,* 1185–1193.

Bar, M., & Biederman, I. (1998). Subliminal visual priming. *Psychological Science, 9,* 464–469.

Baron, J. (1999). *Thinking and deciding* (3rd ed.). New York: Cambridge University Press.

Baron-Cohen, S. Burt, L., Smith-Laittan, F., Harrison, J. (1996). Synaesthesia: Prevalence and familiarity. *Perception, 19,* 1073–1080.

Barron, F., & Harrington, D. M. (1981). Creativity, intelligence, and personality. *Annual Review of Psychology, 32,* 439–476.

Barsalou, L. W. (1983). Ad hoc categories. *Memory and Cognition, 11,* 211–227.

Barsalou, L. W. (1988). The content and organization of autobiographical memories. In U. Neisser & E. Winograd (Eds.), *Remembering reconsidered: Ecological and traditional approaches to the study of cognition* (pp. 193–243). New York: Cambridge University Press.

Bartlett, F. C. (1932). *Remembering: A study in experimental and social psychology.* New York: Macmillan.

Bass, E., & Davis, L. (1988). *The courage to heal: A guide for women survivors of childhood sexual abuse.* New York: Harper and Row.

Bates, E., Devescovi, A., & Wulfeck, B. (2001). Psycholinguistics: A cross-language perspective. *Annual Review of Psychology, 52,* 369–396.

Battig, W., & Montague, P. (1969). Category norms of verbal items in 56 categories: A replication and extension of the Connecticut category norms. *Journal of Experimental Psychology, 80,* 1–46.

Bauer, M. I., & Johnson-Laird, P. N. (1993). How diagrams can improve reasoning. *Psychological Science, 4,* 372–378.

Bedau, H. A., & Radelet, M. L. (1987). Miscarriages of justice in potentially capital cases. *Stanford Law Review, 40,* 21–179.

Behrmann, M. (2000). The mind's eye mapped onto the brain's matter. *Current Directions in Psychological Science, 9,* 50–54.

Bellezza, F. S. (1982). Updating memory using mnemonic devices. *Cognitive Psychology, 14,* 301–327.

Beluggi, U., Klima, E. S., & Siple, P. (1974). Remembering in signs. *Cognition, 3,* 83–125.

Berntsen, D. (1996). Involuntary biographical memories. *Applied Cognitive Psychology, 10,* 435–454.

Berntsen, D. (1998). Voluntary and involuntary access to autobiographical memory. *Applied Cognitive Psychology, 6,* 113–141.

Berrios, G. E. (1995). Deja vu in France during the 19th century: A conceptual history. *Comprehensive Psychiatry, 36,* 123–129.

Besner, D., & Stolz, J. A. (1999). Unconsciously controlled processing: The Stroop effect reconsidered. *Psychonomic Bulletin and Review, 6,* 449–455.

Besner, D., Stolz, J. A., & Boutilier, C. (1997). The Stroop effect and the myth of automaticity. *Psychonomic Bulletin and Review, 4,* 221–225.

Besson, M., Faita, F., Peretz, I., Bonnel, A.-M., & Requin, J. (1998). Singing in the brain: Independence of lyrics and tunes. *Psychological Science, 9,* 494–498.

Best, C. T., & Avery, R. A. (1999). Left-hemisphere advantage for click consonants is determined by linguistic significance and experience. *Psychological Science, 10,* 65–70.

Best, C. T., Hoffman, H., & Glanville, B. B. (1982). Development of infant-ear asymmetries for speech and music. *Perception and Psychophysics, 31,* 75–85.

Biederman, I. (1987). Recognition-by-components: A theory of human image understanding. *Psychological Review, 94,* 115–147.

Biedermann, I. (2000). Recognizing depth-rotated objects: A review of recent research and theory. *Spatial Vision, 13,* 241–253.

Biederman, I., & Cooper, E. E. (1991). Priming contour-deleted images: Evidence for intermediate representations in visual object recognition. *Cognitive Psychology, 23,* 393–419.

Biederman, I., & Gerhardstein, P. C. (1993). Recognizing depth-rotated objects: Evidence and conditions for three-dimensional viewpoint invariance. *Journal of Experimental Psychology: Learning, Memory, and Cognition, 19,* 1162–1182.

Biederman, I., Mezzanotte, R. J., & Rabinowitz, J. C. (1982). Scene perception: Detecting and judging objects undergoing relational violations. *Cognitive Psychology, 14,* 143–177.

Bisanz, T., Bisanz, M., & Korpan, J. (1994). Inductive reasoning. In R. J. Sternberg (Ed.), *Thinking and problem solving* (pp. 179–213). New York: Academic Press.

Bjork, R. A., & Whitten, W. B. (1974). Recency-sensitive retrieval processes in long-term free recall. *Cognitive Psychology, 6,* 173–189.

Blanchard, I., Pollatsek, A., & Rayner, K. (1989). The acquisition of parafoveal word information in reading. *Perception and Psychophysics, 46,* 85–94.

Blanchette, I., & Dunbar, K. (2000). How analogies are generated: The roles of structural and superficial similarity. *Memory and Cognition, 28,* 108–124.

Blaney, P. H. (1986). Affect and memory: A review. *Psychological Bulletin, 99,* 229–246.

Block, N. (1995). On a confusion about a question of consciousness. *Behavioral and Brain Sciences, 18,* 227–287.

Bohannon, J. N., & Symons, V. L. (1992). Flashbulb memories: Confidence, consistency, and quality. In E. Winograd & U. Neisser (Eds.), *Affect and accuracy in recall: Studies of "flashbulb" memories* (pp. 65–91). New York: Cambridge University Press.

Boon, S. D., & Griffin, D. W. (1996). The construction of risk in relationships: The role of framing in decisions about intimate relationships. *Personal Relationships, 3,* 293–306.

Bothwell, R. K., Brigham, J. C., & Malpass, R. S. (1989). Cross-racial identification. *Personality and Social Psychology Bulletin, 15,* 19–25.

Bowden, E. M., & Beeman, M. J. (1998). Getting the right idea: Semantic activation in the right hemisphere may help solve insight problems. *Psychological Science, 9,* 435–440.

Bowen, R. W., Pola, J., & Matin, L. (1974). Visual persistence: Effects of flash luminance, duration, and energy. *Vision Research, 14,* 295–303.

Bower, G. H., Black, J. B., & Turner, T. J. (1979). Scripts in memory for text. *Cognitive Psychology, 11,* 177–120.

Bower, G. H., Clark, M. C., Lesgold, A. M., & Winzenz, D. (1969). Hierarchical schemes in recall of categorized word lists. *Journal of Verbal Learning and Verbal Behavior, 8,* 323–343.

Bowers, G. H., & Schacter, D. S. (1993). Priming of novel information in amnesic patients. In P. Graf & M. Masson (Eds.), *Implicit memory: New directions in cognition, development and neuropsychology* (pp. 303–326). Hillsdale, NJ: Erlbaum.

Bowers, K. S., Regehr, G., Balthazard, C., & Parker, K. (1990). Intuition in the context of discovery. *Cognitive Psychology, 22,* 72–110.

Boyce, S. J., & Pollatsek, A. (1992). Identification of objects in scenes: The role of scene background in object naming. *Journal of Experimental Psychology: Learning, Memory, and Cognition, 18,* 531–543.

Brandimonte, M. A., & Gerbino, W. (1993). Mental image reversal and verbal recoding: When ducks become rabbits. *Memory and Cognition, 21,* 23–33.

Bransford, J. D., & Stein, B. S. (1993). *The IDEAL problem solver* (2nd ed.). New York: Freeman.

Bregman, A. S. (1990). *Auditory scene analysis: The perceptual organization of sound.* Cambridge, MA: MIT Press.

Brewer, W. (1986). What is autobiographical memory? In D. C. Rubin (Ed.), *Autobiographical memory* (pp. 25–49). Cambridge, UK: Cambridge University Press.

Brewer, W. F. (1988). Memory for randomly sampled autobiographical events. In U. Neisser & E. Winograd (Eds.), *Remembering reconsidered: Ecological and traditional approaches to the study of memory* (Emory Symposia in Cognition, vol. 2, pp. 21–90). Cambridge, UK: Cambridge University Press.

Brewin, C. R., Christodoulides, J., & Hutchinson, G. (1996). Intrusive thoughts and intrusive memories in a nonclinical sample. *Cognition and Emotion, 10,* 107–112.

Briere, J., & Conte, J. (1993). Self-reported amnesia for abuse in adults molested as children. *Journal of Traumatic Stress, 6,* 21–31.

Brigham, J. C. (1990). Target person distinctiveness and attractiveness as moderator variables in the confidence-accuracy relationship in eyewitness identification. *Basic and Applied Social Psychology, 11,* 101–115.

Broadbent, D. A. (1958). *Perception and communication.* London: Pergamon Press.

Brooks, L. R. (1967). Spatial and verbal components of the act of recall. *Canadian Journal of Psychology, 22,* 349–366.

Brooks, L. R. (1978). Nonanalytic concept formation and memory for instances. In E. Rosch & B. B. Lloyd (Eds.), *Cognition and categorization* (pp. 169–211). Hillsdale, NJ: Erlbaum.

Brooks, L. R. (1987). Decentralized control of categorization: The role of prior processing episodes. In U. Neisser (Ed.), *Concepts and conceptual development: The ecological and intellectual factors in categorization* (pp. 141–174). Cambridge, UK: Cambridge University Press.

Broome, J. (1991). Utilitarian meta-physics? In J. Elster & J. E. Roemer (Eds.), *Interpersonal comparisons of well-being* (pp. 70–97). New York: Cambridge University Press.

Bross, M., & Borenstein, M. (1982). Temporal auditory acuity in blind and sighted subjects: A signal detection analysis. *Perceptual and Motor Skills, 55,* 963–966.

Brown, A. S. (1991). A review of the tip-of-the-tongue experience. *Psychological Bulletin, 109,* 204–223.

Brown, A. S., & Murphy, D. R. (1989). Cryptomnesia: Delineating inadvertent plagiarism. *Journal of Experimental Psychology: Learning, Memory, and Cognition, 15,* 432–442.

Brown, E., Deffenbacher, K., Sturgill, W. (1977). Memory for faces and the circumstances of encounter. *Journal of Applied Psychology, 62,* 311–318.

Brown, J. (1958). Some tests of the decay theory of immediate memory. *Quarterly Journal of Experimental Psychology, 10,* 12–21.

Brown, R., & Kulik, J. (1977). Flashbulb memories. *Cognition, 5,* 73–99.

Brown, R., & McNeill, D. (1966). The "tip of the tongue" phenomenon. *Journal of Verbal Learning and Verbal Behavior, 5,* 325–337.

Bruce, D. (1989). Functional explanations of memory. In L. W. Poon, D. C. Rubin, & B. C. Wilson (Eds.), *Everyday cognition in adulthood and later life* (pp. 44–58). New York: Cambridge University Press.

Bruce, V., & Young, A. W. (1986). Understanding face recognition. *British Journal of Psychology, 77,* 305–327.

Bruck, M., & Ceci, S. J. (1997). The suggestibility of young children. *Current Directions in Psychological Science, 6,* 75–79.

Bruck, M., & Ceci, S. J. (1999). Children's suggestibility. *Annual Review of Psychology, 50,* 419–439.

Bruck, M., Ceci, S. J., & Francoeur, E. (2000). Children's use of anatomically detailed dolls to report genital touching in a medical examination: Developmental and gender comparisons. *Journal of Experimental Psychology: Applied, 6,* 74–83.

Bruck, M., Ceci, S. J., Francoeur, E., & Renick, A. (1995). Anatomically detailed dolls do not facilitate preschoolers' reports of a pediatric examination involving genital touching. *Journal of Experimental Psychology: Applied, 1,* 95–109.

Brysbaert, M., & Vitu, F. (1998). Word skipping: Implications for theories of eye movement control in reading. In G. Underwood (Ed.), *Eye guidance in reading and scene perception* (pp. 125–147). Amsterdam: Elsevier Science.

Burke, D. M., MacKay, D. G., Worthley, J. S., & Wade, E. (1991). On the tip of the tongue: What causes word finding failures in young and older adults? *Journal of Memory and Language, 30,* 542–579.

Burton, M. A., & Bruce, V. (1992). I recognize your face, but I can't remember your name: A simple explanation? *British Journal of Psychology, 83,* 45–60.

Cain, W. S. (1979). To know the nose: Keys to odor identification. *Science, 203,* 467–470.

Calvert, G. A., Bullmore, E. T., & Brammer, R. (1997) Activation of auditory cortex during silent lipreading. *Science, 276,* 593–596.

Calvert, G. A., Bullmore, E., Brammer, M. J., Campbell, R., Iversen, S. D., Woodruff, P., McGuire, P., Williams, S., & David, A. S. (1997). Silent lipreading activates the auditory cortex. *Science, 276,* 593–596.

Campbell, R., & Dodd, B. (1980). Hearing by eye. *Quarterly Journal of Experimental Psychology, 32,* 85–99.

Caramazza, A., & Brones, I. (1980). Semantic classification by bilinguals. *Canadian Journal of Psychology, 34,* 77–81.

Carmichael, L., Hogan, H. P., & Walters, A. A. (1932). An experimental psychology of the effect of language on the reproduction of visually perceived form. *Journal of Experimental Psychology, 15,* 73–86.

Carreiras, M., Gernsbacher, M. A., & Villa, V. (1995). The advantage of first mention in Spanish. *Psychonomic Bulletin and Review, 2,* 124–129.

Carrier, M., & Pashler, H. (1992). The influence of retrieval on retention. *Memory and Cognition, 20,* 633–642.

Carroll, D. W. (1994). *Psychology of language* (2nd ed.). Pacific Grove, CA: Brooks/Cole.

Carver, R. P. (1971). Pupil dilation and its relationship to information processing during reading and listening. *Journal of Applied Psychology, 55,* 126–134.

Ceci, S. J., & Bruck, M. (1993). Suggestibility of the child witness: A historical review and synthesis. *Psychological Bulletin, 113,* 403–439.

Chang, T. M. (1986). Semantic memory: Facts and models. *Psychological Bulletin, 99,* 199–220.

Channon, S. E., & Baker, J. E. (1996). Depression and problem-solving performance on a fault-diagnosis task. *Applied Cognitive Psychology, 10,* 327–336.

Chapman, G. B., & Bornstein, B. H. (1996). The more you ask for, the more you get: Anchoring in personal injury verdicts. *Applied Cognitive Psychology, 10,* 519–540.

Charness, N. (1976). Memory for chess positions: Resistance to interference. *Journal of Experimental Psychology: Human Learning and Memory, 2,* 641–653.

Chase, K., & Ericsson, W. G. (1982). Exceptional memory. *American Scientist, 70,* 607–615.

Chase, W. G., & Simon, H. A. (1973). Perception in chess. *Cognitive Psychology, 4,* 55–81.

Cheesman, J., & Merikle, P. M. (1984). Priming with and without awareness. *Perception & Psychophysics, 36,* 387–395.

Cherry, E. C. (1953). Some experiments on the recognition of speech, with one and with two ears. *Journal of the Acoustical Society of America, 25,* 975–979.

Chi, M. T. H., Feltovich, P. J., & Glaser, R. (1981). Categorization and representation of physics problems by experts and novices. *Cognitive Science, 5,* 121–152.

Chomsky, N. (1957). *Syntactic structures.* The Hague: Mouton.

Chomsky, N. (1959). A review of Skinner's *Verbal behavior. Language, 35,* 26–58.

Chomsky, N. (1965). *Aspects of the theory of syntax.* Cambridge, MA: MIT Press.

Chomsky, N. (1975). *The logical structure of linguistic theory.* Chicago: University of Chicago Press.

Chomsky, N. (1986). *Knowledge of language: Its nature, origin, and use.* New York: Praeger.

Christiansen, S.-A. (1989). Flashbulb memories: Special, but not so special. *Memory and Cognition, 17,* 435–443.

Christiansen, S.-A. (1992). Emotional stress and eyewitness memory: A critical review. *Psychological Bulletin, 112,* 284–309.

Chu, S., & Downes, J. J. (2000). Long live Proust: The odour-cued autobiographical memory bump. *Cognition, 75,* B41–B50.

Claparede, E. (1951). Recognition and "me-ness." In D. Rapaport (Ed.), *Organization and pathology of thought* (pp. 58–75). New York: Columbia University Press. (Reprinted from *Archives de Psychologie,* 1911, *11,* 79–90.)

Clark, H. H., & Haviland, S. E. (1977). Comprehension and the given-new contract. In R. O. Freedle (Ed.), *Discourse production and comprehension.* Norwood: Ablex.

Clemen, R. T. (1991). *Making hard decisions: An introduction to decision analysis.* Boston: PWS-Kent.

Cohen, G., & Faulkner, D. (1986). Memory for proper names: Age differences in retrieval. *British Journal of Psychology, 4,* 187–197.

Cole, J. (1995). *Pride and a daily marathon.* Cambridge, MA: MIT Press.

Cole, N. S. (1997). *The ETS gender study: How females and males perform in educational settings.* Princeton, NJ: Educational Testing Services.

Coleman, E. B., & Shore, B. M. (1991). Problem-solving processes of high and average performers in physics. *Journal for the Education of the Gifted, 14,* 366–369.

Collins, A. M., & Loftus, E. F. (1975). A spreading-activation theory of semantic processing. *Psychological Review, 82,* 407–428.

Collins, A. M., & Quillian, M. R. (1969). Retrieval time from semantic memory. *Journal of Verbal Learning and Verbal Behavior, 8,* 240–247.

Collins, A. M., & Quillian, M. R. (1970). Does category size affect reaction time? *Journal of Verbal Learning and Verbal Behavior, 9,* 432–438.

Coltheart, M. (2001). Assumptions and methods in cognitive neuropsychology. In B. Rapp (Ed.), *Handbook of cognitive neuropsychology.* Philadelphia: Psychology Press.

Coltheart, V. (1993). Effects of phonological similarity and concurrent irrelevant articulation on short-term memory recall of repeated and novel lists. *Memory and Cognition, 21,* 539–545.

Conrad, C. (1972). Cognitive economy in semantic memory. *Journal of Experimental Psychology, 92,* 149–154.

Conrad, R. (1964). Acoustic confusions in immediate memory. *British Journal of Psychology, 55,* 75–84.

Conrad, R., & Hull, A. J. (1968). Input modality and the serial position curve in short-term memory. *Psychonomic Science, 10,* 135–136.

Conway, M. A. (1990). *Autobiographical memory: An introduction.* Buckingham, UK: Open University Press.

Conway, M. A. (1991). In defense of everyday memory. *American Psychologist, 46,* 19–26.

Conway, M. A. (1997). In M. A. Conway (Ed.), *Cognitive models of memory.* Cambridge, MA: MIT Press.

Conway, M. A., & Bekerian, D. A. (1987). Organization in autobiographical memory. *Memory and Cognition, 15,* 119–132.

Conway, M. A., Cohen, S., & Stanhope, E. (1991). On the very long-term retention of knowledge ac-quired through formal education: Twelve years of cognitive psychology. *Journal of Experimental Psychology: General, 120,* 395–409.

Conway, M. A., & Pleydell-Pearce, C. W. (2001). The construction of autobiographical memories in the self-memory system. *Psychological Review, 107,* 261–288.

Conway, M. A., Pleydell-Pearce, C. W., & Whitecross, S. E. (2001). The neuroanatomy of autobiographical memory: A slow cortical potential study of autobiographical memory retrieval. *Journal of Memory and Language, 45,* 493–524.

Conway, M. A., Turk, D. J., Miller, S. L., Logan, J., Nebes, R. D., Meltzer, C., & Becker, J. T. (1999). A positron emission tomography (PET) study of autobiographical memory study of autobiographical memory retrieval. *Memory, 7,* 679–702.

Cooper, L. A. (1975). Mental rotation of random two-dimensional shapes. *Cognitive Psychology, 7,* 20–43.

Cooper, L. A., & Lang, R. (1996). Imagery and visual-spatial representations. In E. L. Bjork & R. A. Bjork (Eds), *Memory* (pp. 129–164). New York: Academic Press.

Cooper, L. A., & Schacter, D. L. (1992). Priming and recognition of transformed three-dimensional objects: Effects of size and reflection. *Journal of Experimental Psychology: Learning, Memory and Cognition, 18,* 43–57.

Cooper, L. A., & Shepard, R. N. (1975). Mental rotation in the identification of left and right hands. *Journal of Experimental Psychology: Human Perception and Performance, 1,* 48–56.

Cornoldi, D., & de Beni, R. (1991). Memory for discourse: Loci mnemonics and the oral presentation effect. *Applied Cognitive Psychology, 5,* 511–518.

Corteen, R. S., & Wood, B. (1972). Autonomic responses to shock-associated words in an unattended channel. *Journal of Experimental Psychology, 94,* 308–313.

Cosmides, L. (1989). The logic of social exchange: Has natural selection shaped how humans reason? Studies with the Wason selection task. *Cognition, 31,* 187–276.

Courtois, C. A. (1997). Delayed memories of child sexual abuse: Critique of the controversy and clinical guidelines. In M. Conway (Ed.), *Recovered memories and false memories* (pp. 206–229.). Oxford: Oxford University Press.

Cowan, N. (1988). Evolving conceptions of memory storage, selective attention, and their mutual constraints within the human information-processing system. *Psychological Bulletin, 104,* 163–191.

Cowan, N. (1995). *Attention and memory: An integrated framework.* New York: Oxford University Press.

Cox, S. D., & Wollen, K. A. (1981). Bizarreness and recall. *Bulletin of the Psychonomic Society, 18,* 244–245.

Craig, J. C., & Rollman, G. B. (1999). Somesthesis. *Annual Review of Psychology, 50,* 305–331.

Craik, F. I. M. (1986). A functional account of age differences in memory. In F. Klix & H. Hagendorf (Eds.), *Human memory and cognitive capabilities: Mechanisms and performances* (pp. 409–422). Amsterdam: Elsevier-North-Holland.

Craik, F. I. M., & Lockhart, R. S. (1972). Levels of processing: A framework for memory research. *Journal of Verbal Learning and Verbal Behavior, 11,* 671–684.

Craik, F. I. M., & McDowd, J. M. (1987). Age differences in recall and recognition. *Journal of Experimental Psychology: Learning, Memory, and Cognition, 13,* 474–479.

Craik, F. I. M., Moroz, T. M., Moscovitch, M., Stuss, D. T., Winocur, G., Tulving, E., & Kapur, S. (1999). In search of the self: A positron-emission tomography study. *Psychological Science, 10,* 26–34.

Craik, F. I. M., & Tulving, E. (1975). Depth of processing and the retention of words in episodic memory. *Journal of Experimental Psychology: General, 104,* 268–294.

Craik, F. I. M., & Watkins, M. J. (1973). The role of rehearsal in short-term memory. *Journal of Verbal Learning and Verbal Behavior, 12,* 599–607.

Cristofanini, P. Kirsner, K., & Milech, D. (1989). Bilingual lexical representation: The status of Spanish-English cognates. *Quarterly Journal of Experimental Psychology, 38A,* 367–393.

Crowder, R. G. (1976). *Principles of learning and memory.* Hillsdale, NJ: Erlbaum.

Crowder, R. G. (1993). Short-term memory: Where do we stand? *Memory and Cognition, 21,* 142–145.

Crowder, R. G., & Morton, J. (1969). Precategorical acoustic storage (PAS). *Perception & Psychophysics, 6,* 365–373.

Cutler, A., & Butterfield, S. (1992). Rhythmic cues to speech segmentation: Evidence from juncture mis-perception. *Journal of Memory and Language, 31,* 218–236.

Cutler, A., & Carter, D. M. (1987). The predominance of strong initial syllables in the English vocabulary. *Computer Speech and Language, 2,* 133–142.

Cutler, B. L., & Penrod, S. D. (1989). Moderators of the confidence-accuracy relationship in face recognition: The roles of information-processing and base rates. *Applied Cognitive Psychology, 3,* 95–107.

Cutler, B. L., & Penrod, S. D. (1995). *Mistaken identification: Eyewitnesses, psychology, and the law.* New York: Cambridge University Press.

Cutler, B. L., Penrod, S. D., & Martens, T. K. (1987). Improving the reliability of eyewitness identifications: Putting context into context. *Journal of Applied Psychology, 72,* 629–637.

Daneman, M., & Merikle, P. M. (1996). Working memory and language comprehension: A meta-analysis. *Psychonomic Bulletin and Review, 3,* 422–433.

Darwin, C. J., Turvey, M. T., & Crowder, R. G. (1973). An auditory analogue of the Sperling partial-report procedure. *Cognitive Psychology, 3,* 255–267.

Davis, P. J. (1999). Gender differences in autobiographical memory for emotional experiences. *Journal of Personality and Social Psychology, 76,* 498–510.

Deakin, J. M., & Allard, F. (1991). Skilled memory in expert figure skaters. *Memory and Cognition, 19,* 79–86.

Deese, J. (1959). On the prediction of occurrence of particular verbal intrusions in immediate recall. *Journal of Experimental Psychology, 58,* 17–22.

Deffenbacher, K. A. (1980). Eyewitness accuracy and confidence: Can we infer anything about their relationship? *Law and Human Behavior, 4,* 243–260.

de Groot, A. D. (1978). *Thought and choice in chess.* The Hague, Netherlands: Mouton. (Original work published 1946.)

Dell, G. S. (1986). A spreading-activation theory of retrieval in sentence production. *Psychological Review, 93,* 283–321.

Dell, G. S., Chang, F., & Griffin, Z. M. (1999). Connectionist models of language production: Lexical access and grammatical encoding. *Cognitive Science, 23,* 517–542.

Demers, R. A. (1988). Linguistics and animal communication. In F. J. Newmeyer (Ed.), *Language: Psychological and biological aspects* (pp. 314–345). Cambridge, UK: Cambridge University Press.

Desor, J. A., & Beauchamp, G. K. (1974). The human capacity to transmit olfactory information. *Perception & Psychophysics, 16,* 551–556.

D'Esposito, M., Detre, J. A., Aguirre, G. K., Stallcup, M., Alsop, D. C., Tippet, & Farah, M. (1997). A functional MRI study of mental image generation. *Neuropsychologia, 35,* 725–730.

Deutsch, J. A., & Deutsch, D. (1963). Attention: Some theoretical considerations. *Psychological Review, 70,* 51–61.

Dewsbury, D. A. (2000). Comparative cognition in the 1930s. *Psychonomic Bulletin and Review, 7,* 267–283.

Diamond, A., & Doar, B. (1989). The performance of human infants on a measure of frontal cortex function, the delayed response task. *Developmental Psychobiology, 22,* 271–294.

Diamond, R., & Carey, S. (1986). Why faces are and are not special: An effect of expertise. *Journal of Experimental Psychology: General, 115,* 107–117.

Di Lollo, V. (1980). Temporal integration in visual memory. *Journal of Experimental Psychology: General, 109,* 75–97.

Dodson, C. S., & Schacter, D. L. (2001a). "If I had said it, I would have remembered it": Reducing false memories with a distinctiveness heuristic. *Psychonomic Bulletin and Review, 8,* 155–161.

Dodson, C. S., & Schacter, D. L. (2001b). Memory distortion. In B. Rapp (Ed.), *The handbook of cognitive neuropsychology: What deficits reveal about the human mind* (pp. 445–463). New York: Psychology Press.

Dominowski, R. L., & Jenrick, R. (1972). Effects of hints and interpolated activity on solution of an insight problem. *Psychonomic Science, 26,* 335–338.

Donders, F. C. (1969). On the speed of mental processes. *Acta Psychologica, 30,* 412–431. (Originally published 1868.)

Driver, J. (2001). A selective review of selective attention research from the past century. *British Journal of Psychology, 92,* 53–78. (Also online at http://web5.silverplatter.com/webspirs/doLS.ws?ss=British-Journal-of-Psychology+in+SO"\t"wsr".)

Dror, I. E., & Kosslyn, S. M. (1994). Mental imagery and aging. *Psychology and Aging, 9,* 90–102.

Druckman, D., & Bjork, R. A. (1991). *In the mind's eye: Enhancing human performance.*

Dunbar, K. (1995). How scientists really reason: Scientific reasoning in real-world laboratories. In R. J. Sternberg & J. E. Davidson (Eds.), *The nature of insight* (pp. 369–395). Cambridge, MA: MIT Press.

Duncker, K. (1945). On problem solving. *Psychological Monographs, 58,* 1–112.

Eals, M., & Silverman, I. (1994). The hunter-gatherer theory of spatial sex differences: Proximate factors mediating the female advantage in recall of object arrays. *Ethology and Sociobiology, 15,* 95–105.

Eich, E. (1980). The cue-dependent nature of state-dependent retrieval. *Memory and Cognition, 8,* 157–173.

Eich, E. (1984). Memory for unattended events: Remembering with and without awareness. *Memory and Cognition, 12,* 105–111.

Eich, E., & Metcalfe, J. (1989). Mood-dependent memory for internal vs. external events. *Journal of Experimental Psychology: Learning, Memory, and Cognition, 15,* 443–455.

Einstein, G. O., & McDaniel, M. A. (1990). Normal aging and prospective memory. *Journal of Experimental Psychology: Learning, Memory, and Cognition, 16,* 717–726.

Einstein, G. O., McDaniel, M. A., Richardson, S. L., Guynn, M. J., & Cunfer, B. (1995). Aging and prospective memory: Examining the influences of self-initiated retrieval processes. *Journal of Experimental Psychology: Learning, Memory, and Cognition, 21,* 996–1007.

Ellis, A. W. (1984). *Reading, writing, and dyslexia: A cognitive analysis.* London: Erlbaum.

Engle, R. W. (2001). What is working memory capacity? In H. L. Roediger, J. S. Nairne, I. Neath, & A. Surprenant (Eds.), *The nature of remembering: Essays in honor of Robert G. Crowder* (pp. 297–315). Washington, DC: American Psychological Association.

Erikson, E. H. (1950). Growth and crises of the healthy personality. *Symposium on the healthy personality,* 91–146.

Erickson, R. P. (1982). Studies on the perception of taste: Do primaries exist? *Physiology and Behavior, 28,* 57–62.

Erickson, R. P., Priolo, C. V., Warwick, Z. S., & Schiffman, S. S. (1990). Synthesis of tastes other than the "primaries": Implications for neural coding theories and the concept of suppression. *Chemical Senses, 15,* 495–504.

Ericsson, K. A. (1985). Memory skill. *Canadian Journal of Psychology, 39,* 188–231.

Ericsson, K. A., & Charness, N. (1994). Expert performance: Its structure and acquisition. *American Psychologist, 49,* 725–747.

Ericsson, K. A., Chase, W. G., & Faloon, S. (1980). Acquisition of a memory skill. *Science, 208,* 1181–1182.

Ericsson, K. A., & Kintsch, W. (1995). Long-term working memory. *Psychological Review, 102,* 211–245.

Ericsson, K. A., & Polson, P. G. (1988). An experimental analysis of the mechanisms of a memory skill. *Journal of Experimental Psychology: Learning, Memory, & Cognition, 14,* 305–316.

Ericsson, K. A., & Simon, H. E. (1980). Verbal reports as data. *Psychological Review, 87,* 215–251.

Ericsson, K. A., & Simon, H. E. (1984). *Protocol analysis.* Cambridge, MA: MIT Press.

Evans, J., Williams, J. M., O'Loughlin, S., & Howells, K. (1992). Autobiographical memory and problem-solving strategies of parasuicide patients. *Psychological Medicine, 22,* 399–405.

Fabiani, D., Stadler, R., & Wessels, F. (2000). True but not false memories produce a sensory signature in human lateralized brain potentials. *Journal of Cognitive Neuroscience, 12,* 941–949.

Farah, M. (1992). Is an object an object an object? Cognitive and neuropsychological investigations of domain specificity in visual object recognition. *Current Directions in Psychological Science, 1,* 164–169.

Fernald, A. (1985). Four-month-old infants prefer to listen to motherese. *Infant Behavior and Development, 8,* 181–195.

Fernald, A., & Simon, T. (1984). Expanded intonation contours in mothers' speech to newborns. *Developmental Psychology, 20,* 104–113.

Fillmore, J. (1968). The case for case. In E. Bach and R. T. Harms (Eds.), *Universals of linguistic form* (pp. 101–190). New York: Holt, Rinehart, & Winston.

Fink, G. R., Markowitsch, H. J., & Reinkemeier, M. (1996). Cerebral representation of one's own past: Neural networks involved in autobiographical memory. *Journal of Neuroscience, 16,* 4275–4282.

Finke, R. A., & Pinker, S. (1982). Spontaneous imagery scanning in mental extrapolation. *Journal of Experimental Psychology: Learning, Memory, and Cognition, 8,* 142–147.

Finke, R. A., & Pinker, S. (1983). Directional scanning of remembered visual patterns. *Journal of Experimental Psychology: Learning, Memory, and Cognition, 9,* 398–410.

Finke, R. A., & Shepard, R. N. (1986). Visual functions of mental imagery. In L. Kaufman, J. P. Thomas, & K. Boff (Eds.), *Handbook of perception and human performance,* Vol. 2: *Cognitive processes and performance* (pp. 1–55). New York: Wiley.

Finley, G. E., & Sharp, T. (1989). Name retrieval by the elderly in the tip-of-the-tongue paradigm: Demonstrable success in overcoming initial failure. *Educational Gerontology, 15,* 259–265.

Fischhoff, B., Slovic, P., & Lichtenstein, S. (1977). Knowing with certainty: The appropriateness of extreme confidence. *Journal of Experimental Psychology: Human Perception and Performance, 4,* 552–564.

Fisher, R. P., & Geiselman, R. E. (1992). *Memory-enhancing techniques for investigative interviewing: The cognitive interview.* Springfield, IL: Thomas.

Fivush, R. (1991). Gender and emotion in mother/child conversations about the past. *Journal of Narrative and Life History, 1,* 325–341.

Fivush, R., Gray, J. T., & Fromhoff, F. A. (1987). Two-year-olds talk about the past. *Cognitive Development, 2,* 393–409.

Forsterlee, L., & Horowitz, I. A. (1997). Enhancing juror competence in a complex trial. *Applied Cognitive Psychology, 11,* 305–319.

Foss, D. J. (1969). Decision processes during sentence comprehension: Effects of lexical item difficulty and position upon decision times. *Journal of Verbal Learning and Verbal Behavior, 8,* 457–462.

Foss, D. J. (1970). Some effects of ambiguity upon sentence comprehension. *Journal of Verbal Learning and Verbal Behavior, 9,* 699–706.

Frazier, L., & Rayner, K. (1982). Making and correcting errors during sentence comprehension: Eye movements in the analysis of structurally ambiguous sentences. *Cognitive Psychology, 14,* 178–210.

Fromkin, V. A. (1973). *Speech errors as linguistic evidence.* The Hague: Mouton.

Gardiner, J. M. (1988). Functional aspects of recollective experience. *Memory and Cognition, 16,* 309–313.

Gardiner, J. M., & Parkin, A. J. (1990). Attention and recollective experience in recognition memory. *Memory and Cognition, 18,* 579–583.

Gardner, B. T., & Gardner, R. A. (1975). Evidence for sentence constituents in the early utterances of child and chimpanzee. *Journal of Experimental Psychology: General, 104,* 244–267.

Gardner, H. (1983). *Frames of mind: A theory of multiple intelligence.* New York: Basic Books.

Gardner, H. (1985). *The mind's new science: A history of the cognitive revolution.* New York: Basic Books.

Garrett, M. F. (1975). The analysis of sentence production. In G. Bower (Ed.), *The psychology of learning and motivation: Advances in research and theory* (Vol. 9). New York: Academic Press.

Garrett, M. F. (1988). Processes in language production. In F. J. Newmeyer (Ed.), *Language: Psychological and biological aspects* (pp. 69–96). Cambridge: Cambridge University Press.

Garrett, M. F. (1992). Disorders of lexical selection. *Cognition, 42,* 143–180.

Garry, M., Manning, C. G., Loftus, E. F., & Sherman, S. J. (1996). Imagination inflation: Imagining a childhood event inflates confidence that it occurred. *Psychonomic Bulletin and Review, 3,* 208–214.

Gazzaniga, M. S. (1985). *The social brain.* New York: Basic Books.

Gazzaniga, M. S., & Smylie, C. S. (1984). Dissociation of language and cognition. *Brain, 107,* 145–153.

Gazzaniga, M. S., Ivry, R. B., & Mangun, G. R. (1998). *Cognitive neuroscience: The biology of the mind.* New York: Norton.

Gazzaniga, M. S., Ivry, R. B., & Mangun, G. R. (2002). *Cognitive neuroscience: The biology of the mind.* New York: Norton.

Gentner, D. (1989). The mechanisms of analogical learning. In S. Vosniadou & A. Ortony (Eds.), *Similarity and analogical reasoning* (pp. 199–241). New York: Cambridge University Press.

Gernsbacher, M. A. (1989). Mechanisms that improve referential access. *Cognition, 32,* 99–156.

Gernsbacher, M. A. (1991). *Language comprehension as structure building.* Hillsdale, NJ: Erlbaum.

Gernsbacher, M. A. (1997). Two decades of structure building. *Discourse Processes, 23,* 365–204.

Gernsbacher, M. A., & Hargreaves, P. (1988). Accessing sentence participants: The advantage of first mention. *Journal of Memory and Language, 27,* 699–717.

Gibson, J. J. (1950). *The perception of the visual world.* New York: Houghton Mifflin.

Gibson, J. J. (1966). The problem of temporal order in sensation and perception. *Journal of Psychology, 62,* 141–149.

Gibson, J. J. (1987). *The perception of the visual world.* New York: Houghton-Mifflin.

Gick, S., & Holyoak, W. (1980). Analogical problem solving. *Cognitive Psychology, 12,* 306–335.

Gick, S., & Holyoak, W. (1983). Schema induction and analogical transfer. *Cognitive Psychology, 15,* 1–38.

Gillund, G., & Shiffrin, R. M. (1984). A retrieval model for both recognition and recall. *Psychological Review, 91,* 1–67.

Gilovich, T., Medvec, V., & Savitsky, K. (2000). The spotlight effect in social judgment: An egocentric bias in the estimates of the salience of one's own actions and appearance. *Journal of Personality and Social Psychology, 75,* 332–346.

Gilovich, T., Vallone, R., & Tversky, A. (1983). The hot hand in basketball: On the misperception of random sequences. *Cognitive Psychology, 17,* 295–314.

Gisiner, R., & Schusterman, R. J. (1992). Sequence, syntax, and semantics: Responses of a language-trained sea lion (*Zalophus californianus*) to novel sign combinations. *Journal of Comparative Psychology, 106,* 78–91.

Glenberg, A. M. (1974). Influences of retrieval processes on the spacing effect in free recall. *Journal of Experimental Psychology: Human Learning and Memory, 3,* 282–294.

Glenn, C. G. (1978). The role of episodic structure and of story length in children's recall of simple stories. *Journal of Verbal Learning and Verbal Behavior, 17,* 229–247.

Gobet, F., & Simon, H. A. (1996). Recall of rapidly presented random chess positions is a function of skill. *Psychonomic Bulletin and Review, 3,* 159–163.

Godden, D. R., & Baddeley, A. D. (1975). Context-dependent memory in two natural environments: On land and underwater. *British Journal of Psychology, 66,* 325–331.

Goel, V., Gold, B., Kapur, S., & Houle, S. (1998). Neuroanatomical correlates of human reasoning. *Journal of Cognitive Neuroscience, 10,* 293–302.

Goff, L. M., & Roediger, H. L. (1998). Imagination inflation for action events: Repeated imaginings lead to illusory recollections. *Memory and Cognition, 26,* 20–33.

Goodwin, D. W., Powell, B., Bremer, D., Hoine, H., & Stern, J. (1969). Alcohol and recall: State dependent effects in man. *Science 163,* 1358–1360.

Goodman, G. S., Quas, J. A., Batterman-Faunce, J. M., Riddlesberger, M. M., & Kuhn, J. (1994). Predictors of accurate and inaccurate memories of traumatic events experienced in childhood. *Consciousness and Cognition, 3,* 269–294.

Gopnik, A., & Sobel, D. M. (2000). Detecting blickets: How young children use information about novel causal powers in categorization and induction. *Child Development, 71,* 1205–1222.

Graesser, A. C., Singer, M., & Trabasso, T. (1994). Constructing inferences during narrative text comprehension. *Psychological Review, 101,* 371–395.

Grant, H. M., Bredahl, L. C., Clay, J., Ferrie, J., Groves, J. E., McDorman, T. A., & Dark, V. J. (1998). Context-dependent memory for meaningful material: Information for students. *Applied Cognitive Psychology, 12,* 617–623.

Gratton, G., Corballis, P. M., & Jain, S. (1997). Hemispheric organization of visual memories. *Journal of Cognitive Neuroscience, 9,* 92–104.

Greene, R. L. (1992). *Human memory: Paradigms and paradoxes.* Hillsdale, NJ: Erlbaum.

Greenfield, P. M., & Savage-Rumbaugh, E. S. (1990). Grammatical combination in *Pan paniscus:* Processes of learning and invention in the evolution and development of language. In S. T. Parker & K. R. Gibson (Eds.), *"Language" and intelligence in monkeys and apes: Comparative developmental perspectives* (pp. 540–578). Cambridge: Cambridge University Press.

Greenwald, A. G., Spangenberg, E. R., Pratkanis, A. R., & Eskenazi, J. (1991). Double-blind tests of subliminal self-help audiotapes. *Psychological Science, 2,* 119–122.

Grice, H. P. (1975). Logic and conversation. In P. Cole & J. L. Morgan (Eds.), *Syntax and semantics,* Vol. 3: *Speech acts* (pp. 41–58). New York: Seminar Press.

Griggs, R. A., & Cox, G. R. (1982). The elusive thematic-materials effect in Wason's selection task. *British Journal of Psychology, 73,* 407–420.

Groninger, L. D. (1971). Mnemonic imagery and forgetting. *Psychonomic Science, 23,* 161–163.

Gruneberg, M. M., Smith, R. L., & Winfrow, P. (1973). An investigation into response blockaging. *Acta Psychologica, 37,* 187–196.

Haber, R. N. (1983). The impending demise of the icon: A critique of the concept of iconic storage in visual information processing. *Behavioral and Brain Sciences, 6,* 1–54.

Habermas, T., & Bluck, S. (2000). Getting a life: The emergence of the life story in adolescence. *Psychological Bulletin, 126,* 748–769.

Halpern, D. F. (2000). *Sex differences in cognitive abilities* (3rd ed.). Mahwah, NJ: Erlbaum.

Hampton, J. A. (1993). Conjunctions of visually-based categories: Overextension and compensation. *Journal of Experimental Psychology: Learning, Memory, and Cognition, 22,* 378–396.

Han, J. J., Leichtman, M. D., & Yang, Q. (1998). Autobiographical memory in Korean, Chinese, and American children. *Developmental Psychology, 34,* 701–713.

Hanley, J. R., & Cowell, E. S. (1988). The effects of different types of retrieval cues on the recall of names of famous faces. *Memory and Cognition, 16,* 545–555.

Hanson, V. L. (1982). Short-term recall by deaf signers of American Sign Language: Implications of encoding strategy for order recall. *Journal of Experimental Psychology: Learning, Memory, and Cognition, 8,* 572–583.

Harley, T. A. (1995). *The psychology of language: From data to theory.* East Sussex, UK: Taylor & Francis.

Harris, D. A. (1999). *Driving while black: Racial profiling on our nation's highways.* Washington, DC: American Civil Liberties Union.

Harris, J. E. (1980). Memory aids people use: Two interview studies. *Memory and Cognition, 8,* 31–38.

Harrison, J. E., & Baron-Cohen, S. (1997). Synaesthesia: A review of psychological theories. In J. E. Harris & S. Baron-Cohen (Eds.), *Synaesthesia: Classic and contemporary readings* (pp. 109–122). Oxford: Blackwell.

Hastie, R., & Dawes, R. M. (2001). *Rational choice in an uncertain world: The psychology of judgment and decision making.* London: Sage.

Hastie, R., Schkade, D. A., & Payne, J. W. (1999). Juror judgments in civil cases: Hindsight effects on judgments of liability for punitive damages. *Law and Human Behavior, 23,* 445–470.

Hayes, J. R., & Simon, H. A. (1977). Psychological differences among problem isomorphs. In N. J. Castellan, D. B. Pisoni, & J. R. Potts (Eds.), *Cognitive theory.* Hillsdale, NJ: Erlbaum.

Hayward, W. G., & Tarr, M. J. (1997). Testing conditions for viewpoint invariance in object recognition. *Journal of Experimental Psychology: Human Perception and Performance, 23,* 1511–1521.

Hebb, D. O. (1949). *The organization of behavior: A neuropsychological theory.* London: Wiley.

Herman, J. L., & Schatzow, E. (1987). Recovery and verification of memories of childhood sexual trauma. *Psychoanalytic Psychology, 4,* 1–14.

Herman, J. S. (1992). *Trauma and recovery.* New York: Basic Books.

Herman, L. M., Kuczaj, S. A., & Holder, M. D. (1993). Response to anomalous gestural sequences by a language-trained dolphin: Evidence for processing of semantic relations and syntactic information. *Journal of Experimental Psychology: General, 122,* 184–194.

Herman, L. M., Richards, D. G., & Wolz, J. P. (1984). Comprehension of sentences by bottlenosed dolphins. *Cognition, 16,* 129–219.

Herz, R. S., & Cupchik, G. C. (1992). An experimental characterization of odor-evoked memories in humans. *Chemical Senses, 17,* 519–528.

Hicks, M., & Marsh, J. (1999). Attempts to reduce the incidence of false recall with source monitoring. *Journal of Experimental Psychology: Learning, Memory, and Cognition, 25,* 1195–1209.

Hintzman, D. L. (1986). "Schema abstraction" in a multiple-trace memory model. *Psychological Review, 93,* 411–428.

Hintzman, D. L., Block, R. A., & Summers, J. J. (1973). Modality tags and memory for repetitions: Locus of the spacing effect. *Journal of Verbal Learning and Verbal Behavior, 12,* 229–238.

Hitch, G. J., & Baddeley, A. D. (1976). Verbal reasoning and working memory. *Quarterly Journal of Experimental Psychology, 28,* 603–621.

Hockett, C. F. (1960). The origin of speech. *Scientific American, 203,* 89–96.

Hogan, R. M., & Kintsch, W. (1971). Differential effects of study and test trials on long-term recognition and recall. *Journal of Verbal Learning and Verbal Behavior, 10,* 562–567.

Holbrook, M. E., & Schindler, R. M. (1989). Some exploratory findings on the development of musical tastes. *Journal of Consumer Research, 16,* 119–124.

Hollingworth, A. (1998). Does consistent scene context facilitate object perception? *Journal of Experimental Psychology: General, 127,* 398–415.

Hollins, M., Faldowski, R., Rao, S., & Young, F. (1993). Perceptual dimensions of tactile surface texture: A multidimensional scaling analysis. *Perception & Psychophysics, 54,* 697–705.

Holtgraves, T. (1997). Politeness and memory for the wording of remarks. *Memory and Cognition, 25,* 106–116.

Holyoak, K. J., & Koh, K. (1987). Surface and structural similarity in analogical transfer. *Memory and Cognition, 15,* 332–340.

Horwitz, B., Rumsey, J. M., & Donohue, B. C. (1998). Functional connectivity of the angular gyrus in normal reading and dyslexia. *Proceedings of the National Academy of Sciences, USA, 95,* 8939–8944.

Howe, M. L., & Courage, M. L. (1993). On resolving the enigma of childhood amnesia. *Psychological Bulletin, 113,* 305–326.

Howe, M. L., & Courage, M. L. (1997). The emergence and early development of autobiographical memory. *Psychological Review, 104,* 499–523.

Howe, M. L., Courage, M. L., & Peterson, C. (1994). How can I remember when "I" wasn't there: Long-term retention of traumatic experience and the emergence of the cognitive self. *Consciousness and Cognition, 3,* 327–355.

Hubel, D., & Wiesel, T. (1979). Brain mechanisms of vision. *Scientific American, 241,* 150–163.

Hull, C. (1943). *Principles of behavior.* New York: Appleton, Century, Crofts.

Hyde, T. S., & Jenkins, J. J. (1969). Differential effects of incidental tasks on the organization of recall of a list of highly associated words. *Journal of Experimental Psychology, 82,* 472–481.

Hyman, I. E., & Pentland, J. (1996). The role of imagination in the creation of false childhood memories. *Journal of Memory and Language, 35,* 101–117.

Hyman, I. E., & Rubin, D. C. (1990). Memorabeatlia: A naturalistic study of long-term memory. *Memory and Cognition, 18,* 205–214.

Hyman, I. E., Husband, T. H., & Billings, F. J. (1995). False memories of childhood experiences. *Applied Cognitive Psychology, 9,* 181–197.

Intons-Peterson, M., & Fournier, J. (1986). External and internal memory aids: When and how do we use them? *Journal of Experimental Psychology: General, 115,* 267–280.

Irwin, D. E. (1992). Memory for position and identity across eye movements. *Journal of Experimental Psychology: Learning, Memory, and Cognition, 18,* 307–317.

Iverson, P. (1995). Auditory stream segregation by musical timbre: Effects of static and dynamic acoustic attributes. *Journal of Experimental Psy-*

chology: Human Perception and Performance, 21, 751–763.

Jacobs, W. J., & Nadel, L. (1998). Neurobiology of reconstructed memory. *Psychology, Public Policy, & Law, 4*, 1110–1134.

Jacoby, L. L. (1983). Remembering the data: Analyzing interactive processes in reading. *Journal of Verbal Learning and Verbal Behavior, 22*, 485–508.

Jacoby, L. L. (1991). A process dissociation framework: Separating automatic from intentional uses of memory. *Journal of Memory and Language, 30*, 513–541.

Jacoby, L. L., & Dallas, M. (1981). On the relationship between autobiographical memory and perceptual learning. *Journal of Experimental Psychology: General, 110*, 306–340.

Jaffe, J., & Feldstein, S. (1970). *Rhythms of dialogue.* New York: Academic Press.

James, W. (1890). *The principles of psychology.* New York: Holt.

Jenkins, J. J. (1979). Four points to remember: A tetrahedral model of memory experiments. In L. S. Cermak & F. I. M. Craik (Eds.), *Levels of processing in human memory* (pp. 429–446). Hillsdale, NJ: Erlbaum.

Johnson, M. K. (1988). Reality monitoring: An experimental phenomenological approach. *Journal of Experimental Psychology: General, 117*, 390–394.

Johnson, M. K., Nolde, S. F., & Leonardis, D. M. (1996). Emotional focus and source monitoring. *Journal of Memory and Language, 35*, 135–156.

Johnson, M. K., Foley, M. A., Suengas, A. G., & Raye, C. L. (1988). Phenomenal characteristics of memories for perceived and imagined autobiographical events. *Journal of Experimental Psychology: General, 117*, 371–376.

Johnston, W. A., & Heinz, S. P. (1978). Flexibility and capacity demands of attention. *Journal of Experimental Psychology: General, 107*, 420–435.

Jones, G. V., & Langford, S. (1987). Phonological blocking in the tip of the tongue state. *Cognition, 26*, 115–122.

Just, M. A., & Carpenter, P. A. (1987). *The psychology of reading and language comprehension.* Boston: Allyn and Bacon.

Just, M. A., & Carpenter, P. A. (1992). A capacity theory of comprehension: Individual differences in working memory. *Psychological Review, 99*, 122–149.

Just, M. A., Carpenter, P. A., & Masson, M. E. J. (1982). *What eye fixations tell us about speed reading and skimming.* Pittsburgh: Carnegie-Mellon University.

Kahneman, D. A. (1973). *Attention and effort.* Englewood Cliffs, NJ: Prentice Hall.

Kahneman, D. (1991). Judgment and decision making: A personal view. *Psychological Science, 2*, 142–145.

Kahneman, D., & Tversky, A. (1973). On the psychology of prediction. *Psychological Review, 80*, 237–251.

Kahneman, D., & Tversky, A. (1981). Choices, values, and frames. *American Psychologist, 39*, 341–350.

Kako, E. (1999). Elements of syntax in the systems of three language-trained animals. *Animal Learning and Behavior, 27*, 1–14.

Kanwisher, S., McDermott, B., & Chun, S. (1997). The fusiform face area: A module in human extrastriate cortex specialized for face perception. *Journal of Neuroscience, 17*, 4302–4311.

Kapur, S., Craik, F. I. M., Tulving, E., Wilson, A. A., Houle, S., & Brown, G. M. (1994). Neuroanatomical correlates of encoding in episodic memory: Levels of processing effects. *Proceedings of the National Academy of Sciences USA, 91*, 2008–2111.

Kebbel, M. R., & Wagstaff, G. F. (1998). Hypnotic interviewing: The best way to interview eyewitnesses? *Behavioral Sciences and the Law, 16*, 115–129.

Keenan, J. P., Freund, S., Hamilton, R. H., Ganis, G., & Pascual-Leone, A. (2000). Hand-response differences in a self-face recognition task. *Neuropsychologia, 38*, 1047–1053.

Keenan, J. P., Wheeler, M. A., Gallup, G. G., & Pascual-Leone, J. (2000). Self-recognition and the right prefrontal cortex. *Trends in Cognitive Sciences, 4*, 338–344.

Keenan, J. P., McCutcheon, B., Freund, S., Gallup, G. G., Sanders, G., & Pascual-Leone, A. (1999). Left-hand advantage in a self-face recognition task. *Neuropsychologia, 37*, 1421–1425.

Kelley, C. M., & Lindsey, D. S. (1996). Conscious and unconscious forms of memory. In E. L. Bjork & R. A. Bjork (Eds.), *Memory* (pp. 31–63). New York: Academic Press.

Kellogg, R. T. (1994). *The psychology of writing.* New York: Oxford University Press.

Kemp, S. (1988). Dating recent and historical events. *Applied Cognitive Psychology, 16*, 181–188.

Keppel, G., & Underwood, B. J. (1962). Proactive inhibition in short-term retention of single items.

Journal of Verbal Learning and Verbal Behavior, 1, 153–161.

Key, B. W. (1973). *Subliminal seduction.* Englewood Cliffs, NJ: Prentice Hall.

Kihlstrom, J. K. (1998). Exhumed memory. In S. J. Lynn & K. M. McConkey (Eds.), *Truth in memory* (pp. 3–31). New York: Guilford Press.

Kimball, D. R., & Holyoak, K. J. (2000). Transfer and expertise. In E. Tulving & F. I. M. Craik (Eds.), *The Oxford handbook of memory.* New York: Oxford University Press.

Kimble, G. A. (1985). *Psychology and learning.* Washington, DC: American Psychological Association.

King, A. (1991). Improving lecture comprehension: Effects of a metacognitive strategy. *Applied Cognitive Psychology, 5,* 331–346.

Kintsch, W. (1974). *The representation of meaning in memory.* Hillsdale, NJ: Erlbaum.

Kintsch, W. (1988). The role of knowledge in discourse comprehension. A construction-integration model. *Psychological Review, 95,* 163–182.

Kintsch, W. (1998). *Comprehension: A paradigm for cognition.* Cambridge: Cambridge University Press.

Kintsch, W., & Keenan, J. (1973). Reading rate and retention as a function of the number of propositions in the base structure of sentences. *Cognitive Psychology, 5,* 257–274.

Kintsch, W., & van Dijk, T. A. (1978). Toward a model of text comprehension and production. *Psychological Review, 85,* 363–394.

Kirby, K. N. (1994). Probabilities and utilities of fictional outcomes in Wason's four-card selection task. *Cognition, 51,* 1–28.

Kirsner, K., Smith, M. C., Lockhart, R. S., King, M. L., & Jain, M. (1984). The bilingual lexicon: Language-specific units in an integrated network. *Journal of Verbal Learning and Verbal Behavior, 23,* 519–539.

Klatzky, R. L., & Lederman, S. J. (1995). Identifying objects from a haptic glance. *Perception & Psychophysics, 57,* 1111–1123.

Klatzky, R. L., Lederman, S. J., & Metzger, V. A. (1985). Identifying objects by touch: An "expert system." *Perception & Psychophysics, 37,* 299–302.

Klatzky, R. L., Lederman, S. J., & Reed, C. (1987). There's more to touch than meets the eye: The salience of object attributes with and without vision. *Journal of Experimental Psychology: General, 116,* 356–369.

Klein, G. S. (1964). Semantic power measured through the interference of words with color-naming. *American Journal of Psychology, 77,* 576–588.

Kleunder, K. R., Diehl, R. L., & Killeen, P. R. (1987). Japanese quail can learn phonetic categories. *Science, 237,* 1195–1197.

Kohler, W. (1925). *The mentality of apes.* New York: Harcourt Brace Jovanovich.

Kohnken, G., Milne, R., Memon, A., & Bull, R. (1999). The cognitive interview: A meta-analysis. *Psychology, Crime, and Law, 5,* 3–27.

Komatsu, L. K. (1992). Recent views of conceptual structure. *Psychological Bulletin, 112,* 500–526.

Koriat, A. (1991). How do we know what we know? Exploring a process model of feeling of knowing. Paper presented at the international conference on memory, Lancaster, England.

Koriat, A., & Lieblich, I. (1974). What does a person in a TOT state know that a person in a don't know state doesn't know? *Memory & Cognition, 2,* 647–655.

Kosslyn, S. M. (1975). Information representation in visual images. *Cognitive Psychology, 7,* 341–370.

Kosslyn, S. M. (1981). The medium and the message in mental imagery: A theory. *Psychological Review, 88,* 46–66.

Kosslyn, S. M. (1994). *Image and brain: The resolution of the imagery debate.* Cambridge, MA: MIT Press.

Kosslyn, S. M., Ball, L., & Reiser, B. J. (1978). Visual images preserve metric spatial information: Evidence from studies of image scanning. *Journal of Experimental Psychology: Human Perception and Performance, 4,* 47–60.

Kosslyn, S. M., Chabris, C. F., Marsolek, C. J., & Koenig, O. (1992). Categorical vs. coordinate spatial relations: Computational analyses and computer simulations. *Journal of Experimental Psychology: Human Perception and Performance, 18,* 562–577.

Kosslyn, S. M., Murphy, G. L., Bernesderfer, M. E., & Feinstein, K. J. (1977). Category and continuum in mental comparisons. *Journal of Experimental Psychology: General, 106,* 341–375.

Kosslyn, S. M., Reiser, B. J., Farah, M. J., & Fliegel, S. L. (1983). Generating visual images: Units and relations. *Journal of Experimental Psychology: General, 112,* 278–303.

Kozar, B., Vaughn, R. E., Lord, R. H., Whitfield, K. E. (1995). Basketball free-throw performance: Practice implications. *Journal of Sport Behavior, 18,* 123–129.

Kramer, J., Buckhout, A., & Eugenio, R. (1989). Weapon focus, arousal, and eyewitness memory: Attention must be paid. *Applied Cognitive Psychology, 14,* 167–184.

Krueger, L. E. (1992). The word-superiority effect and phonological recoding. *Memory and Cognition, 20,* 685–694.

Kuhl, P. K., Williams, K. A., Lacerda, F., Stevens, K. N., & Lindblom, B. (1992). Linguistic experience alters phonetic perception in infants by 6 months of age. *Science, 255,* 606–608.

Kutas, N., & Hillyard, S. A. (1970). Reading senseless sentences: Brain potentials reflect semantic incongruity. *Science, 207,* 203–205.

Lachman, R., Lachman, J. R., & Butterfield, E. C. (1979). *Cognitive psychology and information processing: An introduction.* Hillsdale, NJ: Erlbaum.

Lakoff, G. (1972). *Women, fire, and dangerous things.* Chicago: University of Chicago Press.

Lakoff, R. (1975). *Language and woman's place.* New York: Harper & Row.

Larsen, S. F. (1996). Memorable books: Recall of reading and its personal context. In R. J. Kreuz & M. S. MacNealy (Eds.), *Empirical approaches to literature and aesthetics* (pp. 583–599). Norwood NH: Ablex.

Lawless, H. T. (1997). Olfactory psychophysics. In G. K. Beauchamp and L. Bartoshuk (Eds.), *Tasting and smelling* (pp. 125–174). New York: Academic Press.

Lawless, H. T., & Engen, T. (1977). Associations to odors: Interference, mnemonics, and verbal labeling. *Journal of Experimental Psychology: Human Learning and Memory, 3,* 52–57.

Leahey, T. H. (1992). *A history of psychology: Main currents in psychological thought* (3rd ed.). Englewood Cliffs, NJ: Prentice-Hall.

Lederman, S. J., & Klatzky, R. L. (1990). Haptic classification of common objects: Knowledge-driven exploration. *Cognitive Psychology, 421–459.*

LeDoux, J. (2002). *Synaptic self: How our brains become who we are.* New York: Viking.

Levelt, W. J. M. (1983). Monitoring and self-report in speech. *Cognition, 14,* 41–104.

Levelt, W. J. M. (1989). *Speaking: From intention to articulation.* Cambridge, MA: MIT Press.

Lewald, J. (2002). Opposing effects of head position on sound localization in blind and sighted subjects. *European Journal of Neuroscience, 15,* 1219–1224.

Liberman, A. M., & Whalen, D. H. (2000). On the relation of speech to language. *Trends in Cognitive Sciences, 4,* 187–196.

Liberman, A. M., Cooper, F. S., Shankweiler, D. P., & Studdert-Kennedy, M. (1967). Perception of the speech code. *Psychological Review, 74,* 431–461.

Liberman, A. M., Harris, K. S., Hoffman, H. S., & Griffith, B. C. (1957). The discrimination of speech sounds within and across phoneme boundaries. *Journal of Experimental Psychology, 54,* 358–368.

Lichtenstein, S. (1978). Judged frequency of lethal events. *Journal of Experimental Psychology: Human Learning & Memory, 4,* 551–578.

Lichtenstein, S., & Slovic, P. (1971). Reversals of preference between bids and choices in gambling choices. *Journal of Experimental Psychology, 89,* 46–55.

Lichtenstein, S., & Slovic, P. (1973). Response-induced reversals of preference in gambling: An extended replication in Las Vegas. *Journal of Experimental Psychology, 101,* 16–20.

Lichtenstein, S., Slovic, P., Fischhoff, B., Layman, M., & Comb, B. (1978). Judged frequency of lethal events. *Journal of Experimental Psychology: Human Learning and Memory, 4,* 551–578.

Lindsay, D. S. (1998). Depolarizing views on recovered memory experiences. In S. J. Lynn & K. M. McConkey (Eds.), *Truth in memory* (pp. 481–494). New York: Guilford Press.

Lindsay, D. S. (1990). Misleading suggestions can impair witness' ability to remember event details. *Journal of Experimental Psychology: Learning, Memory, and Cognition, 16,* 1077–1083.

Lindsay, D. S., Ross, D. F., Smith, S. M., & Flanagan, S. (1999). Does race influence measures of lineup fairness? *Applied Cognitive Psychology, 13,* S109–S119.

Lindsay, R. C., & Wells, G. L. (1985). Improving eyewitness identifications from lineups: Simultaneous vs. sequential lineup presentation. *Journal of Applied Psychology, 70,* 556–564.

Linton, M. (1975). Transformations of memory in everyday life. In U. Neisser (Ed.), *Memory observed: Remembering in natural contexts* (pp. 77–92). San Francisco: Freeman.

Loftus, E. F. (1975). Leading questions and the eyewitness report. *Cognitive Psychology, 7,* 560–572.

Loftus, E. F. (1976). Unconscious transference in eye-witness identification. *Law and Psychology Review, 2,* 93–98.

Loftus, E. F. (1979). *Eyewitness testimony.* Cambridge, MA: Harvard University Press.

Loftus, E. F. (1991). The glitter of everyday memory . . . and the gold. *American Psychologist, 46,* 16–18.

Loftus, E. F., & Ketcham, K. (1991). *Witness for the defense: The accused, the eyewitness, and the expert who puts memory on trial.* New York: St. Martin's Press.

Loftus, E. F., & Pickrell, J. E. (1995). The formation of false memories. *Psychiatric Annals, 25,* 720–725.

Loftus, E. F., Feldman, J., & Dashiell, R. (1995). The reality of illusory memories. In D. L. Schacter (Ed.), *Memory distortions: How minds, brains, and societies reconstruct the past* (pp. 47–68). Cambridge, MA: Harvard University Press.

Loftus, E. F., Miller, D. G., & Burns, H. J. (1978). Semantic integration of verbal information into a visual memory. *Journal of Experimental Psychology: Human Learning and Memory, 4,* 19–31.

Logan, G. D. (1988). Toward an instance-based theory of automatization. *Psychological Review, 95,* 492–527.

Logan, G. D. (1997). The automaticity of academic life: Unconscious applications of an implicit theory. In R. S. Wyer (Ed.), *The automaticity of everyday life, Advances in Social Cognition, 10,* 157–179.

Logothetis, N. K., Pauls, J., & Poggio, T. (1995). Shape representation in the inferior temporal cortex of monkeys. *Current Biology, 7,* 645–651.

Loring-Meier, S., & Halpern, D. F. (1999). Sex differences in visuospatial working memory: Components of cognitive processing. *Psychonomic Bulletin and Review, 6,* 464–471.

Lovelace, E. (1987). Attributes that come to mind in the TOT state. *Bulletin of the Psychonomic Society, 25,* 370–372.

Lubart, T. I. (1994). Creativity. In R. J. Sternberg (Ed.), *Thinking and problem solving* (pp. 290–323). New York: Academic Press.

Luchins, A. M. (1942). Mechanization in problem solving—the effect of Einstellung. *Psychological Monographs, 54,* 95.

Luo, C. R., Johnson, R. A., & Gallo, D. A. (1998). Automatic activation of phonological information in reading: Evidence from the semantic relatedness decision task. *Memory and Cognition, 26,* 833–843.

MacDonald, S., Uesiliana, K., & Hayne, H. (2000). Cross-cultural and gender differences in childhood amnesia. *Memory, 8,* 365–376.

MacKay, D. G. (1987). *The organization of perception and action: A theory for language and other cognitive skills.* New York: Springer-Verlag.

MacWhinney, B., & Bates, E. (1989). *The cross-linguistic study of sentence processing.* New York: Cambridge University Press.

Madigan, S. (1974). Representational storage in picture memory. *Bulletin of the Psychonomic Society, 4,* 567–568.

Maier, N. R., & Burke, R. J. (1967). Influence of timing of hints on their effectiveness in problem solving. *Psychological Reports, 20,* 3–8.

Maki, R. H. (1998). Predicting performance on text: Delayed vs. immediate predictors and tests. *Memory and Cognition, 26,* 959–964.

Malt, B. C. (1989). An on-line investigation of prototype and exemplar strategies in classification. *Journal of Experimental Psychology: Learning, Memory, and Cognition, 15,* 539–555.

Malt, B. C., & Smith, E. E. (1984). Correlated properties in natural categories. *Journal of Verbal Learning and Verbal Behavior, 23,* 250–269.

Mandler, J. A. (1987). On the psychological reality of story structure. *Discourse Processes, 10,* 1–29.

Marcel, A. J. (1983). Conscious and unconscious perception: Experiments on visual masking and word recognition. *Cognitive Psychology, 15,* 197–237.

Marian, V., & Neisser, U. (2000). Language-dependent recall of autobiographical memories. *Journal of Experimental Psychology: General, 129,* 361–368.

Marks, L. E. (1987). On cross-modal similarity: Auditory-visual interactions in speeded discrimination. *Journal of Experimental Psychology: Human Perception and Performance, 13,* 383–394.

Marr, D. (1982). *Vision.* San Francisco: Freeman.

Marsh, R. L., Landau, J. D., & Hicks, J. L. (1997). Contributions of inadequate source monitoring to unconscious plagiarism during idea generation. *Journal of Experimental Psychology: Learning, Memory, and Cognition, 23,* 886–897.

Martindale, C. (1991). *Cognitive psychology: A neural-network approach.* Pacific Grove, CA: Brooks/Cole.

Martino, G., & Marks, L. E. (1999). Perceptual and linguistic interactions in speeded classification: Tests of the semantic coding hypothesis. *Perception, 28,* 903–923.

Martino, G., & Marks, L. E. (2001). Synaesthesia: Strong and weak. *Current Directions in Psychological Science, 10,* 61–65.

Massaro, D. W. (1972). Preperceptual images, processing time, and perceptual units in auditory perception. *Psychological Review, 79,* 124–145.

Massaro, D. W. (1975). *Experimental psychology and information processing.* Chicago: Rand McNally.

Massaro, D. W. (1994). Psychological aspects of speech perception: Implications for research and theory. In M. A. Gernsbacher (Ed.), *Handbook of psycholinguistics* (pp. 219–263). New York: Academic Press.

Massaro, D. W., & Loftus, G. R. (1996). Sensory and perceptual storage: Data and theory. In E. L. Bjork & R. A. Bjork (Eds.), *Memory* (pp. 67–99). New York: Academic Press.

Matin, E. (1974). Saccadic suppression: A review and an analysis. *Psychological Bulletin, 81,* 899–917.

Mattingly, I. G., & Liberman, A. M. (1987). Specialized perceiving systems for speech and other biologically significant sounds. In G. M. Edelman, W. E. Gall, & W. M. Cowan (Eds.), *Auditory function: Neurological bases of hearing* (pp. 775–793). New York: Wiley.

Mayer, R. (1992). *Thinking, problem solving, cognition* (2nd ed.). New York: Freeman.

McBurney, D. M. (1974). Are there primary tastes for man? *Chemical Senses and Flavor, 1,* 17–28.

McBurney, D. M. (1986). Taste, smell, and flavor terminology: Taking the confusion out of fusion. In H. L. Meiselman & R. S. Rivlin (Eds.), *Clinical measurement of taste and smell* (pp. 117–125). New York: Macmillan.

McClaughlin, G. H. (1969). Reading at "impossible" speeds. *Journal of Reading, 12,* 449–454.

McClelland, J. L., & Rumelhart, D. E. (1981). An interactive activation model of context effects in letter perception, I: An account of basic findings. *Psychological Review, 88,* 375–407.

McClelland, J. L., & Rumelhart, D. E. (1985). Distributed memory and the representation of general and specific information. *Journal of Experimental Psychology: General, 114,* 159–188.

McClelland, J. L., Thomas, A. G., McCandliss, B. D., & Fiez, J. A. (1999). Understanding failures of learning: Hebbian learning, competition for representational space, and some preliminary experimental data. In J. A. Reggia, E. Ruppin, & D. Glanzman (Eds.), *Progress in brain research* (vol. 121). Amsterdam: Elsevier.

McCloskey, M., & Zaragoza, M. (1985). Misleading postevent information and memory for events: Arguments and evidence against memory impairment hypothesis. *Journal of Experimental Psychology: General, 114,* 1–16.

McCloskey, M., Wible, C. J., & Cohen, N. J. (1988). Is there a special flashbulb-memory mechanism? *Journal of Experimental Psychology: General, 117,* 171–181.

McConkie, M., & Rayner, K. (1976). What guides a reader's eye movements? *Vision Research, 16,* 829–837.

McDaniel, M. A., & Einstein, G. O. (1986). Bizarre imagery as an effective memory aid: The importance of distinctiveness. *Journal of Experimental Psychology: Learning, Memory, and Cognition, 12,* 54–65.

McDaniel, M. A., Pressley, & Dunay, (1987). Long-term retention of vocabulary after keyword and context learning. *Journal of Educational Psychology, 79,* 87–89.

McDonald, J. L., & MacWhinney, B. (1995). The time course of anaphor resolution: Effects of implicit verb causality and gender. *Journal of Memory and Language, 34,* 543–566.

McGurk, J., & MacDonald, H. (1978). Visual influences on speech perception. *Perception & Psychophysics, 24,* 253–257.

McKoon, G. (1977). Organization of information in text memory. *Journal of Verbal Learning and Verbal Behavior, 16,* 247–260.

McKoon, G., & Ratcliff, R. (1992). Inferences during reading. *Psychological Review, 99,* 440–466.

McLaughlin, G. H. (1969). Reading at "impossible" speeds. *Journal of Reading, 12,* 449–454, 502–510.

McMackin, J., & Slovic, P. (2000). When does explicit justification impair decision making? *Applied Cognitive Psychology, 14,* 527–541.

McNamara, H. J., Long, J. B., & Wike, E. L. (1956). Learning without response under two conditions of external cues. *Journal of Comparative and Physiological Psychology, 49,* 477–480.

McNamara, T. P. (1992). Theories of priming, I: Associative distance and lag. *Journal of Experimental Psychology: Learning, Memory, and Cognition, 18,* 1173–1190.

McNamara, T. P. (1994). Knowledge representation. In R. L. Sternberg (Ed.), *Thinking and problem solving* (pp. 81–117). New York: Academic Press.

McNamara, T. P., & Altarriba, J. (1988). Depth of spreading activation revisited: Semantic mediated priming occurs in lexical decisions. *Journal of Memory and Language, 27,* 545–559.

McNeil, B. J., Pauker, Sox, H. C., & Tversky, A. (1986). On the elicitation of preferences for alternative therapies. In K. R. Hammond & H. R. Arkes (Eds.), *Judgment and decision making.* New York: Cambridge University Press.

Medin, D. L., & Coley, J. D. (1998). Concepts and categorization. In J. Hochberg (Ed.), *Perception and cognition at century's end* (pp. 403–439). San Diego, CA: Academic Press.

Medin, D. L., & Heit, A. (1999). Categorization. In D. Rumelhart & B. Martin (Eds.), *Handbook of cognition and perception* (pp. 99–143). New York: Academic Press.

Medin, C., Lynch, J., & Solomon, H. (2000). Are there kinds of concepts? *Annual Review of Psychology, 52,* 121–147.

Melton, A. W. (1963). Implications of short-term memory for a general theory of memory. *Journal of Verbal Learning and Verbal Behavior, 2,* 1–21.

Melton, A. W. (1970). The situation with respect to the spacing of repetitions and memory. *Journal of Verbal Learning and Verbal Behavior, 9,* 596–606.

Merikle, P. M. (1988). Subliminal auditory messages: An evaluation. *Psychology and Marketing, 5,* 355–372.

Mervis, C. B., & Rosch, E. (1981). Categorization of natural objects. *Annual Review of Psychology, 32,* 89–115.

Metcalfe, J. (1986a). Feeling of knowing in memory and problem solving. *Journal of Experimental Psychology: Learning, Memory, and Cognition, 12,* 288–294.

Metcalfe, J. (1986b). Premonitions of insight predict impending error. *Journal of Experimental Psychology: Learning, Memory, and Cognition, 12,* 623–634.

Metcalfe, J., Schwartz, B. L., & Joaquim, S. G. (1993). The cue-familiarity heuristic in metacognition. *Journal of Experimental Psychology: Learning, Memory, and Cognition, 19,* 851–861.

Metcalfe, J., & Weibe, D. (1987). Metacognition in insight and noninsight problem solving. *Memory and Cognition, 15,* 238–246.

Metzger, R. L., Boschee, P. F., Haugen, T., & Schnobrich, B. L. (1979). The classroom as learning context: Changing rooms affects performance. *Journal of Educational Psychology, 71,* 440–442.

Miles, F., & Hardman, G. (1998). State-dependent memory produced by aerobic exercise. *Ergonomics, 41,* 20–28.

Miller, G. A. (1956). The magical number seven, plus or minus two: Some limits on our capacity for processing information. *Psychological Review, 63,* 81–97.

Miller, G. A. (1990). The place of language in a scientific psychology. *Psychological Science, 1,* 7–14.

Monti, L. A., Gabrieli, J. D. E., Wilson, R. S., Beckett, L. A., Grinnell, E., Lange, K. L., & Reminger, S. L. (1997). Sources of priming in text rereading: Intact implicit memory for new associations in older adults and in patients with Alzheimer's disease. *Psychology and Aging, 12,* 536–547.

Moore, C. M., & Egeth, H. (1997). Perception without attention: Evidence of grouping under conditions of inattention. *Journal of Experimental Psychology: Human Perception and Performance, 23,* 339–352.

Moore, T. E. (1996). Scientific consensus and expert testimony: Lessons from the Judas Priest trial. *Skeptical Inquirer, 20.*

Moray, N. (1959). Attention in dichotic listening: Affective cues and the influence of instructions. *Quarterly Journal of Experimental Psychology, 11,* 56–60.

Morris, C. D., Bransford, J. D., & Franks, J. J. (1977). Levels of processing versus transfer-appropriate processing. *Journal of Verbal Learning and Verbal Behavior, 16,* 519–533.

Motley, M. T. (1985). Slips of the tongue. *Scientific American, 253,* 116–127.

Motley, M. T., & Baars, B. J. (1979). Effects of cognitive set up laboratory-induced verbal (Freudian) slips. *Journal of Speech and Hearing Research, 22,* 421–432.

Mousty, P., & Bertelson, P. (1992). Finger movements in Braille reading: The effect of local ambiguity. *Cognition, 43,* 67–84.

Murray, D. J. (1968). Articulation and acoustic confusability in short-term memory. *Journal of Experimental Psychology, 78,* 679–684.

Murray, W. S., & Kennedy, A. (1988). Spatial coding in the processing of anaphor by good and poor readers: Evidence from eye movement analyses. *Quarterly Journal of Experimental Psychology: Human Experimental Psychology, 40(4-A),* 693–718.

Murray, J. E., Young, E., & Rhodes, G. (2000). Revisiting the perception of upside-down faces. *Psychological Science, 11,* 492–496.

Nadel, L., & Jacobs, W. J. (1998). Traumatic memory is special. *Current Directions in Psychological Science, 7,* 154–157.

Nadel, L., & Zola-Morgan, S. (1984). Infantile amnesia: A neurobiological perspective. In M. Moscovitch (Ed.), *Infant memory* (pp. 145–172). New York: Plenum Press.

Nairne, J. S. (1983). Associative processing during rote rehearsal. *Journal of Experimental Psychology: Learning, Memory, and Cognition, 9,* 3–20.

Nairne, J. S. (1992). The loss of positional certainty in long-term memory. *Psychological Science, 3,* 199–202.

Nairne, J. S. (1996). Short-term/working memory. In E. L. Bjork & R. A. Bjork (Eds.), *Memory: Handbook of perception and cognition.* New York: Academic Press.

Nairne, J. S. (2002). Remembering over the short-term: The case against the standard model. *Annual Review of Psychology, 53,* 53–81.

Nairne, J. S., & Walters, V. L. (1983). Silent mouthing produces modality- and suffix-like effects. *Journal of Verbal Learning and Verbal Behavior, 22,* 475–483.

Nathan, D., & Snedeker, M. (1995). *Satan's silence: Ritual abuse and the making of a modern American witch hunt.* New York: Basic Books.

Navon, D. (1977). Forest before trees: The precedence of global features in visual perception. *Cognitive Psychology, 9,* 353–383.

Navon, D., & Gopher, D. (1979). On the economy of the human information processing system. *Psychological Review, 86,* 214–255.

Neath, I., Surprenant, A. M., & Crowder, R. G. (1993). The context-dependent stimulus suffix effect. *Journal of Experimental Psychology: Learning, Memory, and Cognition, 19,* 698–703.

Needham, D. R., & Begg, I. M. (1991). Problem-oriented training promotes spontaneous analogical transfer: Memory-oriented training promotes memory for training. *Memory and Cognition, 19,* 543–557.

Neely, J. H. (1977). Semantic priming and retrieval from lexical memory: Roles of inhibitionless spreading activation and limited-capacity attention. *Journal of Experimental Psychology: General, 106,* 226–254.

Neisser, U. (1967). *Cognitive psychology.* New York: Appleton-Century-Crofts.

Neisser, U. (1978). Memory: What are the important questions? In M. M. Gruneberg, P. E. Morris, & R. N. Sykes (Eds.), *Practical aspects of memory,* New York: Academic Press.

Neisser, U. (1988). What is ordinary memory the memory of? In U. Neisser (Ed.), *Remembering reconsidered: Ecological and traditional approaches to the study of memory* (pp. 356–373). San Francisco: Freeman.

Neisser, U., & Harsch, W. (1992). Phantom flashbulbs: False recollections of hearing the news about Challenger. In E. Winograd & U. Neisser (Eds.), *Affect and accuracy in recall: Studies of "flashbulb" memories* (pp. 9–31). New York: Cambridge University Press.

Nelson, E. L., & Simpson, P. (1994). First glimpse: An initial investigation of subjects who have rejected their recovered visualizations as false memories. *Issues in Child Abuse Accusations, 6,* 123–133.

Nelson, K. (1993). The psychological and social origins of autobiographical memory. *Psychological Science, 4,* 7–14.

Nelson, T. O. (1984). A comparison of current measures of the accuracy of the feeling-of-knowing predictions. *Psychological Bulletin, 95,* 109–133.

Newell, A., Shaw, J. C., & Simon, H. A. (1958). Elements of a theory of human problem solving. *Psychological Review, 65,* 151–166.

Newell, A., & Simon, H. (1972). *Human problem solving.* Englewood Cliffs, NJ: Prentice Hall.

Nisbett, R. E., & Wilson, W. (1977). Telling more than we can know: Verbal reports on mental processes. *Psychological Review, 84,* 231–259.

Norman, D. A. (1981). Categorization of action slips. *Psychological Review, 88,* 1–15.

Norman, D. A. (1988). *The psychology of everyday things.* New York: Basic Books.

Norman, D. A., & Bobrow, D. G. (1975). On data-limited and resource-limited processes. *Cognitive Psychology, 7,* 44–64.

Norman, D. A., & Bobrow, D. G. (1979). On the role of active memory processes in perception and cognition. In C. N. Cofer (Ed.), *The structure of human memory* (pp. 114–32). San Francisco: Freeman.

Norman, K. A., & Schacter, D. L. (1996). Implicit memory, explicit memory and false recollection. A cognitive neuroscience perspective. In L. M. Reder (Ed.), *Implicit memory and metacognition* (pp. 229–259). Hillsdale, NJ: Erlbaum.

Nosofsky, R. (1984). Choice, similarity, and the context theory of classification. *Journal of Experimental Psychology: Learning, Memory, and Cognition, 10,* 104–114.

Novick, L. R., & Holyoak, K. E. (1991). Mathematical problem solving by analogy. *Journal of Experimental Psychology: Learning, Memory, and Cognition, 17,* 398–415.

Nyberg, L., Cabeza, R., & Tulving, E. (1996). PET studies of encoding and retrieval: The HERA model. *Psychonomic Bulletin and Review, 3,* 135–148.

Olton, R. M. (1979). Experimental studies of incubation: Searching for the elusive. *Journal of Creative Behavior, 13,* 9–22.

Olton, R. M., & Johnson, D. M. (1976). Mechanisms of incubation in creative problem solving. *American Journal of Psychology, 89,* 617–630.

Orne, M. T., Soskis, D. A., Dinges, D. F., & Orne, E. C. (1984). Hypnotically induced testimony. In G. Wells & E. F. Loftus (Eds.), *Eyewitness testimony: Psychological perspectives* (pp. 171–213). New York: Cambridge University Press.

Ostergaard, A. L. (1999). Priming effects in amnesia: Now you see them, now you don't. *Journal of the International Neurological Society, 5,* 175–190.

Ostergaard, A. L., & Jernigan, T. L. (1993). Are word priming and explicit memory mediated by different brain structures? In P. Graf & M. E. J. Masson (Eds.), *Implicit memory: New directions in cognition, development, and neuropsychology* (pp. 327–349). Hillsdale, NJ: Erlbaum.

Paivio, A. (1971). *Imagery and verbal processes.* New York: Holt, Rinehart and Winston.

Paivio, A., & Csapo, K. (1969). Concrete image and verbal memory codes. *Journal of Experimental Psychology, 80,* 279–285.

Palmer, S. E. (1975). The effects of contextual scenes on the identification of objects. *Memory and Cognition, 3,* 519–526.

Palmer, S. E. (2002). Perceptual grouping: It's later than you think. *Current Directions in Psychological Science, 11,* 101–106.

Park, D. C., Hertzog, C., Kidder, D. P., Morrell, R. W., & Mayhorn, D. (1997). Effect of age on event-based and time-based prospective memory. *Psychology and Aging, 12,* 314–327.

Park, D. C., Smith, A. D., & Cavanaugh, J. C. (1990). Metamemories of memory researchers. *Memory and Cognition, 18,* 321–327.

Parsons, L. M. (1987). Imagined spatial transformations of one's body. *Journal of Experimental Psychology: General, 116,* 172–191.

Pashler, H. (1998). *The psychology of attention.* Cambridge, MA: MIT Press.

Pashler, H., & Carrier, M. (1996). Structures, processes, and the flow of information. In E. L. Bjork & R. A. Bjork (Eds.), *Handbook of perception and cognition: Memory* (pp. 3–29). New York: Academic Press.

Patterson, K., & Besner, D. (1984). Is the right hemisphere literate? *Cognitive Neuropsychology, 1,* 315–341.

Pavani, F., Spence, C., & Driver, J. (2000). Visual capture of touch: Out-of-body experiences with rubber gloves. *Psychological Science, 11,* 353–359.

Pepperberg, I. M. (1999a). *The Alex studies: Cognitive and communicative abilities of grey parrots.* Cambridge, MA: Harvard University Press.

Pepperberg, I. M. (1999b). Cognitive and communicative abilities of grey parrots. *Current Directions in Psychological Science, 11,* 83–87.

Petersen, S. E., Fox, P. T., Posner, M. I., Mintun, M., & Raichle, M. E. (1988). Positron emission tomography studies of the cortical anatomy of single-word processing. *Nature, 331,* 585–589.

Peterson, C., & Bell, M. (1996). Children's memory for traumatic injury. *Child Development, 67,* 3045–3070.

Peterson L., & Peterson, M. J. (1959). Short-term retention of individual verbal items. *Journal of Experimental Psychology, 58,* 193–198.

Piaget, J. (1929). *The child's conception of the world.* New York: Harcourt Brace.

Pickering and Traxler (1998). Plausibility and recovery from garden-paths: An eye-movement study. *Journal of Experimental Psychology: Learning, Memory, and Cognition, 24,* 940–961.

Pillemer, D. B. (1984). Flashbulb memories of the assassination attempt on President Reagan. *Cognition, 16,* 63–80.

Pillemer, D. B. (1992). Remembering personal circumstances: A functional analysis. In E. Winograd & U. Neisser (Eds.), *Affect and accuracy in recall: Studies of "flashbulb" memories* (pp. 236–264). Cambridge, UK: Cambridge University Press.

Pillemer, D. B. (1998). *Momentous events, vivid memories.* Cambridge, MA: Harvard University Press.

Pillemer, D. B., Picariello, M. L., Law, A. B., & Reichman, J. S. (1996). Memories of college: The importance of specific autobiographical episodes. In D. C. Rubin (Ed.), *Remembering our past: Studies in autobiographical memory* (pp. 318–337). New York: Cambridge University Press.

Pillemer, D. B., & White, S. H. (1989). Childhood events recalled by children and adults. In H. W. Reese (Ed.), *Advances in child development and behavior* (Vol. 21, pp. 297–340). San Diego, CA: Academic Press.

Pinker, S. (1990). Language acquisition. In L. R. Gleitman (Ed.), *Language: An invitation to cognitive science* (Vol. 1, pp. 199–241). Cambridge, MA: MIT Press.

Pinker, S. (1991). Rules of language. *Science, 253,* 530–535.

Pinker, S. (1994a). *How the mind works.* New York: Norton.

Pinker, S. (1994b). *The language instinct.* New York: Morrow.

Pinker, S. (1996). Letter to the editor. *Science, 276,* 1178.

Pinker, S. (1999). *Words and rules.* New York: Basic Books.

Pinker, S., Choate, P. A., & Finke, R. A. (1984). Mentefectal extrapolations in patterns constructed from memory. *Memory and Cognition, 12,* 207–218.

Plous, S. (1993). *The psychology of judgment and decision-making.* New York: McGraw-Hill.

Polusny, M. A., & Follette, V. M. (1996). Remembering childhood sexual abuse: A national survey of psychologists' clinical practices, beliefs, and personal experiences. *Professional Psychology Research and Practice, 27,* 41–52.

Polya, G. (1957). *How to solve it.* Garden City, NJ: Doubleday Anchor.

Poole, D. A., Lindsay, D. S., Memon, A., & Bull, R. (1995). Psychotherapy and the recovery of memories of childhood sexual abuse. *Journal of Consulting and Clinical Psychology, 63,* 426–437.

Posner, M. I., Goldsmith, R., & Welton, K. E. (1967). Perceived distance and the classification of distorted patterns. *Journal of Experimental Psychology, 73,* 28–38.

Posner, M. I., & Keele, S. W. (1967). Decay of visual information from a single letter. *Science, 158,* 137–139.

Posner, M. I., & Snyder, C. R. R. (1975). Facilitation and inhibition in the processing of signals. In P. M. A. Rabbitt & S. Dornic (Eds.), *Attention and performance* (pp. 669–682). New York: Academic Press.

Premack, D. (1970). A functional analysis of language. *Journal of the Experimental Analysis of Behavior, 14,* 107–125.

Premack, D., & Premack, A. J. (1983). *The mind of an ape.* New York: Norton.

Proctor, R. W., & Fangini, C. A. (1978). Effects of distractor-stimulus modality in the Brown-Peterson distractor task. *Journal of Experimental Psychology: Human Learning and Memory, 4,* 676–684.

Proust, M. (1960). *Swann's way.* (C. K. Scott Moncrieff, Trans.). London: Chatto & Windus. (Original work published 1922.)

Pugh, K. R., Mencl, W. E., Shaywitz, B. A., Shaywitz, S. E., Fulbright, R. K., Constable, R. T., Skudlarski, P., Marchione, K. E., Jenner, A. R., Fletcher, J. M., Liberman, A. M., Shankweiler, D. P., Katz, L., Lacadie, C., & Gore, J. C. (2000). The angular gyrus in developmental dyslexia: Task-specific differences in functional connectivity within posterior cortex. *Psychological Science, 11,* 51–56.

Pylyshyn, Z. W. (1973). What the mind's eye tells the mind's brain: A critique of mental imagery. *Psychological Bulletin, 80,* 1–24.

Pylyshyn, Z. W. (1981). The imagery debate: Analogue media vs. tacit knowledge. *Psychological Review, 88,* 16–45.

Pynoos, R. S., & Nader, K. (1989). Children's memory and proximity to violence. *Journal of the American Academy of Child and Adolescent Psychiatry, 28,* 236–241.

Quinn, D. M., & Spencer, S. J. (2001). The interference of stereotype threat with women's generation of mathematical problem-solving strategies. *Journal of Social Issues, 57,* 55–71.

Radford, B. (1999). The ten-percent myth. *Skeptical Inquirer, 23.*

Rajaram, S. (1993). Remembering and knowing: Two means of access to the personal past. *Memory and Cognition, 21,* 89–102.

Rappold, V. A., & Hashtroudi, S. (1991). Does organization improve priming? *Journal of Experimental*

Psychology: Learning, Memory, and Cognition, 17, 103–114.

Rastle, C., & Burke, M. (1996). Priming the tip of the tongue: Effects of prior processing on word retrieval in young and older adults. *Journal of Memory and Language, 35,* 585–605.

Rawson, K. A., Dunlosky, J., & Thiede, K. W. (2000). The re-reading effect: Metacomprehension accuracy improves across reading trials. *Memory and Cognition, 28,* 1004–1010.

Rayner, K. (1998). Eye movements in reading and information processing: Twenty years of research. *Psychological Bulletin, 124,* 374–422.

Rayner, K., & Morris, R. K. (1992). Eye movement control in reading: Evidence against semantic preprocessing. *Journal of Experimental Psychology: Human Perception and Performance, 18,* 164–172.

Rayner, K., & Pollatsek, A. (1983). Is visual information integrated across saccades? *Perception & Psychophysics, 34,* 39–48.

Rayner, K., & Pollatsek, A. (1989). *The psychology of reading.* Englewood Cliffs, NJ: Prentice Hall.

Rayner, K., & Well, A. D. (1996). Effects of contextual constraint on eye movements in reading: A further examination. *Psychological Bulletin and Review, 3,* 504–509.

Rayner, K., Foorman, B. R., Perfetti, C. A., Pesetsky, D., & Seidenberg, M. S. (2001). How psychological science informs the teaching of reading. *Psychological Science in the Public Interest, 2,* 31–74.

Rayner, K., Foorman, B. R., Perfetti, C. A., Pesetsky, D., & Seidenberg, M. S. (2002). How should reading be taught? *Scientific American, 287,* 85–91.

Reason, J. T. (1984). Lapses of attention in everyday life. In R. Parasuraman & D. R. Davies (Eds.), *Varieties of attention* (pp. 515–549). New York: Academic Press.

Reason, J. T., & Lucas, D. (1984). Using cognitive diaries to investigate naturally occurring memory blocks. In J. E. Harris and P. E. Morris (Eds.), *Everyday memory, actions, and absentmindedness* (pp. 53–69). New York: Academic Press.

Reed, G. (1974). *The psychology of anomalous experience.* Boston: Houghton Mifflin.

Reese, E., & Fivush, R. (1993). Parental styles of talking about the past. *Developmental Psychology, 29,* 506–516.

Reicher, G. (1969). Perceptual recognition as a function of meaningfulness of stimulus material. *Journal of Experimental Psychology, 81,* 275–280.

Repp, B. H. (1984). Closure duration and release burst amplitude cues to stop consonant manner and place of articulation. *Language and Speech, 27,* 245–254.

Richman, C. L., Mitchell, D. B., & Reznick, J. S. (1979). Mental travel: Some reservations. *Journal of Experimental Psychology: Human Perception and Performance, 5,* 13–18.

Rips, L. J. (1974). Inductive judgments about natural categories. *Journal of Verbal Learning and Verbal Behavior, 14,* 665–681.

Rips, L. J. (1989). Similarity, typicality, and categorization. In S. Vosniadu & A. Ortony (Eds.), *Similarity and analogical reasoning* (pp. 21–59). Cambridge, UK: Cambridge University Press.

Rips, L. J. (1990). Reasoning. *Annual Review of Psychology, 41,* 321–353.

Rips, L. J. (1994). Deduction and its cognitive basis. In R. J. Sternberg (Ed.), *Thinking and problem solving* (pp. 149–178). New York: Academic Press.

Rips, L. J., Shoben, E. J., & Smith, E. E. (1973). Semantic distance and the verification of semantic relations. *Journal of Verbal Learning and Verbal Behavior, 12,* 1–20.

Risset, J. C. (1991). Speech and music combined: An overview. In J. Sundberg, I. Nord, & R. Carlson (Eds.), *Music, language, speech, and brain* (pp. 368–379). New York: Cambridge University Press.

Robertson, D. A., Gernsbacher, M. A., Guidotti, S. J., Robertson, R. R., Irwin, W., Mock, B. J., & Campana, M. E. (2000). Functional neuroanatomy of the cognitive process of mapping during discourse comprehension. *Psychological Science, 11,* 255–260.

Robinson, J. A. (1980). Affect and retrieval of personal memories. *Motivation and Emotion, 4,* 149–174.

Rochat, P. (1999). Direct perception and representation in infancy. In E. Winograd, R. Fivush, & W. Hirst (Eds.), *Ecological approaches to cognition: Essays in honor of Ulric Neisser* (pp. 3–30). Mahwah, NJ: Erlbaum.

Rock, I. (1984). *Perception.* New York: Scientific American Books.

Roediger, H. L. (1980). The effectiveness of four mnemonics in ordering recall. *Journal of Experimental Psychology: Human Learning and Memory, 6,* 558–567.

Roediger, H. L. (1990). Implicit memory: Retention without remembering. *American Psychologist, 45,* 1043–1056.

Roediger, H. L., & Bergman, E. T. (1998). The controversy over recovered memories. *Psychology, Public Policy, and Law, 4,* 1091–1109.

Roediger, H. L., & Guynn, C. (1996). Retrieval processes. In E. L. Bjork & R. A. Bjork (Eds.), *Handbook of perception and cognition: Memory* (pp. 197–236). New York: Academic Press.

Roediger, H. L., & McDermott, K. B. (1995). Creating false memories: Remembering words not presented in lists. *Journal of Experimental Psychology: Learning, Memory, and Cognition, 21,* 803–814.

Roediger, H. L., Meade, M. L., & Bergman, E. T. (2001). Social contagion of memory. *Psychonomic Bulletin and Review, 8,* 365–371.

Rogers, T. B., Kuiper, N. A., & Kirker, W. S. (1977). Self reference and the encoding of personal information. *Journal of Personality and Social Psychology, 35,* 677–688.

Rosch, E. (1973). Natural categories. *Cognitive Psychology, 4,* 328–350.

Rosch, E. (1975a). Cognitive reference points. *Cognitive Psychology, 7,* 532–547.

Rosch, E. (1975b). Cognitive representations of semantic categories. *Journal of Experimental Psychology: General, 104,* 192–233.

Rosch, E. (1978). Principles of categorization. In E. Rosch & B. B. Lloyd (Eds.), *Cognition and categorization* (pp. 27–48). Hillsdale, NJ: Erlbaum.

Rosch, E., & Mervis, C. B. (1975). Family resemblances: Studies in the internal structure of categories. *Cognitive Psychology, 7,* 573–605.

Rosenbluth, R., Grossman, E. S., & Kaitz, R. (2000). Performance of early-blind and sighted children on olfactory tasks. *Perception, 29,* 101–110.

Ross, B. H. (1987). This is like that: The use of earlier examples and the separation of similarity effects. *Journal of Experimental Psychology: Learning, Memory, and Cognition, 13,* 629–639.

Ross, B. H., & Spalding, T. L. (1994). Concepts and categories. In R. J. Sternberg (Ed.), *Handbook of perception and cognition,* Vol. 2: *Thinking and problem solving* (pp. 119–148). San Diego, CA: Academic Press.

Ross, D. R., Ceci, S. J., Dunning, D., & Toglia, M. P. (1994). Unconscious transference and mistaken identity: When a witness misidentifies a familiar person. *Journal of Applied Psychology, 79,* 918–930.

Roth, E. M., & Shoben, E. J. (1983). The effect of context on the structure of categories. *Cognitive Psychology, 15,* 346–378.

Rothman, A. J., & Salovey, P. (1997). Shaping perceptions to motivate healthy behavior: The role of message framing. *Psychological Bulletin, 121,* 3–19.

Rozin, P. (1982). "Taste-smell confusions" and the duality of the olfactory sense. *Perception & Psychophysics, 31,* 397–401.

Rubin, D. C., Groth, E., & Goldsmith, D. J. (1984). Olfactory cuing of autobiographical memory. *American Journal of Psychology, 97,* 493–507.

Rubin, D. C., Rahhal, T. A., & Poon, L. W. (1998). Things learned in early adulthood are remembered best. *Memory and Cognition, 26,* 3–19.

Rubin, D. C., Wetzler, S. E., & Nebes, R. D. (1986). Autobiographical memory across the lifespan. In D. C. Rubin (Ed.), *Autobiographical memory* (pp. 202–221). Cambridge, UK: Cambridge University Press.

Rumbaugh, D. (Ed.). (1977). *Language learning by a chimpanzee: The Lana project.* New York: Academic Press.

Rumelhart, D. E. (1975). Notes on a schema for stories. In D. G. Bobrow & A. M. Collins (Eds.), *Representation and understanding* (pp. 211–236). New York: Academic Press.

Rumelhart, D. E., & McClelland, J. L. (1986). *Parallel distributed processing: Explorations into the microstructure of cognition.* Cambridge, MA: MIT Press.

Sachs, J. (1967). Recognition memory for syntactic and semantic aspects of connected discourse. *Perception and Psychophysics, 2,* 437–442.

Sacks, H., Schegloff, E. A., & Jefferson, G. (1974). A simplest systematics for the organization of turn-taking in conversation. *Language, 50,* 696–735.

Saffran, J. R., Aslin, R. N., & Newport, E. C. (1996). Statistical learning in 8-month old infants. *Science, 274,* 1926–1928.

Salaman, E. (1970). *A collection of moments: A study of involuntary memories.* London: Longman.

Saldana, H. M., & Rosenblum, L. D. (1993). Visual influences on auditory pluck and bow judgments. *Perception & Psychophysics, 54,* 406–416.

Saufley, W. H., Otaka, S. R., & Bravaresco, J. L. (1986). Context effects: Classroom tests and context independence. *Memory and Cognition, 13,* 522–528.

Savage-Rumbaugh, E. S., & Brakke, K. E. (1996). Animal language: Methodological and interpretive issues. In M. Bekoff & D. Jamieson (Eds.), *Readings in animal cognition.* Cambridge, MA: MIT Press.

Savage-Rumbaugh, E. S., Rumbaugh, D. M., & Boysen, S. (1980). Do apes use language? *American Scientist, 68,* 49–61.

Schab, L. (1990). Odors and the remembrance of things past. *Journal of Experimental Psychology: Learning, Memory, and Cognition, 16,* 648–655.

Schacter, D. L. (1989). *Memory.* In M. I. Posner (Ed.), *Foundations of cognitive science.* Cambridge, MA: MIT Press.

Schacter, D. L. (1996). *Searching for memory: The brain, the mind, and the past.* New York: Basic Books.

Schacter, D. L. (2001). *The seven sins of memory: How the mind forgets and remembers.* New York: Houghton Mifflin.

Schacter, D. L., & Moscovitch, M. (1984). Infants, amnesia, and dissociable memory systems. In M. Moscovitch (Ed.), *Infant memory* (pp. 173–216). New York: Plenum Press.

Schacter, D. L., Cooper, L. A., & Delaney, S. M. (1990). Implicit memory for unfamiliar objects depends on access to structural descriptions. *Journal of Experimental Psychology: General, 19,* 5–24.

Schacter, D. L., Norman, K. A., & Koutsaal, W. (1997). The recovered memories debate: A cognitive neuroscience perspective. In M. A. Conway (Ed.), *Recovered memories and false memories* (pp. 63–99). Oxford, UK: Oxford University Press.

Schacter, D. L., Cooper, L. A., Delaney, S. M., & Tharan, M. (1991). Implicit memory for possible and impossible objects: Constraints on the construction of structural descriptions. *Journal of Experimental Psychology: Learning, Memory, and Cognition, 17,* 3–19.

Schank, R. C., & Abelson, R. B. (1977). *Scripts, plans, goals, and understanding: An inquiry into human knowledge structures.* Hillsdale, NJ: Erlbaum.

Schank, R. C., & Cleary, C. (1994). Making machines creative. In S. M. Smith, T. B. Ward, and R. A. Finke (Eds.), *The creative cognition approach* (pp. 229–247). Cambridge, MA: MIT Press.

Schegloff, E. A. (1972). Sequencing in conversational openings. In J. J. Gumpetz & D. Hymes (Eds.), *Directions in sociolinguistics: The ethnography of com-*

munication (pp. 346–380). New York: Holt, Rinehart and Winston.

Schiano, D. J., & Watkins, M. J. (1981). Speech-like coding of pictures in short-term memory. *Memory and Cognition, 9,* 110–114.

Schmidt, H. P., & Boshuizen, H. G. (1993). On the origin of intermediate effects in clinical case recall. *Memory and Cognition, 21,* 338–351.

Schmidt, S. R. (1991). Can we have a distinctive theory of memory? *Memory and Cognition, 19,* 523–542.

Schmidt, S. R. (1994). Effects of humor on sentence memory. *Journal of Experimental Psychology: Learning, Memory, and Cognition, 10,* 953–967.

Schmolck, H., Buffalo, L. R., & Squire, L. R. (2000). Memory distortions develop over time: Recollections of the O. J. Simpson trial verdict after 15 and 32 months. *Psychological Science, 11,* 39–45.

Schneider, W., & Shiffrin, R. M. (1977). Controlled and automatic human information processing, I: Detection, search, and attention. *Psychological Review, 84,* 1–66.

Schooler, J. W. (1994). Seeking the core: The issues and evidence surrounding recovered accounts of sexual trauma. *Consciousness and Cognition, 3,* 452–469.

Schooler, J. W., & Eich, E. (2000). Memory for emotional events. In E. Tulving & F. I. M. Craik (Eds.), *The Oxford handbook of memory.* New York: Oxford University Press.

Schooler, J. W., Bendiksen, M. A., & Ambadar, Z. (1997). Taking the middle line: Can we accommodate both fabricated and recovered memories of sexual abuse? In M. Conway (Ed.), *Recovered memories and false memories* (pp. 251–292). Oxford, UK: Oxford University Press.

Schulster, J. R. (1996). In my era: Evidence for the perception of a special period of the past. *Memory, 4,* 145–158.

Schusterman, R. J., & Krieger, K. (1988). Artificial language comprehension and size transposition by a California sea lion (*Zalophis californianus*). *Journal of Comparative Psychology, 100,* 348–355.

Schweickert, R., McDaniel, M. A., & Riegler, G. (1993). Effects of generation on immediate memory span and delayed unexpected free recall. *Quarterly Journal of Experimental Psychology: Human Experimental Psychology, 47,* 781–804.

Searlemann, A., & Herrmann, D. (1994). *Memory from a broader perspective.* New York: McGraw-Hill.

Seidenberg, M. S. (1997). Language acquisition and use: Learning and applying probabilistic constraints. *Science, 275,* 1599–1603.

Sekuler, R., & Blake, R. (1994). *Perception* (3rd ed.). New York: McGraw-Hill.

Selfridge, O. (1959). Pandemonium: A paradigm for learning. In D. V. Blake & A. M. Uttley, (Eds.), *Proceedings of the symposium on mechanisation of thought processes* (pp. 511–529). London: H. M. Stationery Office.

Serafine, M. L., Crowder, R. J., & Repp, B. H. (1984). Integration of melody and text in memory for songs. *Cognition, 16,* 285–303.

Sergent, J., & Signoret, J. L. (1992). Varieties of functional deficits in prosopagnosia. *Cerebral Cortex, 2,* 375–388.

Shapiro, P. N., & Penrod, S. (1986). Meta-analysis of facial identification studies. *Psychological Bulletin, 100,* 139–156.

Shepard, R. N., & Metzler, J. (1971). Mental rotation of three-dimensional objects. *Science, 171,* 201–203.

Shiffrin, R. M., & Nosofsky, R. M. (1994). Seven plus or minus two: A commentary on capacity limitations. *Psychological Review, 101,* 357–361.

Shriberg, L. K., Levin, J. R., McCormick, C. B., & Pressley, M. (1982). Learning about "famous" people via the keyword method. *Journal of Educational Psychology, 74,* 238–247.

Siegler, R. S. (2001). Unconscious insights. *Current Directions in Psychological Science, 9,* 79–83.

Simonton, D. K. (1994). *Greatness: Who makes history and why.* New York: Guilford Press.

Simonton, D. K. (2000). Creativity: Cognitive, personal, social, and developmental aspects. *American Psychologist, 55,* 151–158.

Singer, M. (1980). The role of case-filling inferences in the coherence of brief passages. *Discourse Processes, 3,* 185–201.

Singer, M. (1990). *Psychology of language.* Hillsdale, NJ: Erlbaum.

Sloboda, J. (1986). *The musical mind: The cognitive psychology of music.* London: Oxford University Press.

Sloman, S. A. (1996). The empirical case for two systems of reasoning. *Psychological Bulletin, 119,* 3–22.

Smith, E. E., Langston, C., & Nisbett, R. E. (1992). The case for rules in reasoning. *Cognitive Science, 16,* 1–40.

Smith, E. E., Shoben, E. J., Rips L. J. (1974). Structure and process in semantic memory: A featural model for semantic decisions. *Psychological Review, 81,* 214–241.

Smith, E. R., & Branscombe, N. R. (1988). Category accessibility as implicit memory. *Journal of Experimental Social Psychology, 24,* 490–504.

Smith, M. A. (1983). Hypnotic memory enhancement: Does it work? *Psychological Bulletin, 94,* 387–407.

Smith, R. S., Doty, R. L., Burlingame, G. K., & McKeown, D. A. (1993). Smell and taste function in the visually impaired. *Perception & Psychophysics, 54,* 649–655.

Smith, S. M. (1979). Remembering in and out of context. *Journal of Experimental Psychology: Human Learning and Memory, 5,* 460–471.

Smith, S. M. (1988). Environmental context-dependent memory. In G. M. Davies & D. M. Thomson (Eds.), *Memory in context: Context in memory.*

Smith, S. M. (1995). Getting into and out of mental ruts: A theory of fixation, incubation, and insight. In R. J. Sternberg & J. E. Davidson (Eds.), *The nature of insight.* Cambridge, MA: MIT Press.

Smith, S. M., & Blankenship, S. E. (1991). Incubation effects. *Bulletin of the Psychonomic Society, 27,* 311–314.

Smith, S. M., Ward, T. B., & Finke R. A. (1994). *The creative cognition approach.* Cambridge, MA: MIT Press.

Snyder, M., & Swann, W. B. (1978). Hypothesis-testing in social interaction. *Journal of Personality and Social Psychology, 36,* 1202–1212.

Sperling, G. (1960). The information available in brief visual presentation. *Psychological Monographs, 74,* 1–29.

Spiegel, D. (1994). Dissociative disorders. In R. E. Hales, S. C. Yudofsky, & J. A. Talbott (Eds.), *The American Psychiatric Press textbook of psychiatry* (2nd ed., pp. 633–652). Washington, DC: American Psychiatric Association.

Squire, L. A. (1987). *Memory and brain.* New York: Oxford University Press.

Squire, L. A., & Zola-Morgan, S. (1988). Memory: Brain systems and behavior. *Trends in Neuroscience, 11,* 170–175.

Squire, L. R. (1993). The organization of declarative and nondeclarative memory. In T. Ono (Ed.), *Brain mechanisms of perception and memory: From neurons to behavior.* New York: Oxford University Press.

Squire, L. R., Knowlton, B., & Musen, G. (1993). The structure and organization of memory. *Annual Review of Psychology, 44,* 453–495.

Sternberg, R. J., & Ben-Zeev, T. (2001). *Complex cognition.* New York: Oxford University Press.

Sternberg, R. J., & Davidson, J. E. (1995). *The nature of insight.* Cambridge, MA: MIT Press.

Stevens, J. C. (1992). Aging and spatial acuity of touch. *Journal of Gerontology, 47,* 35–40.

Stevens, J. C., Foulke, E., & Patterson, M. Q. (1996). Tactile acuity, aging, and Braille reading in long-term blindness. *Journal of Experimental Psychology: Applied, 2,* 91–106.

Stevens, J. C., & Hooper, J. E. (1982). How skin and object temperature influence touch sensation. *Perception and Psychophysics, 32,* 282–285.

Stevens, S. S., & Newman, E. B. (1934). The localization of pure tone. *Proceedings of the National Academy of Sciences, 20,* 593–596.

Stolz, J. A., & Besner, D. (1999). On the myth of automatic semantic activation in reading. *Current Directions in Psychological Science, 8,* 61–65.

Strayer, D. L., & Johnston, W. A. (2001). Driven to distraction: Dual-task studies of simulated driving and conversing on a cellular telephone. *Psychological Science, 12,* 462–466.

Stroop, J. R. (1935). Studies of interference in serial verbal reactions. *Journal of Experimental Psychology, 35,* 643–662.

Sulin, R. A., & Dooling, D. J. (1974). Intrusion of a thematic idea in retention of prose. *Journal of Experimental Psychology, 103,* 255–262.

Symons, C. S., & Johnson, B. T. (1997). The self-reference in memory: A meta-analysis. *Psychological Bulletin, 121,* 371–394.

Tanaka, J. W., & Farah, M. J. (1993). Parts and wholes in face recognition. *Quarterly Journal of Experimental Psychology, 46A,* 225–245.

Tannen, D. (Ed.). (1993). *Gender and conversational interaction.* New York: Oxford University Press.

Tarr, M. J. (2000). Pattern recognition. In A. Kazdin (Ed.), *Encyclopedia of psychology.* Washington, DC: American Psychological Association.

Tarr, M. J., & Bülthoff, H. H. (1995). Is human object recognition better described by geon-structural-descriptions or by multiple-views? *Journal of Experimental Psychology: Human Perception and Performance, 21,* 1494–1505.

Tarr, M. J., & Pinker, S. (1989). Mental rotation and orientation-dependence in shape recognition. *Cognitive Psychology, 21,* 233–282.

Terr, L. C. (1979). Children of Chowchilla: A study of psychic trauma. *Psychoanalytic Study of the Child, 34,* 547–623.

Terrace, H. S., Petitto, L. A., Sanders, R. J., & Bever, T. G. (1979). Can an ape create a sentence? *Science, 206,* 891–902.

Thomas, E. L. (1962). Eye movements in speed reading. In R. G. Stauffer (Ed.), *Speed reading: Practices and procedures* (vol. 10). Newark: University of Delaware, Reading Study Center.

Thompson, W. C., Clarke-Stewart, K., & LePore, S. J. (1997). What did the janitor do? Suggestive interviewing and the accuracy of children's accounts. *Law and Human Behavior, 21,* 405–426.

Thomson, R., Murachver, T., & Green, J. (2001). Where is the gender in gendered language? *Psychological Science, 12,* 171–175.

Thomson, D. M., & Tulving, E. (1970). Associative encoding and retrieval. *Journal of Experimental Psychology, 86,* 255–262.

Thorndyke, P. W. (1977). Cognitive structures in comprehension and memory of narrative discourse. *Cognitive Psychology, 9,* 77–110.

Tinker, M. A. (1939). Illumination standards for effective and comfortable reading. *Journal of Consulting Psychology, 3,* 11–19.

Tinker, M. A. (1958). Recent studies of eye movements in reading. *Psychological Bulletin, 55,* 215–231.

Tolman, E. C. (1948). Cognitive maps in rats and men. *Psychological Review, 55,* 189–208.

Tolman, E. C., & Honzik, C. H. (1930). Introduction and removal of reward, and maze performance in rats. *University of California Publications in Psychology, 4,* 257–275.

Treisman, A. (1960). Contextual cues in selective listening. *Quarterly Journal of Experimental Psychology, 12,* 242–248.

Troutt-Ervin, E. (1990). Application of keyword mnemonics to learning terminology in the college classroom. *Journal of Experimental Education, 59,* 31–41.

Tulving, E. (1962). Subjective organization in free recall of "unrelated" words. *Psychological Review, 69,* 344–354.

Tulving, E. (1972). Episodic and semantic memory. In E. Tulving & W. Donaldson (Eds.), *Organization of memory.* New York: Academic Press.

Tulving, E. (1983). *Elements of episodic memory.* New York: Oxford University Press.

Tulving, E. (1991). Memory research is not a zero-sum game. *American Psychologist, 46,* 41–42.

Tulving, E., & Pearlstone, Z. (1966). Availability vs. accessibility of information in memory for words. *Journal of Verbal Learning and Verbal Behavior, 5,* 381–391.

Tulving, E., & Schacter, D. L. (1990). Priming and human memory systems. *Science, 247,* 301–306.

Tulving, E., & Thomson, D. M. (1973). Encoding specificity and retrieval processes in episodic memory. *Psychological Review, 80,* 359–380.

Tulving, E., Kapur, S., Craik, F. I. M., Moscovitch, M., & Houle, S. (1994). Hemispheric encoding/retrieval asymmetry in episodic memory: Positron emission tomography findings. *Proceedings of the National Academy of Sciences USA, 91,* 2016–2020.

Tversky, A., & Kahneman, D. (1971). Belief in the law of small numbers. *Psychological Bulletin, 76,* 105–110.

Tversky, A., & Kahneman, D. (1973). Availability: A heuristic for judging frequency and probability. *Cognitive Psychology, 5,* 207–232.

Tversky, A., & Kahneman, D. (1974). Judgment under uncertainty: Heuristics and biases. *Science, 89,* 1124–1131.

Tversky, A., & Kahneman, D. (1981). The framing of decisions and the psychology of choice. *Science, 211,* 453–458.

Tversky, A., & Kahneman, D. (1983). Extensional vs. intuitive reasoning. The conjunction fallacy in probability judgment. *Psychological Review, 90,* 293–315.

Usher, J. A., & Neisser, U. (1993). Childhood amnesia and the beginnings of memory for four early life events. *Journal of Experimental Psychology: General, 122,* 155–165.

van der Kolk, B. A. (1994). The body keeps score: Memory and the evolving psychobiology of post-traumatic stress. *Harvard Review of Psychiatry, 1,* 253–265.

van Dijk, T. A., & Kintsch, W. (1983). *Strategies of discourse comprehension.* New York: Academic Press.

Van Orden, G. C. (1987). A ROWS is a ROSE: Spelling, sound, and reading. *Memory and Cognition, 15,* 181–198.

Vecera, S. P., Vogel, E. K., & Woodman, G. F. (2002). Lower ground: A new cue for figure-ground assignment. *Journal of Experimental Psychology: General, 131,* 194–205.

Vicente, K. J., & Wang, J. H. (1998). An ecological theory of expertise effects in memory recall. *Psychological Review, 105,* 33–57.

Vokey, J. R., & Read, J. D. (1988). Subliminal messages: Between the devil and the media. *American Psychologist, 39,* 1231–1239.

von Eckardt, B., & Potter, M. C. (1985). Clauses and the semantic representations of words. *Memory and Cognition, 13,* 371–376.

von Frisch, K. (1967). *The dance language and orientation of bees.* Cambridge, MA: Belknap Press.

von Restorff, H. (1933). Uber die Wirkung von Bereichsbildungen im Spurenfeld, *Psychologische Forschung, 18,* 299–342.

von Wright, J. M. (1972). On the problem of selection in iconic memory. *Scandinavian Journal of Psychology, 13,* 159–171.

Voss, J. F., Vesonder, G., & Spilich, T. (1980). Text generation and recall by high-knowledge and low-knowledge individuals. *Journal of Verbal Learning and Verbal Behavior, 19,* 651–667.

Vroomen, J., van Zon, M., & de Gelder, B. (1996). Cues to speech segmentation. Evidence from juncture misperceptions and word spotting. *Memory and Cognition, 24,* 744–755.

Wagenaar, W. A. (1986). My memory: A study of autobiographical memory over six years. *Cognitive Psychology, 18,* 225–252.

Wakefield, H., & Underwager, R. C. (1994). *Return of the furies: An investigation into recovered memory therapy.* Chicago: Open Court.

Walker, P., & Yekovich, K. (1987). Activation and use of script-based antecedents in anaphoric reference. *Journal of Memory and Language, 26,* 673–691.

Wallace, W. P. (1965). Review of the historical, empirical, and theoretical status of the von Restorff phenomenon. *Psychological Bulletin, 63,* 410–424.

Wallas, G. (1926). *The art of thought.* London: J. Cape.

Warren, R. M. (1970). Perceptual restoration of missing speech sounds. *Science, 167,* 392–393.

Warrington, R., & Weiskrantz, A. (1970). Amnesic syndrome: Consolidation or retrieval? *Nature, 228,* 628–630.

Watkins, M. J. (1990). Mediationism and the obfuscation of memory. *American Psychologist, 45,* 328–335.

Waugh, N. C., & Norman, D. A. (1965). Primary memory. *Psychological Review, 72,* 89–104.

Weisberg, R. W. (1992). Metacognition and insight during problem solving: Comment on Metcalfe. *Journal of Experimental Psychology: Learning, Memory, and Cognition, 18,* 426–431.

Weisberg, R. W. (1995). Prolegomena to theories of insight in problem solving. A taxonomy of problems. In R. J. Sternberg & J. E. Davidson (Eds.), *The nature of insight.* Cambridge, MA: MIT Press.

Weisberg, R. W., & Alba, J. W. (1981). An examination of the alleged role of "fixation" in the solution of several "insight" problems. *Journal of Experimental Psychology: General, 110,* 169–192.

Weiskrantz, L. (1986). *Blindsight: A case study and implications.* Oxford, UK: Oxford University Press.

Weldon, M. S. (2000). Remembering as a social process. In D. L. Medin (Ed.), *The psychology of learning and motivation* (vol. 40, pp. 67–120). New York: Academic Press.

Wells, G. L. (1993). What do we know about eyewitness identification? *American Psychologist, 48,* 553–571.

Wells, G. L., & Bradfield, A. L. (1998). "Good, you identified the suspect": Feedback to witnesses distorts their reports of the witnessing experience. *Journal of Applied Psychology, 83,* 360–376.

Wells, G. L., Malpass, R. S., Lindsay, R. C. L., Fisher, R. P., Turtle, J. W., & Fulero, S. (2000). From the lab to the police station: A successful application of eyewitness research. *American Psychologist, 55,* 581–598.

Wells, G. L., & Murray, D. M. (1984). Eyewitness confidence. In G. L. Wells & E. F. Loftus (Eds.), *Eyewitness testimony: Psychological perspectives.* New York: Cambridge University Press.

Wells, G. L., Ferguson, T. J., & Lindsay, R. C. L. (1981). The tractability of eyewitness confidence and its implications for triers of fact. *Journal of Applied Psychology, 66,* 688–696.

Wells, G. L., Leippe, M. R., & Ostrom, T. M. (1979). Guidelines for empirically assessing the fairness of a lineup. *Law and Human Behavior, 3,* 285–293.

Wells, G. L., Rydell, S. M., & Seelau, E. P. (1993). On the selection of distractors for eyewitness lineups. *Journal of Applied Psychology, 78,* 835–844.

Wells, G. L., Small, M., Penrod, S. J., Malpass, R. S., Fulero, S. M., & Brimacombe, C. A. E. (1998). Eyewitness identification procedures: Recommendations for lineups and photospreads. *Law and Human Behavior, 22,* 603–647.

Wenger, S. K., Thompson, C. P., & Bartling, C. A. (1980). Recall facilitates subsequent retention. *Journal of Experimental Psychology: Human Learning and Memory, 4,* 210–221.

Wickens, C. D. (1984). *Engineering psychology and human performance:* Columbus, OH: Merrill.

Wickens, C. D., Dalezman, R. E., & Eggemeier, F. T. (1976). Multiple encoding of word attributes in memory. *Memory and Cognition, 4,* 307–310.

Wiley, J. (1998). Expertise as mental set: The effects of domain knowledge in creative problem solving. *Memory and Cognition, 26,* 716–730.

Wilkins, M. C. (1928). The effect of changed material on ability to do formal syllogistic reasoning. *Archives of Psychology, 16,* (102).

Williams, J. M. G. (1996). Depression and the specificity of autobiographical memory. In D. C. Rubin (Ed.), *Autobiographical memory: Studies in autobiographical memory.* New York: Cambridge University Press.

Williams, J. M. G., & Scott, J. (1988). Autobiographical memory in depression. *Psychiatric Medicine, 18,* 689–695.

Williams, J. M. G., Ellis, N. C., Tyers, C., Healy, H., Rose, J., & MacLeod, C. (1996). The specificity of autobiographical memory and imageability about the future. *Memory and Cognition, 24,* 116–125.

Williams, L. M. (1994). Recall of childhood trauma: A prospective study of women's memories of childhood abuse. *Journal of Consulting and Clinical Psychology, 62,* 1182–1186.

Willingham, W. W., & Cole, N. S. (1997). Research on gender differences. In W. W. Willingham & N. S. Cole (Eds.), *Gender and fair assessment.* Hillsdale, NJ: Erlbaum.

Wilson, M., & Emmorey, K. (1997). A visuospatial "phonological loop" in working memory: Evidence from American Sign Language. *Memory and Cognition, 25,* 313–320.

Wilson, M., & Emmorey, K. (1998). A "word-length effect" for sign-language: Further evidence for the role of language in structuring working memory. *Memory and Cognition, 26,* 584–590.

Wittgenstein, L. (1969). *On certainty.* New York: Harper & Row.

Wood, N. L., Stadler, M. A., & Cowan, N. (1997). Is there implicit memory without attention? A re-examination of task demands in Eich's (1984) procedure. *Memory and Cognition, 25,* 772–779.

Woodworth, R. S., & Sells, S. B. (1935). An atmosphere effect in syllogistic reasoning. *Journal of Experimental Psychology, 18,* 451–460.

Wyer, T. K., & Srull, R. S. (1989). *Memory and cognition in its social context.* Hillsdale, NJ: Erlbaum.

Yarmey, D. A. (1973). I recognize your face, but I can't remember your name: Further evidence on the tip-of-the-tongue phenomenon. *Memory and Cognition, 1,* 287–290.

Yates, F. A. (1968). *The art of memory.* Chicago: University of Chicago Press.

Yates, J. F., Lee, J., & Shinotsuka, H. (1996). Beliefs about overconfidence, including its cross-national variation. *Organizational Behavior and Human Decision Processes, 65,* 138–147.

Yates, J. F., Lee, J., Shinotsuka, H., Patalano, A. L., & Sieck, W. R. (1998). Cross-cultural variations in probability judgment accuracy: Beyond general knowledge overconfidence? *Organizational Behavior and Human Decision Processes, 74,* 89–117.

Yin, R. K. (1969). Looking at upside-down faces. *Journal of Experimental Psychology, 81,* 141–145.

Young, A. W., Ellis, A. W., & Flude, B. M. (1988). Accessing stored information about people. *Psychological Research, 50,* 111–115.

Yuille, J. C., & Paivio, A. (1969). Abstractness and recall of connected discourse. *Journal of Experimental Psychology, 82,* 467–471.

Zaragoza, M. S., McCloskey, M., & Jamis, M. (1987). Misleading postevent information and recall of the original event. Further evidence against the memory impairment hypothesis. *Journal of Experimental Psychology: Learning, Memory, and Cognition, 13,* 36–44.

Zattore, R. J., Evans, A. C., Meyer, E., & Gjedde, A. (1992). Lateralization of phonetic and pitch discrimination in speech processing. *Science, 256,* 846–849.

Zimmerman, D. H., & West, C. (1975). Sex roles, interruptions, and silences in conversation. In B. Thorne & N. Henley (Eds.), *Language and sex: Differences and dominance* (pp. 105–129). Rowley, MA: Newbury House.

Credits

Name Index

Subject Index

Note: Italicized page numbers refer to the definition of the term in the chapter glossary.

absentmindedness, 131–133, 255, *293*
absolute threshold, 73–74, *111*
abuse. *See* sexual abuse
access consciousness, 94
accessibility of memories
 definition of, *251*
 vs. availability, 226
accommodation, 74–75, *111, 419*
accuracy
 of autobiographical memory, 305,
  327–328, 329–330, 332
 definition of, *69*
 as measurement tool, 41–42
 of perceptual processes, 92–93
 in problem representation,
  490–491
 speed-accuracy tradeoff, 42, *71*
acquired dyslexia, 438, *477*
action potential, 57, *69*
action slips, 131–133, *158*, 417
active touch, 81, *111*
acuity, tactile, 81, *113*
additions (speech error), 417, *426*
ad hoc categories, 194, *206*
advantage of clause recency, 468, *477*
advantage of first mention, 468, *477*
aerial perspective, 76, *111*
affirming the antecedent, 531
affirming the consequent, 531
aging
 and language, 371
 and memory retrieval, 249–250
 and tip-of-the-tongue (TOT)
  phenomenon, 370–371
"Aha!" experience, 512–513. *See also*
  insight
alexia, 188, *206*
algorithms
 definition of, *521*
 in problem solving, 497
AM. *See* autobiographical memory
American Psychological Association
  (APA), 292
American Sign Language (ASL)
 animal language and, 388, 389

articulatory loop and, 150–151,
  152
amnesia, *251. See also* childhood
  amnesia
 implicit memory in, 237, 239–240
 indirect memory and, 213–214
amygdala, 63, 287
analog representation, 372–379
 methodologies for studying,
  372–376
 reality of, 372, 376–379
analogy
 definition of, 499, *521*
 as problem-solving heuristic,
  499–503, 537
anaphor(s), 454–455, *477*
anaphoric reference, 454–456, *477*
anchoring-and adjustment heuristic,
  549–552, *564*
anchoring category members, 198
angular gyrus, 441–443
animals
 face recognition in, 189
 language and, 385–390
 visual processing in, 172
antecedent(s)
 in conditional reasoning, 531–532
 in discourse, 454–456, *477*
anterior (rostral), 59–60, *69*
anthropology, as cognitive science, 6
anticipations (speech error), 417, *426*
APA. *See* American Psychological
  Association
aphasia
 Broca's, 449, *477*
 Wernicke's, 449, *478*
arbitrariness of language symbols,
  383, 385, *426*
A (simple) reaction, 41, *69*
argument, in proposition, 467
arrangement problems, 483, *521*
articulation. *See also* speech
 as language production stage,
  416–419
 phoneme production, 395

phonemes, 394–395, *427*
 slips of the tongue, 417–421, *427*
articulatory loop, *158*
 articulatory suppression and,
  151–152
 in deaf persons, 150–151, 152
 physiological basis of, 152–153
 in working memory, 149–153, 156
articulatory suppression, 151–152
articulatory suppression task, 151,
  158
artificial categories, 192, *206*
artificial intelligence, research areas
  of, 5–6
ASL. *See* American Sign Language
associated activation errors, 132–133
association, laws of, 6, *32*
association areas of cortex, 60–61
Atkinson-Shiffrin model of memory,
  103
atmosphere effect, 528, *564*
attention, 115–126
 capacity theory of, 116, 121–123,
  158
 characteristics of, 116
 definition of, 2–3, 115–116, *158*
 divided, 117, 121–123, *158*
 early-selection theory of, 117–120,
  158
 filter model of, 117–120
 as gateway, 116, 117–121
 late-selection theory of, 121,
  158–159
 long-term memory encoding
  and, 215
 multimode theory of, 123–125, *159*
 selective, 117–125, *159*
 sensory overload and, 116, 117
attenuation theory, 120, 121, *158*
audition (hearing)
 in blind persons, 85
 interactions with vision, 87
 sound localization, 76–77
auditory coding, 139
auditory grouping, 78

603